1

Hillbilly Thomist

ALSO BY MARION MONTGOMERY

---

*John Crowe Ransom and Allen Tate: At Odds About the
Ends of History and the Mystery of Nature* (McFarland, 2003)

*Eudora Welty and Walker Percy: The Concept of
Home in Their Lives and Literature* (McFarland, 2004)

Hillbilly Thomist

Flannery O'Connor, St. Thomas and the Limits of Art

MARION MONTGOMERY

Volume 1 : Preface, Chapters 1–13

Bruce: This in celebration of our long friendship, with best wishes.
Marion
april 21, 2007

McFarland & Company, Inc., Publishers
Jefferson, North Carolina, and London

1

Reprinted by permission of Farrar, Straus and Giroux, LLC:
Excerpts from THE HABIT OF BEING: LETTERS OF FLANNERY O'CONNOR
edited by Sally Fitzgerald. Copyright © 1979 by Regina O'Connor.

Excerpts from "Introduction" by Flannery O'Connor from A MEMOIR
OF MARY ANN by the Dominican Nuns of Our Lady Perpetual Help
Home. "Introduction" copyright © 1961 by Flannery O'Connor.
Copyright renewed 1989 by Regina O'Connor.

Excerpts from MYSTERY AND MANNERS by Flannery O'Connor.
Copyright © 1969 by the Estate of Mary Flannery O'Connor.

Excerpts from WISE BLOOD by Flannery O'Connor. Copyright © 1962
by Flannery O'Connor. Copyright renewed © 1990 by Regina O'Connor.

LIBRARY OF CONGRESS CATALOGUING-IN-PUBLICATION DATA

Montgomery, Marion.
Hillbilly Thomist : Flannery O'Connor, St. Thomas
and the limits of art / Marion Montgomery.
p.   cm.
Includes bibliographical references and index.

ISBN 0-7864-2283-1 (2 volume set : softcover : 50# alkaline paper) ∞
ISBN 0-7864-2626-8 (v. 1 : softcover : 50# alkaline paper)
ISBN 0-7864-2627-6 (v. 2 : softcover: 50# alkaline paper)

1. O'Connor, Flannery — Criticism and interpretation.   2. Thomas, Aquinas,
Saint, 1225?–1274 — Influence. 3. Place (Philosophy) in literature.
4. Southern States — In literature.   5. Christianity and literature —
Southern States — History — 20th century.   6. Catholics —
Southern States — Intellectual life.   I. Title.
PS3565.C57Z786   2006   813'.54 — dc22   2005036409

British Library cataloguing data are available

On the cover: Florence Thomas, *Creston Methodist Church*, oil on canvas, 22" × 28", 1980s.

Manufactured in the United States of America

McFarland & Company, Inc., Publishers
Box 611, Jefferson, North Carolina 28640
www.mcfarlandpub.com

This tribute of one hillbilly Thomist to another
is for the Spiritual Diaspora of the Restless Young
in Quest of Community

Acknowledgments

The Earhart Foundation has been supportive, not only of this work, but of many of my works over the years, so that here I wish to express appreciation to it, but particular gratitude to David Kennedy, president emeritus; and to his successor, Ingrid Gregg; and to Anthony Sullivan, longtime secretary and director of program; and to his successor, Bruce Frohnen.

Contents

——— Volume 1 ———

——— Volume 2 ———

Preface

"'We go to the Father of Souls, but it is necessary to pass by the dragon.' No matter what form the dragon may take, it is of this mysterious passage past him, or into his jaws, that stories of any depth will always be concerned to tell, and this being the case, it requires considerable courage at any time, in any country, not to turn away from the storyteller."

— Flannery O'Connor, "The Fiction
Writer & His Country"

In the early 1950s my wife and I (newlyweds) joined with three other couples, already our social friends, in an informal salon, having discovered common literary and philosophical interests. I was a very junior instructor of freshman English, busily concerned with sentence fragments, verb agreement, pronoun reference. The husbands of the other couples were senior professors in disciplines from Shakespeare and Milton to Southern literature. What we undertook was Anton C. Pegis's *Introduction to Saint Thomas Aquinas* (1948), his anthology from Thomas' *Summa Theologica*. We met once a week. By turns as host and hostess, each couple was to present an article or articles, explicating and defending Thomas on the question at issue. There were lively exchanges all along the way. We came to speak of ourselves to curious friends and colleagues as the "St. Thomas Aquinas and Rabbit Hunters Club," apt metaphor given how quickly we discovered that we "jumped" more rabbits than we could run to ground, so rich the Thomistic briar patch. Not that the title was merely metaphorical, since in actuality some of us went rabbit hunting and held an occasional barbecue of the small creatures, or a "mull" — to the puzzled curiosity and perhaps even envy of some of our neighbors and colleagues.

We met, the eight of us, for many years, engaging not only St. Thomas, but Dante's *Divine Comedy* and Dostoevsky and Teilhard de Chardin. And on one memorable occasion, we even risked a dramatic reading of Clifford Odets' *Awake and Sing!* each taking parts, for reasons now quite vague. But what is still vividly memorable is that Conn West, the wife of our distinguished Shakespeare and Milton scholar Robert Hunter West, brought a level of comedy not intended by Odets — she undertaking the role of a New York Jewish grandmother with her very Southern Nashville voice.

It was Conn West as well who first called our attention to Flannery O'Connor, she having encountered stories in *Harper's Bazaar* and elsewhere. The Wests were already old friends of the Brainard Cheneys with whom Flannery was already in correspondence. And there was Professor Thomas Stritch of Notre Dame, Cardinal Stritch's nephew, who had been on the

sports staff of a Nashville paper with Professor West when both were young. Tommy became a very close friend of Flannery. It was inevitable, then, that we should close the circle with Miss Flannery, who by then was back home at Milledgeville, not far from Athens.
What I learned later was that, while the St. Thomas and Rabbit Hunters Club was wrestling
with Thomas' *Summa Theologica* in Pegis's Modern Library anthology, Flannery was also
reading that text, among other of Thomas' works, marking passages in it which we shall
presently engage.

    We were all very much taken with her fiction, so that we lured her to a reading at the
Chapel at the University of Georgia — though we did not advertise our sponsorship as the
St. Thomas Aquinas and Rabbit Hunters Club, lest the wary and skeptical shy away. Mine
was the pleasure of introducing her to a gathering of students and faculty and townspeo-
ple. At last emboldened, I ventured to her a typescript of an essay I had underway: "The
Sense of Violation: Notes Toward a Definition of 'Southern' Fiction," and not long after-
ward came her response: "I sure do like this…. We ought to be on the same program and
reinforce each other's views sometime." This in October of 1962, not long before she died.
We had exchanged some letters in the interval, as when in December of 1960 she responded
to a poem of mine in *Dry Lightning.* "The next time I see Craig Orr I am going to ask him
what he calls himself doing in a book of poems. His wife is our cousin." I had borrowed
Craig's name as too good not to remember, he also an old friend of the Wests, though I
hadn't known his wife Flannery's cousin.

    Flannery and I kept in touch sometimes indirectly through Tommy Stritch and other
mutual friends. And though I occasionally encountered her (at the Georgia Writers Association gathering on one occasion), we never had opportunity to "be on the same program."
Now, after all these years, perhaps what follows may prove something of a substitute program, though perhaps a problematic one. In this respect, perhaps this present work may
suggest something of the nature of the "hooraw" with the popular spirit that she had made
from the beginning. The term *hooraw* and a promise came to me in her last letter to me
soon before she died. She wrote to say that my novel *Darrell,* just published, "took some of
the curse offen the Baldwin County Hospital and eased my bed of affliction generally after
I got home." But, she added, she was under doctor's orders "not to have a lot of hooraw
going on." She was "not stout enough yet for a full-fledged comment à la Orville Prescott
or the gent in the Journal-Constitution" on *Darrell.* Nevertheless "I reckon I could do as
well as either if my blood weren't low." In preparation she had acquired "an electric type-
writer like I saw a picture of James Jones at and I hope to be creating my own hooraw in a
month or two." In a month or two she was dead.

    And so if the pages that follow prove problematic because of my presumption in some-
times speaking for her here with my own hooraw, it is an attempt at a tribute to a brave and
resolute soul, a tribute from one "hillbilly" Thomist to another. Perhaps it may serve in recovery of her view about human nature as she understood it from her Thomistic perspective, her own firm response to the "popular spirit" engaged as (in her phrase) "a prophet of
distances." That the popular spirit seems clouded now more than ever, good reason to summon her as a living presence to our spiritual circumstances on the threshold of this new
millennium. Of course, she has here no opportunity to enlarge upon nor demur from my
speculative colloquy with her. But a reader's common sense is nevertheless a sufficient corrective, I trust. This is an undertaking out of my confident belief that she and I, in the light
of St. Thomas, believe together in the sacredness of life, so that with Dame Julian of Nor-

wich I would affirm for us both that "all manner of thing shall be well" in the light of eternity.

It has been over a quarter of a century since I attempted a tribute to Flannery O'Connor, which I intended more than a tribute. In her two novels and two collections of stories, she had devoted her life as a maker of stories to her responsibility as a "prophet of distances," as she put it. I had attempted a similar responsibility as critic, exploring the relation of her art to prophecies implicit in those stories and novels. In the sense she means that phrase "prophet of distances," she intends that her fiction recall us to known but forgotten things. She does not presume anticipation of future events. What she would recall us to, in dramatic actions attending those known but forgotten things, is an abiding truth: We are created creatures; we are intellectual souls incarnate. And we are such as revealed to us by that condescension (in the root sense) called Revelation.

And so I wrote my trilogy in the 1970s, *The Prophetic Poet and the Spirit of the Age*. First came *Why Flannery O'Connor Stayed Home* (1981), followed by *Why Poe Drank Liquor* (1983) and then *Why Hawthorne Was Melancholy* (1984). They were written in the decade just after the turbulent 1960s in the middle of which Flannery O'Connor died (in 1964). I was finishing the last of my trilogy when our great national celebration began, declaring recovery from the current century's ills: 1976, our 200 anniversary year, in which as a nation the attempt was to recover known but forgotten things about our founding. Nevertheless, we seemed careful to dwell on the surfaces of our history, in contrast to O'Connor's concern for depths that neither history nor nature if taken at that surface could adequately recover. She had said directly and by the implications of her fictions that for us nature had already suffered a radical removal from grace, requiring of her a more distant view of that separation than afforded if we only look back to 1776. G. K. Chesterton puts it, in his little book on Chaucer, "A certain break or sharp change in history can hardly be sketched more sharply than by saying that up to a certain time life was conceived as a Dance, and after that time life was conceived as a Race." It is the tensional pull in us between the Dance and the Race, at the spiritual dimension of our existence, that Flannery O'Connor dramatizes in her fiction.

The title of my first volume was my own, *Why Flannery O'Connor Stayed Home*. But the title to the next two were phrases adapted from one of her talks on "The Teaching of Literature." I had hoped that, by such hinting, I might signal an intended unity of my own concern, taking the perspective O'Connor herself held. She spoke in resisting the growing popularity in the academy of teaching literature as to be accounted for by the psychological as literature's end, whether uncovered by a teacher in the fictional characters as dissected by explication, or in the maker of those fictional characters. The relation between the author and his characters was to be seen largely at the level of the psychologically "personal," whether with the assurance of Jungian myth or Freudian theories of sexuality. Hers, to the contrary, was a concern for spiritual depths, of which the psychological might be symptomatic but not definitive. The psychological, then, was a limited point of departure, but not an acceptable end. Jung and Freud at most spoke to the surfaces of the spiritual dislocations of persons, in her reasoned reckoning. Her intellectual mentor, St. Thomas Aquinas, had revealed to her unmistakably the spiritual depths of that discrete creature in creation, the person. It is in relation to St. Thomas' teaching, then, that she becomes comfortable in her "place," Andalusia, that small farm just outside the small town Milledgeville, in middle Georgia.

And so in respect to both history and geography, her concern is for place as truly seen in the immediacies of things and persons. As she believes, out of Thomas' teachings, it is in place that it is still possible to recover a recognition of creation's relation to grace. But most centrally, her concern is for that relation as abiding to an intellectual recognition out of human nature itself, evidenced in a person's responses to *this* place at *this* time. In that recognition one comes to know that spiritual life exists in an abiding present, to be recognized by the intellectual soul here and now.

Her concern as a prophet of distances, then, was to recall us from our considerable distance from reality — from a spiritual deracination out of a pride in self-sufficiency. We had become blinded to the presence of grace in the things immediately at hand. She makes her fictions out of her own recognition of that presence, under the auspices of reason and not out of vague "religious" feelings. That is a point she insists upon, on the authority of St. Thomas Aquinas. But she must do so, and not only in response to the challenge to herself as *this* maker of fictions, required to engage the guidance of her reason over feeling in recognition of the limits of her gifts: a formidable enough challenge. For, if that is her primary responsibility as maker and not creator, there is yet another challenge to her making: the *matter* with which she makes proves to be the "popular spirit" of her moment, with which popular spirit she is at odds, given her prophetic vision. Here lies an inherent antipathy suited to fiction's dramatic tension within her perspective, an antipathy challenging to her gifts as she would govern them by a visionary truth larger than reason's confident authority. Reason is necessary to understanding, crucial to the making of art, but it can never be comprehensive of truth, given man's intellectual finitude. That is a truth widely ignored by the popular spirit, as it has been actively rejected by an authoritative *gnosis* presuming intellectual autonomy over truth itself. Unacceptable as well: the "romantic" counter elevation of "feeling" in rejecting reason. Only by the virtue of prudential humility, she believes, are feelings to be ordered under reason to an understanding of the limits of intellect itself.

Hers is an age unsympathetic to such prophetic poets as she, who would recall us to such known but forgotten or rejected truth. She is devoted to the truth of things as speaking the cause of truth itself, that Cause called Truth or Love vouchsafed by visitation to mankind called the Incarnation. And so she depends upon reason as understood by St. Thomas, as opposed to reason as reduced to rationalism through presumptuous pride (as she remarks) in the spectacles of thought now remembered as the Enlightenment, that 18th century Age of Rationalism. Her own age, she discovers, is one which is not simply careless in forgetting known things. It has been very active in rejecting those known things which she would recover to recognition — truths deeper than the psychological surfaces of human nature which we have used to mold and contain human nature itself through what we shall call a Modernist apotheosis of the "self." Ours was in her day (and continues in our own to be) an age seduced by various Modernist ideologies which assure us that our "self" is the centering point of the whole universe, to be maintained as sovereign and absolute by the power of an intellectual autonomy which caters persuasively to random self-desires, collectively tolerated as the "popular spirit." What she recognized is that community had become reduced from members to a multitude, in which multitude rise conflicted ideologies contending for power over a "popular spirit," most often by encouraging "feeling" as sufficient to whatever vague "desire" in persons disoriented from the reality of their own natures. That is the Modernist strategy, a condescension quite other than that of the Incarnation. It is *condescension* in its pejorative sense, with intent to seduce through "feelings" an allegiance to ideology, as if this particular version of truth were the means to satisfy random desires. Seeing this distortion of common sense in the multitude by Modernist strategy, she engages both as intellectual errors. But in doing so she gains, especially from the ideologue, the epithet that she is "anti-intellectual." Meanwhile, convenience and comfort (whether that of the "feeling" multitude or the strategizing gnostic ideologue intent on power) require exaltation of sovereign rights to the increasingly isolated "self," those illusional "rights" becoming a bond justifying power over nature for both the ideologue and his enlisted multitude. Theirs becomes a new faith which requires denial of the dragon that sits by the side of the road, of whom St. Cyril of Jerusalem speaks in our epigraph — the full text of which O'Connor sets as epigraph to her first collection of stories, *A Good Man Is Hard to Find*. Those proved to be stories at once confusing and captivating, many of her readers caught between laughter and a smoldering anger, and not always having the courage she says necessary *not* to "turn away from a storyteller" who is concerned with "this mysterious passage past" the dragon. For her, that dragon lies at the side of whatever road each of us as pilgrim takes through this world.

Such, then, that second challenge to her as a maker of fictions: the resistance of her reader, who if not knowingly at least intuitively recognizes himself in her stories. The reader is somehow implicated in the tensional drama of the stories. As for herself as poet — as storyteller — hers is (again, as St. Thomas insists, regarding the making of art things) a primary responsibility to the good of the thing she makes. No slight demand upon her gifts, this responsibility. But she commits herself as maker with a continuing and increasing joy, which is not the same thing as happiness. She understood the gift of joy as a more complex state of the soul than our popular and vague "pursuit of happiness," the pursuit of which we declare our constitutional "right," "legal" constitutions having replaced moral responsibility through a Modernist consent to the letter of the law — positive law divorced from natural law. Joy is commingled inevitably with pain and suffering, she knows. Happiness proves again and again a surface contentment, good "feelings" demanded by us if we are to continue self-righteous in a devotion to our desires as "inalienable rights," litigiously certified by the mechanics of logic in the keep of specialists in the "law." That will prove in the end to require a "psychological" adjustment of the "self," as if it were something of a machine. The social and political intentions we think promising our rescue are the ones against which her Misfit will react in a last defense of the remnant of humanity he finds left in him: his propensity to evil. A shocking suggestion, this, and quite baffling to some of the readers of that story. It speaks our difficulty in recognizing a *good* man no less than that of distinguishing joy from happiness. A good man is so hard to find because we have forgotten the nature of goodness itself, upon which evil as parasite depends. The Misfit's violence is a dark paradox, in that it speaks through paradoxical indirection in witness to the good we have denied.

And so the two challenges we shall explore in these pages, first O'Connor's personal sense of responsibility to her gifts as maker, through which she is committed by reason to the good of the thing she makes. That is for her always the primary concern. In the exercise of that responsibility, St. Thomas reminds her, she is not responsible as poet for the moral rectitude of her reader. The second challenge nevertheless depends upon — depends from — the reader as she understands his state at her moment. Her most likely reader is isolated to the conveniences of the "self" as the highest good to be pursued. And yet he is spiritually distraught, frantic in his pursuit of happiness. She is challenged to an understanding of that *matter* to her making. It is the soul in its Modernist state of deracination, a soul which has become "lost in the cosmos" as her friend and fellow fiction writer Walker Percy puts it. Out of that lostness (again, as Percy puts it) we have become not simply the Age of Alienation but the Age of the Theorist-Consumer, the one feeding upon the other in what proves a reciprocal cannibalism of the intellectual soul, usually justified by a science demonstrating the incarnate dimension of human existence as the ultimate reality. The body and its conveniences determine the possibility of happiness we declare by new faith in science. Or so we are encouraged to believe as citizens in a popular "spirit."

Her overriding responsibility: the good of the thing she makes as craftsman, according to her calling. In turn her story is made as a gift of her talent, to be perfected and returned as offering (as she says) to God, to use or not use as he sees fit. There is a disturbed response by some readers nevertheless, since in being offered up, the stories enter the public domain. There, the reader often finds himself stirred beyond aesthetic virtues of her fiction. The stories disturb us, and in ways unaccountable by aesthetic philosophy as argued in defense of Modernist sensibilities. That is one of the possible uses perhaps to which God (if he will) may put her offering within this world — this disturbing of our Modernist sensibilities. But as poet one never "proves" anything with a story she says. It is nevertheless in response to this effect on us that she will say, in her "Novelist and Believer" (*Mystery and Manners*), that "Today's reader, if he believes in grace at all, sees it as something which can be separated from nature and served to him raw as Instant Uplift." That is, as a magic potion. "This reader's favorite word is compassion. I don't wish to defame the word. There is a better sense in which it can be used but seldom is — the sense of being in travail with and for creation in its subjection to [our] vanity. This is a sense which implies a recognition of sin; this is a suffering-with, but one which blunts no edges and makes no excuses. When infused into novels, it is often forbidding. Our age doesn't go for it." Intent upon "*Instant Uplift*" in the name of happiness, we may forego that joy which is a "suffering-with," which is beyond conveniences to the autonomous self. In that acceptance of happiness over joy, we instead have declared our constitutional "rights."

O'Connor lived just outside Milledgeville on the little farm her mother made a going concern and which Flannery, with a degree of her playful mischief, named Andalusia. Now, at the beginning of our new millennium, we may look across the road from Andalusia: a Holiday Inn, where busy passengers rest a night and then depart for unknown places. They are largely no doubt imbued with the "spirit of the age," in transit and staying no place very long. Perhaps they are more akin to Mr. Shiftlet of "The Life You Save May Be Your Own" than they might at first recognize since more happily possessed of things than he — credit cards and new automobiles. But in these travelers — as in Mr. Shiftlet and even in the Misfit if seen from Flannery O'Connor's vision of our spiritual nature — there rises a longing to get home, a longing which is more unsettling than the road map we consult next morning as we "check out" from an overnight respite from the race. A desire stirs in us as person, hinting itself more fundamental than last evening's relief in finding convenient respite in a strange place after a long day on the road. That desire seems to draw us to some object yet unnamed on current maps, though intuitively known as more promising than the objects of those desires agitating us at the level of the "psychological."

Flannery O'Connor will declare that such a sense of restlessness in us, this buried desire, is closer to the "psychological" surface of the Southerner's life as she knows that Southerner. If he is not "Christ-centered," she says, he continues "Christ-haunted." It is to an exploration of her vision of man as thus haunted, reflected in her made stories, that we shall be interested to explore what "goes-on" in them, in characters, toward whatever possibilities of a recovery of joy from the mere conveniences of happiness as popularly pursued in this age of the Theorist-Consumer. At least this may be a secondary use of my own current offering, which is itself primarily made to that Cause of our deepest desire. As so offered openly, this work too becomes a part of community property. Or so we may hope.

What remains, before our setting out, is some notation on this present roadmap. It intends to be helpful to our recognizing, without confusing, those two waystations so proximate to each other: the motel with its neon sign advertising "vacancy" and (almost unnoticed) Andalusia just across the road — now somewhat run-down and neglected. That is our point of departure, with signs anticipated along the way — some hardly familiar to our current proficiencies in reading maps devoted to life as a race. Unnoticed or neglected signs from O'Connor's perspective upon our journeying, which perspective she sees necessary that we hold them in common. They point toward the possibility of our recovering some sense of Chesterton's Dance, lest we collapse short of home, exhausted by the circling Race. In that recognition through signs we know she read widely and gave long, long thought to the readings of old signposts in what seems so much a desert to many of us. We must not be misled, then, by her self-deprecation as but a "hillbilly" Thomist. Hers is a highly sophisticated mind, an inconvenience to some of her Modernist readers who wish to dismiss her as "anti-intellectual." Indeed, what sets her on caustic edge in some of her words at times is the "pseudo-intellectual" whom she encounters, especially in academic and cultural waystations. We must not confuse the neon signs promoted by pseudo-intellectuals as designating the right way on our intellectual maps with her signs as more carefully crafted.

And so what we shall attempt in the pages of the map ahead — rather ambitiously undertaken — is to reveal something of the social, philosophical, theological context out of which has evolved a Modernist religion in the post-Renaissance history of Western intellectual travels down to this new millennium. Her vision in retrospect is counter, she being a "realist of distances." We shall discover how soundly knowledgeable she is in the geography of this world whose realities belie our false signposts along the way in this present. How unwavering her faith, and how steady her insistence on the presence of grace within that geography of creation.

It has been a geography overlaid by quick pavings, intellectual highways and superhighways cluttered with temporary accommodations to one-night stands, convenient to desires of the moment in respite from the race to home as a Nowhere. But she insists that always there is a presence of grace itself in creation, even in those roadside stops — however much distorted by neon signs tempting us to an arrest or luring us to a further racing along ambiguous ways. Always, she argues there is that intersection on our limited horizontal plane, a geography we take to be a race track. For always *here* is that vertical intersection by grace, discovered as pervasive of our horizontal illusions about the temporal as if the temporal defines limits to the race toward a vague "horizontal happiness." To understand something of her counter vision requires our own "suffering-with," at the level of a labor by the intellectual soul itself, for which necessary labor there is no instant relief sufficient to absolve us as person — as *intellectual soul incarnate* — of the restless desire in us for home as more than a temporary respite from the race.

— Crawford, Georgia
Advent 2005

"Everybody who has read Wise Blood *thinks I'm a hillbilly nihilist, whereas I would like to create the impression ... that I'm a hillbilly Thomist."*

— Flannery O'Connor, Letter to
Robie Macauley, May 18, 1955

"I read [the Summa Theologica*] for about twenty minutes every night before I go to bed. If my mother were to come in during this process and say, 'Turn off that light, It's late,' I with lifted finger and broad blank beatific expression, would reply, 'On the contrary, I answer that the light, being eternal and limitless, cannot be turned off. Shut your eyes,' or some such thing. In any case, I feel I can personally guarantee that St. Thomas loved God because for the life of me I cannot help loving St. Thomas."*

— Flannery O'Connor to
"A," August 9, 1955

1

Settling In at Andalusia

"Catholic or Protestant, the believing writer is equally unhappy. He feels like Lancelot in search of the Holy Grail who finds himself at the end of his quest at a Tupperware party."

— Walker Percy, "How to be an American Novelist
in Spite of Being Southern and Catholic"

It is with something of Walker Percy's playful indirection that I chose an epigraph from Percy as a beginning to this revisiting of Flannery O'Connor in her home country. Both Percy and O'Connor share a sense of being challenged as writers because both are Southern and Catholic, at a point in cultural history when to be either is likely to be suspect and so requiring of them as poets an indirection in respect to their own beliefs. It is an indirection always appropriate to the making of a fiction in accord with the necessities of art, even of pagan art when it is good in itself as art. But it seems even more a necessary strategy to them as poets resident in an unbelieving world. Neither is reluctant to be direct about his belief as Christian, of course. As for their sharing a double jeopardy in being both Southern and Catholic, however, they differ in an important circumstance to their separate journeying of the unbelieving world, each as *homo viator*— as persons on separate but companionable ways. Unlike Percy, Flannery O'Connor seems to have discovered this challenging double jeopardy to her gifts from about the time she was baptized in infancy. Percy on the other hand had to work harder to discover the difficulties. He is, by comparison, late in coming to terms with his "Southerness," as he is also late in his conversion to Rome.

We may discover yet another difference. Though both recognize the common jeopardy to them as fiction writers, Percy's term "unhappy" hardly seems apt of Miss Flannery. Given Percy's playful wit when he is in social circumstances — lectures and the like, especially when before the variety of his audiences as may be remembered by many of us — it may seem something of a surprise that he would think of himself as unhappy. It is not likely that his audience down at the University of Southwestern Louisiana where he spoke the words of our epigraph would have put much weight on his word *unhappy,* so delightfully playful their guest, though deeply serious in his argument for that occasion. We discover by asides and private remarks from time to time that nevertheless he had rather be at home in Covington, even though as on this occasion he speaks to homefolks largely Southern, though not largely Catholic. (They were likely largely Baptists.) He proves genially and mannerly, whether in Louisiana or New York or Illinois, perhaps especially so to audiences out of the South who in turn if not Southern are largely Catholic. Enough to make him long for Covington.

Percy is almost always mannerly, even if on occasion not necessarily genial. With Flannery O'Connor it seems most often otherwise. On similar public appearances, she is likely to be reserved, cautious — appear even timid. Until some silly question is put to her, at which time she may respond in a most prickly manner. She knows the virtues of manners, remarking famously that bad manners are better than no manners at all. Speaking at a Southern Writers Conference at my own university, and to would-be writers for the most part, she was very blunt in warning: "I have a very high opinion of the art of fiction and a very low opinion of what is called the 'average' reader," of whom she encountered many along her way. One suspects she may also here mean average writers who are romantically engaging a dream of becoming writers, a calling she sees as a spiritual and intellectual labor most demanding of personal risk. As that conference dragged on with its "workshops" (as I remember it), she excused herself. She had to get back to Andalusia to feed the chickens before dark, she said.

I think it true enough to suggest, then, that while Percy was more social when necessity required it of him, he was as a person nevertheless in degree more unhappy than she, public manners sometimes suggesting the contrary.[1] Flannery O'Connor is seemingly reserved and cautious in any country other than perhaps that abutting Andalusia, her mother's farm in central Georgia. Sometimes not even a comfortable presence there was possible. There was an increasing stream of random visitors awash on the premises. She is given to a comic wit Percy appreciated, at home or away — used sometimes as a manner of self-protection, though on occasion turned into incisive judgment. She did not always suffer fools gladly, even on her front porch. Her wit may be caustically tempered to sharpness, then, as when she responds to a correspondent from a university asking her searching questions about one of her stories. She responds shortly about his academic manner of treating a story like "a frog in a bottle." It was not always easy for her to be charitable, though she knew herself obligated to be so. Let us say she was especially tried by naïve responses to her work, but most especially so when such naiveté came across to her as sophisticated nonsense — that is, as it may be disguised in academic clothing. Most especially caustic at times when it came across at her on the front porch at Andalusia, borne at her by an unexpected stranger. Not that she couldn't be somewhat gentle with the spiritually naïve. Still, gentleness was sometimes trying for her.

There is an anecdote concerning what we might take as her attempt to be generous-spirited to an old naïve friend. The friend had come home from Greenwich Village, way up there in New York City, all excited by what she had seen and heard and done. Thus enlightened, she was home for a visit and came out to Andalusia to share her adventures with Flannery, whom she supposed entrapped by the provincial South. Calling on her old acquaintance and friend out at the farm, the two of them talked and rocked on the front porch, the friend recounting high adventure among poets and artists. The visitor at last fell silent for a spell, the two of them still rocking. Then, looking out over the pines and pastures, peacocks and chickens pecking about the yard — perhaps even seeing the jackass Flannery had bought for her mother as a Mother's Day present — she exclaimed to Flannery: "Oh, Flannery! If only I could take you out of all this!" And Flannery, rocking a minute and then in her nasal voice: "Out of all *what*?"

There is another story, shared with me by a mutual friend and complementary of this challenging visitation upon Flannery by a friend — New York imported to central Georgia. This mutual friend arrived by bus from South Georgia for a visit. She was let out at the dirt road leading up to Andalusia — to find Flannery meeting her half way down the road, hobbling on her crutches, to share account of an act of country charity granted Flannery the day before. She couldn't wait to share it. A man, visiting Miss Regina (Flannery's mother) on farm business, was walking and talking with Mrs. O'Connor when he realized that Flannery was trailing along behind them on her crutches. The visitor felt obligated to include her, poor cripple that she was. He stopped, reached down at his feet, and caught up one of Flannery's chickens. Then he threw it high up in the air and the chicken, squawking and fluttering, managed to land safely a few yards away. Turning to Flannery like a considerate uncle, he said, "It don't take much to give a chicken a good time." Charity toward small things like a chicken, shared charitably with a hobbling girl — but also to impress her bargaining mother no doubt. A mother, incidentally, who was a rich burden to Flannery as writer, though Flannery recognized herself as well to be a burden on her mother's patience. Not easy to run an orderly farm with a poet-daughter hobbling along, attuned like Dante on his pilgrimage to collecting incident and phrases to consequential comic dramas of fallen man. It could not have been easy for Regina to accommodate to Flannery, an indirect acknowledgment of which perhaps is in that story "The Enduring Chill," in which Asbury is a deliberate irritant to his mother who loves him anyway. Flannery, of course, recognized depths more remote than the comic surface of such encounter, concerned as she was with her obligation to her calling as a "prophet of distances." Something more profoundly afoot than might be recognized by someone treating one of her stories like a "frog in a bottle" to be sealed safely in a piece of academic Tupperware, the research paper container professionally sterilized for a journal.

It is nevertheless impossible to escape the Tupperware party, she discovered, even on her own front porch at Andalusia. But that, too, was a lesson Flannery seems to have been born knowing: in Greenwich Village or in Milledgeville or even out at the farm, human nature fallen is human nature, whatever its spectacle of color. As she became more and more known for her fictions, the challenge of intrusion became exacerbated, though it also proved rich provender, amenable matter, to the making of fictions, as any clever Dante discovers. Whenever and wherever, she knew very well she could not escape those who see the world with *provincial* eyes, *provincial* being a concept understood quite differently by Flannery O'Connor on her front porch and by many of her visitors — whether a stranger from parts unknown like Mr. Shiftlet or an old acquaintance returned from the big city bearing imported light. Especially, she suspected, someone venturing South from a Northern place or a Southern venturer to the North now come home with tales of a fabulous Greenwich Village, a more romantic place than allowable in central Georgia at Andalusia. And Flannery would know an essay on provincialism by an old acquaintance, Allen Tate. "Provincialism," Tate says in it, is an attitude which "is limited in time but not in space." It is "a state of mind in which regional men lose their origin in the past and its continuity into the present, and begin every day as if there had been no yesterday." Northerner or Southerner — either may prove to be provincial.

For both Tate and Miss Flannery, no solution is whole which does not embrace the material and legal order within a spiritual vision. *Programs* and *rulings* in the name of the *common good* are but temporary — temporal: solutions always in decay, requiring an acknowledgment of spiritual dimension to any viable hope for the common good. Otherwise provincialism obtains. Such provincialism is to be seen (Tate says) in contrast to "the classical-Christian world, based upon regional consciousness, which held that honor, truth, imagination, human dignity, and limited acquisitiveness, could alone justify a social order, however rich and efficient it may be. We have become largely provincials," Tate adds, and so we "do not live anywhere," having committed ourselves "to seeing *with,* not *through,* the eye."[2] That Flannery O'Connor recognizes what Tate calls *provincialism* as the Modernist mode of deportment to creation is indicated in her address to a sometimes popular condition of mind much celebrated in fiction and poetry in her day. Hers was the century which seemed almost to pride itself as the "Age of Alienation." And so of that malady of spirit embraced as if a virtue of mind O'Connor says, in her "The Catholic Writer in the Protestant South": "Alienation was once a diagnosis, but in much of the fiction of our time it has become an ideal. The modern hero is an outsider. His experience is rootless. He can go anywhere. He belongs nowhere. Being alien to nothing, he ends up being alienated from any kind of community based on common tastes and interests. The borders of his country are the sides of his skull." Such the dead end waiting the provincial, the Modernist, spirit.

Tate's words were written at the end of World War II, just before he entered the Church in which Flannery O'Connor was at home from her cradle. (Anyone who has raised children knows what an ambiguous phrase — this *at home* — proves to be, churched or not.) It was Jacques Maritain who sponsored him. And it had been Jacques Maritain long before who had written a small book summoning Western artists to the virtues of Thomism in recovering a proper deportment to their making. Maritain's *Art and Scholasticism,* the second edition of it in 1927, coincided with T. S. Eliot's "Ash-Wednesday." And already by the 1920s, Tate and Eliot had become friends. Tate's wife Caroline Gordon, a close friend of the Maritains, was later to become an insistent mentor to Flannery O'Connor — whether Flannery would or no. There occurred, this is to say, a continuity in some Western letters of the Thomistic aesthetics signaled by Maritain's little book. That book became a touchstone to a small but vital diaspora of artists. It was centrally important to Eric Gill, who published its first English edition as *The Philosophy of Art* at Ditchling in 1923, the year after Eliot's *Waste Land.* It was important to David Jones, whose *Anathemata* (1952) has yet to be recognized as the considerable poem it is, rivaling at least Pound's *Cantos.* Maritain's small book was important to G. K. Chesterton and that circle remembered as the Distributists, and to some of the Fugitive-Agrarians, partly through T. S. Eliot. It was important to Eliot, who translated and published in his *Criterion* some of Maritain's work. And of course, it was important to Walker Percy and Flannery O'Connor as representative of that strange phenomenon: Southern Catholic Writers of Fiction.

Maritain's *Art and Scholasticism* was of special importance to Flannery O'Connor, coming to her with recommendation from several respected quarters. Out of it, and from St. Thomas' own words which she read almost nightly, she came to understand as poet the importance of the local to her art, but more importantly she had confirmed her own intuitive recognition of the importance of seeing *through* the eye, rather than *with* it, as if making the eye merely an instrument of intentionality in service to the art of making. That is, to see through the eye is to surrender in communion with the thing seen. She, unlike Eliot had been at her age, could never have thought of "myth," for instance, as "simply a way of controlling, of ordering" art, as Eliot says concerning Joyce's use of myth in *Ulysses.* For her, the eye is not an instrument to be used as a technological convenience evolved by accident in the flesh, serving the intellect as if detached from personal communion with reality here and now through the flesh. In that distortion and in the interest of intellect detaching itself from reality to serve art, one thus chooses "not to live anywhere." The choice will then become to flit along the surface of creation, being careful not to become entangled in any place. The mere spectacle of reality becomes sufficient unto the moment of the self-awareness of the artist, who thus mistakes himself as primary over his obligation to the good of the thing he makes, his story or poem.

If the particularities of things speak more than spectacle, we are unavoidably in the presence of a mystery about *being* itself. And a prudential deportment in the presence of a mystery unresolved requires a responsible deportment to things in response to their recognizable particularities. *This* thing is not simply *a* thing in a reductionism to generalized concept, become abstract formulation through our intellectual deportment. It is *this thing in itself.* Prudence responds properly to a dignity inherent to it because it exists as the thing it is. Our manner of deportment may lack reason's formulations such as this one here underway, but we recognize intuitively a responsibility to a proportionate dignity of the thing, though willfulness may reject that responsibility. By the very rejection, we nevertheless affirm the dignity inherent to the existing thing. This is the moment of intellectual response out of which grows the history of philosophy itself as so variously manifest in what Yeats called "monuments of unaging intellect." Not only the Thomism which is our (and O'Connor's) concern — but the philosophy of Socrates' nemesis, the Sophists, or the Stoics, or the Positivistic Materialist of our age, and on and on.

As for the maker of stories, this point of departure in a manner of response to recognized existences here and now is crucial to the relation of *action* to *spectacle* as addressed by art. And so for the artist *manner* of response to a *thing* as actual, whatever the thing responded to, becomes *matter* to his making. It becomes centrally important to art in a making with signs, with words, as O'Connor is very much aware. There is a phrase of hers made into a celebrated title to her speculations on this matter, her *Mystery and Manners.* It is most apt as title, given the nature of her reflections. She sees that, since *human nature* in action, revealed through spectacle and articulated by signs, is the matter proper to drama, this action becomes the theme in the matrix of O'Connor's speculation about the mystery spoken by things in themselves to her opened eyes and ears. It is through *manners* that as *persons* we respond to *things,* and that is the essence of drama. (On this point, Aquinas reminds us that art is not an imitation of *nature per se* but an imitation of the *action* of nature — an important distinction in that it relates art to the *possible* or *probable* rather than to the *actual,* which is the province of history as opposed to art.) That response is always made in *a* place and at *a* time, always *here* and *now,* though it will in a next moment be remembered as *then* and *there.* Art is of necessity local. Manners, speaking the *manner* of a person toward things known here and now, will prove larger by implication than as if merely a matter of history's accidents, a matter of mere spectacle remembered. This is to suggest that manners run deeper than, though they are conspicuous at, the level of spectacle. For the *ground* of spectacle itself as encountered in things here and now is larger than the mere history of things as known and remembered. (That is why William Butler Yeats's comfort in "monuments of unaging intellect" proves at last inadequate, his confidence in art's rescue of the artist through such monuments being a very ancient Romantic illusion.)

We conclude that manners speak a communal deportment defined by spectacle in the cultural matrix of this place at which we stand within this place's "history." But it is *man-*

ner in respect to the particular person so standing that is central — his manner in response to things existing now, though also to be remembered as existing *then* (i.e., as "history"), whether the *then* be but yesterday or centuries ago. For the things to which we respond exist always anterior to our response. Manners, this is to say, have to do with tradition and the responsibility of *this* person here and now to the sorting of his tradition *as measured by the truth of things known.* That is a lesson O'Connor takes from Thomas Aquinas, leading her to declare that so important are manners for her that even bad manners are better than no manners at all. That recognition leads her to the virtue of a prudential humility not often understood by those who are intellectually imprudent and so likely to set humility itself aside. (See Appendix E.)

Of course, we usually think of manners as merely common gestures made within a community out of convenience — as if but traffic signs to avoid social accidents. Or as evolved by a particular community through a common consent over time, the consent become mere habit — vestigial like our appendix. Among "Southern" manners one still celebrated pretty much in this understanding of manners — at least on what passes for the comic on television — is that of hospitality. But hospitality (for O'Connor and many others) is more anciently as it is more presently viable than as if but a residual habit in a geographical location, history's detritus. Out of a piety of manner toward things in themselves, we anciently supposed we might be entertaining gods or angels unaware. That is a "tradition" to which O'Connor is attuned, particularly suited as a dramatic matter still available to her, though perhaps only residually present to a dwindling remnant — in "Southern" culture, that is, whatever the geographical coordinates. But there is a lingering implication whereby even in bad manners, and perhaps evident elsewhere (even in Atlanta or New York), there is reflected still the history of *manner*, to be recovered and made acceptable by a community in a place as a mode of piety.

We are speaking here, then, of *tradition* — of some version of tradition accepted knowingly or unknowingly and reflected willy-nilly in our manners good or bad. Manners (or their absence) are spawned by intellect, out of or supported by each person's deportment toward things. And it is notable that our *manner* revealed in our *manners* is evident through signs, received by *a* person from *a* person, whether signs approving of or rejecting things, including persons. By consent through such signs, there may be recognized a community in which *this* person is *member,* however much fallen. The manner may indeed be seen in manners toward things that are not persons. That is a deportment of the person which we may not ordinarily recognize as requiring or implying a *communal* deportment, as it does for O'Connor. As Flannery O'Connor is writing her fiction, there is a very popular distinction being made in respect to *manner.* It is out of Martin Buber, who distinguishes between a manner of communion with things which is not an "I-it" but an "I-Thou." And this distinction is in her repeated concern for our having separated grace from nature as a gambit to the conquest of nature itself, especially human nature.

It is indeed a difference we emphasize in O'Connor's fiction. Recall her grandmother in "A Good Man Is Hard to Find," who at the story's close responds in an act of love, a gesture of manner deeper than manners, made *toward* but in a vulnerable openness hardly usual to her and so surprising. By careful reflection we discover it not really "out of character." The gesture is toward the Misfit, accompanied by her exclamation: "Why you're one of my babies. You're one of my own children!" It is at once a confession and an expression of love delayed, as we reflect on it within the story's context under our rubrics of *manner* and *manners.* There has been a comical fore-telling of this resolving communal gesture, fore-shadowing the dire consequences to the grandmother, in a preliminary eruption anticipating her death. The grandmother has smuggled her cat Pity Sing along on this expedition, carefully guarded against detection as a stowaway. One might import here Flannery's own attitude toward cats, she a "bird person" as it might be popularly put, though this biographical point isn't necessary given the long history of the cat's association with the occult and its dark practices. When we see Pity Sing rubbing against the Misfit's leg at story's end, taken up and coddled by him, we might suspect here an agent of the devil, cozening even the Misfit. (*Pity Sing*— that is baby talk for *pretty thing* as a "Southernism," carrying an ironic resonance in the context of the story.) There seems a bond implied from the beginning between the Grandmother and her cat, the Grandmother naïve in her deracinated spiritual manner, superficial in her concern for place in relation to orientation in history and nature. She "misses" the comfort of tradition, to which the rest of her family prove increasingly not only indifferent but hostile.

A certain irony perhaps attaches, then, to the Grandmother's attachment to Pity Sing, as if a bonding impossible to her with her natural and civil family, with her son and his wife and her three grandchildren, all seeming to her foreign to her own desires for some recovery of the comfort of a remembered place in distant "east Tennessee." From the outset we recognize a family in which manner hardly speaks manners, a gathering of misfits one to the other by accidents of nature as it were. The grandmother has led the expedition astray in pursuit of a "tradition" that she dreams might be restorative of dignity, first to herself and perhaps then to this chaotic family of a tradition long neglected. She is innocent of place, and so they all look in the wrong place. Realizing her error, she upsets the valise hiding Pitty Sing. And the cat, snarling and displaced, sinks claws into Bailey's shoulders (he, the grandmother's son, the driver), causing a wreck. Such the circumstances, the dramatic context. We may wonder, after the story's end: Is there a communal relation of the grandmother to the cat, as if the cat might enable her to some love hardly evident among these people as confined by a "natural" history of a family on the road from nowhere to nowhere? Their manners are used to the convenience (largely) of selfish isolation, each with his own agenda for this "vacation," as opposed to the Church's traditional retreat which perhaps O'Connor has in her own mind at least as ironic contrast. Alienation is writ small in this family, though large in its suggestiveness as it speaks to an absence of love. There is that small saving gesture of Bailey's wife, protecting the baby as they wreck, but it seems only a fleeting spectacle in the story. Having read the story, we are not likely to be moved by pity for those here slaughtered (except by sentimentality for the infant perhaps). Especially not moved for those nasty brats — the one named for a Hollywood star, the other for a long forgotten evangelist to the Georgia colony (June Star and John Wesley). By their collective unmannerliness, we are at least tempted to indifference at their fates. Such a response on our part may say something of our own manner toward creation, as again O'Connor is sufficiently aware as the story's maker. She knows her audience well, and sometimes "plays the devil" with it as we say in Georgia.

Manner is revealed through manners, then. But most tellingly revealed in the manners of one person to another, as in the resolution effected through the Misfit and the grandmother. For, though manners imply community consent in *common,* governing the deportment of a person within community at large as signifying his participation in a body, it is in the actions of person to person that manners may be regarded as good or bad at last. One might explore this point at length in O'Connor's dramatic uses of *manners* in story after story. Remember that contest of manners under the pressures of manipulative chicanery, that contest between Mr. Shiftlet and Mrs. Lucynelle Crater in "The Life You Save May Be Your Own." Good or bad manners, either may prove adaptable in a subversion underway. Mr. Shiftlet displays a piety of manners with an intent to deceive, against another person, Mrs. Crater, who proves more wily than he. (It is a comic play of manners which we might find Chaucer delighted by.)

Whatever the dramatic deployment of manners in relation to her drama, O'Connor does not lose sight of an important aspect of reality: Manners distorted by intent neverthe- less speak acknowledgment of the actuality of the person against whom bad manners are being deployed. That actuality speaks a context of a present moment, defining a local arena in which human nature displays itself. It is out of this recognition that O'Connor attempts on one occasion to reassure a contemporary Southern writer who has become uncomfort- able with her own "Southerness." She writes Cecil Dawkins, implying a truth about Dawkins's Alabama by indirection. No place can be all bad in its persons, and certainly not as a place. For herself, speaking of her Middle Georgia place at Andalusia, she says, "It is great to be at home in a region, even this one." It is a "home" at her moment much ma- ligned by cultural condescensions out of Atlanta and New York, she knows, especially by provincialized intellectuals. After all, everybody has to be somewhere, and no place is ever an Eden recovered to any wandering or sedentary person by his manners good or bad. How ironic to the ears of an O'Connor then, that advertising slogan that Atlanta is a city "too busy to hate." "Taulkinham" indeed.

As for that condescension of one "culture" to another — of Atlanta or New York to rural Georgia out of sensibilities supposed the more refined — O'Connor evens the score some- what in making Atlanta her Taulkinham of *Wise Blood*. Haze Motes in that novel, in press- ing bad manners to the level of blasphemy, discovers that one can't blaspheme what doesn't exist, so that his very attempt at impious rejection becomes a proof of the existence of that which he attempts to deny as existing at all, in her words, that "ragged figure" in the "back of [Haze's] mind," Christ. That discovery leaves Haze's new-founded "Church without Christ" a shambles. He has attempted a blasphemous forcing of his intent by reducing the local to random insignificance, but that is not possible even when that local is the corrupted City of Man (Taulkinham), as both Flannery and St. Augustine might name it. There is something inherent in the local that bites Haze at the nexus of his intellect and will, in the arena of dramatic action: consciousness. That action calls attention to the spiritual impli- cations of the local, even as the local may be experienced in a Taulkinham née Atlanta, to- ward which community in its disarray Haze conducts himself with intellectual condescen- sion.

Not Flannery but Haze is that "hillbilly nihilist" she finds herself charged with being. As for her, believing as she does in the inclusive actuality of natural grace — which by its continuous action sustains the local — she believes as well in the actuality of the devil as an implicit agent encouraging intellectual man to a nihilistic rejection of the good that is in some degree evident in the actual. (Whatever is *actual, is* and therefore is *good*, Thomas re- minds us.) She dramatizes the contention of good and evil as joined by Haze's will, within the arena of Haze's soul. In her prefatory note to the reissue of the novel she reminds us that "For the author Haze's integrity lies in his not being able to ... get rid of the ragged figure who moves from tree to tree in the back of his mind," Christ. She realizes, observing the reception of *Wise Blood* on its first appearance, that the challenges to her are great, given the disparity of her vision and the contentment with spectacle with which her skeptical audience is happy — that audience largely ignorant of the possibilities of grace. For her, grace is always in contention with the devil within the arena of conscious intellect itself. That is the arena of the *signified,* the dramatic action toward which spectacle itself points, as Aristotle suggested long ago. Spectacle derived from context is required to mediate this intellectual action of a character between poet and audience — often the spectacle of violence and often (as she knew) a violence mistaken for the truly significant action of the intellectual soul itself, as opposed to symptomatic psychological spectacle. We are not simply intellectual soul, as Plato and old Socrates would have it. For O'Connor it is intellectual soul *incarnate,* to be perfected in a simple unity as *person,* which means the necessity of orderly accommodation of spectacle through participation in creation as incarnate soul. If Plato inclines to reject creation as a drag upon the spirit away from its possible perfection, especially creation as evidenced by our body, St. Thomas argues the body itself the special medium, a gift in our nature through which grace proves operative upon the intellectual soul through the senses. It is the senses that allow the person a bonding in the local with all creation. The rejection of that bonding is a denial of stewardship. Thus Adam fell, bequeathing a complicating violence — and O'Connor suggests that violence may either rescue or damn us consequent to Adam's fall, as Flannery's second novel announces in its title, *The Violent Bear It Away.* Here the *it* is the Kingdom of Heaven in a Biblical text from *Matthew.*

In her prefatory note to the reissue of that first novel, *Wise Blood,* she will affirm with confidence her own conviction of the reality of grace to nature, so that nature itself proves mediator (through our senses) to the uncertain will, raising in will a concern for prospects of rescue by perceived truth of things. Hers is a vision largely rejected by our world, the world in which she finds herself. Still she affirms her vision, as shocking as it may be to Modernist sensibilities: "[F]ree will does not mean one will," she says, "but many wills conflicting in one man. Freedom cannot be conceived simply. It is a mystery and one which a novel, even a comic novel, can only be asked to deepen." It is within the limited consciousness of *this* person as an actual intellectual soul incarnate that this dramatic tension of will occurs — the will responding to the devil on the one hand and yet sustained by grace on the other. In this respect for the action of drama, she as maker is Aristotelian, though hers is that Aristotle baptized by St. Thomas as it is sometimes said. *Spectacle*, Aristotle argues in his *Poetics,* must be distinguished from *action,* though it is with spectacle engaged by the means of our sensual nature that we may come to recognize action as an immaterial reality — the movement of the will immeasurable by any physics or biology. Action is spoken necessarily by indirection, then: through masks, through the dance, through all the intellectual "play" rising out of human nature to the level of spectacle through intellect as the summoning instrument to the soul. Intellect is itself an immaterial reality, spoken as a reality by that indirection called spectacle perceived through the body — acknowledged or denied through manners signaling manner. For Flannery O'Connor as dramatist, this proves a challenge which she must address long after that parenthesis of Western intellectual culture bracketed between Sophocles and Dante, that inheritance still spoken of as a "Classical Culture" once informing community. For that is a tradition long since rejected at the time she comes to write.

Art, up through Dante, was largely and more commonly understood in relation to this distinction between spectacle and action. O'Connor, however, must attempt to recover to her art some persuasive common ground suited to her dramatic intentions in order to reveal unexpected spiritual action through spectacle as commonly taken as if reality itself. The concrete, local — that which is immediate to the senses — has meanwhile itself been distorted through cultural circumstances of community gone awry through its separation of grace from nature. Community is itself disrupted from the reality of existential reality as actual in itself, as a communion of persons as a body. The challenge is that she must nevertheless use those cultural circumstances gone awry, the dislocation made evident through spectacle — a spectacle which suggests existence as randomly chaotic — whether made Nominalistically collective as "nature" or "person" or "community." She must work toward a recovery of spiritual action as the most significant responsibility to the person as he exists here and now in community and in nature at large. What she knows to be missing is any common understanding of the meaning of the cultural circumstances in relation to a vision which may be more or less held in common. The formal understanding possible in relation to myth, for instance — that myth held common between Sophocles and his audience — gave Sophocles a purchase in revealing action through stylized spectacle. But that common point of departure for art, binding poet and audience, no longer obtains.

Her response to this initial challenge lies in a comic enlargement, given that comic or tragic masks no longer signify any common intellectual consent of an audience to a dramatist. Nor could she, as could Dante, depend upon allegorical complexities of signs to the structuring of a story. O'Connor recognized such modern allegorical attempt as failing by degree in her favorite American writer, Hawthorne. She favors Hawthorne in that she shares with him a belief that man is fallen and that man by his fallen nature inclines to sinfulness. (I have explored this theme at length in my *Why Hawthorne Was Melancholy.*) She as a Catholic novelist "believes that you destroy your freedom by sin." But she also knows that "the modern reader believes ... that you gain it that way." How then make believable a gesture or action by a character that reveals his willful action as that of a self-diminution, though "read" as if its opposite — as if self-reduction were the means to absolute freedom? It must be, she says, signaled (signed) by an art in a gesture or action "which is totally right and totally unexpected" in the character. It must be at once "in character and beyond character," so that it may speak at an analogical level of a spiritual reality beyond any formal allegorical structuring of a story. To accomplish this is "to suggest both the world and eternity," that level at which occurs both "the Divine life and our participation in it." That is why she sees the concept of epiphany in relation to her fiction as quite other than as understood by James Joyce, a difference we shall presently explore under the auspices of St. Thomas.

It is to this end that she would be, as poet, a "prophet of distances," though that is an office usually unnoticed or aggressively rejected by her audience. That means for her the necessity of a "realism" more profoundly persuasive than the mere "naturalism" which is ordinarily understood as defining the usual country of the "serious" novelist. For her the very real spiritual country has been distorted by dogmatic naturalism, making art itself a documentation of a provincialism certified as psychological realism. By that certification, art becomes itself prohibitive boundary excluding any passport to the transcendent. And so hers must be a strategy as maker through which she may overcome in the reader his own provincial spirit as it flits randomly on the surface of spectacle in a deportment of intellect which allows the person to mistake spectacle as the only significant arena to "realistic" action. How telling then a coincidence of violence at both the level of spectacle and at the level of Mercy's terror when Tarwater at once drowns and baptizes Bishop in *The Violent Bear It Away.* And how puzzling to her audience.

We need only to this point recall the constant use of and so decay of the term *tragedy* as we hear it announcing random automobile wrecks on the highway, made the more "newsworthy" when there is a "pile-up." In "The Nature and Aim of Fiction" she attempts some recovery of a degree of common ground more than that of spectacle, of random "pile-ups." First is the necessity to recover the local as a point of departure in recovering viable community. She says that the "longer you look at one object, the more of the world you see in it; and it's well to remember that the serious fiction writer always writes about the whole world, no matter how limited his particular scene." We may thus come to remember that, in recovering the gift to our nature of seeing *through*, not *with*, the eye, we may yet come to seeing through our intellect as well as an "ensouled" creature. We may, this is to say, have moved somewhat toward a recovery of integrity as person, no longer more or less divided like Gaul into intellect, soul, body. In this respect, St. Thomas argues intellect *informed* by the truth of things experienced, his *informed* bearing a literal meaning. His argument suggests a deeper mystery to our experience than the level of the spectacle of things might lead us to conclude. And so in "The Fiction Writer and His Country" O'Connor enlarges: "To know oneself is to know one's region. It is also to know the world, and it is also, paradoxically, a form of exile from that world." How different a *person* is from an *object,* when the person as an integrity is recognized as intellectual soul incarnate. For, though a book cannot be at once on the table and off the table, in O'Connor's vision of him the person may well discover himself in two places at once — in the immediate here and now of *this* place as citizen of nature and local community; but within that same present place also beyond it, in a "country" discovered at last as permeating this very here and now. That is the abiding mystery within reality whereby grace and nature cohabit, so to speak, however much Modernist man has labored at that disjunction of grace from nature.

If she finds this truth about human nature explicated reasonably by St. Thomas' scholasticism, his is a rational witness to experience as she has already known it. Nevertheless, St. Thomas serves as prophetic philosopher companiable in his witness to that known mystery, lest it be forgotten. Flannery O'Connor knows this to be true by her experience of this place, a place to which her ecstatically romantic friend returns from Greenwich Village wanting to rescue her from a reality misunderstood as dead — as "provincial." Miss Flannery could but recognize a further witness to this reality, not in rational explication of experience such as that she reads in St. Thomas but as witnessed by a specific event in a distant time and country. Dame Julian of Norwich holds a hazel-nut on her open palm and — that small object seen *through* the eye in an openness of love — she discovers it to be held from collapsing into nothingness, even as she too is so held. She shares with that small thing in a suspension from nothingness — through *connaturality* St. Thomas would say. They are sustained in *being* by an all-sustaining Love.

In that suspense, in a moment of an epiphany, the person makes a discovery which Josef Pieper expresses in his small and marvelously cogent book *In Tune with the World: A Theory of Festivity*: *"To celebrate a festival means: to live out for some special occasion and in an uncommon manner, the universal assent to the world as a whole."* The epiphany in such a festive moment is to see the whole world present in a festive offering of that whole world through objects ceremonially raised. The offering may be only a hazel-nut on the open palm, or it may be bread and wine offered to transforming Love. Such an epiphany is most often private, in contrast to communal festivity. In such a private moment, through the eye and through the object, the person discovers the "world as a whole," in Tate's phrase. In

Pieper's phrasing, this is to discover that "Existence [*all* of the *world*] as we know it … does not just 'adjoin' the realm of Eternity; it is entirely permeated by it." That is the experience of mystery Flannery O'Connor has in mind when she says that the longer we look at an object, the more of the world we see in it. It is a recognition that comes early for Flannery O'Connor and continues with her, evident to her always in things themselves. When such things are borrowed to the task of incarnating her fiction, they thereby bear with them an interior light of grace within her made story.

Through that recognition she sees that as an intellectual creature whose peculiar gift calls her to the making of fictions, hers becomes a demanding responsibility to that gift that allows little leisure for any self-satisfaction grading into pride such as so often tempts the artist, either as presumptuous creator (as opposed to maker) or as intentional savior of mankind by his art. Hers is a vocation, a calling, so that she reminds us (and herself) in her "Catholic Novelists and Their Readers": "Vocation is a limiting factor, and the conscientious novelist works at the limits of his power and within what his imagination can apprehend. He does not decide what would be good for the Catholic body and proceed to deliver it." Or if he attempts to do so, he is likely to end up writing what she calls on another occasion that "depressing new category" of fiction, "light Catholic summer reading." Or he may end up writing ideological tract, presuming his own godhead. Not that she fails to see that even bad art may serve God's good ends, for "God can make an indifferent thing, as well as evil itself, an instrument for good." To do this, however, "is the business of God and not of the human being." Such is the mystery of evil's dependence upon and eventual service to the good, but it is to be accomplished only through God's intentionality — that is, by grace, not by the artist in assuming power as if creator.

Meanwhile, as Thomas says (*Summa Contra Gentiles,* Book III, Ch. 11), "Moral evil is based on the good rooted in human nature," in contrast to that seeming evil that "springs from the nature" of a thing in itself, a deprivation of the thing's formal actuality such as a blindness of the eye as organ, as opposed to that willed blindness of the eye in denials that human nature is fallen in this person and needing that rescue which grace alone can accomplish. But for her, that is action beyond the story, a mystery which art can only deepen. Note Flannery O'Connor's response to the question of whether being crippled affected her writing: no, she says, since she writes with her head, not her feet. It is in her recognition of this distinction between the evil possible through willfulness and the evil that "springs from the nature" of things —fires or lions, storms or serpents. Or lupus, that old secret wolf in nature. Hence she will (with what one is tempted to call ironic mischief) adapt even poor art as suited to the effecting of grace, using that poor art, made poorly in a context of moral evil. She will use it as matter to her own better art. Thus that complex reality of moral evil and bad art, accomplishing in the actions of her story a rescuing action of grace to Mr. Head and Nelson in "The Artificial Nigger." The action comes through that decaying kitsch statue of that "artificial nigger" in that famous story.

Such, then, is the unwavering presence to her of Revelation, which makes her declare that (as she wrote to "A") "the present reality is the Incarnation." That is the abiding mystery, an abiding Presence she encounters when she looks long and deeply into the reality of any actual thing perceived through her incarnate nature. Hence that remark that "the longer you look at one object, the more of the world you see in it," by which seeing one comes "to know" himself. And that, she also says, proves paradoxical in that it proves as well "a form of exile from the world," in that in the world one journeys toward his proper end. She, as does Dame

Julian of Norwich, sees that without that Presence the thing she looks at long and hard would fall to nothingness. It cannot be rescued solely by her own desire that it not fall to nothingness. She is relieved by that certainty, a certainty to which one must return through things themselves along the way, since certainty is not unwavering in fallible human intellect as besieged by the fallen will. Not even the saint always avoids the nagging intrusion of doubt, however intent upon certainty. For the saint is first of all a person, and as person fallen. Even St. Augustine prays fervently, as has St. Peter before him after that experience of denial of Christ: "I believe. Help thou my unbelief." That is an Augustinian moment of a contingency in the will to believe — and so of wills in conflict within one person. Perhaps it is conflict more continuous for Walker Percy than for Flannery O'Connor as persons. But for both, that is the arena to the centering action underlying the level of spectacle in their fictions — their *made* things as necessarily dependent upon givens.

2

In Company with Good Country People

"St. Thomas called art 'reason in making.' This is a very cold and very beautiful definition, and if it is unpopular today, this is because reason has lost ground among us. As grace and nature have been separated, so imagination and reason have been separated, and this always means an end to art."

— Flannery O'Connor, "The Nature
and Aim of Fiction"

Perhaps the steady certainty of faith held by O'Connor proves a more considerable challenge to her as writer than might be true were she more wavering as writer. Uncertainty energizes the desire for certainty, and when one's calling as *homo viator,* "on the way," is that of a maker of stories, the dramatic contingencies in uncertainty are more immediate to that maker of a story. Dostoevsky discovers as much in attempting to write the "story" of a perfectly good man, whose analogue is Christ. Flannery O'Connor from the beginning recognizes that it is the "Christ-haunted" who prove more persuasive as characters, none perfect because all are sinners. Her "Christ-haunted," while kin to her in their common nature as sinners, are not kin to her in the degree of spiritual perfection of belief, for she is resolutely Christ-centered. Dostoevsky remarks Don Quixote as the closest fictional attempt yet upon making a good man, Cervantes in that concern finding it necessary to resort to the satirically comic — to an exaggeration which we recognize as "grotesque," though without the dark implications of the grotesque which Dostoevsky found he must deal with in making his "Idiot," Prince Myshkin.

Concerning this challenge, Dostoevsky says: "The chief idea of the novel [*The Idiot*] is to portray the positively good man. There is nothing in the world more difficult to do, and especially now [in the 1860s when Nihilism is setting fathers against sons in Russia]. All writers ... who have tried to portray the positively good man have always failed.... The good is an ideal, but this ideal, both ours and that of civilized Europe, is still far from having been worked out. There is only one positively good man in the world — Christ." Certainly a good man is hard to find as fictional protagonist, though Mark Twain as Dostoevsky's contemporary, more brash as nonbeliever than Dostoevsky as believer, may be said to attempt a fictional shortcut by arresting an adolescent, Huck Finn. Twain will attempt it once more in his version of Joan of Arc, another arrested adolescent doomed by the world, before Twain himself turns to those dark works of his old age such as *The Man Who Corrupted Hadleyburg, The Mysterious Stranger* (Twain's invocation of the Devil as it were) and that work of his spiritual nadir, *What Is Man?*

And so for Flannery O'Connor believing in one good man — that is, believing that Jesus is the Son of the Living God — attempts a dramatic representation of man as fallen, who because fallen continues haunted by that Son of the Living God. She finds herself living in an age which not only rejects Christ, but which finds its intellectual comfort in declaring Jesus to be as dead (if he ever existed) as any man. It is an age which further declares that God Himself is dead. That is a conclusion intellectually elevated in the gradual rejection of the older intellectual tradition maintained at its height by St. Thomas Aquinas. It is St. Thomas' vision of man in his fallen state that O'Connor accepts and maintains as a time-less understanding of human nature itself, so that she is not drawn toward repeating Dos-toevsky's impossible attempt to dramatize a "positively good man," knowing how hard it is to find and hold to the one good man. The challenge that faces her as fictional dramatist, indeed, is to recover a recognition of man as conflicted by good and evil in a world which now assumes itself beyond both good and evil. It is an attempt she makes out of her faith, and at risk as artist she makes it within the intellectual arena of non-believers.

In such confines, the common belief is that God is dead. It is that principle which has been evolved by an intellectual rationalism confident of autonomy, and that is her point of departure as fiction writer. Her characters reflect this highly sophisticated self-confident con-clusion about the nature of man as but an accident in an accidental cosmos. She engages that presumption at a very local level, in unlettered protagonists as native to Middle Geor-gia's rural culture. An aspect of her wit and humor lies in showing this Modernist malady as having seeped down into such a removed cultural milieux, after having been distilled from nature intellectually by removing nature from grace through process, over several hundred years of imprudent intellectual action. Alas, many of the West's best minds in philosophy and then in science have labored in distortion of reality to a self-interest. And from that labor has followed spiritual erosion, the "Western" disease rejected by Dostoevsky, and by Tolstoy, though Tolstoy's response lies in a Manichaean rejection of both nature and grace.

The Russians sound alarm a hundred years before O'Connor comes to engage that spir-itual disease as the challenge to her making of fictions, complications to her art complex at both the philosophical and the naturalistic surfaces of reality as advanced by Modernist phi-losophy and science. She engages the cultural matrix at the local, as she experiences the local as native Georgian in the mid–20th century. The particularities of the cultural and histor-ical "local" seem at once (in any critical presumption from a distance) as limiting her to a provincialism — in the popular pejorative sense of *provincialism.* For such a grounding of art, most especially of dramatic art, could hardly seem promising of "intellectual" substance that could speak the universal. Hers must then be a somewhat sophisticated genre of "local color," its literary antecedent such works as those of Augustus Baldwin Longstreet's *Geor-gia Scenes,* though with an art sophisticated beyond Longstreet's crudeness.

How odd, then, that she should think of herself as a Thomist. For in such limited cul-tural *matter* as her fictional matrix, she could at most expect to be a satiric local colorist. Nietzsche may prove impressive in arguing the death of God, fascinating to an H. L. Mencken, who pronounces the South the Sahara of the Beaux Arts out of his Nietzschean faith. How, then, such a semi-literate son of a Georgia sharecropper as protagonist, drift-ing Georgia backroads on his way to that shining city, Atlanta (christened "Taulkinham" in *Wise Blood*)? How comes a Haze Motes to such self-elevation as autonomous rationalist? The nihilism attributed to Haze Motes must therefore speak a nihilism in his more sophisticated maker, Flannery O'Connor, who has the advantage over her Haze of having sojourned to

Iowa to a Creative Writing school and then spending some time in New York and Connecticut. Such, an early critical conclusion.

What Flannery O'Connor is certain of, however, out of her faith as reasonably expounded by Thomas Aquinas, is that as intellectual creature man must act intellectually by
nature in his response to experiences, in an immediacy to existential reality here and now.
He does so, and can no other, since he is by nature an intellectual creature existing as such
as *incarnate,* as embodied, however limited may be his knowledge of the cosmos adjacent
to his local response, his manifestation as a person in an immediacy of intellectual action.
As person, he responds as this *particular* person, as an intellectual soul incarnate, though in
being *particular* he must differ by degree in his intellectual gift from other persons. As particular person, he can exist only by virtue of the limits of his peculiar given nature as *this*
person. But as such, he must also act intellectually.

It is within the limits of his givenness that he acts, his peculiar gifts limiting him and
defining as well the arena within which he acts toward the good or away from the good.
O'Connor, believing this true of each person as person, sees the *possible* intellectual actions
suited to fictional drama as not requiring of the protagonist that he be a Nietzsche or a
Socrates. Indeed, within the enveloping intellectual history of the West, she will recognize
and with some mischief suggest dramatically, that one need not be highly trained as intellectual in order to commit errors of intellectual action, most especially that action whose
proper name is "sin." Ph.D. or illiterate countryman share in such failure as persons. She
believes, for instance, that the governing sin of all sins is Pride, an intellectual failure to seek
the good in a reductionist prudential interest in the self. For by willfulness, a person
may become obsessed with a self-love. That is the high theme of Dante's *Divine Comedy,*
whose matter is not available to her in the state it was for Dante to his dramatic making.
Dante's cultural milieux, Florence, perhaps approximates Dostoevsky's Skotoprigonyevsky,
the "town" setting of *The Brothers Karamazov,* which approximates in turn O'Connor's
Milledgeville and its environs — the point being that all such towns are inhabited by
persons. What Dante and Dostoevsky and O'Connor recognize is the inclination in man
to fall from vision, though enabled by his own nature to respond to the proximate
reality of "nature." If that was an understanding more general to community in Dante's
day, it has become considerably diminished by the time of Dostoevsky and O'Connor,
by which time *homo viator* — man on his way — discovers himself increasingly lost in the
cosmos.

If O'Connor's eye and ear are acutely attuned to the local whereby she sees the actual,
that but further confirms her own visionary certainty about man and his nature in any place
at any time. She is also very widely read in the intellectual history of the West, of course,
particularly that since the Renaissance. Her mentors are diversely present on her book
shelves, some heavily marked as she reads them. What she recognizes, concerning her own
age, is that it is an age intellectually governed by convenience to each person, according to
the growing pursuit by intellect of intellectual and bodily comforts, inclined to set aside response to the mystery of man's nature and of the nature of creation itself. She marks a passage in St. Thomas' *Summa Theologica* that proves central to her conclusion (I, q. 14, a. 8,
Reply Objection 3):

> Natural things are midway between the knowledge of God and our knowledge: for we receive
> knowledge from natural things, of which God is the cause by His Knowledge. Hence, just as
> the natural things that can be known by us are prior to our knowledge, and are its measure, so

the knowledge of God [whereby those things *are*] is prior to them, and is their measure; as, for instance, a house is midway between the knowledge of the builder who made it, and the knowledge of the one who gathers his knowledge of the house from the house already built.

That is a passage alerting her to her proper intellectual relation to things, here and now, as experienced in Baldwin County, Georgia. The complex of "natural things that can be known by us" as builders, as makers, requires a "reason in making" in order that we accommodate to our limited gifts of making as dependent upon realities antecedent to our desire to make. Thus alerted, she finds the local helpful to her dramatic making.

She also recognizes an analogy between herself as *maker* to God as *creator,* concepts speaking similarity but speaking as well an insurmountable distinction between man's Creator and man himself as maker, the reality of proportionality addressed by St. Thomas. (See Appendix C.) She is, she believes, created in the image of God, and so therefore limited as maker. It could but be presumptuous to suppose herself "creator" of anything. It is the "prior" reality that reminds her of this distinction, reminding her as well that as maker her "matter" pre-exists her making. Always, there is created nature antecedent to making things as mediator of her relation to the Cause of that given matter to her making upon which all making depends. And especially one antecedent "matter": her own limited gifts as inherently limiting because she exists by the grace of givenness as *this* person and no other. Form, to be derived from creation to the making of a story, is possible only as consequent to the world of "natural things" *informed* by Love and therefore actual, despite recent Cartesian confusions. Hence she comes upon that major error in Modernism, whereby the Modernist man would establish to his convenience, by a distorted intellectual action, a world of his own "creation." That is, he would separate (as she says often) "grace from nature" to the convenience he intends, as if thereby becoming creator. In doing so, he would become the Lord of all nature, which requires his denial of the Lord as antecedent to Nature itself, as "prior" to things. The Modernist, however, declares God dead in the interest of his own intellectual autonomy over nature, his own "knowledge" usurping the antecedent knowledge of God whereby (Thomas argues) he *is.* The delusion thus derived is that of his own absolute freedom as a particular intellectual creature self-created, effected through presumption of his own absolute autonomy. Thus in the convenience of a false freedom, man may believe himself his own cause.

If such is the Modernist end, out of an intellectual revolt formalized in philosophy and science through several centuries, it does not require of the autonomous intellectual creature that he be intimately knowledgeable of the long history of that decline. (We are calling this decline Modernism, a concept I have explored as emerging since the Renaissance in my "Modern, Modernism and Modernists," *The Truth of Things,* 1999.) The Modernist intellectual action is toward self-salvation, a self-love, justified as an autonomous freedom, and that deportment toward creation may be witnessed in more local than merely abstract academic displays at the local college or state university. O'Connor's Bible salesman, for instance (in "Good Country People") insists that he was born believing in nothing. That principle becomes his passport to an autonomous freedom self-conferred, in contrast to his victim Hulga's attempt to gain that passport through her "formal" academic training. And so O'Connor's fictional characters, unlettered though they may be, prove to be acting intellectually, though not necessarily persons called "intellectuals." They share our common nature, whatever the variety of their worldly circumstances, for each is an intellectual soul incarnate. Mr. Shiftlet of "The Life You Save May Be Your Own" or Mr. Head of "The

Artificial Nigger" may seem only comic as "intellectuals," but they act according to our common fallen human nature as not yet rescued, though seemingly absorbed by petty local concerns as seen by liberated "intellectuals." What they reveal in the spectacles of their actions is a commonality with more celebrated "intellectuals" who seem persuasively rationalistic in an intent to use creation to autonomous convenience. If there is a difference in magnitude between Shiftlet's deviousness in possessing Mrs. Lucynelle Crater's derelict automobile and the Enron executive's bilking thousands of their savings, magnitude does not obscure (at least for Flannery O'Connor) the common destructiveness to the soul of a Shiftlet or to the soul of the Enron executive. For the petty tyrant or the tyrant of magnitude are still tyrants.

It becomes of some importance to the reading of O'Connor's fictions to make such distinctions, especially given that they affect us very much as she dramatizes them while at the same time puzzling us. That we are puzzled, we may tentatively suggest for exploration, is because they remind us of known but forgotten things about ourselves as intellectual souls incarnate — things set aside through careless concerns for "personal" convenience in refusing intellectual responsibility out of our experiences of the things of nature. In this respect, we discover ourselves largely Modernists, and may in the end be somewhat shocked to find that O'Connor is aiming with her devilish wit at us as such — almost as if she is called as maker to the task of disturbing us. In her letters, she observes that Nihilism is an intellectual infection we breathe every day, though hope is not therefore denied to us. She writes a correspondent (Ben Griffith, March 3, 1954), defending her protagonist Haze Motes of *Wise Blood*. It is a novel "that no one but a Catholic could have written," she says, in that it is "entirely Redemption-centered in thought." It is difficult to see this for most readers, perhaps "because H. Motes is such an admirable nihilist." And to her editor Elizabeth McKee she writes (June 29, 1955): "Of course, I think of Haze Motes as a kind of saint. His overwhelming virtue is integrity," which virtue in her view brings Haze at last into a Presence against which he has resisted his calling as a prophet of redemption.[1]

As for the nature of this Modernist deportment, we all breathe it daily she says, though few of us reveal Haze's virtue of integrity. For us as Modernists, we find convenience preferable to integrity, justified in a sentimental conclusion that we are pretty much our own cause, victim or conqueror of mechanistic nature. As conqueror, we prove worthy of whatever convenience possible. By a will unwavering, the Modernist concludes himself to be already what he wishes to be, possessing a freedom absolute by intention, since we can be "whatever we want to be," the shibboleth taught our young. Thus a "learned" response through intellectual sentimentality. But as response it is necessary to declare an absence of grace from our given nature as *this* person, except the false grace of intentionality may be supplied by him. How much more comfortable to abandon integrity of intellect to the assumption that existence is but a random "materialism," accidental in origin. Thus occurs an intellectual problem which leaves the Modernist haunted though he is uncertain of what it is that haunts him. And thus the Modernist dilemma. By "intellectual" conclusion, the Modernist must account himself as also but a random accident of random materialism. That is a disturbing conclusion to be shied away from. He must deny all *givenness,* even accident itself as a given. For to admit as prior certain "givens" he will but the more intensify the haunting question of a Giver. How *convenient* a principle nevertheless: to deny any cause antecedent to my own present actions of freedom — myself thus made absolutely free. And still the haunting ambiguity in the confusing contradiction of "freedom" out of a nothingness, a "self" declared into being by his own intentional will — wherever that *free will* comes from. Such is the intellectual morass of Modernist thought which does not require of the thinker any sophisticated vocabulary or a rationalized system to persuade him that his confusion is beyond repair by finite intellectual system. It is a present possibility to any person, lettered or unlettered, the dead end at which Haze Motes arrives. Such is the world Flannery O'Connor makes *material* to her *actions* as a maker of a fiction, anchored in her local middle Georgia culture.

In so anchoring those fictions in the concrete world immediate to her, she reveals her protagonists as disturbed — "haunted" — by the logical conclusion from such a "processing" of the self as person. How unsettling, the *intuitive* (if not rational) recognition that each person *depends* necessarily upon what is purported by "sophisticated" intellectuals as uncaused accidental "realities." As for mind itself, the latest science insists on its ultimate authority in the measure of man, especially measure by psychological system derived from this uncaused accident man. It is by random selectivity that this present psychologically disturbed person seems at least made to exist, an accident. Advanced biochemical formulations when rationalized in support of psychological phenomena, however, hardly seem to resolve random social accidents by the imposition of systems. Such has been the attempt, as the Misfit sees it, in "explaining" him to himself in "A Good Man Is Hard to Find." The story echoes new sciences as intrusively applied by formulations of social behavior over the past hundred years. The Misfit has been assured by the experts of several social and political sciences that he is not responsible for the terrible acts he commits. He must free himself of "guilt," since there is no such reality as sin. Such experts, we reflect, must maintain their own intellectual freedom by a transcendent remove from the materialistic swamps in which the hapless victim they would rescue flounders. They must speak from a point of dry ground decreed a safe remove from the swamp. By faith in the certainties of their science, they as experts maintain (if but for a moment) the transcendentalism of an angelism — removed to a tentative safety by means of the abstractionism that fuels their angelism. A radical and formidable "matter" to deal with in art, then — from O'Connor's orthodox perspective — this pseudo-mystical version of human nature as intended to self-apotheosis beyond good and evil.

Among her challenges as a writer of stories — given her perspective on this intellectual "matter" to her making — are the repeated questions about what she intends as a "Catholic" to "prove" by her fictions, as if moral rectitude were the implicit necessity to the artist as Catholic, a consequence of Catholicism as but one "system" among many. She will respond on occasion with some irritation, but it is with a controlled impatience that she writes Cecil Dawkins regarding that question so often put to her. "It's not a matter in these stories of Do Unto Others," a matter to be found "in any ethical culture series." Instead, her concern is for "the fact of the Word made flesh," a fact for her which she would make a haunting challenge, a "Christ-haunting" challenge in one of her formulations. "As the Misfit said, 'He thrown [the story puts it *thown*] everything off balance and it's nothing for you to do but follow Him or find some meanness.'" By her faith she finds herself allowed a certain detachment as artist, but it is not an indifference to man in his pilgrim plight. She is herself always aware that hers is a detachment as artist, not as an angelistic agent imposing order upon community.

There is in consequence not only a mischievous wit at work in her art out of this partial detachment, but a humor as well. It is in respect to humor that we may discover it a counter to other and more resolute detachments of wit as unleavened by humor. The humor signals an acceptance by Flannery O'Connor of her own condition as fallen person, a condition shared with all humanity. It is in this respect, then, that we find a difference between her as artist and James Joyce or the younger T. S. Eliot, for whom ironic wit serves as a protection of the person of the artist against too close an association with the world, a concern Eliot engages in arguing that the poet must be "impersonal" in his making. (Eliot comes to a quite different judgment of his personal relation to his calling as poet following his later spiritual crises that leads to his conversion.) The answer to the dilemma of uncertainty about finite gnosis as absolute resides in the moral responsibility of the particular person himself to himself in response to the circumstances of his journeying, whereby he is tensionally moved to the good on the one hand and on the other tempted to "meanness" in its various guises of self-centeredness. But even that intention, as St. Thomas argues, proves an intention to the good. It is an intention confounded nevertheless in that it is a willful election of a lesser over a greater good, self-love over love of God. (We are obligated by our nature as *given* to love ourself proportionally that we may love our neighbor and creation proportionately toward the greater love of God.) As artist sharing this tensional reality as a person, O'Connor insists, that does not mean that she as poet bears a responsibility requiring her to make an "ethical cultural" message her primary concern. Art's responsibility is not to teach "Do Unto Others." It is in witness of the truth of things, primarily the truth of *possible* actions out of human nature, that she makes stories.

Such is the intellectual context within which St. Thomas makes a companionable and confirming witness to her situation as maker. Reason becomes important as guide on her way. Thomas says for instance (*Summa Theologica*, I-II, q. 57. a. 3) that "Art is nothing else but *the right reason about certain works to be made*" (his emphasis). It is also through reason that the person has come to understand himself as artist, though he may have known that calling intuitively already. It is through knowledge confirmed by reason that he comes upon that mystery of mysteries: his participation in existence in which both himself and the world are *givens*. Most discomforting to his convenience: the *obligations* attending that givenness. By knowing the object immediate to intellect, through the senses — whether a hazel-nut on the open palm if a Dame Julian in a vision or (if one is Flannery O'Connor) a peacock's proud and beautiful display made by such a pea-brained creature. By that knowing, the poet as person recognizes the whole of creation as permeated by and sustained by that grace called Love, whose continuous act of Love is spoken in the givenness called creation. That is the theme engaged by Flannery in her essay "The King of the Birds." In that essay, she reports with delight having been visited at Andalusia "at least once a year by first-grade school-children," adding a satiric note on the "educationism" she sees as suffocating the children intellectually. They have been brought to the "farm" no doubt to "learn by living" she says.[2] She and the children are delighted by a sudden surprise, no surprise to her. "I am used to hearing this group chorus as the peacock swings round [its tail magnificently erect], 'Oh, look at his underwear!' This 'underwear' is a stiff gray tail, raised to support the larger one, and beneath it a puff of black feathers that would be suited for some really regal woman — a Cleopatra or a Clytemnestra — to use to powder her nose."

That is the children's response to the peacock's backside which they "learn by living," startling to them perhaps more than the splendor of the display of the spread tail as seen from the front since it is somehow secretly closer to them as its "underwear." The discovery seems an unexpected return to common reality. No doubt they themselves came to

Andalusia with clean underwear, demanded by fussy mothers for such a "field trip." Who knows when they might have an accident on the highway? No doubt as well that they might cause some teachers discomfort, at least long ago in the 1950s, exclaiming about the peacock's "underwear." Our progress since then has been such, however, through movies and TV and rap-songs aimed at grammar school sensibilities, that no such difficulty would now attend. One wonders as well how many field trips to Andalusia are now likely, a moot question — for high-schoolers are being taught that her fiction is "politically incorrect," if it is taught at all save by a rebel mind here or there. Then — in the 1950s — O'Connor recognized the children to be responding at some depth to the *being* of this particular creature, a depth which speaks more, or hints at more, than the spectacle of its strutting display, though they lack sophisticated ways of naming what they have suddenly seen and respond to as poets by metaphor. Theirs has been an epiphany for them not yet intellectually digested. Such a poet as Flannery could but be delighted at such a moment of the children's recognition, though they can only speak as incipient poets of the gathering mystery to them as intellectuals, signaled by the peacock's "underwear." They are on the verge of a mystery deeper than Freudian exposition can account for, moved intellectually out of response to the spectacle of the peacock but moved closer by an intuitive response to the *essence* of this thing. So moved, although such a *concept* as *essence* — necessary to reason's metaphysics out of such physics — lies yet before them on their intellectual way. What O'Connor — and St. Thomas — would say is that such truth is known from experience long before reason accommodates to it through concepts ordered.

Flannery knows that these children are most likely to be corrupted along their way by a social world which dwells on spectacle at the expense of essence, the hidden "underwear" of reality. Perhaps there is even a future Misfit among them, a prophet who may go right or wrong. But they live in a world which itself has become unable to distinguish between what Thomas calls *accidents* as certain because born of *essence*, as distinct from accidents of *randomness* in the spectacle of a confluence of natural things. Such certain accidents are *inherent* to the *essence* — to the essential *givenness* of *this* thing as it now exists discretely. Those accidents signal to us as *particularities* this thing. And those inherent accidents are made manifest to us through our senses, known as peculiar to *this* thing in itself. It is through such accidents that we respond with gifts discretely peculiar to man himself. We respond initially through our perception of that which is other than our self — knowing its *otherness* intellectually before we know its name.

Accident as mere randomness is quite other: those effects of the confluence of things within that arena to things which we come to speak of long after the experience as within the "time-space continuum." Random accident, not always innocent of the *inherent* accidents of the essences of things as encountered in confluence at the level of spectacle signaled through our senses, nevertheless speak a deeper mystery as *essential* accidents, requiring reason's sorting of *accident*. In such experiences resonates yet unnamed depths unaccounted for by randomness, requiring that sorting. Nevertheless randomness has taken intellectual precedence since the Renaissance, particularly in Western thought, as if the sum total of randomness were the whole of reality. And it is through this distortion of the *inherent*, by the *random* as if absolutely determinate of reality in full, that *spectacle* has come to replace *essence* in our thought, eventually leading to illusions that spectacle is itself the cause of even any vaguely recognized inherent accidents.[3] Indeed, that is the necessary principle to any Darwinian "progress." That is as well the culminating conclusion advanced by Sartrean Ex-

istentialism, in displacing the Creator with the "accidentally manifest" person as empowered over nature by intentional consciousness. *Myself* as autonomous may through my intentionality as an action cause my own being.

Such encounter with a peacock's underwear may leave the hapless child in precarious
intellectual circumstances. One evident likelihood: Most of them, alas, are not likely ever
to distinguish *tragedy* from *random accident* on the highway, or to discover and hold to any
metaphysical possibilities attending true tragedy when they encounter it — as encounter it
they must as fallen man. The pervasiveness of the "educationism" O'Connor remarks in the
phrase "learning by living," the naively present principle all along their way from kinder-
garten, rises to its high point in that safety slogan she makes the title of a story: "The Life
You Save May Be Your Own." In the story an automobile *figures* (in the poetically technical sense) somewhat as Hulga's wooden leg figures in "Good Country People." In both stories there is a comic address to the prospects of a spiritual tragedy, so that the humor in the
story-telling manner as O'Connor deploys it is both humorous but by implication also *comic*
in Dante's sense of that term as applied to his great epic: a possible progress from misery to
bliss.

Dante could, we have said, in his *Paradiso* address the possibility of bliss more directly
than can she, so that she must address our rescue through grace as only a *possibility*, leaving her protagonists suspended as it were between Hell and Purgatory. She is careful to avoid
the judgmental, never confining her hero either to Hell nor giving him a release into Paradise, knowing as she does that, with our sense of evil "diluted or lacking altogether," we
want either our "senses tormented … or spirits raised." We desire to "be transported, instantly, either to mock damnation or a mock innocence." (The words are from her early address to "Some Aspects of the Grotesque in Southern Fiction.") Such are high concerns for
her, she no doubt aware of a sense of the obligation of adults to "suffer the little children."
Listening to those children exclaim over the peacock's underwear, she must fear for them
that they will become only the more "conditioned" through an inherent diabolism easily
buried in such words as "learning by living." In the confluence of things which they encounter, they are likely to become less and less able to recognize each thing to be the thing
it is by the grace of givenness to each of them. Theirs are potentials to their own limited
perfection, the gift freely given by Love whereby each is the person he is. They *are*, but not
by accident as if accounted for by pure Kantian concept. Yet in our world, random accident
has become the only tragedy admissible through the intellectual distortions of reality by
philosophical angelisms. Those are distortions appropriated to Positivistic science increasingly since the Renaissance. The end becomes the safety of the literal biological *body,* to be
protected from random accident as the primary salvation possible to man. And so for those
first-graders (O'Connor as poet must anticipate) there is unlikely prospect that they ever
understand either the *tragedy* or the *comedy* implicit in the mystery of creation. Nor are they
likely to understand random accident for that matter. Lacking understanding potential to
their intellectual nature, random accident can but haunt them as a dark evil, tempting to
some magic as its solution.

She (and Thomas) understand as consequent to our fallenness the likelihood of our increasingly willful refusal of rescue such as that she dramatizes in Haze Motes. Meanwhile,
those first-graders may be taught that to "learn by living" attaches only to spectacle — even
to that of a Clytemnestra or Oedipus — should they by accident be formally taught Greek
tragedy in current academic manner. They will likely miss the significant action underlying

spectacle: the supporting "underwear" to the illusion of self-love called pride, in which self-autonomy occasions wills at war in intellect. For each, willy-nilly, makes his way as *this* person. This is to speak once more of the intellectual arena within which any significant action occurs, a point made by Aristotle in his *Poetics* concerning drama, but a reality to our actual natures as intellectual souls incarnate — a reality to be experienced at any moment of our actual journeying. Here occurs that tension when the will is drawn between the good and (to borrow once more O'Connor's Misfit to the point) "meanness." Or, in Thomas' distinction, between inclination to lesser over greater good. It is the arena within which virtues are properly operative in removing obstacles to grace, as St. Thomas also argues. Those children, given the pervasiveness of Modernist thought in our culture, are more likely to be taught that virtue lies in their brushing their teeth twice a day and seeing a certified dentist twice a year. They will be taught the virtue of "buckling up," of not "driving while drinking," the principle reason being that the life they save may be their own.

It is the Misfit's recognition of this pervasive deflection of virtue from the necessities of the intellectual soul, through Modernist doctrine institutionalized, that makes him cling to his violent excess. For he finds himself reduced as *person,* though he cannot name this symptom in his "social" malady. He has been reduced by a denial of the reality of evil itself. He responds reasonably then to the Grandmother's mouthing of false shibboleths as she attempts to dodge the inevitable and (in the story) an actual bullet. She insists he is "a good man," that he must "come from nice people." Society has "made a mistake," especially that "head-doctor" who "institutionalized" the Misfit, though the Misfit acknowledges that they had the "papers" on him. The Misfit intuitively knows that explaining away evil, asserting as the only good a social accommodation to the positive "letter" of the law, has somehow been a violation of his person. Here, as in several stories, O'Connor plays the civil, secular "courthouse" law against sacramental incorporations of law. She does so in our moment as insistently as St. Paul might. For ours has become increasingly a law reduced to the positive as convenient to moral neutrality, an inevitable effect when grace has been denied to nature — when both God and the Devil are therefore declared out of existence. The Misfit at least has his "meanness" left, seemingly all that is left to him as *person.*

There is, in the midst of our dislocated age, an accompanying and paradoxical sense of exile which O'Connor speaks of as her own experience from time to time. It accompanies an epiphany in which a person may see the mystery of the whole world spoken by the single object when that object is looked at long and hard in an openness of love, whether in a moment as long ago as Dame Julian's hazel-nut on her palm or O'Connor's posturing peacock always underfoot at Andalusia. That is a mystery to be contemplated with an accompanying light of reason, in response to the grace of such recognition. Such is the experience to which she gives a dark and comic side in her Misfit. Unlike the Misfit — by nature meant to be a prophet she suggests — she herself understands her own sense of exile as requiring of her not a "meanness" (though she is sometimes given to mischief), but an ordinate response to the local in its variousness — the manifestations of things local and immediate to her experiences. It is always within the local that we discover a discomforting sense of aloneness, of somehow being in exile, despite being also comforted by the known local through which we come to know ourselves as persons. One may have a sense of exile, then, even when circumstances seem to speak us most at home. Or alternately, that sense of homelessness may be exacerbated by our being some place other than at our nominal home. But that, too, is still an experience in *some place* which as *place* intensifies the mystery of homesickness. Not even being "at home" resolves spiritual and intellectual discomfort insofar as the pilgrim does not recognize the home he desires. Such, we may speculate from long reading of O'Connor, must have been her own experiences at the University of Iowa Writers School or at that writers colony at Yaddo, and even in residence with her life-long friends the Fitzgeralds in Connecticut before coming home with the burden of her lupus. Only as she is recovered to an understanding at Andalusia could she experience that joy (as opposed to happiness) implicit in her sense of exile as *homo viator*.

Here, too, is further mystery to be engaged: that inescapable mystery of myself as person in desiring an accommodation to the local (wherever that local) through a proportionate — an ordinate — love of *this* place as I may know it here and now. What is to be desired is an escape from that radical resolution of the mystery about which O'Connor speaks from time to time — a possessive clutching of *these* things in *this* place. Her term for one radical resolution of the dilemma of homelessness in the world is *Manichaeanism*, a failure of love manifesting itself in two ways that are seemingly distinct but essentially (in relation to our peculiar *essence* as *this person* willfully inclined) the same. The one is of ancient notoriety. It embraces its own exile of the self as a disembodied ideal, rather than clasping things here and now as seemingly the only alternative. In the end comes the resolution to reject all creation as evil. In its extremity of rejection, it may even embrace actual suicide, destroying those "inherent accidents of essence" as localized in the body itself. Thus an illusion allows the rejection of the person's *incarnate* nature as if the body were a foreign antagonist. Such a rejection may range from a vague uneasiness in this world, through formal asceticism, to actual suicide in studied deprecations of the body. Indeed, a species of this perversion in a secular mode fuels a very large industry conspicuous to all — those dietary concerns whose object becomes the perfection of the body itself as a thing self-consciously possessed as a detached thing. (See the cosmetic ads on the evening news, and dietary ads as well.) That is an alternative to that more ancient species of Manichaeanism, the rejection of (rather than the perfection of) the body in the name of spiritual perfection. On either hand, the distortion is in rejection of a proportionate relation within the discrete gift to *this* person as a specific and integral creature — an intellectual soul incarnate. Anciently, the casting of the body into outer darkness, presently the elevation of the body as our ultimate good. These "two ways" of distortion of the "material" givenness of person reveal the perversion Dante speaks of as self-love. But the consequence of self-love on either hand proves to be self-destruction, in that the action (always an intellectual action) denies the mystery of personhood as both a complex and a free gift from a Loving Cause to *this* discrete person in his singularity — in his possibly unified simplicity as intellectual soul incarnate. Certainly, this is Flannery O'Connor's belief.

And that is the belief that leads her to such stories as "A Temple of the Holy Ghost," whose protagonist — unusual in her fiction — is a pre-adolescent girl, on the threshold of puberty. The story plays the hermaphrodite on display for ticket holders in a traveling carnival against the mystery of the Host raised at the altar. The child has only heard report of the hermaphrodite, but she is present at the Elevation of the Host at Mass. Her antagonists? Two giggling girls just become very much aware of their bodies and now "boy crazy," who on their weekend visit (an escape from the convent school at Mount St. Scholastica) dress in red skirts and loud blouses instead of their school uniforms. They are "beside themselves" with hilarity in calling each other "Temple One and Temple Two." The child, unwelcome intruder when the boys Wendell and Cory call on the school girls, is baffled by the comic contest between the boys' guitar hymning ("I've found a friend in Jesus") and the convent school girls' retort in Latin, St. Thomas' hymn "*Tantum ergo Sacramentum.*" Wendell, one of the boys, declares it "must be Jew singing," at which the girls collapse in laughter in response to such provincialism. The child, angry at their ridicule of the "country boys," shouts at Wendell, "You big dumb ox! ... You big dumb Church of God ox!" Flannery's implications are that the boys are closer to what is happening than is either "Temple One" or "Temple Two," echoing that epithet similarly hurled at Thomas Aquinas, himself as a "country boy" from Italy at school in Paris, that "Dumb Ox" whom G. K. Chesterton has so engagingly given us in his book with that epithet as subtitle. The protagonist, the child, ignorant of St. Thomas, nevertheless recognizes as much, her anger toward Wendell defensive of him out of intuitive sympathy for him against the older girl's teasing. For intuitively the child and Wendell are closer to that "Jew" celebrated by St. Thomas' hymn, closer to Thomas' own intellectual humility in praising "so great a sacrament" as that sacrificial one reverenced in the elevation of the host at the Mass. The boys and the child, this is to say, are intuitively closer to creation as itself sacramental than the convent girls. (The "present reality is the Incarnation," O'Connor declares.) The child, after attending mass with her mother at story's end and on the way home at sunset, herself now knows far more than she can *understand*. The story's conclusion makes that point, the Incarnation seen resonant in the local. The child looks out the car window, "out over a stretch of pasture land that rose and fell with a gathering greenness until it touched the dark woods. The sun was a huge red ball like an elevated Host drenched in blood and when it sank out of sight it left a line in the sky like a red clay road hanging over the trees."

O'Connor, before she writes this early story, would have encountered a dramatic representation of intellectual spiritual arrest in self-love, incipient in her "Temple One" and "Temple Two." The dramatic rendering is of a highly sophisticated "self-love," adolescent in respect to the spiritual implications of that illusional love. T. S. Eliot dramatizes his "lounge lizard" J. Alfred Prufrock as intellectually pretentious in his self-love. We might suggest that Flannery O'Connor much later than her "Temple of the Holy Ghost" will engage in a protagonist the insufficiency of self-love that might be taken in counterpoint to the Prufrockian intellectual asceticism in Eliot's poem. It is a story counter in that there is a stirring of hope to a spiritual pursuit through art in a character intuitively seeking his spiritual rescue beyond art but first through art. That story is O'Connor's "Parker's Back." It at first seems a story so far removed from Eliot's J. Alfred Prufrock as protagonist that our juxtaposing O'Connor's O. E. Parker appears unlikely in correspondences. But remembering O'Connor's own sophistication in matters spiritual, and remembering as well her certain delight in mischief as poet, we might discover the difficulties to O. E.'s spiritual quest pitting him against a world given over to self-love by persons not so cultured as Prufrock. Indeed, to an unwary sophisticated reader, the spectacle of O. E. Parker as "culturally deprived" may be baffling when pursued beyond his appearing as if a "local color" character satirically rendered, rather than as sympathetically rendered as he is intended by O'Connor.

For both J. Alfred Prufrock and O. E. Parker, there lies the spiritual difficulty to accept the complex givenness of themselves as persons, a givenness summoned by an ironically given name to signify an intellectual soul incarnate. For both, it is the biological body which proves the complicating presence confounding an ascetic intent, misunderstood in its spiritual implications by both. From our perspective as witnesses to their dramas of pursuit, J. Alfred Prufrock seems to bear a name better suited, at the level of spectacle, to a banker than to a lover. And O. E. Parker, embarrassed by his own name, senses that his name bears dangerous implications for him that yet escape him. He operates in the name of his initials, O. E., *Obadiah Elihue,* an outlandish Hebrew name, a "Jew" name in his cultural circumstances, designating him a prophet unrecognized. That is, he is by name a worshipper of Yahweh, that I AM in whose image O. E. is created. (His "funny" name is plausible, and was given him by literalist fundamentalists, his surrogate parents.) Whispering his name to his simple, fundamentalist wife through the door she has closed against him, he opens himself to her fury over his "idolatry" in having paid for a Byzantine Christ tattooed on his back. Severely scourged by her with her flailing broom, he is last seen by his wife Sarah Ruth (much safer Old Testament names): the man "who called himself Obadiah Elihue," she reflect scornfully. He is leaning against a tree in the dark and "crying like a baby." (Except ye be born again…?)

A long journey his, since the moment as a child when O. E. Parker saw a tattooed man in a traveling show. From that moment he is infected with a spiritual disquiet hardly recognizable through the journeying he makes. But the seed planted by that visitation festers in growing toward his recognition of that which seems at last as "out of the ordinary," the inescapable "fact that he existed" as unself-caused. That is also the thorn in J. Alfred Prufrock's flesh as well. Prufrock recognizes himself as wasting bodily, responding to his own grotesqueness as aesthetically disquieting, his wasting limbs and balding head. His fastidiousness for the latest correctives of decay, through the latest fashion in words and sartorial appointment, cannot conceal that decay. If he is not tempted to tattoos, he nevertheless fantasizes about walking on the beach clad in the latest fashion. "I shall wear the bottoms of my trousers rolled" in that latest fashion. Meanwhile, he submits to tea parties where "the women come and go/ Talking of Michaelangelo," they no doubt more sentimentally drawn to the *Pieta* than to *The Last Judgment.*

Widely separated, J. Alfred and O. E., in their cultural, social, intellectual responses to the mystery of a reality undeniable: that each person exists anterior to his gnawing recognition that he exists antecedently to his recognizing the problem of his *givenness* as a spiritual mystery, now struggling to accommodate to that mystery of givenness. Each exists as *given.* J. Alfred laments that he "should have been a pair of ragged claws," a body arrested below the burden to body of an intellectual soul. It is as if Flannery O'Connor attempts in her story to present a reduction in her protagonist almost to that level of Prufrockian "ragged claws," dramatizing the reduction as not thereby erasing out of O. E.'s gift as existing any relief to him from his inherent intellectual nature. For he struggles intellectually in pursuit of fulfillment of his rather limited givenness. He seeks his true calling, announced by the accident of his awkwardly given name. Thus must we each seek, whether as a J. Alfred Prufrock or an Obadiah Elihue, or even a Sarah Ruth: such is the implication of the fiction in its dependence upon a vision that "the present reality is the Incarnation."

O'Connor, with some mischief in the subtleties of her imaginative making, echoes names of Old Testament persons famously remembered as exiles in specific places. The temptations to intellectual and spiritual arrest prove most variable, according to the limits of the gifts to each. (We must remember *Enoch* Emory here.) For each person as person exists beyond the "ordinary" limits of those things connatural with persons — the *all* contained in the *here* and *now* through which each person journeys. As "intellectual" creatures, (as here comparatively juxtaposed) there can be no comfort of arrest for O'Connor's O. E. Parker such as that which is sought by J. Alfred Prufrock. Prufrock can neither accept nor exorcise from his consciousness his sense of himself as a limited given, as *this* being who is by the nature of gift an intellectual soul incarnate, and therefore denied by nature any unselfconsciousness such as that of a pair of ragged claws. The proportionate acceptance necessary to him would require, as is requires of O. E. Parker, a prudential humility which must at last be regardless of the peculiar — of the limiting — parameters to his specific and particular, and so limited, existence as person. Those parameters, the limits of existing as *this* person, are revealed in the inherent accidents of the discrete givenness itself— accidents *inhering* essence. What is required to a recovery is not an arrest, as if one might be but a crab scuttling silent seas, but an opening toward — a sacrifice of the self *through* the limits of givenness — a being born again in an act of sacramental openness.

In this respect, it is Obadiah Elihue Parker who more appropriately removes obstacles to grace than can J. Alfred Prufrock. Thus the irony — playful in O'Connor, uneasily witty in Eliot — is signaled in their titles. We discover Eliot's "singer" to be possessed by self-love, protecting himself by ascetic wit from any action — action always possible only in *this* moment in *this* place. Prufrock is unrelieved by any recognition of his intellectual adolescence. But Parker is turned back, through his awkward actions, to the ground of reality itself, to a recognition of the mystery of his existence as beyond any possible, merely artful or sophisticated, understanding. Neither he, nor Prufrock for all his cultured learning, can articulate the spiritual dilemma. Prufrock as "intellectual" shares his failure with several of O'Connor's characters, with whom she seems less sympathetic than she is with Parker, who gives his all. Parker's "all" (comparatively) seems very little when set beside such sophisticated intellects as Prufrock. Not surprisingly, then, we find Prufrock more satirically echoed as protagonist by such of O'Connor characters as Asbury ("The Enduring Chill") or Julian ("Everything That Rises Must Converge"). What these reject as surrogate persons (all of them pretentious intellectuals) is prudential humility, through which they might properly and proportionately love themselves. That is a virtue necessary not only to intellectuals as the world identifies them but to each person: poet or scientist or philosopher; teacher or bookkeeper or garbageman. And as well by such lowly pilgrims as Parker or Haze Motes — to the confusion of some readers of O'Connor, since they prove resonant of personhood to a degree discomforting if taken as more than caricature.

Prudential humility is wisdom in relation to ordinate love, a virtue implicit throughout St. Thomas' work, but it is in O'Connor's work as well. In the discovery of this responsibility to the self as a given — to myself as person (I write because I'm good at it, O'Connor says) — the person is first moved by awe, which is to be pursued by *reason,* toward *understanding* out of the *wonder* born of awe. That is the burden of responsibility to the intellectual soul. It is a circumstance to the person's reality as person, evident in a tensional experience effected by the intellect as both *intuitive* and *rational.* The effect may prove that communal one we have already spoken of as the recognition by a person of his *connaturality* as person with things. The two modes as consonant may be properly grounded in reason's signs: *This thing is. I am.* In that tensional recognition of an active participation in reality, *I* may come to know the limiting gifts to this *thing* and therefore of myself as I also exist by limit. Each *is* by the creating action of Love, of the Creator, but each exists only in a limited givenness.

At least such is the understanding of the particular experiences of the person as held by St. Thomas as he explores our journeying as *homo viator.* And it is held also by O'Connor as well. Her faith recognizes that things *are* (including herself) and that a reality spo-

ken by the plural *are* exists under the auspices of Creating Love — making prudential humility the virtue properly governing the intellectual soul, whatever its peculiar limits in *this*
person. It is within this understanding, then, that O'Connor knows herself to be a *maker*
not a *creator,* a truth she welcomes as unraveled to her understanding by St. Thomas.
O'Connor speaks of this understanding of *connaturality,* though not using the term as does
one of her favored authors, Jacques Maritain. In looking at "one object" with the openness
of love, one begins to see "more of the world in it" as con-joined in the thing by love, apt
summary of the experience of connaturality. That is to begin at last to understand oneself
as *this* peculiarly given creature. "To know oneself is to know one's region," through things
known locally. And that, too, is to know more fully "the world." It is also "paradoxically, a
form of exile from the world," in that the person comes to recognize his proper end to be
con-union beyond created things with the Cause of the world, not a union with the world
itself as if that were the limited end assumed in the new Modernist religion so pervasive of
the popular spirit.

It is by that unraveling, then, that one may approach an affirmation of an *ordinate* self-
love such as that spoken in that commandment to us that we are to love our neighbor *as we
love our self.* From Thomas' perspective, indeed, that is not only a commandment: it speaks
the abiding reality of a *continuous* measurement of our love of our self — whether it is ordinate or inordinate. A false love of one's neighbor is already a measure of a false love of oneself. And that reality, in relation to circumstantial contingencies to our actions toward creation in general (and toward other persons in particular), proves rich in its dramatic irony,
as any true poet or philosopher may know. It is marvelously exhibited by our poet O'Connor when the Misfit in "A Good Man is Hard to Find" experiences, as if for the first time,
an action of active love for him by the Grandmother at story's end. The old woman's is a
gesture Flannery talks about in relation to the story when she says that such an action in a
story must be "both totally right and totally unexpected." It must be "both in character and
beyond character," we have heard her say, for then it may "suggest both the world and eternity." (*Suggest,* not *prove.*)

All through that story, the Grandmother mouths a concerned love for her family, present and past. The encounter with the Misfit is brought to pass by her insistence on visiting
an old home place, in actuality that home place a state away geographically. The encounter
with the Misfit occurs with a little help from Pity Sing — the smuggled cat as grace's stowaway, mayhap. Only in the last moment of her life is the Grandmother able to reach out in
genuine sacrificial act of love — to the Misfit. How unexpected! The gesture plants a seed in
the Misfit's heart (Flannery speculates) which may as a *possibility* turn such a creature as even
the Misfit toward his becoming the prophet she imagines him as intended to be from inception. That foreshadowing of him as prophet is planted in the story. The Misfit recalls
that his Daddy spotted him at once as a "different breed of dog from my brothers and sisters," saying of him that "it's some that can live their whole lives out without asking about
it and it's others has to know why it is, and this boy is one of the latters." That seed of love,
planted by the Grandmother's gesture, has its first fruit in the recognition by this prophet-
to-be in his final words: "She would have been a good woman ... if it had been somebody
there to shoot her every minute of her life." There is at least a hint that the Misfit intuitively
recognizes a possibility that a good exists to which his present evil is counter.

It is in this speculative context out of and concerning our spiritual nature that we
may encounter the terror of Mercy as actual. Mercy — an unexpected means by grace to

accomplish in us a spiritual potentiality through willed consent. There may follow a becoming which is always potential to us as Thomas says — a prospect of becoming a good man or good woman. Without that recognition and amendment through consent to the good (as the Misfit laments, echoing Thomistic metaphysical reality) we are left desolate. Then "It's no real pleasure in life." In the paradoxical sense of exile, though the person may feel at home in the presence of things he properly loves by his experience of the local, he may discover himself to be nevertheless *homo viator*. That is, he is man on his way toward a home lying in an anticipated country larger than and inclusive of the merely local. Hence the sense of exile, even when he feels largely "at home" in the world. However much "rooted" in place, he is yet on his way. That is the root cause of the "pain" in the Misfit, the pain which his incarnating maker O'Connor suggests may be a pain sufficient "to turn him into the prophet he was meant to become." To that speculation she adds that this is yet "another story," and that other story she undertakes to tell of young Tarwater in *The Violent Bear It Away*. We observe on this point that Tarwater is himself a murderer, drowning the idiot Bishop even as he baptizes the boy. (Haze Motes, O'Connor's own admired protagonist of *Wise Blood*, is also a murderer — as are some of those whom Dante encounters on the slopes of Purgatory, to the bafflement of sophomore readers.)

Though haunted with a sense of exile, a person may find himself most at home in this world as (in Allen Tate's distinction) a regionalist rather than a provincialist. We heard Tate observe that "provincialism is that state of mind in which regional men lose their origins in the past and its continuity into the present, and begin every day as if there had been no yesterday." That is a distinction to which O'Connor is attuned, recognizing it as evidence of our limited citizenship in this present country. But that local and wandering citizenship in this world does not prevent our participation as citizen of a country existing in quite another dimension to our given nature as person. Young Tarwater is presented as an awakening intellectual soul through his growing sense of that other "country," a country not abutting but permeating the one through which he moves on his quest. In O'Connor's understanding of this reality of man's given nature, she holds that the intellectual soul incarnate is gifted by his very nature with a seemingly dual citizenship, his acceptance of one citizenship always contingent to his present moment as citizen in creation.

That one is by grace potential citizen of a country seemingly other than this present place may prove spiritually shocking when suddenly recognized. That is the dramatic comeuppance for Mr. Head and his grandson Nelson in "The Artificial Nigger," as it is for many of O'Connor's agents, in varying degrees of their recognitions. We have remarked it in the Misfit, in young Tarwater, and in Haze Motes. Each experiences (by degree) the terror of Mercy. Mr. Head will recognize it as unmerited by him, and as well a reality still beyond his understanding as merited *to* him. He cannot articulate this mystery of Mercy as Thomas does, in relation to the Incarnation. Mr. Head's is a recognition that comes to him as he and Nelson stand in a country far from his putative home in the Georgia countryside from which they set out to "educate" Nelson about the City. They stand before that "artificial nigger" (Mr. Head's term for the statue as *art*). They are lost in a semi-affluent neighborhood of walled lawns in the City of Man, a City divorced from Augustine's City of God. In the moment, Mercy envelops Mr. Head, to his spiritual confusion — let alone to his intellectual inadequacy to account for his epiphany. What O'Connor's art discovers to us as not "artificial" is the reductionism of actual things, actual persons, in her dramatic unfolding of the *possible* actions of human nature itself.

The statue of the "artificial nigger" is a violation of personhood, as it is additionally poor art. In this dramatic unfolding Mr. Head nevertheless has revealed to him through it his dual citizenship inherent to his givenness as this person. The dual citizenship is to be discovered as valid, as certified by the Incarnation for O'Connor. And that is a recognition contingent to recognition even in the City of Man, though that city would deny the other country within which it is itself but a finite province. This, a reality of human nature despite denials such as the City of Man may express in its charter or articles as a secular "incorporation." That process alone, the "artificial incarnation" of community, can only effect "artificial" persons by secular "embodiment" or "incorporation" of a City if presumed a creature "created" by man through his autonomous intellectual process to his merely social convenience. At our moment, as it was in Flannery's day, there is a growing conflict centering in this dual membership's validity, under the rubric of the "separation of Church and State" as the problematic principle to social order, a phrase increasingly ambiguous since the 1960s, when it emerged as a political cause by being divorced from spiritual causes.

That object before which Mr. Head and Nelson stand is a piece of decaying bad art, the statue. Though it reflects a social and political baggage accusatory of injustices in addition to its being also bad art, it becomes nevertheless the instrument of grace to the wayfarers, to Mr. Head and Nelson. It becomes a medium of Mercy especially to an unjust and disoriented intellect, Mr. Head's, and a prophetic forewarning to Nelson in his green youth as *homo viator*. Mr. Head proves an "intellect" not at home in any place, though only by unmerited grace does he discover the terror of Mercy despite his willful self-displacement from grace. He finds himself enveloped by a Mercy excruciating to bear. That Mercy is engulfingly incommensurate to his willful rejections, consuming even his pride. How devastating such an experience to any provincial, whatever his place or in whatever time he journey — or before whatever object he may stand defiantly, whether in Middle Georgia or Atlanta or in Greenwich Village. Or perhaps even more anciently and far removed, in a moment before a small fire made against an evening chill, before which Peter warms himself as he denies Christ. That too is an event we are to recall in the story's broad sunlight as Mr. Head denies ever having seen his grandson Nelson before that moment, after Nelson has knocked down a "respectable" woman and scattered her groceries on the city pavement.

Whatever place or time, a point to be emphasized. For what Flannery O'Connor hopes we may discover as persons, aside from our responses to her art as art, is that provincial pride is not reserved to semi-literate Georgia country folks. It may even be found in those sophisticated persons who look from Greenwich Village windows across the Hudson River toward the South, down into Middle Georgia, seeing that remote place as if it were only a wilderness. From that provincial perspective, there have been launched many expeditions with missionary intent to rescue the provincial South (by social activists, novelists, sit-com entrepreneurs, government agencies). Those various intents to rescue leave the imputedly provincial Southerner wary. A public concern to save lost "social individuals" or to profit from their lostness by force or guile, devolves increasingly into political concerns for a positive law declared absolute, making the rescuers but the more suspect to the forlorn Southerner, though the Southerner himself may lack understanding of what is amiss in the salvational manner that so disturbs him. His situation then is akin to that of the Misfit. Not so Miss Flannery, who through St. Thomas recognizes the Modernist strategy whereby the positive law is intentionally divorced from natural law, as natural law is understood by St. Thomas. By that divorce positive law becomes an instrument with which to promulgate corrective realignments of social order divorced from spiritual reality of persons in community. It is an inevitable corollary, she sees, of our having divorced grace from nature.

Such speculators on the nature of the *good* (or so that wary lost social entity, the Southerner, sometimes suspects) seem seldom to recognize wildernesses closer home. Flannery O'-Connor as one such entity will suggest that they look to their own local wildernesses. She declares, for instance, that New York critics are an "unreliable lot, as incapable now as on the day they were born of interpreting Southern literature to the world." Not that she isn't aware as well of home-grown versions of such critics, paying her respects to them in letters and in talks along the way. Most devastatingly, she does so through such characters as her Hulga Hopewell of "Good Country People." Hulga is a "Southerner" who sees herself entrapped in the wilderness of the South, its citizens best analyzed by a thought most foreign — by Sartrean Existentialism. Hulga as intellectual thus proves to be a spiritual scalawag, seeing her *place* with philosophically specialized eyes that distort her vision of the realities spoken by place. Hers proves consequently the most destructive provincialism possible: it stifles her own spiritual nature.

O'Connor's epithet ("good country people") is ironic, but increasingly sardonic in Hulga's mouth. It seems almost a just punishment (or so the festering irony suggests) that Hulga has been born of such provincials. She is other than as she might have been, had she been born in the shadows of the Sorbonne. Hulga's becomes an intellectual self-laceration that gives her a wicked pleasure as she attempts to scandalize her mother and neighbors by seducing the Bible salesman. How "totally right and totally unexpected," then, the arresting rebuke delivered to Hulga by this ambiguous agent of grace walking up and down among these good country people as if a devil sent by God, and especially to test Hulga. He may be said paradoxically to be grace's agent, though seemingly a Satanic presence as a "Bible salesman," as Satan is agent of grace to Job. He tests provincial spirits such as Hulga. Indeed, Mr. "Pointer" bursts the protective bubble of Hulga's Existential autonomy, even as he tests as well a variety of local provincial spirits, including Hulga's mother. But it is Hulga as a presence, Job-like but in antithesis to Job, who is the centering soul of this trial. She "suffers" her provincial place but has no god to charge with her suffering. The devilish delight here lies in Pointer's having compromised Hulga, revealing to her that her rejection of persons as but hypocritical provincials proves a consequence of a self-reflection, of her having rejected herself as person. That is a failure as ancient as Adam and Eve.

Hulga has, as a sophisticated intellectual schooled in the latest philosophy, embraced Sartrean naiveté in a pretense to the self-sufficiency of an Existentialism which she believes her only possible rescue. Even Walker Percy, we note, seems at first tempted toward such a conclusion as poet. He is at first fascinated by the Sartrean vision of human nature as suited to a fiction of ideas. At the outset, he intends to deploy ideas in the dramatic matter of his *Moviegoer*. But that proves for him as person (rather than as novelist) a very dangerous undertaking — like conjuring the devil to see whether he does actually exist.[4] As for O'Connor's Hulga, out of her faith in nothingness as a revenge against her mother, she sets out to seduce the Bible salesman to scandalize such good country people, supposing Mr. Pointer also one of these naïve and stupid provincials. He is so in one sense. That is, he is as a person man fallen, as are they all, including even the intellectually naïve Hulga. He seems to stand (as antagonist) most especially in the need of grace perhaps, seemingly more fallen than some. And so his actions partake of the diabolic, if one is reluctant to grant him as a "Pointer" to be one of the satanic legion. Hulga's assumption of his simplicity because he is unsophisticated, "unlearned," proves her devastating mistake, and it is she who is seduced. She is not simply seduced by the Bible salesman in the hayloft at the level of sexual spectacle, for hers has been a self-seduction long underway through Sartrean presumption of herself as intellectually autonomous. She would create herself by actions over things, in a willful disregard of that existential reality of things as we have argued them understood by O'Connor and explicated by Thomistic philosophy.

How devastating, then, the Bible salesman's final judgment of Hulga as but an "intellectual" provincial. He is leaving in triumph, with Hulga's false leg as trophy. His most wounding act of all is his last word: "You needn't think you'll catch me because Pointer ain't really my name. I use a different name at every house I call at and don't stay nowhere long." His name, this is to hint by New Testament allusion, is "legion." ("Behold, I stand at the door" are Christ's words, easily mimicked by the Devil.) Flannery reminds us in one of her talks that the devil must be made to name himself most particularly, lest he escape through an alias, mimicking Christ. Hulga has failed to make this devil name himself, for all of the intellectual sophistication which should make her acutely attuned to names. Hulga knows the power latent in Nominalistic manipulations, as when she chooses for her own "public" name *Hulga,* her mother having named her *Joy.* That is intended to be an affront which might pain her mother. How could her mother not be embarrassed among her peers, those good country people like Mrs. Freeman, by such an "ugly" name. *Hulga,* a name almost as wounding to her mother as a bullet, and certainly a blow delivered by a "Misfit," Hulga. Even the Misfit of "A Good Man Is Hard to Find" might be fleetingly amused by Hulga's "meanness." For Hulga herself, the worst is yet to come, tempting a reader to an unexpected pleasure of that *worst,* hardly able to avoid some pleasure at Hulga's expense. The Bible salesman, adding Hulga's false leg to his collection ("one time I got a woman's glass eye this way."), leaves her to endure a devastating truth: "you ain't so smart. I been believing in nothing ever since I was born!" He needed no formal "academic" training to arrive at her dead-end. That is where he started from.

Hulga will have difficulty hereafter, in the light of such devastating news about Nothingness. Perhaps she (and certainly we) are left to reflect on her mother's judgment of this stranger, Mr. Pointer. Her mother stands with Mrs. Freeman, watching the Bible salesman make his way across a meadow from the barn toward the highway. He seemed a "nice dull young man," she says. He "must have been selling Bibles to the Negroes back in there. He was so simple," Mrs. Hopewell says. She adds, "but I guess the world would be better off if we were all that simple." To which Mrs. Freeman: "Some can't be that simple.... I know I never could." Hers is a righteous simple-mindedness that has all along served to sharpen Hulga's teeth. None escape the need of grace, obstacles to which may be removed only by a prudential humility that is lacking in those "good country people"— including Hulga. Indeed, Hulga seems the furthest removed of all from our true country, as perhaps she may now discover thanks to Mr. Pointer. Grace as dramatically present to such characters seems a rather remote possibility to most of us, but especially to the likes of a Hulga we might say. For O'Connor unwaveringly, grace is always inherently present to persons in reality, so that who knows what Hulga, née Joy Hopewell, will make of all this? That is not the poet's responsibility. O'Connor is not to *conclude* as poet either Hulga's salvation or her damnation, as she knows well and says often, though she feels free to speculate in such questions as raised out of the demands of her art. As person, she is not precluded from venturing suggestive reflections, in contexts of concern other than her primary responsibility as artist for the inherent validity of the thing she has made, her story. Having made it, it becomes an offering out of the devotion to her gifts. And in her offering up a story, the story itself joins — as a property, as an existing thing — our cultural matrix to which even its maker responds.

Here lies an important distinction to our reading of her essays and letters as distinct from her stories. She insists that, in the labor of making, her responsibility has been for the good of the thing she is making in an accord to the limits of the material she has chosen in pursuit of a form proper to that chosen matter. It is surrendered as offering within our cultural history as a corollary gift to us. Meanwhile, she is confident that in her choice of "matter" from complex reality there are already inherent limits to her vocation. As person, as Mary Flannery, she recognizes and believes that "the ultimate reality is the Incarnation," which is as well the "present reality," so that there are limits to her appropriation of matter because it is dependent upon ultimate truth of the Incarnation. *All*, she says, is the Incarnation, echoing Georges Bernanos (*The Diary of a Country Priest*): "All is grace." She believes this true, even though "nobody believes in the Incarnation," at least none of "the people I am conscious of writing for." Yet their failure to see does not determine reality, despite Modernist indoctrinations to the contrary.

These are words spoken by O'Connor of the "good country people" she is aware of writing for — the likes of whom are not hard to find even in Atlanta or New York. Her words are worth pondering, at whatever here and now to us. And so perhaps a Hulga may be imagined as doing so in relation to that devastating blow of words from "Mr. Pointer." For surely from O'Connor's perspective, even a Hulga is not irreparably lost, Pointer's words perhaps having planted a seed which if nurtured by reason may recover Hulga as an "ex-suicide," to use Walker Percy's term for that possible recovery as so intimately known by him as person. Or, to borrow the Misfit's version, a trumping "meanness" by Pointer may fester in Hulga's soul bringing her into a new life. As for the term *ex-suicide*, that is an epithet Percy playfully explicates in something of a self-confessional manner in his Augustinian work, his *Lost in the Cosmos: The Last Self-Help Book*. For Percy, like St. Augustine in his *Confessions*, is such a recovered ex-suicide. He will remark a recovery underway in him as he was writing *The Moviegoer* though he did not at first recognize it. Intending a Sartrean guidance to his making, he subsequently discovers the change underway, much later articulating it in looking back at the experience of making his *Moviegoer*.

We may discover, then, that Percy's protagonists (like O'Connor's) are at last left on this threshold of a *possible* recovery, as by retrospection he discovers himself on that threshold. They are left at a point of contingency to future actions, human judgment thus suspended in a deference (whether intuitively or reasonably conceded) to the transcendent Judgment properly reserved to the Cause of all creatures. That is a judgment not to be exercised by those beings themselves in a presumptuous absoluteness of conclusion. This reserve, whether or not one is a gifted maker of imitations of the intellectual and spiritual actions *possible* to human nature as are both Percy and O'Connor. As persons, they affirm justice the province of God, to whom we appeal for mercy. Who would be so bold as to judge that Obadiah Elihue Parker on the one hand or Hulga Hopewell on the other are either "saved" or "damned"? That would be a presumption defying the actions of free will to actual persons in the contingencies of circumstances to such "possible" persons in fictional contingencies conceding the actuality of persons. A necessity of prudential humility in regard to any possible transcendent rescue obtains, whether we are speculating on the eventual fate of a fictional character more certainly than of actual persons known to us —

especially of our own self as person, the most certain creature at risk in contingencies. For in this respect, presumptuous in pronouncing justice, we are at each moment "in the dock." Through our contingent actions of love toward or refusals of love toward things within the range of immediate possibilities of our openness to them, we judge at risk.

Walker Percy, himself comfortably companionable with his friend Flannery O'Connor on such questions and mysteries, hints this contingent action as always a present challenge allowing actual persons *possible* action toward the good. In a retrospection, a talk given on receiving the "Richard M. Weaver Award," he examines himself as the "Physician as Novelist." Looking back on that first, and perhaps most celebrated of his novels, *The Moviegoer,* he speaks of himself in the third person, in the manner of Henry Adams in his *Education of Henry Adams* rather than of St. Augustine's first person in his *Confessions.* In writing the novel, he remembers, it became "almost by accident … a narrative of the search, the quest. And so the novel, again by accident — or was it accident? — landed squarely in the oldest tradition of Western letters: the pilgrim's search outside himself, rather than the guru's search within. All this happened to the novelist and his character without the slightest consciousness of a debt to St. Augustine or Dante. Indeed, the character creates within himself and within the confines of a single weekend in New Orleans a microcosm of the spiritual history of the West, from the Roman patrician reading his Greek philosophers to the thirteenth-century pilgrim who leaves home and takes to the road."

No accident, this. Or so Percy's friend and fellow Southern Catholic writer Flannery O'Connor would say of his discovery. It evidences the abiding presence of grace to him, enabled by his own open surrender to the good of the thing he makes, his *Moviegoer.* At a level of the personal, dangerous to our intrusive speculation though it may be, we may suppose the openness effected through the agony of spirit out of which Percy emerges as himself an "ex-suicide," the concept playfully rendered in a passage of his *Lost in the Cosmos.* For he comes to see more clearly the very "matter" to his making of *The Moviegoer,* selected to the limits of "a single weekend in New Orleans" (as Joyce analogously is selective to a single day in the life of his Stephen Dedalus in the Dublin of *Ulysses*). Thus an arena to his made thing, a microcosm. But out of the selection from reality of the "matter" he must then *inform* it in imitation of the actions possible to human nature. There enters into his making a residual presence beyond any merely "naturalistic" limits of the chosen matter, the concretely actual that serves his incarnational art as ordinately reflective of the natural New Orleans environment. It is in retrospect that he discovers something about himself as pilgrim person within his actions of making. Flannery O'Connor seems to have been acutely aware of such discovery as always underway, even before her own actions as maker. Such a knowing, we remarked at the outset, seems to have been hers almost from her cradle.

3

Glimpsing a Peacock's Underwear

*"Since the eighteenth century, the popular spirit of each succeeding age has tended
more and more to the view that the ills and mysteries of life will eventually fall before
the scientific advances of man, a belief that is still going strong even though this is the
first generation to face total extinction because of these advances."*

— Flannery O'Connor, "Some Aspects of the
Grotesque in Southern Fiction"

Having suggested by anecdotes one aspect of Flannery O'Connor's challenge as writer, that front porch experience with her friend returned from New York City and the local farmer tossing a chicken up in the air to instruct her, we must engage a second challenge which is tandem. She is very much aware that her audience and her fictional material prove largely though not self-evidently the same. The "matter" to be dramatized are those intellectual actions possible to human nature, revealed through actions of actual persons in response to circumstances of their encounter with the actual world, here and now. Her task as dramatic poet: to dramatize the *possible* actions of response to *possible* circumstances, through imaginative makings. The challenge to her is the given correspondence between her fictional "matter" and the intellectual state pervasive of her audience, reflecting the "popular spirit" of our age. But what degree of detachment from her making is necessary, so that she not violate either the reality of our condition as intellectual souls incarnate or the art thing made through her dependence upon that reality? That is the challenge we find reflected in her speculative concerns in essays and talks and in her letters.

This is a delicate, and so perhaps a subtle aspect of her art difficult to articulate. But we see that, were she but satirist of the human condition, as some of her sophisticated readers suppose, she might assume an audience sharing with her in an ironic detachment more easily served by wit, the mode on which such sophisticated delight very often depends. That she is more largely committed as dramatic poet, as a realist of distances, is nevertheless (and for some of her readers disturbingly) evident in her sympathy for such of her characters as Haze Motes and both the Tarwaters, and even for the Misfit. And there is even a seeming tolerance on occasion toward other, less haunted characters such as Mr. Shiftlet in "The Life You Save May Be Your Own." In response to such possible realities of human action, she is committed not simply to wit in her making but as we have observed to a wit moderated by humor.

Where there is humor in art, we may be drawn to conclude, there is an implication that the maker himself concedes to sharing in a common humanity with his characters — a lesson not to be missed in the fiction of William Faulkner, for instance. To say this is to suggest that O'Connor is not so presumptuous as to detach herself from a share in human nature by a judgmental aspect of a strictly ironic satire, the end of which in art is so often caricature of personhood. Her delight in that incident we recalled earlier, that of the man who for her instruction threw the chicken in the air to give it "a good time," might serve as a parable lesson to the point. O'Connor was attuned to the effects of practical, even pragmatic, domestications, studying it as poet in those creatures she kept underfoot, with some irritation to her mother, Regina. (See Flannery's "The King of the Birds" in *Mystery and Manners*.) Chickens can't fly, at least not very far. As for those peacocks with the cock's gorgeous plumage, neither can they. They even have to labor to get up on a roosting place high enough to be somewhat safe from foxes, the peacocks' and chickens' "dragon" always by their road. Both creatures, held close to a ground zero of their existence, exist as they do by their limited natures, even as does man for all his dreams of a transcendental flight by his autonomous will. And even that child, seeing the sunset as elevated Host descending, with notices that the light leaves a line in the sky "like a red clay road hanging over the trees" in that story about "The Temple of the Holy Ghost," knows intuitively a necessity of rescue. But it might also even suggest a road leading not only to the sun but from the sun into those "dark woods."

We are returned always to the here and now, even by a desperately squawking chicken flapping its wings in fright or a red road lost in a dark wood. Not that such metaphorical ventures into the realities of human nature might be fully shared with one's neighbor, especially a neighbor liberated from his or her supposed "provincialism" by a period of residence in sophisticated Greenwich Village. And so the more evident that such parables are likely to escape the attention of those "New York critics," O'Connor's generic term for those she sees as given to the secular provincialism defined by Allen Tate. For her as poet, however, there lies an irony in that secular stance: it seems to turn its devotee to a dream of flight beyond his own secularized, material world in some species of an angelism, seeking transcendence of that world — as if by intellectual action the "self" could throw itself up into the air toward an illusional "good time" called absolute freedom.

Concerning that species of provincialism, she will treat it as fictional matter but in gradations — from the pseudo-sophistication of an Asbury or a Julian in stories like "The Enduring Chill" and "Everything That Rises Must Converge," down to a "country" version of that sophistication in a Mr. Shiftlet in "The Life You Save May Be Your Own." A part of her strategy as a realist of distances, then, is to treat the pseudo-intellectual deportment of intellect itself as evident in gradations. She will see the "pseudo" as an inheritance within the popular spirit of our age as most immediately given to us out of 18th century Rationalism, filtered most variously into the "feelings" exhibited by that "popular spirit." (Rationalism and Romanticism are not so easily exclusive of each other in the reality of a person as analysis may make it.) It is even likely that she was amused by the irony of the response of her "New York critic" to her fictions as if her stories were satiric representations of "Southern" provincialism, when to her thinking such a critic was himself intimately implicit in her "Southern" characters. The continuing critical fascination with her work, attempting to limit it to such a restriction as satire, suggests a mystery in that fiction not yet critically resolved. That continuing struggle may even evidence such critics in a surprised response, as if having suddenly been confronted by reality's "underwear" sustaining fictional spectacle, as those visiting children to Andalusia suddenly see the hidden support of the peacock's spectacular display. But how name that disquieting but unresolved discovery?

If she appreciated the immediacy of the children's awe, grading into wonder about the mystery of the earth-bound peacock, she knew as well a certain childish (not *child-like*) propensity in us which "since the eighteenth century" at least has reduced our wonder about the mystery of existence itself. From her perspective, intellectual vision becomes more and more tenuous through unearned sophistications of intellect in pursuits of that absolute freedom beyond awe and wonder, into pseudo-certainties of intellectual autonomy that would declare the "self" out of Nietzsche beyond good and evil. And so she began to recognize as an established tradition a sophisticated provincialism which we have and shall speak of as that of the "Modernist" spirit. It rose rapidly in the Renaissance, becoming a pursuit of power over things through specialized rationalizations, the intended end a conquering of things through an increasingly complex technology. How seductively does technology allow the conqueror his ever-increasing power over the whole world — he the empirical master of "nature," who need no longer act with a piety recognizing nature as permeated by grace. That was the spirit ascendant, becoming pervasive of Western thought as socially and politically consolidated since the eighteenth century by a Positivistic rationalism which abjured any intuitive response to creation. We lose the speech of creation, its witness to a sustaining Presence to any discrete thing. By a pious deportment to things (if one respond as does Dame Julian of Norwich to the hazel-nut on her palm) the whole world is discovered to witness increasingly its Cause as a Presence within creation itself, though a mystery unyielding to any rationalism divorced from the intuitive knowing of that Presence. That Modernist spirit became consolidated in Western philosophy in the 18th century, in anticipation of *reason* as allowing *being* to be subjected to systematic control and manipulation, *being* having substituted for it as cause random *accident*—spectacle replacing substance.

That is the tradition O'Connor refers to in our present epigraph. It was this Modernist spirit which proved an appropriate, even an inescapable, matter to the form in her fiction, treated as an inherited but false tradition distilled out of creation by the rationalistic reduction of "nature" to but materialistic accident. In that climate of Modernist thought now become general among us, her critics at first (and some of them still) must suppose her (insofar as they wish to grant a sympathetic critique of her fiction) to be merely a satiric "realist" of the local. Her uses of the grotesque must be judged primarily as aimed at backward provincials cut off from the Enlightenment progress which promises to conquer both the "ills and mysteries of life" through "scientific advances." That is the presumption which she addresses incisively in "Some Aspects of the Grotesque in Southern Fiction," the satiric objects in that essay the presumptuous Enlightenment descendents, the Modernist popular spirit become pervasive of community. Her fallen "country people," then, are not limited from humanity by her detached irony, though they are seen as having proved susceptible to Modernist doctrine. We may notice, however, the more direct target of her irony in her *Mystery and Manners,* that gathering of her talks and essays: the pseudo-sophisticated intellectual who presumes himself "shed of" the virtues of prudence, humility, and piety by his pursuit of an absolute angelistic freedom. That freedom O'Connor registers initially in her down-home Modernist, Haze Motes, as a point of departure in dramatizing a *possible* rescue out of that angelism whereby Haze declares himself "clean" by the declaration itself.

Her aim covers more targets, then, than the "New York" type of the provincialist, the critics she remarks in "The Regional Writer" as "an unreliable lot" when it comes to "interpreting Southern literature to the world." There is her figure of a Southern intellectual provincial, the semi-educated and so the more presumptuous intellectual called Asbury in

"The Enduring Chill," or Julian in "Everything That Rises Must Converge." These protagonists suffer the temptations of exile in reverse, each forced to return "home" as an unwanted species of exile from their sophisticated freedom, uneasy in the small but native Georgia communities where they were born. Their local suffering they enjoy as a secular form of martyrdom to sophistication itself, experiencing nevertheless a vague sense of guilt whose cause they attribute to having been born with such cultural origins. Theirs is a cultural inheritance not yet fully exorcised, to be accounted as but another of the accidents to be overcome by angelistic intellect — if only these good country provincials would submit *en masse* to a cultural exorcism. They see themselves as "cultural" victims, their accidental origins the source of the lingering sense of guilt in them. They do not, short of a pending shocking encounter, suspect the depths of the gnawing sense of guilt in them. It lies (in O'Connor's perspective) in their common fallen aberrant nature, the aberrant cultivated by their intellectual pride in reducing their own existence to mere accident. (If only Hulga had been born in the shadow of the Sorbonne we said.) Even so, from O'Connor's perspective such spiritual provincials may yet be recovered through grace, if shocked into an openness of love that might remove pseudo-intellectual obstacles to grace. This side of death in this world, rescue continues contingent to a moment of a possible action out of love such as that of the grandmother in "A Good Man Is Hard to Find," or that by Julian's mother on the bus ride in the City of Man in "Everything That Rises Must Converge."

How excruciating to Julian, such a spiritual circumstance, but it seems to him a pain at the level of social embarrassment. Grudgingly, he makes that trip with his mother on a common bus with the hoi poloi. And how condescending his mother appears to him to be in her exchange of small talk with that small black boy, to whom she gives the only coin she can find, a shiny new penny. Neither Julian nor the boy's mother can recognize beneath that surface spectacle of the old white woman's gesture to the black child an echo of that parable of the widow's mite, not recovered and saved in the story but spent with a gesture larger than might be measured by spectacle alone, by the worldly value of the coin. Julian picks his mother up, after the black woman has struck her with her red pocketbook as she shouts "He don't take nobody's penny." Only then does he begin to discover that more than the mere penny as a gift offered is unfolding to him. Picking up his mother's hat off her lap as she lies sprawled, he sees the penny lying on the sidewalk. Then, as if to rebuke her, intending to be as severe to his mother by his gesture as the effect of that pocketbook that had struck her down. He had noticed the pocketbook "bulged ... as if it were stuffed with rocks." He dangles the penny over his mother's open pocketbook and lets it drop back in, a more devastating gesture than the blow that felled her in his reckoning. How petty a gesture, but as well how near to perdition it brings Julian if seen in the light of the mystery of our existence as intellectual soul incarnate.

Julian's mother meanwhile is insistent that they turn back home. "I hate to see you behave like this," Julian says in rebuke. "Just like a child. I should be able to expect more of you." It is then that his mother suffers a stroke, Julian responding to her face in an agony he seems never to have experienced before. Her one eye, "large and staring," moves as if "become unmoored." The other eye "remained fixed on him, raked his face again, found nothing and closed." This intellectual Misfit has cried out to her "Mamma! Mamma!" And now he runs, calling for help. But from whom? A "tide of darkness seemed to sweep him back to her, postponing from moment to moment his entry into the world of guilt and sorrow," a world he has never recognized before. Whether that token penny as a gift, made with intuitive love to the small black child, will speak to him thereafter is left in suspense. But it was a love offering, effecting a surprising sacrifice by his mother, an action akin to that of the old grandmother in "A Good Man Is Hard to Find" toward the Misfit — each having made a gesture of love that triggers death for each of them. It is almost to suggest that Julian might be a good man if his mamma could be around to die in front of him every day of his life.

How mysterious, then, the actions of love possible to us, given that we have become lost in the spectacles of cultural frictions. But that is a point not easily recognized by the intellectually sophisticated who have removed themselves from reality, as Julian seems to have become removed by his little bit of an education. Even in the seemingly trivial moments of the story's action, a Presence hovers — to which Julian appeals in his panic, not knowing what name to call. What we begin to discover as we read O'Connor's fictions carefully is that her protagonists again and again prove to be provincials akin to each other, however diverse in degrees of sophistication. But they are provincials, not according to geography, but to their spiritual displacement from the realities of *any* here and now. They are dramatized in their responses to persons and things immediate to their present and contingent moment of a possible action of love beyond the mere spectacle of event. What proves a turning point in their provincialism as dramatic denouement is an encounter with the terror of mercy, always contingent as grace to a human action. In its *possible* effect an unspectacular action of love (giving a bright coin to a child opening to the wonder of his world) allows a recovery to "regional" consciousness out of that willful "provincial" consciousness in which the habit of a neglect of reality rules, alienating that consciousness from the Presence abiding through things encountered here and now. O'Connor's protagonists have become detached from this immediacy within their here and now, until out of that contingent reality some violent intrusion upon a provincialist habit shatters their pride of detachment.

It is in depths within that immediacy, the depths of the givenness called creation, that O'Connor's protagonists encounter sudden terror, then, often violent terror but more arresting than the violence of spectacle — even than of murder. For they are affected in their spiritual being. They come to a threshold, to cross which may be to see at last *through* the eye country which has all along been *within* the present local country to their provincial habits as intellectual soul, they challenged only by surface spectacle. How delighted Julian, for instance, to discover his mother's hat exactly the hat worn by her assailant-to-be — that "large, gaily dressed, sullen-looking colored woman," the child's mother, who gets on the bus with the little boy. (The boy appears to be about four, and so perhaps still capable of a response in joy to the offered "new" penny, as he might also recognize that peacock's underwear.) Julian's mother and the boy — one might suppose it possible — in such a moment commune in a mutual recognition of the country opening to them through the gesture of love given and openly received, though such gesture may be confused and largely confounded by the cultural debris of history encrusting such actions. It is the encrustation to which Julian and the black mother respond in an "equality" that is oblivious to the spiritual dimension of this small drama. We should note here, of course, that Miss Flannery is not condescending to blacks, for despite misunderstanding by some critics she treats them as also inheritors of Original Sin and therefore possibly sinful. That is, her manner toward Julian and his companion in Modernist deployment, the boy's mother, does not discriminate by spectacle of black and white.

Given the critical reception Flannery O'Connor experienced with the publication of

Wise Blood and *A Good Man Is Hard To Find*— some of those New York critics taking her
for a hillbilly nihilist rather than hillbilly Thomist — she recognized but the more the challenge peculiar to her gifts: the pervasive and perversely radical reading of human nature as
black and *white* by a pseudo-intellectual condescension awarding absolution as if a recovered prelapsarian innocence gained by system rather than by love — an innocence awarded
by egalitarian reductionism to the black or white citizen if committed to Modernist versions of grace as conferred by abstract "social justice." Not in respect to good and evil as
possible action by *any* person fallen from grace, whether black or white. Instead much of
the critical attention given her work reached only the surface of cultural spectacle, her point
of departure in making. Her critics (many of them) have been more or less oblivious to the
depths of her concern for our common, our *given*, human nature in its fallenness.

By distorted reading of situation as limited to spectacle, the critic in his interest in the
"popular spirit" has been led to the growing authority of "situational ethics," the antagonistic spirit O'Connor engages in her fictions. Recognizing this new order, the critic would
enlist her either in social commentary or, if she be too conspicuously reluctant as artist to
subordinate her gifts to that cause, she must be accounted for as writing witty satire aimed
at social injustices practiced by a part of humanity against the rest of it by citizens arrested
in a cultural primitivism. That is to see justice reduced to the level of cultural history in
O'Connor's view and not as a reality of human nature as *spiritually* fallen. Charity as a virtue,
by this Modernist account of her work, becomes the concept of a corrective abstraction to
be measured impressively on thermometers on the public square, as by those signs with rising red showing monetary contributions to the "Community Chest." Charity becomes a sum
deducted on income tax returns. Such charity can be signified only by material redistribu-
tion, not as properly to be a recovery in our true country by an openness of love in community as a body, in a membership one to another signifying (pointing toward) the material world as but secondary.[1] Community Chest thermometer on public square — Yes. A
cross speaking communal sacrifice in response to Christ's sacrifice on that public square? No,
with an absolute civil positive law prohibitive of such witness.

How tempting as matter to art, this recognition by a visionary artist, O'Connor, this
almost universal temptation to pseudo-intellectual reductionism. A temptation as well endangering that fundamental principle to art, the artist's responsibility to the good of the
thing he makes instead of to social commentary. For his is not a responsibility to effect "moral
rectitude" in his audience as the primary concern of art, the distortion of art inevitable to
Modernist thought. (Here we mean by *pseudo-intellectual* that deportment denying any
spiritual dimension to our actuality as person.) Such sophisticated intellectuals, disoriented
by their alienation from reality, themselves demand more appealing characters in her fictions,
wanting their heart lifted up. How formidable a challenge to the head, especially if one recognize that state of intellect as pervasive of the social and cultural fabric with which the poet
must content in his moment of selecting concrete elements of spectacle as a point of departure in a fiction. For it is false vision that is the necessary texture out of which intellectual
action itself might provide drama. A character *possible* out of such current intellectual context would respond to impinging things and persons, reflecting possible actions of human
nature as recognizable to an audience, though the poet find himself not sharing sympathetically with his audience the surface understanding of the causes of such actions. For
O'Connor, those false causes are rooted in human nature gone astray from what Dante recognizes in the opening lines of the *Divine Comedy,* a state of spiritual deracination in which

the person is "confused by ways" that are "at strife with the straight way," and so finds himself lost in a "dark wood."

Strife consequent upon this deracination is conspicuous in our world, though our experiences of it and recognition of it as actual are not understood as Dante does. A poet like O'Connor (or Walker Percy or T. S. Eliot or Dostoevsky) may see our spiritual confusions within the here and now as the very old intellectual confusions of ways at odds with the straight way since Adam. But for most of us there is a temptation out of such a confusion of ways to presume sophistications of intellect justifying our disoriented intellectual entanglements. Yet such confusion makes possible comic actions (in Dante's sense of *comic*) within a fiction such as O'Connor's. A reader need not necessarily recognize the "historical" origins of what has become the thoroughly established tradition we call Modernism, locating its explosive influence on the popular spirit in the 18th century Enlightenment philosophy as O'Connor does. It may nevertheless help to know that Richard Weaver argues earlier origin in Occam's Nominalism (in his *Ideas Have Consequences*), and that Gilson finds it already underway in Abailard's "logicism" as philosophy's dominant principle. (Gilson makes this argument in his William James Lectures, *The Unity of Philosophical Experience*, at about the time of the Fugitive-Agrarian awakening to Modernist dislocations in *I'll Take My Stand*.)

Such are, for O'Connor as a "Southern" writer, the "historical" challenges in their intellectual dimension to her fictions, engaged by her indirectly through the persuasive immediacy of her characters in her local place. Neither place (as community) nor characters (as her active agents within community) seem to recognize their "historical" conditionings by an increasingly wayward philosophy out of disoriented intellectual actions. What knows a Haze Motes of Nietzsche, or the Bible salesman in "Good Country People" of Jean-Paul Sartre? O'Connor's fiction shares, then, with Biblical texts that characteristic of a "hiddenness" within it, whereby she speaks of herself indirectly as a "prophet of distances." Through her deployments of characters in grotesque manifestations of their actions, that hiddenness is the more obscured in our initial encounter of her fiction, in that as intellectually educated we are generally "smatters," to borrow a term from Solzhenitsyn suggestive of correspondences between Soviet and American "educationism." Walker Percy is more direct and open in his uses of the Modernist history of philosophy as it affects the making of his fictions than O'Connor. But both Percy and O'Connor share (by degree) recognition of our intellectual wanderings from the true way since Dante as to be approached indirectly in making fictions. They do so as persons concerned for the recovery of that way necessary to our recovery as persons.

Though the one (O'Connor) is more "country" in the matter chosen for her making than the other (Percy, whose fictional arena is suburbia), she proves the more subtle "hillbilly Thomist," treating a "hillbilly nihilism" become pervasive of the popular spirit out of pseudo-intellectual sophistications high and low in cultural measures. That is the inherited "intellectual history" we all breathe with which she must contend. It is a tradition exacerbated out of Descartes' "doubt" about certifying his own existence as a "consciousness," a doubt subsequently made intellectually respectable to our deportment toward things and persons. And it is a tradition leading increasingly to our isolated consciousness as we react to things and persons as made "intellectually" acceptable by Kantian "universalisms" spawning "transcendentalisms" of various species — from Emerson's version to Madam Blavatsky's. Such ventures into the angelism of self-sufficiency gradually supercedes the matter-of-fact, down-home nature of the old responsibility of the person to his proper stewardship here and now, a responsibility once held by a faith operative at the level of immediacy in *this* place at *this* moment — the arena within which common sense allows a sorting of the confused ways lest as person we presume to an absolute freedom of wandering. In contrast, our world has made a virtue of being intellectually divorced from reality itself, though thereby we become increasingly lost in the cosmos.

Such tangled ways prove malleable and manipulatable under the auspices of the growing Nietzschean skepticism maintained by a specialized intelligentsia. Skepticism encourages the will to power over nature — over *being* itself as Eric Voegelin says. Old signposts within the entangled ways may be variously adapted, posting false millages to Utopias as based on survey maps of reality from Abelard to Occam to Descartes, enlarged by Kant, Hobbes, Hegel — by Comte and Marx. For the "popular spirit" must be enlisted to such wanderings. Or so the critiques of Voegelin, Gilson, Maritain, and others reveal. Such reductionist intellectual map-making would guide the Modernist on his rambles through reality, distracting him from the realization that he is lost in the cosmos. Many of these critiques are known to O'Connor in relation to her own concerns, for she is widely read in our intellectual history. She puts her conclusion summarily and simply as we know: we have separated grace from nature in a pursuit of Utopian desires to satisfy self-love. Her summary point, one might say, allows as footnotes the considerable explorations of our intellectual dislocations, explicated in such works as that of Eric Voegelin in his *From Enlightenment to Revolution;* of Gerhart Niemeyer's *Between Nothingness to Paradise;* of Gilson's *Methodical Realism.* In her own fiction as art, incarnated from the here and now, O'Connor reflects the *possibility* of recovery toward a way increasing lost since Dante to our community.

O'Connor as poet, then, takes her point of departure in the established Modernist resolution that God is indeed dead, and that therefore evil in relation to good is but a relativistic relation to be accommodated in convenience to this moment, parsed by explaining away evil and thereby leaving good itself a highly relativistic "idea," suited (i.e., "dressed") as may be made most attractive to self-sufficiency. Nietzschean skepticism allows a growing presence in us of a cynicism superadded to dreams of an absolute freedom as Superman — until we reach the increasingly shocking effects upon community in the 20th Century. We become panicked to discover the "self" — the discrete consciousness — alienated from both nature and community! But it had already long since become alienated from that Cause once called a Love transcendent of self and of any discrete consciousness. The detritus of recent history lies starkly accusatory, signified by names: Pol Pot, Hitler, Stalin. On and on our recorded ruins named for super-saviors.

Such is the current reality to the discrete person as intellectual soul incarnate in O'Connor's vision of our given human nature, she as a maker of fictions engaging the Modernist malady at its local level. (If she tried a fiction foreign, she says, her characters would still sound like Herman Talmadge.) What she discovers as maker is that this reality of circumstances in the current world can be dramatized without the heavy presence of philosophical speculation focused in ideas. Her own considerable awareness of the history of our spiritual disease may be hidden by indirection in her fictions in such a way as to allow us some recognition of the fictions as parable-like. Perhaps that is what she has somewhat in mind when she says that the stories are primarily the issue of her talents multiplied as an offering to God, to use or not use as he sees fit. As for her indirection in making, she knows her readers to have been nurtured especially by the academic uses of literature in such celebrated literary movements as "Realism" and "Naturalism." That literary ground is a point for her own departure into a fiction that may prove somewhat baffling since insufficiently accounted for by "movements," yet persuasive in effect. Her comic exaggeration, popularly ascribed to her as her use of the "grotesque," is in her adaptations of the "realistic" and the "naturalistic." She has a quick eye for the surface of things (images of things and dialogue) which is impressive to a naïve response to spectacle, a response as if spectacle were indeed essence. But when she goes deeper than spectacle, the naïve reader, conditioned by formal "Realism" and "Naturalism" in his "education" as a reader, discovers that he must learn a new way of reading. How else come to recognitions of the deeper realities of such "grotesque" figures in her fiction as a Haze Motes, or Old Tarwater and Young Tarwater? Or of a Misfit as an intuitive anti–Modernist? Or of a Mrs. Turpin or O. E. Parker in their awkward quests for the true name of Truth Itself in order to recover their true way?

Such an amalgam of thought, of "ways," O'Connor recognized as the intellectual ground in which the Modernist academy had re-founded itself, wherein it grows new disciples of Modernism such as she refers to in one of its species of professionalism as that "unreliable lot" of critics — to be found not only in New York but in Taulkinham, née Atlanta, or even in Milledgeville, Georgia. As for the latest prophet of that Modernist version of man, and especially evident in the academy when she became a student in a "writers' workshop" at Iowa: Jean-Paul Sartre, whose position intellectually is the obverse of St. Thomas.' One makes oneself by his own action, Sartre maintains — becomes a *substantive* being as an effect of willful action, so that action precedes being. That is the principle which had become intellectually respectable to radical intentionality, a "progressive" improvement upon the more pallid Emersonian arguments for the self-made man as a social entity — Emerson the pre-eminent academic "cultural guru" of that "way." That had been a way increasingly acceded to by the academy, just after World War II, the academy itself increasingly assaulted by an emergent Nihilism in the young, with a chaotic effect not only upon the academy but upon community as remote as that in middle Georgia.

That this is very much O'Connor's reading of her challenge as maker out of Modernist circumstances is evident. It is, incidentally, sometimes openly indicated by her in "talks" such as her "Regional Writer." There she reports news from a Wisconsin friend. That friend had been reassured by the man attempting to sell her a house for her move South, a house in Atlanta suburbs. "You'll like this neighborhood," he said. "There's not a Southerner for two miles." To which news Flannery remarks that "at least we can be identified when we do occur." No report by this agent to his Wisconsin customer on whether there might be, on such a suburban estate, perhaps a cast-concrete statue of an artificial "Negro." It is in relation to this anecdote that she remarks as well that, "no matter how favorable all the critics in New York City may be, they are an unreliable lot, as incapable now as on the day they were born of interpreting Southern literature to the world," that Atlanta real estate agent himself member of the "New York" tribe. Had she been still with us in 1970, when Tom Wolfe published his *Radical Chic & Mau-Mauing the Flak Catchers,* she would have recognized the work as something of an adumbration of her suspicions of the isolated, provincial intelligentsia settled in its version of a "compassionate" community in New York high-rises, with selected blacks but perhaps no Southerners for miles around — except the more notorious ones invited to tea-party gatherings. (*Pace* Prufrock.)

She sees a common relation between those New York critics she has in mind and that real estate agent in Atlanta who is concerned to protect his clients from Southerners. Both

are unreliable witnesses to the significant realities of man's circumstances in the world because man is a spiritual creature. Both tend to be arrested, intellectually and spiritually, at
the level of spectacle. She is attuned to that peculiar Modernist contentment with surfaces,
believed to be sufficiently satisfying to conveniences of the moment but not recognizing the
fostering of provincial emptiness to both intellect and spirit. For one may become an intellectual carpetbagger *or* scalawag, both modes intellectually mobile in surfing spectacle in the
moment's convenience. Of course, such judgments as hers are hardly likely to endear her to
New York critics — or to Atlanta real estate salesmen — as she knew quite well. But as also
certain, she means those judgments to name as specific the "devil" of the moment, to characterize a species of provincials very general in the current world as they have always been
evident throughout human history: the deracinated intellectual soul become indifferent to
time or place. Greenwich Village or high-toned suburbs of Atlanta may reveal concentra-
tions of those given to provincial distortions of *this* place *now.* But they are, we have said,
to be met as well on her front porch in Andalusia. Reading Ralph McGill's Atlanta *Constitution,* she not only found accounts of actual "misfits" suited to her prophetic art. She could
as well but be aware of a certain cultural pretentiousness pervasive of the world "culturally"
established as Taulkinham — good for a tourist trade emphasizing Georgia as the "Empire
State of the South"— a sycophantic echo of that progressive Empire State of the North, New
York, Taulkinham so progressive that it is "too *busy* to hate," its logo declares. No "Southerners" of her ilk need apply for visas. She knew well enough, then, the century-long process
of imitation of that successful Empire State, an imitation inaugurated by Henry Grady in
prophecy of a "New South" in his lectures and as an early editor of that Atlanta paper.[2]

Given her Thomistic perspective upon man as *homo viator*— man on his way toward
a final end as person — she knew that provincial failures on that necessary journey may be
found at every hand, in whatever place we gesture toward or resist with our signs. In
Milledgeville, Georgia, as well as in Atlanta or New York. From her perspective, provincialism is a symptom of man as sinful, as failing to be in tune with the reality of the immediate world — that reality which is always proximate to his journeying of the larger world
as intellectual soul incarnate. Provincialism as symptom speaks spiritual malady, a condition of self-love. If we treat "alienation" by the intellectual elevation of it to a universal virtue,
believed suitable to poets or novelists (as she says), the alienated person as fictional hero is
hero because he is rootless, belonging nowhere, his country limited to his own consciousness, to "the sides of his skull" in her phrase. But as she puts it, we ourselves by worship-
ing such heroes become limited to a country whose borders prove to be "the sides of [our
own] skull."

How odd that such sophisticated readings of current circumstances to the *person* should
not recognize local provincialism as but itself a symptom of an alienation that is spiritual,
though in the popular sense of the term *spiritual* we tend to use *provincialism* to designate
only a local "country" which traps us culturally in the geographically local, usually inhabited by "good country people," a phrase allowing *good* as only ironic. In that popular use,
provincialism appears characterized by a limited tribal ("cultural") withdrawal into a restricted locale. How ironic from O'Connor's perspective, that Prufrock's tea party or Tom
Wolfe's cocktail parties in New York drawingrooms prove as "tribal" in their circumstances
as Hulga's family to her in Middle Georgia. Hulga would see Boston or New York gatherings as liberated from the provincial culture she must endure as best she can by cynicism.
In such a climate, the alienated hero, whom O'Connor remarks as being "alien to nothing,"

ends up "being alienated from any kind of community based on common tastes and interests" that are deeper than as merely suited to social notices in the New York *Times,* and — she will add — indifferent to manners either good or bad in local manifestations of manner.

In her fiction O'Connor will again and again put this aspect of sophisticated provincialism in tensional opposition within a "self" who is responding to a *here* and *now,* often in a reactionary way disdainful of the particular place. We saw this in Hulga in "Good Country People." O'Connor nevertheless sees ripe *possibilities* of grace even to such a provincial person, though that person be almost blind and hard of hearing — not yet so poor as if dead. How conspicuous to this point the dramatic play she makes of the intellectual provincialism of an Asbury in "The Enduring Chill," and in a better figure Julian in "Everything That Rises Must Converge." In such a protagonist we have the pseudo-intellectual in a condescending deportment to persons in a place. Each dismisses his native place as culturally impoverished, the dismissal centering in the mother of each protagonist as antagonist. In her deployment of Asbury as protagonist, there is a satiric wit afoot at Asbury's expense. Perhaps it is less successfully accommodated to her spiritual vision than as artfully modulated in her unfolding of Julian. The "shiny penny" which Julian must deal with on the rest of his journey is more artfully effective to that story's spiritual tensions than those ceiling stains as medium of a "purifying terror" settling on Asbury. The dramatic context allows full unfolding of the pseudo-intellectual, to which the two protagonists Asbury and Julian seem a progressive preparation, in Rayber in *The Violent Bear It Away.* In Rayber there is an intensity of consequences to his distortion of love, the love stirred in him validly toward truth but refused — as we recognize though he does not. He is increasingly confounded by his experiences of local things in their immediacy, his response a rejection of such experience as speaking a pathological disorder genetically inherited. He cannot hear in them a call to acts of openness to things. Still, those experiences raise a terror in him which his rationalism cannot absolve. He experiences an action of love toward things despite his will's refusal, cowed by terror at the prospect of Mercy itself. And so there is little hope left for him as there is for Tarwater — or for Mr. Head or for Julian. Rayber cannot respond to any proffered mercy. It is a dramatic circumstance to him as person, as antagonist to Young Tarwater, highlighting the alternate possibility which Tarwater pursues in the novel's resolution.

O'Connor may indulge herself on occasion perhaps in whimsical mischief, as when in *Wise Blood* she has Haze Motes contending with the cultural matrix of the City of Man, made concrete as "Taulkinham," whose geographical and historical manifestation is Atlanta, Georgia. Enough to mislead a critic into supposing hers a satiric intent as her primary concern in respect to that local cultural matrix. For it is difficult to suppose that the *spiritual* alienation of Haze Motes himself is her centering concern, at least difficult to those who no longer believe in the soul. And so there may be lost to such a reader some of the irony of Haze's restrictions as *homo viator* within the "cultural" matrix of an unbelieving city, against which he initially attempts reaction we might call that of a Nihilistic Manichaeanism. The textual envelopment of character by the cultural spectacle of the City of Man (Taulkinham) reveals that city's rejection of man himself as a spiritual creature self-created as self-made. It thus proves a mirror in which Haze at last sees himself, a reflection of his own personal intellectual failure as made culturally general. Haze cannot at last deny his own arrogant intellectual deportment, though as an intellectual creature limited culturally by his natural origin he can articulate his recognition of exile only ambiguously. Through much of his journeying of Taulkinham, he has insisted that he is sinless, that there is no such thing as sin, his insistent pronouncement being that he is "clean." At the end of his worldly journey, however, he declares the contrary, almost as if he were the only "unclean" citizen in the City of Man called Taulkinham.

It is now a long time since Walker Percy observed that American critics "are still baffled by O'Connor and generally can't make head or tail of what she is about." The bafflement continues after all the expense of ink spent on her work since then. A recent evidence: that action by one of the Princes of her Church to which we have alluded, a transplant to Percy's Louisiana,[3] who forbade the teaching of her "Artificial Nigger" in a parochial school on the grounds that it is racist. He is in an embarrassing position, at a public surface level accused of that horror of horrors to the Modernist spirit, that of censor. But at a level more profound, given his office as shepherd, he is oblivious to the obvious in the story itself, unable to read her careful signs. O'Connor's blacks are signified as *persons* by her art, not idealized in condescending images of them, as if by blackness made martyred saint, each and all. That is, they are not caricatures of the black such as those demanded by the dislocated guilt serving self-pity in the new sentimentality of the popular spirit. The blacks in her story's enveloping action are not presented as if drawn by racist ideology, pro or con. There is implicit, for instance, a devastating judgment of that counter species of provincialism represented in the false art of the statue that is the center of the Bishop's concern. But the blacks as characters drawn from reality itself (O'Connor eschewing condescension) and the searing reality of that false art which treats them in caricature prove an unfolding, a foreshadowing, of a grace immanent to the shallow "racist" Mr. Head and his grandson Nelson, the central characters. In being well-made, the story is a rebuke to our distortions of signs through sentimentality. Standing before the arresting object, the "artificial nigger," Mr. Head and Nelson cannot see whether it is intended by its "artist" to represent a person "young or old," though it is "meant to look happy because his mouth was stretched up at the corners." There is a chipped eye, and the angle of his vision "was cocked," giving him "a wild look of misery" despite a provincial fillip to the making: "[He] held a piece of brown watermelon." Observe the suggestive, inevitable erosion of the art by time itself, as if a rebuke of a false message its maker intends — red watermelon now faded to brown. (Antique dealers would of course "devalue" such a work of art were its owner to recolor the watermelon red.) The very details serve to suggest a mirror of Mr. Head and Nelson by the "art object." It reflects them to themselves as a devastated image of man. They see themselves, though they could not articulate what they see in this image of their arrested vision. The boy appears suddenly old, the old man seems as if "an ancient child," their differences "dissolving ... like an action of mercy."[4]

When the immediate sources of the material she chooses to inform her art proves challenging to her as person (because the *truth* so revealed is of a *falseness* which is antipathetic to her own vision of reality), no wonder the constancy of a temptation possible to her as maker. It could but be difficult to avoid giving primary attention to that antipathetic false spirit of the age so variously manifest in wide-ranging species of provincialisms. How tempting to submit to the "politically correct." Perhaps in this respect the talks she gave (sometimes reluctantly) and the letters she wrote enabled her to recall the truth proper to her calling: Her responsibility is to the good of the thing she would make. The "matter" which she would "inform" — make fictionally "incarnate" (a term she uses about her art) — is the *possible* action of free intellect in response to the immediacy of created reality. That intellectual action, at the level of the popular spirit of her age, can only see spectacle as does Mr. Head. Spectacle itself seems to such a spirit sufficient to appetitive desires, which have become focused in the body as the ultimate cause of desire, rather than an inherent spiritual desire in soul as informing body through a knowledge ordinately addressed by reason.

The soul's deepest desire is beyond the material limits to personhood, the body, she believes. She believed as well that this deepest of our desires is still resident in the person, however much distorted by him in his willful rejections of or avoidance of that desire, so long as he is alive — *on-living* as *homo viator* a Chaucer might say in praising celebrative dance rather than obsessive race. Hence "the possible" might be dramatically restored by cataclysmic event, some shockingly violent event at the level of spectacle but reaching deeper than spectacle. Such violence may prove arresting to the provincial protagonist in a dramatic resolution — which resolution does not promise us of course that he is "saved." Hence that principle to her making she underlines in relation to her audience in saying that for "the hard of hearing you shout, and for the almost-blind you draw large and startling figures." She does not render a cataclysm such as the pile-up on the highway (her Tarwater remembered by his Uncle Rayber as born in such a wreck). For out of surface spectacle the lesson preached by the Modernist spirit is that the only life one saves may be his own, if only he make a habit of seatbelts. That use of reason does not support the "habit of being" that is most important to the intellectual soul. Hence, given her perspective, we discover her fictional vision speaking only the *possibility* of a rescue of an Asbury or Julian or Hulga or the Misfit at a story's end. Rather certainly, we are left with only the *possibility* of a spiritual rescue of Mr. Head or Nelson.

Given her vision, her faith in a residual hope still extant if buried in even the most reprehensible "provincial" in his actuality as person, the challenge to her as maker of fiction becomes intense at a personal level. That is, it is a challenge to her as a *person* whose peculiar calling as *this* person is to the making of fictions true to the contextual realities from which she chooses a matter in pursuit of form. The reality with which she must deal is the false vision held by an unbelieving audience, a miss-taking of actual reality by denying its *givenness*. That is a truth inescapable to her, determinate at last of the limits of the good of the thing she would make. Since the truth evident in the material immediate to her making is that man is not only fallen but in this late moment of his history also intent upon making a virtue of his fallenness, she becomes attuned to our age's programmatic removal of grace from nature as necessary to a pursuit of an apotheosis of the "self" through willed autonomy. That is the truth of the circumstantial reality with which she must deal, knowing that only God can make "any indifferent thing, as well as evil itself, an instrument for good" as she says. As for her relation as "Catholic Novelist" to her readers as themselves largely seduced into the Modernist reduction of personhood: "I submit that to do this [to make good that which is evil or indifferent] is the business of God and not of any human being," including most specifically herself as a maker of fictions.

Understanding herself as limited person, then, she understands the better her responsibility to, and the difficulties of, dealing with the truth of things as artist. She *makes* under the necessity of reaching (through reason) an accord of her given limits as *this* intellectual soul incarnate through responsibilities inherent to her gifts as a maker. As incarnate, she is asked on occasion whether her crippled body (she a "victim" of lupus) affects her fiction. We heard her reply: No, she says, because she writes with her head and not her feet. A seemingly flippant response, but one out of a metaphysical understanding of her nature in its

givenness. In addition, perhaps such a response to shallow question might even stir the
naïve questioner to reexamine his own question in relation to his own reality as an intellectual soul incarnate. By such response to her making of fictions, disoriented questions rising
in spiritually deracinated persons, she knows the likelihood that she will be taken as writing only a satiric "naturalism," seemingly directed against a regional provincialism. She may
be thus read as if engaging a deprivation in "Southerners," especially those a tourist might
encounter in Middle Georgia as culturally deprived.

How challenging indeed, given her understanding of herself as a "realist of distances,"
to make persuasive an art out of such radically antipathetic material as that she meets at
every hand — the ideological Modernist actions of provincial man whose provincialism is
not caused by his "cultural deprivations," whether his *here* and *now* be in the North or
South. Such readings of the human condition encourage national actions through government programs of recovery, formulated by "academic" research in support (she would say)
of a sentimentality about persons. To that intellectual sentimentality she responds with
ironic understatement in letters and talks. And so it is well for her that she may be stead-
ied in her calling by being a "hillbilly Thomist." As such in her deportment to reality, the
first necessity to her — perhaps clarified for her by her earlier outland sojourn to Iowa and
its "Creative Writing" program — was to better understand herself and her gifts as those of
a maker rather than of a creator. That is the distinction spoken to incisively by Thomas
Aquinas, again and again.

With the authority of the Church's "angelic doctor" Aquinas, that position was explored
by Maritain in his *Art and Scholasticism*, in which O'Connor finds encouragement to her
intuitions as maker as complemented by those rational assurances of Thomas which Maritain explicates. That influential little book clarifies for her those suspicions of pretenses to
"creating" acts, a term very popular at her moment at Iowa among her peers and teachers
in the writing "workshop" for fiction writers. In respect to the artist as would-be "creator,"
that is a deportment that requires the assumption of intellectual omnipotence at least, often
paraded in robes of omniscience provided by recent Western philosophers and scientists in
their elevating man through an apotheosis of intellect, whereby man may presume himself
in a position beyond both good and evil. How radically divergent her own position from
that popular intellectual sentimentality about the "self" as autonomous, made increasingly
popular by the academy. She to the contrary believed her gifts as *person* were given, and by
that givenness properly reminding her not only of her limits as maker, but of her continuing dependence from the Lord and Giver of life itself as a person. The same she believed
true of the whole contextual creation, within which her gifts must be realized through actions not only intellectual, but spiritual. Thus reason concludes that intellect is a subordinate servant to the soul of the person on his appointed (his *possible*) way to an ultimate end
beyond the temporal manifestations of the proximate good within which as person each may
easily become lost and wandering in circles, tethered by a false assumption of the self as the
only dependable reality, served by the cosmos as its center.

And so it was reassuring to have St. Thomas confirm her intuitive recognition, in support of her rational confirmations of her vision as contrary to an engulfing intellectual Modernism. As persons, St. Thomas argues, we are endowed by our given nature to be *makers*
of "the particular" he says. (And the principle applies to mankind in general as makers, not
just to philosophers or scientists or poets, as O'Connor affirms.) As makers, we are necessarily dependent intellectually upon the pre-existing things which we experience through

their own particularities. We *know* things, though we know them in a limited and not a comprehensive manner. We know them initially by intuitive intellect, Thomas says, as things in themselves, that knowing mediated to intellect through the senses out of an immediate encounter of a thing, to be remembered as immediate as well to reason's ordering of many truths of things known. By such knowing we may move toward an understanding of the known, through reason's pursuit of universals as governing known particularities within the orders of being. That is the manner proper through an intellectual perfection (a coming-to-be) of intellect as a limited gift, *to be* understood as such by that inherent intellectual nature in us which Thomas calls *natural law*. That is the concept Thomas advances out of Aristotle in response to his own faith in Revelation.

Thus knowing things intuitively serves a larger knowing which is to be gained through the auspices of the rational intellect. And so we begin our journey of knowing, toward understanding, by responding to the self-evident: We as person *depend* by limit from our pre-existent givenness as *this* person. Only by a willful presumption may we claim the title of *creator,* as if thereby to become independent of the mystery of givenness. It is out of this self-evident point of departure that St. Thomas will argue that as person we are "not able to draw forth ... form without material determined and presupposed from another."[5] Necessarily, the person is a *maker*— the making of things his proper habit of existence as person. He must recognize that his responsibility is to draw forth form appropriate to his made thing in relation to the limits already pre-existing in the givenness of things — the matter chosen within his own limits as person in making — the province of his stewardship. There will come to him a shocking recognition: the starting matter for the *poet* proves to be himself as a person, himself a given "thing" existing as a discrete nature through unmerited grace. Thus any claim to be a "creator" by his actions as independent of his own givenness proves most problematic to reason itself, insofar as reason demands an honesty of our will in the pursuit of truth.

Thomas' view of the maker is almost the obverse of the view held by that Modernist artist whom Flannery O'Connor recognized as a dominant presence in her world. She goes against the flow of theory derived from *deterministic* versions of man's own nature as resting in accidents as the ultimate cause of all things. (The theories are worse than the furies, she will say.) Nor did she miss the irony of an arrogant assertion of a determinism presumed by intentionality of the willful intellect, as if by will a "self" thus becomes its own "creating" principle in an absolute freedom. Intentionality is thus presumed the cause of truth itself. How inevitable out of such presumption that evolution of "situational ethics" as a principle of a popular "philosophical" deportment to creation in her day, subverting thereby the intellectual gift of a Thomistic natural law to the accommodation of a deportment to positive law under the governance of that natural law. The separation of grace from nature, she recognizes, denies natural law in favor of positive law as made absolute by intentionality. Intellect itself in this perspective must be logically concluded an accident of the body nevertheless — which is itself an accident of the confluence of the randomness of things "evolved" over infinite time: All things, including this intentional "self," are thus but accidental. Therefore positive law, in respect to social law, must be a formulation out of an intellectual relativism as the principal and cause of any acceptable "truth" as beholden ultimately to random accident. Relativism becomes the necessary "metaphysics" allowed to materialism, out of the "logical" accountancy by Positivistic science of man himself, logic itself (Gilson suggests) born of Abelard's "logicism."

What richer ground, given her own vision of man, for her ironic drama, then? For however confidently asserted may be that Modernist conclusion — in a self-contradictory absolute relativism — no person is easily comforted by it. It is a principle exasperating any person's intentions to his own transcendent autonomy in seeking an escape through intentional alienation from all other than the "self," embracing at last as the only absolute self-love. How inevitable a figure of such an intellect in act then is O'Connor's protagonist Haze Motes, a country Nietzsche! Through dramatizing such a figure, O'Connor explores the origins of self-contradictory conclusions in Haze himself, the tension in him between an illusional freedom which in truth is but self-enslavement by his intellect, as if mechanistically "determined" by his will. She looks closely at that possible drama as most truthful about the reality buried deep in the spectacles of the world at hand, and known (however much denied) within our own consciousness as an intellectual soul in the guise of a "self." How interesting then that, like Dostoevsky, her "researches" for matter welcomes the daily press with its evidences of spiritual malady made popular through spectacles of self-desire out of Modernist doctrine. How naïve, that sophisticated doctrine which declares that the only health possible to the "self" is a willed determination to self-love. Its consequences blossom as symptoms, epidemic in the popular spirit as revealed symptomatically in local incidents of violence, in a "natural" irony often as random violence. The news media proves exponentially ravenous of such a spectacle as denied spiritual origin.

Not only Dante, but a lesser and closer poet to Flannery O'Connor is concerned with the intellectual and spiritual cul-de-sac into which Modernist man attempts to escape the challenges of reality to his spiritual nature. In her *Mystery and Manners,* we find her talking more of Nathaniel Hawthorne than of Joyce or Henry James, though she recognizes a difference between the one (the "romantic") and the other two (the "realists") at the level of their craftsmanship. In her reflections in "Some Aspects of the Grotesque in Southern Fiction," she suggests that "When Hawthorne said that he wrote romances, he was attempting … to keep for fiction some of its freedom from social determinisms, and to steer it in the direction of poetry." He attempted that rescue because he "knew his own problems and perhaps anticipated ours when he said he did not write novels, he wrote romances." That we have paid Hawthorne's observations scant attention in academic concerns, particularly in respect to his "poetry," seemed evident to her. "Today many readers and critics have set up for the novel a kind of orthodoxy. They demand a realism of fact which may, in the end, limit rather than broaden the novel's scope."

That is an imposition upon the complexity of reality by a determining orthodoxy of fact as the instrument to power, an imposition of intentional form to be imposed upon reality rather than grown out of it. Thus the mystery of givenness, upon which depends the artful drawing forth of form, is obscured, the intentionality becoming more and more limited to the *spectacle* of reality as appropriated on the authority of the willful intentionality to *impose* form rather than draw it forth from chosen matter as *possible* action. If Hawthorne was no metaphysician, he nevertheless recognized a perversion underway, a perversion which could only elevate an Alymer (of "The Birthmark") as reigning intellect. Since then there have accrued destructions from the Alymers's experiments of trial and error in the separation of grace from nature, a Positivistic science now established in triumph. It is this fatal intellectual error of separating grace from nature that O'Connor, herself a pilgrim on her way, discovers as the cause of an active self-isolating consciousness whose "freedom" seems possible only in an escape of reality. It is this Modernist consciousness, then, that she takes as point of departure in making her fictions. She will express concern for a sentimentality effected out of perversions of nature, issuing in the dark blossoms of Auschwitz and Dachau. Such horrors, she suggests, occur when we celebrate "tenderness" in a justification of abstraction as derived from facts separated from the inclusive reality of a thing in itself. Persons thus are depersonalized in the most destructive way, though a self-justified action usually made in the name of the common good as to be decreed by some ideological tribe. Always that rational "tenderness" is advanced, at least publicly, in the name of that "common good." Thus a totalitarian power out of "a tenderness which, long since cut off from the person of Christ, is wrapped in theory." But "When tenderness is detached from the source of tenderness, its logical outcome is terror. It ends in forced-labor camps and in the fumes of the gas chamber."

That is her conclusion in speaking of our distortions of reality. She remarks it as evident in Dostoevsky's Ivan Karamazov, having just spoken of Hawthorne's anticipation of such an end to power when it is exercised against nature in the name of tenderness — our example that in Hawthorne's "The Birthmark." What O'Connor reminds us of is that "The Alymers whom Hawthorne saw as a menace have multiplied. Busy cutting down human imperfection, they are making headway also on the raw material of the good." Ivan Karamazov becomes self-victim in his distortions. Such is her argument in her "Introduction" to *A Memoir of Mary Ann,* the book written by the Sisters of Our Lady of Perpetual Help Free Cancer Home in Atlanta in celebration of a child's heroic and even joyful endurance of terminal cancer. They are remarks as well, we recognize, that Walker Percy adapts to his mystical priest in the Louisiana firetower, his Father Smith of *Thanatos Syndrome.* We may remember that Flannery was especially appreciative that the order of nuns memorializing Mary Ann had been founded by Hawthorne's daughter, Rose Hawthorne — Mother Alphonsa.

4

From Lethe to the Mississippi: Shall We Gather at the River?

> *"You know [that Our Lady of Perpetual Help Free Cancer Home in Atlanta] was founded by Hawthorne's daughter? My evil imagination tells me that this was God's way of rewarding Hawthorne for hating the Transcendentalists. One of my Nashville friends was telling me that Hawthorne couldn't stand Emerson or any of that crowd. When one of them came in the front door, Hawthorne went out the back. He met one of them one morning and snarled, 'Good Morning Mr. G., how is your Oversoul this morning?'"*
>
> — Flannery O'Connor, Letter to "A," March 10, 1956

Whence such would-be saviors of humanity as the Alymers of our world? Flannery O'Connor recognizes one of them in a neighbor of Hawthorne's, as Hawthorne had himself recognized that dangerous local intellectual who is still revered uncritically by our own intelligentsia. Ralph Waldo Emerson argued consistently for the separation of grace from nature, so that nature might itself be subdued to the material service of man, allowing in man an intellectual consciousness, a vague aura of a "transcendental" superiority to the givenness of nature. Of Emerson, O'Connor observes (in her "Novelist and Believer") that "when Emerson decided, in 1832, that he could no longer celebrate the Lord's Supper unless the bread and wine were removed, an important step in the vaporization of religion in America was taken, and the spirit of that step has continued apace. When the physical fact is separated from the spiritual reality, the dissolution of belief is eventually inevitable." We need only a cursory recovery of Emersonian arguments to see what she means.

Emerson is particularly concerned for *facts* as an empowerment of man over nature, his facts distilled in a reduction of things to formulae. It is his constant theme, preached for instance on his elevation of the "American Scholar" as man deified by himself as autonomous. And in respect to his "Doctrine of the Soul," he puts that point: "Our life is indeed nothing but an endless procession of facts or events like the pulsations of the head or the beats of the pendulum." It is through possession of facts, out of events of encounter with nature and man, therefore, that the "Self-Made Man" becomes Emerson's ideal, his version of Nietzsche's Superman. Man is to be self-made in acquiring power over nature, for "He who knows that power is in the soul, that he is weak only because he has looked for good out of him and elsewhere, and so perceiving, throws himself unhesitatingly on his thought, instantly rights himself, stands in the erect position, commands his limbs, works miracles."

T. S. Eliot will make a devastating aside on this remark in a parenthetic quatrain of his "Sweeney Erect": "(The lengthened shadow of a man/ Is history, said Emerson/ Who had not seen the silhouette/ Of Sweeney straddled in the sun)." Sweeneys no less than Alymers are possible ends of gnostic intentionalities to autonomous existence, a realization increasingly discomforting to Eliot himself as skeptical intellectual, he having discovered himself to have given consent to that principle as a young intellectual adolescent at Harvard.[1] How dangerous to intellect when liberated to the false-freedom of autonomy by Emersonian assurances that the only virtue necessary is "Self-Reliance." For, Emerson says, "Nothing is at last sacred but the integrity of our own mind." It is in "self-trust" that "all virtues are comprehended."[2]

With that assurance recovered, one can say with self-assurance that "The world is nothing, the man is all; in yourself is the law of all nature" ("The American Scholar"). One need hardly observe that the law of all nature as here propounded is Emerson's version of the "self" as ultimate authority over truth. It carries none of the meanings St. Thomas gives to "Natural Law." For Thomas, natural law is a gift implicit as providential guide to intellect, *in* the "self." In his *Summa Theologica*, II-II, q. 91, ad 2 is that key passage to be recovered and meditated upon in these pages. St. Thomas says that "Among all others, the rational creature is subject to divine providence in the most excellent way, insofar as it partakes of a share of providence, being provident both for itself and for others. Thus it has a share of the Eternal Reason, whereby it has a natural inclination to its proper act and end. This participation of the eternal law in the rational creature is called natural law." The difference from Emersonian self-providence lies in Thomas' insistence that intellect partakes of a *share* in Providence Absolute, proportionate in that man is a finite created creature. Thus man's participation is a limited grant out of the loving largesse of his Creator. Emerson is quite adamant in arguing the contrary, so that the only Divinity admitted by him is that of the self, made Divine by its own intentionality. In that declaration he foresees the coming of a new age, "the age of Introversion," a turning of the self upon itself in an ultimate apotheosis. That will be the final liberation of intellect to its autonomous authority over all else, intellect made the centering cause of truth by its command of fact as wrested from creation. And so creation itself must be declared accidental in a final conclusion, save as ordered by the intentionality of autonomous intellect. That is the conclusion popularized by that later "Emersonian" intellect, Jean-Paul Sartre, in a more shocking version of the "Transcendentalism" dear to Emerson, now popularized as formal philosophy a hundred years after Emerson as Existentialism. Dante (and O'Connor) would declare such "Introversion" as Emerson advocates to be the willful act of self-love such as has (subsequent to Dante) increasingly arrested us pervasively by a popular consent to the holiness of the "self," the doctrine self-rendered in self-justification, whose consequence haunts us as forlorn in our alienations.

What Dante discovers by his journey, first into Hell where he discovers self-love treated as the "Introversion" he calls perverted love, is that he became lost in this world through such introversion, confused by him with what might have otherwise through intellectual openness been a valid love of Beatrice. (See her sharp rebuke of him at the top of Purgatory Mountain on this point.) That perversion of love had led to his becoming lost in this world's dark wood, he having strayed from the "true way." Hence he is required that agonizing journey, in which first he had to recover his proper intellectual nature before he could be enabled to love. That is a lesson learned under the tutelage of Virgil as mentor to reason. Dante's great poem *The Divine Comedy*, we discover, is enlightened for us when we understand the relation of knowledge in intellect to its proper end, namely a love to be exercised by the soul when reason is made ordinate by intuitive openness to things through "natural law" whereby we are. Dante's initial failure had been the same isolating (alienating) one which is to be dramatized in Eliot's Prufrock. For Eliot's famous poem — though called by Eliot "The Love Song of J. Alfred Prufrock"—dramatizes false love, that is *self-love*.

This failure of love is the same perversion dramatized by Flannery O'Connor in her *Wise Blood,* her Haze an activist version of Prufrock's self-love as Haze himself comes to realize at last. Haze experiences a Purgatorial moment, though one hardly comparable to that ritualized epiphany of Dante's spiritual rescue at the summit of Purgatory. Haze sits self-blinded with three strands of barbed wire about his chest in a cheap boarding house room. In the last sentences of the novel he is already actually dead in body, though his landlady (who is "not religious or morbid" she says) thinks him still alive and to be rescued by her possessive care. It is as inconceivable to her that he might be dead as that he might blind himself. That act committed makes him for her "off" in his head. The landlady has discovered that Haze has also lined the bottoms of his shoes with "gravel and broken glass." Haze clearly (for her) needs someone to take care of him she concludes. But she must move quickly, "must get him now while he was weak." That is, she wants him to marry her, making her legal inheritor of whatever goods may yet remain when he dies.

Haze at novel's end has escaped into a night of icy rain in Taulkinham before being brought "home" by two indifferent policemen. Mrs. Flood had already made a formal "legal" complaint that he has not paid his rent and so had him arrested. His last words spoken to the policemen are: "I want to go on where I'm going." And so wanting "no trouble" with Haze, the two policemen take him home to Mrs. Flood and prop him up in his room, they knowing him already dead. Mrs. Flood (the landlady) carries on a scolding reprimand to the corpse, leaning closer to stare into Haze's burned-out eye sockets. There being no response, she shuts her own eyes and sees a "pin point of light but so far away that she could not hold it steady in her mind," she being no realist of distances. But even so, she feels that she at last has "finally got to the beginning of something she couldn't begin" until now. Haze seems to her moving farther away "into the darkness until he was the pin point of light." She is very far from being Dante's Beatrice, though a consistently ironic suggestiveness about Haze is that he himself has moved closer to Purgatory's peak as *homo viator*. The "concrete" imagery of this final scene is unlike that garden on Purgatory Peak: the dreary room in a rundown section of Taulkinham in which Haze's final encounter is by that would-be Beatrice, Mrs. Flood. But Mrs. Flood experiences the beginning of a reversal of her version of "Introversion" as it has trickled down even into the slums of Taulkinham. It leaves her stranded on the shore of a Styx of no name in her vocabulary, to put it metaphorically in Dante's terms. She finds herself at "the beginning of something she couldn't begin," at least not quite yet.

Hers, too, has been a self-love through the willful "Introversion" which Emerson has pronounced as leading us into a new age through the action of separating grace from nature in the interest of fact. He will announce triumphantly in his *Nature*: "One after another [man's] victorious thought comes up with and reduces all things, until the world becomes at last a realized will — the double of man." Emerson, unlike Hawthorne, is oblivious to such a "silhouette of person" as a Mrs. Flood, huddled before the dead Haze in his rented room. He cannot see through the eye, only with the eye, because "Nature" for Emerson is "always the effect; Mind the flowing cause." The mind he has in mind is most exclusively his own. That is a view possible to Emerson (and to a legion of his continuing disciples) because "the whole frame of things preaches indifference…. We live amid surfaces, and the true art of life is to skate well on them…. Life itself is a mixture of power and form." Thus Emerson's argument in his "Experience," whose conclusion is that the "world" is "nothing," that the man is "all."

How may Hawthorne engage such a radical violation of reality by his neighbor down the road? For alas, Hawthorne by circumstance did not have comfortably available to him such counsel as that of St. Thomas, to whose arguments concerning knowledge and love we turn once more. In his *Quaestiones disputatae de veritate* (18, 2, ad 2), a treatise on the nature of truth, Thomas reminds us that "Since the senses are the first source of our knowledge, it follows that all things upon which we pass judgment are necessarily related to the senses in some way." And that is most evident in respect to *knowledge* as an initial perfection of, an *in-forming* of, intellect toward guiding the soul to its proper end. He cautions us however to remember that "The human intellect is measured by things so that man's thought is not true on its own account but is called true in virtue of its conformity with things." Conformity to the nature of things as experienced through the senses: that is the principle which must be rigorously overthrown by Modernism, beginning at least with William of Occam (as Richard Weaver points out in his *Ideas Have Consequences)*. In respect to this "Puritan" distrust of the senses though appropriated to Modernist doctrine, Emerson is acutely wary of the body and its senses, so that there is an incipient Manichaeanism in his thought. In him it is a doctrine on its way toward a secularization which Hawthorne recognizes and which O'Connor speaks of under that old name. Hawthorne (unlike O'Connor) may not have had readily to hand the term *Manichaeanism*. Though unnamed, he nevertheless sees it rather clearly as a reality in Emerson. What he can recognize is the intentional confusion of knowledge in intellect with its object, the resolution of which is to declare intellect the formal cause of the object. To the contrary, the object is to be loved proportionately as good by its given nature, as Hawthorne knows intuitively and as St. Thomas explicitly argues. The denial of this responsible relation to things allows what Eric Voegelin (one of Flannery's mentors) calls a "gnostic intellect" its power through fact used manipulatively against the thing itself. Thus follows an imposition of abstract systems, a pursuit of power through Emerson's "facts." (See Appendix A.)

Thomas sorts *knowledge* from *love* in a way reassuring to O'Connor. Thus in his *Summa Theologica,* I-II, q. 28, a. 1, ad 3, he suggests that "Knowledge is perfected by the thing known becoming one with the knower as [the thing known's] image." A transcendent Love, however, *causes* the very thing itself that is loved to become a one with the lover "in a certain way." The difference we might put in a common experience. We hold in our hand a photo of our Beloved, whether wife or child or (if particularly blest) of both together in a photo. The image in our own mind conforms to the photo but it transcends it as well. The limited object (the photo) corresponds to but lacks the fullness of our knowing, a knowing which can be but partially shared with a friend to whom we may show the picture of endeared persons. (A friend, by exuberance of response, may attempt compensation for the difference, with *oohs* and *ahhhs*.) But how much more precise a recognition of the Beloved by the lover himself in this experience, for the casual person sharing the photo cannot share in Thomas' "certain way." The friend cannot have that two-fold relation through image in our memory as a continuing communion *actual* in the moment of sharing the photo. There is in our intellect a very real presence of the Beloved which we as lover enjoy, even when the Beloved is not present — even though she (or they) may have been removed by death. That is the possible "beginning of something" fleetingly experienced by Mrs. Flood in a quasi-epiphany, seeing Haze as the "point of light" and so discovering to herself as a possibility a recognition that she has till this point been lost in that jungle, Taulkinham. (Again, Beatrice's rebuke of Dante on Purgatory Mountain is very explicit about Dante's failure of a continuing communion with her as Beloved after her death.) There is a *unity,* a continuing *communion with,* effected by love as distinct from mere knowledge of the Beloved as represented by such a "fact" as a photo. What a distance then between the billfold snapshot and the photo of a wanted fugitive on the wall of the Post Office, remembering nevertheless that the fugitive may himself be the beloved of someone to whom he is more particular than for those passengers buying stamps to send messages to some far off place, to those whose image may be a warm presence as they drop a letter in an indifferent mail-slot.

In this respect, we are to remember (from Thomas) that knowledge is itself a perfection of the knowing intellect through its act of knowing, its act of openness *toward,* but toward ends beyond a mere knowledge as reduced to "facts." The proper end is love's communion. Love is (as a resonance of knowledge) a means toward perfection of the soul through its active openness to the good, whereby there occurs a consummation within the lover's own soul which his mere knowledge cannot account for. For knowledge is, by its lesser nature to intellect, limited if taken only as a sufficient "accountant" of reality as measured by "fact." Love is rather an action effecting an *almost* comprehensive unity, effected with the Beloved in a reality beyond knowledge as mediated by the senses. There is a *oneness* spoken of by St. Thomas, a *con-union* with, which for O'Connor means that her making of a fiction involves a "suffering with" humanity. When knowledge itself becomes the will's primary object *as if* it were an act of love, then that "natural" love in the person becomes willfully perverse in response to whatever "Beloved" thing experienced. Any "Beloved" becomes reduced to an object by a pursuit of power over its being. Thus knowledge as but facts commanded by will becomes the ultimate end for the intellectual soul incarnate (the person). That is the Emersonian sense of *inversion* in operation, prophesied by Emerson with his high expectations of a triumph of the self as the cause of the object now possessed by "Introversion."

Thus it is that gnostic intentionality is likely to come to center upon the self as the ultimate Beloved. A little earlier in the *Summa Theologica* (I, q. 108, a. 5, ad 3) as we have seen in a comment worthy of further emphasis, Thomas argued that "Knowledge takes place in the degree in which the thing known is in the knower, but love takes place in as much as the lover is united with the real object of his love." And so we may conclude that *selfishness,* which we all both exhibit and experience from time to time, is but another name for *self-love,* an inversion of love whereby the self-lover has become disjoined in some degree from a specific thing, and ultimately from any thing in creation other than himself — that which is not the self thus reduced to object. By that perversion of love, he has as well become the more separated from the Cause of creation, God. Self-love is therefore a turning toward Nothingness (one of the names of the Evil one) in an action which effects the diminution of the self by the removal of that self from creation and therefore necessarily a self-removal from the Creator. It is the spiritual state which Eliot dramatizes in its psychological spectacle in his Prufrock. Prufrock, for instance, is at first prideful of his body as an object to be used as a mask against creation, his body distancing him from those women who "come and go" in the confines of the tea-party. His body is a protective shell like that of a crab, against his being drawn by love out of his "self" into a communion, even perhaps — horror of horrors — into a sexual union with some Beloved. But as he looks in a mirror, he is disturbed to notice his hair growing thin, his arms and legs wasting away, his protective shell in rapid decay.

And so what of Hawthorne and his dilemma in response to the encroaching gnostic reductionism he sees in Emerson? Again Thomas reminds us that "Since that which is according to nature ordered by the divine reason, which ought to be imitated by human reason ..., sin and evil is whatever is done by human judgment contrary to the order which is commonly found in natural things." Human reason is guided by the natural law, through which man is active in sharing with Divine Reason, though only diminutively so in a proportionality which separates man as created from God as his Creator. Man by his nature is thus said to be an "image of God." Hawthorne, in being true to his own experiences of reality, will as maker reveal the dramatic consequences of sin and evil as reflecting the willful violations of the *true* and the *good,* names inherent to the reality of things in themselves insofar as they *are* for Thomas, with a necessary distinction between the *good* and the *true.* For the *true* is a property *of* the *good* in itself as that good may be held by intellect. It is truth, not the actual good of the thing in itself, that *in-forms* intellect, though willful intellect may presume itself in possession of the good when it actually holds purchase in an actual thing only as a truth in intellect. Thereby the particular intellect is itself made good in respect to its limited potentialities — as the thing it is within the peculiar limit of its own becoming by its nature, by its *essence.* That is the heart of Hawthorne's drama, as revealed again and again, though not put in terms as Thomas does as philosopher. (This distinction is the theme of my *Romantic Confusions of the Good: Beauty as Truth, Truth Beauty.*) We need only recall "Young Goodman Brown" or Dimmesdale in *The Scarlet Letter* to recognize intellectual actions of failure to relate the *true* as known to the *good* of the things known. Young Goodman Brown naively distorts reality in response to things in themselves by a knowledge subverting love itself, even as does Dimmesdale. That is, Young Goodman Brown takes spectacle to his comfort as if it were his own possession of the good. The well-ordered village with its painted yard fences speaks good village people, until his dark vision that comes to him in the New England woods in which he has become intellectually lost.

Henry James is uncomfortable with Hawthorne, recognizing his gifts but rejecting Hawthorne's emphasis upon "sin." T. S. Eliot meanwhile, in his early liberated sense of himself as a Modernist, found himself at once fascinated by, though uneasy with, Hawthorne. How antiquated that concept "sin" to Eliot as a young intellectual dandy. And so perhaps Hawthorne were better treated as a "psychological" writer in a "literary" rescue of him by criticism. That address would in the end prove unsatisfying to Eliot, but just why it should be unsatisfying is revealed to him only later on his journey. For there is a considerable journey to be made by Eliot between his engagement of Prufrock at a "teaparty" salon and that gathering Eliot dramatizes in his play *The Cocktail Party,* which he calls in Dante's sense a "Comedy." In the play, at a turning point, we hear an exchange between Celia Coplestone, a liberated young woman finding herself troubled in ways that psychology cannot account for. She talks with Sir Henry Harcourt-Reilly, initially an "unidentified guest" at the party. Celia, as the play at last reveals, is destined to martyrdom on an ant hill in the Pacific. But in the moment of this exchange with Reilly (whom a Dostoevsky might term a *starets),* she attempts to find a name suited to her discomfort. She experiences a disquiet, she says, which she can name only as a "sense of sin."

Sin is a strange and most foreign name to Celia, though not the thing thus named. For what was once called *sin* until now had "seemed to *me* abnormal." How could it be other, given her rearing, which had been "pretty conventional." Not that "sin" was ever mentioned in her family, because "anything wrong, from our point of view,/ Was either bad form, or was psychological." But now she suffers a sense "of emptiness, of failure/ Towards someone, or something, outside of myself," leading her to feel that she "must … *atone*— is that the word?" Unlike what Prufrock supposes of the women who "come and go" at the teaparty, Eliot's characters in *The Cocktail Party* find themselves talking of something more deeply profound, bearing implications of a "country" larger than (though inclusive of) merely art or social and political order. And indeed, despite the separation of cultural contexts between Eliot's play and Flannery O'Connor's *The Violent Bear It Away,* between Celia's and Rayber's sense of emptiness and failure, their concerns are very like. That is, both are troubled by the mystery of love.

It is that known "country" yet unknown by name of which we are citizen by nature. That is the "country" O'Connor addresses dramatically in *The Violent Bear It Away,* with young Tarwater most reluctant — indeed violently opposed — to his natural right of citizenship in it. Charged by Old Tarwater to baptize the idiot Bishop, he recognizes that by such an act he will have crossed a boundary beyond return to the world as constricted by Rayber. So long as citizen only in Rayber's world, by autonomous intent he might maintain a separation from both worlds. But he is haunted by a "silent country," which appears to him "to be reflected … in the center of [Bishop's] eyes, … and "stretched out there, limitless and clear." It threatens him each time he considers his charge to baptize the idiot child. And despite his violent denials, he draws closer to "the clear grey borders of the country he had saved himself from crossing into," at last attempting to deny himself passage forever by the act of murdering Bishop, whom Rayber has declared after all only a "mistake of nature."

In the willful act of drowning Bishop, Tarwater also pronounces baptism, to his utter confusion. From that point in this world he is drawn and himself draws toward "that violent country where the silence is never broken except to shout the truth," he discovering himself sustained now "in a line of men whose lives were chosen to sustain it"— "through time and darkness" in this world. At last he finds himself bound to "wander in the world." He will be perceived in this world, in which he now experiences himself an exile, a "stranger" from that far country — that country Tarwater has first encountered as inescapable in Bishop's idiot eyes. He must as exile "warn the children of God" in this world "of the terrible speed of Mercy." O'Connor's, then, is a violent context in its spectacle, which violence speaks a "silent" country perceived by Tarwater as prophet. A similar violence will speak the reality of that same country to Celia in Eliot's play as she moves toward that remote anthill. Her martyrdom on a Pacific island is prophetically anticipated, but from within the context of a seemingly serene social gathering in an English drawingroom, echoing Eliot's enlargement of Prufrock's tea-party through his own magnified understanding of the relation of this world to that larger "silent country" that is always at hand.

Perhaps, then, Hawthorne's return to the mystery of sin as a failure deeper than psychological explanations can resolve proves prophetic, recalling some (Eliot among them) to things known but stubbornly ignored. It is that prophetic aspect of Hawthorne's work that O'Connor speaks of in praising him for keeping open to us our spiritual prospects. For he "knew his own problems and perhaps anticipated ours when he said he did not write novels, he wrote romances." In writing "romances," he attempted "to keep for fiction some of its freedom from social determinisms, and to steer it in the direction of poetry." In James, in Joyce, in the early Eliot, there is (in her view as here implicit) an easy (because intellectually convenient) concession to determinisms which became increasingly the purview of psychology. Psychology becomes a new science devoted to symptomatic difficulties to consciousness, considered by an increasingly deterministic Positivism to rise out of biochemical closures that reduce the person to temporal and material limits. And so mistakes of nature in such closure are to be "scientifically" righted.

Not that Hawthorne's stories do not often tend awkwardly as art to become parable, though born of his immediate experiences in the social, political, and natural ground he inhabits. He observes that ground shifting under social limits being busily redefined in both the individual and the community of which the individual is a part. For that is the purported "natural" ground chosen by Emersonian "Introversion" out of which a person is to be reduced to a part of a mechanism called society, rather than recognized as a member in a body called community. Hawthorne's are actual experiences in an actual place, Concord (with Emerson just down the road), at Brook Farm and in the Salem Custom House. Understandable weaknesses perhaps in his fiction — his inclination to parable with allegorical techniques of art. Especially so, given that there no longer exists in that "social" community a common vision of human existence sufficiently supportive of allegory as there had been for Dante. That ground lost, how challenging to a story writer if he would counter the growing dominance of Modernist doctrine. It is the challenge J. R. R. Tolkien will address, at the same time Flannery does in her "grotesque" fictions, in his *The Lord of the Rings*. Tolkien rejects that "Southern" (i.e., the Mediterranean) inclination to allegory conspicuous in Dante, but with an imaginative boldness which would recover a "Northern" myth to ends very like Dante's. (*Southern* becomes a pejorative cultural term for Tolkien.) A daring attempt, including his making a sophisticated language that we are invited to share with his characters. (Tolkien in his essays and letters is adamant in rejecting the infection of literature by allegory out of "Classical" origins.) And so Eliot and Tolkien and O'Connor: variously pursuing ends commonly held — Eliot through a Jamesean social context in his play; Tolkien through a myth he believes possible to the recovery of the spiritual dimension of human existence. And O'Connor: attuned to the local, to a socially derelict language spoken by derelict persons in Baldwin County, Georgia — or so they seem derelict (provincial) as taken by "Northern" critics (her epithet we remember not reserved to any geography).

Flannery O'Connor, as if forewarned by the awkwardness in Hawthorne's "romances," his allegorical inclinations, speaks of that "realism of fact" in Emersonian thought as insufficient alternative. For such an address can serve art only by restrictions of truth itself rather than as both broadening and deepening the *possible* in service to the unresolved mystery of human nature as made particular in each person in those tensional poles of love: the pole drawing to self-closure (self-love) or to celebrative openness to the good. If on the one hand allegory seems outlandish and to be rejected by modern sensibilities that have become dislocated from reality, on the other the dominant Modernist sensibilities that feed on fact alone must be rejected as well and for the same reason: fact's disjunction of the intellectual soul from reality by gnostic intentionality. Indeed, considering that Modernist sensibilities have been conditioned by a Positivism which provides the physics of fact as a willed substitution for a metaphysics suited to the mystery of things in themselves, the challenge to her seems all the more difficult to resolve by reason's service to her making. Out of Positivism, for instance, has grown that dependence upon the doctrine of relativism to which her Rayber clings as if his only life-raft. Nature thus reduced to power through facts depends upon the *relative* power in the individual intellect as its only possible rescue. But as Young Tarwater is quick to see, Rayber's is a mediocre mind, timidly dependent upon a relativism as self-assuring.

Such relativism is, to put the point ironically, the allegory of Positivism as fitfully practiced by a Rayber. When art is made to serve fact, commanded by a rationalistic intent and in obedience to the reigning principle of power over nature, art itself is left with spectacle as its only "matter." That is made a point emphasized in that other mediocre intellect, Asbury in "The Enduring Chill." Such an artist, like the Positivistic scientist, is left to skate on the surface of reality in an illusion of thus being free, unencumbered by reality — as Emerson has advised us all to skate on the surface of things as our self-justification. In such a limited arena, the Alymers inevitably emerge as saviors of the world. They are often intellectually gifted beyond such pathetic minds as Rayber or Asbury possess, and therefore prove the more frighteningly destructive of the world's body — as a cursory survey of 20th century history reveals. (Among the descendents of Hawthorne's Alymer in our moment, consider some of the popularly celebrated genetic engineers.) For the intent is to programmatic imposition of system, made sentimentally acceptable to the "public spirit of the age" by a scientific "tenderness" devoted to a purported "common good." Such programs, for instance, are not only like those Nazi gas chambers; they become increasingly socially acceptable programs to be formalized as positive law, the "rights" of abortion and euthanasia, which in respect to "facts" already dwarf gas chamber statistics.

Hawthorne intuitively, O'Connor both intuitively and rationally, recognize the truth which St. Thomas explicates as our dependency upon givenness in a two-fold respect to man's nature as maker — as artist. Not only must the maker deploy his gifts in response to the givenness of things he has experienced as pre-existing his own deployment of a knowledge of them. He must as well recognize as a "thing" already pre-existing, in limits actual and potential, *himself* as an active consciousness, recognizing his own givenness as that of an intellectual soul incarnate, created as such by a loving God. In addition, he is haunted by the discovery that he already possesses experiences of things when reason in awakened to wonder. He already knows things when he knows that he knows, as St. Augustine says. So both O'Connor and Thomas insist as well. Things known exist before rational intellect is roused in a self-awareness to engage the known as by nature a knowing creature, at which point comes an arresting discovery. Intellect already possesses truths before reason's concern for truth, out of which knowing the reason is turned thereafter to a pursuit of universals appropriate to *this* person's limited gifts of understanding what it knows. His intellectual quest becomes to discover his own ordinate relation to things through active love — active by coordinate, complementary modes of the intuitive and rational intellectual soul. As maker, the poet — a Hawthorne or O'Connor — *makes* out of this complex of givens in a dependency which requires of them the virtue of a prudential humility. That is a virtue conspicuously absent from Emerson's assumption of givenness as accidental — as a mere surface upon which to skate intellectually in order to "create" out of the friction of intellect and thing — intellect believing its own power sufficient to its apotheosis in a "transcendentalism" through "facts" possessed absolutely. By a denial of givenness, however, through a willful separation of grace from nature, the ultimate effect (from the Thomistic perspective) is not primarily upon external nature, but upon his own nature by gnostic reductions of his givenness. By gnostic strategy, there can be no such thing as the self-made man of Emerson's dream. There can be only the self-unmade man — the shocking revelation that Haze Motes comes upon in *Wise Blood*.

It is by her own rejecting of such distortion that O'Connor engages the personal challenge to her of *becoming,* through actions of making with the gifts allowed her. She makes stories, discovering that she is good at it. And as well she recognizes that this same truth about things is common to us, though by degree accorded in the boundaries of the given nature peculiar to each person. That common experience of the truth of things effects our bonding in a community as persons, through the diverse gifts to us by grace which makes us each a peculiar person, but also *member* in a body of community. It is in response to that commonness of known truths bonding community that O'Connor draws from the manifestations of a current community gone astray — persons gone astray — in her moment. Such is the tensional matter to her making. We have been radically affected by the likes of Emerson she realizes — Emerson here our surrogate figure for Modernist man. (We are using Emerson, this is to say, as emblematic, though remembering the legion of contributors to the intellectual dislocation of Western thought since the late Middle Ages.) Hers, she concludes, is a responsibility to the perfection of the gifts providentially given her, whose ground is common to us in the callings so various to us. If we are not makers of stories, we are makers of chairs or gardens or walls, of houses and civil neighborhoods. She, as must we, would maintain a prudential humility as maker through devotion to her peculiar gifts. Making, then, is an intellectual deportment required of persons as persons in deference to their givenness, lest there occur a presumption that man is himself the Creator, not maker. How wounding to self-esteem (*pace* Emerson) — to our self-saving pride — this necessity that we defer to limits as maker, rather than to presume an authority absolute as creator! But that is not a wounding understanding of limit to Flannery O'Connor of course, and so here we need to make a distinction about her deportment to that recognition.

In response to her own calling, she is dogmatic about responsibility to the good of the thing she makes, though she is not committed "for art's sake" — that phrase a popular justification of the poet out of his growing disregard for persons and community. She makes the point to "A" (November 25, 1960): "You do not write the best you can for the sake of art but for the sake of returning your talent increased to the invisible God to use or not use as he sees fit." She nevertheless, given the "matter" to her making — i.e., persons dislocated spiritually through distortions of givenness — must speak directly to that condition in letters and talks because "the human comes first." It is in a respect for the "human" in relation to the Giver of our humanity that she recognizes the necessity to her as artist of an indirection to her audience. But that is an indirection which does not allow a judgment built into the thing she makes, as if to serve an intentional advocacy as primary to her making. Hence for her an irony unleavened by humor in such indirection bears a severity which is insufficient. For such irony becomes easily judgmentally presumptuous. As maker, then, she observes an indirection quite separate from an active subtlety of advocacy in relation to the contingency of the possible, lest she compromise her art by judgmental resolution.

One does not "prove" anything by a story, she will say. But beyond that possible impropriety as artist she knows another danger. How easily by advocacy she might be tempted to intrude upon God's prerogative, a presumption she sees clearly in Ivan Karamazov and his uses of art in his celebrated "poem" "The Grand Inquisitor." Her primary responsibility therefore is to the perfection of her gifts in making by a surrender to the good of the thing she makes. In that devotion nevertheless, something happens to her as a person through her actions of a responsible surrender to the limits of making. She says (again to "A" in December of 1961): "Writing is a good example of self-abandonment. I never completely forget myself except when I am writing. It is the same with Christian self-abandonment. The great difference between Christianity and the Eastern religions is the Christian insistence on the fulfillment of the individual person," a fulfillment through self-abandonment in the act of a surrendering love. That fulfillment comes through a grace responding to a self-abandonment which has removed obstacles to grace. We have been (and shall be) speaking *passim,* not of "self-abandonment," but of the act of an openness of love *toward* that which is not the "self," making possible to the person a "fulfillment" as "individual person."

There is inevitably an implicit testimony in good art, a witness to reality, independent of the artist's intentionality, since art is antecedently limited by the truth of things chosen to "matter" a "form"—to make a *thing*—as we might say of that melding action out of "self-abandonment." The artist's responsibility continues to be to the making of the *possible*, his selected "matter" limiting the form he may draw forth to a perfection as artifact. (This differentiation, we must remember, is common to our several makings, whether we make a garden or chair, a poem or story.) Speculative intellectual action: imaginative engagement of the possible by making. That is a principle that requires the obedience of the maker to the *possible* as it relates to the actual, engaged by reason's deference to its own limited givenness in the maker. As maker, the person acts in a *self*-forgetfulness—a "self-abandonment"—through his gifts. How often, failing this recognition of responsibility, does the would-be poet become entrapped by the actuality of his "autobiographical" experience, unable to deploy his actual self "history" toward the *possible* in a liberation by art from the undeniable actuality of himself and of his "history." It is out of this spectacle of the "personal" that so often springs initially to the maker his "inspiration" to a poem or story, but often as well he responds as if the thing he would make is determined by that actuality at the expense of the imaginative *possible*, he confusing history with art.

O'Connor understands from the beginning, with an intellectual maturity sometimes confusing to both admirers and adversarial critics alike (given her "youth"), this limit to her making. But the limit proves paradoxically also a liberation to making in consequence of surrender to the good of the thing to be made. Such recognition is hinted at again and again to us as we respond to her accounts of life with her mother on that small farm in central Georgia. Sometimes we seem to detect echoes of Regina in the dominant and domineering matrons of her fictions, as if made out of autobiographical history. How tempting to conclude her mother Regina the protagonist of "The Displaced Person" for instance—as if by art O'Connor would take a secret revenge on Regina. What she knows as a responsibility by virtue of her calling, however, lies beyond possible cost at the level of the personal, especially given that undeniably close relation between Flannery and her mother Regina. Regina seems never to have quite understood Flannery's calling as writer, with sometimes amused and sometimes irritated response from Miss Flannery. Not easy to explain to such a practical and active presence as Regina, who (Flannery reports in a letter) "plumbs even upon the Sabbath."

From Regina's perspective of course there is scant likelihood of active help about the farm-premises from that poet underfoot. But Flannery knows beyond such personal cost of misunderstandings the necessity to her of making on the premises. She must set aside the personal in a "self-abandonment." Hers is a "calling," she insists, in response to which she may well discover that in that figure of a Mrs. McIntyre of "The Displaced Person" there may seem correspondences to Regina, given how well Flannery knows her mother. But that is to respond to Mrs. McIntyre from our own remove, although even Regina might on occasion have some suspicions of satiric intent within the art thing once it is made. There is no "meanness" afoot as primary intent on Flannery's part. Or if so, we must grant as well some evening of score in a "meanness" directed at O'Connor herself as the poet underfoot at Andalusia, as in Asbury of "The Enduring Chill." That is, from Regina's perspective, Asbury may appear an adaptation of Flannery as an "artist" come home from Connecticut with actual lupus to Regina's cattle farm. The personal as intimately known may be borrowed to art beyond the personal, in pursuit of the *possible* in response to known creatures such as Regina and Flannery by the poet's action of "self-abandonment."

In such recognitions as maker, reflections on the cost of responsibility as poet, one might discover compensations nevertheless. How hard, Christ's commandments to his immediate followers that they give up home and family and follow him. Indeed, that was the hard commandment the Misfit wrestles with, unable to surrender in a personal abandonment that might make him the prophet O'Connor says he "was meant to be." The obstacle to his discipleship has been a seeming conditioning by circumstances, those circumstances empirically distorting the mystery of experience itself through Modernist dogmas about human nature. In the story, such distortion effects a present blindness in the Misfit, as it does in Haze Motes. Here we remember Saul on his road to Damascus, who himself had not been witness to the Resurrection. The Misfit declares that if he had been there at the Crucifixion and Resurrection, he would know. Had he witnessed firsthand Christ as Christ, there would have been nothing left for him to do but to follow Christ. As it stands however such "historical" witness has only "thown everything off balance" as he sees it, turning him to violence in response to Modernist demands that he deny both good and evil, save as relative. The Misfit is hungry, it appears, for the absolute. That is the theme Miss Flannery will pursue in her *The Violent Bear It Away* long after "A Good Man Is Hard to Find." It is a truth anchored in the mystery of free will, whereby faith moves toward a *possible* that lies beyond entrapment by free will of the undeniable actual known as if *comprehended* by finite intellect. That is the mystery O'Connor embraces by faith as a "prophet of distances" through her "self-abandonment."

Concerning this gathering of art's possible out of actual witness of the nature of persons, from within seemingly circumscribed circumstances to our poet Flannery O'Connor at Andalusia, we make two borrowings from her very personal letters, now become a general public property to the curious critic. One is a report to "A" of an experience in Davidson's Department Store in Atlanta, a store famous all the way down to Milledgeville. In Flannery's own words, a small O'Connor story, undeniably hers and with herself as protagonist:

> An old lady got on the elevator behind me and as soon as I turned around she fixed me with a moist gleaming eye and said in a loud voice, "Bless you, darling!" I felt like the Misfit and I gave her a weakly lethal look, whereupon greatly encouraged, she grabbed my arm and whispered (very loud) in my ear. "Remember what they said to John at the gate, darling!"

An encounter of an actual person, whose manners we have met in Mrs. Turpin in that story "Revelation." Flannery, in downtown Taulkinham, gathers matter to her making beyond an initial temptation to surrender to an anger "exactly like the Misfit." She gets off at the first stop. ("I suppose the old lady was astounded at how quick I could get away on crutches.") Later she asks "a one-legged friend … what they said to John at the gate. She said she reckoned they said, 'The lame shall enter first.'" Flannery's reflective conclusion to "A": "This may be because the lame will be able to knock everybody else aside with their crutches."

Flannery, taking sides with Mary Grace against Mrs. Turpin and with the Misfit against the grandmother, sees them intrusively kindred spirits to that intrusive woman on the elevator. But she recognizes as well possible circumstances to proffered grace. Flannery's account of her experience in Davidson's Department Store in Taulkinham does not deny her irritation with that elevator "neighbor." But in a felt-balance recovered, she is approving of the resolute testing of God's mercy in her kindred spirit, Haze Motes — or in her Mrs. Turpin as well. Enough to confuse many of the best of the New York critics, oblivious to the mystery of grace in relation to spiritual pursuit of that freedom which is a paradoxical "perfect service" to the Cause of all creation. What, indeed, could one's mother make of such concerns as reflected in her child's stories as so palpably made — so recognizably made out of the intimately local known to both Regina and Flannery? But the stories reach beyond such manifestations by their art's appropriations of the immediate natural and social world at hand.

In the long history of fiction, there are many echoes of personal history in fictional disguise, so that it is not simply reserved to the Modern poet. Even Homer as actual poet intrudes his presence in Odysseus as a poet singing his own praises as a man "of many devices" at the court of King Alcinous, Homer reminding his hearers as well of the poet's prerogative at the feast to a proximity not only to the King but to the King's wine bowl. (How philosophically subtle as well, Plato's elevation of the philosopher-poet as *philokalos*— the music and erotic soul — in his *Phaedrus*.) There is, closer home though a hemisphere away to O'Connor as poet, that relation of fathers to sons in the world of lost spirits engaged by Turgenev in his *Fathers and Sons,* as Dostoevsky recognized. And, given Dostoevsky as a son of that "liberal" generation of "fathers" precipitating political Nihilism in their sons, is there perhaps something of the inescapable "personal" in his own work? Indeed, one may even suspect intellectual affinity between Dostoevsky and his Ivan Karamazov, remembering that Dostoevsky is of that generation of Nihilist sons, somewhat late as well in his recovery from Nihilism as signaled in his turning by *Notes from Underground.* But if one is Flannery O'Connor, try to explain such intricacies to one's mother, who labors to maintain a daughter, even tempted to "plumb upon the Sabbath," while that somewhat strange daughter continues to make strange stories that hardly speak (from Regina's perspective) a devotion to her God-given talents. At least, however, Flannery reads St. Thomas at bedtime. Still, those continue baffling stories to those most close to her as family, perhaps especially to her strictly devout Roman mother. For what has Thomas Aquinas to do with a Misfit or Haze Motes or Hulga or Mrs. Turpin?

That may be a burden to Regina's understanding. But it is also an agonizing burden carried at personal cost by Flannery. Thus Flannery, in a closely personal correspondence with Cecil Dawkins, reports Regina as impressed by Dawkins's having sold a piece to the *Saturday Evening Post.* "It sure has impressed my mother" she says. Regina brings Dawkins's postcard home to Flannery, announcing the news, of course Regina having read it on the way from the post office. And then, "The other day she asked me why I didn't try to write something that people liked instead of the kind of thing I do write. 'Do you think, she said, that you are really using the talent God gave you when you don't write something that a lot, a LOT, of people like?'" Regina is somewhat like that reader in California who objects to Flannery by letter since her heart isn't lifted up by the stories when she comes home tired from a day's work. Kindred bafflements, but one of them daily at hand, at moments no doubt testing charity in Flannery, who is devoted as if a nun to her calling to write stories. Thus Flannery's confession to Cecil Dawkins: "This always leaves me shaking and speechless, raises my blood pressure 140 degrees, etc. All I can ever say is, if you have to ask, you'll never know." Of course, one doesn't say to one's devoted mother what Flannery would say of that "old lady in California" in "Aspects of the Grotesque in Southern Fiction"—"that if her heart had been in the right place, it would have been lifted up." In her talk Flannery adds that if we multiply that Californian by "two hundred and fifty thousand" then "what you get is a book club." Alas, one likely member of such a club might even prove most local. Could she not try to write something very like that new genre Flannery is at the very moment of Regina's admonition reviewing for their diocesan paper, "fictionalized apologetics" which makes "a depressing new category: light Catholic summer reading." (Her letter to Cecil Dawkins is dated April 3, 1959, the review published in June 1959.)

As we have heard O'Connor say, her understanding of her manner in making stories when at its best is that of a self-abandonment to the action of making, a deportment difficult to make understandable except perhaps to another fiction writer. And for O'Connor more than for many poets, she understands her calling that of a religious, though she responds to it from within a world which sees such deportment as at best "quaint." Meanwhile, one might (with terms popular in critical circles at the time of her letter) talk of the necessity of detachment in the making, lest the "personal" intrude upon one's art and compromise reason in making. Eliot had talked that way earlier in defining his "objective correlative" as the means to a poet's "impersonality." The poet must choose "a set of objects, a situation, a chain of events" which might serve as "formula" for a "*particular* emotion." Art thus approached analytically may be freed of the personal and so better suited as medium to the rousing of a controlled "feeling" in a reader as corresponding to the "*particular* emotion" which is intended by the poet to arouse his reader's response. It was an argument which Eliot will himself suspect as spurious after his own conversion, a conversion during which as we have noted he is reading St. Thomas.

Flannery will echo Eliot's famous definition of the "objective correlative" in "The Nature and Aim of Fiction," though we should notice how she adapts that critically popular concept (much discussed at the Iowa workshop) to her own personal concern as maker. It had been a concept taken from Eliot by academic critics. But (as O'Connor is increasingly aware) it is so taken by an age in which "grace and nature have been separated" with a consequence (in her words) that "imagination and reason have been separated, and this always means an end to art." The artist, then, must use reason toward a restoration. But for him "to be reasonable is to find, in the object, in the situation, in the sequence, the spirit which makes it itself." Not a *formula,* as Eliot would have it, whose end is to rouse a "*particular* emotion" through deliberate manipulation of the reader's *feelings.* Instead, her concern is for the spiritual implications in the made thing whereby it is made the "thing it is." Insofar as it is well-made, it speaks a good. From her Thomistic perspective it can be made good only "by the violence of a single-minded respect for the truth" in the artist himself. Hers, then, becomes a considerable challenge as artist, since she lives in an age that has largely concluded truth only relative, an age in which a person is encouraged to consent to be determined as a convenience to the particular self in respect to his present desire as reduced to vague feeling—even if that "self" should be that of a poet.

If there is an echo in O'Connor's argument of the early Eliot as father of the New Critic, she makes the echo resonant through her own concern for art's *spiritual* witness to the truth of things, effected when the made poem or story is well-made despite the poet's possible intention to disarm such witness because fearing a "personal" entrapment. Hers is a witness

she declares intended as an offering made to the Father of truth itself. And so her deportment as seen with Modernist eyes is likely to be taken as a strange act of violence. She insists, that is, that truth measures reason in its act of making and not the other way round.
Her age to the contrary holds truth indifferent to the machinations of relativistic intellect.
How could it be otherwise to an age which denies the Father of truths, though amused and
entertained by the Father of lies? How aptly deployed become her suggestions of the presence of the Father of Lies introduced as busily attempting to subvert truth in her fictions.
Looking at the surface texture of her stories, her work appears built on a violence to be critically catalogued. It is a fiction of the "grotesque." The Father of Truth, the Father of Lies?
Those are but quaint borrowings from outmoded superstitions about this accidental cosmos, both God and the Devil now dead — as we have been assured by philosophers citing
Nietzsche, and psychologists and psychiatrists citing Freud and Jung. For we congratulate
any self that has progressed beyond good and evil. The spiritual? That is a term misapplied
to psychological manifestations of neurological activity in the brain — the brain a material
organ operating with mechanical efficiency or deficiency, very like the computer we are told
and if in need of repair requiring only a reprogramming.

Eliot's early concern was to engage his audience as poet by mediating "objective correlatives." O'Connor's is a concern to witness to the truth of things themselves, upon which
things her "objective correlatives" allow a "mattering" of her "form." She does not reject an
audience. She rather intends to put it in a proper relation to the thing as made in relation
to the good of the thing itself. By that devotion her made thing will not likely be a book
club selection, given the current age. For selections appropriate to an enlisted "club" must
cater to an easy passage beyond thought, as if thereby allowing a settled conscience — a still-
ing of that sense of "sin" that so resolutely haunts self-consciousness. That disquiet in us, a
sense of guilt, we would attribute to "history," escaping present responsibility as person. Indeed, it is a requirement even of "fictionalized apologetics" such as that fiction suited to "light
Catholic summer reading." But for O'Connor, to take that direction as poet is to be "used"
by audience, a strategy no more acceptable to her than to use art as a means to manipulate
an audience toward gnostic ends, for instance to control a reader's "feeling" by objective correlatives used as a "formula" to effect a "*particular* emotion" to political and social ends as
final. That is the direction in which art had increasingly been steered since Marx's pragmatic adaptations to power out of Descartes and Kant. One of the conspicuous symptoms
of art's misdirection we find in present manifestations of our sophisticated advertising, a
point O'Connor did not miss. Advertising proves to be an appropriation of art in celebration of the godhead of the self. (The Marxist celebration of the *state* through art is a kindred species, the recognition of which kinship stirred those Fugitive-Agrarians to their reaction against both species of art as anti-communal.)

O'Connor does not reject the possibility that the story when well-made — when brought
to the perfection possible by her gifts as maker in service to her "single-minded respect for
the truth" — may be acknowledged by the maker himself as well-made. It may as a good story
even allow an effective service to community beyond and even separate from its realities as
art. That is, such made things may serve the spiritual and intellectual concerns of man as
homo viator. But that is a service of the good story as God might use art or not. Indeed,
God (as Milton argues in *Paradise Lost* as does St. Augustine and St. Thomas) may use as
well even poor art, since his is a power that may bring good out of failed good, even out of
the evil spread by the Evil One. But the primary concern of the artist *as artist* must not be

intended primarily for the possible rescue of his reader, except as that rescue may prove a secondary effect from the artist's perspective, if God so choose. Not an easy truth to make evident to an audience seeking easy transport into a mock damnation or mock salvation through art. Just try to explain that to a good, devout, caring presence — to one's mother perhaps, who is urging the artist to consider whether she is really using "the talent God gave" her. She might better "write something that a lot, a LOT, of people like." It takes a considerable strength of spirit, a steady practice of piety toward one's God-given talent in service to a single-minded respect for the truth within one's limits as *this* person, to resist a self-inflicted violence. In such a challenge to commit false art one might indeed be subject to a rising blood pressure.

What is required (in O'Connor's view) is a steady attention to the thing being made by a sacramental act, and as a sacramental offering. Who — how many — among those aware of or even close to Flannery O'Connor can be attuned to this dimension of her "self-abandonment"? For her, the thing becomes, when made, a gift to be offered first to the Giver of all gifts — lifted up — only secondarily surrendered to the contingent world of persons. That is O'Connor's understanding of the proper use of her gifts. It is not likely that, in the steadiness of her devotion to her gifts, she will be guilty then of a book club adoption. Nevertheless, her made thing may continue in the world, even as a primary witness to perceptive philosopher or theologian — or even to a social critic if he read it aright. For once made, the story or poem exists in itself, though "historically" dependent upon the givenness of the poet at a point in time and place, a poet who has drawn form that is *possible* out of the actions of human nature in its givenness. It is, from the poet's perspective (as O'Connor sees it) only after the making that a story may be used or not used within the inclusive economy of God's creation. And so, since art depends from truths as experienced by the maker in knowing things, truths independent of the artist, then those made things become a part of creation itself. And when made by such an artist as O'Connor, who is given to "the violence of a single-minded respect for the truth" as she declares herself to be, it may even speak in concert with the authority of philosopher or theologian in witnessing to the truth of human nature. That is a reality of making which she addresses in saying that even the strict Naturalistic fiction writer, insofar as he is true to what he holds in his *limited* vision and even despite his belief in some deterministic "naturalism," may write more prophetically of that larger truth than he may himself recognize.

Hers, then, is a position which embraces possible uses of her gift when ordinately borrowed by her reader in support of his own vision of reality, since it may (in dealing with art's *possible*) reflect the implicit and larger reality in the matter chosen to that art's ends as antecedent to the made thing. Art itself may thus prove prophetic beyond the merely "naturalistic" which the poet himself may suppose its limit. In that address she sees herself in company with companionable pilgrims on the way, whether by their callings they be poet or scientist, theologian or philosopher — all of them measured in their made things by truth and not themselves autonomous measurers of truth. She shares with these in a concern for man's proper end, about which she speaks in letters and "talks," signs made separate from her more limited responsibility to the making of stories with signs. She may by this less formal deportment of letters and essays and talks concern herself as citizen within community as a body possibly recovering from the intellectual folly long festering in it. In her own day at every hand is that body rapidly disintegrating as community. Hers is, as person rather than artist, a concern that we recover a vision of our ultimate end, through recovering a vision of that presence of grace in nature upon which the vitality of community always depends. For there is a consuming and infusing Presence to community to be recognized both *through* and actively *in* both nature and community. She is, as Christian pilgrim, therefore not indifferent to our indifferent submissions to randomness, to the "personal" convenience of reducing truth itself to accidental randomness of nature as preached to us by the likes of Emerson, but as poet she knows the limits proper to art.

I think that if we hear O'Connor's letters and talks with care, we discover that she sometimes speaks not as artist but as a person in community — a community she recognizes as having become disoriented from reality. She does so without assuming special authority because she is increasingly recognized as a writer. Nor does she suppose herself authorized, by her acknowledged credentials as writer, to speak as philosopher or theologian. One might imagine her reaction, given our fascination with congressional committees before whom celebrities as "expert witnesses" testify because they are celebrities. In our new millennium, were she still with us, she might even be approached as witness on the authority of her treatments of "family," given her "A Good Man Is Hard to Find" or "Good Country People." How comic a prospect: Flannery O'Connor before a congressional committee. Or she might be called as expert on the question of the "homeless," given her Haze Motes in *Wise Blood* or Mr. Guizac in "The Displaced Person."

Not that she declines all responsibility as an "expert." If not sociologist or philosopher or theologian, she does know her own craft and its demands. She speaks openly concerning the practice of her gifts as story maker. She recognizes, this is to say, as valid the offices proper to her as person according to her gifts, in proportion to her labor of perfecting them by a devotion to those peculiar gifts. She will defer, for instance, to theological authority as established by the Church, in that the Church's and her own concern is for her spiritual obedience to the truth of things, toward a recovery of community as the body of the Church Militant whose head is Christ. That requires of her as person a perfection of the several virtues to the soul's rescue as taught by the Church, not simply the virtues peculiar to her specific gifts as poet. But she would speak as "expert" only on the latter, though through prudential humility knowing that virtues remove obstacles to grace, allowing effectual grace to her as *this* person within that body of community. The authority in such matters is her Church. Virtues guide us as personal habits of spiritual and moral rectitude, *personally*, even privately. These virtues are to be engaged, she believed, under that authority toward the spiritual rectitude of *this* person, herself.

It is quite other, we suggest, when she speaks from that authority of her special calling as maker of fictions. In that limited authority, she seldom minces words. She will summon witness to that authority as well, as she does to her "personal" spiritual concerns. But it is a witness for her more certainly tested by the truth of her own experiences as a maker of stories. Thus she will recognize virtues *possible* to surrogate persons, to "fictional" persons who may even seem bound to perdition. Similarly of the makers of such surrogate persons, as in her judgments of a Joyce or Henry James as artists amenable to her own gifts — teachers of craftsmanship in *making* to be acknowledged and respected for their gifts, and especially recommended out of her own experiences to would-be writers. That is a concern quite separate from the question of their own conclusions about the possible ends as persons, as intellectual souls incarnate. St. Thomas proves the steady authority to O'Connor in this distinction to her sorting of her responsibility by prudential judgment. If it is through Thomas that she reconciles her own givenness as *this* person, she does so as a gifted poet obligated to the witness of truth in her actions of making. Consequently, hers becomes a responsibility to a clarity in her art such as Thomas speaks of.

We shall presently engage this concern for *clarity* in relation to Joyce's Stephen Dedalus as speculative aesthetician. Clarity, effected through form commensurate to the truth-bearing matter borrowed to her making: that is a most considerable challenge to her, but differing as challenge from that to Dante at his point in history. Dante as poet lived at a point at which Christendom begins to turn away from Christ, though yet in community as formally Christian as O'Connor's community is not. Meanwhile for her, in respect to a distinction between her responsibility to herself as person and the demands of her art in a nonbelieving age, she will show no sympathy for the sentimentalized, romantic version of the artist as if he were by his calling also of a nature peculiar and separate and misunderstood by lesser pilgrims. Very early in her devotion as maker, in "Some Aspects of the Grotesque in Southern Fiction," she is clear on the point: The "writer has no rights at all except those he forges for himself inside his own work." She reads Maritain's *Art and Scholasticism* at a moment of her "exile" at Yaddo and then at the Fitzgeralds before turning home to Regina. And so she understands that her "rights" as a writer depend upon truth known, upon the inherent good possible to the thing she would make. She discovers as well that by the very making — no inconsiderable labor — those "rights" reveal themselves as properly executed only through a self-abandonment to the work itself.

Form, she knows, is the writer's peculiar responsibility. Imagined form (the *possible*) is challenged by the existential (*material* and *immaterial*) limits circumscribing the maker's choice of form. He is limited by the very matter he has chosen to make "incarnate" the thing he would make. That is a concern that is primary over any other, regardless of what a critic might say of the formed thing — whether that critic be established in New York or Atlanta or in a distinguished academy. But she is especially wary of the "scientific" critic as heavily present in the academy at the time, the critic whose address to a story treats it (as she says to one of them) as if it were "a frog in a bottle." Her surety as maker in the light of Thomistic metaphysics is such that she argues hers the greater freedom over a critic whose faith is founded in Modernism. For through her faith in creation itself as speaking with a quietness that can seem but silence to the Modernist ear, she affirms the continuous presence of the Incarnation as spoken by things in themselves, on the authority of St. Thomas as a doctor of her Church. She rejects the Modernist version of reality as governed by the variety of determinisms that have been raised to pseudo-authority through separating grace from nature, most especially the separation of grace from human nature in pursuit of an absolute freedom declared by intellectual autonomy.

From the Church's perspective, insofar as it is orthodox in its concern for the truth as expounded by St. Thomas, the contrary Modernist version of truth proves both wrong and inherently contradictory in declaring that orthodoxy encroaches upon the artist's "rights" as artist. What she holds to by her faith is that any made thing by its dependence upon antecedent matter can only in some degree reflect truth, however intentional may be the poet's denial of the givenness he uses. Creation reflects truth larger than such a poet may either see or by reductionist doctrine approve of, for willy-nilly he depends upon the immediacy of impinging reality upon him. This will be so, even though he argue the only reality to be random, uncaused accident, as Haze argues the only truth to be that there is no such thing as truth. St. Augustine had made this point long ago in his *Confessions* by dramatizing his own "Modernist" progress toward this recognition. St. Augustine this is to say was, before this recognition, something of a highly sophisticated Haze Motes. Only after recovered vision can he assert, "Love God, and do what thou wilt." For through the love of God, the will is made "right" and clarifies the limits of "rights" as rights are properly to be governed by truth. One wills the good, the responsibility thereafter an intellectual one of distinguishing proximate (lesser) good from ultimate good. (We might remember that Augustine himself won an award for his poetry before this recovery of himself as person.)

As a professing Manichaean, a "literary" critic in the academy of his day, Augustine will leave the academy with reservations about it which we find faintly echoed in Flannery O'Connor. But he will argue also, after his conversion to Christianity, that "pagan" literature itself speaks toward the truth of the Christian perspective on reality. For art speaks truth insofar as the pagan poet engages openly the reality of things, however fancifully he may delude himself in mistaking grace in nature as if a pagan *élan vital*. Insofar as the pagan poet is drawn to a communion with, a con-union with, things in themselves, his art must in some degree reflect the truth of the things, drawing the poet thereby to what long after may be apotheosized as "Nature" by continuing Pagan sensibilities, though that truth whose cause (St. Augustine declares) is the creating God descended into "Nature" in the Incarnation. (St. Augustine's perceptive explications of texts both Christian and Pagan incidentally, reveal him to be an unacknowledged father of that "New Criticism" which we tend to credit as if invented in the 1920s and 1930s.)

To *will* the good is not to *cause* the good, but it may be to *consent* to the good as anterior to the willing consent. That is the mystery of spiritual freedom as expressed in a prayer for peace to the soul, a prayer which addresses God as he "whose *service* is *perfect* freedom," and it is to this service through her gifts that O'Connor devotes herself. The challenges to O'Connor at the level of her existence as *this* person, whose responsibility is that of her limited freedom perfected, constant in the challenge to her as the *limits* of her gifts as maker. She accepts limit, and she deals with it more and more comfortably. As a maker of fictions, she did attend that "Creative Writing" school made famous at the University of Iowa, having the good fortune (she would call it a gift of grace) to go there just as Andrew Lytle as fellow Christian appeared as a "writer in residence." As a graduate of that program, with that experience on her *vita*, she had henceforth to respond to an inevitable question, inevitably repeated: Can "creative writing" be taught? Her sometimes acerbic answer: "Yes, there is a kind of writing of fiction that can be taught. It is the kind that you then have to teach people not to read." And again, "Everywhere I go I'm asked if I think the universities stifle writers. My opinion is that they don't stifle enough of them. There's many a bestseller that could have been prevented by a good teacher," perhaps such a teacher as Lytle. What concerns her is a growing "academic" supposition that technique learned in experimental laboratories for writers can produce good fiction.

In her view, that supposition made authoritative can only lead to the story as a well-made machine — working in all its parts but lacking art's species of "life," a persuasive imitation of the *actions* of nature as opposed to the mechanics of nature, especially "psychological" mechanics. Abstract mechanical formulae as art's end she sees as the enemy of art. That is the error Eliot will come to regret as having led him in his early concern. In that early essay "Tradition and the Individual Talent," he reduces art to a metaphor for *making* drawn from chemistry, in order to argue the necessity of exorcising the "personal" from his poetry. What has been lost thereby in such reduction, in O'Connor's perspective, is the poet's visionary consent to making as beyond the limits of mere craft through grace, in a freedom of vision which mechanical form as imposed by process prohibits. She is adamant that craftsmanship is a prerequisite discipline, of course, but that is not the same as mechanical process. She believes as well that the *person* of the maker may be rescued as person through a visionary consent to the possible through "self-abandonment," though it is not his art that rescues him. The art made by self-abandonment to the good of the thing made partakes of that sacrifice necessary in removing obstacles to grace. The "grammar" of art is required, but if that grammar becomes the end of art, then the artist foregoes vision in the interest of making his artifact "technologically" perfect by a *process* of making. It will as art be a dead machine. In such a procedure the supposition is — to borrow Eliot's unfortunate analogy — that the "mind of the poet is the shred of platinum" as catalyst, through whose actions the poem or story is an effected "sulphurous acid."

O'Connor opposes, then, the trickle-down effect upon art of technology, academically derived and centered as process in reductive makings by mere mechanics as the measure of perfection. It is a process borrowed from analytical science as evolved from Enlightenment rationalism. Such science divorces both viable art and viable science from the realities of creation and by separation distorts truth itself. In art, it is the distortion of the reality of human nature as art's matter, very often an intentional effect in the interest of reformulations of reality, usually in order to "prove" a theory. That is an intellectual spirit broadly extant in her world, one which she engages as the matter to her own explorations of human nature become derationed from its proper grounding. One need only read her words in *Mystery and Manners,* her book reviews in *The Presence of Grace,* her letters in *The Habit of Being* to discover that the intellectual history of the West since Thomas is of a fundamental interest to her in her concern to understand the radical dislocation of community which has occurred since St. Thomas by the systematic denial of grace to nature, to the detriment of art. It is of interest since that is the recent "history" of her chosen matter, Modernist man lost in the cosmos.

The strategy necessary to the denial of givenness has been widely imposed upon nature by an intellectual action presuming intellect itself autonomous in an absolute sense. And, although a pride in autonomous intellect is as ancient as Adam, she sees that it has been largely in the post–Renaissance world made the principal virtue of a supposedly "new intellectual correctness" out of which evolved our present Positivistic distortions of reality as issuing more and more in positive law separated from natural law, a necessity to the Modernist intent to declare as transcendental a new political principle: the "politically correct" now pervasive of the popular spirit. Again, this is the antithetic "matter" to truth which O'Connor chooses as starting point in varieties of its manifestations within the local. In it she pursues viable form compatible with the truth of human intellectual failures from truth. The person as intellectual soul incarnate in his Modernist wanderings, more and more lost in the cosmos however constrictive to him his "place," is nevertheless (she declares as prophetic poet) a creature created "in the image of God." That is a truth which she never abandons. She would not deny it as possible to even Mrs. Lucynell Crater, a stickler for the "politically correct" positive courthouse "law."

5

Sorting Truth at the Surface of Things

"Receive thy new Possessor: One who brings
A mind not to be changed by Place or Time.
The mind is its own place, and in itself
Can make a Heav'n of Hell, a Hell of Heav'n."

— Milton's Lucifer, thrown from Heaven,
rallying the fallen angels in Hell

"I preach there are all kinds of truth, your truth and somebody else's, but behind all of them, there's only one truth and that is that there's no truth.... Where you come from is gone, where you thought you were going to never was there, and where you are is no good unless you can get away from it.... Nothing outside you can give you any place."

— Haze Motes preaching in *Wise Blood*

If it were not a necessity to O'Connor's faith that she pay the expense of being artist *because* she is a Catholic in an age of unbelief, she might well have taken a refuge as artist like that she recognizes James Joyce to have taken. Joyce is one of those masters of technique from whom she learned so much in respect to craftsmanship, but he is as well an artist whose vision of reality is quite other than hers. From her perspective, she must recognize Joyce as radically divergent from her own understanding of both human nature and of the role of the artist in his response to human nature as the matter of fiction. Joyce, like his young Stephen, rejects his own Catholic spiritual heritage, though adapting its intellectual heritage to the conveniences of an art he makes independent of the Church's authority. Both Joyce and O'Connor, this is to say, are as artists "Romanists," but of quite different deportment toward St. Thomas as doctor of the doctrine to which O'Connor gives her full consent. Joyce is hardly orthodox as O'Connor insistently is. Her faith envelops her as a maker of fictions.

Joyce appropriates and modifies to his own intent as poet the Thomistic doctrines he learned under the severe tutelage of a Jesuit schooling. O'Connor, unlike Joyce, accepts the Thomistic witness of that angelic doctor which she comes to independent of the "educationist" doctrine heavily secular in her middle Georgia world. Especially, she learns from Thomas' treatise on truth and from his two *Summas*, the *Theologicae* and the *Contra Gentiles*. Of especial interest to her is her copy of the *Questiones disputatae de veritate* published by Henry Regnery, as her letters make evident. These are works which both Joyce and

O'Connor engage to establish an understanding of the relation of faith to art, though they come to quite different conclusions and radically different dependencies upon Thomas' logical expositions of that relation. The difference appears in the arguments Joyce projects in young Stephen in *The Portrait of the Artist as a Young Man,* in which the qualifying phrase ("as a young man") seems to distance Joyce as artist from his "personal" closeness to Stephen. In respect to aesthetics, they prove much closer than sometimes critically allowed. Joyce's novel is published as World War I is raging (in 1914), long before Flannery O'Connor is born, but in the half century interval before she emerges as fiction writer that smallish novel had become the work to know for any would-be writer.

In the novel, Joyce provides Stephen a devoted straight man for the dialectical gamesmanship Stephen would advance concerning aesthetics. It is a fictional strategy as old as Plato's dialectical dramas, but there is no present Socrates as mediator of the argument underway as there is in the *Ion.* Cranley, for instance, puts to "young" Stephen (as if Stephen were his Socrates) the question whether faith is important to Stephen as artist. With youth's expected arrogance (as ancient as Socrates' engagements with his young disciples), Stephen rejects such a silly proposal, rejecting specifically the "God of the Roman Catholics." He confesses nevertheless an influence, since he fears for himself as artist if he abandon reason in favor of feeling — the "protestant" deportment. For if not a psychological influence there is to be admitted at least a "chemical action which would be set up in my soul by a false homage to a symbol behind which are massed twenty centuries of authority and veneration." It is only by a radical intellectual rejection of that "cultural" burden called the Catholic "tradition" that he may escape into the freedom he dreams necessary to him as artist. To which argument Cranley puts a question: "You do not intend to become a protestant?" Stephen replies: "I said that I had lost the faith ... but not that I had lost self-respect. What kind of liberation would that be to forsake an absurdity which is logical and coherent and to embrace one which is illogical and incoherent?"

What O'Connor perceives here in such a young artist, let us say, is a species of intellectual arrogance intent on the authority of his own autonomy as the only absolute that can allow him to declare himself to be "creator" as artist and not merely a "maker." Such was the very popular deportment of "young artists" (many of them already noticeably aging) at the Iowa Writers Workshop which Flannery attended. (It was a common deportment still when soon after her residency I too attended that same program in the mid-1950s.) There was a division evident, however, between those taking Joyce (and Flaubert and James) as patron saints and those more activist disciples of Hemingway — though with some common recognition of technical affinities in the works of each. For both Joyce and Hemingway, there was a "creative autonomy" as the principle to the writer, sometimes slavishly followed. (Hemingway pays credit to Joyce, if with some reluctance, in *A Moveable Feast.*)

There were a few peripheral "creative" students, some like Flannery herself, some of whom held reservations about the formal academic teaching of "creative writing" as requiring this assumption of intellectual autonomy. And as well, by the 1950s, the Iowa School had earned the derisive attention of extra-academic writers, some of them increasingly forming a motley movement to be found in cafes and coffee houses adjacent to the academy. By migration, usually Westward and largely from New York City and the "East" as cultural center, those soon became popularly called the "Beats," whose literary capital was San Francisco as the most adaptable refuge. This, just as Flannery is settling in at Andalusia after her own brief exile from Georgia to Iowa and for a brief time into New York at Yaddo and then

Connecticut with the Fitzgeralds. The "Beats" had by then made their version of the Dantesean journey "on the road"—often with campus itineraries—by the early 1960s. Among
them, some like Kenneth Rexroth focused upon the literary skirmishes along the way between the "Beats" and what he called the "Corn Belt Metaphysicals," an epithet popular at
the time for the Iowa writers. With the advantage of our own perspective of hindsight, we
may recognize this "metaphysical" aspect in American literary history as emerging from earlier manifestations of academic literature in the 1950s and 1960s, literature studied as "American Romanticism" or "American Realism" or "American Naturalism" but with little concern for philosophical dimensions critically engaged Those courses were often arbitrary in
demarcations, not only by historical dates but in particular works isolated from any grounding in philosophy, and thus suited to academic specializations of emerging "literary" au-
thorities in the academy. Flannery O'Connor was very much aware of this concurrent intellectual fare at that academic moment as she undertook her Masters of Art in Creative
Writing at Iowa.

We have cited her suspicions of "creative writing" courses as leading to the sort of writing (she says) which makes it then necessary to teach people not to read it. And we have
heard her caustic view of Emerson as apostate Puritan becoming prophet to a secular rationalism as the dominant faith of the Western intelligentsia, the two closely related from
her perspective. Aware of the Beats as well, she was also well aware of Walt Whitman as
their God-father, sponsor of their species of autonomy dependent upon feeling as the dominant reaction to the "reason" accepted as justifying autonomy in the academy. There was
abroad at that moment a "dissociation" of intellectual "sensibilities" joined in warfare. Whitman had proved puzzling to Emerson, who nevertheless wanted Whitman in his own camp
since both were committed to self-autonomy. A strange affinity, then, between that good
grey poet Whitman and Emerson, for reasons we might perhaps discover in rereading them
alongside each other. Emerson's poem "Brahma" (second only in fame in the popular spirit
to his "Concord Hymn") and Whitman's "Song of Myself" might prove revealing; or Emerson's "The River" in relation to Whitman's "Out of the Cradle Endlessly Rocking," though
in either comparison we most likely concede the laurel wreath to Whitman.

Emerson and Whitman alike, though in prosody and rhetoric so different, pursue intellectual autonomy toward a self-godhead, a process requiring the rejection of the Puritan
faith in a transcendent God, which faith if held must override any intentionally transcendent "self." But Emerson, unlike Whitman, would maintain a respectable "logical and coherent" deportment (to echo Joyce's Stephen), suited to a respectability within the academy
or in the social community bordering the campus, in contrast to Whitman's radical embrace
of chaotic, spontaneous thought. President Charles M. Eliot at Harvard had in fact found
Emerson good ally in his program of reconstituting the academy. (One cannot imagine
President Eliot inviting Whitman as "visiting poet.") Not, of course, that correspondences
don't appear between Emerson and Whitman for reason already pronounced. I contradict
myself, says Whitman. Very well, then I contradict myself. And there is Emerson's famous
remark that a foolish consistency is the hobgoblin of little minds. But Emerson's is a concern for a *sublime* inconsistency through *autonomous intent* to self-empowerment—an intentionality that would reorder creation in a manner that proved suited to "academic" concerns, as President Eliot recognized of him. Neither Emerson nor President Eliot would
submit to the flow of things such as that submission that pleases Whitman. No surprise,
then, that President Eliot of Harvard celebrates Emerson.

Whitman on the other hand had to wait until World War II to become somewhat acceptable to Harvardian academies, by that time (the 1940s) President Eliot's reconstitutions of the academy having trickled down as influence even unto provincial academies. (Consider the gradual strangulation and death of the "Liberal Arts" in the American academy between World War I and the Vietnam War.) Whitman's acceptance by the academy brought him into that academic reservation which had increasingly separated itself from the people in the street by mid-20th century — the academy thereafter (and ironically) rapidly becoming a refuge for the increasingly displaced intellect in its service to itself. That had been the fate of the American academy that Eliot and Pound resisted. The American academy of the mid-20th century quickly made Whitman an acceptable guru to the islanded "self" on those refuges, wherein to pursue "feeling" was made the highest intellectual calling. Subsequently the academy made welcome the Beat manifestation of self-centeredness, in the name of intellectual diversity — as presently it would welcome as well the intellectual anarchy called critical "Deconstruction," born of a "New Criticism" become senile in a premature old age on that academic reservation. A turning inward upon the self becomes the principle of an intellectual solipsism commonly accepted as an "academic right." Ezra Pound, despite his scornful rejection of the American academy all along (for many good reasons) had prepared for Whitman's acceptance as a guru presence in the academy, as he himself rapidly became. After all, very early he had made "A Pact" with Whitman, whom he calls his "pig-headed father." They both share "one sap and one root" which Pound never rejects, a faith in the "self" as autonomous. Indeed, that becomes one of the ironies of Pound's recent history when he is declared a "traitor" at the end of World War II — escaping an actual trial only through a plea of "insanity" forced upon his fierce spirit on the evidence of his poetry. For how embarrassing it would have been to hold a Federal trial with Pound's possible execution, given the moment's euphoria out of victory over Fascism. Execute a poet? Unthinkable, given no persuasive Plato or Socrates to examine the anomaly of justice. As for the nature of Pound's "insanity" it is seen by many of his own disciples as making him quintessential "American," as he insistently declared himself to be.

Such then the intellectual climate to the poet just after World War II, when Allen Ginsberg as the latest disciple of Whitman goes to Italy, visiting Pound in his exile as his own "pig-headed father." Such the climate, when Flannery O'Connor ventures out of rural middle Georgia to the academic enclave in which flourished for the would-be writer an intellectual climate feeding "Cornbelt Metaphysicals." If, then, the Corn Belt Metaphysicals seemed more acceptable to the intellectual community in those immediate post-World War II days than their Beat cousins, they were so less because truly metaphysical than because they were less rowdy in their principles of autonomy than were the Beats (until, of course, the late 1960s). Some of them might be amused by Allen Ginsberg's dancing on a table in a coffee shop, disrobing as he chanted a poem — and perhaps even secretly envious. Pound, too, had performed similarly in a London shop long before Ginsberg, though Pound's dress was more shockingly antique, closer to the Renaissance courtier's dress than to Las Vegas's studiedly outlandish sexual strip-tease such as Ginsberg adapted to reveal his "self." Pound is remembered as shouting out his "Sestina: Altaforte" beginning with a sentiment to be embellished by the Beats, "Damn it all! all this our South stinks peace" and ending "Hell grant soon we hear again the swords clash!/ Hell blot black for always the thought 'Peace'!"

Hardly so raucous as Pound or Ginsberg — Emerson's conclusion to "Brahma." But that poem nevertheless reflects a kindred inclination: "But thou, meek lover of the good!/ Find me,

and turn thy back on heaven." The two earlier "Romantics" then, out of the same "metaphysical" devotion to self-autonomy as the only absolute: Emerson, more nearly "house-broken"
and so better suited to the halls of academe; Whitman a wanderer of city slums, embracing
life's sordidness with a self-centered profession of charity whereby he takes everything into
himself, becoming the savior of all things by absorption. (See "Song of Myself.") Emerson is
concerned with a gnostic sense of nationalism as a secularized Puritanism. He finds himself
comfortably removed by circumstances incipient of what will presently become for James (as
literary "Realist") a drawingroom context in which to discuss high cultural concerns for humanity. Thoreau will speak caustically to the point. In jail for "civil disobedience" Thoreau
has a visit from Emerson. "What are you doing in there?" asks Emerson. "What are *you* doing
out there?" Thoreau is said to have responded. Whitman as radical social libertarian engages
battlefield gore as hospital man, far removed from Emerson's Concord comforts.

　　Such diversities of self-autonomy as manifest in diverse circumstances comes to an iron-
ical displayed long after in a drawingroom tea party setting dramatized as a social political
moment in the West: Tom Wolfe's *Mau-Mauing the Flak Catchers* is an ironic portrait of
Emersonian "Transcendentalism" juxtaposed to Whitmanesque "social libertarianism," the
setting New York high-rise drawingrooms as the latest version of Brook Farm at that moment of our intellectual history. It is a scene in which, as it were, Sweeney enters Prufrock's
tea party, the conversation no longer limited to sophisticated talk about Michaelangelo. As
for Emerson's "logical and coherent" arguments (to borrow once more Stephen Dedalus's
phrase) as appropriated by President Eliot to academic programming toward secular ends,
Emerson speaks authoritatively in "The American Scholar" or *Nature* or "Self-Reliance."
In these, Emerson's version of autonomy lacks only the rowdy spectacle needed for a poetic
"revolution" such as the Beats will proclaim.

　　For O'Connor, her brief journey to Iowa and then to Yaddo and then down into Connecticut must have been a series of strange encounters of disparate intellectuals committed
to the virtues of self-autonomy. For that Georgia girl from the little town of Milledgeville,
now far from home, it proved fiction fodder to feed her own "metaphysical" vision growing out of St. Thomas. From such encounters may well have been born "A Good Man Is
Hard to Find" and *Wise Blood,* whose metaphysical underpinnings are the Modernist doctrines of self-autonomy dramatized in their failures. The conflicted intellectual climate at a
creative writing school must have seemed oblivious to such possibilities as she discovers, and
so its patrons as "metaphysicals" of technique could but be much puzzled by her arresting
fiction, though often no doubt uncertain of what element of it occasioned their confusions
about it. Since Flannery was a continuing, if puzzling, delight as remembered a decade after
her "workshop" presence, perhaps we may justify a personal anecdote. Myself as a Georgia
boy in that strange world, I met the director of the workshop, Flannery's thesis director, for
a first interview when I arrived — to be greeted by a question I didn't understand: "How's
Human?" It took a while to realize his an imitation of "Southern" speech, perhaps his version of Miss Flannery's late presence from the Georgia flatlands. (All Georgia was flatland
to him.) "How is Herman Talmadge" — our then notorious governor-senator, who from the
director's perspective was a caricature of the Southerner as a Shiftlet. Whereupon there followed some of his recollections of Flannery as student. He had "directed" the thesis of stories, though it had been Andrew Lytle as visitor who encouraged Flannery to hold fast to
her own metaphysical address to art that allowed her ironic perspective upon such strange
encounters as those made in her pursuit of an "M.A. in Creative Writing."

I remember as well what was for me still a puzzle a decade after O'Connor's residence in Iowa. By then she had become a famous "ex-student" of the school, which took much credit for her. She was already being likened to Eudora Welty in a few critical quarters, with hinted kinship to Faulkner as well. The leader of my own writing group, an Eastern writer of growing reputation, assigned for class discussion Welty's "Why I Live at the P.O." There followed a general bafflement. What is it about this "Southern" literature that is so engaging and yet so difficult to talk about? The class and the instructor alike were baffled by Welty's story, knowing two things: that they were very much engaged by it, and that it was a "famous" story. It hardly submitted itself to analytical reduction to "theme" to say nothing of its strange outlandish humor. It was a very "foreign" species of short story, at last abandoned out of puzzlement since it proved unsubmissive as "a frog in a bottle."

Perhaps we may better understand Miss Flannery's odd situation within the intellectual climate of the Iowa workshop as reflected in her early story "The River," if we consider it in relation to the continuing "Emersonian" presence in the academy, largely unrecognized in the local intellectual climate at Iowa, which held rather that Henry James, James Joyce, T. S. Eliot (before the *Quartets*) were more respectable academic presences. Consider the uses O'Connor makes of her river in contrast to Emerson's uses in his "religious" poem called "The River." Not that O'Connor has the poem in mind in her story, but she does have a recognition of the Emersonian inheritance, the burden of his poem's self-centeredness, in mind as she engages a local matter "naturalistically" in respect to rivers and woodland. These for her are actual in themselves as borrowed to the context of the story's unfolding. What we might see (in our perspective of hindsight) is that Emerson's poem proves a weakened version of Wordsworth's "lines" written a few miles above the ruins of Tintern Abbey on the banks of the River Wye—a setting intimately local to Wordsworth. But Emerson "sees" with a detachment from the local, giving his poem a burden of pathos such as Wordsworth will come to a little later in his more famous "Intimations Ode" which laments Wordsworth's alienation from the local.

Emerson's poem becomes an expression of a sentimental regret over "nature's" inexorable decay, mirrored as an inevitability to the responding "voice" itself, Emerson's own voice as poet. His is a state of mind we shall see intensified in its psychological pathos by Eliot out of his own detachment, Eliot as poet cautious in his technique of the literary "mask" as in his portrait of the self-lover J. Alfred Prufrock or in that deracinated "voice" of his "Preludes." In Emerson's poem, the external world is observed from a similar intellectual detachment, concluding in a hopelessness. His perspective upon "nature" as prophetic to the "self," he concludes, bears relation to the civil dimension of himself in community as placed "side by side," as "coeval with my ancestors,/ Adorned with them my country's primitive times." What is spoken by that juxtaposition is an inevitable decay of both. His Puritan ancestors were doomed by nature's primeval decay, to which "soon" will be also given "my dust," abandoned within this "funereal shade" of the existential world, the world as a shadow of nothingness. "Nature," then, is not a Platonic shadow speaking transcendence for Emerson, but that inverted Platonism of the "self" as ultimate but doomed to Nothingness.

How unlike Emerson's reading of those shadows we find reflected in the violence of a similar river in O'Connor's story "The River." The boy Bevil seeks a baptism by water promised by the fundamentalist doctrine he hears from an evangelist's lips. In the naïve hope of youth he commits himself to the inexorable river. Bevil intends "not to fool with preachers any more" but to baptize himself and to keep on going this time until he finds the King-dom of Christ in the river. Submitting to the river, though at first struggling against it, he at last plunges under it, the "current" catching him "like a long gentle hand," pulling him "swiftly forward and down." He "was moving swiftly and knew that he was getting some-where," so that at last "all his fury and fear left him." It is a moment to the boy anticipa-tory of what proves more dramatically arresting to us in Haze Motes or in Young Tarwater. Bevil's is a point of a possible beginning we see in Haze's landlady in her response to the point of light she sees when she closes her eyes, for Bevil's is not a suicide. It is, as Walker Percy might say, a consent through which Bevil (as do Haze and Tarwater) may rather pos-sibly become an "ex-suicide" in the mystery of death. For death here speaks more than an Emersonian "dust" within a "funereal shade" of nature. The things of nature as seen by Emer-son speak at most a residue of history to his present mind in doomed memories of his ex-perience, whether of the wasting water before him or the dust of his ancestors.

Our concern in this comparison is not affected by the differing genres, a story vs. a poem. It is a concern for the "poet's" manner toward creation as the matter to his making reflected in his made thing. How evidently different, then, do things in themselves speak to Emerson and to O'Connor. O'Connor's child Bevil would escape that "life style" of Emersonian self-sufficiency as that life-style has become settled into "suburban" manifesta-tions to be shown in sordid detail on the evening television. It is the Modernist life-style that affects Bevil in his own suburban "place," so that he is fascinated by the itinerant preacher when his "baby sitter" takes him to the gathering at the river. ("Shall we gather at the river?" asks a famous "Baptist" hymn O'Connor knows.) Mrs. Connin, Bevil's "sitter," is charged with Bevil for the day while his parents recuperate from a night's "life-style" of partying. They visit the healing preacher, whom Bevil hears preaching "the Kingdom of Christ" in the river. Standing in the water to baptize his converts, the preacher sings an old Baptist hymn "in a high twangy voice." And, though the boy is drawn to that Kingdom in the river, he intuitively suspects the preacher to be a charlatan. Not the Kingdom, but its messenger is false. And so he chooses "to baptize himself." Later, alone at last, freed of his parents and of Mrs. Connin and the preacher, he becomes intent upon that task. But at first the river threatens to betray him as well. He suddenly finds himself "treading on nothing," giving a "low cry of pain and indignation" as the river "sweeps him under." His is certainly not an Emersonian distance from the river. But in his last moment (O'Connor suggests) he knows that he is "getting somewhere." He surrenders "all his fury and fear."

Bevil's experience in this early story is like that more fully engaged by O'Connor in Tarwater's drowning and baptizing of Bishop. The point of yoking these two O'Connor char-acters here is to emphasize a contrast to the secularized use Emerson makes of his river in his pseudo-"metaphysical metaphor." In a comfort of detachment, Emerson laments, he an adult mind using metaphor to a self-comforting quite other than the use of metaphor by O'Connor. As such, however, he is an arrested adolescent intellect. She speaks to the con-trary of a possible rescue by water as metaphor, speaking *toward* a larger mystery of Cause as both beyond and in nature, a Cause which Emerson (like Joyce and Joyce's Stephen) re-jects. For Bevil, the river is a river first of all. But as it is also for O'Connor, it is as well res-onant beyond naturalistic limits. Bevil as child cannot understand the rite of passage un-derway for him, though he is presented as intuitively embracing it. The suggested possibility, suspended in the resolution of the story, is that death means far other than a reduction to merely dust or to a water-sogged body washed up downstream of the "baptism."

What is left open is the question beyond that reductionist determinism that declares death the only finality possible to a person. O'Connor would leave open (as she will do more skillfully in *The Violent Bear It Away)* a mystery of possibilities larger than "nature's" reduction of a person to but history's detritus, the reduction of person to an Emersonian "dust" with one's ancestors as the final end. Thus O'Connor speaks to "A" in a letter, declaring of her remarking "the present reality" of "the Incarnation" in nature, that she would not be misunderstood on the point. Subsequently she writes "A" lest she be misunderstood: "Remember," she writes (January 1, 1956), "that I am not a pantheist and do not think of the creation as God, but as made and sustained by God." Hers is not the closed world Emerson takes creation to be in his pursuit of a transcendent escape through intellectual angelism. But neither is it the world as increasingly embraced by the Neo-Paganism of a New Age "life-style" in pursuit of self-pleasure, speaking such spectacle of life-style as that to which Bevil's parents have succumbed. "Nature" is not God, but neither is it the self as self-loved. That was a sophisticated argument made popularly acceptable by Bergson's conclusion about an immanent "spirit." Following Bergson's revolutionary assertion of an *élan vital* in nature, Bergson will declare that "The universe is a machine for the making of God" (*Morality and Religion*), a progress to be made in a species of "Emersonian" Transcendentalism.

Emerson has his Thoreau (as Stephen his Cranley), encouraging Emerson's rejections of the orthodox Christianity he knows in its Puritan constrictions. Indeed, Thoreau proves highly adaptable to New Age paganisms in the post–World War II world. Before then, Emerson will adapt the Puritan constrictions to his own intentionalities. The Puritan by intent would reduce nature to a matter suited to building a tower toward Heaven, whereby man as perhaps his own agent summoning grace as an autonomous intellect might climb a manmade Jacob's ladder toward Heaven through conquest of "Nature." (See Emerson's essay under this title.) Emerson himself, however, rather builds toward a transcendent platform above Nature, eschewing what he sees as the Puritan's illusion of "Heaven." That, in order to allow himself an intellectual "transcendentalism" over nature as an autonomous "right." Thoreau, we remember, is at least more independent in his own dialectical encounters with Emerson than is Cranley with young Stephen, though we might remember as well — given as we have been to romanticizing Thoreau's *independence* as witnessed by his *Walden*— that the Walden property was loaned rent-free to Thoreau by Emerson, who "owned" it. This is to remind ourselves that Thoreau's circumstances are hardly those of the formidable wilderness through which pioneers were struggling Westward, they often desperate pilgrims in desperate circumstances "on the road" Westward. Even Whitman as "pioneer" intellectual is more comfortably compatible to subsequent intellectual pilgrims than is Thoreau, being as he was at greater risk in his independence from the "dust" of his ancestors. Or at least that seemed so to some of the later "Beats" and their disciples in search of heroes, turning to Whitman more than to Thoreau or Emerson. It is a period in the history of our poets when it seemed particularly difficult to choose some recent Virgil as guide. What O'Connor sees in the Beats, then, and remarks it as setting them somewhat apart, is that they at least risk the "river," though she believes them mistaken in their premises and therefore in the ends toward which they risk themselves.

To the necessity of a "transcendentalism" whereby intellect might gain an angelic detachment from nature (we are arguing), Emerson proves to have secularized the Puritan's *tendency* toward Manichaeanism in their response to "Nature," their address to proximate existence by reducing "nature" as inherently evil. (Out of that Puritan inclination will rise activist "movements" as various as that of the "Temperance League" and "Spiritualism.") Hawthorne recognizes this gambit by the Puritan intellect as underway earlier in Governor Endicott and dramatizes it in his "The Maypole of Merrymount." So too does Emerson recognize it, but instead of simply rejecting Endicott, he adapts the Governor's Puritan perspective in taking the road traveled by the "Alymers" whom Hawthorne characterizes in "The Birthmark." Those are intellectuals intent on gnostic reformulations of existence itself from an intellectually "transcendent" platform above nature, from which presumed transcendence is allowed a purified apotheosis of intellect itself, largely out of Kantian "pure" reason.

Consider Emerson's characterization of life as "a mixture of power and form." By that formulation the things of nature may be reduced by separation through abstractionism, yielding fact and thus enabling power to the "transcendent" intellect in its imposition of form on conquered "nature." For if power and form are to be executed by man as "the law of nature" as he says — a law unbeholden to any participation in creation by Providence — then "fact" becomes the instrument to the imposition desired, that of the intentional *form upon nature* in a radical transformation of *being*. All required to that presumption is a power sufficiently gathered to the reduction of things toward ends serving gnostic intent. It may be made acceptable to the popular spirit when advertised as a convenience under the rubric of the "common good." Theory, supported by promises of an inevitable paradise to consumers, becomes systematized. Intellectual power becomes the only grace to nature itself, once the old Providential grace of God has been denied. And, let us remember, this is the intellectual ground which President Eliot of Harvard establishes in the academy, whereby the academic end is to be the specialization of intellect. Existence assumed as accidental is to be reconstituted according to intentionalities to the convenience of the intellect, in support of its own autonomy as engineered by specializations deploying fact and promising an Eden in some species, to be not recovered but *created* by man's will. Thus man becomes the lord of all power — though some men prove more powerful than others, as the histories of the wars of the 19th and 20th centuries make abundantly evident.

We hear Flannery O'Connor remark, seemingly in passing, that when Emerson rejects "the Lord's Supper unless the bread and wine were removed" there occurred "an important step in the vaporization of religion in America." It is, in the light of our exposition, a telling remark, requiring of us the recovery of that Emersonian thought's destructiveness if we are the better to understand the dramatic ground of her own fiction. It is within that ground that her protagonists struggle with this principle when it has become official social and political doctrine, a new religious doctrine that has proved seductive of the human will in its collective manifestation as the "popular spirit." In the act of denying givenness as the point of departure for philosophy, this is to say, there is implied that separation of grace from nature, a separation which runs deeply through American intellectual history, having been made respectable to the American intellectual by such a declaration as that of Emerson in 1832. What Emerson presages is the more systematic disjunction of positive law from natural law by intellect itself, evidenced in our social and political world and consequently affecting social and political developments at the level of political power. The transformation is empowered by the consent of the popular spirit. Thus positive law intellectually removed from reality becomes increasingly arbitrary to whatever intentional order of community, decreed at whatever moment occurs a sufficient empowerment by the current popular spirit.

That "spirit," appealed to as an abstraction and measured by the latest opinion poll, is declared by a philosophical sophistry to be the ultimate authority in determining the truth of the moment. In response to this gnostic shell-game, played with truth as the purported hidden "pea," O'Connor remarks caustically. She concludes her "The Teaching of Literature": "... a view taken in the light of the absolute will include a good deal more than one taken merely in the light provided by a house-to-house survey."

Here we mean *community* in both its social and political hierarchy, from local to state to national arenas, within which occur the impositions of power upon social, political, and (increasingly of late) upon our religious sense of the nature of community. By that imposition, technique (derived increasingly from Positivistic science) becomes an official intellectual grace to be imposed upon nature to correct nature's mistakes, but particularly upon human nature — thus establishing increasingly by arbitrary form the imminent and divine right of finite intellect through its new religion of power as Positivistically declared. What occurs is the vaporization of Christian orthodoxy. In its stead is established that new religion, a Modernism based in a new divinity: the autonomous intellect empowered by popular consent. Flannery O'Connor might well have argued (if hers were a calling to the explications of our intellectual history) that Emerson's patron and advocate, Charles W. Eliot, succeeds in establishing the foundations of this new religion of intellectual autonomy at Harvard, that school becoming the Vatican to the subsequent deployment of systematized gnosis throughout the American academy. The academy nationwide becomes seminary to the official state religion, in President Eliot's phrase, "The Religion of the Future."[1]

The intellectual climate Flannery O'Connor encountered as "graduate student" at Iowa in the "specialized" creative writing school had been nurtured by this religion. In Emerson's proposition that "the world is nothing," that "man is all" through man's intellectual transcendence, one has an inherent principle which President Eliot pronounced explicitly as "The Religion of the Future" to that gathering of Harvard's Summer School of Theology in 1909. His distant cousin, T. S. Eliot, is on campus at the time as an undergraduate, attempting (among other tasks) to complete his now famous poem, "The Love Song of J. Alfred Prufrock." That "Religion of the Future" had its scholastic grounds already prepared by President Eliot in his long tenure as president since the 1860s, by an imposed system in reformulation of education to specialized ends: systematic form imposed by fact. The object of that exercise is allowed in the name of the "common good" of Americans. In order for those Americans to recognize their own common good, however, they must adapt to the new religion, already incipient in social and political institutions — the principles of that religion enumerated in President Eliot's specific rejection of the Christian tradition. His address outlines his new doctrine to those theological students. There is to be no acceptance of "authority, either spiritual or temporal," given that our "tendency towards liberty is progressive, and among educated men is irresistible." There must therefore be "no worship, express or implied, of dead ancestors, teachers, or rulers," in order that life's end may be designated as "service to others, and ... contributions to the common good." There must be especially removed from our understanding of stewardship as individuals the illusions of any "primary object" of "personal welfare or safety ... in this world or the other." Especially, this "New Religion" is not to be "propitiatory, sacrificial or expiatory." The Emersonian view argued in "The American Scholar" underlies this "Religion of the Future," and by 1909 has been rather thoroughly established in Harvard's new system of education and to be "progressively" imitated subsequently by public institutions, academic and political, across the country —

reaching down even into Milledgeville, Georgia, where O'Connor encounters it in her undergraduate study. But it becomes more blatantly evident at the graduate level as she discovered at Iowa, where for the would-be writer of fiction James Joyce is declared the writer's Virgil.

If the Jesuit-trained Joyce is acclaimed supreme as artist by the literary cognoscenti of the post–World War II world, the Puritan-trained secularist Emerson is celebrated in academic courses for his "Transcendentalism." Each is crucial to specializations as seen from the perspective of a Flannery O'Connor. For either Joyce or Emerson, any Orthodoxy (whether that of Joyce's Irish Church or Dostoevsky's Russian Church or that of Emerson's fragmenting Puritan Church) is to be rejected by this latest orthodoxy. It is O'Connor's understanding of orthodoxy turned upside down, to the private intellectual convenience of the poet no less than for other intellectual specializations. Religion is appropriated to secularized uses, in part as mediated by such poets to the popular spirit. It is in this academic intellectual climate (which rejects both God and Satan, both Good and Evil) that O'Connor finds herself challenged as a maker of fictions. She becomes but the more stubborn in her resistance. Such intellectual advocates of autonomy, consequently, become an adversarial intellectual "matter" with which she would deal as maker. As adversarial, they have proved conspicuously prevalent in the ranks of the sophisticated intelligentsia, as she knows. But she knows as well that this new religion of the intelligentsia has become pervasive of the popular spirit as well, having already settled into persons she encountered in such local places as Milledgeville, Georgia, or even on the farm at Andalusia. Formidable challenge to her as a maker of fictions indeed, though in response to querulous questions she will assert that "When people have told me that because I am a Catholic, I cannot be an artist, I have had to reply, ruefully that because I am a Catholic, I cannot afford to be less than an artist" ("The Church and the Fiction Writer").

There is that other and more personal challenge to her to which we have alluded. She must discover the limits of her personal participation in the world as both beyond and yet also inclusive of her calling as poet. For if hers is a responsibility to the good of the thing she makes, she must as well maintain her belief as *person* in the Cause of all good, by which belief she is inescapably a member of community, though a community not only fallen but in a free-fall toward Nothingness. On either hand, as person or as poet, she must avoid presumptuous judgment of the ultimate fate of those now holding the Modernist doctrine so contrary to community. Her own contrariness to them, this is to say, must not be allowed to distract her from responsibility to either the making of stories or to an ordinate participation in the body of community itself, the latter responsibility perhaps the most trying to her — especially given the current nature of the intellectual community. In her own view, her own "vision," the contrary position that she personally rejects speaks unrelentingly a pervasive command over the "territory" of reality by Modernism. That is the circumstance that leads her no doubt to declare it a territory largely occupied by the Devil himself. How shocking a conclusion to a community which religiously denies the Devil's existence. That is her understanding of her circumstances, as we see in her manner of putting the old argument by Milton's Satan in Hell in a form as it might be spoken by her Haze Motes, the juxtaposition of our epigraphs above underlining the recognition.

Hers becomes, then, an obligation as a believing maker of fictions to discover the limits of her own power through words to draw forth aesthetic form suited to these *givens* with which she must work, the realities of the social context to any struggling persons in an unbelieving age. She must do so, resisting as she may any inclination as fiction writer to succumb to tractarian distortions of her art — as if hers were a primary responsibility of shouting warnings to us to save us, to jerk a ripcord lest we smash spiritually into Nothingness. The givens are the cultural aspects of the Modernist world, of a community gone astray in having willfully wandered, whether knowingly or in vagaries of unknowing. For such is the peril in having accepted as an operating principle to community the diabolical perversions of truth about creation itself in the interest of autonomous convenience. She accepts as *matter* to her making these given circumstances to *homo viator* in the 20th century, his willful distortion of perceptions of the nature of community. The deportment of the popular spirit could hardly seem promising to her, precisely because she is orthodox Catholic. But she insists that it is precisely because of her belief that she cannot avoid the evidences of depths beneath the surface pleasures that are everywhere being celebrated by disoriented community in perversions of sacramental deportment.

Nor may she simply treat those present circumstances with an ironic wit, excoriating satirically the popular spirit at its play on the surface called "social reality," accepting mere spectacle as ultimate in its disorientation. She does not dismiss persons by summary indictment as if of no personal concern to her, though she is not presumptuous in agonizing over them. That is a mode she sees operative in much of the poetry and fiction contemporary to her. She sees it, for instance, in the agonizing irony of the rejection of current culture by the Beat poets who (she says) are right in their reactions to that culture but have no sense of the nature of the spiritual recovery necessary to themselves as persons. In contrast to such surface response, hers becomes the task as a maker of fictions (in her words) to "forge a unity of form and matter" through reason as "governed from within [her] own work." That is a necessary work underway here and now, in seemingly unpropitious circumstances to her. Hers is the response of a delicate accommodation to the necessities of art in relation to the vision granted her by a grace whereby she believes herself called as a "prophet of distances." Those distances are necessarily implicit (she believes with St. Thomas) in the very matter with which she makes, and not to be forced upon her made things by art used instrumentality by her will. She must see her responsibility as artist therefore as far other than that imagined for himself by that arrogantly self-confident artist, James Joyce's young Stephen, in his sophisticated philosophical version of the Emersonian moment of willed autonomy as artist.

For Stephen, we see this in the moment of play between a mischievous Cranley and the pretentious Stephen as would-be artist. In their dialectical exchange about art and the artist, Stephen asserts that he will allow himself only "silence, exile, and cunning" in pursuit of his self-calling as artist. (Two of those strategies Stephen shares with the Beats one might conclude, setting *silence* aside.) To do so, Stephen becomes a creator, intent upon his task: namely "to forge in the smithy of my soul the uncreated conscience of my race." What Stephen does not recognize is that, in the actuality of his deportment he is already rejecting the reality of his own soul, electing by his will to create out of the "uncreated conscience" of his "race" an acceptable *soul.* As artist he proposes himself as creating savior. He will forge, will the force of words, a common conscience obedient to will (his will) through art. His own actions are presumed to precede his own being, his own self-evident membership in community as antecedent denied. He must therefore, as intentional savior of conscience itself, reject and purge himself of any consent to participation in community. His "personal" being, this is to presume, is effected by an active intentionality to be exercised from an angelistic remove. That is a point that will be argued and popularized by Jean-Paul Sartre not long after Joyce's novel.

By the time O'Connor begins to make her stories, Sartrean Existentialism has become pervasive of the academic community, evident in the increasingly "activist" criticism of literature that follows out of Sartrean arguments and begins to command participation in social and political affairs as well. In this respect, Sartrean thought almost possesses literary sensibilities, its principal rival a more intellectually simplistic Freudian psychology. But both Freud and Sartre prove later adaptations of the fundamentalist principles to intellectual autonomy as already well established since Descartes. They adapt the philosophy of "transcendentalism" of the "self" as declared through intellectual autonomy as the centering principle of all reality. Joyce's work, from several decades earlier than O'Connor, has already fallen persuasively into the emerging doctrinaire ideological climate of an Existentialism which by the mid–20th century largely sustains the intellectual community. And so Joyce's art proves marvelously persuasive, prophetic of this latest philosophy. It is an art which becomes a principal measure of fiction in academic criticism, in that it is compatible to the intellectual climate of the moment, even that of the Beats, though Joyce proves too much a "cornbelt metaphysical" for the emerging "Beat" generation of poets and novelists to celebrate their affinity though their literature profits from his techniques. Whitman, not Joyce, becomes their conspicuously chosen Virgil.

We may remember here that the famous author of *On the Road,* Jack Kerouac, was himself initially a professing Catholic, turning in revolt against the Church no less than against the corrupted world of getting and spending which he sees as the Capitalistic world. He becomes a popular figure of the writer as *homo viator,* better suited to the emerging Beat ideal than Joyce could be — despite Joyce's also having elected exile from the arrested "conscience" of his race. And here Kerouac may serve in contrast to Flannery O'Connor, who as a believing Catholic chooses an increasingly less traveled road at mid-century in their concurrent journeying. Jack Kerouac provides limited analogies to James Joyce as well, since both attempt as autonomous intellects a self-sacrifice as artists toward self-salvation as persons. But neither Joyce nor Kerouac will consent, in young Stephen's words, to address creation as it has been honored by that "false homage to a symbol [Christ] behind which are massed twenty centuries of authority and veneration." Theirs is a rejection very like the one made by O'Connor's Haze Motes, though in Joyce there is a less violent rejection than by Kerouac.

A part of O'Connor's mischief as maker lies in Haze Motes's "history" as an unlettered pilgrim who requires no academic training in gnostic Modernism to turn to a pursuit of Nothingness as self-justification. (O'Connor will put the point very directly in the words her Bible salesman will speak to Hulga in "Good Country People": "I been believing in nothing ever since I was born!") But a play of satiric wit on the surface of the spectacle of modern society is hardly sufficient to O'Connor's concerns. That is a play by the artist which she observes underway closer to home than in Joyce or Kerouac or Allen Ginsberg, much closer home in a species of a less intense concern than that of the wayward "Beats." It is evident to her in the two self-exiled Southerners, Carson McCullers and Truman Capote, of whom she speaks more scorchingly on occasion than of the Beats or of Joyce. We may deduce something of why she would be disappointed by that new "genre" of writing — history as fiction — as in that celebrated work Capote comes to in his *In Cold Blood.* If we put in antithesis to Capote's concern for his "murderer" her Haze Motes of *Wise Blood,* we discover distinctions reflecting perceptions of human nature by O'Connor and Capote difficult to reconcile in respect to any "Southerness" they may otherwise share. As a literary genre, Capote's new "fiction" pretends toward the actual in a presumption of judgmental certitude about his murderer, though Capote carefully protects himself by an ironic sentimentality for his murderer — a victim of deterministic social forces. The pretense is of a psychological history told with the authority of fiction, shielding Capote as participating in that history as himself a like person. He is but instrumental to art, assuming the reader largely conditioned by the sentimentality breathed by that reader as member of the conglomerate "popular spirit" of the time. That reader's intellectual state (as Joyce recognizes) may be exploited by wit's irony.

It is not, of course, that Capote is "artless" in his new genre. Indeed, so sophisticated his artfulness that critical attention makes welcomed this new genre with considerable celebration. It is work rich with promises of academic exegesis, given the academy as so largely centered in intellectual concern for social culture. Certainly the possibility of "sin" as a cause of violation by one person of another (leading him to murder) hardly obtains, as O'Connor's Misfit learned to his confusion in being treated as a social animal — he intuitively concerned with the nature of good and evil. This new genre, this is to say, tends away from any Thomistic understanding of man's nature, as it also tends away from Thomistic understandings of a maker's responsibility to the "science" of art — of signs governed by reality itself, whereby truth measures signs and not signs truth. The Thomistic "science," a knowing by reason, accepts truth as limiting the measure possible by the word, rather than presuming the word the measure of truth as derived by the poet's disoriented desire to champion autonomous intellect. For Thomas as for O'Connor to the contrary, there is a relation of the word to the Word, requiring of intellect in its uses of words a prudential humility.

In this context of our differentiation of the sense of the word for Capote and for O'Connor, we suggest that an event which is actual (a murder perhaps) has increasingly been taken by a Modernist response as speaking an increasingly ravenous appetite, wrong (disturbing to social order) because of its excess only. The "media" in our present moment proves symptom of an increasing hunger for spectacle demanding enlarged parameters of excess. Thus there appears, to a growing delight in dissatisfaction in the popular spirit (cynicism), an emerging "myth" suited to full funding of its faith in the art of surfaces. That growing faith distorts the *sentiment* proper to human nature in response to creation, until sentimentality emerges and concedes to feeling as superior to thought, opening by the gates of feeling the flood of excess. Thus we become intellectually addicted to this world through a growing appetite for spectacle. Hence may grow in us a perverse hunger, which Dante might suggest is that of the she-wolf he encounters on the mountain just before he reaches Hell's gate: the wolf Avarice — *appetite* ravenous to consume this world, the curse of which addiction is that by the malady of appetite that wolf is but the more famished in its craving by its gluttony. The philosopher Aristotle, rather than the poet Dante, might put it analytically in its consequences not only to the person but to his art as well. For if by tragedy's *catharsis*, both *pity* and *terror* are purged, by a *pathos* out of self-pity both pity and terror are left to cloy the intellect. Unpurged by a turning in the openness of a consenting love to things in themselves, we suffer pity and terror as festering in intellect, yielding not recovery to true sentiment, but an exacerbating sentimentality fed upon by self-love. The more ravenous, the more subject the intellect becomes to a sentimentality demanding spectacle.

By the distortions of reality through sentimentality, and in respect to the art desired by that deportment of intellect, there emerges a new literary "hero" suited to the condition of self-pity. In the post-World War II critical arena, he became known as the "Anti-hero," though despite the violence of the spectacle sometimes accompanying him in his literary presence, he is to be understood as a victim — usually as victimized by the deterministic forces born of a conspiracy between abstract *nature* and *society*. What O'Connor might argue to the contrary (as is by implication suggested in her art) is that neither pity nor terror can be resolved by the Anti-hero. Self-love almost palpable as self-pity is a symptom of pride, manifest in consciousness as sin. Pride freed of humility allows no genuine sorrow for transgressions through pride. Nor may terror be relieved by self-love as it may be through an enduring — a suffering with — in a love out of faith and hope. That is the charity of *suffering* as Dostoevsky dramatizes *love* in his later fictions by the term *suffering*.

As for the new art of which Capote's new journalism is a particular species, it depends upon feeling, not thought, encouraging a surface response that elevates the surface of reality (spectacle) as if spectacle were essence. The humanity of the person is thus cut off from essential spiritual depths, in Thomas' sense of *essential* in respect to the actual nature of this *actual* thing, this *person*. And here we mean by actual thing that which we know as self-evident — our own "self" as *this* person. No longer persons, we are encouraged to know ourselves only as victims in response to a new species of violence against reality itself. That violence against our nature, however, we justify as a self-defense antithetic to "suffering with," O'Connor's phrase. Dante would call it perverted love, self-love. The acceptable burden of art, consequently, becomes the "feeling" called *pathos,* roused in us by surface appropriations to art of the spectacles of community in its decay. For Thomas or O'Connor, what is thus evidenced is symptomatic of the spiritual disorder of the person. Its consequent effects, collectively manifest, are the disorders in community. It is a symptom but one which we address as if "essential" cause of our disorder.

This new art, then, usually credited to Capote as "father" of it (sometimes called the "new journalism") is worth attention as symptom of spiritual disorientation. It may choose whatever widely popular fad of the moment as a convenient myth, adapting art's response to current "fad," attracting the popular spirit in ways pleasing to both the sophisticated and unsophisticated faddist. It may employ especially an irony in which sentimentality is raised by wit against an undefined or insufficiently identified antagonist, giving a satiric ambiance whose ground is intellectual indifference. But such irony proves amorphous, lacking a common consent to a measure of visionary expectations, the irony speaking an intellectual sophistry regardless of that old communal truth: Without vision a people perish. It becomes difficult to discover the identity of the antagonist against which such satiric ambiance is directed, though its collective designation is but an accidental determinism when we refuse to force the devil to speak his name. We may grant a determinism (by "feeling") as an indeterminate force, the indeterminate made more persuasive by sentimentality vested out of feeling when the refusal of intellectual responsibility is disguised as a helpless victimization. Not a new gambit by the artist. We remember Stephen Crane's story "Open Boat," a protest against such forces as indeterminate. For, that story suggests, there is no longer a "Church" or a God against whom to protest that unnamed X's inhumanity to man.

It is this ambiguity in circumstances that is convenient to a Tom Wolfe as "new journalist," as for instance in his early address to the "Beat" scene in its effects upon New York sophisticates. That is a matter he extends from his *The Kandy-Kolored Tangerine-Flake Streamline Baby* (1965) through *Radical Chic & Mau-Mauing the Flak Catchers* (1970) to the mock-heroic *The Right Stuff* (1976). And it leads Wolfe gradually back toward fiction out of his practice of the new journalism: He writes his *Bonfire of the Vanities* (1987), then a decade later *A Man in Full* (1998). Perhaps his portrait of the hero test-pilot Chuck Yeager had been a haunting preliminary to the second novel, in whose protagonist there is echoed that "right stuff'" so popularly appealing to us in Chuck Yeager. At any rate, Wolfe undertakes the second novel as set in Haze Motes country rather than among the sophisticates of New York City whom he saw moved by sentimentality to do the right thing in search of the right stuff.

This, our aside into the literary phenomena of a new journalism. But it enlarges our recognitions of cultural circumstances with which O'Connor had to deal as a believing poet. That new and exciting genre had come at a time, for instance, when the short story is declared a dead form by some critics, the novel itself also dead. There follows a disappearance of fiction from "quality" periodicals (some of them nevertheless publishing a story or two of O'Connor's). Fiction increasingly seemed to survive only in paper "Romance novels" and in "pulp" magazines. This, just as O'Connor is setting out to make her stories. At the same time of course there flourished widely in academic courses, leading to specialized degrees, that now fabled "Southern Renaissance." We have remarked already O'Connor's awareness of the uncertain literary climate of her time, in which climate her critics tended to take her as a minor figure whose "specialization" was a satiric local color as evidenced by her *Wise Blood*. But at the "cutting edge" of criticism, her work seemed hardly the serious, even high-minded, attempt to rescue a dying literature such as that made by Capote in his *In Cold Blood,* a work critically sensational when it first appeared.

What we remark now long after, in our present critical concern, is that her sense of *blood* as an incarnating image for fiction is hardly *cold* for her as in the psychologically pathological concern of Capote. How integral to action and how intricate in suggestiveness is blood as a "motif" (in a jargon term popular to academic criticism at that moment). Beginning with her title as a clue to what she is about, she pursues the difficulty Haze has in dealing with his blood, counterpointing Haze's obsession with truth as no truth to Enoch Emory's fascination with the mystery of his own blood "knowledge." How quickly Enoch recognizes Haze's "Jesus" with no blood to shed since there is no such thing to shed it for, or because of, as sin. The bloodless mummy in the Taulkinham museum is precisely what Haze calls for, and its Advent is executed by Enoch as a suitable wise man to the "thought" of Haze as a prophet against truth. Enoch is stoned by Haze, a first martyr to Haze's new "Jesus," and in that moment Enoch is fascinated by his own blood as real. As Enoch regains consciousness, he touches his forehead, his fingers becoming "streaked with red." He sees a drop of his blood on the ground beside him, and it seems to widen "to a little spring," staring into which Enoch hears "his blood beating, his secret blood, in the center of the city." An epiphany which he is inadequate to riddle, though in donning a guerilla suit stolen from a movie promoter later on, we see Enoch (lost in the park) sitting in the ape suit in a stance perhaps echoing that famous work "The Thinker." Enoch is Narcissus, his "self" a throwback toward animalistic origins in our abolition of man.

For O'Connor the secret of blood lies in the bonding of intellect and soul through that rescue denied by Haze so vehemently, the Incarnation, Crucifixion, Resurrection. O'Connor knows, as does Walker Percy, that the academic mind has become obsessed with the present cultural moment as the most promising to society since that Industrial Revolution born of Enlightenment intentions to power over nature. In respect to fictional attempts at "man in full," how fruitful to compare Tom Wolfe's version of his "Haze Motes," the very rich entrepreneur Charlie Croker of *A Man in Full* not simply to O'Connor's Haze but to Percy's more hapless protagonist Will Barrett of *The Last Gentleman* (Will also the protagonist of Percy's *Second Coming*). Tom Wolfe, we remember, is (like Carson McCullers and Truman Capote) a "Southern" writer by natural and social origin, though his work is that of an expatriate to any "place." But we here suggest that his novel might be tried and found wanting when read not only in relation to Dostoevsky's or O'Connor's concern for a good man. It fails especially if tried against Walker Percy's pursuit of a "man in full" in that novel *The Last Gentleman,* an advantage in the comparison that both Percy and Wolfe are satiric writers.

There is a difference worth noting, as O'Connor no doubt would notice, between Percy and Wolfe. At the surface, Percy's pursuit of a "man in full" is grounded in spectacles of event or fad accepted as pleasing to "New Age" sensibilities, a ground shared somewhat with Wolfe. That is, for both writers there is a purchase in details from a common historically current culture. New Age culture supplies matter to Percy's particular concerns for a New Age life found in the American suburbs, in which Percy sees self-isolating cultural enclaves, whether in New Orleans or in New York salons. Percy's characters, that is to say, are more culturally sophisticated (as are Wolfe's) than are O'Connor's country folk. But the reflections we have out of Wolfe and Percy of similar cultural spectacles yield quite different conclusions. To make several distinctions we take a brief excursion into Wolfe and Percy to underline Percy's advantage as akin to that of O'Connor, differing radically from Capote or Wolfe in their uses of similar "matter." The differences shed some light on the common vision held by Percy and O'Connor, despite any "provincial" limits that distinguish her fictional milieux from Percy's. For O'Connor shares with Percy a concern for spiritual depths in her characters, though in arenas yielding distinct imagery and dialect.

We recall O'Connor's insistence that as Catholic she cannot "afford to be less than an artist," remembering her understanding of "Catholic" in relation to her seemingly "Protestant" characters. For hers is an understanding of "Catholicity" which some within her own Church find unsettling. That she cannot be "less than an artist" because she is Catholic, in fact, is a remark she makes in defending some of her "fundamentalist" Protestant characters, especially those like old Tarwater in *The Violent Bear It Away.* "When you leave a man alone with his Bible," she wrote Sister Mariella Gable, May 1963, "and the Holy Ghost inspires him, he's going to be a Catholic one way or another, even though he knows nothing about the visible church." For, she adds, "Theologically our differences with [the Fundamentalist Protestants] are on the nature of the Church, not on the nature of God or our obligation to him."[3] In such differences, then, Percy and O'Connor are close to each other as "Catholic" writers, though he chooses as matter to his fictions the more popular and "sophisticated" cultural climate of his day, a suburbia inclined to placelessness shared with Wolfe. What our reflections on these likenesses and differences may reveal is that Percy and O'Connor see with a like understanding of reality, though the little worlds they limit to their fictional concerns may seem quite disparate in respect to textual spectacle.

With such cryptic prelude, too briefly put perhaps, our juxtaposition of those two "Southern" writers as satirists — Percy and Tom Wolfe — in order to cast light by indirection on Flannery O'Connor's work. In an interview of Percy, included in his collected essays, *Signposts in a Strange Land*, Percy reaches a point where he insists upon asking himself a question his interviewer hasn't thought to ask. "*Question*: Since you are a satirical novelist and since the main source of a satirist's energy is anger about something amiss or wrong about the world, what is the main target of your anger in *The Thanatos Syndrome?*" The question as Percy himself puts it makes satire dependent upon some *belief* of the satirist which has been offended by "something amiss or wrong" in the world about him. Percy's response to his own question is a long one, completing that already long 1987 interview. But the beginning of his "Answer" is succinct. What offends him is the "widespread and ongoing devaluation of human life in the Western world — under various sentimental disguises: 'quality of life,' 'pointless suffering,' 'termination of life without meaning,' etc. I trace it to a certain mind-set in the biological and social sciences which is extraordinarily influential among educated folk — so much so that it has almost achieved the status of a quasi-religious orthodoxy. If I had to give it a name, it would be something like the 'Holy Office of the Secular Inquisition.'"

Percy poses an either/or which requires our taking sides, and he does so with a discomforting insistence. We either agree with him or oppose him. That is his intent as satirist, but in respect to art this offended satirist must control his anger if he is to be artfully effective. Percy defines his vision of the "Western world" as one which is shared with O'Connor, each of them recognizing, as firm and orthodox Catholics, a world gone astray. We may observe, in relation to Percy as satirist, a difference between him and O'Connor as Southern Catholic writers. As we have discovered, O'Connor emphasizes her primary concern as writer in an accord with St. Thomas: the good of the thing she makes to be used however God may choose. Percy is himself concerned to make a thing good in itself, but increasingly, as he comes to himself as not simply a "Southern" writer but an Orthodox Catholic writer, he seeks an immediacy of effect of his work. If they share a common vision, Percy increasingly intends to unsettle his audience as satirist, especially those intellectuals serving the "Holy Office of the Secular Inquisition." Not only his essays, but public letters such as those to the New York *Times* suggest as much. No surprise, then, his witty and devastating rebuke of Modernism in *Lost in the Cosmos: The Last Self-Help Book.*

Percy is satirist very deliberately, intensifying that aspect of his work as he becomes more and more comfortable with his "Southerness" in the corrective of that cultural tradition through orthodoxy, sorting his cultural inheritance. (This is the matter to my "Walker Percy's Quest for the Word Within the Word: A preliminary," *Eudora Welty & Walker Percy: The Concept of Home in Their Lives and Literature.*) And so O'Connor and Percy differ, though mutually supported in a common vision not only as Catholic but as Southern, both of them eschewing the status of expatriate from the South, though O'Connor early and more easily settles into Andalusia than Percy in Covington. Both understand themselves to be Southerners but not determined in their vision by cultural tradition. And both recognize as well their cultural circumstances as enriching the visionary felt balance they would maintain in response to the local. That is a support rejected by the "ex-patriate," choosing as the term has it to be "out of his native land." ("Oh Flannery, if only I could take you out of all this.") An expatriate like Capote may on occasion speak apologetically for having been born in the South, the embarrassment O'Connor dramatizes in her would-be expatriate Hulga of "Good Country People." We are not likely to encounter in Tom Wolfe as disciple of Capote that lingering sense of guilt we suspect in Capote, Wolfe having written no "Christmas Memory" out of an Alabama childhood to haunt his self-liberation. (Perhaps some expiation for Capote, then, in *Breakfast at Tiffany's.*) We emphasize in contrast to the expatriate escape of native place that O'Connor and Percy embrace the viable here and now, but in a perspective as devout Christians, believing man fallen, wherever and whenever he may come to himself in this world's dark wood. They do so in part from recognizing their concerns to be those also approached by most of those Southern Fugitive-Agrarians once famous in academic courses in the post–World War II world. (Especially famous in Southern academies we observe, though now largely found in European — especially Scandinavian — academies.) Nor had those poets coming to themselves in a dark wood all shared with Percy and O'Connor an approach through a clarity of religious vision common among them. Those Fugitive-Agrarians nevertheless prove immediate forebears to O'Connor and Percy, though Percy will find himself often very uncomfortable by any association with them as a "movement." For Percy there is an uncertainty lingering long, a demanding question requiring reason's sorting. *Where,* given his gathering perspective on the Western world, is the "prophetic poet" to *stand?* In the *South* is not for Percy an adequate answer, but that had been the answer given in those controversial essays by "Twelve Southerners," *I'll Take My Stand,* as critically interpreted to the popular spirit in its Modernist sensibilities.

Percy as prophetic poet, discovering his own place to stand, depends upon the satiric as his fictional mode, then, since the Western world has so largely lost any recognition of its own origins antecedent to its latest "mind-set" of Modernist ideology defended by its Positivistic philosophy. But how may he rescue that remnant presence of an old "mind-set" that he has gradually repossessed for himself, his Catholic faith? For Flannery O'Connor, the place to stand is among those who, if not Christ-centered, are still Christ-haunted. She finds them actual, a continuing if increasingly besieged remnant among those peopling her local South in the vicinity of Andalusia.[4] Percy is much taken with O'Connor's phrase "Christ-haunted," repeating it several times in the reckoning of his essays toward discovering his own place to stand. For he finds himself in a Western "desert" as he says, as a "survivor of theory and consumption," as a "wayfarer, like St. Anthony." He desires a *place* which is beyond mere place, the desire which moves Haze Motes in *Wise Blood*.

This is to suggest that the labor for Percy in discovering his own place to stand is more difficult for him than it seems to have been for O'Connor, Percy relatively late in coming to terms with his South. He will come to an accommodation at last in recognizing that the larger desert enveloping the West since Descartes has increasingly centered threateningly upon the isolated "self." The Modernist view rejects any culture in which there yet lies a remnant unsubdued by the shifting intellectual sands of relativism which Modernism welcomes. The "suburban" culture promoted as a "life style" encroaches in a "final cultural solution" less spectacular in its deadly consequences than Nazism (which Percy observed in Germany in the 1930s) but as deadly in spiritual consequences. How then find any place, given that Modernist intellect chooses the shifting sands of theory that isolates the "self" by "life style" in its new faith in self-autonomy? As for such a theorist, Percy observes him confident of explaining away the mystery of existence itself, though the theorist cannot explain himself as person. Percy makes a point, which was made earlier by C. S. Lewis, who suggested more than a half century ago that "Freudianism," for instance, can explain everything except Freud. In that perspective upon the enveloping desert, with a witty satiric eye leavened by humor, Percy will say (in his "Diagnosing the Modern Malaise"): how curious that "the scientist, in practicing the scientific method, cannot utter a single word about an individual thing or creature insofar as it is an individual but only insofar as it remembers other individuals ... whether the individual is a molecular of NaCl or an amoebae or a human being."

And so as a "wayfarer, like St. Anthony," Percy becomes at last more comfortable in Covington, Louisiana, where there is a "Southern" comfort more evident with things in themselves. He can do so because as yet Covington appears to the outer world to be a "nonplace," he says, though pilgrimages by those seeking Percy in his "place" may have become increasingly intrusive as his work has become more widely known, making Covington a "tourist attraction" as O'Connor's Andalusia has become. If so, it can no longer be a comfortable "nonplace" in the world's eye as starred at least on academic maps. But in some compensation it has become starred also on the maps of pilgrims who were themselves moved "as was St. Anthony," a diasporas seeking to recover place who would be some consolation to Percy no doubt. Earlier, before Percy's death, he could declare Covington "A perfect place for the writer!" For it lies "on the border between the Bible Belt and the Creole-French-Italian-German South," a placement whereby tradition might be recovered to himself as a writer, though he had been born on a country-club golf course in a suburb of Birmingham, Alabama. It is in that recovery of his own history as pilgrim person, made possible to him in a place through his Christian vision, that he becomes the more effective as satiric witness to pilgrims who discover themselves lost in the Western desert in which he had discovered himself lost. And because he had become more comfortable in place, he could be more effective in his literary witness.

Percy's, then, becomes an address quite other than the "satiric" address of a Tom Wolfe, whose *Bonfire of the Vanities* appears the year after Percy's *Thanatos Syndrome*, Percy's last novel, in which is reflected a comfort in place that had been less possible to him earlier. He is at home in Covington, as O'Connor was early in her spiritual life at home on that small farm she called Andalusia, though aware as well that for a time at least she would also be in exile. Satiric irony proves a strategy used with a considerable popular success by Wolfe in his first novel, an adapted mode out of his earlier satiric prose such as that in his *The Electric Kool-Aid Acid Test* (1968) or *Radical Chic & Mau-Mauing the Flak Catchers* (1970). Those works had established him as a delightfully wicked observer of the decadent social world he encountered in that much-celebrated "place," New York City. As Capote moves from fiction to the new journalism, Wolfe moves from the new journalism back to fiction. But he is satirist, whether making books in the genre of fiction or of social commentary. And here is the locus of the difference between him and Percy. One does not detect in Wolfe that sense of restlessness, uncertainty, that is in Percy. Instead, Wolfe cultivates a public "personal" image of indifference, of separateness, reflected even in his sartorial appointment reminiscent of the deportment of some of those Beats, a means to public attention as we may encounter it in *People Magazine*, except with precisions of dandyism reminiscent of the 1920s. (The distance obscuring this sameness lies in the sartorial spectacle, between white linen suits and no clothes at all for Ginsberg. A last gentleman dress, circa the 1920s, to Ginsberg's strip tease nakedness as the emperor of the Beats may speak as symptoms of a social placelessness by intention.) Impeccable sartorial protection might indeed remind as well of the self-protection dear to Prufrock, for whom the most daring gesture of a Gins-bergian nature for Prufrock would be to walk upon the beach with the "bottoms of [his] trousers rolled."

For Wolfe, then, placelessness has protective advantages, which he sees from his species of provincialism as requiring indiscrimination in regard to his reaction to impingements of any *here* at this *now* upon consciousness. But then there intrudes upon him, more than as a reportorial necessity of fiction in making here and now in fiction, the challenge of things in themselves to his incarnational responsibilities to places and persons in the new fictional journalist. Following his *Bonfire of the Vanities,* that challenge becomes more insistent in his second novel, *A Man in Full.* There is a history to its making that speaks this challenge. Wolfe had at first intended its setting to be also New York City as had been the setting of his first novel, but he shifts it to Atlanta — to Flannery's Taulkinham — at the request of his editor. (Or so it is reported.) But though born in Virginia, Wolfe had (by the 1990s) been long away from the South. In any event, in his second novel he proves not closely attuned, even to the distance between Richmond and Atlanta — let alone between New York and Atlanta. But he is even less attuned to the distance from Atlanta to Southwest Georgia, a region which may be more remote from Taulkinham than even Flannery's Milledgeville. That is the "country" he ascribes to his protagonist.

And so Wolfe can hardly be attuned to differences between deep South Georgia folks, say, and the pseudo-Marxist culture of the New York social elite he has treated in his perspective upon that "Radical Chic" world and fictionalized subsequently in *Bonfire of the Vanities.* Of course that Radical Chic world is imitated by kindred spirits in Atlanta, the capitol of the "Empire State of the South," making his shift of setting seem suitable from a New York firetower upon cultural bonfires in Atlanta. But both are too far removed from the hardscrabble world out of which he would present his protagonist as emerging as a "man in full." We remember once more O'Connor's anecdote of the Atlanta real estate dealer to a pilgrim client, who would love this place in Atlanta suburbs since there isn't "a Southerner for two miles." O'Connor, unlike Wolfe, knows first hand Haze Motes's origins, whereas Wolfe must attempt an incarnation of his protagonist at a level deeper than spectacle, but out of an unfamiliar "blood knowledge" with his own protagonist — that blood knowledge dependent upon a cultural participation in place such as was most native to O'Connor. There emerge problems in the enveloping, the "naturalistic," spectacles of the text. The protagonist become rich has become also a knowledgeable herpetologist, a collector at facilities on the deep-South plantation where he began as "poor white trash." But he finds coral snakes native to that place which is foreign to them. He has encounter with a rattlesnake in unlikely circumstances, the unlikely presented as if likely. And in a moment of bravado, showing off to his Atlanta guest on a quail shoot, the man in full bets he can kill two cock quail on the rise with one shot — and does in the novel, a feat impossible even to a computer save with computerized quail. There is a discomforting, library-research aspect to such details, research not accurately read but presented as if natively experienced by the protagonist. If not discomforting as detail to the unwary reader it is symptomatic of an indifference to, a reduction of, the true nature of man in full.

In a similar challenge to fiction as "incarnational" in respect to persons fictionalized, Henry James handles more convincingly his treatment of a "Southerner" in his *Bostonians* than Wolfe can do for his remote (and to him foreign) Southwest Georgian as protagonist. Wolfe's protagonist then proves more nearly an idea which he must attempt to incorporate fictionally. The difficulty perhaps lies in the spectacle of the fictions necessary to both James and to Wolfe, but both are in contrast to O'Connor. Yet James is at least attuned to a conflict of two aristocratic cultures, one of them removed from his experiences and requiring his cautiously perceptive attention absent in Wolfe — the residual Cavalier tradition of James's planter Mississippian. Basil Ransom, late citizen of the Confederacy, is to be put in dramatic tension within the Brahmin culture of Boston that was more personally familiar to James. James as satirist in his *Bostonians* plays Ransom against that Brahmin cultural righteousness, whose "religion" requires an activist intent to a reconstitution of culture, particularly the Southern culture of which James's Ransom is native. (That is a matter in Brahmin consciousness in the 1870s and 1880s referred to as the "late unpleasantness" of 1861–65.) James makes the friction of cultures persuasive in dramatic ironies of encounter, in part perhaps because his Ransom as an ambiguous outsider is of a genuine interest to James, given his own "native" cultural origins with which as person he finds himself increasingly uncomfortable, but which as a native he is reluctant to reject — though he finds himself more comfortable in English than in Boston drawingrooms.

But how difficult for James to feel at home anywhere, as at first it proved for Walker Percy. The raw American, having lost his European cultural roots, becomes the emerging figure in conflicted cultural wars between Europe and America for James. That becomes his fictional matter as "Realist." His travel accounts (*English Hours, Italian Hours*) are, however, more decidedly "Romantic" than he could know. Meanwhile, on the American continent there continue echoes of that recent civil war, a "late unpleasantness" disturbing to drawingroom manners, dramatized in his *Bostonians* in the fictional tensions between the Brahmin social Bostonians and a recently defeated Southern gentleman, Ransom. As a Southerner, there lingers in Ransom's manner traces of English high culture though now in defeat. As vanquished, Ransom proves an inviting *possible* character for James, though Ransom's residual culture seems hardly comfortably viable to James. It seems little promising to any recovery of the Brahmins nearest and (by blood) dearest to James as himself an uneasy "American." Nevertheless, James seems curious about and drawn to Southerners, though disappointed in the Southern culture as he knows it. It is too shallow in its historical roots for him, as he had already found New England Puritan culture too shallow. We discover as much in the nuances of his account of a Southern venture recorded in his *American Scene*.

In contrast to James, Tom Wolfe depends upon accidental encounter as sufficient to his interests of the moment, stirring in him no "historical" concerns for the cultural roots of such encounter. That is an aspect of Wolfe as "journalist" sufficient unto the cultural spectacle of the moment, with little concern to plumb spectacle even to the depth of cultural history. For Wolfe as he writes, World War I and II are already fading into ancient history in the cultural awareness of the popular spirit, North or South. James to the contrary plumbs spectacle, prompted by his disquiet with history's cultural residue as he knows it most intimately in Brahmin, upper class, society. James reaches further back than to the Revolutionary War which seemed history's starting point for some Brahmin sensibilities. If that defeated part of America — the "Old South plantation" part as known from a Bostonian Brahmin height — was now no more, James seems to have suspected there might be lingering in it cultural artifacts suggesting more ancient origins than merely manifestations of Southern *manners* speaking a shallow cultural *manner*. An older manner seemed desperately needed, North and South, in the emerging "Gilded Age." Otherwise, culture as the patina of history could but be overlaid by false gilding.

We may observe in passing that this recognition of Southern cultural inadequacies is common to both James and that frontier, border pilgrim Mark Twain. Twain is a cultural libertarian of the "self." Imagine Twain and James in the same drawingroom in London (as an old professor of mine reported), James in one corner surrounded by the women (perhaps talking of Michaelangelo) and Twain in another surrounded by men, (Twain telling jokes.) James's concern, more than Twain's, is that of the artist for whom America seemed to offer less than the sufficient cultural matrix he believed necessary to the making of fictions.

Even Puritan New England was too young he concluded. This is a level of James's aesthetic concern important to him. He seeks a culture steeped in history till yielding an acceptable aroma and body, to be quaffed deeply by art, though not down to the settled leaves speaking that *givenness* which is so fundamental to O'Connor. To drink to the dregs means a very personal endangerment. Perhaps that was what led Hawthorne for instance into his concern for sin as the deepest residue of history still coloring the cultural moment, a venture James rejects as naïve.

Our attention to James here as father of "American Literary Realism" helps us know the cultural and critical circumstances for O'Connor. She learned from James — as she learned from Joyce and Eliot and many of the "Moderns" rising out of "Realism." Caroline Gordon was particularly insistent that she learn from James as the "master," and we need only a cursory glance at O'Connor's copy of *The Future of the Novel* (1956, edited by Leon Edel) to see her interested in James. The anthology gathers from James's "Prefaces" to the New York edition of his novels and from the considerable body of his essays about novels and novelists. The 1888 essay "Guy de Maupassant" is rather heavily marked by Flannery in her copy. Given her temperament, one suspects O'Connor learned form James almost in spite of Caroline Gordon's insistent monitoring, but though Caroline was herself a devout Roman (in her insistent deportment in that respect no doubt reminding Flannery of her mother Regina) one wonders whether Caroline appreciated James's own spiritual and (for O'Connor) philosophical weaknesses as poet. His was, from a Thomistic perspective, a limited vision. That is evident to O'Connor in her remarking James's version of "mystery" on that railway siding at Savannah on his way from Charleston to Florida. She cites that incident from *The American Scene,* and in one of her talks she associates herself with that Charleston porter who set James's attaché case in a mud puddle, helped James into the carriage taking him to the station for the trip further South, and then set the muddied case in James's lap. (James complains of the poor training of Southern servants.) Flannery accepts that servant role as writer, and with mischief she says she intends to set muddy stories in our laps.

Not that she is unaware of a pathos in James, his continuing sense of not having yet located himself at a place, though already a considerable writer and knowing himself exceptional as such a master. He could but admit (as does Flannery) that he is good at it. James's speculations on writing are out of his considerable confidence of a mastery of fiction. Even so, James seems (wherever he finds himself) somehow on the periphery of the cultural community, not at its center and ordering, feeding, the present culture into a new life. Hence we may suspect an aspect of Prufrock in James as by allusion we suggested in contrast to the frontier sensibilities of Twain. One of James's admirers, Ezra Pound, reacts to such displacement, putting himself insistently at the center of the decaying culture as poet-philosopher. (We have cited Pound's self-epitaph as anathema pronounced upon Western culture in his *Hugh Selwyn Mauberley,* a poem both Jamesian and Whitmanesque.) At one point in James's travels, reflecting on the sad estate of American society in its cultural decline, he remarks: "so much life, and so little living." Perhaps there may have been at least a pretense to *living* in the recently emerging "Old South" culture, with which he could only be peripherally acquainted. Or so he may have wondered, leading him to a sympathy with Basil in *The Bostonians.* But he was disappointed on that visit with Charleston friends to discover how small their cultural works, they seeming oblivious to the larger European culture, fascinating to James in its hints of a possible cultural Eden. There is an irony in James, a sense of pathos as counterpointed by his "romantic" highs in the presence of Italian art on his travels. But wherever he found himself he felt on a periphery, never quite at home, whether in a London or Boston drawingroom, in an Italian cathedral, in a Charleston world still very "Southern" as a cultural backwash, having recently somewhat escaped the full destruction of that late "unpleasantness" that had destroyed Atlanta and Columbia and threatened Savannah.

James as tourist in the South is already attuned to the newly emerging "American" spirit that has not yet invaded the South despite that late bloody encounter of cultures. He is somewhat uneasy about the emerging symptoms of the Northern victory (the Gilded Age) as if he were himself implicated in its triumph. He is also uneasy in the cultural backwash of an isolated Boston Brahmin culture. It is difficult for James as artist to determine any place on which to stand. Yet he can prove defensive of that emerging "American" spirit when pressed by the condescension of Europeans who "feel" themselves culturally superior. That becomes the "matter" of his *The American,* engaged as well in his *The Ambassadors.* It is as if James could never feel himself *member* in any *body.* From O'Connor's reading of his concern, it might well have appeared to her to have been caused by James's limited vision of community *as* a body, he seeing rather only its social limits at the level of history's lingering spectacle. And so his deportment appears as a social reserve, perceived as a manner of detachment. How tempting, then, to a Charleston porter to set a muddy valise in his lap, the circumstance permitting the porter's own wily social detachment which James reads as but a poor training of a servant. No surprise to us then that Miss Flannery would take that Charleston vignette as parable to express her own deportment to the "body politic"— to the popular spirit — as a realist of distances.

If Basil Ransom has been dislocated from "living" by that late unpleasantness of 1861–1865, in James's rendering he is somewhat hard-pressed to see any lively "living" going on in the spectacles of the Boston circle that would rescue him by its self-righteous convictions about "life." James in his sympathies to the fictional tension of *The Bostonians* seems drawn to Ransom (a dangerous possibility as he knows to his making). Still, there may be possible Cavalier elements in the fading ambiance of "Southern" culture to be reflected in such a character, the roots of which might indeed reach not only back to King Charles's England but further back to Renaissance Rome and Florence. That might speak surviving remnants at least of a culture sufficiently encrusted by history, even though a culture considerably chipped and battered in transit. More resonant nevertheless of a fullness of cultural "living" than that strict, prim porcelain "life" which some of the "Bostonians" are themselves becoming restless with in James's unfolding novel — that culture increasingly set on a shelf as an inherited antique. For Brahmanism seems to sterilize "living" into an arrested "life," though increasingly appearing attractive, as if it might be purchased by the nuevoriche — the "New North" spirit which Twain will satirize as "the Gilded Age."

Tom Wolfe's Charlie Croker will prove an image somewhat of that spirit as imported and "cultured" in "Southern" life. That too is an irony, given that Wolfe intended initially to present his "Croker" in New York City rather than in Atlanta, assuming the setting inconsequential. How difficult from James's concerns, then, Tom Wolfe's *A Man in Full* as seen in relation to James's *The American.* Or we might consider Wolfe's Charlie Croker as protagonist of Wolfe's novel in relation to James's Basil Ransom of *The Bostonians,* Ransom as James's surrogate representative in his concerns for a growing cultural desert. Both characters prove radically disparate as "Southerners," not only separated by an interval of time —

from the 1860s to the 1960s — but more fundamentally separated by the visions held in their making as surrogate persons by James and Wolfe. Croker is proposed as a character to be a "Southerner," evolved from his Southwest Georgia boyhood out of "poor white trash" in saw-grass country. Croker is a clever entrepreneurial "American," a Yankee of the spirit, who has made his fortune getting and spending. Being now one of the "filthy rich" (as an admiring "American" phrase has it), he would create a plantation, to which he retreats as lord and king. As we read Croker as a surrogate person, he seems hardly promising as man "in full," especially if we think of him in relation to that surrogate person of a similar imagined origin, Haze Motes, presented in Haze's pursuit of a fullness possible only by a perfection of his limited gifts as *Haze Motes,* in which as person resides his possible dignity and integrity in O'Connor's vision of man.

We have been exploring both the literary and cultural context to which Flannery O'Connor responds as a prophet of distances in order to distinguish her own uses of reason in making, her distinctions about "life" and "living." She, as did James, became aware of a "New North" and a "New South," both liberated from responsibilities to the immediacy of place. She sees that new liberty born of the Modernist doctrine that declares "place" limited at last to the sides of the autonomous person's skull. That is a dimension of her recognition already sensed by James, but not engaged by him as a prophet of distances, though he pursues it in history. All about him, James could see that "New North" emerging, pushing cultural Boston with its brief history into a backwater, its last refuge perhaps now Martha's Vineyard, long since purchased by the *nouveau riche* with whom Wolfe's "Southern" Croker might find himself compatible in social trappings of Modernist ideology. The Boston Brahmins from James's day to ours have been a culturally endangered species, rescued in an additional irony by Bostonians rising to "cultural" dominance out of Irish immigrants once convenient as Brahmin servants. (See Eliot's "Aunt Helen" in relation to the family history of the Kennedy clan and the New Camelot.) James touches upon such a theme dramatically in having a company of those Brahmins visit New York City with Basil Ransom in company, they encountering New York slums, an experience for them exacerbating the tensional friction between a dying Brahmin culture and a dying "Southern" culture.

Before and after his *Bostonians* (1886), James seems in quest of some "American" in full as a new phenomenon in history whom he might celebrate, toward himself perhaps becoming such an American. Yet he continues disquieted by the intentional severance of that possible "American" from cultural roots. He cannot be encouraged by the withering of culture in the Brahmin remnant, as he can be but by degree irritated at the sophisticated English and Continental corruption of that older cultural tradition. (Contrast Mark Twain, who is hardly cautious in his response to that European condescension.) The Brahmin culture and the European culture — both in a decay seemingly irreversible. In sum, James is concerned as pilgrim *homo viator* with the cultural effects on sensibilities, the symptoms of which he discovers in the conflicted spectacles of community. Still, there is something at issue he has not yet grasped, but whose reality must be a secret of history itself. Or so he suspects. Culture's golden bowl, if not broken, is certainly cracked, and the cultural fault seems widening, perhaps to be restored but only by recovered cultural history.

Concerning James's encounter of "Southerness" out of his New England Puritan heritage as modified by Brahmanism, then, O'Connor cites the passage from James's *The American Scene* to which we have alluded, remarking "James deploring the loss of a sense of mystery [in] the section on Savannah," Flannery's birthplace. (This in a letter to "A.") In that passage James speculates on a cultural depravity reflected in a fleeting scene remembered, a thirty-minute stop at Savannah on his way from Charleston to Jacksonville. He recalls, in his words, "fleeting instants of Savannah as the taste of a cup charged to the brim," but he lacks the leisure to sup or savor it as it were, so brief the pause on his journey. In the passage, James brings his imaginative concerns to focus on persons seen at some distance, they walking on the platform: young men and women, local hawkers of wares, and so on. There is a "mystery" about them, James says, but the mystery seems conjured by his own speculative conclusions about those persons, imagined by James as residents of a cultural backwash. For him they are therefore persons deprived — not materially but culturally. He speaks with self-deprecation of his temptation to such speculative conclusion, for he is "with [his] preposterous 'position,' falsely beguiled, pitilessly forsaken, thrust forth in my ignorance and folly." For what can he know on such scant evidence "about manners or tone, about proportion or perspective, about modesty or mystery, about a condition of things that involves, for the interest and grace of life, other forms of existence than this poor little mine..."? How interesting, this Jamesean address to "manners and mystery" in self-deprecation, the context of the passage allowing James to imbue fleeting figures as themselves poignantly lost because culturally deprived. What they are lost from, to his speculative concern, is "the tragedy of their social, their cruel exposure, that treachery of fate which has kept them so out of their place." Here *place,* for James, does not mean that actual location in Savannah, "a mere railroad matter" to his "fleeting instants of Savannah." His fantasy of the lostness of persons glimpsed on the Savannah siding includes in it his memory of that recent visit with friends at Charleston, who in their own cultural enclave are far removed from the larger world. They, too, had struck him as "unformed, undeveloped, unrelated above all — unrelated to any merciful modifying terms of the great social proposition" as he says of them.

Here is James as a poet aware of (in Flannery's words) "the loss of a sense of mystery" as deeper than cultural circumstances that had kept these persons fleeting, perceived by James as "out of their place." He seems in the moment haunted, but he is also inclined to impose his own proscription of culture against the loss in those persons seen in a fleeting moment on an actual railroad siding in a country not his own. One might be reminded of a similar experience which T. S. Eliot remembers from a sojourn from Harvard to France to hear Henri Bergson lecture, after which out of his own sense of removal from immediate reality he at last completes his "Prufrock" — having as we remarked been introduced to Dostoevsky's work on that visit to France. "Why," Eliot asks much later, "for all of us, out of all that we have heard, seen, felt, in a lifetime, do certain images recur, charged with emotion, rather than others?" He lists some of his own experiences from that journey on the eve of World War I, including "six ruffians seen through an open window playing cards at night at a small French railway junction where there was a water-mill...." He raises this question of memory much later than the experience itself in his *The Use of Poetry and the Use of Criticism,* a personal experience we recognize already embedded as image in his "Journey of the Magi." By the time of his lecture at Harvard in the 1930s, Eliot understands better the "Why." It has to do with a self-recognition out of his personal journeying as *homo viator.* An understanding follows the recovery of his consent to the reality of his own spiritual nature. For by the time of his lecture, to the puzzlement of some and to anger of others of his former literary peers, he comes to profess himself Christian. (William Carlos Williams remembers in his *Autobiography,* 1951, that "out of the blue *The Dial* brought out *The Waste Land* and ... wiped out our world as if an atomic bomb had been dropped upon it," for which Williams never forgives Eliot.)

Eliot by that time (the late 1920s and after) better understands his anomaly as a second-generation "Brahmin," come East to Harvard from a St. Louis childhood. His earlier uncertainty about his cultural origins in relation to his intellectual desires are evident in a sequence of small poems in *Prufrock and Other Observations*: "The Boston Evening Transcript," "Aunt Helen," and "Cousin Nancy," all in the "family" of his cultural origins. In them Eliot reflects a Jamesean discomfort with Brahmin social manners as dependent upon an inherited culture unexamined — as he had not himself examined it in depth when he wrote the poems. There is Cousin Nancy Ellicott on the verge of liberation. She rides across the "barren New England hills" and breaks them, "Riding to hounds/ Over the cow pastures." She "danced all the modern dances," to the puzzlement of her aunts who are "not quite sure how they felt about it," sitting in parlors in which, staring down from "glazen shelves," are the old guard: "Matthew" (the English Matthew Arnold, guardian of literary culture?) and "Waldo" (the American Emerson of Transcendentalist fame?) — "guardians of the faith,/ The army of unalterable law." Or so the ironic suggestiveness by allusion to cultural decay, a decay which Eliot will come to declare a tradition unrescued by an orthodoxy reaching deeper than any current spectacle, artifacts of a residual cultural history no longer sufficient.

Early on, Eliot is more direct, less intimidated, in his own striding and riding across those barren New England hills, being actively skeptical in a more radical way than James will indulge himself to become. Eliot on his way (though innocent of the course immediately before him) is discovering that history divorced from grace is inadequate to a viable culture as he will come to believe. He engages the Jamesean uncertainty out of a new faith in liberated "American spirit," presently focused for him in his *Murder in the Cathedral*. If bound for Little Gidding as a recovering shrine (see his *Little Gidding*) that is a waystop to Canterbury quite unlike a stopping by Canterbury seen by James as a cultural curiosity on an "English Easter" remembered in *English Hours*. James gives us a tourist account of the visit to Canterbury Cathedral, he whimsically amused to remember Chaucer's pilgrims as having also made that journey from London. He finds "The place now given up to dust and echoes," the echoes those of history only. There is a "special sensation of the place" as he stands "on the spot where [Thomas à Beckett] was murdered," his accompanying guide pointing out "a bit of the pavement that caught the blood-drops of the struggle."

Amidst "great rumbling gusts and rain-drifts ... sweeping through the open sides of the crypt" of Thomas, James has come at last through "a magnificent maze of low arches and pillars" through which he "groped about till I found the place," the crypt. He reports an epiphany: "the darkness which seemed to deepen and flash in corners and with the moldy smell, made me feel as if I had descended into the very bowels of history." Into *history*, this descent by James, with an ironic suggestiveness if we remember the account in relation to Dante's pilgrimage into a dark region of old history with Virgil as "verger." Here is reflected a "Romantic" James, especially if we remember Eliot's own April as the "cruelest month" of an Easter in England before it was recognized by Eliot as an Easter journey. In the aftermath of World War I, Eliot echoes the earlier April of Chaucer's pilgrims enduring "sweet showers." A surface history for James for whom those "blood-drops of the struggle" are hardly those in Eliot's *Murder in the Cathedral*. (Flannery in a letter from "Baldwin Memorial Hospital as usual" (*stet*) has been reading *Murder in the Cathedral,* the nurses concluding her "a mystery fan." She ends, "It's a marvelous play if you don't know it, better if you do.")

A recognition of and recovery of the spiritual property of the person as person is missing from Henry James's engagement of his own memory. St. Augustine (or Thomas — or

O'Connor herself) might call it a failure to hear or feel intuitively a resonant dimension in his response to those strangers at a railroad siding in Savannah, Georgia. Nevertheless, James bears some intuitive recognition of his own sense of exile as echoed in his response to cultural conflicts, though not recognized as resonances deeper than simply that of a cultural dissociation "imagined" upon anonymous persons on that railroad platform. How restless James always is, unable to name the cause of his sense of exile. It is a sense of exile which both Eliot (late) and O'Connor (early) would recognize as speaking hope of spiritual recovery, though for Eliot the recognition comes to him late, he having been first victim of that "atomic bomb," his own *Waste Land*, which he later will remember as a "personal grouse."

Perhaps, then, O'Connor recognizes in this fleeting sense in James that James glimpses at least a spiritual relation to cultural manifestations, though reluctant to name it as spiritual. It occurs in a specific place, one more foreign to his experience than is London or Rome. It is, she says, a sense of "the loss of a sense of mystery" by James. Not that such a loss may not be encountered within familiar places, as she knows well. We heard her say that "To know oneself is to know one's region and to know the world," but she adds that in such a knowing there is paradox: it is "a form of exile from the world." It is this "knowing" that she uses to resolve Mr. Head's encounter with Mercy in "The Artificial Nigger." In that story's conclusion we see Mr. Head and Nelson step down off the train at the small junction where they had boarded that morning, come home from the City of Man, back into a familiar "place" that is now forever changed for them, but most especially for Mr. Head. In the cinder-strewn rail yard all the "things" of that place speak a Something yet unnamed by Mr. Head speaking through their very being as never experienced before.

In looking back at her story, O'Connor remarks of her resolution that in that brief space of words she has "practically gone from the Garden of Eden to the Gates of Paradise." Eliot, as his "Journey of the Magi" reveals, would understand what she means. But as both he and O'Connor might recognize in relation to James's experience of that Savannah railroad-siding encounter, it is as if James can only respond at the level of cultural spectacle, though moved by a vague sense of some unnamed loss. Something is missing. And so the experience, he concludes, speaks to his dream of a "great social proposition." There is consequently in James a continuing haunting spiritual pathos in his words out of a pathos in him, only somewhat alleviated by a distancing through irony in his juxtaposing cultural tensions yet unresolved through any "social proposition." Culturally, persons can be seen only as limited to the arena of history — to mere tradition. James is suspended between his "American" experience and his somewhat romantic inclination to European culture, a suspension which one might conclude is rebuked by the somewhat baffling immediacy of his Savannah "moment" which O'Connor might take as a summoning of him by grace beyond cultural limits.

What we might say, in resolving our venture out of Percy into Tom Wolfe and Henry James in their kindred dislocations from place, is that Wolfe seems oblivious to such tensional drama in himself as person as James is not. Wolfe is protected in his dissociation by the rhetorically ascetic, removed from immediacy under the auspices of his clever and versatile wit. Such tensional recognitions lead to deportments that set Percy, Eliot, O'Connor (and even James to a more limited degree) quite apart from Wolfe as (in O'Connor's phrase) "serious writers." Why is the serious writer drawn to those images so haunting in our memory, the writer's own experiences of particularities engaged at moments in which there is a suggestion of epiphany not understood? It is a question more fully answered perhaps by O'Connor's words: "The writer operates at a peculiar crossroads where time and place and eternity somehow meet." At such a juncture when recognized as a "triangulation" of reality, one looks at things more deeply than when their presence proves limited to experiences of surface spectacle. They seem quite other when looked at in the light of eternity. The "longer you look at one object, the more of the world you see in it," whereby one recognizes the object not adequately accounted for (to Percy and O'Connor and Eliot) on that horizontal plane where consciousness engages an object, a plane which may be enlarged and yet limited to the horizontal by a denial that is nevertheless intersected by the transcendent Cause, the Incarnation, as O'Connor suspects evident in James's experience at his Savannah stopover. Within the limited plane of denial, cultures clash with little hope of resolution, though always a hint of possible resolution through attending grace in O'Connor's view.

James, we have suggested, comes to the threshold of this deeper mystery again and again, though we are hard pressed to find instances where he risks crossing that threshold into another country. One instance worth recalling, in part for its relation to Eliot's "Prufrock," is the elegiac story "The Beast in the Jungle," very probably held in mind by Eliot in relation to his making his poem along with (as we have speculated) Dostoevsky's *Notes from Underground*. Eliot finishes his poem just as World War I erupts, in a period when he is reading much of James. A little later he writes a brief "In Memory" for *The Little Review* when James dies in 1916. In his tribute he declares James's a "critical genius" in that James reveals a "baffling escape from Ideas; a mastery and an escape which are perhaps the last test of a superior intelligence. He had a mind so fine that no idea could violate it." High tribute to an intellectual detachment, from a skeptic who is himself maintaining still his own detachment. But this is at a point of his own journey when Eliot is increasingly pressed to defend his declared high skepticism, maintained lest by some commitment he should compromise his own intelligence with an "idea" believed transcendent of reason itself.

Perhaps James's metaphor proves more apt at last: Not ideas, but a resonance of things as speaking realities, speaking "mystery," though it prove beyond the reach of ideas as endangering an openness demanded of reason. Metaphorically, James remains too easily content to sip, to "taste of a cup charged to the brim" with a spectacle untransformed by any response to the mystery of essence in the tea he sups. But from O'Connor's perspective it is through such risks that community itself reaches a viable cultural accommodation to reality. It requires of the poet (as Eliot is at last able to affirm) the responsibility of "purifying" the "dialect of the tribe." For a tribe's signs must be viable, continuously revived here and now as the community's bonding in its intellectual "blood." That must be a blood transformed beyond tradition which by Modernism is reduced from the *intuitive* to the *instinctive* in a devolution of community — transformed, that is, beyond a blood knowledge James sees on that pavement at Canterbury. Or that blood knowledge that fascinates and distances but the more an Enoch Emory in *Wise Blood*. Henry James does not refuse the cup, but neither does he find in it that hidden terror O'Connor calls Mercy, a Mercy infusing and sustaining the world, even this actual tea in this actual cup: to be recognized in that cup when held as Dame Julian holds her hazel-nut. O'Connor will learn from James as craftsman, then, but it is Hawthorne in whom she finds a more "real" response to the mystery in things, confirming her intuitive recognition the more in seeing Hawthorne as a writer of *spiritual* romances about *homo viator*.

Our reservation about Tom Wolfe as a maker of fiction, made especially of his *Man in Full*, is not simply to his assumption of an aesthetic distancing from the matter of his fiction, we must observe lest misunderstood. For we may say (along with O'Connor) that just as the naturalist as naturalistic purist (insofar as he is governed by a respect for the things he uses "naturalistically" in his making) may write more largely than he himself may recognize. Even the strict Positivist despite his intellectually restricted action may reveal more than he knows from his position of an intentional distancing from things—from a connaturality with things as actual which he escapes by angelistic transcendentalism. What is more serious about Wolfe's deportment is his self-confident indifference to the realities of things in themselves upon which his fiction purports to depend. That is a deportment content to adapt the surfaces of reality to his satiric mode, protecting himself thereby from any commitment to any persons as persons or things as things, not Positivistically "objective" but indifferent. No temple for him against which to throw his ironic brick of words, that absence of no importance to him. The tendency encourages him to a caricature of reality whose aesthetic pleasure lies at best in the satiric detachment itself. Put in the terms which Percy uses in his question to himself, Wolfe as satirist has no "anger" as a summoning cause to his satiric engagement of the world as artist. He seems little exercised as is Percy by "the widespread and ongoing devaluation of human life in the Western world," whether observed in New York or Atlanta. We may put Wolfe's position bluntly, as he himself puts it in his recent commencement address to graduating students at Duke University (Spring of 2002), perhaps as a late disciple of President Eliot's "Religion of the Future." For Wolfe life itself is meaningless, except as it might be reckoned, not by metaphysical vision but by microphysics such as particle physics or genetic microbiology, to whatever advantage accrues therefrom to the "self."

"Let's not kid ourselves," Wolfe said to the students, "We're all concatenations of molecules containing DNA, hard wired into a chemical analog computer known as the human brain, which as software has a certain genetic code. And your idea that you have a soul or even a self, much less free will, is just an illusion." How conspicuous a disciple, then, of President Eliot's "Religion of the Future." But what we might remark here as well is that Wolfe's summary bears striking echoes of that sermon delivered by Haze Motes on the streets of Taulkinham, preaching that "there are all kinds of truth ... but behind all of them, there's only one truth and that is that there's no truth," existence itself an accident yielding an illusion of thought At that point of Haze's pilgrimage, should he have occasion to respond to Wolfe's commencement address, Haze might nevertheless rebuke Wolfe as the Bible salesman does Hulga in "Good Country People": "you ain't so smart. I been believing in nothing ever since I was born!"

The report of Wolfe's commencement address is in *The New York Times* (June 2, 2002), but we do not know whether he smiled when he said these words. It is as it stands in this report of it a rather succinct statement of what Percy calls "a quasi-religious orthodoxy" requiring of us a particular mind-set derived from "biological and social sciences" as now increasingly patrolled by positive law to enforce the dogma about man decreed by the "Holy Office of the Secular Inquisition." By juxtaposition of Wolfe to Percy we discover Percy's *Last Gentleman* to be more persuasive of the reality of human nature as we ourselves experience it than Wolfe's *A Man in Full*. Percy's novel is as well more persuasive in its artistry, for though Wolfe's novel is both cleverly and entertainingly ripe with current topical matter, it is the topicality which predominates. To reread it now, only a few years after first publication, is to reread an old newspaper not yet dignified by the yellowing of history. It is Percy then, by contrast, who honors reality the more convincingly in suggesting to us dramatically what constitutes a "good man," so that Wolfe's self-filled Croker appears a cari-

cature of man when compared to Percy's Will Barrett. To say this is to be prophetically reminded that caricature signifies only by its dependence upon a reality known and definitive
of the caricature as measured by reality. Nor is the difference we here emphasize made simply to account for a difference in the magnitude of gift to the two novelists. What is spoken is their manner of response to reality.

Percy knows through his experiences of the world, whatever the place encountered, a
range of the *possible* to human nature itself, which range seems of no interest to Wolfe. One
honors Percy as artist, whether he is dependent upon matter from his New York or Athens,
Georgia, or Covington, Louisiana, experiences. And how widely removed from each other,
the responses to and uses of place by Percy and O'Connor on the one hand and by Wolfe
(or Norman Mailer or Gore Vidal or Carson McCullers or Truman Capote) on the other.
These two "Southern Catholic" writers recognize themselves at a "crossroads where time and
place and eternity somehow meet." They are enjoined by that recognition to a using of signs
toward whatever mediate ends they may, but they discover as well an obligation to signs as
properly oriented to the truth of things, lest signs be reduced at last to Nominalistic whim
for the private pleasure of the poet. It is at this crossroads that O'Connor deploys the limits of her powers as maker through words, toward discovering the possible unity of form
and matter suiting the thing she makes. By that proportionate relation, reasoned in the making of a story, she believes the story therefore will be made better in itself as a thing. How
reassuring to her will be Thomas' encouragement in his *Summa Theologica*: "art is nothing
else but the *right reason about certain works to be made*."

Here, then, let us turn from the more fascile art of a Tom Wolfe to a more serious writer
of fictions from whom O'Connor learned, one from whom Wolfe himself has learned in respect to technique. James Joyce particularly engages our own general concern to understand
O'Connor as a poet responding to antecedent truth. He does so, by the degree of his own
inescapable obligation as poet through his art, responding to things, engaging the givenness of creation itself, however much reluctant to concede givenness. Joyce's young Stephen
Dedalus knows well this passage from St. Thomas' *Summa Theologica* just quoted, a passage which pronounces the principle that a *right reason* is necessary to the artist's making.
But Stephen as "young" artist wills a gnostic intent as artist to deny his own givenness. He
rejects the Giver, God, in order that he may presume himself thus enabled to dream that
he is empowered by autonomous intellect to the creation of that "uncreated conscience of
his race," self-empowerment by his signs. His explicit motto as artist? Satan's *non servium*.
For Stephen, St. Thomas' right reason is "right" according to his own determination, not
derived through finite reason's participation (according to natural law) in the Eternal Reason whereby truth must govern reason and not reason truth. How awkward for the poet's
pride to concede himself existing as but an image of God.

Stephen (and Joyce) could but know (given Joyce's Jesuit training) that the natural law
is considered by Thomism an inescapable property of human intellect, but a given which
binds the person and creation in the disparateness of things, proportionate in degrees of
givenness. That binding speaks the creation of things, whereby they *are* in that commonality called *being*. Thomas' assertion counters the Emersonian-Charles Eliot intention to a new
religion centering in the community as secularized, by which assumption community is reduced to a civil object to be worshipped (as opiate of the intellectual himself). Community
in this perspective is a projected image of gnostic man as god. In that new religion, intellect is an idol, requiring the mythology of the State — as Marx recognized and preached in

furthering this new religion. It is a religion in part fed by residual sentiments of nationalism. But that is a country of thought appropriated most persuasively out of the illusion of self-sovereignty as assumed by a willed dissociation of intellect from creation by each person. Self-sovereignty therefore must be argued a common property, in the interest of a vested power out of the "popular spirit," granted in differing degree to be exercised by a specific sovereign intellect at the level of existential reality, on the horizontal plane. The power is granted to Voegelin's gnostic "director," since some intellects are more equal than others in the emerging Animal Farm. On that plane, by positing ideas of a future Eden that Eden is made technicolored by such a director, accepted by the popular spirit as just "down the road." The New Eden's micro-physical theology has been summed by Tom Wolfe for those graduating students at Duke University as we have seen.

Thomas' rubric to the contrary, especially as we find it applied to art, implies a two-fold dependence of the artist as maker precisely because he is not sovereign. His is a dependence avoided only by radical denial of *any* givenness. The buried principle? Haze Motes's only truth that there is no truth, freeing intellect by relativism. In pursuit of the delusion thus created by the individual intellect as its own self-salvation, relativism becomes infinite. What O'Connor recognizes, and makes a matter to her drama, is that such a sense of freedom is indeed an illusion, however cleverly appointed by rhetoric, by logic. But to hold it requires no sophisticated intellect, as her Bible salesman demonstrates to Hulga Hopewell. That illusion, when projected upon the world by the poet as his operative principle, leads to a false *in-forming* of art itself. That is the challenge facing Stephen Dedalus as "young" sophisticated artist, willfully pursued by his presumption that as artist he is the cause of truth. By logic and arresting rhetoric Stephen is impressively witty to fellow adolescent intellectual companions. It is only by such illusion that one can declare, as Emerson our exemplary Modernist artist as an old man does, that by power over nature the "world" is to be made an image "of man himself" through his own "victorious thought." That is to intend an exercise of power, principally over man's own being, whereby through intentionality of the will, exercised either by facts "scientifically" deployed (Emerson) or through art (Stephen), thought would "reduce all things" to a power serving the now "realized will," to recall Emerson's phrases. It is thus that (again in Emerson's formulation) the world is made "the double of man."

This characterizes the intellectual matter with which Flannery O'Connor found herself confronted as poet. In her concern as a serious writer she would imitate dramatically these *intellectual* and *spiritual* actions of human nature as perversion of intellectual givenness. And it is a mischief of her wit that she deploys her own grotesque "American Scholars" in such figures as her Bible salesman or Misfit or Haze Motes. Meanwhile, as artist bringing reason to bear upon her making, she knows that *action* must be distinguished from *spectacle* in respect to drama (the insistent distinction made by St. Thomas as it had been made by Aristotle). Intellectual action is the centering ground to any drama of the *person* as *homo viator,* inescapably so within that limit to man of his peculiar givenness as intellectual soul incarnate. So convinced, she must deal as best she may with an audience for whom such distinctions have long been lost. It will mean for her along her way as poet a continuous testing of her own intellectual actions by a hostile and unbelieving audience, sometimes effecting in her a testy response to that audience — a severe testing of her own deportment of prudential humility. (See Appendix E, "Prudential Humility").

Once Flannery O'Connor began to be noticed as a writer, she was noticed as someone curiously distinct among her contemporaries. She began to be "interviewed," the interview having become in her day a popular genre of entertainment for both the popular spirit and for the more reserved intellectual community as detached (in its own estimate) from the popular spirit. Whether questions were put to her formally or informally—whether out of awe in response to a fascinated uncertainty about her work or in a dialectical academic game between writer and critic—questions both subtle or simplistic pursued her as artist. In one simple formulation that was inevitable: *Why* does she even write stories? "Because I'm good at it," she responds. But hers (once more) is not the flip answer it may appear to be, its summary meaning requiring a considerable explication by our reason. There was (and still is) scant opportunity allowed for pursuit of complex meaning, especially in interviews, since ours is so much a world in which questions seek quotable sound-bites rather than exploratory, dialectical, answer in the public arena. Sound-bites are expected, just as multiple-choice questions are to be expected as academic measurement of intellectual maturity in that academy bequeathed us by President Eliot of Harvard. For, as we hear Flannery herself observe, ours has become an intellectual world—high and low—which expects instant uplift by signs that confront realities but only to confirm opinions already held about man's existence as accident. In its relation to art, she says, the reader of a story wants "to be transported, instantly, either to mock damnation or a mock innocence." Such is a conditioning of the popular spirit itself, corollary to the anticipated evolutionary progress of each succeeding age (as she also says in "Some Aspects of the Grotesque in Southern Fiction"). The anticipation is that "the ills and mysteries of life will eventually fall before the scientific advances of man," as had been so confidently promised by Enlightenment rationalism, out of which promise we must "evolve" gnostic systems to determine the limits of truth.

Since O'Connor's observations in respect to art and its uses as demanded by the popular spirit, how thoroughly we have come to surrender common sense. But as that good Thomist Ètienne Gilson observes, common sense is the intellectual ground to any viable philosophy. We instead, by rationalism suspicions of common sense, assume it more convenient to give deference to a magic embraced by faith in expectation of rationalism's salvation of the "self" through magic systems. That is a surrender exacerbated when the popular spirit becomes more and more mesmerized by the spectacular control of facts in a pseudo-metaphysics that pronounces existence but an accidental matter to be made submissive to facts. But that agent intellect, intent on power over being, continues haunted in its pseudo-transcendence of matter, condescending to materialism. Yet by its own presumption, it must admit itself an accident, bearing no substantial reality as intellect save by presumption. It must declare itself substantial as subfused by matter, its body suffering thereafter a fading wonder at its own self-awareness as "alienated." Or so the logic of the illusion requires, whereby only a willed action denying the givenness of will itself must presume a self-substantiation by a circling of self-consciousness increasingly lost in the materialistic cosmos. We come upon an evolved idol out of self-consciousness in this Modernist attempt upon transcendentalism, a seeming respite if not rescue. Now computerized science in varieties of electrical impulses imitative of self-consciousness, mediated by silicone entities, deploy facts to mechanically determined ends desired in reducing the cosmos to finite limit as an intellectual act of transcendence. What wonder that thought should be counted—reckoned—by multiple-choice answers in deconstructing reality to determined solutions, within the limits of sheer fact as the ultimate authority of limit, purging mystery thereby? What wonder that the popular spirit should come to "live" intellectually through sound-bites?

What wonder as well that the popular spirit so conditioned should expect instant rescue to a mock innocence, fearing nevertheless a damnation which is not mock — if there should appear an invading cancer, for instance. But alas, have we not established, as Tom Wolfe insists, that man is but "concatenations of molecules containing DNA, hard wired into a chemical analogue computer known as the human brain, which as software has a certain genetic code"? As such, all that is required therefore is to correct circuitry, on principles derived by rational abstractionism attributed to autonomous intellect as Cause, intellect given a temporary name such as *electric current.* By that solving of the ills of man by a mechanism corrected, by circuitry adjustment, we dream an instant happiness. Enough to make a true poet in her reaction speak through such a figure as Mr. Shiftlet. In "The Life You Save May Be Your Own," Shiftlet speaks with a passion to Mrs. Lucynell Crater: "There's one of these doctors in Atlanta that's taken a knife and cut the human heart ... out of a man's chest and held it in his hand ... and studied it like it was a day-old chicken." Out of the "moral intelligence" Shiftlet claims for himself he declares, "he didn't know no more about it than you or me." Magic cannot overcome mystery, even for such a con-man "intellectual" as O'Connor's Mr. Shiftlet.

In the complexity buried in her answer to the question "Why do you write?" O'Connor's "sound-bite" answer bears by its very brevity a rebuke, the origins of which lie in her faith in the givenness of creation which is refused as answer by the popular spirit confronting her, by her "readers and critics." They demand of her as artist "a realism of fact" (her phrase, not Emerson's). They want the poet to be a magician through signs, the poet a substitute for the sacramental priest. She might have responded that in the 13th or 14th centuries such a question as why she writes would have marked the interlocutor as a strange presence in a company gathered to intellectual concerns, since reason was still understood to require a pursuit of the truth of things based in carefully articulated principles — principles evolved from the self-evident as experienced and initially responded to by common sense. From that beginning, the offices of reason can hardly be satisfied by sound-bites as adequate to genuine wonder.

Even long after those centuries, it would have been understood that an O'Connor wrote in response to her "calling," which as an answer to her contemporary interlocutor could but appear as quaint, at best antique. Not of course that a "calling to" artistry did not become increasingly suspect in the interval from St. Thomas to Flannery O'Connor. One instance, Hawthorne hears an old Puritan response to him as writer, out of the recent grave of religious Puritanism and on the threshold of that new Puritanism rapidly becoming secularized as science. As "romancer" he might as well have been "a fiddler." It is a judgment amenable to a Governor Endicott but also to a Positivist scientist. And in response to this progressive questioning of art after St. Thomas, there began as well a progressive critical justification of art as pragmatic, if it submit to a primary *service* in the ordering of temporal community. By the 20th century, art had become largely reduced to the role of propaganda in service to ideological "religions" of most various manifestations, including (O'Connor remarks) even that new depressing genre of "fictionalized apologetics" — "light Catholic summer reading." Meanwhile "fine art" was increasingly consigned to community sarcophagi called museums. How prophetic of the recovery O'Connor will pursue through the proximity of place is Donald Davidson's "A Mirror for Artists" in *I'll Take My Stand* (1930). His conclusion is that "The artist should not forget that in these times he is called on to play the part of a person and of an artist," the part of person "more immediately important" to his resisting an "infection of our times" whereby there governs "the false gospel of art as a luxury which can be sold in commercial quantities or which can be hallowed by segregation in discrete shrines." As public commodity since Davidson and O'Connor, art comes to trade in the moment's spectacle, but to still disquiet in the popular spirit it does so in the name of "man in full."

Meanwhile the best of our art may linger awhile in "discrete shrines," in museums, unless by a grace (at first taken as accident) a person such as Haze Motes encounters in such a shrine an art object residual of the abolition of man — that severed head in the center of Taulkinham's zoo. Poetry and fiction as "fine" writing may survive in academic courses for awhile, those literary museums for a while yet safely (progressively) housed in specialized curricula, lingering in "English Departments." But O'Connor believes her calling as maker to be quite contrary to such subordinations of art, a discovery about herself and her calling certified to her by her reason through cumulative experiences of making stories. I do this, she is saying, because I am *this* person with *this* calling. Insofar as I exercise reason in pursuit of a perfection of that peculiar calling, I am likely to be good at it, though goodness in this respect is always relative — according to the degree of gift whereby as person I am endowed by *this* peculiar gift. I must recognize that gifts differ not only by species but by degree from person to person according to the mystery of endowment as *this* person, an endowment — a givenness — to be discovered as a calling to which each person is responsible. And so I write these stories, because I am good at it.[5]

6

At Risk in the Wilderness of Theory

"… what has given the South her identity are those beliefs and qualities which she has absorbed from the Scriptures and from her own history of defeat and violation: a distrust of the abstract, a sense of human dependence on the grace of God, and a knowledge that evil is not simply a problem to be solved, but a mystery to be endured."

— Flannery O'Connor, "The Catholic
Novelist in the Protestant South"

"We carry our history and our beliefs and customs and vices and virtues around in our idiom. You can't say anything significant about the mystery of a personality unless you put that personality in a social context that belongs to it."

— Flannery O'Connor to interviewer Betsy Lochridge,
Atlanta Journal and Constitution, November 1, 1959

The lesson spoken to in our epigraphs above would be recognized by Dante as suited to his own concerns as poet. If he is blessed with a magnitude of gift beyond O'Connor's, to which he discovers himself obligated, they share a common vision attending them as persons in a place, Florence and Milledgeville. But as differing in magnitude as poets, O'Connor is not envious of that great poet, instead finding Dante companionable to her concerns, while recognizing as well that the "balanced picture that Dante gave us" (in his territories of Hell, Purgatory, and Paradise) are hardly available to her. For hers is "an age which doubts both fact and value … swept this way and that by momentary convictions." (Her observation is made early in "Some Aspects of the Grotesque in Southern Fiction.") There is for her "no literary orthodoxy … not even that of Henry James, who balanced the elements of traditional realism and romance so admirably within each of his novels." It is in her respect for James's "balanced elements" that she scores several sentences in James's "Guy de Maupassant." In its first paragraph James warns the writer that "However full of faith in his inspiration," he puts himself in danger "when he sallies forth into the dim wilderness of theory." There is also that scored sentence James provides as proper to his audience's demands: "Make me something fine in the form that shall suit you best, according to your temperament," though she might have said "according to the limits of your gifts as maker." She is as poet a citizen in this nonbelieving age and so pretty much on her own, though by differing degree she finds both Dante and James companionable — Dante more supportive certainly than James, given Dante's balanced vision of the world around him in Florence in the light of his faith and not simply in the light of the demands of art.

Indeed, we hear Dante in a certainty about both his vision and his gifts early in the *Divine Comedy*, more direct than James though James is confident of his gifts. Without blushing, exercising his gift, we hear Dante acknowledging himself as pilgrim poet to be not simply "good at" poetry, but superlatively good at it. He is made one of five or six in a gathering of the Western world's greatest poets, including his guide Virgil, to whom he nevertheless continues deferential. Even Homer and Horace, met in that conclave of like-gifted poets in Limbo in a moment aside from the journey, greet Dante as poet and vote him a "sixth amid such intelligences."[1] Though O'Connor recognizes and says that she is good at her gifts, she makes no claim for herself as exceptionally good, even among "Southern" writers. She is aware, and acutely aware, of Faulkner as a giant in the midst of Southern writers: "Nobody wants his mule and wagon stalled on the same track the Dixie Limited is roaring down." It is a remark made early in her career in "Some Aspects of the Grotesque in Southern Fiction," in which she has just observed that "while the South is hardly Christ-centered, it is most certainly Christ-haunted." That is a recognition shared with Faulkner, though as herself a believer and not a skeptic as is Faulkner (whom she might well consider "Christ-haunted"), she gains a perspective on the South which some readers of both these Southerners may find more incisive than Faulkner's, less haunted by the pathos which Faulkner so often rescues by humor.

Our opening epigraphs here suggest the difference. Her address to the South as an "identity" underlines that identity as arising from beliefs and qualities absorbed from the Scriptures and affecting the South's "peculiar" history for over two hundred years. It is that coincidence of belief within history which makes the South congenial to her own gifts. As a believing writer, she will speak of herself as peculiarly a "Southern" writer, though in the third person. The believing writer she says would penetrate "the concrete world in order to find at its depths the image of its source, the image of ultimate reality." It is in this attempt that she shares with Dante, more fundamentally than with Faulkner (or James), in her recognition that "history" as actively present in this moment bears in itself a spiritual center. This alliance with Dante more than with Faulkner or with fellow Southerners like Katherine Anne Porter and Eudora Welty affects her concerns for the temporal and spacious arena to the spiritual pilgrimage she dramatizes in her own "Southern" work. Dante descends into Hell, climbs Mt. Purgatory, rises beyond creation itself into that country of Paradise. Then occurs for him a culminating vision of the Multifoliate Rose of Heaven. All along his way, his immediate cultural circumstances allow a daring in his art that is not possible to O'Connor, though the spiritual matter for each is both immediate and the same, despite their differing cultural circumstances.

O'Connor's present and Dante's present prove radically different to each as poet, differing in spectacle conspicuously given the six-hundred year interval between them as prophetic poets living in separate hemispheres. And so O'Connor peers into nooks and crannies of the concrete world immediately at hand, but in doing so she discovers echoes of affinity between her vision and Dante's in what she discovers. When Nelson in "The Artificial Nigger" looks down into the Atlanta sewer, he is fascinated by a terror suited to the experiencing of Hell by Dante, as that Florentine would recognize from the imagery she uses. Nelson, at least intuitively, is stirred by such an intimation of his seemingly hopeless state, though there is not posted over the Atlanta sewer any inscription warning him: no "Abandon Hope, all ye who enter here." The "concrete" world into which O'Connor looks to discover an "image of its source" implies to her that the world, insofar as it *is,* is itself necessarily good, a recognition shared with Dante. But "If the Catholic writer hopes to reveal mysteries, he will have to do it by describing truthfully what he sees from where he is. A purely affirmative vision cannot be demanded of him without limiting his freedom to observe what man has done with the things of God"— with that concrete world which though in itself good is now generally seen with a distorted vision ("The Church and the Fiction Writer"). In penetrating that world at hand, she herself discovers "the image of ultimate reality," God, as implied Cause. That recognition "in no way hinders [a writer's] perception of evil but rather sharpens it, for only when the natural world is seen as good does evil become intelligible as a destructive force and a necessary result of our freedom" ("Novelist and Believer").

She suggests, then, an abiding if unseen world lying within the material world as perceived through spectacle in our "psychological" response to surface spectacle. An intense attention to spectacle yields depths, requiring of her as *person* a long looking at and into any thing in itself. By that attention she may see more and more of a larger world circumscribing but also permeating the object which intellect enjoins by perception. She moves in both worlds (the material and spiritual) in her vision of the hidden, discovering what Thomas Aquinas would call her kinship with things a "connaturality," a "naturalness" of *existing in being* whereby both the perceived and the perceiver *are.* Thus it is that the longer one engages an object with an opening intellectual love, the more of the larger enveloping and sustaining presence of Love may be seen through it. Her reader might therefore consider (she suggests) that as a "serious fiction writer," she is writing "about the whole world, no matter how limited [her] particular scene" may appear at first encounter of a story. Her encounters of objects (especially persons in their intellectual and spiritual actions within the circumscribing local reality) require a penetrating vision deeper than contentment with spectacle alone can allow, though spectacle proves the necessary point of departure to the making of a story in respect to its textural (its "incarnational") nature. In the concrete nature of a thing, underlying its perceived spectacle, is its essential nature as *this* thing (or *this* person), actual in itself and so substantial beneath the spectacle that speaks its particularities out of its essential nature as the thing it is.

And so she must go deeper than the perception of things at their surface by the senses, perceptions charging reason itself to accommodate beyond sensual response to the immediate world. Man is not simply incarnate, she holds: he is an *intellectual soul* incarnate. Contentment with an appetitive response alone isolates the person as *homo viator* to the surface of reality. There he is arrested, as if the whole of his own essential nature were his body. Nevertheless, to avoid the risk to him of immersion in this place at this time through his body, the pilgrim person may refuse recognition of the concomitant grace to each thing whereby it *is* and therefore proportionately good even in its "carnate" nature. But most especially to himself as *this* person he may refuse that consent. To fail to recognize and engage grace itself as the cause of the good of each thing whereby it actually exists is a spiritual failure. For, insofar as a thing *is* (*exists*) it does so by grace and so is necessarily good, by relative degree both actual and potential. That is a fundamental principle of her Thomism. It is a principle self-evident to Thomas, for a thing is antecedently graced by its *being* in the first place. Both the perceiver and perceived share therefore a connaturality by the reality of existing, the self-evident reality ignored by Descartes, to our age's discontent as intellectual souls.

It is within this connaturality to things that intellect becomes endangered, and in that drama O'Connor engages, as a realist of distances, this centrally important truth. For in the

person's responsibility as this very nature to a specific stewardship in creation lies a responsibility consequent upon his being created in the image of God to his peculiar calling. Even
so, by his very intention to the good he may transgress his own limits, endangering his soul.
Here lies the intersection within consciousness itself in which reason must deal with the problem of evil. Jacques Maritain engages the mystery of evil in a lecture, *St. Thomas and the
Problem of Evil,* just as World War II begins to emerge in all its horrors — in 1942. At once
he sets the parameters of his concern: to engage *moral* evil as understood by St. Thomas
and St. Augustine. Evil, he says, "is neither an essence nor a nature nor a form nor an act
of being — evil is an absence of being; it is not a mere negation, but a privation: the privation of the good that should be in a thing." (Maritain cites to his summary beginning the
texts of Thomas' *Summa Theologica; de Malo; Contra Gentiles; Compendium Theologiae.*)

How ancient, man's complaint that evil is an unjust *privation* (rather than a "mere negation") for as privation there is spoken by implication an agent cause, ultimately God, who
is to be "blamed" for evil in finite intellectual dislocation. Why should God allow my
diminution of good as intellect, my deprivation which from my perspective appears a willful evil visited upon me by God? That is a mystery Thomas pursues in justifying God's ways
to man — that is, revealing reasonably that the privation by limit makes a larger good possible to man through that very privation, the good which we call Mercy as one of God's
names. We might, indeed, lament with Descartes that our intellectual privation as man
means we must *become* intellectually through a gradual discursive knowing. We are as person deprived of that instant knowing of all things at the point of our conception, as Descartes
on one occasion complains. How unjust of God, this privation, and never more sharply re-
gretted than in proportion to the magnitude of our intellectual gifts. The greater our gift
of intellect, the more intense the temptation to revolt, as the "story" of Lucifer reveals. The
greater the created intellectual potential, the more tempted that intellect to indict God for
privation. We have remarked Descartes' inclination (and shall allude to its *passim*) as the
position taken by Dostoevsky's Ivan Karamazov, a position Ivan at last will concede to be
his "romantic" presumption at his spiritual collapse. Hence we well remember that Lucifer,
the brightest and most perfect intellectual soul, instantly knowing on creation, covets the
ultimate *comprehension* reserved to God alone. Lucifer, preeminent intellectual "light-
bearer," falls into a nether opposition — as Satan declaring *non servium* with an intellectual
pettiness familiar to most of us as fallen creatures.

Lest Satan carry this argument with man as intellectual soul incarnate against truth itself, St. Thomas addresses the mystery of evil again and again, a last time in his *Compendium of Theology* just before his death. He argues a distinction of *moral* from *natural*
evil, for "the evil of lameness is caused by a curvature in the leg, not by the motive power
of the soul." Evil out of that "motive power" is a moral evil through a presumption (in some
degree) of godhead — a questioning of God's justice and mercy with an intent to reduce those
mysteries that speak the absolute to the province of autonomous (but ironically) finite intellect. In this strategy will follow various declarations toward an impending Eden, the creation by finite intellect itself in correction of God's "injustice," and at the expense of a person's proportionate providential stewardship. It is evil which gains by an intentional
intellectual dominance over creation under the auspices of autonomous intellect. But Thomas
suggests that "If evil were completely eliminated from things, they would not be governed
by Divine Providence in accord with their nature; and this would be a greater defect than
the particular defects eradicated" (*Compendium of Theology,* I, 142). The most conspicuous,

the greatest defect, would be (could finite intellect make all creation perfect in an absence of any possible privation) that there would be no such property in created man as his own free will. "Consequently," Thomas adds, "it is the concern of Divine Providence, not to safeguard all beings from evil, but to see to it that the evil which arises is ordained to some good." And the *good* ordained to free will as itself intellectual is that it bear its privation, its limits through hope strengthened by love. It may *understand,* but not *comprehend* this mystery of "suffering-with." That is not a negation as rational creature but a grace to man's nature as an intellectual soul incarnate, without which that entity the *person* could indeed be only a mechanically determined "perfect" machine. Indeed, this is a concept most difficult to even imagine by finite intellect — itself as "pure" machine — since requiring of that intellect its "transcendental" removal from creation sufficient to *comprehend* (as opposed to understand) man as a perfect machine transcendent of reality created through angelistic intent.

Given such challenges to reason as those raised by Augustine and Thomas, one might the more admire Flannery O'Connor, who with deliberateness engages the mystery of evil in an age concerned to see evil only as relative in relation to "mistakes of nature," to be resolved by reason's illusion of a "transcendent" position beyond nature itself— beyond both good and evil. That is what O'Connor has in mind when she says that since the 18th century "the popular spirit of each succeeding age has tended more and more to the view that the ills and mysteries of life will eventually fall before the scientific advances of man." In dramatizing her Rayber in *The Violent Bear It Away,* she engages with a daring the distinction Thomas makes between moral and natural evil. The willful rejection of mercy in the name of autonomous justice as decreed here and now by finite intellect is one evil, in part a reaction, a challenge to moral free will in response to "mistakes of nature"—Thomas' "lameness caused by the curvature" of the bone in the leg, or that more challenging confrontation, the idiot Bishop in Flannery's second novel as a "curvature" of nature.

Thomas' example in his distinction of moral from natural evil, then, is a more gentle instance than O'Connor introduces in her novel. Her idiot Bishop must to our limited sensibilities undeniably suffer a privation which our reason must conclude in somewise a mistake of nature. But how then must reason respond to that unfortunate creature in moral responsibility to such a creature? That becomes Rayber's dilemma, he suspended between his reason as fierce in its rejection of nature because seen only as random, requiring Rayber's reason as its corrective of intentionality to determine natural good, that strangely gnawing at the love he has for Bishop. How then, his disturbing hesitancy before reason's solution, a "final solution" of Bishop's challenge to reason: euthanasia? Just how thoroughly converted young Tarwater becomes to Rayber's "idea" about correcting mistakes of nature is evident when he drowns Bishop. Before that action, intended murder, Tarwater takes pleasure in needling Rayber as a "theorist." On the verge of drowning Bishop, Tarwater says (concerning Bishop as a mistake of nature) "I can pull it up by the roots, once and for all.... All you can do is think what you would have done if you had done it. Not me. I can do it. I can act."

How subtly attuned, our hillbilly Thomist, to Thomas' arguments. She understands that the intellectual soul, through the concrete "good" of things as evidenced to us through the body in experiences of things actual in creation, comes to intellect's fundamental recognition of reality. It does so as member in a connaturality with all things created. It may do so, insofar as it exercises an openness toward things. Rayber himself willy-nilly responds to things intuitively, in an openness of love, whose effect on him he can only conclude by his constricted reason an encroaching madness. (Intellect, Thomas argues, can *intend* only the good, its confusion coming in sorting good in the orders of creation in relation to the good of discrete things existing by an Absolute Good, by God's love.) Rayber cannot accept the reality of things whereby in proportionate limits each thing *is* the *thing* it is. Each thing thereby, as specific, is subject to *privation*— not *negation*— as a discrete reality: as the thing it is. Even that idiot Bishop. Understood within the limits of his own finitude, the intellectual creature may come to understand — though not *comprehend* we must emphasize — that things *are,* and therefore are necessarily *good* in being each a limited creature. That is the intellectual challenge Rayber can not resolve. Without limit to *each* thing, indeed, there would be only a "pure" negation, a "never-to-have-been" which can only be spoken of speculatively in a necessary dependence upon antecedent actualities of things in themselves. It requires a measure by what already is. One cannot conceive *nonexistence* independent of *existence* as already known by intellect as a truth *conceived* in intellect.

This *thing* perceived must be concluded therefore necessarily good by degree, prompting reason, out of that intuitive experience of its own good, to pursue the nature of the good as a universal through the multiple beings perceived — the many speaking a One as Augustine argues in abandoning a Platonic confusion of intellect. (See Plato's *Parmenides.*) And that must bring the intellectual soul (through grace) to a point of possible vision. There comes a moment of intellectual consent by reason itself to recognition of a Presence to things, a Cause of the goodness whereby specific natures are because *given* and not random accidents. Nevertheless, evil itself is by its nature a privation "active" against *being* in the range of possible things that *are.* And evil is especially dangerous to the being of the intellectual soul obligated to sorting the *good* by reason as morally responsive to beings. Alas, by a free act of will the intellectual soul may assume itself empowered to elect as a greater good that which must prove at last only a lesser good. That is the moral ground in which literary tragedy flourishes as art. Thus concerning art as "reason in making," O'Connor is deeply lessoned by Thomas. For as Thomas observes, in his *Contra Gentiles,* "Everything evil is rooted in some good, and everything false in some truth." In the same work he says that "It is impossible that any evil should be striven after precisely as evil, either by the natural appetite, or the sensitive, or the intellectual, which is the will." And in his *Questiones disputate de potentia Dei* on the same theme he remarks that "We do not strive toward evil by tending towards anything but by turning away from something."

Moral evil, this is to say, is a choosing of a lesser good by turning away from a greater good. The culminative and cumulative lesser good leaves the intellectual soul isolated in self-love. Willfulness to a self-love as the greater good we must see as evil, O'Connor remarks. It is an evil "become intelligible [to finite intellect] as a destructive force and a necessary result of our freedom" as intellectual creature, she says. Evil in intellect is thus a falling away from universal good as mediated to us by a created reality and therefore speaking an Absolute Good, God as Absolute Love. That universal good of creation is mediated to intellect, not with a necessity that intellect know every created entity in creation. For we may recognize good as universal in the smallest of things, in Dame Julian's hazel-nut on her palm. That is the truth O'Connor affirms in saying that "The longer you look at one object, the more of the world you see in it." But if we begin with denial of the good of this thing experienced here and now, our reason tends toward a necessity out of that error, toward a declaration of reason's own illusional "universal": existence as accidental. In that conclusion lies a denial not only of proximate and universal good to things because they are, but a denial of the Ultimate Good, of God as Love.

That is a "development" engineered by reason, to which T. S. Eliot speaks in his *Dry Salvages* as

> a partial fallacy
> Encouraged by superficial notions of evolution
> Which becomes, in the popular mind, a means of
> disowning the past.

Both Eliot and O'Connor, then, accept the connaturality of finite reason with Eternal Reason (man as existing in the image of God). For both, it is love as a natural inclination to the good which is the motive proper to stewardship of things — even a stewardship by love to that mistake of nature, Rayber's nephew Bishop. In her novel, Rayber comes to love Bishop over all other things, but can see his love only as an intellectual disease. What is diseased is his reason atrophied by willfulness, a moral consent to the evil of his own willed diminution of things to accident. For him, his reason can hold love only as madness, so that Rayber himself becomes the greatest mistake possible in nature — man self-apotheosized by his fallenness — his consciousness suspended between good and evil. That is the diabolical "transcendentalism" of Modernist doctrine. But by his willfulness, he is unable to consent to an act of love relieving that suspension.

Only in consequence of a freedom to turn away from the good, a freedom unfettered by our very givenness as *this* person, may man himself fall away from the good possible to him. That is the mystery of free will. But further, only by that freedom and the dangers to this person attendant upon his freedom may man be concluded other than a determined creature in both body and soul, a mere mechanism. At Flannery O'Connor's moment in history the term *soul* is granted only a pejoratively intended metaphorical sense, a convenient reference perhaps to the age's unresolved desire for the singularity of man, even as man is argued to be a well-ordered machine. It is by a desire distorted by willfulness that our age seeks "a man in full," a "good man," in an illusion of autonomy, the illusion that intellectual freedom must be absolute over both nature and nature's God, thus empowered to correct all of nature's mistakes. In response to the mystery of his singularity in creation as reduced by willed apotheosis, yet troubled by the seeming separation of his body and his "consciousness," the person may attempt to certify himself as beyond the cosmic determining machine, as well as beyond his own body as proximate adversary as limit — the body an unjust negation. Thus his own body seems in "cahoots" with that larger machine he calls the cosmos. How jealous he is of his intellectual freedom as not only independent of God but as well of the cosmos which, by an initiating freedom of intentionality, he would declare only a machine. Life is the noise the machine makes, a noise haunting and echoing in consciousness as the shadowy sound of solipsism.

In such a deportment of thought the Modernist man discovers that his very thought has no locus. There is no *place* to *stand* from which to execute his dissociation from the cosmos. For, although having used the cosmos to customize himself through gnosis (initially his own body the vehicle used in a ranging of time and space), in the end he finds himself as a thinking creature alienated not only from the cosmos but from his own "self," haunted solipsistically. The point of his initial departure toward that dead end, as Eric Voegelin puts it, is the gnostic presumption to a power over being itself, out of an intellectual autonomy assuming the office of an absolute "director" of his own being. (No wonder that O'Connor finds Voegelin a companionable intellect to her own opposition to this Modernist gambit against being, as does Walker Percy also.) Autonomous intellect, self-translated beyond the "machinery" of its own body on the wings of intentionality, would thus en-soul itself by presumption of godhead, in pursuit of power as antithetic to love as understood by O'Connor. By that action of will, the person denies his own particularity save insofar as he may declare it self-created. But in doing so he must deny that givenness whereby he *is*, thus bound in his intention toward the abyss of Nothingness. Haze Motes preaches this intentional ideal, an Emersonian message. He harangues his motley listeners on the streets of Taulkinham: "Where is there a place for you to be? No place. Nothing outside you can give you any place," only your own willed intentionality. Nevertheless, he finds himself at a disadvantage, since, as he says, "I ain't got no place to be."

To solve that problem, Haze buys that "high-rat-colored machine with large thin wheels and bulging headlights," the discarded Essex, declaring that "Nobody with a good car needs to be justified." How very local these details, as well as Haze's speech patterns. O'Connor uses such "local color" but knows that within it is revealed as buried by her clever mischief as maker both the older Jansenist doctrine and its kindred Puritan inclination to an absolute spiritual determinism of nature as separated from grace, deeply infecting Haze's intellect. Since the 17th and 18th centuries there has been prepared therefore the triumph of Positivism through gnostic power, perverting the popular spirit to a doctrine of self-love on the principle that "Nothing outside you can give you any place." That radically distorted judgment of natural creation as "outside you" allows a presumption of a Positivistic purity of rationalism to act against being in a self-election beyond creation itself. But the reality underlying such illusion of power, as we must be momently reminded, proves to be the diminution of the gnostic himself, as Haze discovers when his Essex proves unable to carry him where he is going as if a portable place.

O'Connor, then, rejects the Modernist species of Manichaeanism, the proclaimed determinism of will over being whereby intellectual "consciousness" would be the lord of being. She recognizes in Hawthorne his intuitive awareness of this process of self-apotheosis as becoming more and more prevalent in the popular spirit. It is, in a Puritan aspect of the ancient species, reflected in his "Maypole of Merrymount." That destructiveness to the discrete consciousness is also dramatized in his "Young Goodman Brown." But the gnostically-adapted pseudo–Manichaeanism, prelude to Positivistic dominance over being, is the theme of his "The Birthmark." In an adaptation of that thread of Puritan gnosis to Positivistic science, creation must be reduced by a faith believing the cosmos a material accident to be corrected by gnosis. That becomes a perspective adapted from the distortions of spiritual reality already accomplished by both the Jansenist and the Puritan strains of willfulness. Subsequently, by a rejection of the soul as the shadow of wishful thinking, the body may be elevated as the ultimate end as a "place," to the increasing fascination of the popular spirit.

In that ambient collective consent of the popular spirit to Positivism there lies power sufficient to the reconstitution of being by the gnostic director, of whom there are so many representatives on the stage of our history in the 20th century. But the consequences to that popular spirit, to borrow Walker Percy's term for it, becomes its "thanatos syndrome." It becomes haunted by death as oblivion. Materialism elevated as a pseudo-religion assures only a temporal control over the popular spirit, centralized in that icon-idol, the State, in the worship of which the popular spirit becomes restive and then cynically perverse. That haunting sense of oblivion shadows us, the doctrine of death. In reaction, the doctrine accepted, the popular spirit becomes the more obsessed with desire to reconstitute the body itself as if it might thus fulfill in this moment that old but radically distorted desire for immortality in quest of eternal youth. O'Connor rejects that reconstitution. The challenge to her as poet proves formidable, she sometimes thinking her voice overwhelmed in the spiritual vacuum of the popular spirit. But most resolutely she rejects the view that man is an accident as God's determined toy, an alternative faith out of Jansenism and Puritanism as ancient forms of the Manichaean. She rejects as well "gnostic" intentionalities to reconstitute being by Positivistic authority as but the obverse of the older Manichaeanism, the deterministic agent (the gnostic "director") to be self-made god by his assumption that man is only random effect of cumulative accidents within a closed, material universe but rescued beyond determined machine by intentionality. Thus that director becomes substitute god. Each course is kindred to the other in intellectual presumption of a vision presumed inclusive of reality as made subject to finite will. Both strategies of intellect prove (in her vision) illusions systematized through reductionist principles, whether those of Governor Endicott or of Dr. Aylmer as parable figures. Either reduction is self-evidently inadequate to immediate experiences of an actual thing in itself as she has known things.

How alike, these gnostic extremes, though often pitted against each other in contests for power over nature. But it is a mistake to conclude them as *diametrically* opposed, since both share in manipulations of reality at the expense of reality. Theirs are kindred intents: the apotheosis of man through a reductionism of creation itself, but particularly a reductionism visited upon the intellectual soul incarnate. From O'Connor's (and Thomas') perspectives, what must inevitably prove most radically reduced is man's own given nature, ironically by his intellectual actions as reductionist of himself as an autonomous "self." If our argument is somewhat abstractly put, we must nevertheless attempt to describe the confused intellectual stage built by gnostic contraventions of reality since the Renaissance, upon which Modernist stage those two religious contenders have been increasingly embattled in an increasingly fanatical intent to power, each of them self-empowered by abstractionisms reductive of nature as separated from grace. They are at last ideologies. That is to say, each by intentionally separating nature from grace builds of nature thus sterilized that intellectually jerry-built stage, a platform of departure into angelistic transcendentalism. O'Connor casts her drama on this stage, but not as expected by gnostic Manichaeanisms. She dramatizes these contending intellectual posturings with inevitable comic effect.

As dramatist, she understands *action* as intellectual, however dependent it is in a staging of dramatic representations of spectacle, or however much spectacle itself may be stylized by the selections and deployments of the dramatist. We have attempted some characterization of that intellectual ambiance, the stage as a *consciousness*, in which occur actions of spiritual denials within that dominantly Modernist small world of the "self" which encourages that denial. It is from that world that she draws the matter to a making of imitations of *possible* actions of characters, the possible as governed by the actual — as art is always necessarily governed by the limited largesse (the givenness) of human nature to the making of dramatic things such as Haze's attempt to build his Church of Christ without Christ. What we must keep in mind is that at the very center of that staging for O'Connor is the consciousness of a character, within which consciousness the drama of action occurs. (She underlines in her copy of Henry James's "Guy de Maupassant" a sentence beginning "character, in any sense in which we can get at it, is action, and action is plot...." It is an observation in accord with her rejecting "theme" in favor the larger "meaning" of a story.) In approaching her own version of art's "stylized" action, O'Connor cannot imitate nature in the manner of a Sophocles, nor of a Dante, the current circumstances of community to her as poet being what they are. Her manner depends on the "naturalistic" local, upon the actual as seen here and now, especially as sometimes and alarmingly reported in the local press. (Her "Misfit" she first encounters in a newspaper story.) Through such stylization of the local in the manner perceived as "grotesque" by many, she would dramatize man in his most dangerous exercise of his supreme and most ambiguous gift to him from his Cause: his freedom of will as an intellectual soul. Even the drama of Sophocles, his *Oedipus Rex,* we should notice implies a reality of free will, so that Oedipus is not simply a victim of a coincidence called *fate.* The Classical concept of "fate" is already for Sophocles complex and troubling, a mystery of limit — of intellectual finitudes yet unresolved by logic, as we discover in the resolution of his *Oedipus at Colonus* by a puzzling mystery. For Sophocles desires resolution of the dilemma which for Dante and St. Thomas and O'Connor is resolved by the Incarnation.

The local, then, distorted to our recognitions by Modernist intellectual manipulations of our own nature, trickled down as doctrine even unto the far reaches of Baldwin County, Georgia: that is the climate to uncertain thought within which O'Connor elicits an intellectual action counter to it. Her dramatic manner is that of a counter distortion which she speaks of as "violence," deployed as suited to the particular manner of her "grotesque" figurings of man as haunted by denials of his spiritual nature within a limited, local place. Her figures as she "incarnates" them are very specific. Thus a Haze Motes, a Misfit, loom more largely as dramatic presences than when taken as petty, inconsequential figures drawn out of a laughable provincialism of a place by Modernist sophistications. That may be a more self-comforting way of taking such figures, if the reader is himself isolated within that Modernist intellectual temperament. She chooses the Modernist version of the person, upon whom the Modernist has projected his version of life as reduced to mechanical causes. But underneath that self-imposed form, a surrogate person, her fictional character begins to stir, restive in his intellectual action. The accidental cosmos serves as backdrop against which she projects by art her disturbed figures as protagonists, slowly defeated in the resistance of Modernist willfulness. A protagonist's growing perceptions of reality through the truth of things (particularly the truth of himself as person) struggles with degrees of violence against the Modernist straitjacket woven by his fancy.

Not that all of her protagonists are like her Misfit, a "prophet gone wrong," or like Haze a saint (as she calls him) because of his single-minded pursuit of integrity. Modernist man may be shown to strut ludicrously upon the stage that he has built in order to isolate himself from reality to the conveniences of his fancy, in his attempt to con reality itself. Nevertheless, that separation of grace from nature, O'Connor holds, is possible only through such intellectual con-game. How ludicrous is this delusional action, this pettiness of pretense. O'Connor underlines by comical aspect in some of her protagonists, as we recall in the drama of Mr. Shiftlet. Shiftlet's is a self-delusive pretense, in that his distorted stage is itself nevertheless sustained by the reality he would deny. He pays pious lip service to what in his own mind he denies in an old sophistry. He nevertheless comes to a faint recognition of his emptiness as "intellectual" con-man with that blunt rejection by an embittered juvenile hitchhiker. The boy sees through Shiftlet at once and demands that he "go to Hell," which is where Shiftlet is headed. Haze experiences a similar shock to more healthful effect, devastated by his own logic. For how can he commit the blasphemy he intends if God does not exist? For a Shiftlet or a Haze, self-delusion depends always upon the *givenness* of their nature, especially a givenness as *this* (surrogate) person willing his intellectual actions of self-destruction.

Ah, there's the rub. For free will as an actual and unrestricted gift is a gift nevertheless. But it is a gift to be earned in its perfection through a right reason, lest will turn willfulness. One might make daring comparison to the point once more in our most famous American intellectual. How companionable Emerson is to these very strange fictional pilgrim of O'Connor's such as that provincial Haze Motes. In his *Essays: Second Series,* Emerson includes a brief, whimsical essay called "Gifts" which declares that "It is not the office of a man to receive gifts" since "We wish to be self-sustained. We do not quite forgive a giver. The hand that feeds us is in some danger of being bitten." The moral: "Brother, if Jove to thee a present make,/ Take heed that from his hands thou nothing take." That is Emerson's advice to us. For how humiliating to "a man" to be beholden for his very existence to any "Jove." How, if beholden, can he ever be "a man in full?" Better a final isolation in solipsism as the last desperation toward being "self-sustained."

That is Haze's initial motive in reaction to his own existence, though he does not take refuge in the conclusion that existence itself is but an illusion, that suicide of consciousness with which Modernism flirts though a principle which was refuted long ago by St. Augustine: if I am deluded (St. Augustine argues) as the skeptics (sophists) would say, I must *exist,* since I couldn't be deluded if I did not already exist. This realization marks a point of turning for St. Augustine (he as a highly sophisticated "Haze"), as it also proves to be for O'Connor's surrogate *homo viator* Haze. The delusion that nature can be separated from the active presence of grace, therefore — as advocated by either the gnostic Puritan or gnostic Materialist whom Emerson turns into his own Puritan "self" — does not *effect* that separation. By intent contrary to his own actuality, he can only effect a separation of his own gnostic intellect from grace, and so linger trapped in the body until dust claim it to his doomed ancestors. It is by this willfulness that intellect builds obstacle to a grace that might unify person as intellectual soul incarnate. (St. Thomas is a "fundamentalist" on this point.)

It is indeed at this juncture of nature with its sustaining Cause that the pilgrim discovers his own closest correspondence as person to his Creator, in recognition of which he knows himself "created in God's image." For some persons, that is an unsupportable — a demeaning gift since it requires acknowledging it a "present" which "Jove" gives man. This is the point of dramatic confrontation which O'Connor speaks of as occurring to intellect at that crossroads "where time and place and eternity somehow meet" if and when the person succeeds in "locating" himself in that point. In its reaction to that coincidence of the immanent and transcendent to consciousness, the will may consent to or reject its own gift of unqualified free will from the Giver. What O'Connor recognizes is that such a crossroads is always immediate, is always *here* and *now* to a consciousness which necessarily exists in *this* place at *this* time. The person as pilgrim need not necessarily journey the world's geography or its history to find a single discrete umbilical binding it to creation through an infusing grace. Hence her remark that "all is the Incarnation."

In O'Connor's vision, Bethlehem and the Cross are somehow mysteriously coincident in this place at this time — in Middle Georgia for her — in an actuality to consciousness which her Misfit cannot believe, not realizing himself already presently there could he but see that "all is the Incarnation" as O'Connor believes. Should he come to recognize this, he would become the prophet "he was meant to be." It is a present reality of the Cause of reality, to be recognized in response to *this* thing *now* experienced by my consciousness through my senses, requiring my response to it as actual through an openness of love. O'Connor knows this from old witnesses, not St. Thomas only, but especially also the witness of St. Augustine. It is St. Augustine's discovery at his own crossroads, as we have suggested, turning him from both his obsession with the sensual (Lord, save me from the sensual — but not quite yet, he prays) and his temptations to an obsessive rejection of the sensual in an embrace of Manichaeanism. It is also the point of recognition which St. Paul pronounces as self-evident after his encounter on the road to Damascus: this witness of things to their Cause: "For the invisible things of [God] from the creation of the world are clearly seen, being understood by the things that are made [i.e., created]." Hence mankind is "without excuse," St. Paul says, given such self-evident witness of God to man in the actually existing things perceived here and now.

Free will: A property of person as himself a peculiar gift among created things, to creation a steward having been created "in the image of God" as providential to creation. Though the person by his actual existence is nevertheless *prescribed* in limits, there is yet that mystery of his close kinship in a gift by delegation, his nature. He is special in responsibilities to creation as steward of both himself and of things. In the exercise of free will, always in respect to limit, what may be effected as the ultimate consequence of his proper exercise of free will is first of all the perfection of himself as person, as *this* person. As person he does so by pursuit of an *integrity* of the good possible to him, through his free will. Always, his will is adequate to remove by reason obstacles to the grace necessary to his possible perfection. But alternately, he may effect a diminution of his limits by willfulness, a destruction of both his actual and his possible good in that revolt advocated by Emerson as "self-sufficiency." It is on this stage of action — the interior stage of self-consciousness — then that the will proves deliberate in deployment of reason. And that, once more, is the stage on which O'Connor "makes" her *possible* dramatic action. In the reality experienced by the senses she sees such action, evidenced in the ripening of a person through grace or, alternately, in a withering from grace. The spectacles of both inclinations speak something of an unperceivable reality to her characters. This is to say that for her, dramatic action occurs for each *within* the tensions of will whose "place" is within a consciousness of the self as *this* person. The dramatic play evidenced by spectacle points toward the reality of this interior action, in *possible* imitations of the *action* of human nature by her art.

And so it is a considerable challenge to her as a maker of fiction in an unbelieving age that we have lost recognition of such fundamental distinctions as that between *spectacle* and *action*. It is a loss following our rejection through relativism of a distinction between good and evil except as residual terms that might be applied by "feeling" rather than by "thought" on the surface of reality — in relation to our immediate convenience. That becomes the operative action of intellect when grace and nature are sundered, so that we may skate on the surface of things as Emerson advises us to do. And we have been so largely conditioned to that surface that we "reason" it the limit of reality itself. One might make a figure here, suggestive of O'Connor's difficulty as writer. Most of us know the awkward attempt to call a child's attention to some thing we think might be of interest to the child. We point to it. But it takes some children, perhaps most of them, some experience of habits of perception before they look *toward* what our finger would point out as separate from all other things within the limited horizon of the moment. "Don't look at my finger! Look *there!*"

Something like this is the difficulty she must overcome in her fiction, given the pervasive appetite for surfaces to the "popular spirit," that spirit now long schooled in denials of the *soul's* existence in order that it may deny the existence of *good* and *evil* except as relative to fulfilling a random desire of the moment. That spirit first rejects God as "dead"—a figurative deployment implying he never even *was*. But it may then be the more comfortably asserted that the Devil is only a figure of the imagination as infected by fancy, a residual "thought," vestigial of antiquated superstitions. But, says O'Connor in her own person (as well as in the implications of her art), "Look *there!*" In her art she does so with "large and startling" figures, knowing that her audience is hard of hearing and almost blind to the reality of good and evil. How strange, her insistence to Modernist ears: God *is;* the Devil *is;* good *resists* the diminution by Evil. That is her personal insistence, which in her art she rather puts as a challenge by indirection: *what if* God exists, and the Devil as well? What then?

In this respect, she dramatizes her own challenge through a Haze Motes. And because Haze is so doggedly intent upon an intellectual integrity in his pursuit of truth, at the cost of severely personal suffering, she will remark him a figure suggestive of man as *homo viator* seeking sainthood. For however terrible for Haze the truth may prove, and despite his intellectual confusions effecting in his "wills in conflict" (her phrase for his circumstance as a consciousness), Haze persists into death in pursuit of truth despite its terrors. His soul has been crippled by Modernist ideology, as a child's lungs might be crippled by second-hand smoke. But he continues unrelenting in his quest for truth as purifying and restorative. It will prove a truth, when he comes to it at last, that is more overwhelming and terrifying than he could either imagine or put into words. And so the dramatic parabola of Haze's journey runs from that point at which he can say that the only truth is that there is no truth to the threshold of a recognition of Truth Absolute, a Truth he can neither name nor himself "justify" by his own intellectual nature, so distorted have become his terms: *Jesus, Christ, Incarnation,* let alone *sin* and *repentance.* He comes to that threshold, which when he crosses it may find even a Haze declaring "All is the Incarnation." We must enlarge upon this point if we are to see why O'Connor says of Haze Motes that he is saint-like, a spiritual hero for her. Haze's pursuit, as our hillbilly Thomist might put it in respect to Thomistic modes of knowing truth, is an *intuitive* one out of a spiritual desire for the good (for "truth" Thomas says) but whose fulfillment requires a complete surrender which Haze has been reluctant to make.

St. Paul would put it that Haze as *homo viator* must put off the old man that he may put on the new. But that is an easy "saying" in relation to the cost of the action, as Haze is shown to discover. On his way, desiring a Truth he cannot name, he is an embattled consciousness, the dramatic conflict lying *in* Haze though manifested by spectacle out of his action—spectacle necessary to the "incarnating" responsibilities of art. Even when he has encountered and surrendered to that Truth, in a defeat that is to be seen paradoxically as a victory, he cannot name that Truth itself as St. Thomas might give Truth most various names. (See, for instance, St. Thomas' *Summa Theologica,* I, q. 13, in twelve articles on "The Names of God.") The Truth Haze desires but cannot name leaves him able only at life's end to declare himself "not clean," up to that surrender having insisted he is clean because there is no such thing as sin because the only truth is that there is no truth. He therefore uses derisively the name *Jesus,* declared "a trick on niggers," his derision quickly recognized by the "Jesus-fanatics" he encounters (Asa and Sabbath Hawks as Christ-haunted), marking Haze himself the greater fanatic, "hungry" for Jesus. He declares "Jesus a liar," for if "Jesus existed, I wouldn't be clean." Even the dim-witted Enoch in the street gathering recognizes Haze as bound for an encounter with a new "Jesus." And that would-be prophet Asa Hawks as himself "Christ-haunted" at once declares Haze a "Goddam Jesus-hog." Flannery O'Connor puts it more mildly perhaps in saying that Haze as a "Southerner" is up to his epiphany one of those who are "Christ-haunted," as is Asa.

There is, then, a recognition we come to: that of a sympathetic affinity between O'Connor herself and her fictionally incarnated "Southerners" as "Christ-haunted," so that to suppose her work merely a comic satire as dominant genre, as if out of her detached display in fiction she is self-protected by "local color," misses wide the center of her work. That mistaken reading (sometimes with a critical desperation) is corrected by a more careful attention to the novel's resolution. We begin to understand Haze's "integrity" as it confronts his landlady in a baffling way to her. But even Mrs. Flood responds in a confusion out of her derivative Modernist assumptions. Mrs. Flood stares into Haze's burned-out eyes in puzzlement. Then, closing her own eyes, she finds herself responding to a "pin point of light … far away," within the image she yet retains in her consciousness of Haze's empty eye sockets. (Haze has blinded himself for not "seeing.") We have been prepared for this resolution of the novel in a foreshadowing, as Henry James might say. Earlier in the museum, Haze stares into the mummy's eyes, through his own eyes as reflected on the glass case in that museum devoted to history as dead. The landlady Mrs. Flood stares into Haze's eyes, her own eyes shut, until at last (in the novel's final words) "he was the point of light." A long way yet to Bethlehem and its star for her, but perhaps a beginning — or so she senses with a growing disquiet.

As for Haze, he has struggled for an integrity of will whereby he might resolve his "wills in conflict," the point O'Connor suggests in her prefatory note to the reissue of *Wise Blood*. Freedom (she says) is a mystery which cannot be conceived simply, and so it can only be deepened by the novelist, who must recognize that "free will does not mean one will, but many wills conflicting in one man" — in one consciousness as center stage to dramatic action. On another occasion she reminds a correspondent that our "salvation is a drama played out with the devil, a devil who is not simply generalized evil, but an evil intelligence determined on its own supremacy." That contest takes place within the consciousness of *this* person, so that if for Satan a victory over God is impossible to him, then at least it may be possible to gain a small victory over God's creature man, over God's image. Again, how petty and banal in relation to sublime Truth, that "intellectual" revenge against God out of envy and jealousy — this attempted subversion of the good. And from St. Thomas' perspective, how adolescent an intellect is Satan's. From O'Connor's perspective as a maker of fictions, how comic the Satanic attempt to seduce persons who in turn are thereby tempted to bite the hand of that Gift Giver through whom they *are*. In that attempt, of course, evil requires the collaboration of the particular person, who is at risk of his own undoing through free will.

Out of such observations, and very self-evidently with herself in mind, O'Connor concludes that the believing novelist will have to do the best he can in his travail with the world he has inherited here and now. He may find in the end that instead of reflecting "the image at the heart of things," he has only "reflected our broken condition and, through it the face of the devil we are possessed by. This is a modest achievement, but perhaps a necessary one." Necessary perhaps, in that insofar as the novelist has made his own thing a good thing in itself it bears witness to the reality of "our broken condition." It may prove suited to other uses in the world, though only under the auspices of God himself to the good of his created world. The writer makes a thing good out of "a distrust of the abstract, a respect for boundaries, a desire to penetrate the surface of reality," reaching into that region we have observed which supplies the spectacle necessary to art's drama. Thus he may "find in each thing the spirit which makes it itself and holds the world together." Such is her belief, which we have already somewhat adumbrated through St. Thomas and his concern for the *thing in itself*, to be recognized by the intellect through its complementary intellectual modes, the intuitive and rational modes, in response to the things of the world perceived through the senses. That is at the heart of O'Connor's address to her "Southern" inheritance as writer, a difference distinguishing her from Faulkner. It is a distinction we might footnote, for instance, by reference to Faulkner's own "grotesque" figure, his Popeye, in relation to O'Connor's Misfit.

Neither a Dante nor a Faulkner, she nevertheless shares with both somewhat in manner and intention as a maker of fictions, under the auspices of the "science" to that making called *craftsmanship*. (In that company we must acknowledge Dante *il miglior fabbro* — the better craftsman, in adapting Daniel's tribute to Dante on *Purgatory* mountain — Dante the craftsman himself supplying Daniel's words.) O'Connor is exceptional from them precisely because — being peculiarly gifted but with the question of magnitude of gift set aside — she pursues the perfection of her specific gift quite unconcerned herself with any relative "greatness" among any company of writers. Hers is an intense concern very like Haze's — for a single-minded integrity which as single-minded she speaks of as "violent" for truth. She sees art's concerns as they are engaged by some critics who reduce art to the level of skating contests in which numbers are to be critically registered from 1 to 10 in regard to the surface grace of the contestants. O'Connor instead devotes herself to her gifts with a cloistered intensity of devotion to the making, indifferent to such rankings. It is a deportment to her gifts not easily understood, not even by one so close to her as her mother. It is a deportment suspicious of Pulitzer Prizes or book club selections. She knows, as believer, that instead she is obligated to her gifts in a continuing apprenticeship of intellectual labor, requiring that she learn from Dante and Faulkner and Joyce and James and from many others, though not required by that learning to embrace their visions.

Her concern is neither for a relative ranking as poet, then, nor for the multitude of theories about art that so proliferated about her in the speculative criticism that had so conspicuously exploded in literary journals. We may recall that Walker Percy dubbed his and her age the Age of the Theorist-Consumer, in which the theorist and the consumer are mutually corruptive of the good. O'Connor remarks the theories worse than the furies, for theory freed of intellect tempts intellect to an abstraction intruding upon and disjoining the poet from his obligation to the right word in response to the truth of things experienced. Hence her underscored warning from James in his "Guy de Maupassant" that we cited: a story writer, "however full of faith in his inspiration," endangers himself "when he sallies forth into the dim wilderness of theory." The obligation of the poet is to images of the possible, images echoing human nature in its responses to the truth of things perceived. Dramatic actions are dependent upon images retained from this experience of things. And again her underscored remark in James to the point: "Every good story is of course both a picture and an idea, and the more they are interfused the better the problem is solved." (James's *idea* will not be a sufficient term for her as we shall see.) Through the craft of "incarnational" art, the poet imitates the *actions* of nature, not the same thing (Thomas says) as to imitate *nature* itself, the province of history. In this respect, her understanding of Eliot's "objective correlatives" is quite different from that which Eliot held at the time he formulated his definition. (Eliot of course subsequently rejects his own "theory" about images assumed as mere devices.) That is, the imitation is of the possible, not of the actual. She might have cited Joyce's Stephen as a "theorist" to the contrary.

Let us, in a manner of a Keatsian "negative capability" as if experiencing Flannery O'Connor's coming to herself as poet, imagine speculatively the stages of that becoming as she may have experienced it under the auspices of St. Thomas. If by intuitive intellect she may have discovered her peculiar gifts, it is through rational intellect that she must bring those gifts into a perfection as bounded by the magnitude of the gifts peculiar to her as this person, Mary Flannery O'Connor. She must draw from herself or through herself as person a form of perfection in the made story as suited to the limits of her gifts in response to the matter she has chosen. But she knows that she may do so only through a right reason in the making of that thing, in a continuing apprenticeship toward perfection as poet. Put in another way, in a concern for the delicacy of precision required to her attempt, she is responsible in stewardship to her own gifts. That stewardship is enacted under the auspices of the virtue of a prudence infused with humility, meaning that she must not confuse her gifts of making as those of a "creator" God rather than those of this limited person, Mary Flannery. This is a distinction to be recognized properly through reason, in response to her having recognized and accepted with joy (which is not the same as *happiness,* Thomas reminds us) that she *is* by the virtue of grace. She is an intellectual soul incarnate. Nor may she confuse that virtue of prudence proper to her as person with the virtues of art as peculiar to a calling to make what St. Thomas calls "*certain* things." Consequently the prudence proper to art itself allows her to draw forth form in a story by a right will to the good of the thing she is making. However, she may only draw forth form (so prudence reminds her) from realities pre-existing, borrowed from creation as both actual and antecedent to her, allowing her *possible* service as steward by her art. She is enabled to do so because she is by her nature (as are we all) a reasoning creature. Nevertheless, from her own circumstantial point in time and place — at mid–20th century in middle Georgia — she discovers that among her fellow poets reason is a virtue seldom advocated by or for the poet.

To those not sharing her vision, hers will appear a rather strange deportment, especially so in her repeated adversions to the authority of St. Thomas Aquinas. Is she really a "creative" writer? Perhaps. For after all, she did attend a "creative" writing school. Insofar as her first concern is for her gift as a maker, to be exercised in an accord with her vision as Christian, the puzzlement over her deportment that is held by some of her contemporaries is for her a secondary concern, though she is not indifferent to it. For she is attuned to the general dislocation of her age as shared with community, even though members in it may presume themselves exceptional to and adversarial toward their age, and especially some of her fellow poets. She is exceptional among a companionable remnant of poets in her century in that she will neither ignore nor reject what is for her the vibrant, life-giving spiritual reality spoken — even shouted — by creation itself, and even within particular members adversarial to her vision. She speaks of a grace resonant in nature, never actually separated by a self-blinding intent to that separation so long as the separator is not dead. That recognition of grace is always immediate to her, recognized as from an active Presence to her, her recognition a consequence of that continuous and sustaining action of Love perceived in all things but most immediately evident in herself as *this* person. She could appreciate with a comic eye, though not a severely judgmental one, that most of us are naïve participants in that reality, from within a popular spirit governed at the surfaces of our existence by the new Modernist "religion." We "live" *on* reality at the level of spectacle — or so we seem to intend — parasitically and not communally, despite our connaturality with things in being (in existing) which St. Thomas speaks of as evident *natural law.*

Given that operative level, she recognizes as well the tendency of her peers, especially among "creative" writers, to surrender themselves to theories of art that are quite counter to her own understanding. There is especially a general consent to an "imaginative" flow of signs understood as governed by psychological responses at the level of spectacle, many of her peers embracing Freud or Jung as their Virgil. Thus many of them (encouraged by many critics at her time) had been fed the "theory" of the "subconscious" as the poet's authority in response to spectacle as experienced through the body. As thus limited, they must see the validity of response as focused in the authority of the "self," encouraging an isolating autonomy as a "psychological" self. Such theory pressed by reason, however, may reveal the "psychological" as constricting the mystery of the person's very existence to a determinism defined by Positivistic science in isolating consciousness to the sands of shifting "personality" as the only acceptable foundation to the "self" in an accidental cosmos. And so O'Connor is understandably skeptical of the dependence of some of her fellow poets upon Freud or Jung to their limited visions, as opposed to her own advocacy of St. Augustine and St. Thomas as the better "scientists" of reality. She sees the psychological as a "theory" made falsely promising of the "self's" accommodation to self-consciousness as autonomous, and particularly so as had been advocated by Freud and modified by Jung at 20th mid-century, with the additive of an ambiguous Bergsonian theory of an "élan vital" as Holy Ghost. For Bergson lingered long for the "creative" poet as if some rescue from the solemn cold fundamentalist determinisms of existence as accident declared by Positivistic theory, the theology of Determinism as the god of all being demonstrated by a Positivistic science. It is against this closing of mystery by theory that Walker Percy himself at last revolts, more openly and polemically than does O'Connor, and in part because at first given to that new religion. (His first academic "major" is chemistry.)

What do we remember most of Freud at this late date? He had much to say of art as a symptom of sexual disorder, a theme residual in the popular spirit, sometimes used in justifying pornography as therapeutic art. Jung was rather inclined (in what proved a revolt against Freud) to speculations about "myth" as a psychological residue inherited out of an ancient evolutionary history, still evident as believed at the temporal level in our present moment. For "myth" might prove pragmatically acceptable as a quasi-religious remedy to recover a possible psychological health. Jung, this is to say, theorizes a temporal tradition in its manifestations as historically residual effects that may be imaginatively rendered by art to our psychological health, rather than taking art as but symptom of a sexual pathology as did Freud. And so many poets (Freudian or Jungian) sought scientific (i.e., "psychological") ground to accredit their imaginative flow of signs as poetry. Such "theory" might still the sense of uneasiness as "felt" in response to uncertainty about human origins and ends. Poets might therefore prove channeling instruments of the flow of consciousness, making us (as resident in the "popular spirit" of the age) content with history's flow — perhaps even reassured by such magic phrases as the "Collective Unconsciousness." At least such poets need no longer fear themselves seduced by the devil as they might once have feared, in what by now had become for those "ancient" times before release from the devil by Enlightenment thought. The devil no longer haunted the poet's "ink pot," even less invasive of a "lap-top." God having been declared dead, in God's death there also died that old devil, resolving the uneasy sense to reason of a dichotomy that so long tempted to Manichaean resolutions of intellectual dilemmas about the relation of *good* to *evil* that had plagued art for so long. Besides which, there was now a new theorist in whose name could be actively justified the imaginative flow of art — one who resolutely declared intentionality valid in the creator, the poet. For the active force in "creating" was an *élan vital* centering in the poet. That might prove a way of "transcending" both Freud and Jung.[2]

The poet as creator of the self, here and now: That was an evolved principle which was to become famous among poets and critics alike in that wild-looking and -sounding Frenchman, Jean-Paul Sartre. One might by a willful boldness (he would have us agree) declare himself an Existentialist, reducing all theories to the subservience of human actions as beyond good and evil in service to self-creation — even perhaps beyond the reductionism of Positivistic Science. Good and evil: reduced to sexual disorders (Freud) or partially rescued from the pathological through art's grounding in the "Collective Unconscious" by Jung. These — very strange projections of a new "body of community," especially under the sway in intellect of a newly declared myth, the "Collective Unconscious," even if treated symptomatically as sexual disorder. Alas, poor Oedipus. (Jungian psychology seems to have proved especially encouraging of a neo–Paganism, an elective "life-style" of varied manifestations.) Such were uncomfortable and intellectually confusing solutions as effecting a troubled "Age of Alienation." But with Sartre, the poet may be less troubled since all Gordian knots tied up by Modernist philosophy and science in the imprisonment of the mystery of existence itself are to be severed by intentional action. The *being* thus effected is no longer very troublesome, as it had been from Plato to Aquinas — and even unto Jung and Freud. For existence is declared caused by willed intentionality. One could by an action of *creating* make oneself, intentional action to be declared with an intellectual faith the cause of being rather than the reverse, though just what origin of *intention* unspecified. That was a new dispensation of freedom to the intellect as autonomous. By will thus deployed, man is freed of obligation to any givenness other than what he gives to himself. But what an intellectual labor spent to arrive at that point Mr. Pointer asserts to Hulga; he was born an Existentialist. And how oblivious (St. Augustine might observe) to the anterior intention that speaks an ontological mystery ignored.

What has been discarded by reason in such intellectual shell-games, leading to a generally chaotic discord of intellect with reality in the popular spirit of our age, is the self-evident truth articulated by St. Thomas concerning the relation of *will* to *knowledge*. Reason in making is the proper deportment of the maker, but it necessarily begins with self-evidently antecedent known truths that speak antecedent existences of some aspect. An "Existentialist" pretense of self-creation out of nothingness is therefore necessarily a self-gratifying illusion. Reason's matter is that givenness denied as self-evidently antecedent, which is already in some degree known in initiating self-consciousness into an action of reason. In response to that initiation occurs all intellectual action. Put in another way, common sense, examined by reason in response to actual experience, refutes the errors possible to the common sense as (figuratively) an unlettered reason. The pretense in Sartre that reason over-rides, supercedes, common sense is refuted by the coordinate support in intellect of a common sense born of the *intuitive* response to things stirring *reason* by a self-awareness. That is a recognition which Flannery O'Connor dramatizes in refutation of the intellectual pretentiousness of a Sartre, using the self-evident nature of consciousness itself as matter to her making. It is an aspect of the drama especially in such stories of hers as "Good Country People" and *Wise Blood*.

As for reason supporting common sense in response to actual experiences, Thomas says (*Questiones disputatae de veritate,* 10, 8) that "Nobody perceives himself to know except from the fact that he knows some object, because knowledge of some object is prior to knowledge of oneself as knowing." In this view self-awareness occurs *after* we have experienced things as not only actual but also antecedent to our awareness of our "self" as a "thing." The "self" finds itself to have already experienced things. "Our mind is unable to know itself in such a way that it immediately apprehends itself, but it arrives at knowledge of itself by the fact that it perceives other things." And that means that there are "things" existing as necessarily antecedent to the recognition of even our own mind as knowing, that recognition we term by its effect our self-awareness. That blossoming point of self-awareness becomes also self-evident, not to be denied by the "skeptics of the academy" (St. Augustine's phrase), in that we already know something even before we know that we know. And so we must in somewise *be* before we can know. It is not, therefore, by an act of will that things exist, especially our *self*. It is only a pretense that by a willed act we ourselves come to exist by our will's creative intention to self-gratification — to self-love. That is nevertheless the pretense of Sartrean intentionality, Sartre declaring his action the cause of his own being, a "new" possibility to a delusion of absolute freedom.

That became a popular delusion of the intellectual community just after World War II. Sartre must deny the self-evident truth to self-awareness by an act of his will — an action declaring the pre-existing self a *nothingness* in order to give illusional credence to self-creation. But above all else, it is necessary to deny *givenness,* so that *nothingness* may become the point of departure in making the "self" by an action purporting to be precedent to the *being* of that self-enacted self. What is set aside is the necessarily antecedent *being* of the actor. Common sense alone, though to be supported by reason's logic, requires that recognition, as perhaps Hulga of "Good Country People" may come to recognize. That "something," the "actor," preexists his self-conscious point of departure that precedes his action. But how humiliating to the self-esteem in purporting to be self-created out of nothingness to discover dependence upon a somethingness already "there."[3] It is out of this humiliation that Sartrean violence erupts as quite other than O'Connor's "single-minded violence" for the truth. (Here I have in mind not only the species of violence in Sartre's novels and such plays as *No Exit* and *The Flies* that at first stir Walker Percy toward a recovery, but Sartre's autobiography *The Words*. As well, remember Sartre's more famous *Being and Nothingness,* so devastatingly critiqued by Gabriel Marcel in *Homo Viator: Introduction to a Metaphysics of Hope* in the midst of World War II.) Such is the devastating discovery of Haze Motes, a humiliating recognition by his common sense when trapped by the truth he seeks, a truth which gives rise to a growing humility in Haze at the point of his death. Such might be the inevitable end to the Emersonian dream of that "self-sufficiency" which requires it to bite the hand of Jove, or of Sartre's philosophical "biting" of Jove's hand in perverse violence against reality itself.

St. Thomas' arguments on our first encounter must inevitably strike us as esoteric, given our long separation from the mystery of grace as indwelling nature itself, exorcised from a common sense that once governed any prospect for a "popular spirit." That is a mystery nevertheless encountered necessarily in the initial openness to reality, in an immediacy which is undeniable to actual experience of *a* thing — an openness which does not require Thomas' scholastic assurances, though his assurances are encouraging to native reason. At least it is undeniable to O'Connor. It is an encounter she recognizes in those children visiting Andalusia who are delighted by her peacock's "underwear." Out of such recognitions, how often as a maker of fictions she "makes" figures of adolescents in contention with the "adult" blindness to the reality of the "underwear" of things which is so natively perceived by the adolescent though he may be baffled by what he suddenly knows. Not that the adolescent is able to articulate and affirm what he intuitively knows. He lacks both experience sufficient to the recognition and a reason yet unable to name what he knows according to its true nature. And so as a dramatic figure he is at a point of spiritual endangerment, especially in danger of losing what he knows, as that boy hitchhiker knows himself to be endangered by a Shiftlet.

Recall then once more that stunning rebuke to Mr. Shiftlet in "The Life You Save May Be Your Own" by that boy, who directs Mr. Shiftlet to Hell as if he has glimpsed the diabolical. Or there is the younger child in "The Temple of the Holy Ghost," who recognizes in the girls visiting from the convent school their advanced temptation to an "adult" blindness reflected by shallow responses to present reality. The child knows, though only intuitively, that creation speaks Christ immanent in creation, as the story's resolution in the concluding sentences suggests. There is a more arresting manifestation in Nelson of "The Artificial Nigger." But more especially there is the extended dramatization of that adolescent young Tarwater, in *The Violent Bear It Away.* In Tarwater the intuitive and rational within his consciousness conflict to his endangerment, he confused as *homo viator* just setting out by his own "wills in conflict." And in a more comical rendering, there is that arrested child anticipating Tarwater, the simpleton Enoch Emory, who sees more clearly than Haze can see the "Jesus" in Satan's image that Haze requires for his "Church of Christ without Christ," the bloodless mummy. The adolescent intellect still able to respond to the truth of things is a figure O'Connor returns to, even though it may on occasion be an adolescent consciousness advanced in earthly years.

And so O'Connor discovers in St. Thomas a support of what is self-evident to her from her experiences of persons in the actual world. We need not conclude that Thomas is the primary cause of her vision however. He is rather a clarifying witness, with his formidable reason certifying the validity of her own vision of creation's "underwear." Thomas speaks of what she already knew: "Love is the first movement of the will and of every faculty of desire" (*Summa Theologica,* I, q. 20, a. 1). Again, "Man wills good by natural necessity," in that the "proper object of love is the good," and the good itself is "the proper cause of love." What becomes the concern of Thomas' philosophy, following his own recognition of that truth from his own experiences, is the deployment of reason toward *understanding* the actualities of his experiences of the self-evident. Common sense is the point of philosophy's departure for Thomas, toward a perfection through reason of metaphysical vision. And so St. Thomas' concern is for the mystery of grace evidenced in his experiences of nature, spoken to him by his experience of things as actual — spoken to his intellect through his senses. It is a mystery to resolve by an understanding gained by reason's complementary relation to intuition in ordering the will to the reality of intellect's own given nature. By its own nature, will's perfection rests in recognizing and willing the good *through* not *with* reason, out of an initiating intuitive love of the good, as the soul sees *through* as member not an instrument to see *with*.

This is, we are suggesting, the mystical ground out of which Thomas pursues his metaphysical vision through reason. He does so in a primary interest in his own integrity as *this* intellectual soul incarnate, whose most signal gift proves to be an exceptional reason, distinguishing him from that perfect intuitive nature he concludes to be the angelic property in which man shares. It will lead him to arguments carefully pursued to resolution, the origin of those arguments nevertheless his own initial intuitive recognition of truth about his own self-awareness, a "self-evident" beyond human reason's powers to demonstrate. (Prudential humility is a conspicuous virtue in St. Thomas.) Thus, "The human intellect is measured by things so that man's thought is not true on its own account [and especially "on account" of any "scholastic" thought] but is called true in virtue of its conformity with things." To the contrary, he concludes, God as divine intellect is the only measure of things, not man by his reason, by whose active measure as Cause (called Love) a thing *is* the *thing* it is (*Summa Theologica,* I-II, q. 93, ad 3). That realization about the *real* leads to reflections concerning reality as it may be perceived by finite intellect. The conclusion: "Created things [things that *are* by virtue of the creating action of Love] are midway between God's knowledge and our knowledge, for we receive our knowledge from things that are caused by God's knowledge. Hence ... things that can be known are prior to our knowledge and are its measure," while God's knowledge is "the measure of created things and prior to them" (*Summa Theologica,* I, q. 14, a. 8, ad 3).

Our existence as *this* person, then, is a peculiar gift of Love, as O'Connor believes and finds confirmed by Thomas' arguments. In response to this truth, we participate in providential responsibility to created things through intellect's actions, in a *towardness* to our own proper end called *becoming*. Intellect is a light to will in consciousness, holding evident to consciousness the *true* as derived from the *good* experienced according to our given intellectual nature — truth gained in response to things in themselves experienced through our senses. In respect to this relation of intellect to the reality of things, Thomas speaks as if a poet — an attribute in him not often enough remarked. "The intellectual light dwelling in us is nothing else than a kind of participated image of the uncreated light [God] in which the eternal ideas are contained," which "ideas" we approach by a providential participation in creation itself which must be governed by humility (*Summa Theologica,* I, q. 84, a. 5). This is to speak at last of that mystery confirmed by the Incarnation, certified by Incarnation itself: we are created as person "in the image of God." And if by willfulness we should dim or turn off our intellectual light, the "uncreated light" is not thereby affected. "On the contrary" O'Connor says, "with lifted finger and broad blank beatific expression" as she imagines her own comic encounter with her mother Regina: "the light, being eternal and limitless, cannot be turned off."

For Thomas, then, our reason properly participates in response to the "intellectual light dwelling in us" in a pursuit of *integrity* as person (as intellectual soul incarnate), an integrated — a *simple* reality as *this* person. Reason aids our gaining that integrity, but proportionately, as limited to us as *this* person. It does so in an *understanding* of that relative proportionality of unlikeness in likeness discovered in the orders of nature, for our reason is most especially disproportionate to God as the *comprehensive* Eternal Reason. Thus finite reason must sort actual experiences of things toward understanding the universal, in quest as *homo viator* of an ordinate accord with Eternal Reason. Always finite reason must make a distinction between that Perfect and only Self-sufficient Thing (God) and the created image of that Thing (man) — a radical distinction between God and man. By participation within the limits of a finite givenness whereby he *is* and through prudential humility, this finite person seeks an accord with the Divine Actuality which is its cause. Thus intellect responds first intuitively in an openness of love to some actual thing perceived through the senses as good because it is — an anticipatory action of will toward transcendent Love. The reason's active response is properly complementary, whereby intellect discovers it knows truth self-evidently through intuitive openness, through its natural (i.e., its law of limited nature). Thus things in themselves are known before "mind" knows its own existence in a self-consciousness.

The moral responsibility of intellect is to the proportionate nature of human reason as a gift to existence as person — a responsibility to be exercised through reason by a proportionate participation in creation as in accord with the Eternal Reason. Reason's responsibility (Thomas argues) is therefore to understand universals through particulars, in a movement out of particulars first known intuitively through love. Thus we journey as persons toward beatitude. It is the *conscience* as a presence to intellectual action that commands recognition of proportionality, lest *will* pervert its proper office of love into a self-love. (We hear Haze Motes in a rhetorically violent and specific rejection of conscience.) For, says Thomas, "Conscience is said to be the law of our minds because it is the verdict of reason, deduced from the law of nature." Conscience is the "natural law," then, active in us as persons in relation to which conscience governs. We might say of conscience metaphorically that it is the autogyro in the intellectual soul, itself governed by the gravity of Love, whereby the intellectual soul recognizes its "felt-balance." The person knows, far this side of comprehension of the mystery of Love, an orientation within the limits of his given nature. (On Thomas' principle of proportionality, see Appendix B and Appendix C.)

Hence Thomas can say that our "natural inclination is the beginning of virtue" (*Summa Theologica*, I-II, q. 58, a. 4, ad 3). Reciprocally, the "virtues perfect us so that we follow our natural inclination in a fitting manner" (*Summa Theologica*, II-II, q. 108, a. 2). That natural manner requires of us the ordinate integration of our nature, which by our discursive nature as intellectual creature (as *rational* creature) distinguishes the person as (1) intellectual (2) soul (3) incarnate. By an integrity of such parts into a simple whole (*this person*) we gain that *claritas* proper to our nature and governing our deportment toward the created world. We have known or known of (though seldom encountered) persons whose *claritas* is such that they are judged *charismatic,* a term now appropriated to an electable candidate by political engineers or perhaps further decayed as applied to a rap star, though it once signifying a person believed particularly graced by the Holy Ghost in perfection as person. And though that simple deportment of perfection as person as actively serene is not understood, still we may feel called to seek that state, even expressing ourselves envious of it perhaps if recognized in an actual person. That is a Christ-like deportment foreign to political wars or popular agitations, not properly applied to a *hero* but to a *saint.* (How pleasingly discomforting to us, Mother Teresa.) If not our own deportment, still we gain some small purchase toward that perfection in response to beauty — to a *claritas* in things experienced as good. In response to that *claritas* (Thomas might say) we are encouraged to a bearing toward things in an apprenticeship in this world in quest of possible sainthood. It is a pursuit of an integrity according to the limits of the discrete gifts to ourself as *this* person. In sum, we seek through the beauty of the good our proper end: a simple perfection as *this* person which Thomas calls beatitude. Such is a necessity to the simplicity, to an *integrity* as person, to be fulfilled at last in that ultimate consummation of our given limits we anticipate through hope. Heresy against Love lies in an interior disproportionate intention to self-elevation of given, inherent properties of personhood through willfulness, most conspicuously effecting by willfulness a distortion of reason as reduced by will from its proper nature in a perversion by intent to the illusion of absolute freedom.

The will to a transcendence of intellect itself through gnosis can but distort the integrity of the person, whether in that species of heresy of the Ancient Manichaean or its secularized version which we have illustrated by example in Emerson as our surrogate representative of Modernist man. By that heresy, and in differing species of like heresies, the will initiates action against nature, intent upon a separation of nature from grace. But the most destructive effect, as we would make emphatic, is upon the peculiar given nature of the heretic himself. What proves underway, this is to argue, is a deconstruction of the person by the person himself through his denial of the intimate relation of his intuitive action of love for the good and his rational mode as properly supportive of that action of openness. He becomes (contrary to Emerson's promise) a self-unmade man. For the person's will, by perversion of the intellectual modes would deploy reason in a pursuit of that illusion of absolute freedom as if a self-apotheosis. It is the complementary dependence of a right will upon the intuitive and rational intellect which prevents this spiritual deracination. And so the disjunction of the intuitive and rational modes of intellectual action in the attempt to deny grace to given natures can but erode the unity of person most consequentially. Thus may easily follow, for instance, a submission to appetites of the body in an excess which erodes possible unity as person. Or there may follow an ascetic denial of the body in destruction of that unity.

We may discover here that the separation of our intellectual modes effects in the popular spirit on the one hand "New Age" sensibilities that would elevate the intuitive as not simply initial but primary; or on the other hand the Positivistic rejection of the intuitive through a scientific intellectual asceticism of gnosis that elevates reason as absolute over being itself. These are both curious as well as destructive confusions of our intellectual nature, both of which Walker Percy engages as joined when he calls ours the age of the "Theorist-Consumer," counter but kindred reductionist ideas of a willed disjunction of intellect from reality itself. This is to describe the currently unhealthy deportment reflected in the popular spirit by divided (the "dissociated") modes of intellect as intuitive and rational. But such disjunction is neither unique to our age nor to Western intellectual history, though thoroughly pervasive of culture in our moment of history. O'Connor would remind us of its origin and speak of it as a doctrine of her belief as Original Sin. Here we suggest that division (reflected as a "dissociation of sensibilities") as effecting two kindred, sometimes adversarial, distortions recently more oppressive to us which we have pointed to as dramatized by Nathaniel Hawthorne. Hawthorne's circumstances at mid–19th century make him as a writer of "romances" prophetic of consequences to our cultural "evolution" through sin as reflected in emerging species of a disjunction of sensibilities, represented in Hawthorne's Governor Endicott and his Dr. Aylmer. Henry James as a "realist" emerging from this New England "romanticism" may be embarrassed by Hawthorne's recognition — not of these species themselves but of Hawthorne's attributing their emergence to sin as an actual inclination of the intellectual soul. But that is Hawthorne's virtue which draws O'Connor to him as her favorite "American" writer.

St. Thomas remarks that "If a man deliberately abstains from wine to such an extent that he does serious harm to his nature, he will not be free from blame," a truth concerning our nature hardly acceptable to Hawthorne's Governor Endicott we know. But for St. Thomas, such a "Puritan" reaction by man to the good of things in themselves means that man will have acted sinfully against the good of his own bodily nature. (The virtue of *temperance* is at issue in the context from which these words of Thomas are taken, a concern in four articles for drunkenness as sin in man, not evil in wine, in his *Summa Theologica* II-II, q. 15.) For Thomas, our pursuit of integrity as person requires an *ordinate* fulfillment of our natural inclinations, to be fulfilled in accordance with the good which is proper to the limits of our givenness as *this* person, even in the taking of wine. In the Mass we "partake of the divine nature" of Christ in the wine and bread, as declared by the liturgy of a formal offering of the world through our "self" to its Cause. That was too shocking for Emerson, beyond his endurance as "a self-made man." It is for O'Connor, believing truth explicated by St. Thomas, a necessity to the integrity of a person which may rise within our given nature as incarnate in a spiritual fulfillment of limit. For by our *embodied* presence in the world, we are obligated to fulfill a consequent "natural inclination" through that embodiment, an inclination evidencing, Thomas argues, a law natural to us.

Such is a high moment of our "natural" inclination when properly governed by intellectual will as ordinate to a limited given nature as a person. It is so for Flannery O'Connor. This is the mystery which O'Connor engages in her story "A Temple of the Holy Ghost," to which story one might recover a "thematic" epigraph: Unless we become as little children in an integrity out of surrendering love, we shall be lost. Or so Christ both tells us and witnesses to us in the Crucifixion. Here, then, we engage that obligation in us as our natural law to partake ordinately of this world, in a participation of providential stewardship. The high moment to that stewardship is the Mass for O'Connor. In the Mass (certainly for St. Thomas as for St. Augustine, and so for O'Connor in their common faith) we "partake of the divine nature" of Christ in the wine and bread, as declared by liturgical affirmation. It is a high moment in our lifting up of creation through ourselves as stewards of the whole creation to its Cause, in a restorative participation providential to the world and to ourselves. We do so, lest (as Thomas would have it) we do "serious harm to [our own] nature" and therefore "not be free of blame."

Put in respect to man as an intellectual soul on his way as understood by O'Connor (and by Thomas): through providential participation, man may perfect his simple unity as proper to his given nature as *homo viator,* as intellectual soul incarnate, obligated to a perfection of his given limits in being on his way. While we are in this world we are to seek perfection intellectually by the grace of the Eternal Law, through a natural law native to essential humanity, sufficient to a peculiar limit as *this* person.

And so natural law, we have suggested out of Thomas, is in us as a power of the intellectual soul, a light of Eternal Light by grace in our nature whereby as rational creature we may reason proportionately toward union with the Eternal Reason — toward that perfection of our givenness that Thomas calls Beatitude. In this light of intellect (in proportionate relation of light as that of the moon to the sun), we may better ourselves understand O'Connor's interest in Hawthorne's struggle with his own gift as a writer of "romances." It is "in the light" of this understanding that we discover an intellectual kinship between Hawthorne's Governor Endicott of "The Maypole of Merrymount," that "Puritan of Puritans," and Dr. Aylmer of "The Birthmark," who is intent upon remaking his beloved Georgiana by correcting "a mistake of nature," a blemish on her otherwise perfect body. For Aylmer would by gnosis transubstantiate her into angelic beauty, *miss-taking* the nature of beauty. Both Endicott and Aylmer exhibit violence against their own nature primarily, though affecting the outer world destructively as revealed in spectacle. That is the effect of distorted arguments which O'Connor sees now general to us in our cultural spectacle, against which her fictions run counter, though for most of us her arguments against both species of Manichaeanism no doubt appear strangely foreign to our intellectual conditioning.

It is as a "hillbilly Thomist" that O'Connor reads Thomas steadily, understanding him at a level hardly available to most of us, despite her demurer that she is but "hillbilly" as an intellectual. She expresses her Thomism prudentially, in recognition of its general unfamiliarity to a non-believing world. This is to say that she summons him largely as restricted to her concerns as a maker of fictions. But hers is a concern as well at a personal level for the resolution of mystery to her own understanding through faith as person. From her personal perspective, she perceives our intellectual world in its social and political manifestations as indeed haunted by furies, but they are furies conjured by willful intellectual distortions of common sense by theories leading us into Henry James's "dim wilderness" as more general than as if limited to the poet as poet Our dislocated reason or dislocated "feelings" cloud what we know reasonably and intuitively, despite our having responded to the good of things known before we know our own self as *this* person. It is only by reason's accommodation to that knowing that we may remove obstacles to grace, recover a virtue of "adolescent" openness of response to things toward becoming "little children" of the Father.

It was in an adversarial intellectual climate to her that she set about her apprenticeship, believing unwaveringly that truth is the measure of intellect and not intellect of truth. Hers was a moment in a long intellectual history in which truth itself as proper to art had become distorted by illusion, as if through fancy a benefit to the artist. That made her but the more resolute in declaring that as Catholic she could not "afford to be less than an artist." But if she is unwavering in her commitment to the Christian vision, she knows as well that through a "reason in making" she will be thoroughly tested by her unbelieving age.[4] Hers are untoward circumstances as poet, and she will remark the difference between herself as Christian poet and many of her peers as secular "creators." Her understanding of the general intellectual disjunction in her world from Dante's vision reveals the formidable challenge to her as poet, a challenge raised in that initial alarm by Eliot under his rubric of "the dissociation of sensibility." (We observed that Eliot's own early response will be deepened for him subsequently, in part by his reading of St. Thomas.)

She learns from Dante in her response to cultural disparities, and one of the things she learns is a difference in respect to the accidents of their histories — their personal histories which for any person is always contingent to the immediacies of the *here* and *now*, whether the poet live in the 13th or the 20th century. She speaks of the challenges peculiar to her as requiring of her a "felt balance" in herself, especially as citizen in an unbelieving age. In an early letter to her new correspondent (known in her collected letters as "A") she makes that remark that "One of the awful things about writing when you are a Christian is that for you the ultimate reality is the Incarnation, the present reality is the Incarnation, and nobody believes in the Incarnation; that is, nobody in your audience. My audience are people who think God is dead. *At least these are the people I am conscious of writing for.*" (Our emphasis.)

We observe how carefully she puts the contemporary challenge. She writes *for* such an audience, recognizing the state of literary affairs embraced by the intelligentsia of her moment. It is not that she seeks that audience as the primary responsibility to her calling, and certainly not that she caters to it so that she might draw it out of its peculiar understandings. Hers is a "peculiar" understanding because seemingly provincial as seen from the Modernist's perspective. How ironic that one of the recurring charges made against her, early and late, is that she is "anti-intellectual," for a close reading of her work reveals this an absurd, not to say usually a self-defensive, response. How odd to that antagonistic response that she should reject an intention to be "successful" in converting her audience of the intellectuals, in an age of ideological wars intent on factional conversions. But she has been adequately forewarned by St. Thomas of her responsibility as *artist* as far removed from that concern. Least of all does she anticipate the worldly success of becoming popular through the Best Seller lists of the *New York Times,* now so markedly the newspaper of record for provincial intellectualism. Nor was it likely that her work would be celebrated in a "populist" alliance, she enlisted against adversarial intellectuals. Imagine, for instance, any likelihood that *Wise Blood,* let alone *The Violent Bear It Away,* might be a selection made welcomed on an Oprah Winfrey program.[5]

Even so, she knows it likely that the audience she has is more select than that of a book club, though some among them loyalists of the *New York Times.* She knows equally well that hers is not for the most part a fit audience, though certainly few. It is an audience unreceptive to her vision given the implications in her work — her seeing creation in a manner so contrary to that view of the world held by an audience she is "conscious of writing for," which includes not only those with sentimental concerns for the heart (those who people book club audiences) but especially including those equally sentimental intellectuals concerned for the *head* to the convenience of Modernist distortions of reason — those who constitute much of the Modernist intelligentsia as culture's directors. These latter, she knows, hold to their dearest principle, an intellectual autonomy serving the self, however much that principle may be disguised by "democratic" arguments for the "common good" as an intellectual ploy to allay suspicions of the "intellectual" himself as held by the "popular mind." That is an ancient suspicion of the popular mind, reaching back at least to the trial of Socrates with its uneasiness of the intellectuals as "elitists" rising up against him as a corrupter of youth. (How clever of the Modernist intelligentsia, of a Julian or an Asbury in her fiction, to depict an O'Connor as anti-intellectual.)

O'Connor's vision as by its nature adversarial as detected by her audience she knows a challenge, her audience made up largely of skeptical intellectuals she suspects. She sees them descended from recent philosophers resolutely intent upon a dislocation of reason from any consent to Revelation. The range of philosophers in that evolution of Modernism is formidable, from Occam and Descartes, to Kant and Hume and Hobbes, to Marx and Nietzsche, down to Freud and Jung and Sartre. The tendency in this evolution is ironic in effect: it is a centripetal isolation of consciousness to a "psychological" islanding of the "self." Within the climate cultivated by that intelligentsia in its philosophy and art, at the moment it is Jean-Paul Sartre she sees as serviceable antagonist in her fictions. Sartre is the latest and most rebellious successor to Emersonian self-apotheosis, that Emersonian gentile mode which eschews violence of any aspect. Here we have touched with names points on the "evolutionary" thread constituting intellectual provincialism as it might be seen from O'Connor's perspective, a thread not rescuing the intellectual soul from the maze of wonder but leading to the increasing bafflement by existential reality as a maze in which man has become thoroughly lost, finding no exit. Being lost is now a tradition which would require several volumes to adumbrate in the unraveling of matted threads since Occam. But Sartre appears at the end of World War II in a summary culmination of that tradition just as O'Connor begins to write her stories and, being especially popular with the intelligentsia, he proves serviceable to her as representative philosopher of the current intelligentsia. O'Connor as is by now evident knows much of this rationalistic historical thread of Modernist thought which she says has become dominant "since the eighteenth century." Especially as poet, she knows its effects upon our literary sensibilities, and so she is not surprised by pretentious responses to her work, though on occasion irritated by it for a moment.

From the beginning, we are suggesting, she was attuned to the depths of that malady which Eliot characterized as the "dissociation of sensibility," the "separation of thought and feeling." In a letter to "A" (a month earlier than the one insisting on the Incarnation as "the present reality") she comments on a review of her stories appearing in the *New Yorker,* a review which classifies her as "a Catholic peculiarly possessed of the modern consciousness, that thing Jung describes as unhistorical, solitary, and guilty." A curious combination of terms, for on the one hand she is said to share with the reviewer (as he apparently sees it) that experience of and commitment to "modern consciousness." And yet she does so as "a Catholic," one most "peculiarly possessed" of that consciousness. It is as if the reviewer must therefore take her fiction (as it was largely taken at first) as satiric, dependent upon certain naturalistic representations of the South convenient to her own sardonic humor as so peculiarly a Southern Catholic. She is seen by the reviewer as sharing a "truth" about things Southern, though perhaps a truth somewhat confused by the Jungian malady through which she is "peculiarly possessed." Though possessed of a "modern consciousness," she seems judged not to have been yet freed of being a Southerner nor a Catholic. (In response to this intellectual provincialism reflected in the *New Yorker* review, Walker Percy engages it with wit and humor in his "How to Be an American Novelist in Spite of Being Southern and Catholic.")

In that reviewer O'Connor recognizes the cultural inheritance she uses by indirection in her fiction, an aspect of her "satire" unperceived by that reviewer. That outlander's provincialism assumes as common among Southerners, even if possessed of a "modern consciousness," a cultural poverty. So it must seem to the sophisticated Modernist in his understanding of the political and social history of that vague place he designates as the "South," in H. L. Mencken's famous term "the Sahara of the Beaux Arts." She would see that critical judgment, then, as deeply ironic, though whether she is a Catholic "possessed" by Modernism or a Modernist "possessed" by Catholicism seems ambiguous in the reviewer's judgment. As for her own view of the matter, we do not put too great a burden upon her wit to suggest that she sees in the New Yorker's words a residual Puritan concern for the Satanic as now secularized, accepted, and so turned upside down before being embraced. To be a Catholic must suggest to such a reviewer her own demonic possession by "Catholicism" at this moment of our history, just after World War II. For under the Modernist aegis, a rational intellect must concede that God is dead and that therefore so is the Devil, save perhaps as a cultural residue, strangely turned by the reviewer in this instance into a "possession" of O'Connor because a Southern Catholic writer. The devil in such a view is acceptable only in satiric uses to belabor provincial (Southern) believers.

O'Connor would, in this respect, appreciate St. Thomas' observation that "A devil knows the nature of human thought better than man does" (*Questiones disputate de malo,* 16, 8 ad 7), giving a considerable advantage to the old dragon, usable to acts of Satanic possession of naïve sophisticated intellect, perhaps even that of the reviewer. (She knew, of course, C. S. Lewis's *Screwtape Letters,* in which are cogent observations about Satan as Preeminent Intellectual beyond man.) And so she remarks that brief notice in *The New Yorker* as "not only moronic, it was unsigned." To her the review reveals that "the moral sense has been bred out of certain actions of the population," but for her especially in that section of the sophisticated, liberated intelligentsia confident that God is dead. From her, this "breeding out" makes a convenient entry into "human thought" by the diabolic. (On this point see not only Lewis, but especially de Rougemont's *The Devil's Share,* which O'Connor knew well.) She will use a Lewis-like analogy: By such intellectual breeding a person becomes the Modernist version of the chicken whose "wings have been bred off … to produce more white meat on them." This, she adds, is "a generation of wingless chickens, which I suppose is what Nietzsche meant when he said God was dead." The new intelligentsia, then, like flightless chickens hovering in enclaves away from reality, were increasingly being gathered into academic breedinghouses, which by our century's turn has become the feeding houses for even newer versions of wingless chickens. The person is no longer to be seen in Dante's figure of man as a lowly worm destined (through grace, if he but will) to become angelic butterfly in a spiritual metamorphosis, enabled to that transformation by the Incarnation.

Concerning this generation of wingless chickens, how odd that they should take themselves as realists by their intellectual act of rejecting both God and Satan — both of whom O'Connor defends as actual of course as herself an intellectual. In commenting on the devil's relation to her own work, she insists that "we need a sense of evil which sees the devil as a real spirit who must be made to name himself" — as his surrogate agent the reviewer does not. And "As for Jesus as realist: if He was not God, He was no realist, only a liar, and the crucifixion an act of justice."[6] That is Haze Motes's own insistent position at first, Jesus "a liar," a "trick on niggers." And that is the argument her Misfit makes to the grandmother in her title story "A Good Man Is Hard to Find," the collection responded to "moronically" by the anonymous reviewer for the *New Yorker.* It is the crucial question of all questions about the Incarnation, raised long ago by St. Paul before the Misfit's echoing of it. Nor should we forget that it was Saul — Saul being (from a Christian perspective) a most formidable Misfit — who held the coats for those who martyred St. Stephen, the first Christian martyr.

We imagine Saul standing by, approving of the stoning. But we know him at last more affected by Stephen's deportment than he will understand until he has become the prophet of distances he was meant to become. Stephen's response to his executioners was not unlike the final response the grandmother makes to the Misfit just before she is shot. St. Stephen in an act of love prays for forgiveness of his executioners. The grandmother's, too, is a gesture of love, and it is recognized though not understood as such by the Misfit in shock, though he reacts to it as if he has been bitten by a snake. Her final gesture is the only genuine action of love by the grandmother in the story, but very much "in character" Flannery would argue, though an action "totally unexpected." For the grandmother, too, as surrogate person is inclined toward, though cleverly avoiding, the good up to that final moment. Given such observations, we may better understand O'Connor's remark in *Mystery and Manners* that her Misfit is "a prophet gone wrong," and that the grandmother's "capacity for grace" while not "equal to his" (he more gifted than she as intellectual) may nevertheless serve in his rescue. For, she says, perhaps "the old lady's gesture, like the mustard-seed, will grow to be a great crow-filled tree in the Misfit's heart, and will be enough of a pain to him there to turn him into the prophet he was meant to become."

In regard to O'Connor's "either/or"—Jesus as either God or a liar—we remember a very similar insistence by C. S. Lewis very like the Misfit's, though it is St. Paul that she must have had in mind. Paul, writing to the troublesome church at Corinth, says, " ... if there be no resurrection of the dead, then is Christ not risen: And if Christ be not risen, then is our preaching vain, and your faith is also vain. Yea, and we are found false witnesses of God.... If in this life only we have hope in Christ, we are of all men most miserable." We might as well, in the Misfit's version, give ourselves over to "meanness." It is an either/or worked with an inverse irony in *Wise Blood* when Haze Motes in anger chases down Hoover Shoates and kills him. That is, Hoover betrays Haze's new church of Christ without Christ. Lacking Haze's integrity, Hoover professes himself a disciple in Haze's "Church" as a con game, not as a believing disciple to Haze. How complexly diverse the material Flannery O'Connor finds to make her fictions in our age of disbelief, in which even disbelief seems less and less convincing, leaving us doomed on the cusp of the abyss of nothingness. It is as if, in having to deal with Nietzsche's argument that God is dead, she must anticipate such a proposition as merely "symbolic" for us who make it as if we were believers, made in the interest of hollow intellectual sounds echoing in the Modernist void. And here some of our intelligentsia prove more Hoover Shoateses than Haze Moteses. She would have more sympathy with Nietzsche, then, than with the moronic reviewer for *The New Yorker,* who sees her as a curious anomaly. No wonder that she might choose to present us with a figure of Nietzsche as a country boy, as I have suggested she does in her protagonist Haze Motes. But Haze at last comes to accept his own "wise blood" as more telling of the truth than his willful intellectual rejection of God as dead.[7] Haze is forced by his own wills in conflict toward the good, conflicted in his professed intent to self-justification.

It is out of her recognition that we confuse the center of action in Haze's own intellect with spectacle (whereby we respond to *Wise Blood* as if merely a satiric comedy) that she reacts and sometimes sharply, as she does to that anonymous reviewer in *The New Yorker.* It is in Haze's own conflicted will, she argues, that her novel's center is to be found, even as it is to be found in the Misfit's. She says in that prefatory note to the reissue of *Wise Blood,* as we know: "free will does not mean one will, but many wills conflicting in one man." If man wills good "by natural necessity," as Thomas says, that "first act of the will does not exist in virtue of the command of reason, but in virtue of a natural [intuitional] or some higher cause" (*Summa Theologica,* I-II, q. 17, a. 5, ad 3). That higher cause issues to us as a grace effecting the possibility of recovery of the natural inclination of the will to the good. That is a recovery seemingly immanent to Haze in our last view of him, though it is a spiritual reality easily overlooked in the "realistic" images of him sitting dead, badgered by his landlady as if he were yet alive. (O'Connor would say that only now is he alive.) Haze has been left a dead body on a chair by the impatient policemen, who know him dead. How awkward to account for the dead body of a homeless man—all that paperwork—so that there is great relief in having found his room and left him there in the care of Mrs. Flood, having brought him "home." Mrs. Flood, not yet realizing him dead, responds to the "life" in him which O'Connor suggests at last opened to him by grace. Such is a paradox hovering always in circumstantial spectacle, which we shall see comically effective when Mr. Head and Nelson stand frozen but spiritually thawing before that seated decaying image of man, the "artificial nigger."

7

Out of Essential Displacement, Toward a Felt Balance

"We live now in an age which doubts both fact and value, which is swept this way and that by momentary convictions. Instead of reflecting a balance from the world around him, the novelist now has to achieve one from a felt balance inside himself."

— Flannery O'Connor, "Some Aspects of
the Grotesque in Southern Fiction"

Given the disparity of her vision of reality from the fleeting versions of reality that have sprung from Modernist thought — versions effecting a chaos in community itself— no wonder that Flannery O'Connor through her "grotesque" fictions must maintain her own felt balance. She is attuned to the ironies of disparity as it impinges upon her art. There is for her a necessity to address it under the guidance of her unflinching faith in the Christian vision, a faith she is not always sure is being adequately maintained within the Church itself in her moment, especially given the Church's uses of art. Even within the Church, to quote Pope John Paul II in his retrospective critique, *The Splendor of Truth,* there have risen "theories" that "gain a certain persuasive force from their affinity to the scientific mentality." They "seek to provide liberation from the constraints of a voluntary and arbitrary morality of obligation which would ultimately be dehumanizing." (The Pope's Encyclical at this point of his argument is addressing "*consequentialism*" or "*proportionalism*," under which terms a theological relativism is afoot among the Church's theologians, a relativism that bears ominous moral consequences.)

At every turn of thought and argument, then, O'Connor meets signals of fundamental intellectual disorder, requiring of her a more disciplined address as artist, lest by a response out of irony alone she might be tempted to use her gifts to caricature persons lost in the cosmos with no suggestions of hope of their being found — that condition which Walker Percy will address with such devastating satire in his "Last Self-Help Book," *Lost in the Cosmos.* In her essay concerning the grotesque, though its title is restricted to "Southern Literature," she remarks the concern as more general than as limited to the literary canon, which as she speaks is the historical phenomenon "Modern Literature." Her understanding of and uses of exaggerations of present reality in her art runs deeper in time than history, more widely abroad in the world than can be accounted for by geography. She calls attention to the means to her own talents which are, though more limited than those of Dante, akin to his in her concern for the soul in its progress as echoed by its responses to history and place. That response signifies but does not determine the progress through temporal or spatial finitudes to the person's final end. And so she will say that "when the grotesque is used in a legitimate way, the intellectual and moral judgments implicit in it will have the ascendancy over feeling," particularly over any feeling of a personal irritation at an age which refuses to come to itself in its dark wood, like those children of old lost in a desert but derisive in their revolt against Father Moses.

The grotesque in its "violent and comic" aspects speaks to "our essential displacement," she says, in which phrase she means *essential* in its Thomistic sense — our displacement within creation through a will inclined to the separation of grace from nature, favoring an illusion of convenience to the Modernist "self" through declaring as autonomous its free will. What she sees effected by that illusion is a spiritual deracination of persons and community. But although as intellectual soul incarnate — as person — dislocated by a self-centered and sentimentally valued "angst," there yet abides the possibility of a recovery. Even though we be spiritually disoriented, we have yet a haunting concern for a "redemptive act," reaching the proportions of a demand (O'Connor says) "that what falls at least be offered the chance to be restored." At such a crossroads to *homo viator* as spiritually deracinated, haunted by his desire for rescue, the danger is that he may turn to some false Moses of the moment. Especially in recent centuries he has turned to science as redeemer, largely out of the failures of both philosophy and theology to orient his quest toward abiding truth. In having lost a sense of evil, and of his own participation in evil out of his fallen nature, he responds with panicked demands for rescue nevertheless. He is hard pressed to *name* what he would be rescued *from*. Dare we call this reaction either a naïve or an intentional participation in sin, as Hawthorne or O'Connor might call it?

It is largely out of desperation that we demand rescue, demand that we "be transported, instantly, either to mock damnation or a mock innocence." Sensing our dislocation out of a loss of faith in God as a presence to us in active grace (in the Person of the Holy Spirit, the Lord and Giver of life as St. John witnesses in his gospel and as St. Thomas argues), we but the more demand rescue by science as a worshipped god. We rest an increasingly forlorn hope in psychiatry or in "miracle drugs" to set our body or our psyche right. *Psyche* does not mean for us *soul,* as it might if we were more Greek. Rather it is a term attaching to consciousness as the cumulative neural locus of response to existence in the body's brain, a strange consciousness to be accounted for in origin as a biochemical accident. Concomitant to this reduction of the person from intellectual soul incarnate to a random "self," the virtue of hope is no longer understood as a spiritual virtue, though that old virtue yet stirs tenuous desire abiding in our given nature. We are encouraged to rely on instinct whose issue is "the survival of the fittest," instinct given a pseudo-spiritual character as manifesting an *élan vital.* Hope turns toward a faith in instrumental manipulations of our "biochemical nature" through Positivistic doctrines of intentionality to ends devised as the "bottom line" of systems. And so, hope dislocated, there rises a collective angst in the "popular spirit" demanding rescue under the threat of violence or the vote, supportive of intentional gnostic reconstitutions of our "nature" through the latest authority of Positivistic science.

At our moment "hope" rests increasingly in that latest science, genetic engineering. In the issue, the hope native to man as intellectual soul incarnate is thus relocated in support of a power over nature as freed of intimations of grace. *Instinct* becomes the machinery of the psyche having superceded *intuition* in the intellectual soul. It is out of that dislocation that persuasive programs of progress flourish under promises of instant restorations by systematic mechanics applied to temporal existence, in promise of a sufficient mechanical *adjustment* as substitute for lost innocence. The prospect of rescue through some sequence of "five-year-plans" posits a New Eden as if beheld by a visionary prospect through intellectual determinism. By rationalized dream, the mechanical reconstitutes man's nature and attempts to still the desire native in the person as fallen spiritual creature. But there abides in us by nature (Thomas says and O'Connor affirms) an ineradicable desire through hope of rescue from our spiritual fallenness, an absolution of sin, a reality of our nature. But to that possible recovery through grace, we propose gnostic intellect sufficient, though requiring of us a submissive consent to the proposition that our ultimate end lies in social or political systems, temporal limits declared man's ultimate end. Thus we shall build an accidental community suited to "good" feeling. Rather certainly, this is a summary of the social ambiance out of the Modernist spiritual state as Flannery O'Connor sees it, with which state of reduced human nature she makes her fictions. What seems rather remarkable in her response is that she does not herself abandon hope of a recovery possible to us despite the overwhelming popular consent to this dislocation. An abandonment might indeed have been signaled had she attempted her own escape as poet into merely satiric irony, always an intellectually tempting self-defense out of skepticism affected by a cynicism about human nature.

Irony is of course an element in her fictions no less than in Joyce's. But hers is an irony differing, in that while her principle matter is the Modernist mentality conspicuous in our age, and particularly so within the community of intellectuals, she knows also a desire long buried in our given nature by willfulness — a desire for a real "object" which is always summoning us to acts of love. She would no doubt insist that this native desire for the good lies even in those intellectuals who are most truculent in their gnostic intent to transform human nature to temporal limits in the name of the "common good." It is in them by their very nature, however deeply buried, insofar as they *are*. That is to say that as Thomist, O'Connor recognizes in the distorted Modernist as ineradicable intent to his proper end despite willfulness out of that "natural" inclination to the good which St. Thomas affirms as inherent to his given nature as an intellectual soul incarnate. It is an ineradicable inclination, despite willful rejections of it and is the ground in self-awareness within which occur wills in conflict. In response to innate desire for the good, the will itself may substitute some lesser good for the greater with defiance. But to do so implies nevertheless an abiding dependence on the reality of the good despite a flawed vision of it. That good beckons the soul, despite flawed vision's urging an appetite for a lesser good. That is the dilemma Haze Motes wrestles to his death.

Hope, however much dimmed, remains in a person because he is a person. But in his being as swayed by Modernist principles he seems to have very nearly moved beyond recovery from "our essential displacement" (in O'Connor's phrase). That is a displacement, however, and not a reconstitution of his essential nature. Thomism might cast O'Connor's phrase: by willfulness a person may pervert his given nature toward self-love, but he cannot obliterate absolutely even then his "natural" love of the good. He succeeds only in perverting, in distorting, the inherent good of his own "self" by a willfulness concentrated erosively inward as self-love. Desire for fulfillment through love, though diminished, stirs in him a sense of a *personal* loss, a sense that as intellectual soul this person knows himself unreconciled to his own existence by self-love. In this circumstance to the intellectual soul there rises, to its confusion, reason's confounding of the ultimate good with proximate good, and the most proximate good of all to this intellectual soul becomes itself. How troubling to it, then, its very self-awareness, its continuing sense of loss despite intellect's attempts to force consent to self-love as ultimate — to declare that the most obvious good is the self as ultimate. It finds itself troubled by a sense of exile for which there is no answering name, no country beckoning. And so exile to that dislocated reason speaks only an absolute alienation in despair.

Why a continuing unrest when reason declares "*I* am number *One?*" Why a growing hunger lingering still for recovery? Recovery *from* what, and more challengingly, recovery *to* what? The disconsolate person begins to demand satisfaction. He demands consent to his "inalienable right" to that rescue. But demanded of *whom,* given that he increasingly discovers that social rights decreed by a positive law abstractly sterile and indifferent to the person as this "self" bring no spiritual rest. The person is but the more restless in a displacement, within a certified context declared accidental, existence allowing no authority as actual beyond accident by a dominant Positivistic dogma. "I" as "cosmos" finds the "self" exacerbated in a lostness, with arresting spectacles of violence by nature and society a consequence.

In a conflict of wills within "individual consciousness," unable to accommodate proximate to ultimate good, there rises a spiritual disquiet within a person too easily mistaken as if but animal desire in conflict over appetitive ends, especially as explicated to the "self" by the Modernist principles of our certified experts, the scholastics of Positivism. That is the mistake Haze makes into an expert principle for his "empirical" attempt to *sin* deliberately in order to prove that sin does not exist. Therefore he must be good — "clean." But there is no point of reference to the good for his unsettled reason. How apt dramatically, this confusion for Haze when he seeks out "Mrs. Leora Watts," who announces herself on the wall of a men's toilet as keeping "The friendliest bed in town!" And later Sabbath Hawkes welcomes Haze to her bed with the command "Take off your hat, king of the beasts," sending Haze's hat flying across the room. There is an intricate metaphorical manner in *Wise Blood* of animal imagery played against cultural signs of order, suggestive of an elaborated metaphysical conceit worthy of a term paper on the animalistic resistances to the spiritual. Good manners, for instance, require Haze to remove his hat indoors, a display of manners with a cultural history, but not in order that he may become "king of the beasts." In her fiction, then, is a witty engagement of local cultural spectacle whose "history" is largely lost and so speaking appropriation by Modernist principles, in a variety of her "local" characters. But what is made common to them through wit is that their intellectual actions are made in a manner pointing up their "provincial" kinship to sophisticated Modernist intellectuals, especially those who would treat O'Connor as if but a cultural satirist, a writer perhaps even "influenced" by that academically identified genre of recent "Southern" literature, "Frontier Humor."

In an age of unbelief, this suggests, satire (Southern or other) is possible only at a surface level, directed at a dominant culture's habits from which the satirist retires even in the action of commanding spectacle to make his artifact. This is an intellectual gambit in which irony may be used to protect the artist from his own recognition of lostness in himself, his sense of spiritual exile. And that is rather certainly the strategy practiced by the early T. S. Eliot — as he came to realize after his "nervous breakdown," making him as an actual person in history, though a highly sophisticated one, kinsman with such a surrogate "intellectual" as Haze Motes. It is relatively late that Eliot is able to surrender to the "personal" in hope of rescue, after *The Waste Land*. Taking her to be using a condescending wit at the expense of persons "culturally deprived," making "palpable" instances of inhabitants of a region provincially arrested (the "South"), some of O'Connor's readers can but mistake her incisive, penetrating point, made shocking perhaps by our juxtaposing her Haze to T. S. Eliot. It is *they* who are the most vulnerable objects of her irony, skewered by indirection. But hers nevertheless is an irony which does not surrender hope, not for herself, nor for her reader, even though skewered by an indirection of art. Being fallen, man is born with potentiality to believe in nothing, but he is not determined to that belief save by his own unwavering willfulness to his end in death.

How easily a person may pretend otherwise through self-pity, declaring himself victim of an existence that is meaningless and at the same time demanding that he be rescued. By such declaration, he must rest faith and hope in himself (as Emerson insistently declares), though unable thereby to exorcise either faith or hope by willfulness to *some* good though a lesser good. But the most unexpected object looming for such willful intent is Nothingness, disguised by that dragon waiting at the side of whatever road the person travels as a rich inviting jungle Eden to be possessed by will. That is a dark truth the Bible salesman knows, shared with Hulga to encourage her cynical despair. In our common fallen spiritual state, there is no necessity for graduate study in Existentialism (as pursued by Hulga) so that we may believe in Nothingness. On the other hand, neither is any person protected by merely clinging to cultural virtues, residual history, as if these were virtues determined by a present possession and therefore saving *homo viator* by his "historical" or "family" tradition, as is the manner of Hulga's mother. That is the confusion Hulga rightly supposes in her mother and other "good country people," though wrongly electing Nothingness in her response. And so to subscribe to evil through intellectual willfulness or by naïve confusion about the good are equal opportunities of becoming lost in the cosmos to the person as person — wherever or whenever he becomes self-aware and through whatever symbols may disguise his commitment to Nothingness. How various the range of possible self-diminution through willfulness, whether encouraged or condemned by established "law."

In our perspective on O'Connor's fiction, there will appear a disparity between her reader as person and her surrogate person as fictional character, advanced to us through precisions of local spectacle to her art. How "other" must appear her fictional agents from our more sophisticated sense of ourselves. But we are suggesting that the spectacle she uses allows her a clever opportunity for an indirection. The seeming disparity between our own world and that of her characters is almost a trick she plays on us. How much more comfortable we feel about ourselves as reflected akin to a Ralph Waldo Emerson rather than to Haze Motes, though both as "intellectuals" may conclude God dead. If that provincial Southerner receives his come-uppance in the fiction, Emerson to the contrary emerges as revered father of the American Scholar, in an irony of intellectual history to which O'Connor is attuned. It is the "Emersonian" intellectual whom O'Connor sees as her audience, "the people I am conscious of writing for," who "think God is dead." Theirs is the Modernist deportment toward both creation and creation's God which she plays out dramatically in an action occurring on that interior stage, the consciousness of her "provincial" protagonist. As readers, we discover this evident through the textural, imagistic spectacle of a story made palpably real out of her remembered experiences. We may be shocked, then, to discover (when we have gotten beneath the spectacle) ourselves in "our essential displacement." What a shock: to discover kinship with a Haze Motes or Mr. Head or young Tarwater. Or with Hulga or Asbury or Rayber. But that is a discovery which might prove a beginning of a recovered hope (a possibility to O'Connor at least), making us perhaps more like Mrs. Flood in *Wise Blood,* seeing that spark of light through Haze's burnt-out eyes — if God by grace allow that small opening point of light to us.

In her dramatic resolution of such dramas, it is possible that we may recognize ourselves, then, as potential persons to a rescue through grace, though we too may have lost the way here and now. That is by O'Connor's reckoning of our being lost in the cosmos a possibility to us, in that we are each a person wherever and whenever — regardless of calendar or geographical coordinates. That is a fundamental principle maintained by Thomism as O'Connor believes. For on the one hand, to us as person there continues hope of rescue more profound in nature than our dominant temptations to mere convenience — a hope which may be properly pursued to a proper end out of a natural propensity in us to the good. On the other hand, alas, there is also that habit of convenience so temptingly practiced in pursuit of some instant Eden, anticipated as instant to us and at this present crossroads, especially out of the marvels of our science. We shall be made perfect by gnosis — though only perfect in the sensual property that belongs to us as a "self," the only Jove whose locus is this decaying body. Thus, the lesser good may be transformed by random desire as if the greater. We shall be freed from poverty, from threats of bodily deprivation and decay in an Eden to be built (we are assured) by a mastery over being itself. The mansion of the body is celebrated by our now decaying philosopher Hugh Hefner as a "Playboy Mansion."

We, unlike Dante in his balanced reflection, inhabit an age in which faith in God is no longer tolerable, though still fitfully desired. In consequence, we have become hard of hearing, and almost blind to the truth of things in themselves. If this characterization of the reader as Modernist seems extreme, even shocking, our uneasiness with it might suggest the depths of O'Connor's own uneasiness with our Modernist age, with an audience she is "conscious of writing for." In response to her reading of her age (as she says) she adopts as fictional strategy the grotesque — a means of shouting to the almost deaf, of drawing large and startling figures for the almost blind, through which we may see ourselves as crippled by "our essential displacement" from our essential nature as person. It proves uncomfortable, then, to be shown spiritual depravity as justified in the name of the *relative* good as ultimate, devised to the conveniences of self-love. She would draw such large and startling pictures in order to bear witness of the reality of our spiritual state as become common, her figures (surrogate Modernist persons) in witness to an abiding contingency to rescue by grace. That is a reality to us even in such a seemingly desperate moment of history as ours. Not, however, that this is her primary responsibility in her act of making this story she reminds us and herself, for in that action of stewardship to her gifts her responsibility is always to the good of the thing she is making, though God may choose to use her art beyond art.

She is aware of certain *historical* ironies, of course, remembering Dante in his forced political exile from Florence — sent away from his own small town whose "provincial" circumstances might be seen to bear some correspondences to Milledgeville, Georgia, by a perceptive poet. She sees a relation, but with a difference as well of Dante's actual political exile. Hers is a sense of exile which speaks her transcendent end less threatened in local circumstances than for Dante. (He could have lost his head in a more immediate sense than Mr. Head's loss to Mercy.) Her own sense of exile at Milledgeville, her small town, or on that small farm at its edge, Andalusia, allows a comfort to her as acceptable refuge, but she knows it more than a refuge. That is, she knows a difference between the *circumstances* of her exile and Dante's, though sharing in spiritual exile as person fallen spiritually. And so she feels "at home" in Middle Georgia for the endurance, the duration, in this world, knowing that as artist it is there that she steadily "operates at a peculiar crossroads where time and place and eternity somehow meet." That very concrete crossroads we now mark with an X on tourist maps: Andalusia — now with a Holiday Inn across the highway from it for our convenience.

O'Connor labored to reveal reality through signs speaking the truth about the actions of human nature — always actions here and now — believing she did so most effectively with matter gathered at her own crossroads where time and place were more comfortably intersected for her by eternity than for most of us, wherever we find ourselves. It is at this point of convergence, recognized by this "realist of distances," that she would engage truth as suited to art. But she must do so (she concluded) through "the best modern instances of the grotesque," knowing of course that the truth of our nature as spiritual creatures is manifest in any person in any place at anytime, not simply for her as *this* person at Andalusia in Central Georgia. And so she recognizes that Dante shares in this knowledge with her, theirs a common metaphysical vision of man in the world. Yet Dante could also share in a degree of common knowing with his audience as she could not, including even those of Dante's contemporaries beginning to emerge in Florence whom Allen Tate might call "Yankees of the spirit." Such "Yankees" were already emerging in Dante's day in an increasingly active revolt against that metaphysical vision fundamental to community as he understood that vision at his own moment of history, in part prompting him to his *Divine Comedy*. That sense of *life* as a Dance held by the Christian community was beginning to turn toward life as a Race, to recall Chesterton's version of our Modernist turning. Even so, Dante's audience at least knew the vision against which they revolted, in a knowledge commonly shared at that "cultural" moment of a turning which we have come to speak of as the emerging "Renaissance spirit." That new spirit is celebrated by Machiavelli, a later citizen of Florence than Dante, in his *The Prince* (1513), a work transitional from the doctrine of the divine rights of the Prince toward the secular rights of the sovereign individual. (See Bertrand de Jouvenel's *On Power: The Natural History of Its Growth*, published at the end of World War II [1945] which explores the evolution of democracy into egalitarianism whose principle becomes the absolute sovereignty of the "Self." And for an incisive explication of Machiavelli's contribution to Modernist sensibilities as exercised in the public arena, see also Leo Strauss's *Thoughts on Machiavelli*, 1957.)

The "Yankees of the spirit" with whom Dante had to deal were in their most proximate threat to him the political Ghibellines, the triumphant political party at Florence that sent him into exile. They supported the Emperor against Dante's own "Southerners," the Guelphs, who supported the Pope against the Emperor. In that local "civil war," the battle was over who should be *invested* with power both economic and spiritual. The Emperor or the Pope? In the interval from Dante, we have suggested, the economic and spiritual (the body and soul of community) have been separated concomitant to a separation of grace from nature. For in the West increasingly since the 14th century we celebrate as preeminent the political and economic freedoms, evidenced as progress toward *democracy* and *convenience* as recognized in retrospect. In the post–World War II world we began to recognize anew a collateral damage, especially to family and local community, out of this celebrated progress, against which the Fugitive-Agrarians attempted a warning in *I'll Take My Stand*.

Through this progress occurs, despite conspicuous conveniences to a new "life-style" (indoor toilets, running water, and even into an abstract cyberspace citizenship), undeniable effects of communal erosions culminating in this present "Age" of the "theorist-consumer." It is in retrospect that we begin to uncover the history of how we got here from there, now become uneasy in a creation reduced to a cosmos in which we find ourselves alienated. We begin to perceive our gradual separation from community as persons as we become autonomous as individuals, in a loss of the spiritual relation proper to political and economic freedoms as bonding us in community. That has been the deliberate strategy of separation to any gnostic director of being, he recognizing it as necessary to power. Hence his act of separation of grace in the nature of *person* in order to redesignate *individuals* in a Nominalistic purchase of power. That is a separation necessary to any system as imposed deterministically upon both nature and human nature.

Accompanying the separation of grace from nature, then, is that accelerating temptation to an apotheosis of man himself as a "self" in wooing consent of the popular spirit, under the auspices of a carelessly embraced "Renaissance" spirit whose emerging password to that popular spirit becomes the shibboleth *democracy*. For *democracy* as shibboleth may more easily conceal a buried distortion of the reality of the person himself. The term is made convenient to variable attractions to seemingly "personal" conveniences advertised as "the common good." For, buried in that term, as if a private gnosis to the individual who may pay public deference to the common good, is that egalitarian conviction of an absolute sovereignty of the self which justifies the spectacles of his "rights" in the public arena. Put starkly, the thing which is given Nominalistic term, *democracy,* is an idea reduced to idol, its truest name an *egalitarianism* made to serve some species of totalitarian reduction of person to his own province as a self. By reduction of persons to *identity*, indistinguishable one from another, there may be promulgated in the isolated self a faith in its own "sovereignty."

The person as *individual* collects "rights'" to himself as if he were a sovereign state. Under the dispensation of such a term, embraced to personal conveniences "on the road," the "self" begins to assume its own self-justification. There follows a confusion of feeling in the person self-celebrated as *individual,* as if feeling were thought, so that such selves (collectively called the "popular spirit") depend more and more upon scientific Positivism as the acceptable "scholasticism" of New Age freedoms embraced by sentimentality. Thus thought is delegated to the Positivistic experts in order that by its evolving science some system may be devised to humor feelings of self-sovereignty as well as to solve "the ills and mysteries of life" by the "scientific advances of man" through rationalism. Though briefly put, the complementary progress of scientific Positivism on the one hand (through rationalism) and the progress of an emerging New Age paganism on the other (intent on a personal "life-style") effect a generalized collateral damage to community. In its actualities community erodes as a body from its traditional meaning and justification (and imperfect manifestations as actual) in its proper service to the person in full — as *homo viator.* For each person in that old understanding is by nature a discrete member, a particular intellectual soul incarnate. That is the traditional office of *community,* in a shared "blood knowledge" held in common as tradition binding members. That is a traditional membership which T. S. Eliot argues must be supported by orthodoxy in recognition of the community's responsibility to the person as a spiritual creature, not as an element in the machinery of social order. (Eliot makes this argument in his controversial Page-Barbour Lectures, *After Strange Gods: A Primer of Modern Heresy,* 1933.) At the end of World War II, Jacques Maritain enlarges upon this theme out of Thomistic metaphysics in his *The Person and the Common Good,* lectures beginning at the opening of that war and gathered at its end in 1946.

Certainly there has been a tendency of Modernist system away from orthodoxy as recognized by Flannery O'Connor. Hers is a studious reflection on its recent history, she more learned in that history than sometimes recognized. For her, Tate's "Yankees of the spirit" were those Modernists whose faith, though various according to the species of elected ideologies, rests ultimately in materialism as accidental and therefore suited to gnostic machinations. She does not shy from such terms as *liberal* as epithet to name the tenor of that inclination in her world. And *liberal,* we might notice, is also a term haunting Modernist engagements of political and social and economic categories used pejoratively by Dostoevsky as well. It is in this climate to O'Connor's reflections that she recognizes with approval the Southern Protestant Fundamentalist as a "reactionary," scandalizing the "liberal" by her defending them as inclined to orthodoxy. Both liberal and Nihilist were scandalized by Dostoevsky's defense of the local Slavophiles as many of O'Connor's readers were by her defense of Haze or Old Tarwater. She recognizes in an Old Tarwater, of course, an excess of violence, but she sees as well that his is a violence in defense of the truth of Revelation, however excessive his rational or activist defense. (He becomes for her, after made fixed and certain by her art, almost actual as surrogate person.) The title to her second novel echoes that recognition. St. Matthew puts the point in a timeless way: "From the days of John the Baptist until now, the Kingdom of Heaven suffereth violence, and the violent bear it away." For O'Connor, one species of Matthew's "violent" Fundamentalist is such a figure as Old Tarwater. But she knows also that there are the more sophisticated and subtly violent presences out of gnostic Positivism such as her Rayber. Rayber is more destructive of his own spiritual nature than his mild intrusions support as mere spectacle, as young Tarwater complains. How "violent," Modernist sensibilities wonder, is his speculative reduction of a tree to board feet worth so many dollars the foot, in the interest of money to educate Young Tarwater in our academy? But Rayber would seize truth and make it conform to system, toward a promised illusional Eden down the road. In the unfolding drama of *The Violent Bear It Away,* then, Old Tarwater and Rayber serve as externalized, fictionally incarnate, poles to that central action in the novel in a consciousness joined violently to defend or bear Heaven away: the wills in conflict within the boy Tarwater.[1]

The Fundamentalists O'Connor knows firsthand. She could encounter them locally on radio stations or in local papers — evangelicals whose rhetorical violence is so distressing to the sophisticated "liberal." Nevertheless, her own sophistication as a prophet of distances was quick to recognize in that violence of words a genuine concern for the truth — for that quest of integrity in response to a desire for the truth which she ascribes to her Haze Motes. She could meet such witnesses locally, their common theme the truth of Revelation as the centering burden of concern beneath the wildness of their ranting. It is that obscured truth that she defends, knowing these violent presences to be most certainly Christ-haunted, though not necessarily Christ-centered. There is a corollary to that recognition, concerning the mystery of violence which she expresses in emphasizing the importance of *manners,* the deportment of the person to creation evident in spectacles attending persons. Bad manners, she says, are better than no manners at all. And so she dramatizes violence by winnowing those Fundamentalist intuitions of the truth, dramatizing those intuitions in her Old Tarwater for instance as a figure of what she calls a "natural" or "crypto Catholic." She will present her Misfit as admirable in his "Southern" manners, even as he shoots the grandmother. (How respectful, to take one's hat off to a lady whom one is about to shoot.)

She shares much with Dostoevsky as we are increasingly aware. Dostoevsky castigates his own generation as that born of the *liberals* (his term), his immediate fathers through whose intellectual failures — intellectual violence against truth analogous to those of O'Connor's Rayber — have been spawned their sons, the Nihilists. The fathers through intellectual (and spiritual) failures effect violent reactions, emerging in actual "civil" wars of terrorist destructions of civil order. Such disorder, programmed ideologically after Dostoevsky by Marxism, will affect Eastern and Western history into our own new millennium. The triumph of Nihilism to O'Connor seems to have been largely accomplished in the interval of the hundred years between her and Dostoevsky, a conclusion expressed in a letter to "A" (August 28, 1955). For "if you live today you breathe in nihilism. In or out of the Church, it's the gas you breathe." But she sees a major, and an admirable, resistance to it in those semi-literate Fundamentalists to whom she became increasingly attuned.

Dostoevsky himself turned increasingly to the "fundamentalists of place" after his portrait of the Modernist mind in his *Notes from Underground.* The Slavophiles were (by analogy) Russian "Southerners" opposing their own "Yankees of the spirit," the Nihilists and their liberal fathers. Not that Dostoevsky found himself comfortable with his "Southerners," his uneasiness about the Slavophiles reminding us of both Walker Percy's fascination with Dostoevsky and of Percy's attraction to but uneasiness with the Southern Fugitive-Agrarians. Dostoevsky was attuned to the Slavophiles in their attempts to recover faith through Russian orthodoxy, which they tended to hold indigenous to place, perhaps affecting them more as Christ-haunted than Christ-centered. His discomfort grew, so that in his favorite phrase, "the Russian soul," he feared that at times there accrued too much to the *Russian* over the *soul.* He feared that the Slavophiles would be tempted to abandon the reality of the soul, in being drawn by their resistance to Western ways into a localized species of nationalism.[2] O'Connor, too, was cautious about a balance in the terms of "Southern Fundamentalism." Still, as with Dostoevsky, she found much in the daily press that she could use to incarnate her version of *homo viator* as "Christ-haunted." She thus exposes her own deracinated age through recognizable correspondences between her characters and persons actual in a fiction born of the history underway all about her. Flannery's "Misfit," for instance, is directly out of the daily local press as a textural presence, even as is true of the persons borrowed as characters by Dostoevsky in his *Crime and Punishment* or *The Idiot.* In the latter novel, Dostoevsky's portrait of a "good man," he intends Prince Myshkin to be "God's idiot." But Myshkin as grounded in the local proves to be man fallen, despite Dostoevsky's intention to an abstract naturally good man. That intellectually inept though spiritually hungry spiritual wanderer, Prince Myshkin, must be presented as engaging actual circumstances of the moment as Dostoevsky reads the moment in the local press and he can be made fictionally persuasive only by actual kinship to fallen man, incorporated as the novel's events from Petersburg social affairs. (*Wise Blood* and *The Idiot* afford interesting comparisons to this point.)[3]

Dante, very famously, is also a "realist of distances," but with that advantage over O'Connor and Dostoevsky as poets which we have noticed. That is, Dante could depend upon a commonly shared (if by some grudgingly shared) concession by the popular spirit of his day to the Source of power, to God as more awesome than as reduced either to a measurable natural force or to man's own autonomous intentionality in political and social affairs through self-apotheosis. (Even the social radical in Dante appeals to God for justification of his radicalism.) Power in contention with love had been philosophically adumbrated as anciently as Plato and Aristotle, of course, whose works as rescued by late Medieval and early Renaissance intellectuals certify ancient traditions of belief amenable to a Christian polity, as St. Thomas discovers particularly in Aristotle. But that certification does not appropriate power to be radically imposed, though Dostoevsky concludes this to be the Jesuits' undertaking, leading him by extension to reject the whole Western Church. One devastating instance is his Westernized intellectual Ivan Karamazov as pleased by his "poem" called "The Grand Inquisitor."

For those who were unsubmissive intellectually to that ancient classical authority of the philosopher (Plato or Aristotle), there was nevertheless a shared recognition of the grounds in which authority was declared the reality of power, though rejected. In the West, Christianity reduced to but myth, as opposed to Christianity founded in Revelation as actual reality, were becoming contentious against each other already by the 13th century. But whether a sometimes entertaining myth or an actual reality, those factions yet shared a "grammar" of the matter as Dante's audience. O'Connor could expect no such common grammar to her visionary art. St. Augustine and St. Thomas Aquinas bracket the tradition she holds in their scholastic concern for Christianity as the vision holding community, both these "doctors" of Christian doctrine very much presences also to Dante, though already eroding in authority out of the response to that emerging "Renaissance" spirit, that spirit responding to nature as tempting to power to be exercised aggressively in a new "humanism." Aristotle's *science,* as increasingly suspect to the new science, becomes a convenient wedge driven by empiricism in separating St. Thomas from the new humanism.

After all, Thomas had depended upon Aristotle as "the philosopher," whose "science" is increasingly unacceptable. By the 16th century, the movement toward autonomous intellect as independent of nature was well underway, increasingly under the influence of Machiavelli as ideological poet, the man of letters defining a new "man in full." One of Machiavelli's subsequent epithets calls him "the first realist of politics," a warning flag, though recognized as such in retrospect. Gerhart Niemeyer, in his *Between Nothingness and Paradise,* remarks Machiavelli as "the first political thinker of rank to propose a way of looking at human life that leaves out the question of what ought to be and merely observes 'what is'—a view from without [as if taken from outside reality] reducing political science to an analysis of phenomena." Indeed, by that principle social order is removed from the moral order increasingly by such empirical detachment, questions of morality thus removed by implication from philosophical concerns for justice and thus eventually removed by pragmatic systems justifying social order as virtuous by analogy to a well-oiled machine—the oiler and mechanic the gnostic "political *scientist.*" Eventually, and especially in the West, the gradual erosion of faith in a transcendent Cause brought Revelation itself in doubt as the popular spirit proved increasingly susceptible to the growing flood of Modernist doctrine.

Community thus became at risk of mudslides as nature was denuded of grace. St. Thomas' understanding of the modes of *intuitive* and *rational* intellect are terms that help us see the increasing civil war between those modes. They are characterized by the popular spirit as Rationalism (18th century) and Romanticism (19th century). The rational mode commandeered to Modernist ends would be subsequently celebrated as 18th century "Enlightenment." For it is the rational mode that is deployed increasingly, though by a rationalism increasingly tyrannical as empirical rational "light." Rationalism liberated from prudential humility promises always a power over nature, promising attractive freedoms of convenience to the popular spirit, given the pressures of its current circumstances. A consequence of the tyranny of rationalism we remarked as noticed by T. S. Eliot, though he addresses it in its surface manifestations in literature as the "dissociation of sensibilities," the separation (Eliot says) of "thought" and "feeling." It is out of that separation that we shall come upon rationalism as residual in O'Connor's Rayber, the "schoolteacher,' whom young Tarwater declares to be the thinker as mechanist. "Do you think with that hearing aide?" he asks Rayber. (Rayber has suffered a loss of hearing from that shotgun blast of Old Tarwater, trying to prevent Rayber's "kidnapping" the boy, Rayber having been declared "legal" guardian.) Young Tarwater notices that Rayber is able to respond to trees only as board feet. Rayber's faith rests, then, in mechanistic science, he having been converted by rationalism to believe in the power of intellect over nature. As that power's evangelist Rayber is dedicated to correcting "mistakes of nature." That is the power largely acceded to by the popular spirit, though markedly less amenable to that power are those "Southerners" like Old Tarwater, as Rayber becomes painfully aware, declaring the old man "self-called" as prophet by psychological aberration. Rayber's own self-calling is to bringing that good news of creation as an accident to these benighted locals, especially in an opposition to the likes of Old Tarwater, O'Connor's "natural Catholic."

What lies between these contenders for the rescue of young Tarwater is the policy Rayber advocates out of his separation of grace from nature, policy to be executed by systematic corrections of the accidental mistakes of mechanistic nature. This is the separation made on the authority of autonomous intellect, but in order to do so intellect must first purge itself of intuitive knowing, under a rubric for that mistake in human nature to be called vestigial instinct. Rayber experiences that malady himself, waves of "feeling" overwhelming him in response to actual things. O'Connor understands it rather an intuitive action of love though Rayber can account for it only as symptom of a pathological madness — a family trait (another "mistake of nature"). He sees it conspicuous in Old Tarwater as a religious fanatic. Intellectual perceptions, in the new Modernist dispensation Rayber embraces — O'Connor implies by fictional indirection — must not be taken as rationalism's instructive response to the truth of things in themselves. They are for St. Thomas an intellectual mode by grace to an intellectual knowing, effected through an openness of love toward things by the person, even by a Rayber. That is an intellectual deportment removing barriers to grace. For O'Connor (as for Thomas), Rayber's limit in detached perception is a means to the measure of a thing by rational intellect as unencumbered by the intuitive, in the interest of declaring truth by rational pronouncement. Thus by intellectual fiat, systems may be adduced sufficient to impose truth upon nature, correcting it. Thereby reason (purged of the intuitive) determines not only the truth of things, but it does so in the interest of determining its own progress toward a predicated Eden — always in the future. Along the way to that Eden, however, reason must declare by fiat that the "essence" of a tree lies in the measure of its square board feet. Such are the "facts" determining essence, as advocated by Emerson.

To put that progress so compactly in our summary term *Modernism* depends on the considerable labors of an intellectual remnant, some of whom we have named: Gilson, Maritain, Weaver, Voegelin, Niemeyer, and kindred spirits. And many of these O'Connor read. Some of them she even reviewed for local benefit in her diocesan paper. But what we have emphasized is that her interest in these fellow heretics to Modernist dogma reveals not

merely a surface level of their "influence" on her. Rather, she discovers in them confirmations of her own observations about the spiritual and intellectual state of her age as it is immediate to her experiences. And that such experiences are not merely local to her is especially evident in the range of her intellectual interests in these fellow "heretics," though made
from a point of lookout upon our world at Andalusia, in middle Georgia. How inevitable,
then, in her reading of poets ancient and recent that she recognize affinities to a Dante on
the one hand or to Dostoevsky on the other, differing though both do as prophetic poets.
How inevitable, given her own intellectual virtues, that she should recognize not only her
affinity to Dante, but as well a considerable difference in the cultural circumstances to him
and herself as prophetic poets. But perhaps especially inevitable was her recognition of
affinity with that wild Russian Dostoevsky, who responded in art with defiance of the Western infections imported by the Russian intelligentsia, those Enlightenment invasions of the
"Russian soul." There could but be a recognition that she shared with Dostoevsky in a belief about the relation of evil to good, which common belief made for both of them a persuasive case for the reality of the Devil as now met in a multitude of Modernist guises.

There is an additional correspondence between O'Connor and Dostoevsky to note.
Dostoevsky discovered in his Slavophile friends a recognition he especially shared with his
close friend Apollon Maikov in letters — their common prophetic vision of Modernist dangers to Russian Orthodoxy. Similarly, O'Connor discovered affinity with such "Southern"
presences to her as Richard Weaver, Caroline Gordon, Allen Tate, Andrew Lytle as mutually concerned with the "Southern soul" under siege, and she especially shares reflections
on the concern in those letters to "A." By that recognition of her affinity to the "Southern
soul" she observed as well, with growing sympathetic interest, the fundamentalism still evident at the local level, heard on the radio and witnessed in local newspapers. Here was an
"orthodoxy" she recognizes and to which she pays tribute.

In their circumstances, though separated by that hundred years and by geography and
culture, O'Connor recognized Dostoevsky as a prophetic poet compatible to her Southern
peers — from several of the Fugitive-Agrarians down to Walker Percy. For both Dostoevsky
and O'Connor as for their soul mates, audiences were nevertheless more problematic than
for Dante. We emphasized that Dante's audience, consenting or not to his vision, could at
least recognize by degree what he was "talking about" as poet and so value the philosophical and theological principles informing his great poem, the *Divine Comedy*. Such a sharing in philosophical and theological grounds, whether embraced or not by all of his audience, made possible to Dante a convenience of allegory in his great poem. Dante recognized
as well the importance of "incarnating" his allegorical implications through very concrete
recent history summoned to his art with arresting naturalistic imagery, transporting the local
and recent to an allegorical terrain out of his actual experiences of recent history. (Later, in
Milton's *Paradise Lost,* the diversity of Milton's audience proves a more considerable challenge to Milton as poet than to Dante, leading Milton to acknowledge that he wrote for "a
fit audience though few.")

For Dante a common knowledge of cultural history shared with his audience allowed
him that mode of allegory which so fundamentally *informs* his great poem. But for O'Connor (as for Dostoevsky) such matter shared to the making of a prophetic vision no longer
obtained as common. Her solution to that problem of a common ground with audience
turns then toward adapting recent history and natural realities in a *grotesque* manner rather
than attempting an allegorical one. Disparities, enlargements of the actual at the level of

spectacle, thus are summoned to bear evidence of depths in reality not perceived by her readers. It is of this deployment of the grotesque as the "large" and "startling" signals of the dramatic action of intellect that O'Connor speaks in her "Some Aspects of the Grotesque in Southern Fiction." She gives her talk, made on home ground, at Wesleyan College for Women a few miles from Andalusia, explaining her manner as necessary to her cultural circumstances. By that aspect of her art, reasoned into persuasive drama, she may engage a reluctant audience. Perhaps she may even shock it out of its confused sensibilities — perhaps eventually even wake that anonymous reviewer of her stories for the *New Yorker.* But if this early argument is made in home territory, in local circumstances a few miles from Andalusia, O'Connor makes it out of a more considerable knowledge of Western thought than is at first evident no doubt to undergraduates at a small local college and the few random visitors (among them myself). Her argument is to be understood in respect to her art as a response to the general disorientation of *homo viator,* the increasing intellectual deracination that has occurred since Dante. If O'Connor's audience did not respond with certain recognitions of that complexity at that moment, out of educated remembrances of our intellectual wandering, they did so intuitively — or at least some of them did.

For Dante and his audience, neither the poet nor his readers were yet overwhelmingly threatened by the loss of a common intellectual and spiritual ground still supporting community, given the authority of the Church as explicated by St. Augustine and St. Thomas especially. Though that ground was already being eroded at the edges, it was presently to be plowed over, some ancient plantings in it plowed under. Some of it would become a ground salted by an increasingly radical skepticism declared *de rigueur* for the intellectual progressive, the rationalist. Meanwhile the poet Dante could share with his audience points of reference in very ancient common ground for a moment longer. With the inception of the progressive spirit increasingly associated with "personal" autonomy, there grows the inclination to self-celebration of a self "re-born" in ways quite other than that term as spoken to Nicodemus by Jesus. It rises with intent to social and political power, the suspected agenda for which is that change toward a secular conquest of nature, including human nature, accepted as justified by Machiavelli. And we have suggested a reaction to that tendency which proved more nearly akin to it than the reactionaries recognized. That is, in Europe and in the fledgling New World colonies, by the 18th century there occurs a "Great Awakening," a revolution within Christendom that will be answered out of the Modernist spirit in the French Revolution. The reaction was first directed against sacramentalism and ritualism in the Church. It leads to the founding of Dartmouth, Princeton, Brown Universities, in which at our point of history the old active Puritanism is now secular and anti–Christian.

The Protestant revolution itself prepares a way for an evolution into the secular religion by rejecting sacramentalism in forms maintained by the Church, though in an irony of history the emerging new secular religion will discover a necessity of at least the emptied forms of sacramentalism. The "progress" toward community's deracination from the transcendent lies in a separation of the *intellectual soul* by fiat, in order to reject the soul, but how recover the popular spirit to a collectivity sufficient to power? That becomes a task laid upon the skeptical educators of youth toward a new worship by community itself as the "State." How compatible, then, proves Emerson's refusing of communal worship in any church where bread and wine are present as manifestations of Presence, he restricting nature's wheat and grapes to the province of the human body in its appetitive nature. Only a little earlier than Emerson as our "rationalist," that exciting "Romantic" Jean Jacques Rousseau writes to d'Alembert a formula for the appropriation to political uses of a rationally controlled pseudo-sacramental deportment of community. D'Alembert, we remember, is one of the 18th century Encyclopedists and a principal father of Positivism. Concerning his contribution to Modernism, see Eric Voegelin's examination of him in *From Enlightenment to Revolution,* remembering as well Voegelin's observations of Robespierre's "cult of the *Etre Supreme*" and Comte's "cult of the Grand-Etre" when a century after them will be declared a "right" of equal opportunity to any "self" as sovereign, characterized by Henri Bergson attributable to a universal élan vital in which the sovereign self participates as central.

What Rousseau advises that severe rationalist d'Alembert is that there is a practical advantage of festival in ordering the popular spirit. It is no great challenge to manage an event to that end: "Plant a flower-decked pole in the middle of an open place, call the people together — and you have a fête!" How far such "festival" is from that Maypole at Merrymount as rejected by Governor Endicott in Hawthorne's story. We need only cursory observation, a summoning in memory of that secular Endicott, née, Robespierre of the 1790s. As for an "open place," preferably paved, save for the centering spray of flowers on that pole as the new altar, the nature of place must be sterilized of all grace. Thus gnostic intellect establishes triumph over nature, commanding a worship by the popular spirit of that triumph. There occurs that "Festival of Reason" in Paris (November 10, 1793), in preparation for which the Revolution's newspaper *Le Moniteur* announces that the bells of all the churches are now under new management. When the bells ring, the "populace will fill the streets and public squares, aflame with joy and fraternity"—lest heads by chopped off.

A few months later Robespierre will serve as liturgist at a "Festival of the Supreme Being" gathered to a presence as a multitude around monuments he has commanded raised for the new worship, a principle one the great statue called *Wisdom* (an "artificial wisdom"?). Robespierre's is a cleverness as gnostic director of the social order in his strategy of a seduction of the popular spirit by secularized sacramentalism. He imitates Medieval Christian art with idols of emblematic figures such as those of Wisdom and Justice as if mediating a worship of that *Etre Supreme* whose diabolically hidden reality is the Self as the only God, to be worshipped as beyond good and evil. We observe that this gambit occurs a hundred years before President Eliot at Harvard adapts the emerging new version of man worshipped in the name of a pure but pragmatic reason in his own "The Religion of the Future." And, once more, in relation to our foray here into *festival* see Josef Pieper's *In Tune with the World: A Theory of Festivity,* as compared to Flannery O'Connor's recognition in Hawthorne, who she says "knew his own problems and perhaps anticipated ours when he said he did not write novels, he wrote 'romances,'" thereby keeping open to art "deeper kinds of realism" than that demanded by "a realism of fact."

As the American colonies are politically constituting themselves a Republic in reaction to England as Empire, we recall, there accompanied it that "Second Great Awakening" of evangelical Protestant Christianity. It is underway from the 1790s (as Robespierre is instituting his secular sacraments in worship of the Supreme Being), a reawakening that by the time of Andrew Jackson is becoming increasingly a secularized "Protestantism." Particularly in that interval has been the concerted action in New England Congregational churches of rejecting worship as a communal sacrament celebrated in lifting creation itself in tribute to its Cause. Emerson's rejection of bread and wine we take as emblematic, bread and wine reduced to the conveniences of the body, wine itself even so increasingly suspect in that office, even to the intellectually sophisticated fathers of Brahmin culture gathered discretely as "Congregational." (In the South the distillery tended to be adjacent to the pulpit.) That Second Great Awakening influenced the political moment as an "awakening" in which an intent to power over political and social institutions begins to rise as well, both increasingly opposed to the Roman Church incidentally. At least by analogy, there was a continuing of that old war between Emperor and Pope which sent Dante into exile, though in 19th century manifestation the tension is between an evangelical self-sufficiency of the person and the political-economic centralizations of power in a secular government, requiring for a mutual convenience to each faction the political doctrine of a separation of Church and State.

That secular government will realize a necessity to collective, centralized power to resist the "evangelical" popular spirit, the contentions between those polarities a subject of considerable speculation called "political science,' though seldom put in such terms as we are using. In our address to these polar attractions to the popular spirit, in contest for power over it, we have been arguing that at the heart of each lies a species of Manichaeanism, each advocating an Eden to be built on or out of an "American" ground. By hindsight, awakened now by a sense of having become lost in the cosmos, we may discern a two-fold gradual triumph of Modernism through antithetic but very like Modernist intents to power, skillfully maintained to the wooing of the popular spirit. Each (a Puritan or a Positivistic Manichaeanism) give at least a surface deference to the common good, the one declared a defense of, the other a rejection of, God as the source of the good properly common to community. By such strategy is furthered the dry-rot of intellect itself to *homo viator*.

Meanwhile, the *person* become reduced toward submission in a collective "individualism" is still encouraged to "skate" on the surfaces of reality (to recall Emerson's figurative advice to us). What became increasingly unrecognized as a necessity to any balance on such surfaces was a rootlessness, by which rejection an increasing winter in the soul is less noticeable. But the wandering "self," *homo viator* converted to Modernism and become spiritually deracinated, finds itself waking in a dark winter wood, forlorn citizen of the "Age of Alienation." That was a waking recognition that for some of the stirring intellectual community seemed proof of the fulfillment of Hegel's prophecy of "the end of history." (I have a collection of works sharing as initial title words *The End of,* completed by a subject term to each work of various categories: *Democracy* or *Linguistics* or *Biology* or like subcategorical themes on intellectual "disciplines" gone astray in Modernist doctrines.) We become aware of this dead-end difficult to find a name for in our new age. The "Age of Alienation"? "The Age of the Theorist-Consumer"? Certainly ours is a new age increasingly recognized in frenzied responses to a waking as lost in the cosmos.

In the Renaissance, we have suggested, begins the relocation of the seat of power to man himself, in favor of an emerging self-centered angelism declared on the authority of intellectual autonomy. To say as much is not to say in our opposition as heretics to Modernism that we reject all of the fruits of that "reawakening." Our concern is rather for the sorting of our inheritance by reason as measured by truth, lest we either as "Renaissance Cavalier" or "Renaissance Puritan" intellectuals mistake intellect itself as the measure of truth rather than the other way round. It is by the false selection of surfaces as the primary reality that both the Puritan spirit in its reactionary rejections of this world as but surface and that counter intellectual inversion through a radical skepticism begin to anticipate a shocked awakening at dead end. Out of either of these lost ways, in an increasingly darkening wood, in a last self-defense we are likely to take refuge by a cynical withdrawal. The illusions of progress founder in 20th century decaying Edens, as that century's history shows. As Walker Percy has it of that dead-end century which attempts its own fitful rescue by the epithet "post–Modern," it proved nevertheless "the most scientifically advanced, savage, democratic, inhuman, sentimental, murderous century in human history." That is Percy's summary judgment in answering the question so often put to him, "Why Are You a Catholic," he looking back to Dante and St. Augustine and St. Thomas for any prospect of recovery.

As our recent intellectual history makes evident in its philosophical and scientific as well as its poetic dissociations of sensibilities, there is a belligerent separation of the *rational* and the *intuitive,* separated into warring factions to recruit the popular spirit of the moment and place under varied banners. What ensues are many confusing civil wars, first within specific intellects (O'Connor's "wills in conflict") but breaking out into the public arena in actual civil wars, both within local communities and among nations. By the *intuitive* or the *rational* as separated justifications of factional intentionalities (the intuitive to a "Romantic camp," the rational to a "Rationalistic" camp), each shares a kindred intentionality: an anticipation of an apotheosis of man as autonomous. That self-made godhead of the man as "individual" will be characterized especially by Nietzsche for the Rationalist camp, though he was personally much taken by Dostoevsky's *Crime and Punishment* as prophetic of Nietzsche's own "Romantic" resolution of the mystery of existence, his prophecy of an emerging Superman — man angelistically transported beyond good and evil as Raskolnikov attempts and as Haze Motes attempts. Dostoevsky's protagonist in *Crime and Punishment,* however, at last proves one of his *sufferers,* on his way to conversion — hardly acceptable to Nietzsche. Nietzsche could not approve of Dostoevsky's resolution in the novel's "Epilogue," the concluding sentences prophesying a "new story," the story of "the gradual renewal of a man [Raskolnikov], of his gradual regeneration, of his slow progress from one world to another, of how he learned to know a hitherto undreamed-of reality" borne to him through the suffering love of Sonya, who shares his exile. That is a similar "undreamed-of reality" which O'Connor's Haze Motes discovers at his death as well. And her young Tarwater also makes his uncertain way in a "slow progress from one world to another."

A long journey, then, this from Dante to Dostoevsky and O'Connor, on a way leading deeper into a darkening wood which the poet cannot resolve empirically, only deepen in our awareness by his imaginative vision. It is in that dark wood that O'Connor would have us recover by a flickering light, the flickering within us as intellectual soul perceived in the 20th century despite our having become almost blind to it on our recent journey. It is the light she calls grace, in which light she declares "all is the Incarnation." Dante, given his high intent (announced as a vision occurring to him just as he is finishing his *New Life* and demanding of him his own newer life) recognizes that the local allows some purchase in recovery through the immediacy of things commonly seen as actual in themselves, at the very doors of his flesh and speaking truths to intellect through his experiences of things that affect his possible actions as *this* person beyond being a poet. His will may at this moment embrace or reject such truth. In that immediacy therefore may lie endangerments to the poet as person, his temptation not only to the surfaces of reality as experienced but to his mistaking the "historical" dimension of his experience as determinate of the limits of art itself. That is, he may not distinguish between the *actual* and the *possible* in Aristotle's distinction between history and art as differing in respect to intellectual makings, but not differing as each measured by the truth of things. Most especially, as the poets of the 20th century in particular discovered, there seems an added challenge in the adaptation of the "autobiographical" history to drama, given the loss of humanity understood in common with his audience. For so advanced are those current "civil wars" grown out of history, between the time of Dante and O'Connor, that in the decay of community at this late date the poet seems limited to himself as his most dependable but "private" matter, tempting him to a skeptical swaggering in defiance of a vaguely impinging world. Such was the challenge to poets as diverse as Hemingway, Joyce, Eliot, Pound, as our reading of their literary witness may reveal. Theirs are challenges to the intellectual soul by circumstance and by audience quite other than the challenge to Dante.

Dante's concerns require his accepting the local, which he more than accepts: He embraces the local, not only local incidents but local speech as well, electing the vernacular for his great poem for a "local color." In doing so, he affirms the balance necessary within himself, whereby his reasoned making is more than a "journalism" reflecting a 13th century place, as Thomas' philosophy is more than a history of ideas up to the 13th century. Dante's great poem, this is to say, is larger than "local color," as Thomas' philosophy is larger than an intellectual history of Western ideas, though in respect to art's uses of the local in Western literature and philosophy's uses of what men have thought both Dante and Aquinas are astounding to us in their witness to intellectual inheritances. As poet whose grand work is matter ordered by metaphysics on the one hand and by the "sciences" of art as complement to truth on the other, Dante in his complementary mastery of his matter is widely recognized as a preeminent prophet of distances, even by the skeptic. Any explicator of his *Comedy,* or even a casual reader of it, discovers as much very quickly. Not so widely recognized, O'Connor proves rather like him, though less conspicuously a philosophical poet under the necessity to her craft of indirection in response to her cultural circumstances. What we know as common in their kinship is that both value common sense in intellectual responses to immediate experience. Each believes that the more we look at a thing in itself, an object local and immediate to intellect through the senses, the more we may see of the largeness of the world and of the spiritual implications in that gathering of largeness in this object. Its proximate nature recognized within universal principles speaks its rest in a Cause. And so blessed by metaphysical vision centering upon the local, both Dante and O'Connor are comfortable as persons with the local as most personal to them, encouraging them to reason's locating the particular crossroads at which each stands — at a different time and place in "history." That comfort is greater than any "autobiographical" limit.

Reason in making, attuned to the local, orients each as not only a poet but as *homo viator*— man on his way to his proper end beyond both art and history, a perfection which (in Eliot's phrase in recognition in his *Waste Land*) "is not to be found in our obituaries." In that assurance, either will realize, will *know,* that whether poet or philosopher or scientist the most fundamental point of departure for any person is the local, the immediate world as experienced. Thomas will say of this recognition that *homo viator* begins at a point of personal knowing of things in themselves, known through the senses, but to be ordered in discovering his unique (his "personal") calling. It is by intuitive response to *this* thing known *now,* Thomas says, that a person discovers himself to be actual for the first time. In O'Connor's words, echoing Thomas, "To know oneself is to know one's region. It is also to know the world." But we recall as well her conclusion to such a knowing. Out of experience enlarged to discover herself at her crossroads, here and now, there rises a mystery, a sense of

"exile." In recovering a "felt balance" on that way, the very balance reveals "also, paradoxically, a form of exile from the world" as an effect of the knowing of the local, however dearly
loved. A form of that exile Dante knows is his actual journeying into a geographical, political exile, a lesser species of exile than Flannery has in mind and as Dante discovers through
his great poem.

Dante's actual exile we know is not the same as that O'Connor sees in the popular spirit
of her age, that self-generated angelistic removal from place — from both the region and
world — which is attempted through an intellectual autonomy naively oblivious to that
country toward which O'Connor herself sojourns as pilgrim. (Currently, info-space seems
a more comfortable habitat to a large element of the popular spirit.) Here in this place at
this time, one sees (if one be a realist of distances) beyond the here and now, largely misunderstood by the popular spirit of the moment. And by that perspective it becomes possible to her as pilgrim that she draw form by intellectual reason from truths known here and
now, recovering a larger citizenship than of this world only and more reassuring than that
abstract country of the internet. Thus O'Connor's art, governed by a felt balance between
the intuitive and rational modes of intellectual action, escapes the limits of the topical in
respect to the surfaces of history as reflected by spectacle. Hers is not therefore art as satiric
local color. She knows that she must not, as poet in a present action of making, consent to
the merely topical, neither defending or advancing Church or secular party — neither polemical ally of either our age's Guelphs or Ghibellines under whatever local title they may bear
in this moment in this place.

Flannery O'Connor's concerns as prophetic poet, as a realist of distances, is certainly
not to defend the "South," then, nor to castigate the "North," although she is in her cultural nature very much a Southerner in sensibilities to the local.[4] Dante's circumstances bear
an analogy parallel to Flannery O'Connor's nevertheless, she a "Southern" writer in some
respects as Dante was a "Guelph." The considerable difference to her as poet in contrast to
Dante is that in neither her "North" nor "South" does there seem to be any shared ground
comparable to that which supported Dante's vision as recognizable to both Guelph and Ghi-
belline. As "Guelph," as of the Pope's party, O'Connor can find little common ground
shared locally in terms such as those of St. Thomas, though in respect to recognitions of
man's spiritual nature there was reassuring recognition by local fundamentalism that kept
her local populace at least Christ-haunted. There was that small reading group she was a
part of which bravely undertook reading even Heidegger, strange presence to a local intellectual community feeding the spiritual for her. In her perspective Dante no less than St.
Thomas could prove in some degree welcomed Virgils to her in company with those local
persons, though perhaps not always conspicuous in her acknowledgments.

Eliot discovers, after an early enthusiasm for Dante as but poet, depths he had at first
not noticed, depths suited to encouraging his recovery of hope as he makes his way out of
his local Modernist forest. He will on his death bed remark to his visitor Cleanth Brooks
(as Cleanth remembered it to me), speaking of his intellectual family origin in Unitarian-
ism: "There's not much to it, is there, Cleanth." Earlier Eliot had felt almost comfortable
as skeptical "woodsman" in London as an ambiguous "place" reflected in his *Waste Land*.
He was aware increasingly of London however as a more sophisticated place than, but also
spiritually analogous to, O'Connor's Atlanta as "Taulkinham." His uses of the geography
and history of London provide him signposts ordering the *Waste Land,* though signposts he
at last recognized as having led him in circles. And so how recognizable, in relation to her own

circumstances as poet at Andalusia, would be Eliot's remarks on revisiting Dante soon after his conversion, in his "Dante" (1929): "in Dante's time Europe, with all its dissensions and dirtiness, was mentally more united than we can now conceive." Or there is the more central point discovered on revisiting Dante: "Practically, it is hardly likely that even so great a poet as Dante could have composed the *Comedy* merely with understanding and without belief." Such remarks might well encourage O'Connor. Thus she will say that "When people have told me that because I am a Catholic, I cannot be an artist, I have had to reply, ruefully, that because I am a Catholic, I cannot afford to be less than an artist." The point is not that O'Connor read Eliot on Dante and was "influenced" by his essay, but the essay echoes a personal community to a remnant company of believers in which both Eliot and O'Connor continue as members. As she knew well, she is a member in that continuing company which Eliot calls that of "the living and the dead," a company embracing an active presence in that membership of Dante in his Florence, Eliot in London, Dostoevsky in Petersburg, herself in Milledgeville.

Dante; Dostoevsky; Eliot; O'Connor: pilgrims as poets but not themselves heroes of an epic stature in earth's annals. They are poets called to a prophecy of the *possible* which is inherent to human nature as *given*. But how are they as such pilgrims in the world to deploy the concrete local in unpropitious times — even the unheroic detritus of personal memory itself— as their art's high calling? In the old tradition, thanks perhaps to Homer (who finds a comfortable place for the poet at the King's right hand) the poet's high calling to epic dimensions required the hero to be cast in a high language celebrating high social station, the nature of that high language from Virgil to the Middle Ages requiring classical Latin — given the political triumphs of Rome and its absorption of Greek high culture. *Latin*, to praise as hero a great figure like Aeneas, was apt out of a cultural piety. But to follow the uncertain wanderings of the poet *himself* as a protagonist is rather less arresting in spectacle than to follow an Aeneas or an Achilles. (We remember how cleverly Homer makes Odysseus as hero a poet at a banquet occasion at the court of the Phaeacians.) Colloquial idiom, lacing the vulgar Italian as it had decayed from Latin with a sprinkling of dialectical intrusions? Perhaps some lingering purist in Dante's own day, should he encounter that exiled poet at his making, toting his poem unpublished about with him and perhaps sharing his manuscript as *samisdot* of the day, might be shocked that Dante's high seriousness should be cast in such low language and seemingly about himself. So too may a critic be shocked that Flannery O'Connor casts a Dantesean high seriousness in a low provincial country and in characters and language considered provincial — given such literary benchmarks as those of James and Joyce in their art's arresting elevations of the personal.

In her day there had appeared those self-elected exiles, the Beats, one of whom proclaimed in his own epic himself as hero, presuming thereby to supercede at least Eliot's *Waste Land* by a language more shocking than Eliot's had been to his peers. The poem was Allen Ginsberg's *Howl,* which begins "I saw the best minds of my generation destroyed by madness, starving hysterical naked,/ dragging themselves through the negro streets at dawn looking for an angry fix,/ angelheaded hipsters ..." and on and on in Whitmanesque rhetoric sprinkled with a scatological dressing. A long long way from Virgil in the *Aeneid,* a long way from Dante in the *Divine Comedy*. Even a long way from Eliot's epic beginning in a cruel April for his own lost soul in *The Waste Land*.[5] We may remember that, as an epic for the 1950s *Howl* was published with an "Introduction" by Ezra Pound's old friend William Carlos Williams, whose concluding word of warning to the reader is "Hold back the edges of your gowns, Ladies, we are going through hell." At the time, Flannery's friend Robert Fitzgerald is finishing his translation of the *Odyssey*, and no doubt a juxtaposition of the "heroes" of Homer's *Odyssey* to an Allen Ginsberg as the hero self-celebrated (with a growing "media" attention) were in O'Connor's mind when she responds in a cautionary letter to Dr. T. R. Spivey (June 21, 1959). Spivey's reading the "beat writers" seems "the most appalling thing you could set yourself to do." She thinks, concerning them — on the evidence of what they say about themselves — that one might find "a lot of ill-directed good in them," a sound enough Thomistic judgment in that they at least embrace a lesser good in reaction to a collapsing culture rather than attempting to reject all good. But they do so in order to reject the world about them — a world they would consign to Hell by dragging it there with them — if there were a Hell. O'Connor remarks that the Beats know "a good many of the right things to run away from." But they lack the discipline needed to validate their pretensions to a holiness through the instrumentality of a revolution in manners and language, though bad manners be better than no manners at all. "They call themselves holy but holiness costs, and so far as I can see they pay nothing," she wrote Spivey. They are children of the age, moved by "the conflict between an attraction to the Holy and the disbelief in it that we breathe in with the air of the times," as on another occasion she wrote John Hawkes in a related context. In the context of our own enlargements by pronouncement, but consonant with her judgment of the spiritual effects of breathing such air, we may say that the Beats take refuge in the "self" as the only Holy.

So much for them as vatic heroes to their generation, then. As for the Beats as artists, "You can't trust them as poets ... because they are too busy acting like poets." This, O'Connor's response to the Beats as she is reviewing a book "On Zen and Japanese Culture," seeing in that scholarly work why Zen proves so attractive to that new Beat movement. Her review itself when published concludes that Zen is "non-conceptual, non-purposive, and non-historical, and therefore admirably suited to be exploited by the non-thinking and pseudo-artist." To Dr. Spivey she had remarked, concerning Zen, that if "you took Christ, the Church, law and dogma, out of Christianity, you would have something like Zen left." Better a Haze Motes, who knows (without a Ginsberg's advantage of formal academic training) "the right things to run away from," but who knows as well the necessity of discovering something toward which to run — however terrible the thing may be when discovered. Haze, as a "Southern" version of the "Beat" mentality, discovers (as St. Paul also discovered) that it is "a fearful thing to fall into the hands of the living God." That is a terror deferred, Flannery suggests from Andalusia, if one choose only the sensational "Hell" which William Carlos Williams promised to "Ladies" (implying the current literary establishment) if they should read *Howl*.

Not for her then, the Beat's appropriation of Modernist philosophy from Descartes to Heidegger, partially gathered from their own intellectual dalliance in the academy, on whose outskirts they begin to perform. That vague climate to solipsistic consciousness they lace with Zen. Hawthorne's pilgrim, young Goodman Brown, was shocked to find the good people of his village in a dark woodland at a black mask, at a worship of the devil. But the Beat poets are hard pressed to shock literary "ladies," or even O'Connor, by their role as anti–Courtly Love lovers. Nor were the "Cornbelt Metaphysicians" as another enclave of such "Ladies' to be much impressed by the Beats' overbearing indecorous address, the unseemly presented as if astounding, intending to make their audience (to touch the root meaning of *astounding*) "star-struck" at Beat performances. How then may academic rituals of the literary establishment be turned upside down if the Beats cannot do so? A question pondered indecorously by the Beats in coffee houses adjacent to campuses, those coffee houses increasingly inhabited also by Cornbelt Metaphysicals nostalgic for the ancient coffee houses once attracting old Metaphysical Poets like Marlow and Ben Jonson, perhaps even Shakespeare. The Puritan vengeance against "metaphysics" in several "Great Awakenings" made coffee houses sinful, beginning spectacularly in England's Civil War. But add drugs and sex, especially perverted sex, and the combination becomes (in the 1960s) irresistible even to the academy itself.

Since O'Connor's death in 1964, the inversion has become integral to academic curricula. For who can resist such a metaphysical poetry of the self as that of Ginsberg's "in your face" rhetoric of self-pity? Poetry becomes a ritual modified by "angelheaded hipsters"—a self-sacrament burning in their "ancient heavenly connection to the starry dynamo in the machinery of night" in which feeling seems to vibrate with the magic of incantation — out of whatever private vision of the "self" prompts it. "Mohammedan angels staggering on tenement roofs," after having "passed through universities with radiant cool eyes hallucinating Arkansas and Blake-light tragedy among the scholars of war." (This from *Howl.*) By such violence to the self, if only for a moment, there seems to occur one desired reaction: making the evening paper — having been "expelled from the academies for crazy & publishing obscene odes on the windows of the skull," etc., etc., etc. Until at last will come an offering of "Chairs" in creative writing, superceding those once held by Establishment Cornbelt Metaphysicians.

Try explicating such a passage as this last one quoted from *Howl* without the knowledge that knowledge itself has been in a rapid decline since Descartes into isolating specializations under the auspices of the academy! It is hardly a language spoken by man to mankind, language immersed in reality itself, though such pyrotechnic poetry may prove highly entertaining at the surface of response by "feeling." How shocking for those Ladies holding their skirts aside from the realities implied in such a descent into a hell, imagined in a vengeance as if it were love and so hardly yielding the Hell Dante or O'Connor know. Hell in this random vision is to be made the place of heroes, its celebration heroic in justifying merely "being on the road," aimlessness made a virtue. And protected only within the "borders" of his isolated country, "the sides of his skull" as we have heard O'Connor remark of such pretensions to self-rescue, rendered later by Ginsberg as a "publishing [of] obscene odes on the windows of the skull." For as Ginsberg announces, his special calling is that of publishing such odes as a self-protection against an openness, seeing things through reductionist odes in pretenses of an egalitarian love of all things. Thus one may become a floating provincial, skating on the surface of a reality self-created.

In opposition to this peculiar response to Modernism by the Beats, Flannery holds fast to a principle learned from St. Thomas. For her, "the moral basis of Poetry is the accurate naming of the things of God," as she writes "A" (January 13, 1956). The failure of the Beats, she might argue to this point, requires only our reading Ginsberg in comparison to the attempts at accurately naming the things of God by her favorite poet, Gerard Manley Hopkins. In such confused intellectual circumstances as those seen by the Beats, formal language in rapid decay, there is no common "vernacular" the poet might use to the rescue of language as Dante found still possible. What manner of naming of things, then, is possible to the poet? Surely not by a language such as that of Ginsberg, who in his revolt against sophisticated intellectual pretensions as he sees it registered by the words of Cornbelt Metaphysicals imitates emptiness in parody of rhetoric. Those "Metaphysicals" themselves turn to a language increasingly specialized in a contracting to tribal desires of isolation. There occurs for them similar tribalism increasingly isolating them as the Beats are isolated in their "counter cult" of the "non-thinking and pseudo-artist" in opposition to the pretentious "thinking" of the academic poet — both tribes rejecting as well the smothering political and social "Establishment." (For, in Dostoevsky's term, how "liberal" both the Beats and the "Cornbelt Metaphysicals" become in respect to the body of community.) No pleasure but in meanness, then, as the Beats might say echoing O'Connor's Misfit. Indeed, rejection becomes the primary ideal in response to that intensifying hatred of a vague "Establishment."

That deportment of either the Beat or the Cornbelt Metaphysical is quite other than the pursuit of truth which O'Connor dramatizes in Haze Motes. For O'Connor, Haze's pursuit requires hope of a unifying naming of things in themselves, bonding namer and named if only intuitively known by Haze — a right name discovered under the auspices of the *being* actual to things. In that possible bonding therefore lies for her prospect of community. The name — the meaning? *Form* responsive to the *known*. When O'Connor remarks to Dr. Spivey that the Beats know "a good many of the right things to run away from," her remark suits even her own Misfit, though perhaps in his defense *meanness* is more than the *shocking spite* of the Beats to what the Beats perceive in the Cornbelt Metaphysicals as vacuous elitism. The Misfit's "meanness" is in a paradoxical way we have suggested his defense of evil, a paradoxical witness by indirection "proving" (i.e., testing) the good as actual, an intuitive recognition seemingly foreign to both Beat and Cornbelt Metaphysical.

That civil war contingently current to O'Connor as she writes — that between the Beats and the Cornbelt Metaphysicals (the latter known through her own participation in the Iowa workshop for creative writers) — is a war she sees as a larger civil war within an "unincorporated" randomness of members. Neither "local" side (as measured by eternity) enlists her consent. It unfolds as a civil war within the academy itself over the nature of man, however much disguised by Beat addictions to language celebrating appetite as if ultimate that become "mainstream" in the academy. The war of poets, waged on the surface of reality itself as serving autonomous selves on either side, was a continuation of that old, old war between rationalism and the appetitive instinct, these factional causes to tribalism replacing Thomistic *reason* and *intuition*. It was (and is) a war which in its recent history continues a very old one, symbolized concomitantly in those academic studies O'Connor encounters on her brief academic sojourn which posed surfaces of 18th century Enlightenment against surfaces of 19th century Romanticism. But from her Thomistic position, both these are "romantic" distortions of man's intellectual gifts at their surface, distortions largely made in the interest of an autonomy of the self. On either hand the intent is to an absolute freedom through absolute sovereignty declared to the self. Insofar as the war is waged on the surface of things (remembering that we were advised to "skate" on those surfaces by Emerson) the surface of language becomes the first casualty of naming turned to self-convenience, a Nominalism of feeling replacing Occam's Nominalism of thought. It is a principle appropriated by the residual dependence of Modernism upon that older Nominalism as the governing epistemological principle out of Occam, whether focused as rationalistic logic indifferent to mystery or as a naturalistic instinctiveness governed by feeling.

And so, what is a small-town, even a country, girl like Flannery O'Connor to make of language in her concern as poet? Is that familiar, and even comfortable, country idiom she knows sufficient to her purposes? Perhaps it is not so cut off from its cultural roots as had been "academically" supposed. After all, so sophisticated a poet as Alexander Pope said "jined" for *joined,* and Sir Walter Raleigh at Queen Elizabeth's court may well have said "watermillion." Or so Cleanth Brooks suggested in his academic monograph upon regional dialects of Elizabethan England in relation to the dialect on the Georgia-Alabama border country which is whimsically but also "scientifically" echoed in Joel Chandler Harris's Uncle Remus tales — in O'Connor country. But unless such inherited manners of speech (being busily eradicated in the academy through speech corrections technology in the immediate post–World War II South) — unless dialect in whatever manifestation is governed by an attempt at community through the naming of things, language itself serves only some species of a specialized tribalilzation which increasingly isolates enclaves of community, even physicists or geneticists among other tribal isolations. Is such effect not already evident in the specialized language nurtured by the academy itself, languages requiring initiations of intellect into multiple enclaves of autonomous "disciplines"? A considerable problem, this, to the poet — this fragmentation of community by "neuvo-vulgar" languages of specialization upon which the poet may not depend in his attempt to speak to those disparate enclaves within a dissolving community of humanity.

Perhaps a poet might depend upon the dialect of the good country people at hand. But he must remember as well the ambiguities and ironies implicit in such a seemingly-harmless term as *good.* The phrase *good country people* depends from reality according to truth about reality itself as signified both in and to *people,* in customs and manners, whereby both *country* (*what* country?) and *good* may only further exasperate attempts at *common* understanding. Nevertheless, a possible strategy, at risk in that "dialects" themselves were increasingly becoming mere matter to specialized concerns for language reduced to abstract local systems as empirically categorized. In that concern, the relation of words to the surfaces of reality are presumed not only sufficient to a *beginning* of understanding but believed the *ultimate* end. Etienne Gilson, in 1969 — soon after O'Connor's death — engages this problem in his *Linguistics and Philosophy: An Essay on the Philosophical Constants of Language.* His is a concern for a confusion of philosophy and science in a tendency to abandon metaphysical implications of language in that emerging "science" of linguistics. What disturbs Gilson is that this science pretends to an unwarranted philosophical authority in its address to the nature of language.

Since her neighbors are people, as O'Connor is acutely aware, perhaps the deportment of these good country people to the actualities of existential reality might serve her purposes as poet, their language itself echoing their own reality as persons. She knows that such "folk" (as they might be categorized from an academic distance) do not themselves very likely recognize the rootedness of their inherited dialect as binding generations in a present community. How awkward for the country boy or girl entering the academy out of Appalachian "culture" and speaking with a grandfather's residual Elizabethan English. And how seldom is that country child happily rescued from his backwardness as G. B. Shaw so delightfully manages in his *Pygmalion* at a surface of social satire.[6] Aside from such speech as possible object of "science," with specialized intention to use local speech structures and diction to graph demographics and plot the geography of history, can such local matter serve the poet in the Age of Alienation?

From the critic's perspective — if he be Flannery's New York critic perhaps — how can she be concerned with more than the satiric, perhaps in Shaw's sophisticated ironic manner? Perhaps her "folk" stories, in a language bearing sociological implications like those of

Joel Chandler Harris, may serve linguistic science and even sociology. As such they may prove welcomed accident, historical matter to the science of language as used in Middle Georgia in the 1950s. But surely O'Connor could not intend a genuine sympathy for such backward figures suffering such provincial isolation — their having become so isolated from the "real" social world dreamed immanent through Modernist manipulations. A sociological sentimentality in O'Connor's day was already beginning to concentrate upon such dialect as Harris's to further social restructurings that appear increasingly indifferent to the realities of persons as particular intellectual souls incarnate. There is lively interest in surface differences, reflected by differentiated dialects, which for the common good must of course be dissolved. Those surface differences undeniably bear sociological aspect. Certainly, however, such a writer as O'Connor could not believe her provincial, arrested characters representative of the heroic nor of the "intellectual." And how can she speaks of her Haze Motes, not as an arrested "Georgia Cracker," but as a "saint?" She might as well associate herself with such unrevised concepts as *good* and *evil*.

8

Miss Flannery in Cahoots
with the Devil

"In my stories a reader will find that the devil accomplishes a good deal of groundwork that seems to be necessary before grace can be effective. Tarwater's final vision [in The Violent Bear It Away] *could not have been brought off if he hadn't met the man in the lavender and cream-colored car. This is another mystery."*

— Flannery O'Connor, Letter to Winifred
McCarthy, in *Mystery and Manners*

Fallenness is a condition to our very existence as person, as intellectual soul incarnate. It is this reality of our given nature as a spiritual inheritance, as handicap to the will through Original Sin, which requires a personal, local, immediate engagement of my "self" at risk through my free will. Fallenness cannot be addressed as if it were an abstract philosophical or theological "universal," if by that address we allow ourselves the illusional comfort of the universal as understood by a reason denying the Ultimate Good. Encouragingly remote from me at this place at this moment, "I" (as *this* person) am detached from the world's impinging upon consciousness through my body, removed from it by skeptical speculative reason. Since this is a very deeply personal complication to my nature as *this* person, and because by an abstraction reality may be made seemingly removed from my responsibility to the limits of my "self," this mystery of evil — of the devil's direct participation in my consequential actions of will through my fallen nature — seems hardly actual to me in the moment itself. For I alone am master of my fate through autonomous intellect. Such the tempting presumption.

What becomes necessary to spiritual survival in that moment (as St. John of the Cross speaks of it mystically) is a necessary prevention, a *coming before* of grace to my consent turning me fervent for rescue. That is a mystery abiding, though in the desperate moment it may be mistaken as indifference. What faith and hope may discover is that steady attendance to the pilgrim in his abiding expectation of Love itself. How difficult to reason: Love's unwavering answer to our hope may appear in such a moment an indifference, prompting a demand for instant rescue or damnation in relief from spiritual crisis at O'Connor's "crossroads" at which time and place anticipate fitfully an eternity. The fear of Love's indifference may even tempt reason to declare God's an unwavering determinism, an election to rescue or damnation in Jansenist or Puritan certainties about grace. Spiritual rescue, as St.

169

Augustine or St. Thomas or mystics like St. John of the Cross witness to us, require a painful labor of the intellectual soul, most often a tedious patience in an intellectual labor to remove obstacles to preeminent grace already operative and sustaining of our free will. In that testing moment which St. John of the Cross calls "a dark night of the soul," the dark verge, the margin of the way (felt-balance lost in despair) draws the intellectual soul to the abyss. There comes temptation to rest in the shadow of that old dragon unrecognized as a presence in false green pastures along the way.

In retrospect, St. John might well see such a moment as one from which the intellectual soul emerges through grace as "ex-suicide." That is a point out of arrested spiritual action, one which Walker Percy, more playful as *homo viator* than St. John of the Cross, remembers of himself as an "ex-suicide." O'Connor, however, in a broader perspective will see it a moment shadowed by that old dragon, from which the soul may escape into the terrors of Mercy through a single-minded violence for the truth such as she dramatizes in her Haze Motes. Percy, unlike O'Connor, is reluctant to concede the Devil's participation as an active presence in that dark moment of spiritual danger, for O'Connor always lying "by the side of the road" we travel toward the "father of souls," as St. Cyril of Jerusalem puts it in that epigraph she chose for her collection *A Good Man Is Hard to Find,* stories about "Original Sin" she says.

It is in O'Connor's engagement of the mystery of evil actively encouraged in her agents under the auspices of the Devil as actual that her stories diverge from Walker Percy's, though they share an opposition to the Modernist reductions of evil to the merely psychological or pathological. How subtle, her echoing of Freud in that confused prophet gone wrong as she calls him, her Misfit. Standing over the grandmother lying in the ditch, just before shooting her, he reminisces about his own history, which is not unlike that of Mr. Shiftlet in the variety of their "callings" attempted along the way. He has been a gospel singer, a soldier, sailor, undertaker, farmer, railroad worker. He is *homo viator*, finding himself at last in a penitentiary, examined by a psychiatrist who judges from his symptoms that he suffers from an "Oedipus complex." Thus explained, his destructive violence is explained away as an unnatural sexual fascination by envy. "It was a head-doctor at the penitentiary said what I had done was kill my daddy but I knowed that for a lie." As he has said, "god never made a finer woman than my mother and my daddy's heart was pure gold." Besides which he knows that his "daddy died in nineteen ought nineteen of the epidemic flu and I never had a thing to do with it."

Shocking to Modernist sensibilities, then, that Flannery (in her letters especially) is so steadily insistent not only in her sympathy for her characters — even the Misfit — but insistent as well that many of them in their spiritual sufferings are even heroic in a single-minded pursuit of the truth of things, though truth confused for them by intellectually and spiritually suffocating under the Modernist doctrines whereby they deny Evil's existence. The Misfit is perhaps destined to become "the prophet he was meant to become," she suggests. And Haze Motes emerges, in her estimate, as a "saint." Even the more simplistic O. E. Parker may be discovered, beneath the elementary spectacles of his pseudo-New Age pursuit of viable icons, to be in quest of spiritual rescue, with a flickering hope for him at last. As seen by his literalist wife, out of her own simplistic Manichaeanism with its fundamentalist rigidity, Obadiah Elihue wrestles with a dark angel she knows only as a name. Through the window pane she sees him "leaning against a tree, crying like a baby" at his spiritual nadir which (from O'Connor's own perspective as distinct from ours) is his dark night of the soul, from which he *may* emerge through his unrepentant and so steady hope to "see God."

O. E. a *hero* in quest of *sainthood*? How strange. But how much stranger that O'Connor should speak hopefully of her Misfit, even siding with him in his arguments, though not subscribing therefore to his actions at the level of spectacle — his murdering naïve but not innocent victims in the story. The Misfit, she would counter, has a concern to discover a Good Man, though his seems at best an intuitive concern whose effects as spectacle are murderous acts. He is ill-equipped to articulate that concern, able only to say that "Jesus thown everything off balance." Her characters, we discover, tend to seek the "felt balance" she speaks of as necessary to herself but in a circumstantial world widely dominated by Modernist doctrines of the nature of man. The Misfit muses of Jesus that "It was the same case with Him as with me except He hadn't committed any crime and they could prove I had committed one because they had the papers on me," though they never let him see those papers. The Misfit's engagement of his spiritual state bears little sociological jargon such as the grandmother is inclined to affirm to save her life, though she quickly abandons them as upsetting to the Misfit. There is no philosophical presence in him save at the level of a struggling common sense in his recognizing the reality of an evil denied by his "head doctor."

How confusing as well: Old Tarwater in *The Violent Bear It Away*, who speaks for O'Connor's own position in matters spiritual, as she insists, in a "country" language leavened by King James English. And how difficult for us to celebrate, as does she, Haze Motes's heroic intensity in his pursuit of the truth of things in the unpromising circumstances he engages on the streets of Taulkinham. With such ill-prepared intellectual gifts as Haze's (as they are seen by "civil" authority) he is decidedly a threat to the social order. Must we not conclude, then, that if O'Connor calls him a saint that assertion suggests her of the devil's party — as she herself suspects those Beat poets may prove to be no less than are some of the Cornbelt Metaphysicals she knows? Of the devil's party? That was the charge against her by a contemporary, John Hawkes, who writes on the question for the *Sewanee Review*, publicly suggesting her more on the Devil's side than on God's, more nihilist than hillbilly Thomist. But in the exchange of letters with Hawkes on the "Devil," Flannery makes insistent distinction between the reality of the Devil and any subscription of devotion to him or to his machinations. That Evil exists, which to deny disarms the intellectual soul of defense against proximate evils.

Her concern with the "Devil" is far more than a metaphorical strategy to her fiction. Hawkes to the contrary would rather limit the Devil to the merely symbolic, an appropriation to the convenience of art out of cultural tradition — a myth allowing an ordering of art perhaps. Surely she cannot *believe* him actual to her appropriation. Her fiction grounded in the *actual* existence of the Devil! But Flannery emphatically subscribes to that actuality as a presence in our world. She does so, sometimes to the embarrassment of even some of those within her own Church. In November of 1961, soon after the publication of *The Violent Bear It Away*, she responds to Hawkes, defending the fictional Devil present in the work as having origin in the Devil as actual. "My Devil has a name, a history and a definite plan. His name is Lucifer, he's a fallen angel, his sin is pride, and his aim is the destruction of the Divine plan. Now I judge that your Devil is co-equal to God, not his creature; that pride is his virtue, not his sin; and that his aim is not to destroy the Divine plan because there isn't any Divine plan to destroy. My Devil is objective and yours is subjective. You say one becomes 'evil' when one leaves the herd. I say that depends entirely on what the herd is doing." Implied in her words: it is Hawkes himself who, unsuspectingly, is of the Devil's party, seduced by a pseudo-metaphysics of the "self."

Flannery's Devil believes in, worships, Nothingness, though he knows God's actual existence and God's plan. His principle of action is an active rejection of the Good. It is an intellectual circumstance (since he is an "angelic" intellect) to his action of rejection, as it is spoken to by the Bible salesman as his surrogate. Flannery's Satan assumes the stance of her Bible salesman who was "born" believing in nothing. But that is an unconvincing faith, given that Satan, created the highest intellectual creature, knows God and God's plan with immediacy. Of course, belief and knowledge are not the same. As for the Bible salesman as surrogate to the Devil as actual for O'Connor: The tendency in criticism (after the rise of psychology as a "science") has been to treat any belief in the Devil's actual existence as evidence of some psychological miswiring, traceable to a disordered body most likely, and perhaps even to be located at a place. It is in the nerve-endings and their connections in the physical brain. New mystery replaces the old: Neural synapses — an unmeasured vacuum, a Nothingness as philosophically centered in the brain — across which vacuum "thought" is fired into existence by the small electrical artillery of the nerves. But the "firing" goes untargeted on such evidence, evidence of the accidental nature of both nerves and thought taken as random effect of random accident, evidence of the accidental nature of both nerves and thought — random effect of random accident.

A belief in Satan as actual is quite other. From O'Connor's perspective, one might believe the Devil actual and not thereby deny such "science" as that speculatively made about the biophysical realities of the brain as themselves real. What is to be denied is that such science can account fully for the mystery of thought as but random accident. That organ is a part of the "reality" of our nature as incarnate. It is a small stage upon which (and within which) mysterious actions may occur, neuron to neuron. But that is action at the level of spectacle, as measured impulse on science's limited instruments. That is, science validly measures the spectacle of things — not their essence — with its sophisticated instruments. Such measure is acceptable to metaphysics, though with a philosophical caveat which Positivistic science is reluctant to engage. Science speaks with a limited authority to the *how* of things, but it violates its own limits by presumptions of *why*. In this perspective the Thomist might raise warnings out of St. Thomas. For the Devil's most ancient and effective strategy against the essentially good requires Satan's assuming an active presence and participation in creation, clothed in seeming actualities of creation, often cleverly clothed as spectacle. He adapts spectacle, appropriating it to his intentional reductionism of reality toward nothingness. (How persuasively effective in deception —*possible* deception — of the intellectual soul as dramatized by Dostoevsky in that encounter in Ivan Karamazov of the Devil as a bitter Russian middleclass gentleman.) Perhaps even neural synapses of the brain may prove to be within the organ itself— the brain —a specific crossroads in which meet recognitions of time and place as intersected by eternity. That seems revealed in Ivan, leading to his spiritual collapse, the "local" battleground of Ivan's self-awareness invaded by evil.

This is a crossroads at which *homo viator* as intellectual creature again and again engages that endangering presence spoken of by St. Cyril of Jerusalem, the old dragon, cunningly disguised by spectacle. It is at this crossroads that as writer O'Connor must achieve her own balance, but not one simply "reflecting … the world around" her. The balance possible is within her own "personal" fallen world, as it is for each of us in her view, but in the circumstances to her considerable gift as so radically besieged by that latest religion imping-ing so insistently upon her — the Modernist distortions of good and evil. In that tensional circumstance, here and now, she must stand firm in "a felt balance inside" herself that does not deny the Dragon by our way. And so affirming good, she will insist as well on the ac-tuality of evil. With balanced assurance, the accommodation of the intuitive and rational intellect, as intellectual soul she sojourns the larger contingent world, not limited to the "sides" of her "skull" as is that "intellectual" provincial who would deny both good and evil through the strategy of declaring both concepts "relative" as truth — at most psychological myths as actualities. Those concepts are too generally explained by a shifting relativism as products of whim, residual in consciousness and traceable by the latest sciences as illusions out of biological accidents exacerbated by cultural and natural contingencies.

How relieved we might be from such provincialism as O'Connor's — her assertion of Satan as actual — by summoning a Positivistic science devoted to the *how* as if the *why*. We may take Ivan Karamazov's devil then as but a product of his own nervous disorder. Here we speak of that small devil visiting Ivan just before his "nervous breakdown," not that more popularly "mythical" Grand Inquisitor of that poem with which Ivan so proudly assaults his brother Alyosha. This small devil appears to Ivan in the guise of a bourgeoisie, middle-class "Russian gentleman" with ambitions to a cultural respectability. His ambition is to be accepted as welcomed citizen in the bourgeoisie world. Dostoevsky as artist makes that presence to Ivan difficult as he can to dismiss on simplistic "psychological" grounds. He makes it a persuasive presence to Ivan by concrete spectacle, though as spectacle it is am-biguously perceived by Ivan. How knowledgeable this devil of the realities of the social sta-tion he assumes. And he is so persuasive as a reality that Ivan wrecks his room trying to drive him out as if a physical presence, as if an incarnate *person*. We as intellectual provin-cials may be content to take this little devil as a psychological aberration in Ivan's raddled brain, clothed with images out of Ivan's memory rather than as a spiritual aberration made manifest as a mirror reflecting Ivan's own spiritual state. But Dostoevsky sees him quite differently. Ivan reports his devil actual to his brother Alyosha, and Alyosha does not deny that reality. But in Alyosha's recovering presence Ivan is at last forced to name this presence as the devil in a frenzy as if himself self-victim of a possession by the diabolic, a symptom not lost to Alyosha.

In the implications of Dostoevsky's dramatic strategy, Ivan's very ordinary devil proves kindred spirit to Ivan, Ivan as pretentious intellectual finding himself uncomfortably at large in the provincial small Russian town in which the Karamazovs are prominent and be-come notorious. As a presence, that little Russian gentleman seems to have been precipi-tated out of what Ivan has made of himself by a willful diminution of his intellectual gifts. If Ivan's gifts are more considerable than those we meet in a kindred dramatic presence, Ray-ber of O'Connor's *The Violent Bear It Away,* both figures as surrogate persons prove sufficiently rich as intellectual subjects to a presence of the devil, even to possession in the formal sense. For both Dostoevsky and O'Connor believe the Devil actual, in a relation bor-rowed to Ivan or Rayber as surrogate persons. What these two poets share, then, is a belief in the devil as an actual agent pursuing the diminution of the good of creation itself, hav-ing failed in that old frontal assault on God implied in Dante's *Divine Comedy* and explored in Milton's *Paradise Lost.* Dostoevsky and O'Connor — as do Dante and Milton — under-stand the mystery whereby God brings good out of evil, though none of them declares an intellectual comprehension of that mystery. In this perspective, indeed, the devil might be said (as O'Connor affirms in respect to her own fictions) to accomplish through her textural making "a good deal of groundwork that seems to be necessary before grace can be effective" in her made things as reflective of spiritual reality. For her, both grace and evil are realities inescapably affecting art. In the context of these words, O'Connor makes her point: "Tarwater's final vision could not have been brought off if he hadn't met the man in the lavender and cream-colored car," a fictional manifestation of that devil she believes actual.

For both these poets then, Dostoevsky and O'Connor, the devil is an active and continuous agent in the world, intent upon eroding the good of creation, which creation by the very existence of things in it (including persons) is good insofar as each thing *is*. The diminution possible is a falling away, a lessening of the "is," an erosion of existential good toward nothingness. And the Devil's principle ally to this destruction is the consenting willfulness of the person himself. That consent is the most formidable barrier against grace, since by willfulness the person lessons his natural love of the good. Under the Devil's illusion of absolute freedom, tempting will to its sense of an absolute autonomy, the person as *homo viator* proves self-victim through free will. The person on his way is thus turned from the way to that path leading to the abyss of Nothingness, shadowed all that way by the Dragon. Alas, that is the Devil's only possible revenge against God, a spiteful diminution of the good of this small creature created in God's image, the person. But that is a revenge made possible only through man's free will.

It is the spiritual endangerment of the discrete soul that is the centering concern in both Dostoevsky's later fiction (following *Notes from Underground*) and of all of O'Connor's fictions. As poet, then, O'Connor does not take it that the Devil's participation in preparing her fictional ground for the drama of action in her surrogate persons — her characters — is merely the Devil as an imagined fancy suited to the convenience of art as a fictional device. Nor does she believe the Devil as operative in the world can be explained away by an alternate "fancy" proposed by rationalistic science when the *hows* of reality are declared the *whys,* thus supporting Jungian "collective unconscious" as a residue of nature as accident. In respect to the lingering and increasingly ambiguous "knowledge" of the devil, residual in the popular spirit, she does not conclude it only a pathological illusion or a residual cultural folk "myth" as a lingering echo of the "psychic" evolution of man himself. That is a *how* argued as if a *why*, derived from the reductionist principle that man is himself only an accident of the accidental cosmos. For in this Modernist reading of "evil," the devil can only be accounted for on such a principle as a vague shadow of history cast interspace between hapless neurons.

How then that our neurons continue haunted beyond the genetic history of evolution by that mystery called *evil?* That is the question O'Connor raises against the false light of rationalism that would dispel such shadows as if thereby correcting mistakes of accidental nature through the authority of gnosis. It would do so through a Positivism whose operative process has increasingly commanded the popular spirit through a positive law divorced from natural law. (For O'Connor as for Percy, the evidence of this divorce is evident in the increasing popularity of abortion and euthanasia as false "gospel" of Nothingness as god.) So Tarwater hears Rayber argue unrelentingly this doctrine of Nothingness as the only reality, and taking a devilish delight in chiding Rayber as unable to act on that doctrine. If but a shadow on the accidental cosmos, the devil can only be sufficiently accounted for as a contamination of that pure inter-neuron vacuum, which is itself a *nothingness* to be filled by the autonomous will's intentionalities to correcting the "nature" of man. The mechanistic measures of *how* promise an absolute determinism by the will as empowered over being itself, whereby some gnostic director of being becomes the only *why*. But most destructively, it is the being of *homo viator* that is to be recreated. The person as intellectual soul incarnate is thus tempted to intend his own nothingness as a self, hoodwinked by pride.

If indeed this is accurate characterization of the Modernist "vision" of existence, says the Thomistic metaphysician, then what a clever strategy of the Devil in having gained so general a consent by the intellectual community to this "vision" of man as only the latest accident of cumulative accidents! Thus evil may be denied on the authority of Positivistic renderings of the person as but mechanism. On the point, see once more the dialectical cat-and-mouse game played between Ivan and his visitor, that little Russian gentleman who deploys Ivan's own rationalistic arguments against him to the point of Ivan's collapse. Yet, is Ivan's devil then but his own hallucination? That visitor engages him in fierce Platonic dialogue, in a voice increasingly difficult for Ivan to distinguish from his own. Is that devil but a symptom of physiological malady, a "break-down" of Ivan's mechanistic limits, his neurons misfiring? Is thought itself but illusion upon which Ivan builds an ultimate illusion — himself? That is a solipsism rescued only by symptomatic despair as evidencing to a person his having lost the way and the truth and the life. From Dostoevsky's (and brother Alyosha's) perspective, Ivan's devil is more than a shadow, though perceived in spectacle as a reflection, a shadow upon which a true light casts Ivan's own self-diminution as a shadow by the light of grace. This "ordinary" devil as more than shadow reveals Ivan's consensual perversion of love into presumptuous self-love by his rejection of the true light, a rejection of Love with all its terrors.

O'Connor, in her "Introduction" to that *Memoir of Mary Ann,* remarks Ivan's attempt at revenge against God for what God has allowed to happen to children over the long history of man as *homo viator*. From that perspective Ivan is thus in an awkward position in his rationalistic circumstances of denial, for he also seeks revenge against a God he must deny as existing, under the intellectual influence of Western philosophy since Descartes which has so affected Ivan. How difficult to him to admit his rational actions as themselves dependent upon a faith in the absoluteness of Nothingness, as he has already played out that intellectual shell-game with hidden truth by both a relentless logic and in delight disguising his recognition of pending spiritual collapse conjured by unacceptable premise. And surely as she writes tersely about Ivan in his frustrated dead-end as a rational creature, O'Connor has in mind her own surrogate person in like circumstances self-conjured, Haze Motes of *Wise Blood,* who deports himself intellectually very much as Ivan. Haze's intellectual dilemma is the same, then, as it must be the same for any Modernist seeking a rational power over being by the absoluteness of his rational autonomy. Haze's frustration, too, rises to a frenzy in him as he is forced to recognize that the "blasphemy" he would commit as a denial of Love, of Mercy, is a denial which has no object against which he may blaspheme. If God does not exist, then blasphemy, like Haze's truth, does not exist. Nor does Haze need Ivan's more considerable intellectual preparation in Western philosophy, formally acquired, to isolate himself as person in the Province of Nothingness.

This is the theme revisited by O'Connor in *The Violent Bear It Away* through her surrogate person Rayber, the evangelical Modernist she pits against Old Tarwater. In this respect, Rayber seems to presume himself to be as accomplished an "intellectual" as Dostoevsky makes Ivan. Rayber's self-victimization is dramatically deployed in the novel through his unreasonable address to what he takes as the "accidental" disease in his natural, i.e., in his mechanistic nature. He experiences waves of intuitive love for things as particular to his experience of them through his senses, even of sticks or awkward starlings. How may his reason account for such responses to insignificant things in themselves? He cannot recognize them as *signifying*, as signs to his spiritual nature. And so his reason must insist that intuitive love is but symptomatic evidence of an encroaching madness, out of himself as but a mechanism not yet under the self-healing command of Positivistic "scientific" correction by process through science's *how*.

Rayber concludes that he suffers an inherited condition in his mechanistic nature. His is a defect, making him genetic victim, a "mistake of nature" not yet corrected by his science (short of euthanasia). For love, he contends, because unaccounted for in biochemical rationalizations by terms of evolutionary history, can only be a shadowy evidence of himself as a malfunctioning machine — suffering gear-slippage as it were. That necessary conclusion by his "logic" in its service to Positivistic principles redounds upon Rayber as person. He has advocated, as the most certain and necessary power over nature, his own reasoned actions in voiding all mistakes of nature, euthanasia being the "kindest" service of science to that conspicuous mistake of nature, the idiot child Bishop. How else act for the good of his idiot nephew, his "legal" responsibility? To put Bishop "down" as our euphemism goes, would be a charitable act under the rubrics of Modernistic Positivism. But what meaning can there be for *charitable*? By Rayber's logic, such would be an act of a relativistic "good" to Bishop, to the general good of the cosmos as machine, manifest as a good to the convenience of that more proximate inclusive machinery, civil society. In denying that such an act is inspired by the Devil, as charged by Old Tarwater, Rayber denies the existence of the Devil. For if there is no God, then there can certainly be no devil, a conclusion in which lies implicit but unrecognized by Rayber a granting of a Thomistic argument. (That is, Rayber does not recognize the awkwardness whereby the devil *is* before he can be said *not* to be, a conundrum which St. Thomas engages in quest of the names of God as problematic in our signs' relation to reality.) Rayber's is an argument he is forced to face in its implications, not by Thomistic caveats brought against his intellectual formulations, but by the direct and simple actions of young Tarwater. Tarwater drowns Bishop, to which Rayber's response is his own collapse, not engaged at length in the dramatic action of the novel but sufficiently engaged to suggest Rayber's kinship in Ivan's collapse. By his own action young Tarwater forces the logical issue of Rayber's argument against love.

If Rayber should engage that issue in his own defense through his specious logic, he might be imagined as doing so as if through a subjunctive entertainment of the *possible*. He might put it in terms of *as if*, a favorite rhetorical strategy of O'Connor's in presenting her own implicit belief in truths actual that are rejected positivistically and not subjunctively by Modernist doctrines, made more acceptable to the Modernist reader in signs of *as if*. The *subjunctive* as mode, we might suggest, implies some degree of intellectual humility. Thus, if there *were* a God as Ultimate Good, then there *might be* a Devil as agent of an adverse evil erosive of the good of things. But by that admission might be required the logical antecedent reality of good by reason's logic in attending the *possible* existence of evil itself, of nonbeing as dependent upon being. Such a *cul de sac* to logic. Our final participation with that admirable logician Ivan in his own reckonings about this intellectual conundrum sheds a light on Rayber's refusal of Love which he translates intellectually as a "positive" madness. Of course Tarwater's refutation of Rayber is in respect to spectacle but not to spectacle's own dependence upon essence. Tarwater acts, and with spectacle more violent than Alyosha's response to Ivan. That is, Tarwater drowns Bishop. Contrast Alyosha's response to Ivan after Ivan's clever enactment of his "Grand Inquisitor," in which Ivan's is a full consent to — he for the moment possessed by — the Inquisitor's logic. Alyosha responds to Ivan's enacted poem as if he were the poem's Christ standing actual before the Inquisitor Ivan. Without a word, as Christ in the poem speaks no word, Alyosha kisses Ivan on the cheek as Ivan has his Christ kiss the Inquisitor. It is an act which Ivan at this moment of his journey supposes the only "self" defense of Christ, though Alyosha sees it an act made through grace, an act of love. Such is Dostoevsky's foreshadowing of the inevitable collapse of Ivan from his participating in a diabolic deportment of logic in making his famous "poem" as he calls it. (Ivan charges Alyosha triumphantly with plagiarism.)

There is also a considerable foreshadowing of the diabolic as participated in by Tarwater, up to his violent drowning of Bishop, in which act of murder he speaks concurrent words of Baptism of the hapless child. A paradoxical action rather surely intended by O'-Connor to suggest Bishop's ultimate rescue. For even as an evil priest may perform valid sacraments — in a principle of doctrine in refutation of a famous ancient heresy in the Church — Tarwater fulfills his responsibility to Old Tarwater, who has charged him from the beginning to baptize Bishop. The boy does so as he concurrently murders the hapless child. Ivan Karamazov later, at his dark night of the soul, is frantically insistent to Alyosha that he has just encountered the Devil as actual, palpable as a Russian gentleman, his arguments at first more to himself as rationalist than to Alyosha. For Ivan is experiencing a shocked awakening from self-induced intellectual illusion. He presently comes to confess himself surrogate to the Devil, for as he says to Alyosha, "He is — myself." Having made this confession, Ivan collapses in a scene we may take as Dostoevsky's figurative rendering of St. John's dark night of the soul. Dostoevsky, like O'Connor, certainly believes in the Devil as actual, however much that may embarrass some admirers of his fiction. For "in this day and age" as we say, how uncomfortable and confusing to us, such antiquated beliefs, even if granted only by *as if.*

The Devil, O'Connor insists, is an actual existence, a declaration even more embarrassing to us, given that she takes her position a hundred years after Dostoevsky in the history of our progress. For surely in that interval, there has been a progress in science and philosophy, and even in theology, sufficient to make her insistence patently absurd. And so John Hawkes suggests, in part because of her insistence, that she must be of the Devil's party — if there is a party. *As if* there were such a creature as the Devil! Flannery O'Connor in response might well suggest that to use the Devil as but a fictional device though believed unreal may prove very dangerous. For to take the Devil's name in vain presumption might prove a conjuring act with perhaps unfortunate consequences. At the time O'Connor and Hawkes are debating the Devil's existence, the TV comic Flip Wilson is making that phrase "the Devil made me do it" popular as excuse in his "personal" skits. But is the laughter elicited simply in recognition of the phrase's absurdity as an excuse, made perhaps before a judge rendering the positive law, since as everyone knows — there is no such creature as the Devil?

The O'Connor-Hawkes exchange occurs at a point in our recent history at which it has also become a popular gambit for entertainment to play at the occult. Such games were especially appealing to the naïve young, who were increasingly hard-pressed to find ways to offend those they supposed but staid "Establishment" parents, seen as holding residual moral Puritanism as a measure of their young more than of themselves. But in such gamesmanship, in which both good and evil are increasingly set aside by parents and their young alike, is there a dangerous conjuring underway in a mutual naiveté akin to that of Hawthorne's Young Goodman Brown. How destroyed is Goodman Brown to discover his "good towns-folk" worshipping the Devil as believed real in that dark woodland mass, the town become a ghost town. (For a context to these questions raised, see Fr. Gabriele Amorth's *An Exorcist Tells His Story.*)

From her position, and in response to Hawkes, O'Connor suggests that such logic implies that to insist on the reality of evil is not to endorse evil itself, only to recognize it a reality, the contrary of the faulty argument by Hawkes. The counter: does denying the Devil and evil by that denial make them not exist? That has been the attempt in that interval since Dostoevsky, especially as seemingly encouraged by Nietzsche. How interesting to this concern, then, that Nietzsche should have been so fascinated by Raskolnikov of *Crime and Punishment*! Flannery O'Connor will have nothing to do with such argument, though Hawkes draws her into refutations of his own position.[1] In the context of our own more recent perspective upon the exchange between Hawkes and O'Connor, we have enlisted Dostoevsky for correspondences. By naturalistic "objective correlatives," Dostoevsky presents his little Russian gentleman as a devastating presence to Ivan — a strategy with parallel in O'Connor's. She has thought long and hard on this mystery of evil and of how to engage it steadily in her fiction as both real and to be opposed. She brings that concern to a focus in *The Violent Bear It Away,* we have indicated, a focus in which she carefully dramatizes young Tarwater's encounter with the Devil, recognized by Tarwater certainly as actual, though only in retrospect as he lies sobbing on Old Tarwater's shallow grave. It is from that point that Tarwater slowly begins to emerge from his own dark night of his soul, made imagistically incarnate as a natural nighttime experience on his actual journey to the city where God's children are asleep. As for Tarwater's deciding encounter with the Devil, it has been dramatically prepared, beginning with Old Tarwater's death and exploding at young Tarwater's "crossroads" just after he has at once drowned and baptized Bishop.

Fleeing that event, he does not yet understand what he flees from nor to what. He is first picked up on the road by an "auto-transit" driver, who after attempting to talk with Tarwater exclaims in frustration, "I won't see nobody sane again until I get back to Detroit," away from such Christ-haunted "Southerners" as this hitchhiker. The truck driver's language seems that of a displaced "Southerner," one we suspect now resident in Detroit but not native there. His actions and gestures on this encounter with Tarwater prove background to Tarwater's re-enacting, in a dazed half-sleep, the murder he has just committed. The boy's mumbled words are out of a physical exhaustion whose cause is spiritual, a combination disturbingly baffling to his truck-driver host. (One might compare to this encounter that earlier scene in O'Connor's fiction which concludes Shiftlet's encounter with the boy hitchhiker who is about Tarwater's age.) It is this confused reenactment of the murder as it occurs within the confines of Tarwater's skull that proves prelude to his actual encounter with the Devil in the flesh as it were. But we may already hear somewhat the Devil's own voice as present in Tarwater's mumblings, mingling with Tarwater's own voice — to the confused exasperation of the truck driver. There has gradually occurred a subtle seduction of Tarwater in his reactions to Rayber, tending toward that external spectacle of encounter of that slick "pervert" in the lavender car. But the preliminary and most decisive seduction lies in Tarwater's justifying his violent act, his drowning of Bishop.

In Tarwater's disoriented state, riding with truck driver, it is as if the murder were still a contingent act not already accomplished. It is as if Tarwater's intellectual act were suspended between the murder and baptism as spectacle. That is, Tarwater suspends the already accomplished murder in his wills in conflict. The Devil encourages Tarwater, at that crossroads within Tarwater's consciousness, to an ex *post facto* self-absolution by reason's persuasive justification of his having drowned Bishop — reasons Tarwater echoes in his own defense out of Rayber's teaching. Rayber could *say* the action but could not *do* it, as Tarwater has said earlier in rebuffing Rayber as a hypocrite to his own nihilistic beliefs. In Tarwater, then, there is an evil presence represented as if merely a psychological after-effect of his violent action. So Rayber might explain it. But O'Connor sees it as quite other. She writes Cecil Dawkins (January 26, 1962) concerning Hawkes, who "has a theory that my fictional voice is the voice of the Devil — a good insight as far as this last story ["The Lame Shall Enter First"] is concerned." It is on such evidence, she continues, that Hawkes would put her in the Devil's party, when her concern is rather to recover to us the actuality of both the Devil and of evil in us (sin) as his operative mode toward the diminution of our good, effected against both our potentiality and present actuality as an intellectual soul. Evil is actual, then, and as actual it is a part of art's matter. In her view as a realist of distances, both the Devil and evil have been too long denied as real by a variety of Modernist ideologies.

For O'Connor, more than psychological pathology is afoot in her stories. It is Tarwater's spiritual exhaustion, not his psychological disorder, which has made him susceptible to the Devil's strategy of seduction through his body, violated by that Devil in the flesh driving that lavender and cream-colored "sporty" car. And so she makes the point once more emphatic for the almost blind and deaf in their decayed Modernist sensibilities, even so sophisticated a reader as Hawkes. In that chilling story "The Lame Shall Enter First," we have a Tarwater beyond rescue, an adolescent Iago satanically possessed, whose chief victim is the Rayber-like character Shepherd, Modernist guardian of the child Norton. Shepherd is a sentimentalist holding that the good is a matter of conditioning by scientific and sociological methods to adjustment. Perhaps even that active presence of Satan as an adolescent is to be rescued by Shepherd's good intentions. How diabolically proficient the street-child Rufus Jackson, leading to that final "space travel" of poor Norton, a joint enterprise with Shepherd. Shepherd at that final point of encounter, realizing his unjustness to Norton, would too late be both "mother and father" to Norton. He jumps up from his meditation about Rufus and Norton, rushing upstairs to kiss Norton "and tell him that he loved him." The actual tripod in the story, with its telescope, has become a sign much larger than object, as Hulga's wooden leg becomes. In the boy's room, then, first Shepherd sees the "tripod ... fallen and the telescope ... on the floor." But then he sees a "few feet over it" Norton's hanged body. The "child hung in the jungle of shadows, just below the beam from which he had launched his flight into space" under the diabolic tutelage of Rufus, and the spiritual ignorance of Shepherd as joint "directors" of Norton's "space travel."

She had written Hawkes himself earlier (November 1961) about Rufus Johnson of "The Lame Shall Enter First." Rufus is "one of Tarwater's terrible cousins," who as an agreeable surrogate of the Devil in that story has reached a dead end, unlike Tarwater's quickening at last toward a spiritual life. Now if that man in the lavender and cream-colored car seems but a random encounter by Tarwater as it may at first seem to him, in respect to his spiritual journey up to this point of turning it is rather an encounter in the flesh of what is present to him all along, first indicated in that old "friend" with whom Tarwater is already well acquainted and whom he has unwittingly conjured. Tarwater's friendship with this visitor into his consciousness in the opening chapter foreshadows this late encounter. How susceptible in his nature Tarwater proves at the beginning. Flattered in hearing his great uncle's plans for him as prophet, Tarwater has imagined for himself high heroic actions ahead. The old man shouts sermons at him in their desert country, removed from Rayber's city at least as far as Andalusia from Milledgeville. Tarwater hears himself charged from the very beginning of his journey to "Go warn the children of God ... of the terrible speed of justice," lest none be left to benefit when "the Lord's mercy strikes." But Tarwater's specific charge as prophet is that he baptize Bishop. What a piddling charge. Tarwater rejects it, since God has in mind for him more than "to finish up your leavings" as he tells the old man. Suddenly, in the midst of this argument, the old man across from him at the breakfast table dies before Tarwater's eyes, in a grotesque formidable presence to Tarwater. The old man, slumped over dead, is a mountain of a body suddenly become Tarwater's responsibility to bury. That the old man chooses this moment to die Tarwater sees as evidencing betrayal, an abandonment. Still, he is obligated to "plant" the old man, and he undertakes to dig a grave. But he soon abandons that unheroic labor, going off to the old man's still and getting drunk on moonshine.

It is in his reaction to the old man's death and to the burden of that charge upon him as prophet to first dig a grave that Tarwater gradually becomes aware of a friendly presence. A voice begins to speak to him, in Tarwater's own speaking voice as he recognizes. But then it begins to sound "like a stranger's voice." As he responds to this new, strange voice, he becomes aware that now he is freed of both his Great Uncle Tarwater and of his Uncle Rayber (from whom he has been kidnapped by the old man.) This stranger speaks at times as if an obsequious friend, but at other moments with the insistent authority of the old man himself— always through Tarwater's own voice in this strange experience. Through words there develops a dialectical argument, wills in conflict. Young Tarwater, very like Ivan in his encounter with his own "strange" visitor, attempts to maintain an independence from that strange presence, but he is affected by that stranger's arguments. Tarwater is resolute about "mindin" his own "bidniz," but he is nevertheless affected in this dialectical engagement over the nature of free will as specific to him in relation to both Rayber and to Old Tarwater. That is a dialectical theme running through the novel, prompting the boy to insist repeatedly that his only responsibility is to mind his own "bidnez" as independent from all creation.

And so we are carefully prepared with the help of the stranger, the Devil thus helping prepare for us the ground for Tarwater's final vision. O'Connor summons us to that ground she sees necessary to her fiction, for it is in that ground that the Devil is a presence jealous of the good, salting the earth with his evil. O'Connor adapts this strategy out of her own belief in the actuality of that agent of evil who (she says) must be made to name himself as *this* particular presence in *these* immediate circumstances. She makes that presence almost palpable to Tarwater in the vibrations of his own voice, the stranger speaking in Tarwater in response to the boy's desperate circumstances but speaking with familiar words and tone. There is a growing awareness of that presence as actual to Tarwater, affecting the ordinary — the comfortably known —"environment" within which he attempts and then abandons his gravedigging to get drunk on moonshine.[2] As maker, O'Connor is very careful in her choice of "objective correlatives" to this reasoned making of Tarwater as a surrogate person. In him we are to recognize wills in conflict. Is he to submit to Rayber as the civil au t   h   o   r   i   t   i   e   s expect the Misfit to submit? After all, Rayber is legal guardian and has the papers on

Tarwater. Is he, if necessarily by subterfuge, to baptize Bishop under Rayber's very eyes? The old man was crazy, the stranger urges the drunken Tarwater, intending to prevent that mission. "Ain't you in all your fourteen years of supporting his foolishness fed up and sick to the roof of your mouth with Jesus? My Lord and Savior, the stranger sighed, I am if you ain't." And so Tarwater sees his alternatives clearly for the moment: It is "Jesus or the devil, the boy said." To which the considerate stranger responds like a Dutch Uncle, wryly concerned. "No no no, the stranger said, there ain't no such thing as a devil. I can tell you that from my own self-experience. I know that for a fact. It ain't Jesus or the devil. It's Jesus or *you*." (This "stranger" we have heard speak earlier in Haze Motes's words: Jesus is only "a trick on niggers.") Not that the devil cannot quote scripture. Indeed he must, so that he says at this early stage of Tarwater's journey as *homo viator* a truth: " ... as for Judgment Day, the stranger said, everyday is Judgment Day." What he would have Tarwater conclude, however, is that the boy himself is the only acceptable judge.

We discover Tarwater already intimately knowledgeable of the Devil as met in that friendly considerate stranger at novel's end. The final encounter is of the Devil not merely an inner voice but in the flesh. Not as a presence disguised by his own voice and cadence of words seductive of his will, but in the stranger who gives him that ride in the lavender and cream-colored convertible, that "pale, lean, old-looking young man with deep hollows under his cheekbones," wearing "a lavender shirt and a black suit and a panama hat," with "heavy black lashes." Tarwater has rejected the support of a "good country person," the truck-driver who kicks him out into the road. That truck-driver more or less speaks Tarwater's own language, we might notice, but without the undertow of evil we detect in the more sophisticated words of the stranger in the lavender car. Tarwater rejects the preferred companionship of the Detroit driver, inclining instead to that soothing interior voice now returned in his half-sleep, the voice first encountered at the unfinished grave of Old Tarwater. It is the voice of Evil he is to meet midway his journey as prophet, in the flesh and in a shocking way through his own flesh.

In letters written to Winifred McCarthy (in *Mystery and Manners*), O'Connor suggests that her reader "will find that the devil accomplishes a good deal of groundwork that seems to be necessary before grace is effective." Therefore "we need a sense of evil which sees the devil as a real spirit." Such concepts as *devil, grace, epiphany* do not serve her simply as fictional devices, residual as but myths out of historical cultural origin. They require of us as already a possible concession a suspension of disbelief in these concepts. But they at least name *possible* realities denied by our Modernist principles. For her, these are realities named, not fancy's "concepts" summoned to fictional convenience out of cultural detritus. She remarks to McCarthy that "Tarwater's final vision could not have been brought off [as a "fiction"] if he hadn't met the man in the lavender and cream-colored car." But that is "another mystery" (that of evil) not easily resolved by rational argument alone, though sometimes a mystery which may be convincingly deepened by art. Concerning Tarwater's final vision, opened to him by the violation of his person both physically and spiritually by that newly-met but very old stranger, the vision now opened makes it no longer possible to avoid that "silent country" he has recognized as stretching out "limitless and clear" in the depths of Bishop's trusting eyes. So threatening that country had been to him that Tarwater "never looked lower than the top of [Bishop's] head." Again and again Tarwater is brought to the border of that unnamed country, resisting it, saving "himself from crossing into it" only by the firmness of willful refusal, encouraged by that dark presence of the friendly stranger.

At the point of spiritual arrest with Bishop's death, having traveled from Old Tarwater slumped dead at the breakfast table, Tarwater turns back toward the actual place at
which he had failed to bury the old man, there discovering the grave finished by Buford,
the old black simple neighbor, who in his simplicity has set an awkward cross over it. In
contrition, at last prostrate on the grave, Tarwater is now much older than when he set out
as a boy of fourteen a few weeks before. Once more he experiences himself on the border
of that silent country which now begins to open within him. By its opening it "felt" like a
"crater." Now undeniably he recognizes "the clear grey spaces of that country where he had
vowed never to set foot." And so, lying on the grave, he begins to experience a new and
different hunger, though it is that most ancient hunger of all inside the person as person, a
hunger for citizenship in each person's gift by nature. Now there grows in Tarwater the heed-
less desire for a food to be found only in "that violent country where the silence is never
broken except to shout the truth." Tarwater begins a recovery of his citizenship in that country, which begins now to make him a stranger in that world Rayber declares the only world.
Tarwater's epiphany is his recognition of his calling as prophet, cast now quite differently
from his hearing that calling on Old Tarwater's lips in prophetic alarm over God's *justice*,
to be proclaimed to the children of God as the Old Man had charged him to proclaim it.
From this late point, in a new beginning (though it is yet to be recognized in its worldly
complications by Tarwater), he must henceforth find himself a stranger, an exile in this world,
but with a voice other than the Devil's that had mingled so intimately with his own. (Not
that he is therefore free of that voice as continuing temptation.) It is as a stranger in exile
from that silent country that he is now commanded to his calling: "GO WARN THE
CHILDERN OF GOD OF THE TERRIBLE SPEED OF MERCY." That is a warning Tarwater is to make out of an experience more profound than that pretended by the Devil as
friendly stranger at the outset, the stranger who had assured him that "there ain't no such
thing as a devil ... I know that for a fact. It ain't Jesus or the devil. It's Jesus or *you*."

    O'Connor will be more direct with the doubting John Hawkes: "I certainly do mean
Tarwater's friend to be the Devil" in the novel, she writes him. The violation of Tarwater
in the woods by the stranger is by an agent of Perverted Love, in both Dante's sense of that
epithet and in the more sexually explicit and concrete sense of violation that brings home
to Tarwater the nature of his own rejection of a Love he is called to advocate as violently
Merciful beyond Justice. That is a Love which is also called Mercy, the ultimate terror to a
self-surrender beyond self-love. "I couldn't have brought off the final vision without it"
O'Connor says (December 26, 1959) — without this perverse visitation upon young Tarwater. How "metaphysical" her strategy, if we remember Thomas's insistence that what we know
is truth gained through the senses, however much we may distort truths gained by our
senses' responses to the actualities of creation — or however terrible to us the recognition of
our willful attempt to violate Love by self-love. One of the things we come to know is the
actuality of evil as a subversion of love through our consent of will to our own violation.
Our sensual nature is properly a good accompanying our nature as incarnate, so that perverted love in the clinical sense of the pathology of worldly love effects Tarwater's recognition of his own perversion of spiritual love.

    It is his rejection of the real nature of love, then, that has brought Tarwater to the dark
night of both his senses and (with more terror accompanying it) his soul: his rejection of
God's love. The effect upon him is that he discovers on the very threshold of Hell his mission toward recovery, though there has not been that "neon" sign posted for him as it were

as for Dante: "Abandon hope, all ye who enter here." Tarwater turns from a crossing over into the country of Nothingness, and so toward that haunting "country" of which he has become increasingly aware, as increasingly he will experience an exile in this world from it. He will, paradoxically, become more like Bishop in his citizenship —*perhaps, possibly*. Our last glimpse of Tarwater is in the novel's closing sentences, in which naturalistic details recognized as if palpable to our senses out of memory is an actual midnight. In that dark night of Tarwater's turning, the moonlight touches him as he makes a way among Georgia pines. The moonlight flickers, since he moves along his dark way through the actual woods. It is a light "diamond-bright" when it touches him in falling "between patches of darkness." How like, Tarwater's moonlight, to that more famous to us out of John Keats's attempt to transcend his own dark midnight, borne for a moment on the nightingale's night song. But how far removed from Keats — that melancholy poet arrested in an "embalmed darkness" where (he says) "Darkling I listen." To his arrested listening in darkness, Keats's moonlight sifts through leaves more taunting than beckoning to Keats, who in response confesses himself often "half in love with easeful Death." Death for Keats is the moment of crossing into oblivion, into the country of Nothingness. He cannot turn, cannot become what Walker Percy will call an "ex-suicide."

In O'Connor's conclusion to her novel we discover in Tarwater a growing violence of intent for the truth rather than a Keatsean despair. Now his intent is to an integrity he cannot yet understand, though there is hinted a foreshadowing of his future worldly end — one we might speculate not unlike that of Haze Motes. Tarwater has intimations of a "fate that awaited him" in the dark city — for the Dragon may prove a more formidable presence in that dark city than by the way on which he makes toward the city. "*But,*" says our last words, Tarwater sets "his face … toward the dark city, where the children of God lay sleeping" in spiritual darkness. He responds, despite his disquieting anticipation, to that command now clear in itself, though lacking all detail of circumstance lying before him. It will be his labor to discover and engage those circumstances. He must go and forewarn "THE CHILDREN OF GOD OF THE TERRIBLE SPEED OF MERCY."

By bearing that message, Tarwater has not escaped the violence that always attends the good. For him, "every day" will continue "Judgment Day" as a reality O'Connor's vision sees as that for each person. For her there is a violence deeper than spectacle at each moment of self-consciousness, in that contention in us each she speaks of as "wills in conflict." And so at each conscious moment for the intellectual soul incarnate there is that "crossroads" where time and place and eternity constitute contingencies to the will. Incipient for consciousness in response to the moment's actual "worldly" contingencies is an action of violence, a movement beyond the arrest of consciousness in a stasis of self-content. Action involves a violence, movement between those poles of good and evil *in* us, in the will. Between a turning *toward* or a turning *away from* the good. The action is either that turning away in effecting an erosion of full citizenship in reality as a *person* or toward full citizenship in rejecting an isolation as a *self*. By action the person moves toward or away from that country haunting Tarwater, O'Connor believes. In species of violence by degree as *this* person "the Kingdom of Heaven suffereth violence," that term *suffereth* including most significantly that sense of the Kingdom's *allowing* freedom of action toward or away from Heaven, a Heaven to be "seized" only by the full surrender to it and to its King, "whose service" in that full surrender is "perfect freedom."

9

Coincidence of the Moral and Dramatic Senses

"In the greatest fiction, the writer's moral sense coincides with his dramatic sense, and I see no way for it to do this unless his moral judgment is part of the very act of seeing, and he is free to use it.... It affects his writing primarily by guaranteeing his respect for mystery."

— Flannery O'Connor, "The Fiction
Writer and His Country"

Such serious matters as these, enjoined in their defense by O'Connor in responding to John Hawkes about the Devil, are centered in her vision of man as created an intellectual soul incarnate, through the grace of God, whereby man's nature (as is the nature of all things created) is through a continuous grace. That is a vision which she knows to be largely lost to her own age, in recognition of which loss she deports herself in her letters and in her talks with a wryness received by some as pointed and disturbing because not always understood in relation to her vision. If a reader is drawn into her work by a fascination accompanied often with irritation, his very puzzlement is a consequence of her peculiar perspective through which she uses her moral-dramatic sense in making. She is a writer who (as she says herself) chooses the lowest "social" and "cultural" elements of the local quite deliberately, but in a concern for a high seriousness of art which reaches beyond both fictional satire or documentary reflection of the "social" realities to these deprived, local, provincial citizens in their outlandish country. For many of her readers these folks are disproportionately located in a notorious "South," leaving a reader afar baffled as had been that anonymous reviewer of her stories for the *New Yorker*.

She responds to such miss-takings of her work on occasion, though she is also cautions about the poet's authority in speaking of his own work. Still she had, as "a Catholic possessed of the modern consciousness" (as that early reviewer describes her), very deliberately chosen a seemingly Southern provincialism as her matter, out of a "place" supposedly denied advantages to most of its citizens of that "modern consciousness." (Henry James lamented that "Southern cultural poverty long ago.) But by an intensity out of her vision, she would reveal, not a provincial South, but the whole world of man as evident in the limited local, even in her South. And, as we have heard her say, "because I am a Catholic, I cannot afford to be less than an artist" engaging this challenge to her calling. The burden of her response to some critics is as if in her fictions she were ringing the bells backward quite deliberately, to borrow an ancient metaphor concerned with old alarms signaling barbarian invasion. For when the barbarian invades, the Church bells must be rung "backward" from those accustomed cadences of musical sequences intended to the praise of God in summoning to offices of sacramental celebration. When rung backward, the bells shout to those who haven't heard or cannot see a threatening invader, the music grotesque. Hearing such a violence of music, citizens must then either gird themselves for battle or "take to the hills."

It is in this concern that she makes what seems an unseemly playing upon the inherited music she most values with her grotesque pointings, using a local language that still carries in it a residual burden of old visions of spiritual order, however much decayed toward an opacity to current sensibilities. She points to the cadences of the local as bearing substantive witness, as in Old Tarwater, whom she speaks of as "crypto–Catholic." She will say to an interviewer not long before she died (to C. Ross Mullins, *Jubilee,* June 1963) that "what the Protestant South gives the Catholic novelist is something very good that he doesn't get elsewhere. Judgment is just as much a matter of relishing as condemning." A favorite media sport at that moment, as she knew, was that of condemning the Protestant South as culturally provincial. (A nationwide statistical poll of the religious at that time, however, found that "Southern Baptists" exceeded "Roman Catholics" in affirming that "Jesus is the Christ.") She values in at least some Protestant Southerners then their refusal to abandon what are for her significant and fundamental realities for her, both she and they believing in Christ's Divinity and siding with each other on questions about human nature itself. What they share is responses to circumstantial challenges to their personhood by Modernist ideology in a common deportment, reflected in traditional manner. In that shared manner she recognizes as buried in it, if generally unrecognized, a more considerable grounding in spiritual orthodoxy than in the "main line" churches.

If the Southern "Fundamentalist" does not talk about these concerns in Thomistic terms, nor in terms acceptable to current psychological theories of human nature, he does keep fundamental questions alive, for which she values him. Her many defenses of her Old Tarwater *passim* in her letters shows how highly she does. But as a writer, that "Southerner" interests her additionally. In answering a question put to her about her own seeming "Southerness," by a sophisticated interviewer from the literary department of the dominant daily in her Taulkinham, she observes: "We carry our history and our beliefs and customs and vices and virtues around in our idiom," her "we" principally applying to her Southerners. She knows that she is speaking to a Yankee of the spirit, the interviewer, when she adds, "You can't say anything significant about the mystery of a personality unless you put that personality in a social context that belongs to it" (*The Atlanta Journal and Constitution,* November 1, 1959).

As for the burden she carries as maker, she feels it shared by some of those "Southern Protestants" she encounters. It speaks, for both, to an ancient battle still in progress — that between good and evil in contention for the intellectual consent not of the psychological "personality," but of this specific creature, this person. How odd it may appear nevertheless that she should choose as fictional heroes such strange creatures, handicapped as they seem to be intellectually no less than culturally. But the misunderstanding of what she is about in her concentration upon the "Christ-haunted" as spiritual pilgrim leads to her defense of them as she knows them "in person." To Margaret Meaders ("Flannery O'Connor: 'Literary Witch,'" *Colorado Quarterly,* Spring 1962), she says "The prophet–freaks of Southern literature are not images of the man in the street." That is, man is not an anonymous entity under the auspices of a reduction from person to egalitarian abstraction until he is but an "individual" entity defined by Modernist doctrines. Instead, for her "They are images of the man forced out to meet the extremes of his nature." Those extremes as *possible* lie in his gift of free will. And so in his extremity is discovered the capacity of his limited gifts for both the good and evil as may be embraced by *this* particular person. The actualities of good and evil are in contest over the intellectual soul of this discrete person, circumstances to his actual existence forcing him to contend with his own givenness. That becomes the center of her engagement with John Hawkes over the question of Satan as actual.

The battle O'Connor dramatizes, let us say with a suspension of our disbelief in their actualities, is between the Devil and the Holy Ghost, those subtle (even hidden) presences are the tensional poles to the fictional agent's action, dramatized *within* a consciousness. In respect to the battle in Haze Motes, we heard her speak of Haze's "wills in conflict." The arena of conflict is so *essentially* personal for her in its reality as to prove impervious to the measures of time and space, but it is nevertheless real in *this* place at *this* moment. The actual spiritual battle within a person is deeper in its reality as actual than the spectacle necessary to art's representations of that arena. Spectacle must nevertheless be borrowed from an actual place in an actual time in order to incorporate —*incarnate*— a character as a surrogate person. This spiritual action she sees as a high drama, regardless of necessary trappings of spectacle, for at issue is *this* intellectual soul incarnate whose proper end is Beatitude. It is action, as Aristotle suggested, interior to consciousness and therefore requiring a mediator among minds through common perceptions of spectacle given signs, those signs sometimes spoken of critically as the "concrete detail" that emphasizes the role of perception in art. She draws us to the very edge of a staging of, a dramatization of, a crucial action which is indifferent to the accidents of time and place upon which art necessarily depends, namely spectacle. (Again, the critic in this concern will speak of the necessity to art of "universality" gained in common recognitions of the universal through shared signs.) The poet must deploy spectacle drawn with naturalistic immediacy of images, toward a universality of human nature itself as shared through art, even as the philosopher must pursue a universality through speculative reason in response to the particularities of things on his metaphysical quest. O'Connor draws spectacle from *a* time in *a* place, centering in Andalusia, and the Middle Georgia vicinity. In doing so, however, she knows most surely as a prophet of distances that cultural history and nature's immediacies, however "naturalistically" presented, are insufficient to account for that old spiritual war that is so intimately personal to the knowing person, though he may deny that knowledge. There is a privacy of action within consciousness of the person as *homo viator* beyond instrumental measure, requiring of persons as community (most tryingly) a prudential humility in reconciling mercy and justice to the necessities of community order.

Whatever spectacle attends the surrogate consciousness of man made incarnated by art in her story is drawn from personal experiences of things in themselves known by O'Connor, whether a dialect modified skillfully in dialogue or imagistic "local color" of things like her "artificial nigger," or Haze's rat-colored old Edsel or that strutting peacock's "underwear." Such is the necessity to an art whose intent is the drama within consciousness, a drama common to us all by our common humanity save in respect to spectacle, however differing by degree of reconciliation of spectacle to will's actions. The significant action, as opposed to the spectacle that locates it in consciousness through imagery, is signified by a borrowing of the perceived things to the poet's "incarnating" act of making with signs. Spiritual action, labored through reason into art's "incarnation," occurs on that inaccessible stage of consciousness — inaccessible to the measurements of reason itself as enlisted in service to any sciences of the *how*. Because O'Connor's concern is to celebrate the intellectual soul as grace's particular *given* form to human nature, it is this interior action of affirmation or denial that she sets in polar tension of drama. In our response the spectacle receives its significant (its *signifying*) presence in imitation of the actions of nature experienced on the small stage of our own consciousness. It must be "like" the actual in proportionate imitation of the possible action of the becoming of consciousness itself, a possible action of the intellectual soul recognized as a reality reflected imagistically.

In respect to our response to such art, degrees of our remembrance of actual experiences stirs a consensual response to those possible actions as imitated by the dramatic art itself. Imaginatively, then, the *known* in relation to the *possible* effects in the responding intellectual soul a *re-membering* out of the images already held in the intellectual soul — an imagining of the possible allowed as our own "incarnating" response to art through the willing suspension of disbelief necessary to an intellectual consent. For the possible action is not itself actual action, save in the *becoming* of the responding intellect whereby the possible requires active consent of an imaginatively speculative response in the beholder. Thus, though art does not *prove* the possible, by responsive engagement of the possible intellect is open to a visionary deportment as an intellectual soul on its way. (How reluctant, the fundamentalist Positivist, to grant validity to this *imaginative* dimension of his own becoming as an intellectual soul. The more "puritan" that Positivist in this respect, the more reluctant even to grant validity to speculative history, let alone speculative art, in his *becoming* as an intellectual soul toward his limits.)

In this perspective upon dramatic art, we discover *image* held in intellect out of actual experience, along with other gathered images of other experiences from the continuum of time and place we journey. Memory carries these "notes" as a history of *this* responding intellectual soul. An image engaged by reason becomes a *member* gained from the fullness of the experienced thing itself. That *member* is a truth (in some degree) corresponding to the inherent *accident* of which it is a truth, a particular accident inherent to the *essence* of the thing experienced by the intellectual soul. Reason may with such members *re-member* through speculative wonder (imaginative speculation of the relation of the actual to the possible). What is thus re-membered is that which has become known intellectually from experiences of actual things. Even the "puritan" Positivist as theorist by the very nature of his intellectual soul responds as does the poet, though by intent he may will the possible to become transformed by an intentional power over the possible. Thereby in Positivistic theory of intent, that which *is* the more easily becomes declared an effect of Positivistic theory in operation against nature, against creation, autonomous intellect thereby presuming itself superceding creation. Out of such speculative concern for the nature of intellectual action in response to the actuality of the given as anterior to any active response to given reality (we suggest) is an aesthetic response, the emotional effect of which initially is awe — leading to wonder. It is a present action in the intellectual ground of memory, memory being that mystery of our nature as intellectual soul which St. Augustine addresses at such length in his *Confessions*. (See his "Philosophy of Memory.") There occurs as thought a *re-membering* out of the actual as already experienced in relation to the possible as speculatively opened to reason, echoed in concept. Concept is thence served by art. In this respect what an awe-inspiring poem is Einstein's $E = MC^2$. There is a response of beholding a thing's formal beauty. (What is here presumed of the form is a sufficient *claritas* of the made thing accomplished through "reason in making" by the poet, the presumption of proximate cause in relation to its effect in Thomas' understanding of the nature of the made thing.) In this respect, then, spectacle in dramatic art (our present concern) serves *claritas*— serves the beauty of the thing made — in an analogy to St. Thomas' "accidents of essence" as inherent to a thing in itself. Those accidents have been perceived through the senses from the actualities of a specific thing in itself and abide as truths of things in the memory. For St. Thomas, *image* names a presence in the intellectual soul, collective as memory. Such are images of experiences to be ordered reflectively by reason with intuition continuing in consort toward recovery of a visionary light along the way to be traveled by the intellectual soul to its final end. It is in this perspective that Flannery O'Connor understands (largely intuitively I believe) that spectacle held by the intellectual soul out of experiences here and now, gathered along that way, speaks to the complex necessity to a reason governed by a strategy of signs in any dramatic making — in the poet's concern for analogy, for metaphor. That is the necessity whereby a visionary truth, a point in prospect of distant reality, may be gained to a visionary art. Thus image in relation to images — truth in relation to truths — requires a sorting of *likeness* in the *unlikeness* of things. She recognizes a common grounding of things in *being* as speaking a Loving Cause whereby things are specific, each according to its given nature — according to the limits of its nature whereby it is. One may explicate such a concern to reason through St. Thomas' "natural law." But one may well recall also that, for St. Augustine, it is a recognition intuitively recognized in a seemingly sudden reorientation as *homo viator,* turning St. Augustine himself toward his proper end. It is, he says, the "beauty" of each thing truly seen which shouts "He made us!" From this visionary experience there follow those abiding explications by St. Augustine of the intuitively known, beginning with the *Confessions* and including many treatises, whether on the Trinity or that more celebrated work ringing the bells backward for us to recovery of the true way to his wandering age, *The City of God.*

In recent intellectual history, then, there appears a certain "historical irony" in our prophetic poet T. S. Eliot as he begins to turn in his concern for *image* in relation to the poem as mediated by images drawing the poet and his audience. (Eliot's personal turning point in *The Waste Land* echoes St. Augustine: "to Carthage then I came, burning, burning.") It is through images that the poet deploys signs in the "re-membering" which Eliot speaks of at first — before his *Waste Land*— as "objective correlatives." Images yield "sets of objects ... situations, a chain of events" in his illustrative phrases, signifying critically for him the capturing by the poet of the *possible.* When proportionately deployed, the made thing effects through the re-membered images an aesthetic response in recognition of the validity of an "imaginative" making by reason of a *possible* dramatic action occurring in a surrogate intellectual soul. Eliot must wrestle with the problem of "voice" in his early poetry, sometimes in confusing ways, making us declare him a "hard" poet to read. This, whether that surrogate intellectual soul be the "voice" speaking an ordered sonnet or the diverse "voices" of agents deployed dramatically by the poet in juxtapositions within a context of situations, events, and the like. The challenge to the poet is of a place to *stand* in ordering images. And here we observe as inevitable to such a making of surrogate intellectual souls the inescapable presence of the maker himself, the poet. He is always implicit to his making — however much he may (as did Eliot) fear "personal" implication in the thing he made. (We return to Eliot along the way, then, in that he wrestled with common problems to the poet and resolved many of them to O'Connor's benefit as maker.)

In this speculative argument underway, concerned with the poet's relation to his made thing as himself a presence to the making, we may better appreciate St. Thomas' emphasis to the poet that his primary responsibility is to the good of the thing he makes, for in fulfilling his gift as poet his stewardship is to beauty, requiring a proportionate regard of reason in relating the possible to the actual, a participation as a maker whereby he is an image of the Creator intent upon "the good of the thing made" as Thomas says. In the proportionate accord of elements to an "embodying of"—an *enmembering* of—a made thing (O'Connor speaks of this as an "incarnating" by art), this thing made with signs achieves whatever *claritas* it possesses, through which is effected its beauty in being the thing it is as fixed by signs. Such, then, the circumstances to making which O'Connor understands in relation to St. Thomas' arguments, her centering concern the intellectual actions possible to her intellectual soul incarnate in its actualities. From the beginning of her making, hers is a concern deeper than Eliot's early address to the nature of "objective correlatives" necessary to the beauty of a made thing. And though she recognizes a peripheral concern for the present reality of her "audience," especially since it constitutes so largely the *matter* to her making, hers is not a concern to manage that audience's response to her made thing. Eliot's own initial concern is specifically to control emotional response in a reader by his "objective correlatives." Though already turning out of his skeptical rational detachment from reality, Eliot's initial defense is of his own intellectual independence from reality. Eliot would manage his audience's emotional response to his made thing, though an emotional response is but a surface spectacle of the intellectual response itself.

By a control of the "external facts" to his making, then, Eliot would control an intended effect on his reader, limiting the "emotion … immediately evoked." But if there is indeed an initial emotional effect (controlled or not) in a reader responding "aesthetically" (we are arguing) much more is effected within that receptive intellectual soul as it experiences an artifact — a poem or story. Something deeper than can be accounted for as merely an emotional effect — a surface response — has been made to the "essence" of the poem or story when it is a thing made good by reason out of the unavoidable dependence upon the *givenness* of things, including that givenness of both poet and reader no less than the matter of common human "nature" chosen to the making. It is a response to inherent "accidents of essence" in the fixed and certain thing, existing now as actual. And what may possibly occur as actual in the respondent, in the reader by his own intellectual action in response to the *claritas* of the made thing, is the recognition of its echoing the *possible* in dependence upon the actual. That proves to be an experience deeper than a merely "emotional" response. It is understood as deeper, for instance, by Aristotle, who in his concern for the *cathartic* effect of tragedy — the purging of pity and terror in *Oedipus the King*. By his reason, Aristotle engages the mystery of dramatic effect in the audience no less than in that surrogate person Oedipus. The person experiencing *with* Oedipus his catharsis turns back to his own actual reality as a person affected more deeply than merely emotionally — emotion but a very weak symptom of the more fundamental consequence to the intellectual soul of an intellectual action. The reader or playgoer makes his way back from aesthetic journey into the actualities of his way within the created world. (We recall Rilke's recognition of the aftereffect on that return from his experience of a bust of Apollo: "You must change your life.")

We have been exploring the intellectual circumstances to Flannery O'Connor out of her intuitive and then rational understanding of responsibility to making stories as a "realist of distances," returning from time to time to a reflective concern for whatever discoveries made. The relation of making to creating is the challenging mystery, so that she would welcome St. Thomas' arguments concerning the intimate relation of "art" to "history," St. Thomas building on Aristotle, his beloved "philosopher." By reflection, we remember that both nature and cultural tradition are antecedent to the artist's making and are therefore antecedently actual to making as an intellectual action. To this concern, Thomas reminds the poet that art is not an imitation of *nature*—of antecedent actualities upon which his art depends — the spectacle of things. His is rather an imitation of the *action* of nature, particularized in spectacle by his art as an "incarnating" action with signs. Thus it is the *possible* or *probable* which the speculative imagination "incorporates" as art, given "body" as art from dependence upon whatever *is* and whatever may be perceived. It is with some confidence to her making that O'Connor holds so resolutely to this recognition as the deepest personal circumstance to her dramatic making out of human nature itself. Just how resolutely she holds to this truth as governing her making is suggested by her saying that the "Basis of art is truth, both in matter and in mode" ("The Nature and Aim of Fiction"). In the same talk she argues that "imagination and reason" must be recovered in concert, having been separated by Modernist distortions of reality by an intellectual process, a separation by denial of grace from nature. That is the most considerable challenge to her, in that she must "intrude upon the timeless"—into a country denied by her age — in order to recover the consort of her imagination and her reason to a resonant "meaning" in her made thing. It requires of her she says "the violence of a single-minded respect for the truth," even at the risk of making a spectacle of herself before an age that has so generally abandoned concern for truth in intellect as evidencing nature and human nature existing through active Love, a Love as Lord of a timeless country omnipresent in this here and now. How challenging, then, to finite discursive intellect — this necessity to an indirection for reason, necessary to its nature as limited. For, since that old walking of Adam with Love in the garden to name things — since Adam's "personal" violation of that intimacy—finite intellect's burden is to approach Love as mediated through things in themselves. It is discursive bridging of the gulf between the disproportionate Divine knowing and finite knowing, encouraged by the beauty of things in their shouting "He made us!" No wonder, then, O'Connor's admiration of that figure of man Haze Motes for his own violent single-minded hunger for truth. But in this context of her intellectual and spiritual concern as poet, it must be remembered as well that as poet she knows that her responsibility is not to deliver judgment upon her age. It is rather to prophecy by an art that may at last if well-made witness the abiding and unwavering possibility of the terrible speed of Mercy through proximate good received by finite love as grace. That is the witness Tarwater would bring to wake the children of God from their spiritual sleep, their catatonic intellectual and spiritual sleep.

And so in respect to the drama that concerns O'Connor, she is not as poet to be concerned with judgment, neither of a person nor of her own characters — nor at last of her age as that of the Theorist-Consumer. She knows that to be a concern improper to art and so to her calling. She is neither Moses nor Isaiah. Not that she may not be sorely tempted, as are we all, in responding to conflicted circumstances on our journey, wishing to set the world a-right. But she knows and believes it valid to art, as Thomas insists, that the rectitude of human weakness is never the primary demand to art as art. Not justice, then, not her own limited judgment of any consciousness as conflicted, is proper object to art by intention of the artist — though she as person at times is less hesitant to remark our human failures (even her own) in letters or in talks. Hers remains dominantly as poet-postulant in the act of making a steady sense of responsibility to reasoned uses of the actual as known, the range of judgment proper to art governed by the *possible* or *probable actions* of human nature, in the primary interest of the good of the thing she is making. By that limiting of her concern as poet, she may the better succeed in an artful "incarnation" of surrogate persons — characters made persuasively viable by a dependence upon the truth of persons conflicted between good and evil.

Her attempt as poet is made in the light of such a distinction as that made by St. Thomas, that between *this person* and *humanity* as shared in a body of persons. In respect to *person,* the local serves as incarnating matter to art, which when reason properly governs the making must necessarily speak toward the transcendent in respect to *humanity* itself as a body whose head she believes is Christ. Humanity as a common nature is shared by persons, a universal concept made particular always by the limits of *this* person in which is spoken that common ground of humanity, a shared kinship in *being*—in existing. It is a ground shared proportionately in the necessity of *limit,* whereby any thing is *the* thing it is. For each thing that *is* actual is so by the virtue of its discrete limit, its peculiar nature. As such it may be perceived by a particular creature among created things (man as intellectual soul incarnate in an intellectual way) through discrete perceptions of actual things existing. (*Pace* Descartes.) That is the point from which reason itself departs in a *becoming* of a person as intellectual soul out of his limited givenness as this person. That is what the intellect recognizes intuitively as a truth of its becoming, first recognized in response to a thing actual at a local point of experience — in *this* place at *this* time. In first experience of a drama it is this epistemological "process" which gives rise to wills in conflict within a discrete consciousness, the will conflicted in accepting or rejecting truth known intuitively.

Such is the metaphysical aspect of human experience in respect to Thomistic epistemology, believed unavoidable to the poet in whatever terms he may attempt to accommodate it in O'Connor's understanding. The poet may prefer a spontaneous response to the truth of things, avoiding these speculative concerns as too "scholastic." Rather surely, O'Connor was herself already well on her way as poet, but she recognized the support of St. Thomas to her reason's riddling of her actual experiences of things. Most especially welcomed to her is Thomas' affirmation that *art is reason in making.* In her own experiences of fellow artists, she had discovered increasingly their reluctance to be governed by reason, especially that "romantic" inclination in the "Cornbelt Metaphysicals" close at hand as well as in the self-celebratory Beats to a self-sufficiency presumed by intellectual autonomy.

Not that she will argue her Thomism in explication of her own work as if Thomism is "proved" by her art, certainly not to the degree that we are here doing. She knows beyond that necessity how solidly Thomas affirms her own intuitive knowing as she already pursues this truth about reality in the making of a story. If *this* person is human, St. Thomas reminds us, as person he differs from *that* person, but without forfeiting a shared humanity save through his willful sin. Not that God is what our frontiersmen used to call an "Indian giver," for Love is a Perfect Openness whereby the person *is.* It is only the person himself who can take away from his own givenness by sin, that concept *sin* naming a reality infecting human nature that O'Connor insists an effect of evil to the diminution of the person's good, a common propensity to sin is signified by the Church's doctrine of Original Sin. And so each person exists as particular in Thomistic metaphysics, an effect of Absolute Love whereby he is *this* person by limit of gift in being.

Because particular, a person is known by other like limited creatures as such, sharing as *created* but differing from the other as a discrete person. He shares most conspicuously with other persons in that common ground, humanity, in which sharing lies the ground of community. A person knows persons through their particularities, manifest in the world as accidents of the peculiar essence of each person. We respond to particularities initially by perception, at first to the particularities as spectacle. And so perceived, the perceiver (the discrete responding intellectual soul) sorts particularities by his speculative reason. Nevertheless and always, most central to this knowing (whether of a person or of a thing) it is an intellectual action at the local and immediate place and time in experiences of an actually existing person or thing. Reason properly responds, refining thought toward understanding — toward recognition ordered to thought as universals. It is in this local response to the actual existence of the "other" that the person discovers kinship (whether with persons or things) — a kinship oriented by that most inclusive universal of all, *being itself.* That this thing is! That you are! Thus an intellectual soul responds in a local experience, from which follows (as Thomas says) the accompanying sequential wonder of discovery: "*I* am!" (Such the mystery of perception, properly self-evident but baffling to Descartes in his doubt.)

What the poet through reason knows is that a likeness recognized in unlike persons vitiates neither the unlikeness nor the likeness as distinctions valid to his understanding. It proves instead an enlargement of his understanding the mystery of existence, though the intellectual soul is never absolute in comprehension of that mystery. It is precisely here that misunderstanding may occur in the intellectual soul, especially if tempted to a Manichaean rejection of particularities, in various species of rejection. We are well reminded therefore of O'Connor's recognition of this point. She will speak often in letters and talks of the continuing Manichaean error whereby things in themselves may be rejected outright by what we have called the Puritan version of Manichaeanism native to our "American" culture, or may be rejected by that secular reduction of things by an abstractionism devoted to power over things, the latter a Positivistic species of that older Manichaeanism. (The Positivistic mode declares the ultimate truth to be Emersonian "fact," facts themselves the "skates" necessary to skim the surfaces of truth.)

To counter the Manichaean attempt to resolve the mystery in things by rejecting things, Thomas speaks on one occasion to remind us that at least "sometimes … from the distinctive character of our nature's spirit" — our givenness as intellectual soul incarnate — we discover an ordinate "love" of "intelligible goods." Those "goods" are the distinctive and plural realities of the good of existing things, relative in respect to the given nature of each. In response to likeness in unlike things the poet may bring concert of vision, an understanding in praising the glory of their Cause as a Presence to and in confluent creation itself. (That is the *oneness* in diversity that so much concerned Plato.) Although diverse according to the specific nature given to each thing (one *thing* differing from another in gifts of and degrees of *being*), it is in the very diversity recognized by the intellectual soul that reason pursues the Universal of all universals governing particular things in their concert. It is in this light that the poet's most ancient concern (as it is for the philosopher or the scientist as intellectual soul as well) is the conundrum to reason of *likeness* in *unlike* things which Plato pursued in the conundrum of the One and the Many in his *Parmenides.* When reason engages that conundrum through openness to things in themselves perceived as "natural" to the person (in consequence of "the distinctive character of our nature's spirit," as Thomas says), things as diverse particular things may be seen in an ordinate "conformity with our reason." In this accommodation of reason to the mystery of likeness in unlike things, Thomas concludes that accommodation made by a deportment called love in intellectual action. Indeed, "This love is pure," he says, and quite other than the impurity of reason's distortions through Manichaean manipulations of reality out of willfulness — out of a denial of Love to things as necessarily good in themselves whereby they are.

Our point of reference to St. Thomas's words could be various, but his concern is especially evident in his *Summa Contra Gentiles,* though our quoted phrases above are from his letter to an unidentified Cantor of Antioche, who was sore pressed to defend Rome against both Muslims, the Eastern Orthodox, and the Armenians. He sends the letter East to that Cantor around 1265 a.d. The argument here seems to our ears abstruse, especially as directed so specifically against the Muslims for distorting God's relation to creation in God's act of love, condescending to us in the Incarnation. But the ancient historical circumstances to Thomas's argument do not arrest the validity of his 13th century recognitions, as if the letter were but a footnote in the history of Christendom. (Indeed this old letter proves current to this moment of chaos in the Middle East, where ancient Antioch is still proximate center to wars of conflicted wills in violent spectacles, especially suicide murder in tribute to Nothingness.) O'Connor knows such a Thomistic argument specific to her place and time, though historically removed, geographically in another hemisphere. She knows because she knows persons as actual in her place at this time: those Southerners who (she says) "carry their history and ... beliefs around in their idiom," evidencing thereby "personality in a social context" but as fallen persons. Evidencing, that is, a *personhood* common to humanity in any place or time. But to the person now existing it is always particular, and one aspect of our human history as revealed by social context is out of this most local knowing of the "self," a person's continuing sense of being "Christ-haunted," whatever the term given that sense of exile or whether the Haunter Himself lacks yet a name.

Such then are truths she knows, to be reflected inevitably in her art insofar as her reason deploys the locally known with an attention to present reality. This common likeness in unlike persons, then, signals the limited arena to her dramatic action, not only in a story but within herself as person. It is interior to consciousness in a most personal way, in response to which O'Connor will speak playfully of her affinity to an Enoch Emory or the Misfit are other characters with whom she shares humanity. Because this is true, one of the virtues of dramatic art for her is that (through spectacle ordinarily deployed by reason in the making) the responder to a well-made story may discover that a fictional character echoes himself. There is a nature common beyond spectacle, a kinship in being among persons upon which any persuasive "incarnation" of a fictional character as surrogate person depends. Hence there is to be discovered an unlikeness, though the particularities in unlikenesses may speak a particular beauty out of differences seized upon as sentimental conveniences of identity — to an egalitarian reduction of things to sameness in a species of an Averroist heresy of universalism. (This Averroist distortion is the bad seed planted in Western philosophy by Siger of Brabant, whom Thomas refutes in his *On the Unity of Intellect Against the Averroists.*) In well-made drama, then, a surrogate person, a "character," unfolded out of actual personhoods resonates truths that may be very personal to the beholder in his imaginative participation in a drama. But what a shocking recognition of kinship as a reader to a Haze or even to a Misfit — or to Mrs. Turpin or Mr. Head. Or to Julian, Hulga, Asbury.

That is why O'Connor as prophetic poet forewarns us of that meaning of prophesy, now much distorted by our confusing *mystery* with *magic.* As a realist of distances, the prophet's role is not to foretell the future (as St. Thomas reminds us) but to remind us of once known but forgotten truths. Young Tarwater as waking prophet, then, is charged to waken the sleeping children of God to this remembrance of the truths inherent to what St. Thomas calls our "distinctive character," resident always in "our nature's spirit" as an intellectual self-awareness initiated by perceptions. And so the limited arena of a discrete consciousness proves crucial to our "reading" of a character when that character is made persuasive by the poet's borrowing common *personhood* to his incarnation of a surrogate person by art. As for O'Connor's uses of spectacle as textual matter taken from her immediate world, consider the consciousness of a Mr. Head in "The Artificial Nigger" or of O. E. Parker in "Parker's Back."

And here we may enlarge the point, comparing Walker Percy's treatment of a like problem, Percy himself a "believing" writer. In contrast to O'Connor as prophet, Percy wakes to his calling more gradually than she. He differs as well in respect to his discomfort with "place" in his life reflected in his fiction. His place is largely borrowed from American suburbia, rather far removed from Haze's downtown Taulkinham or from Mr. Head's country cabin, though Mr. Head comes to its border in suburbia in the City of Man, where he encounters the "artificial nigger." Percy's Binx Bolling is attuned to sophisticated New Orleans, its common epithet "sin city." There is also another aspect of Percy's fictional matter differing from O'Connor's. He is more deliberately and dependently concerned in his choices of spectacle upon suburbia with all its recent sophisticated science made companionable to the pseudo-sophisticated "New Age" culture of suburbia that he recognizes as tending to paganism. That is a matter to his spectacle in which he sees a concert of Positivistic Science and New Age paganism, effected in Percy's "place" in what he calls the "losangelization" of the local. It is conspicuous in suburban America at large but concentrated as source of his fictional spectacle to the vicinity of Covington, Louisiana — Covington increasingly drawn toward New Orleans.

Given their like spiritual vision, held by Percy and O'Connor in their Christian commitment, he differs again from her in mode as in matter. His is a witty satiric manner, though he shares with O'Connor a concern for consciousness become deracinated, "lost in the cosmos" in his phrase. One might, in reflective enlargement of Percy's and O'Connor's dissimilar addresses to a common vision, juxtapose the concluding scene of Percy's *Thanatos Syndrome* to such action as that in the last pages of O'Connor's *Wise Blood*. Dr. Tom More at the end of *The Thanatos Syndrome* reports himself "Sitting on the front porch of my office sailing paper P-51s at the martin house" on a "fine warm Louisiana winter day," his "P-51s" those folded paper airplanes boys make in the 3rd or 4th grade. He has just been reassured by Father Smith (a character whose spiritual history is somewhat like that of Haze Motes). Father Smith has said: "I will tell you a secret. You may have a thing or two to add to Dr. Freud and Dr. Jung, as great as they were."

Dr. Tom More, sailing his paper airplanes, is left wondering about Father Smith's words in retrospect. "Did he wink at me?" How do those words fit the considerable change in his own view of the world now come upon him? He is, for the first time, calm and almost serene, in a spiritual state not known before and not understood yet. But in comparison, how seemingly radical, that final scene of Haze Motes propped up dead in a slum apartment in Taulkinham. Yet these closing scenes suggest the writers' kindred vision of our spiritual nature despite the wide divergence of the textual spectacle through which they would speak prophetically toward spiritual recovery. Haze's Mrs. Flood is engaged by a "winking" eye, but it seems to her to become a point in Haze's glazed eyes, a point of light like a star, perhaps a light at the end of her own tunnel-vision of reality. She thinks she is moving toward it—having closed her own unseeing eyes. Dr. More, unlike Haze, is a sophisticated scientist, attuned to and even drawn by New Age culture as he begins in this conclusion to ponder Father Smith's countering "wink" that suggests it possible that he might now riddle the inadequacies of his old Positivistic rationalism through which he had once been comfortable in his New Age pleasures. For Dr. More had supposed Positivistic science as desirable in a consort with the neo–Pagan New Age embraced earlier (in *Love in the Ruins*), "feelings" he had held for the social arena he inhabited. Neither separately nor together can New Age sensibilities or Positivistic certainties account for spiritual encounters with reality such as he has begun to experience at last.

Unlike in contextual details: these closing scenes of books by writers who share in being both "Southern" and "Catholic." It is to our point, this bold juxtaposition of seemingly incommensurate fictional scenes, that O'Connor makes an observation in her "The Fiction Writer and His Country" worth recalling: "In the greatest fiction, the writer's moral sense coincides with his dramatic sense, and I see no way for it to do this unless his moral judgment is part of the very act of seeing, and he is free to use it…. It affects his writing primarily by guaranteeing his respect for mystery." The sense of that mystery is common to each, both to Percy and O'Connor, though her manner of address to that mystery is to make large and startling pictures for those she sees as almost blind, as in that final scene of *Wise Blood*. Percy is more subtle in his modulation of mystery, circumspect in giving an unspectacular representation of Tom More's concluding spiritual moment of *Thanatos Syndrome*. Dr. More sits meditative—sailing paper planes, littering his office lawn.

The reader familiar with Western literature, discovering these writers within that tradition as both committed to a high seriousness about their art, might expect to meet in their work fictional persons of at least some social and cultural magnitude. He may be especially baffled by O'Connor's lowly protagonists chosen to her intent to a high seriousness. Aristotle, after all, points out very reasonably the advantages to high drama of the King as protagonist in service to the larger social community order. (There is some advantage to Percy's Dr. More, given the popular spirit's respect for experimental "doctors.") But the rescue of the very soul from evil (even though the reader should set aside any reality of *soul* or *evil* for art's sake) surely qualifies as a concern for high drama though engaged at a low social and political level. But, asks the skeptical reader wary of a suspension of disbelief, to be played out in the consciousness of a Shiftlet? A Mr. Head? Such confrontations of the reader by purportedly serious fiction seems to suggest a disparity between the fiction's matter and high intent to a skeptical reader, especially if we respond to that art with sophisticated Modernist reactions. The concerns of *Wise Blood* seem hardly comparable to *Oedipus the King*, though we reject kingship as antique.

High drama seems an unlikely concern in protagonists or antagonists as "good country people" such as Haze Motes or Mr. Head, or to Mrs. Turpin, the disparity no doubt contributing to the misunderstanding of O'Connor's work. If she is a social or cultural satirist, very well. But that does not necessarily engage "high" drama, and if she asserts, separate from the stories, that she is concerned with heroic actions of a Haze, or to suggest that for her he is possibly a "saint" seems untenable. Can she be serious about her personal closeness to Old Tarwater as a natural "Catholic"? To Joel Wells ("Off the Cuff, *Critic*, August–September 1962) she says, "I wanted to get across the fact that the great Uncle [Old

Tarwater] is the Christian — a sort of crypto–Catholic — and the schoolteacher [Rayber] is the typical modern man," and she sided with Old Tarwater. To a less sympathetic critic than Wells, to Granville Hicks of the *Saturday Review* (May 12, 1962) she says "I'm not interested in the sects as sects [as might be assumed from New York offices looking South]. I'm concerned with the religious individual, the backwoods prophet. Old Tarwater is the hero of 'The Violent Bear It Away,' and I'm right behind him 100 percent."

Not that O'Connor engaged very publicly in defense of either her characters or her stories or of her position as devout Christian, especially in response to the critical readings of her work. She does not write letters to the *New York Times* as Percy will do, nor to the *Atlanta Journal-Constitution*. She is sometimes more open in her public talks given by invitation, though she does not actively seek a forum. She is usually reluctant to make public appearances to account for herself as fiction writer. On occasion she used her physical difficulties as excuse to avoid public appearances, though her physical difficulties alone won't account for her reluctance. More revealing to us, more open because more private, are those personal exchanges in correspondence, her letters in volume quite impressive compared to her "talks" and "essays." And so her exchanges with John Hawkes about her fiction, or her letters to such a correspondent as Cecil Dawkins or "A," reveal her in her most open deportment concerning what she believes or what she intends in her fictions. They are private, personal, and she seems not to have noticed that those letters might one day become "matter" for public critics, creating problems for an editor as Sally Fitzgerald discovered. The legitimacy of private letters to public critical uses even now proves ambiguously on the border of intrusiveness (including of course our own resorting to them here). That was no doubt a difficulty to Sally Fitzgerald, leading to omissions by editing that some critics charge as dishonest, since as a "public" writer *all* of Mary Flannery O'Connor is taken as a public property.

At risk then of violation in using some personal letters, partaking of them in what might be for a Sophocles or Aristotle even considered *obscene* (i.e., properly off-stage) and to be removed from the critical scene, we have risked intruding, especially upon that private exchange with another serious fiction writer about her concerns and intentions as a writer in relying upon the Devil as actual. John Hawkes had of course published his essay in the *Sewanee Review* concerning her uses of the devil, initiating her response. She feels drawn to persuade Hawkes of how deeply she does believe the devil to be actual, and in respect for him as a serious writer to persuade him as well that spiritual action in her fictions accept that reality as actual and therefore valid matter to art beyond mere device. Spiritual action occurs at that crossroads in consciousness, and that crossroads is within her own self-awareness no less, indeed more than, in Haze's or Tarwater's self-awareness, evil a reality to the *possible* actions of her characters. But it is in self-awareness that the poet as person recovers his own recognition of evil at this crossroads of consciousness itself: of this time and in this place, as intersected by eternity. Within self-awareness, then, occurs the issuing action (*issue* in its sense of a "coming out of") as a concern common to man as intellectual soul and therefore necessarily a concern to the poet. As such, even the actions of the "lowly" proves a high concern, in God's view if not in man's. For Beatitude, the proper end for each person as intellectual soul incarnate is the proper end for each person precisely because Creating Love is "no respecter of persons" in the relativisms of cultural — of social or political or economic — circumstances.

In O'Connor's view, every person engages the prospect of eternity, so that every day is indeed Judgment Day as even the Devil admits. Each does so necessarily at *a* place and in *a* present moment, and he does so by virtue of being this peculiar, this *specific*, intellectual creature. It is so for Mr. Head or Mr. Shiftlet, for Mrs. Turpin or Haze Motes or Tarwater as surrogate persons then. It is so as well for O'Connor or in the light of Eternity for Sophocles in his actions of incarnating Oedipus. Or for Dante in his incarnating himself as Pilgrim. Or for John Hawkes. As figures deployed in *possible* intellectual actions, circumscribed by contextual limits of art, that are nevertheless peculiar to a time and a place, such agents will echo the possible as commonly inherent to persons as actual, wherever and whenever they come to themselves, and by degree according to the vision of the poet. What she must deal with as maker of such a drama, then, is her recognition that this arena to her limited fiction is significant in a decisive way of the necessity of *spiritual* action within that arena. But she recognizes as well how strange and contrary such a truth will appear to the Modernist sensibilities which have dissociated persons from spiritual realities. What has been substituted in obscuring this knowledge is the highly sophisticated strategies of skating on the surfaces of reality — especially sensitive to spectacle as but cultural history or accidents of nature.

Holding this vision of human nature itself, knowing what it has come to for persons lost in the cosmos, she would make the conflict of wills in a consciousness as concrete as possible — to be properly measured by the reader as himself a person sharing a nature akin to her surrogate representative. Her "character" imitates the actions of human nature in the ways possible to that nature. These surrogate persons — characters as an imaginative presence "incarnate" through art as if alive — depend from the actualities known to us because we are persons still alive, recognizing (if but intuitively) as known to us through spectacle ordinately deployed. In well-made surrogates we discover our "self" like them. Though unlike in details of spectacle there is a shared nature. For it is the nature of art to lead us into the arena proscribed for dramatic action toward that decisive crossroads where time and place are measured by Eternity, at which point the pilgrim discovers that every moment is Judgment Moment. In that moment of recognition, even the reader of an O'Connor story may experience a self-recognition, an epiphany which Aristotle speaks of in Greek tragedy as a catharsis. Not always a moment requiring a magnitude of art such as *Oedipus the King,* and we have cited "epiphanies" along our way reflected by art, here recalling once more that one for Ranier Maria Rilke as so radically different from the response of John Keats before a Grecian urn. Rilke stands before a piece of archaic statuary, in response to which he recovers a prudential humility beyond despair. In response, he must change his life.

For O'Connor — as for Rilke or Tolkien or Eliot at last — man's presumptions as "creator" are ironic when seen in a Thomistic perspective. For always antecedent to that presumption is that primary plane of a mediating reality, creation itself, upon which man in his secondary making as artist necessarily depends. J. R. R. Tolkien in his letter to his son Christopher in the midst of World War II writes his soldiering son to recall him lest Christopher have forgotten known things. The "Artist and the Author of Reality" in a "Primary Miracle (the Resurrection)" tells the "true story of all stories" by his active condescension by His Incarnation, allowing the intellectual soul (in Tolkien's words) "a glimpse that is actually a ray of light through the very chinks of the universe about us." Tolkien is giving account of an epiphany experienced on his way, which Thomas (as we have heard him say) would argue mediated by things in themselves, standing as they do between our knowing that that Supreme Artist's absolute knowing.

And how many, the witnesses to such an experience as Tolkien's at which through grace in the moment a person has a glimpse *through* the very chinks of the universe of the reality of that supreme Artist and the Author of Reality. Dante is elaborate in his allegorical attempt to witness his culminating moment as intellectual soul, his vision of that Multifoliate Rose, from which moment's vision he falls earthward once more out of Paradise, in service as witnessing artist and author to that reality in making his *Divine Comedy*. He reenacts his steady but trying journey, opened in that visionary moment to Dante's understanding. Not all art's witness is so grand in magnitude as Dante's. We have recalled that gifted poet as *homo viator* responding to an "Archaic Torso of Apollo" in the small compass of a sonnet. But the action of Rilke's witness is also to an epiphany through grace standing before that small refuse of Classical history. His is an epiphany through surviving detritus of decaying high art, inherited by us as tribute to humanity from that anonymous Greek. It was made in tribute to that most Greek of gods, Apollo, the God of sunlight, prophecy, music, poetry: the God of art to reason in making. Apollo is rivaled by Dionysus, as Nietzsche unsettles us by his reminders. Thus anciently the conflict in will between head and heart — between reason and intuition — in pursuit of the beauty of the good. As for Rilke in his moment opened through reason before that archaic torso to man's reason as a god, its beauty a resonance of truth commands us. The poet Rilke concludes, more to himself than to us: "you must change your life." O'Connor would grant Rilke's epiphany actual, perhaps even very like the one she dramatized, but one in which the mystery of Love is deepened, not resolved through Apollo's gifts as the intellectual god to the poet. So, Mr. Head and Nelson stand before a piece of eroding "low" art if the term *art* be granted at all to that spiritually archaic work hinting Adam. Cast in cement crumbling — that "artificial nigger." O'Connor's difference as a poet celebrating epiphany? She deepens the mystery in our knowing, in the light of the Incarnation — that highest act of all art by the Absolute Artist.

And so in the depths of art, well-made or ill-made, may lie truths recalling us to the once known but now forgotten realities about our "self." For O'Connor, the truth at issue is the significant struggle within our tensional suspension as a self-consciousness at risk between good and evil, the risk to be resolved only by the will's embrace of the one or the other. That is a struggle continuous, short of actual death, and so continuously the intellectual soul finds itself endangered along its way in each circumstantial moment. What O'Connor understands, and dramatizes through her crypto–Catholic Tarwater, is that the Christ-haunted may misunderstand the habit of being necessary to become Christ-centered. What the evangelical as Christ-haunted may have forgotten is that the person is always at risk, is always to be saved or lost. "Have you been saved?" demands the evangelical on radio sermons O'Connor heard often enough, an insistent interrogative accusative in its presumption that by baptism the pilgrim soul is saved once and for, through all time within his continuing circumstances as pilgrim. For O'Connor (as for St. Thomas) any pilgrim's end is always in doubt this side death itself, though always possible through grace. St. Paul's command as evangelical that we put off the old man and put on the new leaves forgotten to some "fundamentalists" Paul's understanding: that new man is always *a-building* in this world, in a *becoming* through will's consent to grace when will is in service to a Christ-centered desire for a perfect freedom called Beatitude. That service is always problematic in the contingent circumstances to the journeying of this world.

And so for O'Connor, even Tarwater's friendly stranger, the Devil as comforter to self-love, must confess an affirmation: "Every day [every moment] is Judgment Day." It cannot be other, since in each present moment of consciousness the person encounters circumstantial challenges to his will. To choose good over evil in the immediacy of present circumstances to this moment requires (in O'Connor's phrase) a "habit of being," the steadiness of a "felt balance" in habitual consent of the will to the good, sorted in the present circumstances by reason. It is in this respect that St. Cyril (not Tarwater's friendly devil though that devil is capable of doing so) reminds us that the old dragon sits always present, in both the circumstances and in the consciousness itself—*consciousness* a term for that arena in which any pilgrim as intellectual soul incarnate "comes to himself" in Dante's phrase. Hence her remark to John Hawkes describing our conflicted journeying. There is always "the conflict between an attraction to the Holy and the disbelief in it that we breathe in with the air of the times."

A significant exacerbation to that breathing seems inevitable to us at our moment of history she believes, in that we have so generally denied that conflict in a rationalistic programmatic way, though there continues the tension in us between the Holy and the Ultimately Profane. In this view of our current historical point to journeying, these "antagonists" to the will prove peculiar in each person as presences. By implication those presences seem a gift in evidence that our will is free. It is first of all stirred in consciousness by that ancient one, the old dragon as we become self-aware, against whose "intellectual" prowess there abides in consciousness also that Presence of Love, antecedent to that stirring in us by our own "friendly stranger." By our very natures the Holy Ghost as Lord and Giver counters antecedently in a stirring life. As antagonists conflicting the will of *this* person, they activate consciousness to tensional conflict in will between love and power. It is in self-consciousness as the arena that the person's will is brought to the test. The actual Good on the one hand; on the other the illusional advocacy of the "self" as if the only ultimate good by that old dragon. How enticing that old dragon can make an illusion to a wavering will, the illusion of an absolute "self" freedom beyond this person's created limits. The horror of the Abyss (popularized by some Modernist poets as if true philosophy) is that for created things (persons) the absolute freedom promised lies only in nonexistence. The Absolute Good on the one hand therefore, but on the other the good distorted through temptations toward Nothingness — as if Nothingness itself were absolute in its proportionate antithesis to the Good. There follows all those accompanying confusions of what philosophy calls *dualism* (the thorn in Western philosophy), however cleverly hidden by Manichaean logic. The ghost of an ancient Manichaean dualism, then, still haunts us — as if the actual and the illusional were co-equal: the Good and Nothingness. (On O'Connor's concern for this lingering Manichaeanism, both within and outside the Church, see Appendix D.)

Within this perspective upon reality as held by Flannery O'Connor as a believing maker of fictions, man is tragically vulnerable through his willed action of denial in separating nature from grace, in his pursuit of an illusion of absolute freedom as power over nature. It is a vulnerability against which we are forewarned by St. Thomas when he says (in his *Questiones disputate de malo*) that "A devil knows the nature of human thought better than man does." If we see the devil (as O'Connor does no less than does Thomas) as the brightest of angels willfully fallen, we must conclude, and be shocked by the conclusion, that the old dragon lies in wait for us whatever our gifts, most threatening always on the borders of our intellect so that every day is Judgment Day. Lucifer become Satan is, among created beings, the ultimate scientist, philosopher, theologian, poet — though knowing more certainly than we that he is limited by his nature, having been created and so not a god co-equal to Absolute Good as his own creator. He knows "human thought better than man does," and one of the things he knows most certainly is our vulnerability when we consent to deny grace to nature. He would encourage that presumption by assertion, to sterilize nature as if thus merely a prime matter, chance's residue, in order that we may presume to reconstitute that residue by our intentional systems.

Thus "nature" — random accumulation — is declared by willfulness the battleground in which lie objects for conquest by autonomous intellect. But history itself hints the trophy at issue, the human soul. Hence those profound warnings against the soul's consent to "the world, the flesh and the devil." For these are a consortium of adversaries to the soul when colored through the aperçu of willfulness to serve limited desire. In that "technicolor" distortion by that prism of distorted desire comes will's denial of the greater good, preferring the lesser good as if it were the greater. How cleverly operative this Manichaean Devil, at least since the eating of the apple. For, as St. Augustine or St. Thomas (and by implication of her persuasive art, Flannery O'Connor) remind us, it is by illusional "gnosis" out of pretense to absolute freedom that Satan can manipulate a right will into willfulness, effecting as if by magic human nature reduced to a playground for illusions suited to disoriented desire. Thus is intellect seduced by such a "virtual" reality. Those playgrounds multiply out of gnosis, each colored Eden-like by self-promises of a "future" reality in time and place suited to man's wishful thinking. That is the illusion sustained by false faith in autonomous intellect which must be dogmatically defended by a gnosis that must allow no dissent. Thus gnosis by willfulness shears the pilgrim person from reality by a totalitarian power.

To say this of the dramatic circumstances O'Connor engages is to be reminded again that in her vision of man, God is "no respecter of persons" in the worldly, comparative sense. Each is an intellectual soul incarnate intended to Beatitude, each discrete and specific as person. The dignity of person, in Christian theology, lies in a fulfillment of the specific limits whereby the person is *this* person, both actual and potential to fulfillment of limits made particular by Love. It is in this perspective of the reckoning of a person, in God's justice and mercy, that the person is quite removed from our own relativistic reckonings of his worth when grace is removed from belief. And so *this* intellectual soul incarnate is by the very gift of his being intended to Beatitude through his willing participation in the perfection of his limits. In this perspective, then, each person is charged, by his very being, with responsibility to that fulfillment, to an *integrity* of his peculiar gifts. It is within these parameters dignity as person has meaning, a dignity to be supported by the members of community.

Within that confluence called community, a bonding of persons in a body, lie advantages to the devil which he intends to manipulate, though it is the particular person he would destroy. He may do so only with the person's consent to his own deconstruction by sin. As for the poet appropriating this strategy to art, we heard O'Connor remark that "A working knowledge of the devil can be very well had from resisting him," spoken as one experienced in resistance. The risk to a Mr. Head or to a Doctor Faustus as surrogate persons may seem almost obverse and they largely are in respect to social magnitude, thus confusing to our judgment as we may be affected by the spectacle of magnitude evident in persons. Confusing, that is, if we abandon fundamental truths about personhood. For such distinction among persons as that of magnitude (consider O. E. Parker in relation to Oedipus) depends so largely upon worldly measures of magnitude, as St. Paul warns us in asserting that every person is properly a *member* of the body of humanity. As member in that body the person is also particular, and by his particularity regardless of magnitude as member affects the wholeness of community of which he is a part. We recall Maritain, who in his *The Person and the Common Good* says that "With respect to the eternal destiny of the soul, society exists for each person and is subordinate to it." That is a conclusion which must follow from St. Thomas' definition of *person* in the *Summa Theologica* (I, 29, 3): "Person signifies what is most perfect in all nature — that is, a subsistent individual of a rational nature," created by Love. As "subsistent," the person's magnitude as member of society is transcended by his (potential) nature when perfected within his created limits, signified as the perfection of *beatitude*. It is within God's love that his perfection ultimately lies — not within community.

The transcendent truth about the person as person is his *peculiar* worth to God, the Cause of each person's specific limits in respect to both worldly (i.e., mundane) and otherworldly concerns — those beyond our worldly judgments of the magnitude of gifts. It is in this light, therefore, that humility becomes a decisive virtue to any person's pursuit of his own simple unity as person within community. In this dimension of a person's *spiritual embodiment,* magnitude becomes largely irrelevant, except as the person addresses his gifts with humility in journeying this world toward Beatitude, his "eternal destiny" in Thomas' phrase. It is in this perspective, then, that scripture assures us that God is no "respecter of persons" in their severalness of magnitude (a "relativity" of gifts) within social or political or intellectual relativisms.[1] Here is the meager but inclusive arena in which God's Love sustains each creature, Himself absolute in Love of the particular created person. To recognize as much is to cross over into that beckoning country that haunts young Tarwater, the country he attempts to deny until he no longer can.

And so there are two countries, the two cities about which St. Augustine wrote his great work. It is out of this understanding of the nature of the person on his way that O'Connor "makes" her Shiftlet, her Haze, her Misfit, her Rayber, her Tarwater. Within this country in which magnitude, deduced by measure of relativisms in Modernist ideologies, is subsumed. We may not deny such unlikenesses among persons as specific creatures as evident in the social confluence of course. Certainly some persons are undeniably more gifted as person than others. But our reason is required to come to terms with (and so to an accommodation with) the orders of being. Beyond making such worldly distinctions, governed by prudential humility, *this* reasoning person discovers himself on his way beyond membership in a merely social community. In this vision, he discovers the true magnitude of his "self" as a person opposed to temptation to self-deification in worldly measurements of the self by its finite intellect. Failing this distinction, we take finite measurement as determining the person's limit according to the reductionism of finite measure. There is a confusing conundrum to intellect when in parsing "by their works ye shall know them" it is assumed that the works are the measure of the person in a primary justification of being. (Again, remember Young Goodman Brown in Hawthorne, who mistook his well-ordered hamlet as demonstrating his neighbors to be good, till that encounter of them at a Black Mass.)

It is out of this recognition of the two countries, not adjoining but the one inherent to the other, that the mystery hinted at by the spectacle of things is to be uncovered by reason. And it is within this vision, as a prophet of distances, that O'Connor adapts the sacrament of baptism as the sacramental opening but not the end, a passport into that larger consuming and inherent country that at first terrifies Tarwater with its responsibilities to a habit of being. Rayber, attempting to "save" Tarwater as a moral duty (though he confuses *moral* duty with *lawful* duty), argues that passport to a far country to have been deceptively forged by Tarwater's Grand Uncle. But Rayber fails intellectually in a very common and popular way: He is never able to distinguish *individual* as citizen of the proximate country from *person* in citizenship as well to that other country beckoning the intellectual soul. Rayber's dream is of a perfection of community as a social machine, adequate to the boy as but an individual. How democratically "liberal" Rayber's intellectual intent, he is oblivious to a totalitarianism inherent in his Modernist principles. Maritain, in the concluding paragraph of his *The Person and the Common Good,* gives a quietly chilling summary of that Modernist principle which has been embraced by the likes of Rayber. Such thinking must reach a sentimental conclusion for a Rayber: a mercy through euthanasia. Maritain says to our Raybers that "the drama of the modern democracies has consisted in the unwitting quest of something good, the city of persons, masked by the error of the city of the individual, which, by nature, leads to dreadful liquidations."

How conspicuous the spectacles of such liquidations in the 20th century, a century conspicuous in mistaking St. Augustine's City of Man as the City of Man as God. These properly integral cities are denied by the strategy of separating grace from nature, by that separation the ground of being itself opens to the Devil's machinations. Thus it is that the Devil prepares the grounds for O'Connor's fiction. If O'Connor believes the Devil salts the intellectual ground by a denial symptomatic in human sentimentality, she believes as well the ground already antecedently exists even as it continues sustained by that Presence, the Holy Ghost, beyond the power of Satan's salting. (Gerard Manley Hopkins remarks as well this "dearest freshness deep down things.") She writes Father John McCown (*James* in Fitzgerald's editing of *The Habit of Being*) that the Holy Ghost is a hidden presence in her fiction. She may only suggest that this Third Person of the Trinity is also a hidden presence even in Joyce's fiction, knowing that Joyce would deny that Presence. For O'Connor, it is the Lord and Giver of life sustaining consciousness itself whereby she makes things, believing as well that necessarily true of Joyce despite his denial.

The antagonist to this Presence in O'Connor's fiction itself is more evident — the one causing John Hawkes difficulty in responding to O'Connor's fiction if he must consent to O'Connor's firm belief that the Devil is an actual perverter of life, engaging manipulatively in a person's particularities insofar as a person is open to his invasion through willfulness. For her part, the Devil is clever in his skillful "coloring" of spectacle. Consider O'Connor's vision operative in her making that scene of Tarwater's baptism of Bishop and the concurrent murder of the boy. In her vision the scene is resonant of mystery through paradox, a more complex rendering of this mystery than in the earlier self-baptism by Bevel in her story "The River." In her challenge as maker, she knows that to speak directly of the presence of the Holy Ghost is even more problematic to a reader than to employ Satan. To engage Good and Evil as presences in contention within the restricted arena of a human self-consciousness requires that she proceed in a "stylized" manner out of known realities. Her stylization differs from that of Sophocles, given the absence of common formalities shared with her reader such as the Greek tragedian shared with his audience. The actualities for her of the Devil and of the Holy Ghost are realities necessary to her making, though but antiquated concepts rejected by the world within which she must write. Sophocles' audience at least knows buskins and masks as symbols of a high station within which the drama's surrogate person contends with a fate signaling magnitude. Yet even for Sophocles, fate becomes a larger antagonist to the possible good of his protagonist than can be certified by reason, whatever the dramatic magnitude of his surrogate persons. Now, in the 20th century, what purchase on such an elusive mystery? Through the Devil? The Holy Ghost? These are precisely the presences for O'Connor herself, occasioning a high drama in the person whatever his station in the orders of humanity. But they are presences allowed no credence by the audience she writes for.

Father McCown understands, and perhaps even John Hawkes might come to understand. But as for most of the readers for whom O'Connor realizes she writes, they are not likely to do so. In her understanding, the conflict of wills in a person (represented by her in reference to Haze Motes), is conflict in response to the pressures upon and attractions to will by the Holy Ghost on the one hand and on the other by the Devil. These are hardly acceptable alternatives within the temporal circumstances in her world, now grown indifferent to or openly hostile to such antiquated mystery in complex reality if to be believed actual to man. Man himself is no longer acceptable as a *spiritual* creature for the Modernist fundamentalist. From her perspective, nevertheless, the person is an *intellectual soul,* that property of his personhood therefore necessarily central to any significant actions as a person existing as incarnate in a created world. That significant center (consciousness become a self-consciousness) is conflicted by will, in a contention between body and soul in an old metaphor as ancient as the Egyptians. As an intellectual soul *incarnate,* the person is integrally involved in creation *through* his body, his will challenged to an ordinate love of creation for us by that Primary Miracle, the Incarnation. It is because of his fallen nature that he resists. This inevitable involvement in creation for the intellectual soul at O'Connor's point in history and place has been distorted by a cultural emphasis on the body, an emphasis serving Modernist dogmas that are quite various, but as differing dogmas they all depend upon one common dogma: the body is the ultimate reality, despite reason's reckoning of it as but an accident of an accidental material universe.

From O'Connor's Thomistic perspective, the challenge to any person is to a *becoming* out of this present cultural decay. And that *becoming* is toward a *simple* singleness as a discrete being — myself as *this* person. When perfected through a right will consenting to grace, the end sought on the way O'Connor would call that state of being through virtuous habits of becoming Beatitude, as does St. Thomas. That is, by integrity as person, a right will allows by grace a melding of the person's given properties as *this* specific nature, a nature increasingly self-recognized in its progressive *becoming* through discursive reflection. The end, through a consort of prudence and humility, is a genuine self-love, made ordinate to creation itself. Such is a prospect toward joy in being *this* person by virtue of essential limit as an intellectual soul incarnate, as *this* person. Self-love in this respect becomes a habit in which there grows increasingly, out of an active participation in existence through discrete gifts, an "unself-aware" love such as O'Connor remarks. To "A" (December 9, 1961) she says, "I never completely forget myself except when I am writing and I am never more completely myself than when I am writing. It is the same with Christian abandonment." Such abandonment speaks the depth of her surrender to her calling, in which calling nevertheless she knows she is "good at it."

That is the pursuit Dante dramatizes toward his own unself-awareness in a perfection of himself, that joyful openness of love fleetingly experienced in his final vision of the Multifoliate Rose. In his elaborate figuring of his circumstance (a figuring by the poet's necessary indirections of metaphor), Dante speaks toward the fulfillment of the simple unity of those triune properties to his personhood — intellect, soul, and body — resolved in the melody of love's consent to limit. This is the *becoming* encouraged by the will's habits of virtue. They are to be recognized as moments of consent toward perfection when self-love is properly oriented to Love Absolute by what O'Connor calls "Christian abandonment."

In retrospect (reflecting on his own gifts as poet) Dante knows the seeming indirection he must take toward God by the stewardship of his gifts, in service to the good shared connaturally with the things of creation. And so the pilgrim having reached the vision of the Multifoliate Rose returns out of Paradise to the contingent created world as poet. His metaphors witness his pilgrim journey by writing his *Divine Comedy.* In that manner of his deportment as person, whose calling in this world is as poet, he has become bonded through creation's orders of being, discovering the joy of the concert of the orders of being, whereby creation itself celebrates the Cause of all existing things. What Flannery O'Connor recognizes here, sharing a recognition with Dante, she dramatizes in her own thematic play of those two "countries," between which in his disoriented loyalties young Tarwater is suspended. That fourteen-year-old boy has not yet recognized the truth O'Connor holds, though drawn to the recognition by his own (crotchety) love. It is the truth aptly put by our Thomistic philosopher Josef Pieper in his own celebratory argument, *In Tune with the World: A Theory of Festivity:* "Existence as we know it … does not just 'adjoin' the realm of Eternity; it is entirely permeated by it." O'Connor (to "A," May 4, 1957) remarks the point, by quoting one of "the Eastern Fathers": "All life is a holy festival."

It is in pursuit of perfection toward joy that the person as Christian (Dante or Pieper or O'Connor) would understand that as person he would make joyful hosannas to the Cause of all by acts of "making," in pursuit of his peculiar calling to stewardship to the good of creation according to his limited gifts — even though those gifts (*pace* Hawthorne's Puritan fathers) should be those of a mere fiddler or a story writer. Regardless as well of the *magnitude* of the made thing as measured, one poet's work against another's, comparatively by finite intellect. Once more a truth now largely obscured or forgotten: It is through such a habit of becoming that the dignity proper to the person as *this* person accrues, unaffected by accidents of circumstance or magnitude of gift. And so in this vision upon human dignity, O'Connor will speak of her Haze Motes as heroic in his pursuit of integrity, describing him as bound toward sainthood through a single-minded pursuit of the truth at whatever cost to him. There follows for Haze (no philosopher nor theologian) a violent self-destruction out of his confused attempt to put aside St. Paul's "old man" as unclean. What is implied, but not certified by O'Connor's art, is that Haze's actions reveal to him at last the proper object of his desire, his final resolution as an intellectual soul incarnate. That possible resolution is only implied as possible, since "Fiction doesn't lie," although "it can't tell the whole truth" as she remarks to "A" (May 19, 1956).

From O'Connor's perspective as believer (as it is from St. Thomas's) significant action occurs, always and in each moment of the journeying, at a crossroads known by each person as a person once self-aware. Here stand I. Crucially, it is the intersection of will and reason as agitated to self-consciousness by transcendent desire. His actions depend for the significant magnitude proper to his limited gifts (the possible magnitude of Beatitude) upon the degree of fulfillment of (the perfection of) *limited* gifts as *this* person in response to obligations to creation consequent to his own givenness — not upon the relativity of the person's social position or economic or political power. It is in this respect that scripture reminds us (as we need momently to be reminded) that God is "no respecter of persons" lest we may presume to measure a person by worldly relativisms. It is in this understanding that O'Connor considers her agents as heroic or unheroic, according to their pursuit of the integrity proper to their limited gifts, which by her labor in making she would effect contextually concrete in the fictions. This, whether her surrogate persons are on their way in quest of integrity or fleeing from it. Along that way they may have been like the Misfit: a gospel singer, in the "arm services," twice married, an undertaker, railroad worker, farmer, even "been in a tornado" or "seen a man burnt alive oncet." But at every point along that way, as we hear even the old dragon admitting to Tarwater, "every day is Judgment Day." For O'Connor, then, as for St. Cyril, the old dragon is always beside the way, endangering each pilgrim in the way toward the truth and the life.

A question is steadily before her as poet. How is she to make such a concern persuasive in art as reflecting the actualities of human "life" to such a serious mind as that of a John Hawkes? Because she acknowledges and even insists, and more than metaphorically, upon the devil's having made ready the ground in her fiction in which the possibilities of operative grace may be dramatized. Hawkes himself suspects her of being of the Devil's party, his suspicion shocking to her. More shocking perhaps than the careless presumption that she is a "hillbilly" Nihilist rather than a "hillbilly" Thomist. In September of 1959 she writes Hawkes about the action in *The Violent Bear It Away,* and of whose side she is really on in the conflict of wills underway in Tarwater. The "burden," she says, "is taken up with the struggle for the boy's soul," for Tarwater's. It is a struggle "between the dead uncle and the schoolteacher. The modern reader will identify himself with the schoolteacher, but it is the old man who speaks for me." She defends the old man a little later to a worried Sister Mariella Gable, who seems to be concerned for Flannery's orthodoxy as Sr. Gable sees it reflected in the fiction. O'Connor responds to that concern in defense of Old Tarwater: "When you leave a man alone with his Bible and the Holy Ghost inspires him, he's going to be a Catholic one way or another, even though he knows nothing about the visible church."

O'Connor is neither of the Devil's party nor of what might appear a party of the Pharisees in her Church itself. For even in the Church may be found those fundamentalists of the law who are so judgmentally rigid as to intrude upon God's prerogatives to reconcile mercy's relation to justice in dealing through grace with *this* person, especially persons like a Haze Motes or an Old Tarwater — or even with a Misfit, as Dante discovers on Purgatory Mountain. As they may appear to us at the level of spectacle, they seem beyond rescue, either by Modernist sentimentality or by the Church itself. But we are not therefore endowed to an absolute but only to a "finite" judgment of them, though in some degree judge we must. Given her circumstances as a believing Catholic in the Protestant South, under siege in a climax of history in which Modernist rejections of those beliefs dominate (and even increasingly invade the Church itself), O'Connor's is at considerable challenge as she knew well to make persuasive by art the soul's magnitude, and especially when she must attempt to do so through "local" spectacle that seems far removed and isolated culturally by "New Age" sentimentality in her audience. It is an age that has abandoned high concern for the soul through self-justifying skepticism. As for wills in conflict, given the world of the 1950s and 1960s it could not have been easy for her to go deeper into that spectacle of our general intellectual deracination in the moment — deeper into the "concrete world" — and make persuasive the reality of the hidden Presence she sees sustaining creation itself, the Holy Ghost. If difficult to persuade the current world of the reality of the Devil, it is very nearly impossible to persuade any Modernist person of the reality of the Holy Ghost. For there has been long underway, through both neglect and through a deliberate deconstruction of reality in the interest of gnostic empowerment to autonomous intellect, that separation of grace from nature that allows no such recognition.

How resolutely she holds her position. For her, the conflict of wills involves a decisive spiritual war, seemingly become general within the arena of social spectacle and occurring in a period of history in which actual wars appear more and more random in their destructiveness. But it is for her as fundamental reality *this* embattled intellectual soul that is at risk. Nevertheless, historical spectacles of violence occur in a world that can no longer believe in the spirit, having systematically distorted the inherent spiritual desire in a person into a sentimentality convenient to Modernist triumphs over human nature. How general has become the destruction of the world's body, but destruction of *this* soul proves most local. In the Modernist distortion, the body of the person must be presented not only as the ultimate end, but desirably so — as a sufficient "opiate" to secular religion through limited appetitive desire. O'Connor puts this point succinctly in relation to Ivan Karamazov's sentimentality by which Ivan justified his intellectual arrogance: his indictment of God over the suffering of children. For her, Ivan becomes a figure representative of a general intellectual sentimentality of the intelligentsia and as well prophetic of the inevitable horrors in the hundred years since *The Brothers Karamazov*.[2] For Modernist activists are descended from Ivan in respect to highly sophisticated intellectual sentimentality in a world in which there is "the absence of faith." In that absence "we govern by tenderness," O'Connor says. It is a tenderness, Eric Voegelin might add, executed through systematic formulae. O'Connor suggests that by "popular pity, we mark our gain in sensibility and our loss of vision." Ours has become a tenderness "long since cut off from the person of Christ," and now "wrapped in theory." But she adds, "When tenderness is detached from the source of tenderness, its logical outcome is terror. It ends in forced-labor camps and in the fumes of the gas chamber."

Such are the circumstances of "pity" as a sentimental salve making acceptable to the popular spirit various pogroms in the name of the "common good." The magnitude of human slaughter in the 20th Century out of such distortion is statistically arresting.[3] Walker Percy observes that a writer, engaging distortions of persons, "traffics in words and meanings" in a world in which "the chronic misuse of words, especially the fobbing off of rhetoric for information, gets on [his] nerve." ("A View of Abortion, with Something to Offend Everybody," Percy's letter to the *New York Times,* June 8, 1981. A later Percy letter on this topic, incidentally, was never published by the *Times.*) As novelist perhaps it may be more effective to recover language by indirection Percy concludes. Hence, in a last word the year Percy died ("Why Are You a Catholic?"), he remarks that "novelists are a devious lot to begin with, disinclined to say anything straight out …, since their stock-in-trade is indirection, if not guile, coming at things and people from the side so to speak, especially from the blind side, the better to get at them." He remarks this indirection necessary for the believing novelist, especially since words like *religion, born again, salvation, soul, Jesus* "tend to wear out and get stored in the attic."

Challenge enough to make Percy or O'Connor think long and hard on their 20th Century circumstances in their search for words. For they find themselves challenged as believing poets to find common touchstones with common names, theirs differing from Dante's challenges in this respect, or from Sophocles' challenges in attempting to make incarnate actions of the possible or probable within an active consciousness through stylized symbolic spectacle. The mystery of the good in relation to Fate will presently occupy Socrates and Plato. Aristotle engages this question concerning art's action in his *Poetics,* as O'Connor was especially aware through St. Thomas' uses of that philosopher ("*the* philosopher" Thomas affirms). Thomas goes beyond the *Poetics* in exploring art's relation to Revelation. How is the poet to make the dramatic thing good, however, if the contingencies to its resolution as necessarily depending from the realities of good and evil is before an audience which denies good and evil or granting them as only relative to convenience as concepts used as device. Especially challenging when those realities in turn must (O'Connor holds) be recognized in a relation to both the Holy Ghost and to the Devil as active participants by indirection in art. For O'Connor, given her unflinching vision of these realities as indeed actual, the contingencies to the dramatic action of her agent character depend for resolution upon at least a willing suspension of disbelief by a doubting audience very much reluctant to grant the possible.

This is a steady concern for O'Connor in respect to an openness she believes always *possible* from an audience, residual if not recognized in its true nature by that audience's forlorn expectation of rescue as person by art. Not that she is not on occasion irritated by that audience for not seeing. But she recognizes as well that hers is an audience almost blinded by the spectacle of things serving its appetite. That audience has also become almost deaf to the resonance of things in themselves as sustained by the Holy Ghost. As for the forlorn desire tempting to despair — made somewhat acceptable to the sophisticated artist as *angst*—she understands terror and pity not as Aristotle did, but as St. Thomas out of Aristotle understands those responses. Such a response speaks mystery as spiritual symptoms, though lacking the catharsis of a grace accepted. Without spiritual healing, pity and terror become a residue in the soul speaking the absence of cleansing Love. The residual pressure of pity and terror upon the soul becomes then, not a *terror* of response to something outside the soul. Nor does *pity* extend to something outside the soul, but rather turns to self-pity out of the terror of self-lostness. The centripetal burden of terror and pity upon the soul becomes spiritual despair. O'Connor would maintain that love yields joy, though she knows as well that joy bears in it always sorrow, the lesson to be learned at the foot of the Cross. That is a reality for her of a joyful sorrow in Christ on that Cross. For sorrow is a soul burden differing in nature from the Aristotelian *pity* and *terror*, sorrow's burden expectation through hope. Hence for her joy includes a "suffering with."

How as prophetic poet may she make sacramental baptism believable beyond the level of a merely residual social custom then? It is a question she poses not only to herself but several times to her skeptical readers. For when grace is denied as a reality possible to the almost deaf and almost blind soul, sacraments depicted in art are most generally taken as but gimmicks serving art, at most seen as sociological *deus ex machina*. They may entertain a reader's intellect as "historical" or as part of a "symbolic" puzzle imposed and to be explicated without commitment, but not operative in relation to spiritual reality itself here and now. How make either Good or Evil palpable through spectacle or believed speaking more than as conceptual devices attributed to fancy as Cause? How make an action of consciousness speak an *epiphany* effected in an agent, an epiphany which proves more inclusive of realities than as a "psychological" change in the character consequent upon his naturalistic experience.

To do so requires a textual spectacle presented as "naturalistically" occurring within the limiting context of existence itself, but to be seen as more than merely accidental. Yet how may the intellectual *soul* as a reality serve as a fictional stage in this Age of Alienation in which that malady of alienation is denied as a spiritual sickness reaching even unto death as oblivion? Kierkegaard attempts to resolve the dilemma. Flannery O'Connor reads his *Fear and Trembling* and *The Sickness unto Death.* And it is especially Kierkegaard as well in whom Percy discovers an initial diagnoses of our disease as spiritual. But Kierkegaard cannot resolve or prescribe sufficiently to prevent that rampant malady as become epidemic. Neither can Jean-Paul Sartre dismiss it by declaring the sickness our ultimate health. Sophocles had it easier. His audience (as Aristotle reminds us) shares with Sophocles at least a myth consented to by an audience for art's uses, a common knowledge of Oedipus as agent in act. The drama Sophocles unfolds rises to a "Classic epiphany" in which that which is already known by both Sophocles and his audience coincides with what Oedipus has *come* to know by dramatized intellectual action of a surrogate person Oedipus. It is almost as if there has been a collusion between Sophocles and his audience, at the spiritual expense of Oedipus.

How radically *other* appears O'Connor's possible collusion with any audience, her initial strategy of indirection granting Modernist circumstances as actual and as the point of departure in her making. *Oedipus Rex* unfolds in suspended stylized spectacle, out of which emerges a high moment with no surprise to Sophocles nor to his audience, but with a soul-rending surprise to Oedipus. Thus a reinforced recognition shared by Oedipus and the audience which Aristotle talks of as a *catharsis,* a dissolving of pity and fear as an infection of the soul. But here lies a mystery unresolved in Classical drama, reflected in that other treatment of Oedipus by Sophocles, his *Oedipus at Colonus.* Oedipus as blind prophet and not king pursues this mystery implied but unresolved by either Sophocles or his audience. That play's resolution hints at a possibility not yet recognized, a resolution for Oedipus which will be declared resolved by Dante in the light of Revelation. For Dante is enabled to engage that mystery beyond Sophocles' intuitive sense of man's soul, beyond this "pagan" foreshadowing of the mystery of the Incarnation. It is Dante, then, who is enabled through Revelation to dramatize a spiritual progress beyond pity and terror in that Light never turned off. In the resolution of Oedipus at Colonus the blind prophet Oedipus, once king, is "assumed" as was Elijah, but not in a drama speaking a shared faith in God as is Elijah's rescue. Even so, that woodland retreat, the copse within which Oedipus disappears leaving no trace of his earthly presence, becomes a sacred shrine in Sophocles' play, with a hint of some mystery commanding awe before that Biblical event (in respect to history) occurs, the event openly and celebratively recorded of Elijah's ascent into heaven.[4]

We look back here as Flannery O'Connor did to the circumstances of a Sophocles or Dante as contrasted to her own. If the one (Sophocles) lacked the grace of Revelation she enjoyed, he had access to what was at his moment a "modern consciousness" (that *New Yorker* reviewer's phrase in judging Flannery). Thus Sophocles could assume some general share with his audience in the myth of Oedipus. And if Dante's world was moving as would become more and more rapidly to a conclusion that life is a race and not a dance, he at least still had some common purchase with his audience through the established Church as still vigorously defending Revelation. Indeed, the most salient contemporary support to Dante as poet is St. Thomas Aquinas, the philosopher. But for Flannery there was neither a common recognition of, let alone belief in, Revelation, nor any common myth holding the popular spirit's attention other than Modernism as an illusional myth in the current "modern consciousness." That illusional myth, widely sustained in the popular spirit by a Positivistic science, supplied spirit to myth at best as the *"élan vital"* announced in Bergson's *Creative Evolution.* That immanent force, the *élan vital,* somewhat alleviates the stark determinism preached in a fundamentalist "Puritan" Positivism which would allow only accident as the cause of existence as random, denying Cause. If uneasily allied with Positivism, Bergson nevertheless encourages a New Age *feeling* that makes acceptable the illusion of having recovered through feeling a reassociation of sensibilities justified at least in part by Positivistic *thought*. There occurs, this is to say, a strange amalgam that will be Walker Percy's primary *matter* in his essays and fictions, confronted by his strategy of "indirection" which differs from O'Connor's by his satiric address to our age as that of the "theorist-consumer." For Percy, these strains are brought together in (and *as*) *The Thanatos Syndrome*.

O'Connor assumes a strategy initially as if journeying with her protagonist in a consent to the "modern consciousness." To characterize that strategy: she engages the Modernist myth, imaginatively assumed as if it were the intellectual perspective of the poet within his making, in a close association of maker with her protagonist — a Haze Motes, for instance. Hers is an indirection of a seeming consent to illusion made through what John Keats might recognize as her "negative capability." It will not follow that her own position as person, distinct from a strategic presence to the making as dramatist, consents to that illusion, though a John Hawkes might suspect the contrary in suggesting that she is of the Devil's party. It is this misreading which leads some critics to conclude O'Connor a "hillbilly nihilist." But, as we heard O'Connor remark to "A" (August 2, 1955), "A working knowledge of the devil can be very well had from resisting him." By such a strategy she is enabled to see the world as it may possibly be seen by her protagonist, usually through that fictional manner Henry James made more available to the novelist, sometimes spoken of as an associated point of view, the "limited third person point of view." In that manner nevertheless, it is the protagonist's sensibilities that are dominant, though we recognize a close hovering presence of the maker of that manner. It is as if the poet as a presence looks at the world through the character's own eyes. Indeed, we might notice how convenient that point of view to O'Connor, even in her talks when she is presenting not a "nihilist" protagonist but the "serious writer of fiction." She speaks of herself in the third person, an indirection allowing her to speak for the very serious writer without an intrusive "I."

By such indirection as fictional strategy, then, she encourages our sympathetic suspension of disbelief, at least a partial suspension by a reader as himself (most likely) in her own view a "modern consciousness." Nevertheless, she will be sometimes surprised that a reader does not respond as does she to a character, not recognizing, for instance, that she is herself behind Old Tarwater a "hundred percent" or that she sees Haze at last as a saint. She does not abandon either irony or humor in relation to her character, but there is a satire afoot more devastating. Hers is a manner of indirection carrying a barb, though the barb is not a central concern as much as it is for Percy. That is, she invites a reader to a condescension to a character that may well prove shocking if that reader should suddenly come to recognize in the character his own likeness. (There is a difference of course in her closeness to Mr. Shiftlet, in contrast to her closeness to Haze Motes.) Hers, then, is a manner of indirection whereby she as maker incarnates a presence of her protagonist (*incarnate* a term she sometimes applies to this manner of art). Through her own sensibilities as a person she thus gains for her characters a concreteness of presence to us. (On occasion, her mother Regina might rebuke her for "talking like" such locals.) Additionally, by such a sharing in "modern consciousness" as a point of departure, with a Rayber in *The Violent Bear It Away*, that challenging character may more nearly seem given flesh and blood presence.

Indeed, one might be surprised to hear her say (to "A") that "Rayber's love for Bishop is the purest love I have ever dealt with. It is because of its terrifying purity that Rayber has to destroy it." Very interesting, this aperçu into a surrogate soul which remains a mystery

even to her. To Alfred Corn she writes that Rayber throughout the book is "fighting his inherited tendency to mystical love," a tendency implicit in each person's nature as person
whereby as intellectual soul incarnate he is by nature encouraged to mystical love by intellect's intuitive mode. Indeed, that is the mystical aspect in her fiction: an ambient desire in
a character's consciousness for recovery of love toward things. By her participation in a
character through the imaginative act of making a story, by her gifts of Keatsian "negative
capability," she makes more real to us both the reality of and the inadequacy of that view
that is dogmatically held by the Modernist consciousness in violation of its spiritual nature.

It is by indirection then that by art she attempts to recover the truth about human nature itself through characters as they may reflect the *substantive* reality of actual persons. She
knows that such reality may be sufficiently named only by a complex of terms for what in
actuality is a simple, indivisible nature: the person as *intellectual-soul-incarnate*. Her indirection out of "modernist consciousness" is a strategy in celebration at last of this mystery,
the point of departure a Keatsian "negative capability" approximating the sensitivities imagined for her surrogate person . What she holds steadily by her faith is the truth that as persons we hold a common desire for an integrity now radically eroded by the contrary Modernist illusion born of intense rationalism. Intellect in its Modernist faith would dissolve
reality in favor of that illusion. Such, then, the disturbing ambiguity in her fiction which
so puzzled that anonymous reviewer about her "modernist consciousness," finding O'Connor (in her own paraphrase of the brief review of *A Good Man Is Hard to Find*) "a Catholic
peculiarly possessed of the modern consciousness, that thing Jung describes as unhistorical,
solitary, and guilty. In sum, then, O'Connor recognizes that by our very given nature and
despite our refusals to acknowledge that reality by reason, we (even if resolute modernist)
continue "christ-haunted" in some degree as intellectual soul so long as we exist by nature
as *homo viator*— so long as we live and breathe. (Concerning this strategy of her *indirection*
in pursuit of an imaginative vision as poet, see Appendix D as further commentary on it.)

10

The Intellectual Air We Breathe
in Skating the Surfaces

"St. Augustine wrote that the things of the world pour forth from God in a double way: intellectually into the minds of the angels and physically into the world of things.... The artist penetrates the concrete world in order to find at its depths the image of its source, the image of ultimate reality. This in no way hinders his perception of evil but rather sharpens it, for only when the natural world is seen as good does evil become intelligible as a destructive force and a necessary result of our freedom."

— Flannery O'Connor, "Novelist and Believer"

Our epigraph here summarizes a repeated emphasis Flannery O'Connor makes: the relation of her perspective on creation to her concerns as fiction writer. We meet it in a variety of ways, not only in her talks and letters but everywhere implicit in the fiction itself when carefully engaged beyond surface spectacle. The artist as artist, responsible as steward to his gifts in response to the goodness of creation, must not deny evil as initiated by an actual, erosive spirit at war with the good. The artist as a figure for man himself is, as a maker since Adam's fall, obligated to restorative stewardship, in witness of his right will to the world. By art (diversely peculiar to persons as makers) he recovers, "penetrates the concrete world" in O'Connor's phrase, in a questing witness out of his desire for truth itself. His quest is for "the image of [the concrete world's] source." But in that deportment he must recognize evil as a "destructive force" adverse to the good immanent in "the world of things." Dante, aware of himself as in the shadow of Adam, dramatizes the stewardship of gifts peculiar to him, his great poem the *Divine Comedy* dramatically emblematic of each person's obligations as maker. Thus the poet himself may be taken as a figure for all persons who would sing life in celebratory song and dance rather than in a race toward the abyss, to recall G. K. Chesterton's remark on our having turned toward Modernist appropriations of the good of "the world of things" at about the time of Chaucer.

In our own figure, we remember Adam and Eve for whom life was seen (from our own fallen perspective) as if a perfect poem beyond the necessities of their making. Only out of the subversive discord of evil, penetrating their native good, does life fall through their willful presumption. They are tempted to a subjunctive distortion by intellect: as if evil itself could fulfill a life otherwise incomplete till man become "as gods, knowing good and evil." Since that moment and to be reexperienced by *homo viator* on his way, occurs separation

211

from natural perfection. "Modernist" diminution since the old Eden, evil continues for us erosive of the good of things through human intellect's deployment of the good by deliberate or intentional willfulness, that propensity in us which speaks Original Sin. Hence, in penetrating the good poured forth from God into the world of things out of that propensity no less than by intuitive love, we discover (or so O'Connor insists) that the Devil is actual and not to be denied by an intellectual angelism.[1] To deny evil, though one may desire the good and seek a good even by such denial, is to become endangered intellectually through will's distortion of and even abandonment of reason. For we do not now exist in perfection though by nature we desire our perfection. The consequence is a deportment toward the good which remains actual, but through reason's failing love we may distort perception of the good by sentimentality. And sentimentality out of disoriented reason proves a depreciation of the good itself. (Again, Appendix C enlarges upon this war in its Modernist aspects.)

Through sentimentality, then, the person very easily turns his natural love of the good into a love of the self, an old recognition which may be hinted in exasperation by the current epithet for such a deportment of person: he becomes a "do-gooder" possessed of a gnostic certainty of what is good. In such a confusion of intellect, a possible end is that the person though intending good may form a fanatic attachment to some lesser good, and may indeed mistake evil itself as good. Again, recall Haze Motes as intentional savior of Taulkinham on his arrival there. And that is the shocking "self-recognition" we find in Ivan Karamazov also. It is within this country of dislocated thought as governed by sentimentality that O'Connor dramatizes her Haze Motes, then, with a subtle difference from Dostoevsky's Ivan. Haze responds in anger, not in anguish as does Ivan, to his recognition of the evil he denies as a reality. Ivan would charge God by logic before the court of justice divorced from reality as if but idea: God culpable "agent" of the suffering of children. Haze in a more severe logic serving intent denies both God and evil, though he becomes enraged by those who violate this truth hypocritically. By denial, he is made "clean," since "sin" does not exist. The good (or evil) as opposed to his truth is a delusion cultivated as a "trick on niggers." So Haze concludes. Ivan would "do good," though his actions in the name of the good will appear at last as radically evil to him. Ivan's is a rationalistic excess of perversion Dostoevsky has earlier explored in Raskolnikov of *Crime and Punishment*. For Ivan, "Everything is permitted to the intelligent man" in his pursuit of the good, the ultimate "Romanticism" certified by reason. Hence even Ivan's cultivation of an evil in his bastard brother Smerdyakov is justified, Ivan making that bastard brother an instrument of murder, honed by Ivan's intellectual dialectic.

In this respect Ivan is in a relationship to his dark brother Smerdyakov which is somewhat echoed by the relation of O'Connor's Rayber to Young Tarwater, though with quite different issues of action. Tarwater proves traumatically effective in Rayber's spiritual collapse in that he acts on Rayber's principle, killing that "mistake of nature," Bishop, the immediacy of Rayber's doctrine made concrete and unbearable, a cruelty to a child, so that Rayber collapses, no longer his own God over nature. Ivan's self-justifying little Russian gentleman in diabolically mirroring Ivan leads to Ivan's collapse, a parallel we here observe in Rayber. Tarwater's destructive words to Rayber as he is about to drown Bishop sting Rayber, even as he cannot yet know why. Rayber can *say* evil, but not *do* it. Rayber rationalizes beyond contradiction to himself the mercy of euthanizing the idiot Bishop because a "mistake of nature," but he cannot kill Bishop. But by his arguments he pushes Tarwater toward that act, as Ivan pushes Smerdyakov toward killing their common father, the dissolute (evil) man. The dramatic fillip in Dostoevsky is that Alyosha, come to bring news to Ivan, listens patiently to Ivan's account of his encounter with the Devil as a little Russian middleclass gentleman. But Alyosha has come at that moment to bring news that their bastard brother, Smerdyakov, a "creation" of Ivan as a weapon against God, has just hanged himself. Ivan collapses at the news as we see Rayber similarly collapse when Bishop is drowned. As we anticipate God's bringing good out of Karamazov evil through Alyosha, so too we may anticipate God's bringing good out of the evil fathered by Rayber in Tarwater through Tarwater.

We remember that Flannery cites Ivan as intellectually naïve, though a highly sophisticated student of the Western philosophy since Descartes. She argues that the position Ivan takes, which he justifies as morally justified on that old Karamazov principle his father bequeathed the brothers, is that anything is permissible to private ends. Ivan maintains his "Westernized" intellectual deportment by a "puritan," a single-minded, intention to the good he would define on his own authority as autonomous intellect and then effect through his sentimentality as the only available agent of grace, God having failed in His office. But Ivan's "god" proves to be instrument to a vendetta against God ill-founded by Ivan's reason on the random sufferings of children in this world. It is this putative high principle in defense of children that justifies for Ivan any action by a self-righteous "self" as defender of human innocence — children having been reduced to abstractions in Ivan's dialectical intensity of indictment of God in denial of Original Sin. How quickly that distortion yields to euthanasia — to gas chambers or the needle — or more violently, that drowning of Bishop.

It is to this Modernist doctrine as held by Ivan that we contrast Alyosha's relation to children, its culmination presented in the novel's final pages. The resolving action of the dialectical contest between Ivan and his brother Alyosha — whom Ivan engages as if Alyosha were a naïve intellectual simpleton — is dramatically resolved by Dostoevsky in the novel's conclusion by Alyosha's "Speech at the Stone" to the grieving children at the funeral of one of their own, the child Ilyyushka — a "good" and "kind" and "brave" boy. Alyosha's resolution: "Do not be afraid of life." That brings the novel to its close in a chorus by the children celebrating life: "Hurrah for Karamazov!" And, given Dostoevsky's intention to a sequel to his *Brothers Karamazov* with Alyosha as protagonist, one might suppose that projected novel might have been an exploration of the inevitable relation of *suffering* to *life*, as perhaps we might also imagine Tarwater in the city of the sleeping children of God in a like unfolding. Dostoevsky's intense concern at life's end has been with *suffering* as necessary to our soul's rescue. It is a suffering intensified by that necessary resistance to the ubiquitous dragon lying always at the side of our personal way, seeking whom he may devour. And that, O'Connor will say, is a "suffering with" in the body of community. Very probably, we might have seen Alyosha as more sophisticated staretz out of his suffering, a part of that suffering already underway in his love for Ivan. He might in sequel have spoken to Dostoevsky's "Russian soul" of the terrible speed of God's mercy, though in ways of speaking and circumstances differing from those facing Young Tarwater as O'Connor's country "boy" differs from Alyosha as culturally sophisticated.

In a further parallel, O'Connor's Rayber differs from Ivan, though both share a common infection of intellect — that Modernist infection whose inception occurs with Adam and Eve bequeathing humanity that spiritual infection, Original Sin. This Modernist presumption of originality out of intellectual autonomy confusingly and too easily disguises an intellectual naiveté. It does so through a sophisticated sentimentality that presumes self-rescue through whatever means as self-justified, and along the way justified as well to rectify whatever mistakes of nature. O'Connor's Rayber operates on the Karamazov principle that anything is permissible to a good end as projected by autonomous intellect — theoretically — including euthanasia. That is the principle raised to startling magnitude by Nazi Germany as surreptitiously pursued through positive law wrested from natural law, in systems of totalitarian action devised in the name of a "common good." O'Connor (and especially Percy) see this self-sophistry as a Western intellectual sentimentality, established through totalitarian rationalism — one of the species of "Romanticism" as Ivan Karamazov recognizes as he collapses.

In relation to Ivan's collapse, he is a self-victim through whose psychological symptoms as spectacle allow Dostoevsky to reveal the raging spiritual fever endangering the "Russian soul" in spectacles of conflict between Dostoevsky's "liberal" fathers and his generational peers, the Nihilists. O'Connor echoes that collapse, though she does not dwell upon it in such directness of spectacle as Dostoevsky's episode of Ivan in contest with his devil in the guise of that little middle class Russian "gentleman," a decidedly "liberal" citizen of the society in decay as Dostoevsky would have it in his defense of a fundamentalist Russian soul. Tarwater's "friendly stranger" is more quietly persuasive. Rayber, become a self-victim of that "stranger," collapses when he realizes that Bishop's death has been intellectually justified by his own arguments for an action he could not himself do. (Again, in parallel to Ivan's manipulations of Smerdyakov, who unlike Ivan can *do* No, killing old Karamazov.) Rayber, like Ivan, can only "talk" about correcting Bishop as a conspicuous mistake of nature as Tarwater scathingly tells him. From O'Connor's point of understanding, in parallel to Dostoevsky's drama of Ivan's collapse, she sees Rayber suffering an agony beyond the "accidental" world's spectacle which Rayber himself has till his collapse taken as the ultimate reality. Hence as Modernist intellectual in good standing, Rayber must conclude his own insanity, evidenced to his reason by inclination to love things in themselves. His collapse is an implosion of spiritual failure which he cannot articulate in its reality, having rejected all terms born as names of man's spiritual reality. For all his "formal" intellectual training, as old Tarwater recognized, Rayber as person is perverted to a worship of Nothingness by intellectual naiveté. As Old Tarwater would put it, Rayber is damned to Hell.

Thus Rayber suffers from an accreted burden of love deferred by its denial, so that O'Connor will say of him as a formidable challenge to her craftsmanship (to "A," March 5, 1960): "Rayber's love for Bishop is the purest love I have ever dealt with. It is because of its terrifying purity that Rayber has to destroy it. Very interesting." Very interesting indeed, so that two years later she will remark to Alfred Corn (July 25, 1962) that "throughout the book Rayber was fighting his inherited tendency to mystical love." So long as Bishop is alive, Rayber thinks his disease of love can be contained, though Rayber has not "thought this through" as we say. Now without Bishop he must face the continuing terror of loving "everything and specifically Christ," in O'Connor's phrase. His reason requires Bishop dead, to which end his inherited inclination to love cannot consent. Rayber precipitates the murder through persuasive arguments which Tarwater turns upon him, so that like Ivan, Rayber must at last recognize his participation in Bishop's death.

It is in this "interesting" conundrum of love that one might well see Tarwater's act of murder as itself a possible mode opening Rayber to a grace of rescue. But unlike that possible spiritual action by the grandmother to the Misfit, Rayber cannot say to Tarwater,

"Why you're one of my babies. You're one of my own children!" Instead he makes (O'Connor says) "the Satanic choice, and the inability to feel the pain of his loss [Dostoevsky's "suffering"] is the immediate result." And then she adds a Dostoevskian note: "His collapse then may indicate that he is not going to be able to sustain his choice — but that is another book maybe." The Rayber-Ivan mystery of love, however, seems to draw both poets less than does a pursuit of the Tarwater-Alyosha dimension of love. It is as if in her novel O'Connor practices a dramatic economy in Tarwater as a consciousness within which appear aspects of all the Karamazov brothers, but especially Ivan and Alyosha in their dialectical conflict. At another level of craftsmanship on occasion she gains dramatic economy by juxtaposing separated generations, a grandparent and grandchild in contention in condensing cultural history, as she does with Mr. Head and Nelson in "The Artificial Nigger.") As was true for Dostoevsky, O'Connor did not live to pursue either Tarwater's invasion of the city or Rayber's suffering his love in another "book." It is a matter present in the novel we do have — a "meaning" she would say — nevertheless very important in a preliminary to that possible third novel, the intricate story published a few months after these observations to Corn, her "The Lame Shall Enter First." (We do not pursue that story here — leaving that "fixed and certain" story for the reader's measure of our argument.)

O'Connor's difficulties in making such dramas lies in the complexities of the psychological symptom so dear to current psychological science as the ultimate cause of a disoriented "psyche." In her understanding, these difficulties are valid in part, but largely as symptoms of the deeper cause, that of a spiritual deracination that requires us "to find at its depths the image of its source." That discovery is to be made (Thomas would hold) in a discovery by the questing "self" as itself an image of that source. For as intellectual creature, man is created "in the image of God," his reason an endowment of finite natural law by his very likeness to Eternal Reason. Meanwhile, that natural law denied, there grows an assumption that existence is an accident. Whatever intellectual magnitude justifying that presumption, there lies in it an ironic contradiction. For as presumed based in that principle — that is, the conclusion that human reason constrained to temporal limit by the rationalistic presumption — intellect must conclude man himself necessarily an accident of cumulative accidents. And so the presumption of autonomous intellect that it is by its unaided willful reaction made self-sufficient (that "Existentialist" illusion) leaves intellect dangling tenuously on the thread of whatever whimsical intent it clings to in the maze of the accidental cosmos. The presumption must therefore at last be declared a pseudo-theology: the self is a god beyond both good and evil. It is a conclusion made through finite intellect self-willed to its own apotheosis by angelistic, gnostic intent, whereby the "self" is transcendent god self-declared.

It is this contradiction that O'Connor initially engaged in that first arresting novel *Wise Blood,* in which Haze Motes is her Nietzschean "transcendentalist," presuming himself beyond good and evil and therefore "clean" and unspotted by the world. It is as well the same engagement we find pursued in *The Violent Bear It Away,* not only as affecting young Tarwater but generating a poignant effect of pathos in the fictional presence of Rayber as Modernist intellectual.[2] It is in a common intellectual ground of Modernism that she engages Rayber as a character "culturally" differing from Haze, both sharing this contradiction by intellectual deracination. Haze is her Nietzschean "transcendentalist" presuming himself beyond good and evil, both knowing and doing that which he asserts neither good nor evil since the only "truth is that there is no truth." But how precisely he engages actions sinful in avoiding actions of love. Nevertheless Haze (we might say) is more heroic in pursuit of truth than Rayber — Rayber's cowardice leading Tarwater to taunt him for a cowardice we cannot charge to Haze.

Out of Haze's anger against God, he pursues in his intellectual blindness the only absolute, the Kingdom of Nothingness. Not intellectually familiar with such concepts as current among philosophers, theologians, scientists at mid–20th century, he is initially a "natural Nietzschian," who with an evangelical zeal insists that the only truth is that there is no truth. How close he comes, then, to Satan's "intellectual" declaration in Milton's *Paradise Lost:* "Evil, be thou my good." The difference is that Satan by his created nature knows the proposition a pretentious lie, knowing God so "personally" as he does. Haze believes it the only truth, becoming single-minded in his pursuit of it. And so he is by degree more engaging of our sympathy as protagonist than Rayber, in that Haze recognizes and opposes a range of hypocrisy among his fellow citizens of Taulkinham, who pretend to believe truth actual but act contrary to that belief. Haze opposes what he sees as hypocrisy at an intellectual and spiritual level, though he does not use those terms. In an act of violence, because Hoover Shoates is "not true," Haze murders the hapless charlatan. (Onnie Jay Holy, neé Hoover Shoates: who would make not straight but crooked the way in the desert of Taulkinham.) Even in his act of violence, Haze is appealing to us in his single-mindedness toward truth, though at that moment his is the truth that there is no truth. In such a species of single-mindedness, he might well embrace evil as if good, so that lest careless sympathy obscure that reality St. Thomas in his treatise of evil reminds us that "A devil knows the nature of human thought better than man does." Not knowing his own mind, Haze teeters on the Abyss of Nothingness.

In recognizing such a thematic concern in O'Connor's fiction, we must recognize just how ambitiously high she sets her dramatic intent. Hers is a concern hardly to be restricted to the arena suggested by the contextual "provincial" spectacle to her dramatic action. (As for provincialism, we remind ourselves once more that Dostoevsky's *Brothers Karamazov* has as its setting a small provincial Russian town, perhaps comparable to Milledgeville and its environs.) It is the precise and loving care with which O'Connor builds a limited place within which to unfold her high dramatic action that she is greeted by an initial critical response to her fictions as but satiric species of "local color." But we have heard her speak more incisively on this point in locating the dramatic center in consciousness itself: "The longer you look at one object" (she says in "The Nature and Aim of Fiction") the "more of the world you see in it." Therefore, the "serious writer" (herself) "always writes about the whole world, no matter how limited his particular scene." It is the possibility of a "whole world" of an intellectual soul incarnate upon which she centers her dramatic concern, in her Haze Motes the little world of her agent hero unwittingly pursuing sainthood.

This is a truth of the possible in each person for her, discovered or rediscovered out of two passages she underlies in a collection from St. Thomas edited by Anton C. Pegis, his *Introduction to Saint Thomas Aquinas.* It is an anthology from the *Summa Theologica,* on her bookshelf or at bedside. The first, which she underscores, is from the *Summa Theologica,* I, q. 14, a. 8. Thomas says that "the knowledge of the artificer is the cause of the things made by his art from the fact that the artificer works through his intellect. Hence the form in the intellect must be the principle of action." But *form* in intellect is not arbitrary, not even (we add) when distorted by fancy in an attempt to free intellect of dependence upon the realities of things experienced in their actualities. Things are known in sequential experience when the thing's form *in-forms* intellect, effecting by truth thus receptively known an actualization of the potentiality of the perceiving intellect. Thus intellect is bonded to things in themselves through the person's experiences of things. It is by *inception* (Thomas argues) that truth is initially acquired through the senses. (It is in this respect that Thomas reminds us that our first movement as intellectual creature toward God is through our senses, an irony in *Wise Blood* in that Haze's first attempts to sin in denial of sin is through his senses.) Out of intellectual responses to experiences of things, the actualization of intellectual potentiality, a willfulness of the fallen intellectual creature may presume his own sovereignty over truth itself, ignoring the reality that the act of knowing (a *becoming* of intellect) is already antecedent reality to the will's intentionalities. Knowing, then, is always partial, never comprehensive though the will may be tempted to presume its reason comprehensive. The act of knowing is not the cause of the thing known. But if knowing is at once both partial and already antecedent to intention, by a right will (a right intentionality) the will may pursue an *understanding* proper to the knowing person's finitude, though never *comprehensively* possessing things known. Will may do so through a prudential humility concerned for the perfection of intellect to the understanding of the intellectual soul, reflectively attuned thereby to the orders of being.

Failure of understanding occurs through willful presumption if the person does not recognizing that *understanding* is not *comprehension*. Finite intellect is by limit denied a full "assumption" of a thing as God assumes it in his Love. Thus is the will tempted to that intentionality of reductionism in its intent to comprehension. A thing is reduced by Amazonian "facts" in a violent intellectual subversion of the thing, presumed thereafter as existing only by the intentionality of the will in its power over a thing through gnosis. Still, *knowing* is necessary if alone it is also inadequate to *understanding*. Failing this distinction, how easily will reaches a conclusion presumed by the facts of knowing to have been made by finite intellect, thus concluded *comprehensive* of a thing. (This is the country dangerous to the "experts" in specializations, upon which the popular spirit so much depends at the expense of common sense.) We have here suggested a *process* of thought under will's false sway, understood by the Church as the heresy of angelism, the active presumption by which will acts as if independent of, yet fully comprehensive of, any thing in itself. It is the process whereby love proper to an intellectual action (governed by prudential humility) is perverted to an intention to power over being. And in our recent philosophy, as O'Connor is acutely aware, this is the presumption advanced as if thereby the only *vitalizing* philosophy. Thus Jean-Paul Sartre becomes one of her sources of fictional matter though seldom mentioned by name as in that story "Good Country People." We recall, therefore, that O'Connor had been well-attuned to this perversion, sometimes as an excited acceptance of Sartre as of Jung and Freud by "Cornbelt Metaphysicals" at the time she began writing, a time at which incidentally Walker Percy himself was also much taken with Sartre as prophetic to him of possible uses of "ideas" in fiction.

Whence that "form in the intellect" with which the artificer works? Thomas says it is gathered from things experienced directly by the finite artificer, and to be sorted under the concept of the *possible* by reason. It is concerning this provision to intellect that Flannery marks a second passage from the *Summa,* I, q. 14, a. 8, Reply Objection 3: "Natural things are midway between the knowledge of God and our knowledge: for we receive knowledge from natural things, of which God is the cause by His Knowledge. Hence, just as the natural things that can be known by us are prior to our knowledge, and are its measure, so the knowledge of God is prior to them, and is their measure; as, for instance, a house is midway between the knowledge of the builder who made it, and the knowledge of the one who gathers his knowledge of the house from the house already built." And here, let us be clear, lest we be chary of a willing suspension of disbelief: The question immediate to our concern is not whether we ourselves subscribe to Thomas' "metaphysics," but with the relation of this maker of a story to her made story. Thomas' argument here is central to O'Connor's reason in her making of stories.

Our concern first and last, in order that we may honor her postulant devotion to art as Christian artificer, is to better understand the effect upon her making of her belief as a Christian for whom St. Thomas is the "philosopher." Her action of making is affected by that belief, especially in relation to her selection and ordering of *matter* to the service of a *form*. In respect to fictions, the conjunction of form and matter toward an aesthetic unity — toward the good of the thing being made — allows to her as poet that dramatic ambiance we ourselves may experience in *this* story as now fixed and certain, an ambiance of "meaning" which we carry with us as an after-effect having read it. That is, our own intellect is in some degree *in-formed* from having read a story. Her understanding from Thomas allows her the recognition of an analogical relation of herself as poet, as maker, to God as Creator. And within that understanding there follows for her a moral sense of responsibility as maker, in act at the secondary level of the analogy. Her *story,* then, is like the *house* in Thomas' metaphor, being "midway" between herself as its proximate cause as builder and the reader who "gathers his knowledge" of the story from the story itself as "already built." But this is a concern at the secondary level of artisanship in respect to the reader's responsibility to judge the beauty of the story according to its being well-made or not, even as he is responsible to judge a house or garden as well- or ill-made. At the primary level of responsibility, the builder's concern must always be for the good of the thing he makes is building, house or story. But our living in a house or in a story for the duration of a willing suspension of disbelief carries a responsibility to us as resident. We must judge whether such a "living" enhances "life" or not.

Whoever the maker, his belief affects his making, O'Connor insists: This is a reality of art regardless of the particular belief held by the artist. (Even indifference to *any* belief is a species of willed belief.) It is this reality to which John Paul II speaks in his encouraging *Letter to Artists* (1999). For, while the "distinction between the moral and the artistic aspects is fundamental" (an allusion to the distinctions we have found in St. Thomas), it is "no less important" to recognize "the connection between them. Each conditions the other in a profound way." Thus the work of art "becomes a unique disclosure of [the artists'] own being, of *what* they are and of *how* they are what they are." While this argument recognizes distinction between moral and artistic aspects of the made thing, it recognizes as well the fallacy of "impersonality" in respect to any making — whether of scientific theorems, philosophical systems, or masterpieces of art. "In shaping a masterpiece," John Paul II continues, "the artist not only *summons his work into being,* but also in some way *reveals his own personality* by means of it" (his emphasis).

It is in recognizing this inevitability to the actions of making that the artist may avoid reducing art to a tract as a means of advocating his belief, a deportment in making destructive to art itself as St. Thomas insists. O'Connor's concern for art's indirection rises out of recognizing this dangerous byway as seductive to the artist, and especially as it may lead to a distortion of truth through misunderstanding the proper relation of the "moral and artistic aspects" in art by the poet. By such misunderstanding the poet commits himself in a reductionist (even a "puritan") service to art, no longer seeing *with* art but *through* art as if reduced to instrumental. That is, he commits himself to some species of a pragmatic intent toward his audience, whether he intends to deny or assert the reality of sin or Satan or of God Himself. It will lead, as she remarks in that review of a poor "religious" novel intending the good, to a "depressing new category," that "light Catholic summer reading." By avoiding evil as actual, or by sentimentally advocating good in an excessive enthusiasm (lest a reader become disturbed by his summer reading) there becomes lost by pseudo-art a sharpened perception of evil in its relation to the good, as O'Connor argues in our present epigraph. By that failure of art, a reader is lulled, and will come to demand (as does Flannery's Californian reader) that his "heart" be "lifted up" at the expense of his "head."

Art as dependent upon the actions of nature is therefore implicitly dependent upon the realities of good and evil. A thing fails to be good — whether a story or a wall, a peach or a person — insofar as it is *not*, whether by an arrested potentiality as a "mistake of nature" or in *homo viator* as intellectual soul by his denial — his *non servium* — preventing potential understanding. Most crucially, then, for the poet or for his reader, is his own willful rejection of his potential good. That is the arena within which drama unfolds as *possible* action. What a shock, then, to discover a failure to acknowledge the moral responsibility to distinguish by reason between good and evil. By mid–19th century, through habitual cultivation of dissociated sensibilities in the popular spirit, the "Victorians" (some of them) could but be suddenly shocked by Alfred Lord Tennyson, that gentle beloved poet up to that late moment, when he declares shockingly that "nature [is] red in tooth and claw." And by then, others of the Victorians were beginning to feel arrogantly comfortable in a more serene putting of the Tennysonian phrase in justification of nature's bloody demeanor: "the survival of the fittest."

It is in this tension between good and evil that a drama may signify beyond the magnitude of the "personal" limits of the artist as an intellectual creature embodying fictionally (i.e., as *possible*) the dramatic action. But by removing obstacles to that recognition, the poet may become a "realist of distances." Even though he think himself rationalistic to the core of his intellect, even taking himself a Darwinian disciple, nature red in tooth and claw may speak through his art a deeper mystery. In O'Connor's words, if his is a "responsibility to the things he sees, he may transcend the limitations of his narrow vision." As for herself as poet, only by a sharpening of vision through reason, she argues, can "evil become intelligible as a destructive force" but also a mystery signaling "a necessary result of our freedom." Hers is a recognition we have suggested as also permeating Dostoevsky's greatest work, in response to which Dostoevsky comes to emphasize *suffering*—a "suffering-with" in O'Connor's phrase — as the virtue which removes obstacles to grace. Closer home to Andalusia, over in Mississippi, Faulkner speaks the name of a virtue to be praised, *endurance*. But in O'Connor's Thomistic perspective mere endurance as a Stoic virtue lacks the spiritual depths of the concern as held by Dostoevsky and O'Connor. Our introducing this Russian as more "Southern" on this point than Faulkner as seen by our "hillbilly" Thomist is occasioned by John Paul II's own summoning of Dostoevsky to support in encouraging artists. It is in Dostoevsky's "profound insight" in *The Idiot* (Part III, chapter 5), the Pope says, that we hear the words, "beauty will save the world." To which John Paul adds that "Beauty is a key to the mystery and a call to a transcendence" far other than that of a Modernist angelism, making the stewardship of beauty the artist's special charge. It does not therefore require, and indeed makes impossible to any recovered beauty, our ignoring evil, either in life or by life's art, since art is an imitation of the *possible* life of the intellectual soul as discovered by the poet. The poet discovers in the actualities of a person's actions in response to the contingencies to his life — the actions thus a "history" in its human manifestations, especially as the poet remembers his own personal experiences of persons. And the most viable person from whom the poet learns most is always himself.

For Flannery O'Connor, the obligations of the maker of things (nature informing art) as understood through Thomas are based in a belief in God as the "architect" of all natural things. It is her knowledge of things in this light which O'Connor must therefore appropriate to her fictions. It follows that *form* in her making is known (or discovered to be already known by her) in her actions of making with reason. That is, her pursuit of form in her art is in response to forms already intellectually recognized from experiences of "natural things," adapted to possible actions of human nature responding to truths in realities, in things actual. Most central to art as a part of creation are those exceptional "things" called persons. Thus the *possible* proves *viable*— proves "life giving" to her made thing. In the light of that understanding, she imitates imaginatively possible actions as learned from actually existing things — from actual persons. But, once more, it is in that actual person most closely at hand in whom the poet discovers the possible as derived from what we tend to call the known "history" of particular persons. Thus — wonder of wonders to the poet in coming to himself as poet — no actual person is closer for that discovery than himself. In the light of such "self" recognition, much of what O'Connor has to say in letters and in talks and essays becomes vibrant of the personal, though most often she expresses it by indirection in the third person about the "writer." (How "personal" her testimony in that remark to "A" that "A working knowledge of the devil can be very well had from resisting him.")

How well O'Connor knows, how personally known to her, that old commonplace that art is local. But in the local there accompanies as well for her vision an abiding mystery attending local matter of those "country" persons she knows. In her perspective the most intimately possible presence to any person — here and now, recognized or not — is the Holy Ghost, through Whom that person continuously *is,* and is therefore in prospect of fulfillment. That presence for her is the Absolutely Personal, through Whom she lives and breathes and has her being. Still, there is that other "presence" she recognizes as well — one always abiding an opportunity in this present moment to some spiritual destruction. No less personal by clever intent, feeding a growing appetite in the person for illusion as he may. This is a presence recognizing that each person is possessed of free will, but a free will which suffers a congenital crack called Original Sin. That is the aperçu — the "crack"— through which Satan may enter a self-consciousness by its consent, intending by subtlety a destruction of the actual and a prevention of the potential good of *this* person at *this* place at *this* time. Here is that crossroads at which the person finds himself in each moment, at which "place" in his being he may or may not recognize the dragon lying in wait for him. How friendly that creature may appear at first: as is Ivan's bourgeoisie devil as a little Russian gentleman who desires acceptance as a middleclass neighbor, or Tarwater's considerate "country" talking devil at the grave of Old Tarwater.

What more revealing person at hand against whom to test the possible than the poet, the maker? Indeed, in literary matters of the 20th century we discover it the most autobiographical century ever. The *matter* of the personal *self* tended in that literature to be heavily autobiographical in providing art's spectacle. Yet in that tendency of art, given the poet's lacking metaphysical reconciliation to creation, the poet tends to treat his personal history as disguised by techniques out of a fearfulness of the "personal" in art. That is a detachment by the poet almost as if he were scientist, even. It may appear a seemingly objective pathology under diagnosis. Consider Ernest Hemingway as big game hunter or as aficionado of the bullfight, or James Joyce as an intellectual undergraduate. There seemed necessary in the circumstances of the autobiographical as matter to art a special attention through technique in adapting the autobiographical as if studiedly "objective" and removed from the poet. It is as if that detachment were as much to protect the poet as to defer to the good of his art. Not, of course, that there was not as well a possible exhibitionism in someone like Allen Ginsberg, or Hemingway in his *Moveable Feast,* the art therefore more conspicuously "personal." T. S. Eliot had argued specifically a necessity to the poet of selecting and controlling his "objective correlatives" in removing the poet as person. That, we have suggested, had been a strategy for Eliot out of a deeply personal dilemma rising in him toward a spiritual crisis. His primary action as poet must be, in the pre–*Waste Land* Eliot, to distance himself from what he knows to be most personal in its origin.

The reacting of the "Beat" poets — and of Ezra Pound earlier — was to what seemed to them only pretenses to the "impersonal" in that strategy. The severance of the poet's "self" from his art is severely pilloried by the Beats in an epithet for the poet's "objective" pretense. He is a "Cornbelt Metaphysical." Epithet thus suggests a cowardice in refusing personal risk by the poet, Ginsberg's *Howl* an intentional counter to Eliot's *Waste Land* in this respect. Pound is satirically indirect, though he very likely had Eliot's stance in mind in early poems, in his "Sestina: Altaforte" for instance as sharply counter to Eliot's mode in "Prufrock." Or remember Pound's brief "Tame Cat," which declares "It rests me to be among beautiful women./ Why should one always lie about such matters/"— this latter poem perhaps bearing in it by implication that familiar name for Eliot among his friends, "Tom." (Eliot will become for Pound later "Parson Eliot." Pound to the contrary is intent on being more an active than a tame tomcat.) As it turns out "personally" for Eliot, his attempt to remove himself as artisan from his own personhood proved for him futile gambit, and so in his "Ash-Wednesday" he faces directly the inescapable personal in a confessional mode much closer to that of St. Augustine's *Confessions.*

We find O'Connor recognizing as immediate to her making the relevance of the personal, reflected again and again in a whimsical or ironic association of herself with a character who had become more or less publicly notorious through her fictions. On one occasion she speaks a playful identity with a character, then finds it necessary to clarify lest misunderstand. Her friend "A" misreads Flannery's speaking of herself as "like" Hulga in "Good Country People." She reminds "A" that she is also like Nelson and Haze and Enoch. She might have put it that, when effective in making a story, she reveals in the "possible" human natures of her fictional characters something of her own potentialities as person. In life itself, given a conflicted will, the possible may appear either desirable or threatening. (It seemed desirable to Pound, threatening to the early Eliot.) Relations of the personal to a thing-so-personally-made in devotion to art, then, may very well reveal something of what John Paul II calls the author's own "inner life," something of his own *"personality."* But in using such a term as *personality,* John Paul II means much more than an impression by spectacle of the author as perceived by others at the surface as popularly understood, the surface of "autobiography." Hemingway is soldier, hunter, lover at the level of his history, sometimes shown with a flair like Pound's shouting his "Sestina: Altaforte" on a pub table.

How like in his several callings to a Misfit or Mr. Shiftlet, one might suggest — this varied
pursuit by Hemingway of becoming a man in full through the surface of things. But O'Connor believes she sees something deeper than those surfaces. In Hemingway, she writes Father McCown (January 16, 1956) "there is apparently a hunger for a Catholic completeness
in life."

O'Connor and John Paul II understand in common that *personality* speaks manifestations of the very specific essence of *this* person as person who makes *this* work. The realities of the *freedom* exercised by a person in intellectual actions may well reveal to the person as writer (if not to the reader of such a "personal" work) the inherent possibilities,
contingent possibilities, to good or evil actions in himself. Dostoevsky is uncomfortably
aware of this truth of the poet's dependence as person upon his own peculiar yet common
humanity, that dependence which opens him to the possible in his drama in compensation
to his calling. How uncomfortable: to find a likeness of the poet to Raskolnikov or to Ivan
Karamazov in oneself, let alone with that narrator of *Notes from Underground,* which work
set Dostoevsky on a new and more personally endangering direction as poet. There is an
anecdote of Dostoevsky at a tea party where the women coming and going were celebrating him, *pace* Prufrock, asking "personal" questions about how he could know such horri-
bly violent things, whereupon he declared himself guilty of having tossed children up to
catch them on a bayonet. Whether they responded "That is not what I meant at all" I don't
remember reported in the anecdote.

If the principle that undergirds our understanding of the relation of the personal to art
is sound — the principle that we are by common nature potential to good and evil acts —
no wonder that a person may find himself "like" other persons in reading a well made work
dramatizing human actions, even though such possibility need not be specific actions registered in the personal *history* of the poet as recorded in the obituary called *Biography of....*
We nevertheless do find ourselves in somewise akin to agents most various in well-made dramas, including even likenesses to an Oedipus or to a Raskolnikov in respect to *possible* actions. It will come as no surprise to Flannery O'Connor, then, to discover actual persons
separate from herself who correspond closely to her own fictional characters, after she has
made characters fixed and certain in a story. Such discovery may be a reaffirming delight,
evidence that the poet has been true to possibilities of human nature. (How common the
disclaimer prefacing novels, that any likeness of a character in the novel to any person living or dead is a coincidence.) It can but be arresting to the poet to discover a likeness of his
character to an actual person encountered long after, an actual person anticipated in a story
already published. We cited earlier that small "O'Connor" story she reports in a letter, that
encounter on an elevator in an Atlanta (Taulkinham) department store of an actual Mrs.
Turpin. This, after having *fixed,* made *certain* by art, her own Mrs. Turpin in "Revelation"
(the emphasized terms from Thomas describing an artifact's limits).

The similarities discovered are more than coincidence, though made the more arresting for O'Connor by the upside-downness of her actual experience in relation to her made
character. For here "life" seems to be imitating art. To have taken the experience and from
it to have made a story — that is the more likely sequence. Indeed, it is a procedure endorsed
by no less than Henry James, who in advocating *character* as the desirable point of departure in fiction intends character as gathered from observations of actual persons. (James is
an inveterate "people watcher.") *Character* thus gathers *situation* to a fiction more persuasively James argues than if the poet first manufactures a situation and then attempts to fill

it with a character. For O'Connor, the moment itself in the Atlanta store may be said to have irked Miss Flannery personally, judging from her report of it. She reacts to the condescending pity of that actual "Mrs. Turpin," who was so concerned for that poor crippled country girl on the elevator whom in charity she tries to help. In reporting her Atlanta experience, once back home at Andalusia, O'Connor provides a smoldering irony in her account, controlling a possible anger such as that already exhibited by that "ugly girl" Mary Grace in "Revelation" who strikes Mrs. Turpin with her textbook from a liberal college, a book entitled *Human Development.*

Such is food for thought, perhaps long hard thought, while recovering from such an experience in an Atlanta department store — once safely back at Andalusia and feeding those greedy aggressive geese and chickens and peacocks. Especially one might puzzle the mystery whereby the lame may enter first, or the top rail find itself on the bottom. No doubt, she says (in her account of the Atlanta venture) the lame enter first because they knock everybody else aside with their crutches. That remark, remembering her own angry flight away from the actual Mrs. Turpin on an Atlanta elevator, might make one appreciate Mary Grace's hitting Mrs. Turpin, though perhaps well-advised to take from the actual experience only a "working knowledge of the devil" gained from a struggle in resisting him in the moment. From such an actual experience in Atlanta, no wonder that Flannery writes Ted Spivey (March 17, 1964), "My idea about Atlanta is get in, get it over with and get out before dark." Mr. Head and Nelson after their visit couldn't agree more.

Of course in such "seeings" of the self, such a knowing of oneself, O'Connor concludes it a way to "know the world." But if thus gaining a more certain knowledge of the world it may in the moment itself be unsettling to discover as well in that self-knowledge something of an "image of ultimate reality" possible to any person, including a shuffling cripple on an Atlanta elevator — alas also fallen through Adam. To do so is to suspect as writer herself as an immediate image of mankind in its fallenness, more certain than comforting knowledge. Nevertheless it is a rich "personal" experience for one whose calling is to dramatize our common fallenness. To recognize this reality about the self as a person may lead to a discovery of the ultimate Cause of this image (myself), that Cause springing up within and hovering from beyond the moment's panic of self-exile by rejecting Grace. And so exile proves not so simple as when reserved to the will and its pursuit of alienation from reality. There is another condition of alienation that continues unrelieved by moving from this place to some other place, whether to New York or London or Paris — or even back to some Andalusia, as some of the "Expatriate" artists of the 1920s were to discover. Such recognition is circumstantial to Asbury in "The Enduring Chill," he accepting his "Joycean" exile as artist with sardonic irony because confining him in a place very like Andalusia, Asbury's only relief from guilt his excuse of having been determined by circumstances. As artist, Asbury is hardly concerned to penetrate "the concrete world in order to find at its depths the image of its source." He rather reflects on his own image in his self-pity as a species of self-love. This manner by a poet in pursuit of placelessness, as if thereby to certify autonomy is notorious as a literary "Movement" in the 1920s, a flow of writers as "Expatriates," taking flight from the Midwest or the South to New York, and then from New York to London or Paris. And so conspicuous this "Movement," indeed, that the phenomenon became matter for books and even academic courses, much talked of speculatively by neophyte writers at the Iowa Writers Workshop in the 1950s — or by a visitor to Flannery, wishing Flannery might be taken "out of all this," i.e., out of provincial Milledgeville and her final hospice Andalusia as Flannery's determining circumstances were perceived by a concerned visitor risking that provincial territory on a brief visit.

O'Connor recognizes a true sense of exile as common to us through Original Sin and unreconciled by mere place. She would see it often manifest in the wanderings of the world by "Artists." That manner of response to exile, she also knew, does not effect any nurture of hope so long as the wanderer does not recognize the course of his feeling haunted by a sense of exile in any place. If not recognized by reason as beyond accidents of history or geography, then hope proves forlorn. F. Scott Fitzgerald, in both his life and his work, plays out this loss of understanding with a pathos as the signal effect in both his life and his work. Such a sense of exile as Fitzgerald's reflects the deeper dislocation of himself as person, deeper than any surface discomforts that might be attributed to geographical place, either to a Midwestern or New York or Paris "place." To wander roads East or West (as Expatriate or as Beat) may serve only to arrest the deeper journeying stirring the wanderer's desire. For that limited sense of *place* attributed to geography and its history proves inadequate placebo, comforting though it may be in the fleeting delusion that surely some "place" in itself may satisfy the sense of a loss — absolve the wanderer if only he find the right place in which to bide. How anciently haunting, this sense of a lost Eden. And how easily transmuted into self-pity out of a sense of exile declared unjust, unwarranted. The unreasoned desire is that by the journeying alone *homo viator* may dissolve from his self-consciousness his sense of dislocation in nature or community which persists as a mystery beyond either history or geography. Perhaps what is required, then, is a magic act devised by intellect to overwhelm such a mystery, effecting a self-rescue beyond both history and geography. By the authority of autonomous intellect, empowered by autonomous intent, by an angelism he would decree pseudo-transcendence. Failing that attempt, *homo viator* may well collapse into despair, as do Ivan Karamazov and Rayber Tarwater.

No manner of "high-stepping" in the liberated 1920s could still the restless spirit, recover spirit to a dance out of the panic of the race experienced by most of the Expatriates. Not even the "Charleston" was sufficient or the mask of dandy or flapper. Ah, memories of the "Charleston," periodically revived. We notice that Eliot, at first himself an Expatriate as Henry James had been before him, settled into place in London, observing the malady he had already experienced more widely acted out in spectacle by his friend Ezra Pound. Pound moves from Idaho to New York, to the continent, to England, back to France, then to a redoubt in Italy, a last gasp attempt upon his own Andalusia. O'Connor, becoming aware of such immediate literary fathers when she goes off to the writing school at Iowa, will quickly know that hope's certification, its healing power, lies in a country far other. Hope lies, not in any Andalusia, but in the Cause of things, binding this place (wherever signified by coordinates) within a "country" beyond both geography's and history's reckonings. For her assuredly there is a recognition of a country beyond "provincial" place, whether an Andalusia called New York or Paris or London or Pisa. Very early she begins to recognize an abiding place beyond Baldwin County, Georgia, or Iowa City, Iowa, a place always close at hand. That is a country spoken to her through her senses, through transcendent Love, a Love speaking always the possible recovery of that lost country. But she begins to know more certainly that it is a country to be recovered always *here* and *now*, whether the place be Andalusia in Middle Georgia or New York or London or Paris or Pisa. And always it is a most *private* possibility to an actual recovery as person on the way, allowing the poet to recognize the mystery of the Word within his own word — if the poet is an O'Connor or Eliot or

Percy. Hope at last begins echoing in consciousness itself, speaking the exile as no longer forlorn since desire now homes toward its Cause.

And so the poet may discover hope spoken to by that beauty to which the poet is responsible as John Paul II reminds us. In doing so he may celebrate at last a Beauty past change. As our allusion suggests, that is the reminder O'Connor encounters in her favorite poet, Gerard Manley Hopkins, citing his "Spring and Fall." (This, a month before she died.) The poem begins "Margaret, are you grieving/ Over Goldengrove unleaving?" The speaker — Hopkins and not a "mask" — is asking a child observed as disturbed by the season's change, the seeming cause of her premature sorrow. The child's tears are not for the leaves fallen to decay, Hopkins says, but for "What heart heard of, ghost guessed," namely that "It is Margaret you mourn for." (The poem as drama is a reflective meditation on a beauty changing, the words not to be imagined dramatically as if cruelly spoken directly to Margaret by the poet.) Understanding — for Margaret on a first awakening or for Flannery nearing her own death — is resolved beyond tears through an intensity of response to a thing, in which response the thing is no longer simply an object perceived — not even those golden leaves of autumn falling to decay before Margaret's troubled eyes.

What Margaret does not yet know, nor can she be told since she must make that journey toward understanding, is that change speaks its cause by change itself as Hopkins believes. For Hopkins that Cause is Sustaining Love, beyond full understanding this side Beatitude. How other is the "meaning" of change for John Keats, who can see only Queen Melancholy as presiding over "Beauty that must die." The fading song of the nightingale encourages in Keats only his projecting melancholy of self-pity, even upon the "Fast fading violets covered up in leaves" at his feet where he stands "darkling." Alas for Keats, even the timely "Goldengroves unleaving" for which Margaret thinks she mourns were already withered in their April bud. By feeling, projected as self-pity upon the larger world, all things turn objects by their dissolving, dissolution speaking Melancholy as sovereign queen over thought. The thinking person doomed as trophy, to be hung at last as but "cloudy" on Melancholy's dark wall. Feeling over thought, in response to change. No wonder that Prufrock will be distraught over that bald spot in the middle of his head.

Here we are a long, long way from change patiently unfolded to Dante by reason — by his guide Virgil — in their steady descent into Hell and the labor of ascending Mount Purgatory. Dante's guide Virgil is critically celebrated as figure for the reason waking in the pilgrim Dante along his way. But only up to a point where Dante is strong enough intellectually to move beyond limited reason. Not that in Virgil as actual poet of his *Aeneid* we do not have Keatsean moments. How poignant is Dido's farewell to that beautiful presence Aeneas sailing away, who will not be kept from his proper end, the founding of a New Troy in time and place. And along that way of Aeneas as journeyman Virgil finds many occasions for acknowledging "the tears of things," Virgil's famous phrase. But reason speaks ends beyond change, change the sad "fate" of all things for Virgil as pagan. Even New Troy must eventually fall. For Dante, then, reason in itself is not sufficient to the recovery of the intellectual soul beyond golden groves and golden lads, all decaying. There is to this point Dante's elaborate pageantry of a sacramental transformation in himself crossing Lethe into that Eden beyond death on Purgatory summit. Dante the pilgrim bearing reason itself as now transformed. Virgil must make his lonely way, his mission over, back down to Limbo where Homer waits and those other great poets.

In literary history between Virgil and Dante, in the spectacles of Western sensibilities, there follows Virgil that formal Stoicism he exhibits so reasonably to Dante on their journey, knowing himself fated to Limbo. We inherit that Stoicism from Marcus Aurelius, persuasively with us still, edition after edition of the emperor's *Meditations* written for himself as lord of creation. How ancient and continuing to us, those meditations on a deportment necessary to control melancholy stirred by the tears of things. Stoicism proves adaptable since Aurelius, particularly in the Modernist world as encouraged by inclinations to intellectual autonomy. In the midst of the rubble of defeat, an endurance of defeat is still possible through Stoical skepticism, the skepticism a protection against sentimentality. Thus Walker Percy will remark a Southern Stoicism born of the history of Southern defeat, suggesting that defeat itself may help explain the blossoming of Southern literature, the "Southern Renaissance." But he will also find Stoicism insufficient to his own intellectual soul's rescue. (See Percy's essay "Stoicism in the South," in his posthumous gathering, *Signposts in a Strange Land*.)

Stoicism proves insufficient to Percy but seemingly well-suited to a pragmatic New England poet as Stoic, Robert Frost. We remarked earlier that Frost takes his Stoic cue in a New England manner as activist poet from reading Henri Bergson, Frost's "West-running Brook" his immediate response on reading *Creative Evolution*. That contrariness of a west-running brook, in that neck of the woods of the cosmos where all brooks run east, speaks a dark message demanding firm, unsentimental Stoicism in response to anticipated hopeless resistance. A dignity is thus gained (as Stoicism out of the emperor argues) though likely known only to the firm resister himself. The brook by its contrariness speaks the "universal cataract of death/ That spends to nothingness," and such dark recognition out of nature's signs might best be kept private, lest the Stoic disturb his Beatrice in her own fading beauty. Besides which (as Frost's poem has it) that New England Beatrice would take the dark truth off to "lady land" in denial. Best to compromise with formidable "nature." Better "One Step Backward Taken," as another Frost poem puts it. How contrary Hopkins proves to Frost's "Stoical" deportment toward the meaninglessness, the nothingness of things swept by cataract to decay. Hopkins in his response to the seeming contrariness of things in decay speaks of a "pied beauty" in things, *piedness* itself a celebration of an unchanging Beauty. For Hopkins, both these beauties are present here and now. That is a recognition O'Connor holds in common with Hopkins, her favored poet.

We have here been suggesting the literary ambiance O'Connor encounters as she ventures into the Midwest then to the East before turning back to Baldwin County. Hopkins not Frost speaks for her when he sees "rose-moles all in stipple upon trout that swim," speaking a vision of Beauty which O'Connor sees in a comic recognition: that awkwardly beautiful peacock strutting its limited glory of beauty in a display whose glory depends upon its hidden underwear, the grace of existing at all. A turning home to her true Home, then, though a turning often read by O'Connor's critics as more than one step backward taken, she submitting to Rome over Andalusia. But she turns things in themselves at hand in Baldwin County, no longer to be taken as objects as they were taken by Keats or Frost. Or as they are at first taken by an Ernest Hemingway perhaps in his reaction of a Stoic forwardness to engage "death in the afternoon" bullfight, yet seeking an epiphany in a rescue O'Connor suspects. O'Connor sees in him instead "a hunger for a Catholic completeness in life."

For O'Connor, then, in that hunger lies a possibility through the immediacy of things here and now by an open response to those things that (as St. Augustine discovered) stand always about the doors of our flesh. That has been O'Connor's steadying faith as maker all along, confident that by that response she could "find at [the object's] depths the image of its source." In that response, she finds confirmed her belief that in the "object"—in the actually existing thing—nature and grace are discovered in a coincident proportionality, speaking a thing companionable in the mystery of being. Insofar as one may gain by his manner, if only partially gain, vision of the "source" of things, he may understand the more fully why St. Thomas insists that the responsibility of the artificer, the person as maker, is primarily to the good of the thing he makes. Moral rectitude as necessary to *homo viator* on his pilgrim way to fulfillment is always paramount to the person as *person,* including the person as artificer. In respect to the responsibilities proximate to the labors of his making in service to beauty, the "science" of that making is peculiar in limits to here and now to his stewardship of beauty. Consequently for the artificer, that thing's own good is primary toward that beauty called (by Thomas) *claritas.*

If moral rectitude is an inescapable concern to the poet as person, the responsibility to the making of a thing in itself is secondary to that end, for stewardship is *toward,* not the *end.* But in the act of making, that act here and now is primary as proximate, in the interest of the good poem or story he *is making.* That thing, through form consonant with matter, may come into being with a *claritas* proper to it thereby. It may well be that, through the exercise of stewardship to gifts at that local level of responsibility, there may consequently follow the maker's own recovered orientation to his proper end as person. The same may follow even for the reader himself— God's uses of the good of things made (poem or story) being beyond the maker's limited power of intent. As well, it may prove that the made thing in the little world of our becoming as person, as we respond to a beauty fixed in the made thing, allows that thing higher office through art as instrumental not only to the maker's but even to a reader's own becoming. But that is a possibility to human action reserved to the grace of God and not to the maker's intent to that end by art. In this devotion to the good of a thing being made, O'Connor recognizes this paradox of grace. Hence she will say "I am never more completely myself than when I am writing," and this because in that devotion "I completely forget myself." The paradox, or mystery, she recognizes: "It is the same with Christian self-abandonment" in the "Christian insistence on the fulfillment of the individual person...."

But first: the concern for bringing beauty out of selected matter by form requires judgment by the maker of the viability (of the particular piece of wood or word he has chosen) if he would make an ax-helve or a poem. That choice made, there must follow actions of release of possible form from the chosen matter—a form consonant with the "engrained" virtues (the essential nature) of the chosen matter. We speak figuratively by terms of concrete matter, of a piece of wood chosen by a craftsman to make an ax-helve, to emphasize that any matter to a making bears essential limits to any form possible to the craftsmanship. For the poet, the potentialities of human nature is the forest from which he selects his wood, recognizing that his choosing according to merely board feet if sawed regardless of grain is to abuse matter in ignorance of the essential nature of the thing as matter, affecting the essential nature of his made thing. An ax-helve properly made by a woodsmith's art suits its rigid ax-head but without violation of the nature of the helve in its strength and resilience. Then the ax may well serve in building a house—or an altar in a house.

By analogy to our argument we may find St. Thomas in agreement that a story well-formed from its matter through reason may subsequently serve also in the recovery of a "temple of the Holy Ghost," to borrow from O'Connor's story of that title, in which story lies the "meaning" we attempt here to articulate, the integrity of this person at his final end. But first comes the ax-helve well-made. First comes the story in itself in that labor of love in self-abandonment to its good. And in respect to either's being well-made — the ax-helve or story — it may bear a perfection even though "made" by a craftsman who is, up to the point of his making, a moral reprobate. And even after his devoted making, he may prefer to continue reprobate. Yet in the act of making itself, insofar as he is devoted to the good of the thing being made, he turns outward in a devotion to its good. The moment of his making, let us suggest, is (by an analogy) a proportionate action in kinship, as "like unto," that moment of the pilgrim's openness to the Good at the lifting of the Host at Mass. That is the recognition O'Connor experiences as we heard her remark in that letter to "A" (December 9, 1961): "In never completely forget myself except when I am writing and I am never more completely myself than when I am writing."

It is a possibility she sees reflected in the art of writers who do not share her belief, their made things reflecting a truth they have seen but not subsequently embraced in the matter used in a making beyond their recognition. Such unbelieving makers, by their devotion to the matter chosen in eliciting a form proper to that matter, may possibly discover a mystery. For, in O'Connor's words once more, what such a writer "makes will have its source in a realm much larger than that which his conscious mind can encompass and will always be a greater surprise to him than it can ever be to his reader" ("The Nature and Aim of Fiction"). For such a writer, though he insist to himself as a "conscious mind" that he is Modernist in his belief, the very matter he chooses bears in it essential accident and by his openness to his making his is an act out of a love for the good of the thing he makes which does not run contrary to the "grain." To our point, we remember that event, the Priest's sacramental action "made" in an offering to God, an action not vitiated even by a reprobate priest as maker. The denial of the validity of such sacraments was long ago declared a heresy by the Church. In this belief, how could O'Connor declare other than that as such a believer she has no choice but to be an artist in response to her calling. Indeed, this is a mystery of a person's becoming which O'Connor engages in "A Temple of the Holy Ghost," she in that story very much on that child's side, her rare protagonist as preadolescent. It is as if in forgetting herself as maker of the story she too becomes as a little child, forgetting herself in making.

In the devotion proper to the good of the thing being made, that "self-abandonment" (O'Connor's phrase) speaks devotion to the good, reaching by that action beyond the maker's finitudes as *this* person. And so we affirm again that there may consequently occur to the maker through such a devotion beyond himself some recovery of himself, toward that integrity which St. Thomas affirms the poet's proper end as person. That possibility to his proper end lies in a larger dimension than of his limits as a person gifted to the making this story in itself. What we would affirm out of Thomas is the possibility that the maker's deportment to his gift may remove obstacles to grace. He may move toward his proper end in a self-forgetfulness, by acts of love in making the thing he makes. His action is a proportionate action, analogous as maker to that unlimited act of Love whereby he *is* as God's image. Hence the possible collateral effect by grace: a degree of perfection of his "personal" potentiality as this intellectual soul incarnate, recovered through devotion as poet. In hope, he may recover himself as congenial — as con-natural to things created and made — according to natural law incipient in his reason. He may become *congenial* in its literal sense through the shared *being* proportionate to things, to both himself and those things created by Unlimited Love.

Such a possible recovery, then, is through the openness of an intuitive consent to that which is other than the poet's "self," an openness of consensual love tending (though it may appear but an indirection, given the in-betweens through which he moves) toward that ultimate Love. The maker's reason may not conceptualize or give a word to that recovered tendency. For grace works in mysterious ways beyond reason's limited commands as made through conceptions formalized as belief and set in signs as if fixed and certain. The formal perfections of limited gifts, though a seeming indirection, may remove obstacles to an enlarging grace, allowing the possibility inherent to the potentiality of this existing thing— this intellectual soul incarnate, this poet — to proper end. That, whether he is called to make an ax-helve, a house, an altar, a poem or story, or whether in a radical refusal of that grace he declare himself "clean," in that the only truth is that there is no truth as Haze Motes attempts to do. Not that such a progress of *homo viator* is an inevitability, then, given that man as craftsman — as maker in his peculiar stewardship to creation — is fallen out of Adam in a long "history" and is also as a free will contingent in acts of willfulness or good will. To recall this truth is to be reminded that O'Connor's devil is present at the pilgrim's side all the way. That recognition is a reminder as well, as young Tarwater's devil assures him, that every day — every moment — is Judgment Day. The contingency of right will or willfulness suspends the final issue from moment to moment. (Hence the obligation to confession, contrition, amendment in habitual deportment of being.)

One so firmly committed to this faith, in a hope born of intuitive love as is Flannery O'Connor, knows that such distinctions are actual to the making of a story good in itself, whether affirmed or not by the "conscious mind." For herself she knows that her "Fiction may deal with faith implicitly" if explicitly it deals only with "faith-in-a-person," as she writes "A" (July 5, 1958). "What must be unquestionable is what is implicitly implied as the author's attitude, and to do this the writer has to succeed in making the divinity of Christ seem consistent with the structure of reality. This has to be got across implicitly in spite of a world that doesn't feel it, in spite of characters [in a fiction] who don't live it." It is when a critic misses this implicit aspect of her fiction, then, that he may well conclude her a "hillbilly nihilist" rather than the "hillbilly Thomist" she is. The naïve poet not sharing her faith, she believes, may nevertheless happen upon such a "revelation" of the relation between the divinity of Christ implicit in "the structure of reality." For by her faith she believes that "all is the Incarnation." We have suggested O'Connor in a kinship with Dame Julian of Norwich, who in a vision born out of that small object on her palm, the hazel-nut, is enabled to assure us that "all manner of thing shall be well." O'Connor in response to her own mystical recognition finds supporting witness to her vision in St. Thomas. For if Dame Julian says "all manner of thing" (not *things*), St. Thomas might be understand, parsing that testimony as metaphysician: all manner of *thingness* (of *essence*) is necessarily good. If, then, the longer we look at one thing we see increasingly the whole world in that thing (as O'Connor suggests) we might come to conclude as does she that "all is the Incarnation." But that is recognition we come to in journeying moment by moment, O'Connor here echoing that mystical Doctor of the Church, St. John of the Cross, who in his *Dark Night of the Soul* reminds us of a nadir likely on that journey, a "Dark Night of the Senses" themselves. Such is for O'Connor an inescapable truth to the journeying pilgrim here and now, and so central to her concerns in making out of her self-surrender to the good of the thing she makes. She, to the contrary of the poet in his late discovery of this truth, seems almost to have been born beyond that naiveté, knowing very early in her intellectual becoming her responsibility as maker to the mystery of a human nature which she shares with all mankind since Adam. Thus her manner of exploring of the *possible* in that common ground called human nature, the matter she would in-form by art by an imaginative *possible*.

That matter is a given, whereas the form she would induce from it requires an exercise of an imaginative consent to that givenness which allows her discovery of possible form through reason. That is art's exercise of what Thomas phrases "reason in making." At issue therefore is not a responsibility to moral judgment, as if requiring a moral rectitude of either the poet or his reader as the *primary* intention of either a beginning or an end in making a story. The responsibility is rather to a prudential judgment of matter as appropriate to the imagined form, to be induced as *possible* to such matter, a governing by reason of the imagined as related to the actual. It is through her own responsibility as poet that imagined form through her vision in making is to be "consistent with the structure of reality." In this aspect of making, she knows that any maker is, antecedently, an imperfect person, perhaps even an evil person, but not thereby incapable of making a thing good in itself through reason's discovery of form consistent with given nature. There is here an implicit analogy of the poet's possible becoming as person to the possible becoming of a made thing by induced form. However innocently oblivious to that relation the poet may be, his action of love in making is, as action of an "image of God," an initiating movement of that image toward its source. Hence her remarking that the rationalistic skeptical Modernist as maker may prove true artist. For he is not absolutely an evil person, short of having become diabolically *possessed* in its theological sense. Pornography as if art, speaks a maker's dangerously verging on that abyss. For the Modernist intellect may of course prove perhaps a probable, even a willing, recruit to destructions of the good, in some degree therefore possessed in the theological sense. Nevertheless, O'Connor argues, a maker though he lack vision of distances may well inform his chosen matter better than he himself can recognize. That is, as she says, the novelist who is committed to beliefs about human nature as accidental, denying transcendent end — who even finds human actions "predetermined by psychic make-up or the economic situation or some other determinable factor" — may yet write "a great tragic naturalism" that transcends "the limitations of his narrow vision."

He may do so, she suggests, if his primary concern is "with an accurate reproduction of the things that most immediately concern man, with the natural forces that he feels control his destiny." For in so doing, those natural forces themselves already bear within them affecting realities into his made thing — more deeply present than his limited vision anticipates or recognizes. They do so at a depth experienced by O'Connor as prophet of distances, the depth in which grace and nature coincide, the depth in which (in Pieper's phrase) Tarwater's two countries are discovered as not *adjoining* existence here and now but the proximate country "entirely permeated by [Eternity]." Any existing thing bears this mystery, and since the artificer (the maker) necessarily uses existing things as his given matter to making, that mystery of reality implicitly affects the made thing when it is well made. It does so since the form possible to the chosen matter is made consonant with the givenness of that matter. If this be true, then well-made works of art speak by degree the complex reality of things actual to the maker's experience, and since that matter of human nature is peculiar to the maker himself his art things, as John Paul II says, "will speak of their authors" as actual persons. The works therefore enable us "to know [the artists'] inner life" through art, a life which for John Paul II and for O'Connor is essentially spiritual.

That is O'Connor's experience in knowing persons through the stories they make. She finds herself (perhaps even surprising to herself) drawn to Hemingway as we have seen as a presence in his work, she responding to something underway in the fiction not to be accounted for by Hemingway's pursuit of a "macho" image of himself. Not long after returning to Georgia she writes Robert and Sally Fitzgerald, commending a current issue of the quarterly *Shenandoah*. It carries not only a review of her work by Brainard Cheney, but there is the more interesting review of Hemingway's *The Old Man and the Sea,* by one William Faulkner: "He says that Hemingway discovers God the Creator in this one. What part I like [of Hemingway's new novel] was where the fish's eye was like a saint in procession; it sounded to me like he was discovering something maybe new for him." Three years later as we know she writes Father McCown, speaking again of Hemingway in whose work "there is apparently a hunger for a Catholic completeness in life." That is a hunger perhaps not recognized or named by Hemingway but it affects his fiction out of dependence upon Hemingway's inner life as he responds to buried realities in creation — in the created things upon which his fiction of necessity depends such as that "fish's eye" — or perhaps to wine or women, bulls or lions in the spectacles we remember of Hemingway's "life." He as writer borrows matter he knows to his making in a dependence not obviated by any "macho" mask in the bravado of autonomy. That is, he borrows more than he recognizes by his necessary dependence upon the antecedently given, in which (though not recognized nor reverently named) grace is joined in the mere "nature" he borrows carrying suggestions of a spiritual restlessness in Hemingway. In O'Connor's reckoning, one of the antecedently givens is Hemingway's own peculiar existence, in which she detects his almost discovering "something new for him" about himself as an intellectual soul incarnate.

Flannery O'Connor's deportment to the making of her own stories is, at every turn, governed by her conscious Christian belief, sustained in her by the coincidence of nature and grace as she experiences things. Grace, being near as well as distant, is an incommensurate agent to that truth called Love that sustains all existence. She understands that in this belief therefore she is required a primary respect for the good of the thing she makes in the stewardship of her gifts, as a "Catholic" having no choice but to be an "artist." And by that grace she is sustained in her actions of making most personally, because as maker she exists in the image of her Cause. By her very self-conscious existence, her Cause is always most immediate and personal to her (beyond her Misfit's uncertainties in that concern). That is the good news of that *condescension* of God called the Incarnation, abidingly close and personal as the Person Christ, two natures in one. Out of this assurance of faith her concern is to explore with speculative imagination the gift of her calling to make possible form, but she must do so through a steady reasoning in her act of making, lest her mystical vision become too much dependent upon mere feeling.

She would do so, then, confident that insofar as the thing she makes is good it is prophetic of a larger good with which as person she is mystically attuned, though that prophecy is not her primary responsibility in the act itself. Rather, art is the habit "to be rooted deep in the whole personality" ("Writing Short Stories") in *knowing* that the source out of which the poet makes lies "in a realm much larger than that which his conscious mind can encompass." And so when the thing is well made, that thing even in the light of her faith "will always be a greater surprise to [her] than it can ever be to [her] reader" ("The Nature and Aim of Fiction"). In pursuit of that habit proper to gifts, then, the writer's responsibility is to the things he truly sees in their present actualities, through which responsibility "he may transcend the limitations of his narrow vision" — whether so narrow a vision as that of the writer affected by Modernist rationalism out of the 18th century or the 19th century inclinations to a sufficiency of "feeling," or of her own visionary faith in the Incarnation. For the truth of things is not dependent upon any person as finite intellectual creature but upon that agent Cause in response to whom she declares "all is the Incarnation." And so in prophecies larger than her imaginative possibilities of form as governed by reason in pursuit of truth, she is often surprised by those prophecies as echoed in a story. They prove larger than her own "conscious mind can encompass." But she declares her fiction can only deepen, not resolve, the mystery of existence itself. For art never "proves" truth to Positivistic expectations.

She is quite aware that, in her imaginative acts of making, she participates in the oldest of all wars, that between good and evil as in contention within the specific consciousness of *this* person. That is the ground of contention for man's free will, in which as drama there emerge wills in conflict. How demanding of her, this vision, in a century blighted by spectacles of destruction consequent upon wills in conflict, in specific and in multiple consciousness, laying such a general waste of persons beyond any numbering of spectacles of actual wars. For the 20th century is notorious for destructive wars debilitating humanity's body. And indeed, hers is a day in which shadows of wars yet to come seem more terrible than those just past. For ours is an age in which (she observes) we possess made-things sufficient to eradicate us from nature almost entirely as she sees it. But her more proximate war is not that one whose uneasy name as she writes is called "Cold," shadowed by the "Bomb," though the inner war in each person that concerns her lies under that same larger unsettling, topical threat.[3] It is the ancient and uninterrupted war out of which (given her prophetic distance) our current wars prove symptomatic so that from her perspective, this ancient war's most local "front" is located always in each consciousness, however noticeable its effects in external history general destruction of community by collective power. The more fundamental war that concerns her is hinted by our popular epithet on the precipice of history's end: the Age of Alienation, speaking the pathos of *this* person separated from all else. We seem more confused than she by that topical history because not recognizing its cause as the progressive dissociation of intellect from reality since Dante, accelerated out of an 18th century rationalism that becomes embraced under the rubric of absolute freedom for the popular spirit, centering upon the sovereign "self." But how disconcerting to this lone, alienated self that our present history should prove so insufficiently accounted for in its current circumstances as an alienated consciousness defending its false sense of freedom. Circumstances at the topical level are nevertheless rich in symptomatics of that error in our "New Age" liberation.

The war for which she becomes a "reporter" more perceptive than Hemingway, then, is the one that Milton had engaged ambitiously in *Paradise Lost*. It is the same war which Dante engaged in *The Divine Comedy* upon finding himself as poet lost in a dark wood, on the brink of despair but fighting his way back to the true way. It is the war Aeschylus and Sophocles bear dispatches from. In sum, it is a war peculiar to the consciousness of any man as *this* person on his way in any time or place, reported long ago in *Genesis:* the war between Good and Evil in which we each as person take sides, either by intention or willful neglect. How interesting then that Milton, concerned with the necessity of a concrete setting for his great poem, attempts to remove that war's beginning from both time and place but is forced nevertheless to "picture" it by dependence upon spectacle familiar to us as necessary to our response as finite intellects. He presents that war as if occurring on concrete plains of Heaven itself. By Dante's day the *place* had been already reduced to the small cities and rural by-ways of Italy, thus closer to *place* as that concept is taken by O'Connor. History — not a pre-history as somewhat fancifully projected in an attempt to "justify the ways of God to man" — requires a measure by reason along those actual ways. Thus history may be made available to and acceptable to man when he "feels" himself a lone, finite creature in nature, lost among the world's ways and strangely longing for a community to which history can only speak ambiguously concerning his haunted sense of being in exile in the world — whatever his time or place.

History is itself inadequate to a completed purchase upon a way out of that old war, as Milton himself knew. As poet, he attempts a visionary "incarnation" of rescue, while at the same time as a Puritan activist he is also somewhat drawn toward a Modernist mode unsettling to his vision. He is summoned under Cromwell as Latin Secretary, not as poet, to help determine history's course for social and political England. Caught in this dilemma to reason, as poet Milton moves increasingly toward a Keatsian melancholy such as that he had rather fancifully engaged very early in his career in his youthful "Il Penseroso." Given Milton as a looming figure of the poet in the recent history of our poetry, largely on the authority of *Paradise Lost,* and given his divided undertaking, we appreciate how it came about that a bright young poet beginning to be troubled by his own sense of exile, T. S. Eliot, would declare that in recent English poetry it is at about that point — at the time of Dryden and Milton he says — that our poetry suffers a "dissociation" of poetic sensibilities. (Eliot will gradually make his way back to Dante, in part through John Donne, for a new beginning of recovery of his own new life.)

We make the point emphatic that the same dilemma to any discrete intellect always was and is, both then and now. In that war's resolution for each person (as Dante dramatizes it) it can be resolved for only a brief reassuring moment on that battlefield of the individual consciousness in its recognition of a possible rescue, each moment threatening a new defeat since every day is Judgment Day. That rescue is natively ("naturally") desired by a person, and desired regardless of the "natural" magnitude of his intellect as confronted by the complexities of impinging circumstances. The war we describe proves, as Milton at least intuitively knows, both timeless and placeless despite the political, social, theological spectacles of an English Civil War. It lies, we emphasize, within the human spirit of *this* person in the deepest of all civil wars, and so it is the placeless "place" much sought by philosophy and poetry, and even by science despite being self-evidently beyond the measures of science. This is the place in which lies possible fulfillment of this person's final end — in that perfection which St. Thomas calls Beatitude. It is as well a place contingent in each moment to creation in this timely world, in which as a consciousness this person stands at a contingent point in place and out of which place he may move to either a dead abyss or a living Center beyond himself. That is a recognition which leads the poet Eliot (after he has come to terms with Milton) to conclude that there is no such thing as a "lost cause" in this world because in circumstantial reality to the specific consciousness here and now, there is no such thing as a "gained cause." In that recognition, Eliot will sing in a chorus of his *Rock,* that "if blood of Martyrs is to flow on the steps [of the Temple]/ We must first build the steps;/ And if the Temple is to be cast down/ We must first build the Temple." Flannery O'Connor, less solemn but no less committed than Eliot, sees this temple as that of the Holy Ghost, this body whose form is the intellectual soul — in sum, this *person.*

We have been attempting to locate this placeless "place" in which O'Connor locates her wars of fictional action, the *possible,* as imaginative form to her made thing. It is the consciousness of the characters with which she peoples her fictions. As fiction writer then, "place" for her in its most profound location is within the discrete agent as she makes an agent *as if* a person. It is there that we are to locate the "peculiar crossroads where time and place and eternity somehow meet" in a *possible* nature, a *possible* person. And as fiction writer, as a prophet of distances, she believes herself charged to "find that location" and make it seemingly palpable, as if an actual crossroads made concrete by spectacle. In that place occurs an intrusive mystery, eternity itself glimpsed in its reality through grace. Time and place in their ordinary sense must nevertheless provide those accidents of spectacle necessary to art. As intellectual creatures, we move toward truth by an indirection suited to our finite natures as persons, responding to things known in themselves Thomas argues. But that spectacle is to be used in the interest of action beyond whatever the spectacle provides as the textual "body" to an imagined action, action itself the essential in human nature in a contingent possibility of a becoming in this place at this time. The intellectual and spiritual action of the discrete character thus becomes persuasively possible as a surrogate of person drawn from the actualities of persons known by the poet. Not by photographic spectacle of the actual person at the level of art, spectacle thus reduced to the instrumental as if art were empirical science or history. Not nature in mirror images, but the *actions* of nature possible, says Thomas. Any poet is more deeply drawn into the common ground we share in being persons existing in possibilities by Creating Love. Art deepens that mystery of reality beyond the capabilities of science alone to arrest life.

As for her own *personal* responsibility as artist, that continues very complex for her. Always (she writes her friend "A," November 25, 1960), the "human comes first. Nor do you write the best you can for the sake of art but for the sake of returning your talent increased to the invisible God to use or not use as he sees fit," a remark worth our repeating. The "human" most evident to her, as we have also said, is herself as person, she speaking out of self-awareness the overriding responsibility to herself as person, not as artist, though by her talent as exercised she is "returning" it increased "to the invisible God." That is a dominant responsibility here and now for her since it is the proximate means to her ultimate end. And it is this *postulate,* Flannery O'Connor, who in devotion to her calling as artist discovers most clearly the correspondence proper between her proximate devotion to art and that devotion to her Cause as her proper end as person. Concomitant *to,* but not always easily discoverable *in* the art she makes (since as artist it must be only "implicit"). Hence she is intent upon discovering the next word suited to the good of the thing she is making.

She will speak of her "personal" recognition of the mystery of her own existence as *homo viator,* out of experience of that "self-abandonment" when she completely forgets herself in making a story. Here "self-abandonment" is richer than when taken only in the casual sense of the term as a derogatory epithet for self-neglect. We say that "So and so doesn't take care of himself." Indeed, this experience points her toward the "great difference between Christianity and Eastern religions," the "Christian insistence on the fulfillment of the individual person." For her, the term means a surrender of her gifts through love in the act of making by reason, an openness to the grace of Love made through actions proper to her nature as *this* person whose gifts are those of a poet. Thomas' insistent point is at issue here: grace is never commanded, though we become receptive of grace when we remove obstacles to it in an openness of love to the good. Through such surrender lies prospect of fulfillment as this "individual person," grace allowing—a full surrender to grace a perfect freedom. For

O'Connor, that is the best "care" of the self possible to her "self" in the light of her faith. But lest "A" mistake her position, she adds a cautionary note. She declares all creation "the Incarnation," within which by "self-abandonment" through making she would surrender her talent in a celebration, by actions of making, to that abiding Love whereby and in which bides that Love in things. But "Remember" (she writes "A," January 1, 1956), "I am not a pantheist and do not think that creation is God, but as made and sustained by God." Therefore for her God is a continuous Presence, recognizable *in* things through the surrender of "self-abandonment," a seeming indirection of knowing things in themselves which by its openness as receptive love of the good removes obstacles to grace.

Here is a difference, requiring the delicate and precise attention of reason to the differences in things. Especially for O'Connor, given her unbelieving age in which faith rests in "feeling" out of which feeling arises a "New Age" species of pantheism that might leave her mistaken as also a pantheism. Reason must affirm distinctions. That New Age perhaps does not think that creation *is* God though it may "feel" that it is. It feels this way as if by an abandonment of thought its consciousness becomes suffused in all the things of "nature" by feeling, with "me" nature's new inhabiting god. Things consequently become mere identities, if the "feeler" should be forced to *thought* despite feeling as a sentimentality eschewing thought. For thought requires engagement by reason of differences. By feeling in Neo-Pantheism, things that are actual in themselves must be denied particularities, lest difference confound a weakened reason as gradually enslaved by the principle of a philosophical egalitarianism reductive of reality. If her New Age audience is thus affected by this subspecies of the Modernist "consciousness" (New Age Paganism), it may well experience a considerably exacerbated disbelief in her vision. Here perhaps is the source of that confused fascination with her art as at once arresting but irritating to Modernist sensibilities, if the secular world attend to her gifts as poet. It is discomforting to her no doubt to acknowledge that same hesitancy about her work within the Church itself on occasion. In a letter to "A" (July 20, 1955) she registers a lament. "It seems to be a fact that you have to suffer as much from the Church as for it," though she is rescued in that suffering by her belief in "the divinity of Christ" as more powerful than all our "human sufferings." (Dostoevsky, as we have suggested, shares this sense of "suffering" as a challenge to faith.)

How difficult for some persons to appreciate, even from within the Church, her position then when she says that her Old Tarwater of *The Violent Bear It Away,* a Protestant Fundamentalist, is a "crypto–Catholic." That seems an alarming sign as read by any formulaic patrolmen within that increasingly unsettled country of mystery still in the keep of the Church. For the offices of the Pharisees are always at work in both ecclesiastical and civil purviews, doctrinaires not unlike (some of them) those ancient patrolmen with whom Jesus contended. There is difficulty with O'Connor's art certainly from the point of view of some in her Church who try to come to terms with this "Southern" Catholic writer on the supposition that *Southern* supercedes the *Catholic.* Some respond to her work and to her arguments, uneasy about her defense of Old Tarwater's "natural" Catholicism as unhoused. A devoted daughter of the Church, that misunderstanding could but be painful to her. But hers is a suffering she maintains within the Church. In addition, circumstances to a misunderstanding of her felt balance were more severe outside the Church. There had been that touchstone to this point in the *New Yorker* review that finds her intellectually "conditioned" by Church dogma though still no doubt a Modernist. In that conflicted circumstance to her "suffering" then, she is most wisely careful in speaking to those outside the Church, especially those who may be drawn to the Church by her work. To one she cautions that her correspondent is wrong to think he should "join the Church," as he expresses an interest in doing. Instead he must "become a Catholic," perhaps even initially we might suppose a "natural" one under the embracing Love of his Creator — given the spiritual confusions both within and outside the Church.

Flannery O'Connor, out of such responses to her work from within and without the Church, however disappointed she may be, will the more recognize that the *matter* to her art reveals these problems as real to *homo viator* yet may prove richly yielding, though her problems differ from those Dante had to deal with. Her fictional persons in an initial engagement are presented as often radically deficient in their knowing the possibility of spiritual life as beyond a merely earth-bound incubation like wingless chickens confined to the ends defined by a "naturalistic" determinism advocated by secularized science. Her challenge is to draw forth form, opening beyond that reductionist "vision" of man as but an accident. Still, her *form* touches implications not likely to be perceived by an intellectually deracinated audience, especially insofar as that audience provides the very intellectual matter she uses in her making. That she calls herself a prophet of distances therefore is a hint to that audience toward a possible self-recognition, shared with that audience at a secondary, not that primary level of responsibility to her as a poet to return her "talent increased to the invisible God" to use as he will. She is precise in dealing with such a term as *prophet* in an age in which magic is dominant over her "antiquated" belief in the mystery of nature as in the keep of grace. Hers is an age in which knowledge is more comfortably seen as an instrument to alchemy, operationally confined to horizontal time and place — especially by the magic of intellectual angelism that holds in thrall the popular spirit by illusion.[4]

Prophecy for Modernist sensibilities is the purview of autonomous intellect in control of cause and effect through process. It has to do with the future of *my* present moment in time as calculated through gnostic intentions to a reconstitution of my own reality to satisify temporal ends tomorrow. The intent is to an illusion of a worldly moment arrested — in the future. In brief, prophecy to the Modernist understanding must serve temporal convenience, the "servers" of Positivistic intent measuring the convenience, ranging in specialties from scientific poll-takers as experts to mere palm-readers as a sub-species of determiners serving suburbs and ethnic enclaves. O'Connor understands that the true prophet is dedicated to the truth of reality as evident here and now, knowing that a corollary effect of her fictions (if it is well made) might be to recall her reader to what he has intuitively known all along but forgotten about himself as *this* person. She holds as prophet a truth: each person — wittingly or not — is here and now a citizen of two countries simultaneously, though most conspicuously to him as a resident at the level of spectacle as the finitudes of creation itself. Those two worlds — two countries to his being: that of this present creation but permeated by eternity at this very present place and moment speaking citizenship in that second primary country in respect to his proper end. It is this recognition which prompts her to declare that "all is the Incarnation." A possible corollary effect of a made thing therefore — her story — may be to recall a reader to his own now abandoned prophetic vision in recovery of what he has known and either forgotten or has rejected deliberately by willfulness. What he may discover with an immediacy of truth is that creation itself speaks and shows his dual citizenship, though he may be almost blind or deaf. That is the possibility of recovery through her story of created reality — if God choose to fulfill it.

Such recognition of a dual citizenship by the artist may raise that dangerous temptation in him to abandon or modify his primary responsibility, the perfection of form in relation to the limits of his chosen matter in a devotion to the good of the thing he makes. For the temptation is to a more heroic intent, that of a rescue of mankind by his art. (Remember young Tarwater bridling at the unheroic command of his Great Uncle that he finish the old man's "leavings," baptize the idiot Bishop, hardly a spectacular action.) But by analogy if one as furniture maker would make a rocking chair, he must do so in the larger light of its end as the comfort of some person whom he may never even meet if his rocking chair be well-made. Nevertheless in his actions of making, his responsibility is to effect *form* drawn proportionate to that proximate end of the good of the thing he is making from well-chosen wood — wood suited by art's form to that proximate intent from which he draws form. What an "unheroic" labor, this making toward a mere chair's final end, someone rocking on a front porch, perhaps at Andalusia. Or perhaps a Dr. More sailing paper airplanes into his yard as he meditates in Percy's rejection of a New Age Thanatos syndrome. In making (Thomas argues), the responsibility is always to the perfection of form consonant within the limits of the givenness of the wood in hand, under a guidance of reason toward its final end, whereby God may use that made thing or not. A concern for some final heroic end out of pride in defiance of limit must not obviate responsibility to the grain of the given oak as governing a possible form quietly imagined.

First then, a proximate concern for the good of this *thing* (the chair) as a thing *in itself* in making. The "rocking" — that is an end to which the finished thing may be surrendered, as a story is surrendered to an anonymous reader. Such is O'Connor's understanding of responsibilities to her own gifts as maker, though she does not put it in our metaphorical way. She makes the same point clear nevertheless in the passage cited from her letter to "A," who at that time is exploring her own gifts as possibly those of a writer. As for "art" — "all it is is working in a certain kind of medium to make something right," the emphatic word being *right*. The artist's "material is no more exalted than any other kind of material and the idea of making it right is what should be applied to all making" (April 6, 1957).

Flannery O'Connor, we are discovering again and again, has little patience with our inclination to self-approval, especially that of a cultivated sentimentality through self-love. That malady of intellect she will on occasion remark in both the poet and in the popular spirit — the intellectual error which encourages a deportment of the person as self-important. The adulation by the popular spirit of "celebrity" — whether of poet or politician — is for her symptom of a spiritual disease. It speaks the inclination to a "romanticism" which follows when intuition is diminished from its openness of love beyond the self to a self-love projected. What may happen spiritually is a delay in acknowledging the reality of evil reflected in the temptation to self-apotheosis — that turning inward by charity falsified till the person becomes addicted to reductionist illusions concerning the truth of things. It often becomes an ideology of the egalitarian *good*— various in the idols raised to it. Thus a partial good is elevated as ultimate, but can only arrive at a diminution of the actuality of things self-evident to reason as within the *orders* of being. A love of the good is not therefore to be reduced to an egalitarian sentiment pleasing to the self, though we daily breathe that sentimentality as sustaining popular spirit out of long habits of avoiding distinctions among things. Emblematic to that deportment: a small dog becomes an arrested child to the convenience of a person, an idol to love more convenient than the more challenging love of a small child. Egalitarian illusions of good, dissolved by a self-awareness, distort self-evident

particularities of things existing disparately in the complex economy of creation. What a relief from reason, the more easily substituting feeling for thought. It seems to relieve as well
a desire for that joy embracing this most disparate creation, in which joy lies also a presence of sorrow requiring a "suffering with." Not that shibboleth *happiness,* then, but a joy
inclusive of sorrow to an enduring of sorrow is the modal deportment of love in this world.
Thus sorrow (Dostoevsky would say *suffering*) is embraced by hope. Such is the challenge
to a genuine progress of *homo viator,* to his *becoming* toward a joy transcending all sorrow.
How wise to this point then is J. R. R. Tolkien's remark in his "On Fairy Stories" concerning fictional making. For him the fairy story (as for O'Connor her stories in which the
grotesque echoes Tolkien's vision) "denies universal final defect and in so far as evangelism,
giving a fleeting glimpse of joy, joy beyond the walls of the world, poignant as grief."

The confusion, distorting intellect from such a deportment to things in responsibility
of stewardship, is an intellectual one, out of inordinate accommodation of intellectual intuition and reason when reduced from their complementary offices to knowing toward an
understanding. The dislocation of intellect, so typical of Modernist doctrine, instead allows us to avoid recognizing in ourselves a propensity to evil in the world through some
species of idol worship, as in that worship of the self as artist. In separating reason from intuition as modes of intellectual action, intuition itself becomes reduced by a rationalistic intent. Intuition is explained as mere instinct for self-preservation by a doctrine which seems
very "reasonable" to thought by its self-celebration. By that self-flattery a person concludes
his separation from "the world of guilt and sorrow" as Mr. Head has long attempted in "The
Artificial Nigger." It is by presumption of self-importance that Mr. Head can see himself
as Nelson's rescuing Virgil, the agent of reason. And so occurs the manifestation of intellectual error rampant in the popular spirit called sentimentality, elevated as if a mode of reasoned intellectual action and most usually pretending a devotion to the common good. It
must lead ultimately, through a relentless system of logic, to the sentimentality of an egalitarianism harnessing power over being. In this distortion, *thinking* becomes instead *feeling*
trained to yield *power*, preparing the community ground for an emergence of the tyrant at
last. That is in the playing out by intellectual denial of the *discrete* particularities of persons
which prevents viable community. We come to pretend to an egalitarian absolution to all
others which proves not absolution but reduction. Particularities thus confiscated to a power
serving the "common good" enables lords of power to their dreams of reconstituting being
itself, those tyrants of varying magnitude according to degrees of power accumulated. And
underneath the reductionism, in a phrase of C. S. Lewis's, is "the abolition of man."

The air we breathe daily to the spirit's possibly thriving or diminishing, O'Connor suggests, is now inescapably toxic since the intellectual climate in our moment (we add) is contaminated. Eliot, coming upon this same problem during World War I, will declare its
symptom: the "dissociation" of our "sensibilities"—a separation of thought and feeling.
Even then Eliot, in his strategy of self-protection against it (as we have suggested) removes
himself as personal behind a mask of irony, as if effecting his detachment from that cor-
rupting air. In a letter to Norbert Wiener on Epiphany 1915 (which day for Eliot was only
a "Bank Holiday") Eliot embraces "the lesson of relativism." It is to "avoid philosophy and
devote oneself to either *real* art or *real* science." For him "philosophy is chiefly literary criticism and conversation about life," in which is to be avoided that drawing of a "sharp line
between metaphysics and common sense," for that would be to commit "metaphysics and
not common sense." No such intellectual judgment "is formally either right or wrong," Eliot

choosing to attempt "to get along without any theory of judgment whatsoever." As a declared skeptic about truth, then, he devises (as poet) a strategy of ironic skepticism, a detached control through "objective correlatives" suited to a sufficient control of a psychological response by his reader to the thing he makes, his poem, in a minor gnostic tyranny. And, in an irony no doubt haunting him after "Ash-Wednesday," he does so in part by defining the poet's mind in action as compared to a chemical reaction, taking metaphor from that Positivistically inclined science.

How evident Eliot as skeptic, an intellectual Misfit he will later conclude. In his "Tradition and the Individual Talent," he argues for what he calls an "Impersonal theory of poetry," developing metaphorically that chemical analogy. "The mind of the poet is the shred of platinum" serving as "catalyst," and as such it effects "new combinations," as when platinum is introduced to meld two gases yielding "sulfurous acid"—the poem by analogy. What is effected on the chemical side of his metaphor is H_2SO_3. In its "natural"—essential—constitution however (the chemist reminds us) that is a weak and unstable acid, used commercially as a bleaching agent. Not an apt figure for the poet as an individual talent unless intent on bleaching existence of particularity. Eliot is responding to a hampering tradition staining the popular spirit—as he would himself agree after his *The Waste Land*—*after* making that poem as a "personal grouse" against his personal circumstances unresolved by skepticism. What we might seek is better analogy in pursuit of metaphorical correspondences between our spiritual nature and the maladies effected in it out of that now dominantly established tradition we have explored under the rubric of *Modernism*. They might be pursued by a prophetic rather than a skeptical poet.

If we think of our spiritual nature in its older traditional association with our breathing (for insofar as we yet breathe, there is yet hope a proverb says), we might consider other gases as correspondences rather than Eliot's liquid bleaching agent, sulfurous acid. We might even venture that the "breathing" of life into Adam was a breathing of an oxygen suited to intellectual life, Adam thus set on his way toward maintaining perfection as a free will. It might then occur to us, given our concern for the atmosphere necessary to the intellectual soul now on its way in a fallen state, that it digest truth by its feeding upon the good in its dual modes, the intuitive and rational. Such a feeding to its life in response to the life of things allows a growing, a becoming toward fulfillment. As an intellectual soul the person responds to most various gases emitted by the essence of most various creatures in the orders of being collectively called *creation*. We might hit upon a relation of two gases rather closely akin but in one manifestation bearing deadly effects as food to the intellectual soul, which even so common sense an intellectual as Eliot does not escape by skepticism. Consider instead of sulphurous acid as the effected poem—intellectual word—two other possible intellectual words as metaphors: carbon dioxide and carbon monoxide.

Carbon dioxide (CO_2) is a natural effect in creation of residual good to our bodily breath by an indirection, one of the gifts of the Holy Ghost to breathing. It is a gas from "animal respiration," absorbed by plants that "recycle" to us from it the oxygen needed as breathing incarnate animals. Suggestive of a healthy relation for the intellectual soul in its circumstances of "connaturality" in the created world, this sharing in being, in the correspondences of our metaphor underway. But what if? What if...? Science says of natural and necessary oxygen to the body (to the intellectual soul in our metaphor) that when we breathe it out it has become doubled (CO_2). Breathing out is in an openness to creation itself (which in respect to metaphorical correspondence is our own small largesse to the plant world). The

green world responds in a greenness of life, emitting in turn the oxygen we need. If, as intellectual soul, intent on reconstituting being, we ignore the givenness of C (carbon) we may
by intent diminish oxygen by a niggardliness of giving. In pursuit of power it becomes CO.
And CO (carbon monoxide) proves in its essential actual nature a colorless, odorless, and
very toxic gas—almost beyond recognition to our givenness as body with senses (our "carbon" base) save by its effects—namely a gas deadly to the actual body as an actual gas and
metaphorically deadly by analogy to the intellectual soul. If then, in a larger perspective by
metaphor, the intellectual soul reduces itself to the body as machine, turning inward as consciousness itself an accident, the intellectual soul increasingly feeds upon its own "carbon
monoxide."

We have, let us say with this playfulness of metaphor in a high serious concern, presented intellect itself as if a formula: I_2: intellect (intuitive-rational). In a dissociation of sensibilities, we observe, occurs a separation, not simply by the poet's mind resting content as
accident of the body, but in the intellectual soul violating its very nature — its calling to making in a stewardship considerate by reason's proportionality of ecological creation whose
ground in commonness — in a connaturality — is the givenness of being (prime carbon). The
conflicting ideologies since the Renaissance emerge, we have suggested, when either the *intuitive* intellect is declared ultimate or the *rational*— by that division infecting the ambient
air breathed by this spiritual creature man (as intellectual soul incarnate), the "popular
spirit" in a collective term. In a becoming that is crippled by what has become almost a colorless, odorless, toxic monoxide, both the person and persons in community are adversely
affected. What proves the more confusing to both *intuition* and *reason* is that as singular in
heretical intent, they can but divide and thus distort the good. That will lead Eliot in part
perhaps, in coming to himself in his dark wood, to remark that the trouble with any heresy
in the intellectual soul is that heresy is *partly* right.

We have engaged in a playfulness of metaphor, knowing from both Plato and St.
Thomas in particular that metaphorical correspondence proves limited from an intellectual
comprehensiveness of truth by analogy. There prove always unlikenesses named in the terms
of likenesses. But in our somewhat extended "metaphysical metaphor" may lie a valid truth.
We are remarking a division whereby the *part* is taken as whole (thus a partial good). It is
a division possible only when the intellectual soul denies or ignores its own "carbon" base
in *being* as an essential givenness, not only as an intellectual soul but as also incarnate. As
such in its actuality, the person is therefore *connatural* to things other, each thing limited
within the orders of being by its essential givenness. In the person's response to the context
of its own givenness, proximate good is good, but not the ultimate good. In an enthusiasm
leading either to a rational intent or to an intuitive intent—each divorced from the other
(giving rise to Rationalism and Romanticism as vague distinctions)—the intellectual soul
may decree either (though each partial) as ultimate Virgil to the journeying. That decree is
justified by the intuitive or by the rational in contentions of an intellectual civil war in consciousness, distorting proximate good. And so our current circumstances (to return to our
metaphysical analogy) are those in which we breathe an odorless, colorless gas, the source
of its generation our intellect divided against itself to its self-poisoning. That self-poisoning we have called self-love.

Now this is the circumstance to the dislocation of the intellectual soul which O'Connor takes as her point of departure, though she speaks of it only as the ambient air which
we breathe daily as spiritual creatures. Ours has been a metaphorical enlargement of the na-

ture of that "air" she has in mind. She in taking this matter as the point of departure in her fiction — seeing it symptomatic of our spiritual malaise — leads some of her critics to mistake what she sees as afoot (or rather in the very lungs of our being) for *homo viator* on his way. What is underway in the journey of a story is the possible departure out of this intellectual error. That departure point may certainly be called "nihilistic," so that she (as she remarks) may be mistaken for a "hillbilly nihilist" by a careless reader, rather than for the hillbilly Thomist she is. She sees that the Modernist circumstances to our "spiritual" breathing becomes erratic as we become the more entrapped in a centripetal diminution of our potential givenness, self-poisoned by self-love. In that closing in upon the self, we attempt some image of rescue raised to idol within entrapment, a *partial* good, as our end. From a Thomistic perspective, that thus becomes heretical attempt against our own nature. We raise up idols of worship of the self in the latest model, the latest "life-style," becoming only the more lost in a wilderness of the orders of nature, unable to see things as other than mirrors. In extremes of desperation, in exacerbated attempts at self-salvation, what wonder that there should arise egalitarian ideologies of such varying aspects, such disparate spectacles of "life" as the latest models of life-style, a dress for the race rather than ceremonial dress for the dance. A reduction of all *other than the self* to absolute equality, denying thereby the truth of things in themselves, gives rise to an illusion that intellect thus effects the self as sovereign beyond the reductionisms of all other than the self. Things thus made opaque become mirrors revealing only the alienated self. That is the social spectacle introduced as confusions about "rights," whereby each person as autonomous declares himself endowed with sovereign exceptionalities to *all other,* in a sham "metaphysics" out of an egalitarian illusion as the strategy to self-empowerment, an intellectual sophistry requiring no schooling in the old Greek- Sophists who were Socrates' antagonists.

The heresy of an intentional good limited to the proximate as absolute gives rise by intentionality of idols raised to the self (*vide* Haze Motes and his "Church without Christ"). The strategy may allow a momentary stay against the confusions encountered by a person on his way, especially the most disturbing recognition of his vague sense of exile — a recognition of my "self" as alienated and deracinated in a creation which is popularly declared only an accidental cosmos. In such a state, the person may seize upon promises of an absolute sovereignty, happy to be called an "individual" rather than person. In that illusion of self-liberation, it is as if he thereby gains absolute freedom beyond limit, with which illusion as breathed daily in our recent history he can but turn community toward chaos. He grows more desperate in pursuit of his "rights" as affirmed by a positive law, by logic conveniently disjoined from natural law. But he festers as person in the illusion of his "individual" freedom as if he were a sovereign entity — self-decreed autonomous. That frenzy seems only to be exercised through the presumption that as an individual he is an entity detached from *all other.*

Certainly to an O'Connor this is the prevalent spiritual disorder of alienation from reality in her day, and becomes the point of departure for her in making a story. Frenzy, spiritual agitation of the isolated "self," despite the person's sacrifice of sentimental "feelings," serves only the despair of isolation she believes, implicit in a randomness of violence to the person. (Remember Asbury and Julian.) That, despite our sacrifice of sentimental feelings, as if to embrace all else is "in truth" an intellectual action out of a pride in the self, a sacrifice embittering the intellectual soul in its exile. In that contradiction has been raised the banner *Egalitarianism,* the idol raised over all the created orders of being (though reserving to the flagman self his own transcendent sovereignty). Ours here are high reflections on the low ends to which *homo viator* may incline through willfulness. But out of her own high concern, O'Connor implies through grotesque figurings of such seemingly low agents, those ends are false. She dramatizes intellectual agents that we are reluctant to concede intellectual creatures — a Mr. Head or a Shiftlet, whose intellectual symptoms nevertheless reveal them to have been long breathing a Modernist air despite their not being aware of an effected spiritual malady until some arresting encounter. In such moments of encounter, grace intrudes upon the ground of consciousness, a grace in the ground which (she suggests) has been already well prepared by that old adversary of man, the Devil. And so for her the dramatic conflict she dramatizes is deeper than the spectacle necessary to our perception, lying within the consciousness of *this* person in his wills in conflict. How shocking, if we discover that person to be our self.

How shocking to discover myself as "like" a Mr. Head or a Mrs. Turpin, more comfortable with Hulga as provincially abused. Yet that possible epiphany to me as reader: beneath the spectacle of provincial "life-stylesm" a family resemblance between me and a Mr. Head. O'Connor's art makes mischief with my New Age Paganism, though in a manner perhaps more subtle than Walker Percy's mischief. More conspicuously, Percy engages the "losangelization" of suburbia in closer proximity to New Orleans than Mr. Head to Atlanta as Taulkinham. To put the shock of recognition more starkly: O'Connor's version of the intellectual soul lost in the cosmos is a Mr. Head or a Mrs. Turpin as untuned to the abiding realities of creation itself— until some violent intrusion of grace rebukes their self-love, a violent intrusion of grace out of an "artificial nigger" or even out of grunting hogs in the latest sanitary hogpen.

11

The Cannibal of Thought: Modernist Theory

"One of the awful things about writing when you are a Christian is that for you the ultimate reality is the Incarnation, the present reality is the Incarnation, and nobody believes in the Incarnation; that is, nobody in your audience."

— Flannery O'Connor, Letter to "A," August 2, 1955

In breathing a cultural air contaminated by Modernist ideology, a person may lose the felt balance otherwise orienting him to his proper end as an intellectual soul. That is O'Connor's reckoning of our present spiritual circumstances as *homo viator,* as a spiritual creature on the way through wandering mazes ideologically systematized. The circumstantial evidences lie about us as consequences of our having lost a common consent to community as a body. We struggle more and more, and at every level of social and political spectacles, to recover community as an organic body out of a mere collectivity in which persons are reduced to mechanical integers. They must consent as "individuals" to an egalitarian status in a conglomeration of power, promised to be used for the common good. Community is a mechanism to be reconstituted by a gnostic transcendence of being itself by centrifugal whirls, despite a counter effect against the smoothness of that imposed gnostic force by residual personhood in persons as integers. For persons purported to be but integers yet desire community — con-union — and in a "self" defense incline to a centripetal resistance to system.

If that experiment by Positivistic thought in reconstituting being itself is to be put in dramatic terms, our metaphors of motion — centrifugal against centripetal — are hardly promising, even as Eliot's rendering of a contrafusion of the poet's actions of making as an "individual talent" resisting "tradition" could not be well served by a metaphor for the "creative process" out of chemistry's making of sulphurous acid. Old terms recovered to proximate actions of surrogate persons, then? Perhaps a misfit person reduced to integer — a Misfit prevented his possible good as a person — might be shown defending at least his evil against common denials by community in the chaos of good and evil. In a confused state of his intellectual soul, he commits violent actions as a large (grotesque) figure. O'Connor's Misfit, she might suppose then, might break through a catatonic consciousness of a reader as large and startling figure.

But such an attempt, made through local spectacles of unsophisticated agents and things, requires of the poet (so O'Connor must reckon) some residual recognition of evil in relation to good however much distorted by current intellectual sensibilities breathing too long the Modernist air of denial. It requires recognizing that a *community* desire, by the very nature of the desiring person, has been now largely prevented, so that the person becomes alienated as an *individual,* denied that resonance of his being declared in the term *person.* His will likely be some form of violence in rejecting that other than himself. In a paradox, manifest in spectacles of irony as seen by a realist of distances, the person has been assured of his expanding as individual, only to discover the contraction of his isolation. The desperation from loss of personhood may well lead the person to a final refuge, as he has been conditioned to expect by the air he breathes: his is a sovereign autonomy against creation in some distorted Manichaean manner. And so in relation to other individuals as integers, rather than as organic members in a body, the person comes to depend upon his "Feeling good about himself" as the contaminating doctrine puts it popularly, in a last hope of his disoriented desire for the good. Not that the person's reason does not whisper the dangers when community loses its binding in membership by fragmentation. But how difficult without vision, any recovery of membership through reason. How problematic the recovery of ordinate dependence of person upon persons, of persons upon person. Out of that old bonding lies some prospect to the person's quest for an ordinate joy, an implicit meaning of that quest in the *Divine Comedy.* Joy to be discovered by reason through the particularities of himself as this person who discovers himself member in the body of humanity, humanity itself "en-membered" through particularities within convergent particularities of the created world. It is in this circumstance to a person's being that he encounters the mysterious complex of "meaning" of existence itself, whether he pursue meaning as scientist, philosopher, or poet. Whatever the particular calling of the intellectual soul incarnate — scientist, philosopher, poet — as pilgrim gifted in being an intellectual soul he must engage that mystery in that most intimate "place" of all — his own self-awareness. Within himself he discovers that crossroads where time and place as contingent to self-awareness may by grace be intersected to his felt balance as pilgrim eternity. Such rather certainly are the parameters of O'Connor's vision in dramatizing a particular consciousness.

We have put the circumstances to the person in his loss of community in radical metaphor, especially centering in physics' term *entropy* as circumstance to self-awareness, emphasizing the danger in a thermodynamic closed system. There occurs in self-consciousness through willfulness an analogous closed system, not physical but spiritual by nature, in which natural love as centrifugal in opening by a right will becomes by willfulness centripetal, turning inward in a festering love of the self. *Person* thus distorted becomes a closed system intending self-generation, with frictional heat a consequence of counter motions of love held internal (closed) within the gradually arrested intellectual soul. Such is the condition of the Modernist for O'Connor, in that consequence to awareness of its "wills in conflict" within its world as a closed consciousness. The borders of that world are the sides of the person's skull, she will say. Once more we identify (in some agony of metaphor suggesting the agony of spirit) the arena within which occurs will's struggle with love, the "stage" of self-awareness for that action which is O'Connor's point of departure in her stories. That inner "distance" proves deeper than psychological spectacle, or physical encounters of person with person can either *comprehend* or resolve. Hence she makes her fiction rather a deepening of that mystery than presuming art a resolution of it. The dramatic paradox with which she deals is more simply put by Walker Percy than our rendering: the person becomes "lost in the cosmos."

O'Connor is acutely aware of this dislocation of person from community as become general at her point in time and place. She understands that deracination is consequent upon the intellectual "air we breathe" as she says. It is her awareness of this distortion of "personality" atrophied spiritually by foul intellectual air which is the ironic ground to her fictions. And so it is the Modernist person she engages initially as surrogate, as antagonist or protagonist, of a story. The dramatic tension in her fiction lies within the surrogate person's struggle with a disparity unnatural to his humanity. Her initial focus is thus upon the consciousness of her surrogate person — her "character" — as severely handicapped intellectually (however much or little formally "educated"). It is because of his spiritual handicap that he becomes confused and baffled, responding with a growing desperation out of which spectacles of violence issue from his intellectual mistakes against human nature itself in his willfulness. In her fiction, the popular scientific "psychology" in its Modernist measure of the nature of consciousness, is both pointed and counterpointed by spectacles of violence such as that we observed in her Misfit. Thus her vision as a realist of distances unfolds in the variations of willfulness out of our spiritual nature as person. Denial of ourself as person is evidenced by symptomatic spectacle which Modernist ideology treats as if it were the essence of man himself. In that surface attention to symptomatics by Modernist dogma, there is promised a "happiness" possible to the individual, especially through psychological "analysis" leading to "adjustment" of an individual as a mechanism to be fitted to the ultimate reality of man as machine. The individual is no longer person, and therefore for his own operational health he *must* be made an *integer* in the accidental community of an accidental cosmos, a machine within a machine. A happy "personality" is to be decreed and then executed by psychological proscription of some system, if necessary through a positive law Positivistically justified. (We always need "papers" on a Misfit.)

We have already remarked this shallow address to the reality of the person as inadequate to a recovery from what is in truth a spiritual malady. Even Mr. Shiftlet, that conman charlatan of "The Life You Save May Be Your Own," knows this to be a truth, though he manipulates it with a hypocrisy which a Haze Motes would likely answer by bashing Mr. Shiftlet in the side of his skull. (Haze does dispatch Hoover Shoates in like circumstance of hypocrisy.) Such violence as an effect upon a deracinated intellect in her protagonist, O'Connor will present as consequent upon his breathing too long what has become a most foul intellectual air to the spirit, subverting the breath of the Holy Spirit. It is the starved intellectual soul which precipitates violence in her protagonists, on occasion starved souls conceived by her imagination as by their givenness imagined into fictional being as intended to be prophets of truth. The spectacle out of spiritual atrophy within the consciousness of such a protagonist proves confusing to some of her readers. It is in relation to the spectacles of violence deployed imagistically in textual surfaces of the fictions that she implies a metaphysical ambiance, to be discovered by a reader through his own awakened reason, if not recognized in an immediacy by intuitive recognition. In this metaphysical dimension, we are surely meant to recognize (though difficult to us according to degrees of our intellectual deracination) that evil is undeniable a parasitic enemy of the good. Evil symbiotically becomes joined destructively to the good, evil's actuality dependent upon whatever the good to which it attaches. As nature itself suggests, mistletoe though beautiful bears poison fruit and may fell a mighty oak. It is this undeniable relation of evil to the good, in respect to the will's inclination to willfulness through Original sin, that O'Connor engages within her protagonist's consciousness his "wills in conflict."

In Modernist dogma, a latest in scientific rationalism speaks of a synaptic space, located as a noplace within the biochemical brain. In our concerns here for O'Connor's understanding of the soul, the Modernist "psyche" thus treats itself as but an accidental phenomenon associated with nerve-endings, thought sparked in a vacuum at synapse, a biochemical interior "space" which is no space. Consider a current denial of the soul's actuality as scientifically rationalized in Joseph LeDoux's *Synaptic Self,* a late argument that is almost as old as Adam — its ancientness disguised by sophisticated spectacles of our scientific progress. In that place-which-is-no-place (synaptic space) we locate the "self," or so we are assured. That "self" occurs at the level of "psychology, culture, and even spirituality, where memory joins with genes to create the ineffable essence of personality." By such argument, the inherent inclination to the good in consciousness may not be quite explained away completely by scientific authority, but it may be manipulated "rationally" as thus divorced from any reason grown out of common sense. Indeed, it is but our latest intent to a divorce, induced through gnostic intention to a power over being such as that Eric Voegelin has explored, and against which occurs an unlearned response of violence by the Misfit. (The Misfit's prophetic commentary: murder in reaction to what John Paul II calls our age's "culture of death.") Voegelin and the Misfit, this is to suggest, each refute this latest version of the abolition of man, Le Doux's *Synaptic Self* (2002), as pseudo-metaphysics.

For Flannery O'Connor, the Modernist denial of the soul is to be addressed initially in its psychological manifestations as a "self" as reduced to a biochemical entity seen by Modernist intellect. This is a fanciful, an *as if,* that she presents as her point of departure as dramatist. *As if* as maker she suspends her own belief in the Incarnation to assume that point of fictional departure. It is a strategy of diagnosis by indirection, beginning from the Modernist distortions of our inherent inclination to the good. Our initial response to reality by intellect, Thomas argues, is through that *intuitive* mode of intellect, but Modernist doctrine reduces intuitive intellect to *instinct* in the interest of rationalistic manipulations of that inclination. For thereby the truly religious inclination of an intellectual soul may be focused upon its *proximate* rather than toward its *ultimate* end as person. Thus the result is, as she says, a "tenderness … wrapped in theory" which allows us — indeed requires of us — that we become "detached from the source of tenderness," Christ. (How perceptive of Modernist doctrine, then, is Haze's attempt to found his Church of Christ without Christ.) This manipulation of intuitive desire by a rationalistic intentionality, she concludes, makes it inevitable that we should be suddenly arrested by such horrors as forced-labor camps and gas chambers.

This is a point of common recognition O'Connor shares with Walker Percy, as we have observed. Percy, for instance, will adapt O'Connor's exposition of evil as enabled by a rationalistic sentimentality she had argued in her "Introduction" to *a Memoir of Mary Ann.* He puts her words in the argument of his own version of his prophetic Misfit now recovered to a true prophetic office in his last novel, his Father Smith of *Thanatos Syndrome.* And it is this same ambiance of Modernist thought which Percy also talks about in essays, such as that one declaring that ours is the age of a reciprocal cannibalistic feeding upon our spiritual nature by the Consumer and Theorist in concert, now made idols in the pantheon of idols to be worshipped by the popular spirit. Flannery O'Connor locates this conjunctive cannibalism within the soul at the immediately personal level of encounter. It involves, for instance, the popular spirit and the theorist feeding to mutual satisfactions upon those manufacturing Modernist doctrines reconstituting persons. Thus she observes that when we multiply the sentimentalist who wants his "heart lifted up" by "two hundred and fifty thousand times … what you get is a book club."

In such an intellectual climate, no wonder the temptation for a writer to enjoy self adulation as "Artist." The happiness is reciprocal between consumer and theorist, the "popular spirit" elevating even some poets among its idols in the desert, along with other pop stars, on occasion making them "universally" idolized. (Elvis is alive, though God be dead.) It is in this service that the publishing "theorist" prospers in cultivating the popular appetite. And with encouragement by theorists, we evolve elaborate rituals deployed through the symbols made in order to cater to a created public "taste," so that an Eric Voegelin might well find correspondences between our world idols and those in the Egyptian world centuries before Christ as embellishing the Pharaoh's robes, though the Egyptian idols nevertheless touch upon desires that the transcendent be somehow brought down to center in the Pharaoh as person transformed by symbol. If that Egyptian world is closed in its cosmology about that worldly center (the Pharaoh), Voegelin suggests, that is history's prelude to an eruption toward Revelation. O'Connor reviews for her diocesan *Bulletin* (November 15, 1958) Voegelin's *Israel and Revelation,* her copy heavily marked, but one passage seemed of particular interest to her: "Through the leap in being [into an awareness of community as a "Chosen People"] … through the discovery of transcendent being as the source of order in man and society, Israel constituted itself the carrier of a new truth in history." That is an eruption out of that closed Egyptian cosmology whose symbols adorn the divine Pharaoh's clothing.[1]

What our reflection suggests is that recent intellectual history effects in the popular spirit a contraction of vision that limits the intellectual soul within a closed cosmology, though the "individual" thereby increasingly discovering himself as Pharaoh lost in the cosmos. The poet as person (for O'Connor), in his pursuit of beauty through ordinate signs, becomes aware of himself as a person who has a particular calling beyond such closure — a calling to be responded to at an intersection of planes of reality at a point within his own consciousness. His difficulty lies in a proportionate accommodation of his gift of making to the larger obligation of his own perfection as a person at that crossroads. How is he to reconcile a proximate primary obligation — that to his acts of making — as lying *within* a larger primary obligation to his proper end? Especially when he finds himself pilgrim in the Modernist desert. For if, as St. Thomas argues, the moral rectitude of the poet's reader is a concern to be set aside in the interest of a primary responsibility to the good of the thing the poet is making, it is also necessarily true for Thomas that moral rectitude is the primary responsibility to the maker himself as *person*. It is that responsibility, even though neither recognized nor embraced by Modernist ideology, which is native to human essence itself.

Because of an ineradicable presence (sometimes called *conscience*) the person finds himself restive in a calling to accommodate proximate and ultimate good. That responsibility cannot account in every instance for the good possible to the thing he makes, of course. That is, the maker failing as person may even so make a good thing, sometimes to the amazement of both himself and his audience. On the other hand even makers rescued as persons may make flawed things. But such is a relativism in respect to specific gifts of making to discrete persons, confusing within the order of community in that it speaks worldly, not spiritual limits as reflected by the person's gifts in making. A good work is not decisive to the rescue of the person to his final end, though such a confusion may be encountered in Puritan addresses to making, as Nathaniel Hawthorne suggests with an ironic humor in some of his stories. (The Puritan's well-kept cottage in a well-kept village is mistaken by Young Goodman Brown, we noted, as certifying the citizen's well-kept soul.) It also emerges in Romanticism in our literature in the 19th century out of a desperate attempt at self-rescue by art itself, as with John Keats and (in a particularly arrogant instance) in Percy Bysshe Shelley as "unacknowledged" legislator of truth as poet. Little wonder that the poet may, out of a self-pity born of such a complication to his calling, take a "romantic" out — retreat from his moral responsibility as person into a self-celebratory exile as "Artist." (Again, recall Shelley — or Ezra Pound.)

The poet may thus pursue glory as awarded by the popular spirit, even though that may come only after he is dead, his art his monument. The meteoric parabola of Dylan Thomas on the American scene at the time Flannery is writing her *Wise Blood* proved not only titillating to an American audience, especially to some of the Cornbelt Metaphysicians, but fascinating to a more general audience because of the disparity between Dylan Thomas' intense poetry and his intellectual and moral collapse played out by the media as spectacle, sensational gossip to the delectation of the popular spirit becoming especially a manifest interest of the academy at the time of his death. Dylan Thomas' own self-evaluation as poet seems counter to his public deportment: "I am painstaking, conscientious, involved and devious craftsman in words, however unsuccessful the result so often appears...." It is more the public Dylan than the poet speaking these words who received celebrity status, made the more notorious by his death through excessive drinking. (Flannery remarks to "A," August 9, 1957, concerning Thomas: "It's awful the way they pick on the dead, feast on the dead," naming Thomas' wife Caitlin among the feasters as evidenced by Caitlin's recent "tell-all" reminiscence of "life" with Dylan.)

It is difficult to the poet to accomplish as maker an ordinate relation between his gifts of making here and now and his proper end as an intellectual soul incarnate, both that proximate and ultimate end so intricately related at a most "personal" level for the poet within his self-awareness. A problem indeed, casting some light of understanding perhaps upon the "Romantic Poet" of popular myth as he finds himself in contention with that Modernist spirit increasingly celebrated as it emerges in spectacles of science out of that 18th century aspect of reason reduced to rationalism. For how fickle the popular spirit, seduced by the conveniences of materialism as advanced through its own growing dependence upon science's mechanistic art in a new addiction. Enough to make a poet an intellectual Luddite! Dostoevsky is acutely attuned to this difficulty. His Dmitri Karamazov is presented as a "romantic," specifically as a Byronic hero, counterpointing his brother Ivan as Enlightenment Prophet. Dmitri would sacrifice himself heroically — if only he could break free of "romantic" entanglements with women. As Byronic hero, he affords Ivan (until Ivan's collapse) a wry pleasure by his Byronic foolishness, as that species of foolishness may be seen by a Positivist like Ivan, who has not yet recognized himself a romantic. (Ivan is forced to admit we remarked — after his ordeal with the devil as bourgeoisie Russian, a middle-class "gentleman" — that he, too, has been and is a "Romantic.")

Flannery O'Connor, far from being tempted to such "Romanticism" — to the comforts of celebrity as "Poet" or "Artist" with capital letter — pursues what was in many of its aspects a rather solitary way among her literary peers, a way baffling not only to them but to persons close at hand, including her devoted mother, Regina. She does not respond to misunderstandings with any self-agony, her irritation more on occasion to a reader's failures (including perhaps even her mother's failures) to see the truths toward which her fictions point. Just home with her lupus, she writes the Fitzgeralds (May 7, 1953) of her mother's response to the Modern Library books Flannery had ordered: "You would get something called *Idiot*. What's it about?" To which, Flannery: "An idiot." O'Connor, then, evidences no sense of a "personal" neglect, knowing how often popular adulation is not the same as love. Love she received most amply, if sometimes irritatingly, from Regina, even amused that her mother is troubled because Flannery does not turn her writing talent to good account. Instead, she pursues her own limited perfection as poet in the light of eternity, or so she would insist. She holds fast — and even joyfully — to the understanding that by her calling as poet she may not violate the truths upon which that calling depends, even at the expense of being misunderstood, and even by her loving mother. She even remarks that, given the initial reception of *The Violent Bear It Away* by some of her own faith, perhaps in fifty years they may begin to see what the novel is about — if they go back to and begin reading the Bible again.

Hers is foremost a sense of obligation to recognize truth, in which she is confident she will discover that abiding Truth more and more, the omnipresent Incarnation. By that obligation accepted joyfully, and though she may be disappointed for her reader's sake, she will not cater to that reader's intellectual and spiritual weaknesses. That would be to make of ordinate sentiment her own deportment of sentimentality, out of the presumption that by art she might rescue a wayward reader. That is his own responsibility for intellectual and spiritual rectitude. Meanwhile, she must keep in mind the limits of her calling as artist. She will say that "all I mean by art is writing something that is valuable in itself and that works in itself." Through that labor, in respect to herself as person, she may return her work as gift — as offering — to the Lord of all gifts, understanding that it may be used or not used as He wills. "The basis of art is truth, both in matter and in mode," she says, and will say the same often in many ways. Her devotion to this relationship of matter to mode is through the act of making, as she reminds us and herself. But her mode is quite separate from any concern for the rescue of the person of her reader — other than of herself. And insofar as she forgets herself in the actions of making, in the habits proper to her calling, she also sets aside that concern for herself in a "self-abandonment" proper to her as Christian writer.

As poet in the act of making, she must forget herself into the making at a plane of intellectual concerns that at once encompasses but does not presume to determine the art itself in an absolutist intent. She must not do so, lest as if by Jansenistic intentionalities of any species she should mistake herself as especially empowered. As artist, she knows, a maker is tempted to force art's ends, becoming thereby presumptuous as if the absolute determinist of the artifact's being. As for the worldly end of such devotion, one might of course imagine an old sinner, rocking in his well-made chair at the end of his life, supported but not determined to rescue by that well-made rocker, in relation to which by metaphor we associated the well-made rocker and well-made story. Such for her is her possible reader of a story she has loved into existence by reason. It may be that the rocker or story shall be used by God in rescue of a reprobate, but that is a concern between the reprobate and God, a circumstance properly quite indifferent to the poet's proper deportment in his making. Even so, reason may engage that mystery whereby the maker stands in a relationship as maker to the world as himself a pilgrim.

As person, then, she is a maker in a mystery of analogy related to God as creator. She is "on the way" to that incommensurate Cause to her as but image of that Cause, in that weak analogy in which she believes herself created "in the image of God." How interesting, that such a mystery provides art the possible drama in a poet's actions of making, especially if that poet be Flannery O'Connor in such an untoward age. And so O'Connor as poet rationally pursues the relation of her given matter to a proper mode in the interest of art's limited truth — her devotion turned to the good of the thing she makes. As person (as she reminds herself again and again), she must not violate the "faculty of spiritual vision." *Simple* knowledge in a *special* sense: the immediacy of recognition of the truth of a thing as preceding any rational accommodation to that truth through her discursive reason in service to her art of making. O'Connor is then (as are we all in her vision) restricted from Comprehensive Knowledge by the disproportion between this finite person and his Cause. For the person, there is an undeniably incommensurate finite limit from the Omniscient, that Omnipotent Love which is present and abiding to the person as the Incarnation.

Put starkly once more: the poet is maker, not Creator. It has been out of the dissociation of the modes of intellectual knowing in man as maker — the intuitive from the rational — that Enlightenment Rationalism implies suspicions of and ultimately antagonism toward intuitive knowing, in reaction to which the Romantic poet is likely to err in response by denigrating his own rational knowledge. Here we emphasize as spiritual in its nature the intellectual civil war observed in the public arena as "history," effecting what T. S. Eliot famously declares a "dissociation of sensibilities," the separation of "thought and feeling." It is consequent to this separation that the "Romantic" poet, forgetting Adam and Eve expelled from the Garden, begins to cultivate a myth of the poet as if unique vagabond, an outcast of community elevated by his own self-pity as the lonely artist in a specialized myth serving the "Artist." O'Connor finds the "myth of the 'lonely writer'" to be "particularly pernicious" in our day. That is the myth "that writing is a lonely occupation, involving much suffering because, supposedly, the writer exists in a state of sensitivity which cuts him off, or raises him above, or casts him below the community around him" ("The Regional Writer").

There is a great distance between such a romantic myth about writing and the realities of the labor required to make a good poem or story or novel. Not loneliness but labor is the burden, for to write well is hard work. She says in "The Catholic Novelist in the Protestant South" that "the writing of any novel worth the effort is a kind of personal encounter, an encounter with the circumstances of the particular writer's imagination, with circumstances which are brought to order only in the actual writing." At the time of her talk, there is a critical debate underway on whether the novel itself is a dead genre, but that is a concern hardly hers. What concerns her most immediately, she says, is whether the one she is working on is dead. (A personal note to the point: I asked Karl Shapiro, who approved of my poetry, to recommend a Guggenheim for me to write a novel, he responding he could not because the novel was "dead." The next year he published his own autobiographical novel.) She grows jealous of her time in resuscitating the work in hand, a personal encounter with it especially as time grows short for her. We might suppose, then, that O'Connor might be amused by Eudora Welty's experiences at Eudora's last days. Miss Welty (the story goes) would be at work in her street-level room at 119 Pinehurst in Jackson, only to be interrupted repeatedly by well-meaning neighbors thinking her lonely.

Though they might suffer such local "dangers," neither Welty nor O'Connor would take refuge in self-exile. O'Connor in this same talk cited above explains why she would not. She must as writer wrestle with that task "like Jacob with the angel," but from within her local context, whatever its disadvantages. For as a poet, she is an integral member of a community, whether the community recognize her as a member beyond a growing popular notoriety as she becomes increasingly a "famous" local writer. The maintaining of membership in community she judges a necessity, considering her perspective upon both the advantages of and necessities to her own writing as certifying her own membership in humanity. In addition, as we have heard her say, "The novelist is concerned with the mystery of personality, and you cannot say much that is significant about this mystery unless the characters you create exist with the marks of a believable society about them." Thus as a "Southern" writer she values the enveloping social context of her local South "in all its complexity," to be observed from within it — and often quarreled with as a member of it. It is "so powerful ... that it is a force which has to be encountered and engaged" — *here* and *now*. Young writers, she warns, make a mistake in supposing that they will be able to write only if "they ... shake off the clutch of the region," whatever the region.

If there is a suffering undergone by the writer, then, it is not that of his being inevitably lonely, seeking solace in a wandering exile and looking for some amenable place. The suffering, insofar as it is actual and significant, lies within our shared community in being persons, to be discovered by the writer in persons within a social context whatever the actual place. From her position the origin of suffering is shared as a common inheritance through Adam and Eve, who go out of the old garden to earn their keep in the larger creation by the sweat of the brow — in labor discovered as requiring of them as persons varieties of art suited to peculiar callings within the seeming "desert" of the "larger social context." We are consequently out of Adam's fall required to a "suffering-with" in O'Connor's phrase. Thus for any person, even the artist, this suffering-with by the self has origin in our gift as flawed by Original Sin and limited further by our finite existence as persons. The person labors in his medium, in the manner proper to his calling, in order "to make something right." Perhaps out of that necessity, even the poet may remove obstacles to grace in some minor expiation of a self-forgetting, through a devotion in making something right. An evidence of that possible effect upon the artist as person — that of removing obstacles to grace in a consent to limits — he then proffers the thing he has made to that ultimate Giver of all gifts. But to presume such gifts to be limited by his own limiting intent to make it right, and most especially if he presume his purpose to be that of restoring the "larger social context," is to risk diminution of the made thing from its potential, making it lesser as an offering.

That is the error reducing art to subservience to temporal social conveniences at the expense of its spiritual implications for the poet in making an artifact good in itself, the moral danger to the poet O'Connor understands through St. Thomas. Most especially so when given the gradual appropriation of art to political and social ends in recent history, from Hobbes through Marx down to the confused circumstances of the poet in society in O'Connor's own day. In that interval, art becomes reduced to serving pragmatic conveniences, whether those of an advertising "industry" promoting consumer goods or the furtherance of some social ideology such as that so skillfully managed by Lenin, executed by Stalin or Hitler. That ideological reduction of art is inevitably accompanied by justifications in the name of the *common good* at both the political and social level, to the particular individual's good as "consumer" reciprocally fed upon by ideological patrons of the popular spirit in devouring persons as but individuals. "This is an expensive perfume or soap or hair restorer" the ad's little drama announces, "But I am worth it." Let us not blink the seduction underway in such an obstacle to vision: The *good* defined by the gnostic directors of community in the moment, whether focused upon the consumer's appetite or upon the elevation of a political state to consume the citizen in a new worship, profits in the seduction of intellect from reality. To oppose that ideological distortion requires of the poet (as O'Connor says) a "felt balance" in himself, one learned only through prudential humility, lest he lose himself in an illusion of gaining the world for the common good to his own convenience as sovereign. In gaining that balance, he may recognize that as poet his "material is no more exalted than any other kind." It is by presumption only that he supposes his material (human nature) exalted by his high wisdom rather than by Love's largesse whereby human nature is. That presumption serves pride in elevating the poet above his own kind (as it may do for any other calling of a person). Not that the artist may as well allow himself to be reduced to serving consumerism through his gifts. (O'Connor would see this evidenced on occasion by a work's being a "book club" selection.) Or he may become an instrument subverting art to social and political ends.

O'Connor in her resistance to the poet's perversion of himself as person insists that the poet must make his artifact as governed by prudential humility, not allowing himself to be exalted because he is an "Artist." For title is not an entitlement, as if by name the poet were transformed in his own nature beyond common human nature. He is as maker (as are all persons), required by that common property of his humanity to "make it right," whatever the "it" proper to his gifts within limits peculiar to him. That is a principle that "should be applied to all making," O'Connor insists, whether to the making of a poem or story, or a garden or ax-helve. Her advice here to would-be writers differs radically from that given by Ezra Pound in shouting: "Make it new!" Since that small book by Pound under that title (1934), followed by his *Jefferson and/or Mussolini* (1935), Pound as poet and court philosopher had come to be declared a traitor. He had been incarcerated in an open cage at Pisa at the end of World War II. By the time O'Connor arrived at Iowa, his *Pisan Cantos* (1948) had occasioned him a *cause célèbre* in the intellectual community, Pound having been awarded the Bollingen Prize under government auspices for those Cantos. Pound waited trial as a traitor in St. Elizabeth's Hospital near the national capitol, a hospital for the insane, one evidence justifying committing him introduced at his hearing his own poetry.

Make It New. The question rests in the meaning of *it,* the authority to the making Pound's having declared Mussolini his anticipated poet-king. Such an argument before the popular spirit might well call both poets and political "kings" in common question. It was endangering to Beats no less than to Cornbelt Metaphysicals, given the popular stir raised by the Pound scandal. That circumstance in our literary history, notorious among intellectuals particularly in the 1940s and 1950s, might well encourage Flannery to consider more deeply Pound's cry to poets to "make it new." Meanwhile, it would seem likely that Pound himself had been caught up in an enthusiasm as poet by his own species of Modernist ideology, self-justified by an autonomous authority as poet. How poignant that moment's self-recognition by Pound later in a fragment of a late unfinished Canto near his earthly end: "That I lost my center/ fighting the world./ The dreams clash/ and are shattered —/ and that I tried to make a paridiso/ terrestre." (This recognition by Pound is a theme in my "Ezra Pound: The Quest for Paradise," in *The Men I Have Chosen for Fathers.*)

The poignancy of recognizing his own dreams as clashing and at last shattering is also perhaps in recognition of a likeness in an unlikeness ignored by Pound as revolutionary poet (though it is this failure itself which perhaps draws Ginsberg on a sympathetic journey to

Italy to visit and interview Pound). Modernist ideology, pervasive of the intellectual community which Pound had declared his enemy early on, manifests itself variously as ideology. And so in terms we have developed, Pound may be said to have discovered himself sharing with that intellectual community he chose as most direct enemy in a common denial of the mystery of the givenness with which he must make his "it." (That fragment of a Canto begins "M'amour, m'amour/ what do I love and/ where are you?"— speaking Pound's inclination to the good through love as yet haunting him, its "object" become obscured for him.) Long beleaguered by social and political adversaries, caught up in ideological wars, there seemed to him even at the end no possible spiritual rescue, his autonomous authority as poet then in shambles.

In our concern for this episode of the poet as *homo viator* (and Pound very much saw himself in analogy as superceding Dante by his own *Cantos*), we return to his battle cry "Make it new," to which there is a response from O'Connor—though she seldom mentions Pound. She writes Robert Lowell (May 2, 1952) to give her regards to Omar, Pound's son, adding "I met a doctor recently who had been at St. Elizabeth's and knew Mr. and Mrs. Pound, and liked them very much." Less sympathetically, she writes the Fitzgeralds (January 22, 1956) that "All my erstwhile boy friends visit Pound at St. Elizabeth's and think he is made and finished — he calls them all funny names and they think its wonderful, touched by the holy hand, etc." Hardly a laying-on of hands she could approve.

And so perhaps for O'Connor, Pound in the light of the critical contests over his relation to his work as person might appear something of the poet as Misfit, especially given Pound's suspicions of "Parson" Eliot long since churched in the 1920s. Whether she knew of the Bollingen controversy so particularly as to know that her friend Allen Tate, defending the award, reaches a point of challenging one of the severest critics of the award to a dual, I don't know, though she might likely have known Eliot's quieter defense of that award. Eliot, with a considerable sadness — a suffering-with — knew a validity in Pound's work as art not to be denied. But Eliot had already engaged Pound's battle cry "make it new," in another perspective from Pound's concern to condition a society in an order through the supreme authority of poetry. Eliot had argued that to seek *originality* as a poet to such ends as Pound dreamed — social order — is a false goal. The poet's responsibility, he had recently declared in his *Four Quartets*, is to "purify the dialect of the tribe." In consort with that judgment O'Connor will declare that the poet's, or any maker's, responsibility is to make a thing "right." For her St. Thomas' metaphysics establishes the meaning of the term *right* in a relation to *truth*. For as she says the "basis of art is truth, both in matter and in mode," O'Connor perhaps suspicious of her "erstwhile boy friends" as championing mode over matter in distortions of truth, pursuing the "new" and feeling justified by Pound as newfound Virgil.

Truth in matter, she recognized, requires reason's recognition of hierarchy through being, a recognition that had proved crucial to Milton himself in his *Paradise Lost*. Particularities speak good most various — within the orders of being. And for O'Connor (and Eliot after "Ash-Wednesday") truth is understood as reflected to finite intellect in those orders of nature, accessible to speculative reason as inevitably reflected in any art. For art must necessarily by form reflect those orders of nature, centering in the echo actions of human nature itself as experienced by the poet specific in persons. Bonded by being and oriented (or perhaps disoriented) by reason's response to likeness and unlikeness in things known in the immediacy of experience, the poet as person proves present in his made thing. It is in re-

spect to order as proportionate in a hierarchy of membership that we consider a community vital, the absence of that order signaling community in decay. When persons in their
diversities begin through reason to engage the nature of order itself in aspects of universality, then divergences of judgment begin to occur tensionally to a community of persons, exacerbated where there is no consent to proportionate order in support of persons as intellectual souls incarnate. Those tensions, however, in decaying communities are less
determined by the magnitude of reason in persons than by that inclination in each person
to a willfulness that tempts an excessive presumption of self-sufficiency. There is a range of
judgments by reason in response to the mystery of reality then, reason properly seeking bonding in community by signs, requiring unceasing labor in purifying "the dialect of the tribe."
Parameters to disorder may range from an egalitarian extremity of intention to dissolve all
particularities into a common, indiscriminate amalgam of being — an order dreamed founded
upon denial of particularity. That has been a tendency we remarked as the "democratiza-
tion" of nature, whereby finite intellect must at last assume itself no respecter of either
things or persons in relation to particularities perceived. The implicit irony of righteous certainty of this principle emerges nevertheless, most notably the self-evident realities of *this*
person in relation to *that* person as most discomforting to *this* person, raising demands for
justice made personal by self-sovereignty. At another extreme, not a reduction to sameness,
to *identity* in the philosophical sense by denial of particularity, but rather there may be presumed by the willed intent of sovereign intellect sufficiently empowered in a moment to declare order by fiat by that willful person's transcending the orders of nature as tyrant. A gnostic hierarchy is thus presumed established determining the positive accord to imposed order,
in an intellectual tyranny empowered. At either extreme, the willfulness operative against
the hierarchy of nature which reflects the givenness of creation (the orders of nature), despite that self-evident truth, is countered by force in a willful denial. How seductive to reason, this willful strategy, whereby natural law is denied, thereby denying reason's participation in that Eternal Law whereby things *are* in themselves despite all willful intentionalities
of fallen intellectual souls, the sons and daughters of Adam and Eve.

Such speculative observation concerning hierarchy may be a fundamental concern if
we are to recognize just how thorough in thought Flannery O'Connor as "hillbilly" Thomist.
Hers is a counter judgment by her vision of the egalitarianism as a principle to one species
of sentimentality dissolving reason on the one hand. Her position is as well counter to the
tyrannical autonomy forced by reason on the other in gnostic tyrannical determinism. These
mark parameters to the dramatic arena O'Connor engages at mid–20th century, hers a truth
about two falsenesses in Modernist dogma she finds evident in the social and political world
about her. These come to climactic crisis for the person as intellectual soul incarnate in social and political spectacles just as she begins to answer her calling as a prophet of distances.
Hierarchy, O'Connor recognizes through St. Thomas, speaks the inherent order of creation,
implying a relation in community order to the natural law. Reason discovers this relation
in response to the natural law *in* intellect itself— in our given nature — the self-evident good
in disparate things seen antecedent to our givenness as person, as intellectual soul incarnate.
Thus reason may discover that it is by Eternal law that things are actual in proportionali-
ties of existence as things in themselves, the recognition of which implies this intellect's special provenance of reason's perfection according to its specific limits through understanding opened to the intellectual soul by its participation with Eternal Reason.

Things are therefore to be seen by reason as consequent upon *being*, though susceptible to either deconstruction by power or to a perfection governed by love. Things made, when sustained in their potentialities through love, reflect the stewardship of art as action proper to the given nature of man as maker, as artist. That is a recognition Dante explores along his way, to his culminating vision of the Multifoliate Rose in the *Paradiso.* The contrary action out of willfulness is to the tyranny over things in themselves by manipulative distortion of the givenness of those things to the pleasure and convenience of the tyrannical intellect. Will becomes intentional to power over being through gnosis dreaming a reformulation of being itself by overpowering things. Ironically, gnostic intentionality in the tyrannical mode profits from the alternate distortion of the true "self" we dubbed egalitarian reductionism in its pseudo-love as an obverse of gnostic power. It is in this light upon the parameters of willfulness that we have suggested that the existence of a New Age paganism proves a complementary servant to any Positivistic tyranny over being, a reservoir of power to Positivistic intentionalities executed in the name of their "common good."

If there seems to occur a climactic moment at mid–20th century in the divergence of social, political, cultural ways for community, O'Connor suggests the moment consequent upon community's having wandered from the true way, a wandering in lostness of persons and community made increasingly notable since the 18th century. She remarks it as a turning from the true way in which "the popular spirit of each succeeding age" becomes addicted to false dreams, tending more and more to the view that the ills and mysteries of life will eventually "fall before the scientific advances of man," as she remarks in "Some Aspects of the Grotesque in Southern Fiction." It becomes a concern for her as poet and so a matter to her art as she looks back upon recent intellectual history. It comes to focus in her allusion to that critical shibboleth borrowed by literary criticism from Eliot, the "dissociation of sensibilities." O'Connor recognizes the dissociation, but recognizes as well that at issue is much more than a judgment of recent literature in the declensions into literary "categories"—Romanticism, Realism, Naturalism. Metaphysical truth is at issue for her, not a ranking by a critical accountancy of the works in the Western canon of artifacts. (Pound characterizes scathingly this "academic" concern as "cause" in World War I: "For two gross of broken statues,/ For a few thousand battered books" possessed in "a botched civilization," by an "old bitch gone in the teeth," costing all those young lives in such horrors as the Battle of the Somme.)

If Eliot points with his famous phrase ("the dissociation of sensibilities") to an eruption in intellect at about the time of Dryden and Milton, he does so as he is seeking his own recovery through those somewhat earlier 'Metaphysical Poets," a conspicuous example to him John Donne. It has become a concern as he finds himself at a crossroads, not yet recognizing it as intersected by eternity. But all along her own way O'Connor has been oriented by those metaphysical depths in her faith, recognizing our having become almost blind and deaf through a spiritual malady. The separation of "thought and feeling" is Eliot's characterization of sensibilities gone awry. What Eliot will at last (as O'Connor almost from her beginning) understand is that the orders of being speak to the intellectual creature man a necessary conclusion, that God is a Loving Cause revealed through things in themselves at each crossroads on the way, despite man's dissociation as intellectual creature. That has been the intellectual territory crucial to the poet in his concern for likeness in unlike things, though not always recognized in his necessities to an indirection by his signs. It had been evident to St. Augustine and to St. Thomas, as it was to poets like Dante or (if more fitfully) to Shakespeare and Donne. It becomes especially intrusive upon Milton as a Puritan intellectual finding himself metaphysically conflicted between being a poet and being a Puritan activist. Milton, composing his *Paradise Lost,* finds himself willy-nilly depending upon the hierarchy in creation as affecting social and political manifestations of community — independent of Puritan inclinations to rigidly counter to "Popish" hierarchy. The Roman theology lies in a Thomistic metaphysics of religious, social, political order that is anathema to Cromwellians, though that metaphysics had influenced English culture down to the Tudors and beyond.

Milton as poet (as opposed to Milton as Cromwell's Latin Secretary) is confronted by orders of being certified by his reason as inherent to both nature and human nature. Though Puritan, as poet he is challenged to relocate hierarchy to the realm of Heaven. How wisely, given his Puritanism, had he abandoned his first inclination to deal with hierarchy in that Arthurian "matter" that fascinates him in his youth. A Puritan inclination of will, let us suggest, may be tempted to autonomous power with dangers to a tyrannical power that would decree order as religious fiat. In an irony of our religious history, the Puritan rejected whatever is "Popish" as theological hierarchic. But that proved an inclination toward a Manichaean separation of grace from nature, nature itself to be conquered most soberly. That is the implicit recognition by Hawthorne in his "Maypole of Merrymount." But already, before Hawthorne, Milton had engaged that same problem, not only as poet but as a prominent Puritan polemicist. He will reach an impasse as Puritan activist, however, requiring protest against his own protesters, in opposition not only to the "forcers of conscience," those Papists, but as well to those would-be "forcing protestants," as he calls them. The dilemma is engaged by Milton in opposition to that attempt by Parliament to decree positive laws of religious compulsion. Milton's response is his *Treatise of Civil Power in Ecclesiastical Causes,* whose subtitle suggests his own dissociation of sensibilities in his relation to the tyrannical civil power of the Protestants no less than to the Papists: The treatise announces in subtitle a "showing that it is not lawful for *any power* on earth to compel in matters of religion" (my emphasis).

To put our point concerning the dissociation of sensibilities in respect to Milton: as poet, Milton depends upon what may be seen as a Thomistic reading of the orders of nature in relation to the proper order of the person to the person's proper end, though Milton will quarrel as polemicist with the "scholastics" in his public Puritan office in service to Cromwell. It is through hierarchy, he knows as poet, that persons are bonded as members in community, under the auspices of a creation that certifies hierarchy itself as grounded in being, requiring reason's sorting of a law "natural" to each created thing as the limit whereby it *is*. As poet he responds to creation, from the orders of angels as intellectual creatures in their full natures, to orders of nature as culminating in man — creation thus reaching upward to angelic natures. Thus one might conclude that hierarchy binds all creation under the auspices of man's stewardship to creation in a "chain of being," from the ultimate (the angel) to the penultimate (man), as intellectual creatures.[3]

If Milton can not avoid hierarchy, though it is discomforting to some of the strictures of Puritan theology in relation to politics and social order, neither could Eliot's friend Ezra Pound. Unlike Milton, Pound as a truculent intellectual would ground hierarchy not in God (as Milton does in *Paradise Lost*) but in Confucian philosophy in his own "epic," *The Cantos.* Indeed, Pound adapts Confucius in a deliberate antithesis to St. Paul (between whom and Milton there are intellectual affinities). Thus (in *Canto* XIII) "Kung gave the words 'order'/ and 'brotherly deference'/ And said nothing of the 'life after death.'" For Pound (on the authority he deduces from Confucius), it is the poet-philosopher who determines order. From a Thomistic perspective upon his position, Pound acts out of a pseudo-transcendent point declared into existence by his autonomous intellect, provided spectacle by a selective cultural history. From Pound's perspective, then, Eliot as an emerging Thomist could but be a disappointment to Pound, affirming as Eliot does the Word within any word, whether overtly summoned or in the word (the made thing) by implication — and whether the poet's or philosopher's or scientist's word, recognized or not by the word-smith in his making.

Such a parting of the ways between Pound and Eliot, both recognized as principal poets at the end of World War II, serves to signify a decided drawing of lines underway at the time, though the metaphysical principles at issue may appear obscure in the social and political re-alignments underway just as O'Connor is bound for the Writers Workshop in Iowa. On either side of this growing divide within the intellectual community, hierarchy is recognized as a necessity to order, though on the one side it is declared established by secular power, while on the other accepted as self-evident on principles of transcendence other than the presumptions of intellectual autonomy. The secular order as established by fiat — by positive law enforced at variance from natural law — will be recognized even by a "hillbilly" Thomist as destructive of community, and is seen by O'Connor as gaining a popular ascendance out of rationalism. But what is destroyed by a positive law decreed by gnostic, secular intellect as contrary to natural law is scientific mechanism deployed in reducing nature. Community is founded out of nature as discretely ordered beings speaking implicitly to reason a hierarchy of creation itself, the orders of nature discerned by speculative reason that is the community increasingly disordered by imposition of mechanistic system. Thus individuals are, by a positive law rejecting natural law, to be reconstituted as cumulative integers commanded by gnostic system, rather than persons bonded in *con-unity* as a body viable in the rescue of the person beyond his merely social or political or economic parameters. Sharing by nature as persons a property of being, made actual out of potentialities to persons through their making (through *stewardship* within and toward creation out of a right will to the good), the member as maker is rather to be required to make "it" (community) new. O'Connor's countering phrase is "make it right" in consonance with the inherent limits of any thing the person would make. It is from this Thomistic perspective that the person may reach an accommodation to that truth which declares that "God is no respecter of persons," but recognizing in the saying that God's active love proves always personal and undivided to *this* particular creature in respect to that creature's possible *integrity* as a person created by Love.

It is in such distinctions as we are making that O'Connor as poet recognizes the metaphysical implications of the most central "place" to the person to which she turns in her making. It is at that crossroads she speaks of in which time and place intersect, but always triangulated in the *person* by the grace of that transcendent Love. St. Paul, not Confucius, advised that it is through a perfection of the person as person that the body of community is to be made vital in its memberships. Persons become *members* of that *body*, differing in gifts as members. It is as member that each person becomes manifest in community as particular within that body, reflecting thereby a hierarchy of relative spiritual and intellectual responsibilities to community, though in its worldly dimensions as community God continues no respecter of persons because of any person's hierarchical manifestation as steward to creation, whether as a laboring arm or a prophetic eye in that body. The dignity of perfection in the person as person is not measured by God's love on a relativistic scale of membership but in respect to the fulfillment of that member in the gifts peculiar to the person's limit as *this* person.

O'Connor finds pernicious the romanticized myths about the writer — the "Artist" — as embraced by the popular spirit out of 19th century inclinations of the poet to a self-pity through which he would set himself aside from humanity as *hoi-poloi,* in effect reserving himself from membership in common humanity, the strategy of pride to self-love. (In that recognition we see as well in the next century that the spectacle of *celebrity* replaces increasingly old distinctions of members as *heroes* and *saints.*) But she finds equally pernicious that other "romanticism" born of 18th century Enlightenment: the systematic diminution of the person effected by a dogmatic rationalism that rejects any intellectual gift of the intuitive, natural, inclination to the good. That is a strategy in the interest of power through autonomous rationalism, commanding "facts" as absolute instruments to the reconstitution of being itself. With Thomas, O'Connor (as does the later Eliot) sees the intuitive intellect as initiating reason's response in the intellectual soul to creation, enabling the person to a deployment by rational intellect to his being "on the way" to a proper end. For that which is intuitively known moves reason toward *understanding.* Given her recognition, she must be wary, lest she too succumb to temptations to a merely pragmatic action of making in an attempted rescue of either the wandering lonely Romantic or the self-assured Rationalist — the one submerged, the other detached, from creation by his intellectual error. The one is pilgrim lost; the other has deluded himself by a "transcendentalism" believed already accomplished through an angelistic reason. The one eschews unlikeness dissolved into the cosmos; the other eschews likeness in being with the cosmos created. The one by angelistic reason declares his own way by autonomous reason, rejecting speculative "emotional" wanderings in the cosmic desert as he observes it as "romantic." Either may reach that intellectual stasis called despair which is an abiding threat to that faith in intellect as its own autonomous god.

Both species of "romanticism" are to be found in O'Connor's audience. She recognizes this as peculiarly consequent out of the current state of the intelligentsia on the one hand and on the other of its inordinate influence on the popular spirit, that theorist-consumer complex Walker Percy addresses. But if she must resist a fictional proselytizing, neither is she required to an indifferent neutrality as artist, since truth is truth however engaged. If she refuses to be lured into a "Catholic" fiction suited especially to be read on vacations at the beach, neither will she engage the Rationalist in a dialectical exchange as a primary emphasis of her fiction, since one never "proves" anything by a story as she says. (On the point, consider Walker Percy's fictional manner in his *Lancelot* as dialectical argument.) Nevertheless, she will take seriously that Modernist sensibility as her matter. She has come to know it omnipresent in the popular spirit, evident in actual persons she knows, both in intellectuals and in good country people. By dramatic attention to this truth concerning spiritual dislocation, she makes drama of the *possible* consequences of spiritual dislocation, adumbrating truths about our given nature as persons in the intellectual actions of surrogate persons. And out of her unwavering faith she holds to such truths as a prophet of distances.

We are hard pressed, then, to conclude whether a protagonist in her fiction is either "lost" or "saved" by the implications of the resolutions of a story, though he will have been dramatized through a series of epiphanies that enlarge upon contingent prospects to be imagined as continuing past a story's end. Such is a dramatic suggestiveness of the *possible* beyond the story itself, whether we recognize it in a simplistic intellectual such as Asbury in "An Enduring Chill" or in that illiterate intellectual simpleton Mr. Head in "The Artificial Nigger." O'Connor will herself speak a prospect upon her Misfit, who may be imagined becoming the prophet she suggests he was meant to be. What these surrogate persons have in common is that they are figures of man fallen from grace through willfulness, revealed as fallen intellectual souls through their *possible* intellectual actions in circumstantial environments made concrete by her art. Whether to be fully rescued by the grace dramatically proffered in the fictions is quite another and a most ambiguous problem, a mystery deepened. For O'Connor does not presume upon God's justice or mercy by resolving in her fiction the *possible*— as if she might *prove* both God's justice and mercy by her own judgment of versions of actual persons as characters. It will not follow, however, that she may not remark their strengths or weaknesses from her own position in respect to contingencies, even speculating on the *possible* for such surrogate persons beyond a story's fixed limits. But such speculations are subsequent to the "incarnation" of her characters in specific fictional deployments of the possible to human nature. She accepts that the story itself, in St. Thomas' terms, remains *fixed* and *certain* when she offers it up.

What is required of her as maker, then, is not a neutrality in relation to the truth of things — as philosophers since the Renaissance have increasingly maintained necessary to the building of systems serving Positivism's dreams, thereby progressively de-winging persons to individuals, flightless chickens in collective flocks that become climactically controlled in henhouses prescribed by gnostic positive law caging the intellectual soul. In the pretense to such neutrality, intellect becomes disarmed critically by its assumed mandatory "objectivity," which intellectual deportment is never possible to man. The prudential humility of O'Connor in her intellectual action is a manner quite other than such a pretense to "objectivity." O'Connor submits to the truth of things as experienced, truth itself the measure of the good of the thing she makes, she in no wise dependent absolutely upon intellectual system as established by a deterministic form decreed to control art. That had been a charge against her as a "Catholic" artist, leading to her insistence that "because I am a Catholic, I cannot afford to be less than an artist."

Not that there will follow for her any comfort as artist from the Church's response to what she writes, or rather response from other persons also within the Church. She puts that recognition in a "bald statement" to her friend "A" (July 20, 1955). She declares herself guilty as charged as it were. She is "a Catholic peculiarly possessed of the modern consciousness," to possess which "*within* the Church" is a considerable burden to her as artist. That is a circumstance to her as *person*, in which she feels "the contemporary situation at the ultimate level." Little wonder that a reader outside the Church — that *New Yorker* reviewer of *A Good Man Is Hard to Find* for instance — can but be baffled by such an independent "modern consciousness" as Flannery O'Connor as a presence in her stories who professes herself as well member *in* the Church. What horror to a fellow modern consciousness outside the Church. Ah, Flannery. If only we could take you out of all this, these stories on "original sin" in which the Devil is acknowledged a presence actually believed a reality by the author. She sees such a reviewer in his angst as a special species of the modern consciousness, a member of a "section" of humanity current, in whom the moral sense has been bred quite out of him, so that he is like one of those chickens whose wings have been atrophied of membership in the whole chicken by breeding — by form imposed.

As member of, member *within*, the Church, then, she must engage "the contemporary situation at the ultimate level." And since, as person in membership she knows it impossible to be comprehensive of truth as a finite intellectual soul, the virtue she must welcome as artist becomes that of prudential humility. Being a maker and not a creator, she must make with reason. Even so, she does not shy from a speculative wonder at her own accomplishment when a story is at last fixed and certain. Especially, we are arguing, there is that persuasive witness to her, a steady and encouraging presence to her reasoning, Thomas Aquinas.[4] She can but love him, she says, because he so loves God. In this light, then, she makes telling speculative observation about the limited virtues of that "naturalistic" writing which had emerged as a "genre" much studied systematically in the academy in her school days. It was a literary genre rising immediately out of the "Realism" of Henry James in reaction to the seeming uncertainty of Jamesian Realism, a genre whose advocates were wary of Hawthorne's Romanticism as James had been. Thus those three "movements" in the 19th century became heavily listed in course descriptions in the 20th century academy: Romanticism, Realism, Naturalism. As critic, one could become a specialist of a genre, having written a dissertation. Naturalism's descent through Realism, she recognized, is out of 18th century Rationalism as lately aided and abetted by Darwinian doctrines. In respect to literary matters it is a movement served by the emerging science called Psychology, especially as that science is increasingly made a corollary to Positivism in philosophy, yielding a dominant Positivistic science which the Naturalist can ignore only at risk of heresy.

What O'Connor observed of Naturalism is that, despite the dangers of its "theories" as derived from and credentialed by Enlightenment thought through Positivistic theory, if the Naturalistic writer is truly naturalistic he may write more largely than he may either intend or recognize. One of her specific arguments we have already cited, from in "Some Aspects of the Grotesque in Southern Fiction." It warrants our quoting it with some fullness:

> Since the eighteenth century, the popular spirit of each succeeding age has tended more and more to the view that the ills and mysteries of life will eventually fall before the scientific advances of man, a belief that is still going strong even though this is the first generation to face total extinction because of these advances. If the novelist is in tune with this spirit, if he believes that actions are predetermined by psychic make-up or the economic situation or some other determinable factor, then he will be concerned above all with an accurate reproduction of the things that most immediately concern man, with the natural forces that he feels control his destiny. Such a writer may produce a great tragic naturalism, *for by his responsibility to the things he sees, he may transcend the limitations of his narrow vision* [our emphasis].

Very probably O'Connor has in mind such a naturalist as Theodore Dreiser, whose signal work of Naturalistic drama is *An American Tragedy,* a work once much discussed in academic literary courses. She would also have known that Dreiser, though a convert to biological determinism, also continued deeply interested in spiritualism, a "spiritual" movement made popular in America by Madam Blavatsky in Dreiser's day. (Concerning Spiritualism as a movement, especially in relation to its origin in Kantian philosophy, see Peter Washington's *Madame Blavatsky's Baboon: A History of the Mystics, Mediums, and Misfits Who Brought Spiritualism to America,* 1993). But such a waywardness from Naturalism into Spiritualism does not obviate the truth of her reckoning some measured truth inevitable to Naturalistic writing, so long as the writer has a "responsibility to the things he sees." The recognition of this truth about Naturalism is inherent to her own fiction, she as comfortable with empirical realities as is the Naturalist. As her old friend Brainard Cheney observed in the *Sewanee Review* (1964), if she was "a true humorist and possessed an unusual gift for the grotesque," she also "resorted to something far more remarkable to reflect her Christian vision to a secular world." She invented a new form of humor which "consists in her introducing her story with familiar surfaces in an action that seems secular, and in a secular tone of satire or humor. Before you know it, the naturalistic situation has become metaphysical and the action appropriate to it comes with a surprise, an unaccountability that is humorous, however shocking, The *means is violent,* but the end is Christian."

That observation by Cheney is incisive. It suggests why O'Connor was (and is) so easily misunderstood. For how is one to deal with a violence recognizable in daily manifestations as a violence that would take Heaven by storm, thereby asserting by implication the reality of Heaven? That is a paradox not easily resolved by any rigid Naturalistic doctrine as cultivated by intellect in a narrow doctrinaire "flightlessness" of spirit, denying any possibility of *transcendence* beyond the limits of man's "naturalistic" finitude as intellectual. Not, we have emphasized, that as maker her primary intent is to *prove* her Christian vision to a secular world of man as a lowly worm *possibly* transformed by grace into butterfly. She is nevertheless acutely aware that her vision and that of the dominant secular world are engaged in mortal conflict, the one almost believing, the other adamantly denying, the intellectual soul. She recognizes as well that there is underway all about her this intellectual civil war, with grave consequences at the naturalistic level (witness the Gulag and the gas chambers). But there is an even graver consequence in her view at a common spiritual level removed from large political spectacle.

This is a recognition perhaps better put concerning the "felt balance" she attempts as artist: insofar as she makes a good story, the story does test though not positively demonstrate her affirmation of the Christian vision. It does so, even though as artist making the story she does not intend to "prove" her vision as if art were science. At a level of indirection in respect to the limits of her responsibility as artist there is a testing of recovery through speculative reason of a *possible* long denied. The secular world may profit by that witness or not, prudence reserved to the individual soul at large in that secular world — at spiritual risk on its own responsibility to that *possible* vision. As a poet engaged in the making of *this* story now underway, she must have no primary concern for the story as a fictional refutation of dialectical materialism, of Positivistic science, of New Age paganism such as settled upon Naturalistic writers like Dreiser or Norris or Balzac and then became popular after them. In this respect let us say that when she is *poet* she is in the act of making a work *now.* Having made it, she becomes a part of her own audience, she as person finding her work, when true in its "matter and mode," a confirmation of the vision she holds as person. That is a position which she would probably defend on the authority of that angelic doctor, St. Thomas Aquinas, by reference no doubt to his careful explications of the virtues to the intellectual soul, *prudence* and *humility*. From her perspective as person, she believes herself enlarged in her vision of distances by her concentrated devotion as maker, the relation of herself as person and as artist thus reconciled in an understanding of herself. That she understands as her spiritual felt balance gained through reason in Thomas' speculative arguments. St. Thomas addresses as philosopher these challenges to the prophetic poet concerned with responsibility to the good of the story to be made. The prudential responsibility of the poet as a person endowed with gifts to her own becoming is to be made ordinate by a humility, recognizing that prudential deportment is not sufficient to her becoming.

O'Connor is quite open, we know in acknowledging Thomas her primary aesthetic mentor in her letters and in the talks she gave by invitation to a variety of audiences in a variety of places. (She was nevertheless always anxious to get back to Andalusia from such sojourns abroad, to "feed the chickens" as she put it.) But the teachings of St. Thomas are present by implication in her work at every turn. That is no doubt one aspect of her work which occasioned invitations to speak at some institutions, as it also lured a steady flow of letters from around the world addressed to Andalusia. And a primary lesson, held as revealed dogma to govern her present actions in making, was Thomas' insistence that man is by his given nature a maker. (Again, I have devoted my *Making: The Proper Habit of Our Being* to this Thomistic principle.) We have quoted Thomas declaring that art is "nothing else but *the right reason about certain things to be made,*" whatever the specific calling of the person as maker. It is in the passage bearing this assertion (*Summa Theologica,* I-II, q. 57, a. 3) that Thomas adds (in his a. 4) a reminder to us as makers: "the good of things made by art is not the good of man's appetite, but the good of those things themselves." For "art does not presuppose rectitude of appetite." It is rather, through art's peculiar limit as a "science" of making, a *reasoned* making of a thing good in itself, to which devotion the maker — the artist — sets himself aside as it were. In respect to its limit, art is nevertheless peculiar in relation to *this* maker's peculiar gift whether he make a poem or rocking chair. The thing made *may* serve in relation to appetite subsequently, even that of the artist and especially to that tempting appetite for fame. But that is a concern at a separate level: the artist's responsibility to himself as person in a present act of making this thing *now* with *these* givens. His sacrifice is that of a self-forgetting which O'Connor speaks of having experienced in the act of writing. We recall again words to "A" (December 9, 1961), "I never completely forget myself except when I am writing and I am never more completely myself than when I am writing."

That forgetfulness speaks to her the nature of "Christian self-abandonment," a self-abandonment native to us as persons, a "natural" openness to the good through intuitive intellect, turning us outward in a self-forgiveness. The poet (O'Connor), reflecting on such experiences as a person may recognize in the consequent act of making a possible good to a thing by the proportionate correspondence of the poet as maker (through love) to that Openness of Love her Creator, in whose image she exists as person. In the act of making there is the immediacy of a limiting responsibility to present actions of making as governed by reason at the level of a craftsmanship undertaken with love. Thus, "rectitude of the will is essential to prudence," St. Thomas says, "but not to art," in respect to which as a virtue "prudence is a virtue distinct from art." The distinction nevertheless lies in a relation to our particular calling as *this* person to a maker by nature, with *these* gifts. Both the virtue of art and of prudence have in common that each is "in the thinking part of the soul" and must be concerned therefore "about things that may be otherwise than they are" (Art 4, Reply to objection 2). The necessary distinction is that, while both prudence and art as virtues depend upon right reason, prudence is concerned "with things to be done" as *person* in that dimension of our existence as intellectual soul incarnate, while art is concerned with "things to be made," in which hierarchy of responsibilities art is secondary. For man as maker (as artist) in his responsibility to "things to be done" exercises a moral responsibility to his gifts — his potentialities — in a becoming to the limits of his specific nature wherein he lives and breathes and has his being. A gift in his exercise of that responsibility is discovered through self-forgetfulness, a *becoming* advanced beyond even his proper sense of moral responsibility through his surrender in love. For one cannot think of the martyr as becoming martyr, simultaneous to an intention to martyrdom, the theme Eliot engages in *Murder in the Cathedral.* What is to be done prudentially, through reason, carries the pilgrim to that point of surrender, but the surrender proves above and beyond prudential responsibility, an entering of a country beyond the creation he sojourns.

Thomas develops the distinction between "prudence" and "art" out of Aristotle's *Meta-*

physics, but he does so in the light of Revelation. *Making,* by this distinction, "is an action passing into outward matter," while *doing* is an action through prudence affecting primarily the perfection of the acting self on its journey to its ultimate end. It will follow that a bad person may, by his attention to the good of the thing he makes, make a good thing, even though he may as *person* be on his way to perdition. The fixed and certain thing he has made will nevertheless continue good in itself. This distinction informs O'Connor's observation about the artist as Naturalist, who by his attention to the good of the thing he makes in response to things *as they are* (at the "naturalistic" level) may in the end have made a thing that transcends his "narrow" vision as person. And that is the point Thomas has emphasized in his Article 3 of our citation. "For a craftsman, as such, is commendable, not for the will with which he does a work, but for the quality of the work." Art is therefore "an operative habit," dependent upon the antecedently given — that upon which art necessarily depends as *matter* and from which the artist induces a form imagined in an accord with that chosen matter. Art as an "operative habit," then, underlines for O'Connor that pretentiousness of the "romantic" artist as longsuffering in the world, a self-pity sufficient on occasion to persuade that suffering artist that he is Creator and not merely a "maker" of things with givens. But always, form depends from given matter in respect to the poet's imaginative limit in making.

In O'Connor's phrase, art's form depends from that "larger social context" she speaks of in relation to her fiction, a context of common humanity to persons. The species of givenness chosen by the artist constitutes form's matter in his pursuit by form, discovered in making of *possible actions* of nature. That matter infuses form as it were, allowing an "incarnational" aspect through the imaginative making of the *possible.* It is in relation to this coincidence of given matter to imagined form executed through reason that the made thing is to be properly measured in respect to its own perfection as an artifact revealing beauty. The art "thing," therefore, is not in its necessities dependent upon the moral rectitude of either the artist or of his reader. The concerns for moral rectitude on the one hand and for the perfections of art things on the other are separate orders of concern in distinctions about the nature of things in themselves as understood by discursive reason. To put the point in a extremity of metaphor, then: The drunken painter may paint a house properly, if he properly scrape and caulk and brush the paint on wood with strokes evenly suited to the wood — provided of course that he chooses the right caulk and paint and scraper and brush — and does not fall off a proper ladder. (*Pace* Dylan Thomas.)

In the cultural climate out of Modernist thought, it is popular usage to speak of *making* as *creating,* since if man is limited to *making* he thereby acknowledges a dependence upon some given or givens, out of which he must make a thing by art. Much grander, the title *creator* than that of mere *maker,* which though the terms have lost the old scholastic precisions yet carry a residual suggestiveness. The artist in pride as creator would create *ex nihilo,* but when confronted by insistent reason's concern for distinction, he must concede that his imagined form depends upon the antecedently given (including that of his own existence). Through an accommodation of imagined form to given matter, Thomas argues, an artifact comes to be actual. And, even though the poet should refuse the implication of Cause in his givens, insofar as he responds to the actualities of those things antecedent to his making, he may prove better maker than his professed theories themselves would allow.

That is the point Flannery O'Connor addresses in suggesting that the poet as self-declared naturalistic determinist — convinced of nature as deterministic machine directing his destiny indifferently out of confluent accidents — as "naturalist" may reflect a vision in his art that is implicit in the very matter he must use, overriding his intention. For O'Connor, it is inevitable that this should be so, insofar as the Naturalistic Determinist as maker of things responds to things in themselves through his perceptions of things actually experienced. That is the first movement toward God, St. Thomas argues: perceptions intuitively received by intellect through the senses And so, actions of making dependent upon the truth of things in themselves speak truths that may be obscured by the maker but not eradicated from the matter necessary to him as maker. Thus, despite his radical intentions or denials, even the "puritan" scientific Positivist we have spoken of cannot "purely" escape dependence on givenness by a Kantian "pure reason" in his angelistic intent to transcendence of givenness. For he is most dependent for his formulation upon the actuality of things — foremost upon the actuality of the puritan Positivist himself. Thomas chooses another maker than the poet as example to this point: "For as long as the geometrician demonstrates [by his speculative art] the truth, it matters not how his appetitive faculty may be affected, whether he be joyful or angry: even as neither does it matter to a craftsman." As artist the geometrician pursues universal truth, though he deny the Cause of that truth. Both the speculative geometrician and the craftsman making actual things may deny the cause of the *given* upon which their differing arts depend, but neither one of them may avoid actual dependence upon givens which provision their speculative or crafted makings. Only as imprudent may either one deny this limiting reality to his making, whether he make a theorem ($E=mc^2$), a poem, or an ax-handle.

We encounter a kindred argument from a different perspective further along in the *Summa Theologica* (II-II, q. 49, a. 6, Reply Objection 2). In this later passage the epistemological relation of the maker to his own givenness becomes more precise. Thomas' principle of the essential unity of intellect to *this* person (against the arguments of the Averroists) holds that the simple intellectual nature of that specific person bears unity in a discrete actuality of a given nature. Intellect as a specific and limited given bonds the person to his Cause. It has as its properties to intellectual action those complementary modes we have named: that of the intuitive mode (Thomas' *intellectus*) properly in consort with the rational mode (Thomas' *ratio*). "The certitude of reason comes from the intellect," he argues. "Yet the need of reason is from a defect in the intellect, since those things in which the intellectual power is in full vigor have no need of reason." The intellectual power to which he refers here is that of the intuitive (analogous to the angelic) intellect. The intuitive intellect receives the truth by simple insight, "as do God and the angels." In man that is the operation whereby one knows what is called the "self-evident."

Thomas responds to an objection to his argument, an objection that prudence is not dependent upon reason since reason is the "operative" mode of rational intellect peculiar to that intellectual creature called man, differing from the angelic intellectual nature. But to the contrary, Thomas says in response, reason in its offices to making differs from reason in its offices of support of the prudential habits proper to man as *homo viator* — as man on his way to his proper end as person. In respect to the habits of art as differing from the habits of prudence, it must be recognized (he says) that in "matters of art, though they are singular [they] are nevertheless more fixed and certain, wherefore in many of them there is no room for counsel on account of their certitudes...." A story or poem once made is "fixed" Thomas says — once it is surrendered by its maker into creation. The artist may subsequently rework a story on recognizing an inadequacy in its fixity. He may *re-fix* it. Thus O'Connor revisits her first published story "The Geranium" at the very end of her life, reworking that story which she had first used to open her master's thesis at Iowa. It becomes "Judgment Day."

There is a relation of prudence in the making of that fixity, but prudence in this sense lies in the concern for a reasoned perfection of the thing made, lest it prove inadequate in itself through a flawed making. If form and matter are not made commensurate to the good possible through form as imagined and brought to execution in making, there is a failed making — an inadequate craftsmanship or an inadequate conception of possible form. Though a fixed thing results, it will lack the good proper to it, this becoming the concern of the critic as prognostician of the possible good of a made thing. The poet himself may, out of his concern for the good of the thing he has made, discover mistake not in nature as matter but a mistake of art insufficient to the material realities of the nature antecedent to his imaginative form in his quest for the possible form of making. When he recognizes the thing flawed, he may wisely destroy that work, though in doing so he in no wise may be said to commit that apostasy against being of which Rayber is guilty in advocating euthanasia as solution to such mistakes of nature as his nephew, the idiot Bishop. The difference most telling for the poet, perhaps relieving the pain of defeat as maker, is that he is maker, not creator, more easily consigning a failed sonnet to flames as made, not created *ex nihilo*, as even Rayber proves unable to consign Bishop to death.

If that poet does not destroy his flawed work, it may survive as "juvenalia" harvested by the curious critic, such as that gathering of Eliot's early work made years after his Nobel Prize. There has been especially evident the publisher's tendency to profit from unpublished work by the famous — an early poem or story celebrated posthumously, though it was judged imperfect and abandoned by the poet and (alas) not burned. "Never before published," a blurb will declare. That it has never before appeared because it was recognized as fixed in its weaknesses is obscured by the poet's notoriety. How profitable, indeed, has been such literary scavenging, in which an honored maker by his name alone gains for a flawed work a moment's reputation. For work made and abandoned by the famous and only now "discovered" excites for a moment. Not, of course, that the poet himself may not participate in the moment's notoriety of a work. Ezra Pound apologizes, for instance, for having (as he put it) dumped his notebooks upon the public, his judgment of much of his early work as flawed products of apprenticeship, appearing as his "shorter poems," *Personae*, exercises he is justified in foisting on the "public" for the sake of his rent and groceries. (Not of course that the poet may not be mistaken in his judgment, as by degree Pound is in wanting to be judged as poet only by his *Cantos*.)

Such reflections are a "critical" aside here, though elements in the literary air of the academy at mid–20th century. Not crucial to what Thomas has as a concern: namely, the fixity and certainty of a thing made as differing generically from the flow of created things in themselves within creation, in their becoming to the limits of their created natures. There is, therefore, a fundamental difference between man as maker of poems or stories, himself created in the image of God, and the "natural" reality of things created by God upon which his making depends. That distinction requires of the maker a prudential humility as steward to created things — as maker — in which office becomes possible his integrity as person. For it is upon his integrity that his ultimate end depends, upon a simple perfection as intellectual soul incarnate. In relation to this distinction, through which we know the *limited* arena to the making of a thing as fixed and unchanging, the poet as person *makes* in collateral becoming of himself, in a changing either diminishing or fulfilling his potential being, depending upon the degree of surrender to making, his self-forgetting in surrender to the good of the thing he is making. How surprised he may be then (as O'Connor was in responding to her own "The Artificial Nigger") to discover that much more than consciously intended or anticipated in the act of her making proves inherent to the fixed and certain thing. And a reader in revisiting a fixed artifact may respond initially in surprise before a familiar poem or story, as if the story or poem has changed since a first encounter. It is either more a failure as a made thing or resonantly larger than when at first experienced. His reason recovers him from that inclination. He recognizes that it is his own capacity of response that is changed. He has been becoming in the interval of his encounter. There has in the interval occurred some degree of an intellectual *becoming,* since intellect itself is not fixed as is the artifact.

The more perfect the fixed thing, the story, the larger its yield to our subsequent experiences of it, which is why we sometimes say of a work that it "stands up to a second, third reading." (Some poems and stories, we judge as better than others.) In truth the work has stood as it is all along, the reader rising to its fixed virtues or failures. We know this at once, when reason is allowed to support our responses to the artifact's fixities. So young Shakespeare seized upon his making, lured as poet to art's immortality. For "So long as man can breathe, or eyes can see,/ So long lives this [poem], and this gives life to thee." (Not, of course, that a clever seduction of the "thee" is not underway as perhaps the chief strategy of the poet as "young" amorous person.) The highschool student reading *Don Quixote* or *Adventures of Huckleberry Finn,* or *The Lord of the Rings;* and then the same student become middle-aged, perhaps reading one of these to his own children: how different the work seems to him. What he may thereby discover on reflection is that in the variousness of his own becoming he has moved (as the text has not) toward a perfection of his gifts as this discrete intellectual soul incarnate. And it may be in this wise that God may use art's fixed things to a good beyond art's limits — as God sees fit. Hence, as the poet may be sometimes supported and enlarged by his making, so too may a reader. For a reader may discover a progress through prudential intellectual concerns as *homo viator* seemingly unrelated to the virtues of art. In devotion of openness to a thing made (Coleridge calls it the "willing suspension of disbelief"), poet or reader may discover himself as having become changed not by aging but under the auspices of grace, recognizing that God uses our gifts or not as he will, indifferent to (unrestricted by) time or place as their necessary proximate occasion.

The poet's responsibility in the Thomistic view is to perfect a fixed certainty, to *matter* a *form,* in relation to a vibrancy of the chosen matter mediating that bonding of reason and Eternal Reason. Thereby the thing itself may be made good in itself. It is in her recognition of this truth about art that Flannery O'Connor, when asked what she is trying to prove by her fiction, responds that "you never prove anything" by a story. For stories in their limited meanings are never comprehensive of the vibrancy of human nature upon which they depend as art's given matter. One does not from the virtues of the well-wrought story effect necessarily either justice or mercy in the realm of the prudential journeying as *homo viator,* anymore than science perverted by gnostic intentionality can necessarily effect a reconstitution of reality to suit gnostic whim, capable rather only of a reductionism. Propaganda pretending to be art, for product or political party, decays. The limits of art, the limits to the artist of his knowing, is an exercise of reason in the making of a certain fixity in devotion to the good. The perfection of the thing he makes lies in relation to the poet's limits of gift as maker in responding to the good. But art alone cannot recover nor reconstitute human nature. The "science" proper to art may test the range of the *possible*, but it does not *prove* (i.e., demonstrate as specific and undeniable) any "truth" in the popular sense of that term *prove* as a term inherited to popular use from Modernist philosophy and Positivistic science. The artist may be said to "test" possibilities as imaginatively perceived out of given truth. He does not thereby *demonstrate* comprehensively truth itself.

To speak of art as "reason in making" does not deny the participation of the intuitive mode of intellect in the poet's making, for he is required not only to reason but to maintain an openness to possibility in the very act of a reasoned making. We remember from Thomistic epistemology that reason is a mode of active engagement of the antecedently — the intuitively — known. (Thomas in his *Compendium of Theology* engages the relation of the "possible intellect" — the intuitive — as a passive mode of receptivity to truth, truth thus *incepted* (in St. Thomas' metaphor) in intellect by actual experiences of things. There is that complementary mode to inception, the rational, or as Thomas calls it in his *Compendium of Theology*, the "agent intellect." Rational intellect is *active* in ordering the intuitively known *toward* understanding universals, toward understanding. Thomas' distinction, while insisting upon the unity of intellect (against those Averroists), emphasizes as well that intellect is modal in its actions. In his *Summa Contra Gentiles* (I, q. 57, a. 8 & 9) he remarks concomitantly that *reason*, as distinguishing man among intellectual creatures from both angels and from God is an *extension* of the *intuitive* mode, though in relation to the angelic intellect (and ultimately in relation to God's singularly comprehensive knowing and surpassing as the Cause of both angel and man), reason is "a certain defective intellect." We suggest this the epistemological context to O'Connor's understanding of herself as story-writer, out of which she adapts Henry James's advice to the would-be writer that, at the practical level of making a fiction, the writer should begin with a *character* born of the writer's actual knowledge of *persons*— not a character projected abstractly by reason to fit preconceived situation.

O'Connor, this is to suggest, recognizes a validity in James's argument, though she understands it at a level of reality deeper than does James. In the light of Thomistic epistemology, this is to say, we respond with that intuitive immediacy as a person experiencing another person, though there follows a necessity to reason to clarify the intuitively known. That is a necessity crucial to the poet under the Thomistic rubric that art is "reason in making." Thus a character gains a validity to a possible "incarnation" by art which is more difficult to the poet when he elects situation, circumstance, as abstractions to possible actions as the poet's primary point of departure. The *situation* out of which he would deduce *character* from human nature tends to make the character from mere spectacle. The reason as "agent intellect" properly digests the intuitively known from actual persons toward an understanding accommodating the known in relation by reason's speculative understandings of the *possible* as anchored in the actualities of persons, not in situations. In such action there may likely rise in the poet an arresting wonder: the *possible* called into *form* seems in itself as if *actual* in his surrogate persons.

How often out of this sense of wonder the poet may speculate on his "character" as if an actual person. But prudential humility reminds him that, in having made rather than having created his character, he never *comprehensively* knows the matter chosen to his form, as if the poet were a creator of persons. James's understanding does not engage this mystery of making at metaphysical depth, though he recognizes that situation evolves more effectively out of character than character out of situation. It is to this aspect of making that O'-Connor speaks in "Writing Short Stories." If "you start with a real personality, a real character, then something is bound to happen; and you don't have to know what before you begin. You ought to be able to discover something from your stories [by the act of making them]. If you don't, probably nobody else will." The experience of discovery is possible to the writer — a learning underway in him about "personality" as born of personhood — through the act of his making. Reason in support of the intuitively known opens upon that mystery of personhood, discovers form suited to matter or to a selection of additional or different matter to a possible form — an accommodation increasingly clarified by the actual labor of making. That free will to a making is the most signal property to the intellectual soul incarnate, particularizing the person of the poet in his becoming — guided by reason.

In the self-forgetting in the act of making lies a "mystery … which a novel, even a comic novel, can only be asked to deepen," not demonstrate, not prove, O'Connor holds. (These words conclude O'Connor's remarks on the "wills in conflict" in her Haze Motes in the prefatory note to the reissue of her *Wise Blood*.) In that discovery, by analogy, the poet may discover that the situation in a story is more "naturally" grown out of character than if his reason choose to pursue making in the reverse, attempting to incarnate character out of situation. Thus does reason accompany the action of imaginative making as a corrective of form's response to the "grain" of reality itself as intuitively known, considering that truth about making which St. Thomas affirms. As "makers of the particular," human beings "are not able to draw forth … form without material determined and presupposed," since human beings are in "their own virtuosity … limited to the form alone, and therefore can be the cause only of this form." (The words are from *Collationes Credo in Deum,* "sermon-conferences on the creed").

Given the poet's limited virtuosity as that of discovering through reason the form proper to material "determined and presupposed" to his choosing, the very act of exploring the possible in such chosen material very often proves a surprise to the poet himself, as O'Connor remarks of her own experiences as writer. That surprise in part lies in the poet's discovery of what he has already known intuitively of the "determined and presupposed" material from which he draws forth an imagined form, the surprise following his act of drawing forth. It is in this address and re-address to the making of a particular thing that is the labor to perfect form. O'Connor is willing to surrender a story to the *fixity* peculiar to the artifact through that labor. And as well, it is out of this labor that she will recognize herself as a maker called to be a "prophet of distances," those distances discovered as already spoken to intellect through the created matter that gives art's echo of life in art. It is matter "determined and presupposed" by its very creation in limit whereby it *is,* borrowed to the possibilities of a form induced through stewardship of the gifts of making by reason, which constitutes the limits of *this* person as poet. As a prophet of distances through making, O'Connor comes to understand the perfection of form consistent with the reality of her chosen material. And for her, a further discovery: that very material upon which her story depends already bears a presence implicit to it, intuitively "in-cepted" by the poet. She borrows that presence to her making, knowingly or unknowingly to her reason, one of the surprises attending her fixed and certain story. That presence echoes into her made thing, into her "in-forming" of what has been natively known through her actual experiences as *this* person, as this maker of things. That is a burden implicit to possible form, though it is not the *primary* responsibility of the poet to reveal it by an intentional form as if to *prove* that presence. For by such intentional form the maker risks the flaw of imposition, perhaps thereby making a thing suited to comfortable "summer" reading. The burden, present of necessity, is truth of things in themselves created and sustained, and therefore perceived and known resonantly as truths. They are not truths "caused" by the poet's form, as he may be tempted to suppose accomplished by an imposed form.

That is why, once more, O'Connor is confident that the poet, though he be a radical "Naturalist" in denial of the ultimate Cause of the "nature" he holds as matter to his making, may write more largely than he can know. He may do so — so long as he is open to things in themselves in their actualities. But it is also in this context to her own thought as a maker that she recognizes how formidable the challenge facing her as this poet in this place and time. The distance between Modernist sensibilities cultivated by denial of "distances," engineered by dislocating intellect from reality, has been accomplished as she says by that separation of "grace from nature," leaving "nature" declared but random and conglomerate accident. By faith she fares to the contrary, confident here and now that *this* intellectual soul (wherever and whenever existing and however dark the woods seem to its present reality as intellectual soul) knows intuitively the good of things in themselves. That is for her self-evident beyond the systematic reductions of truth itself to accident by Modernist ideology. They *are,* so that there is contingent to this knowing of things the possibility through reason of removing obstacles to the recognition of grace in nature against the will's disinclination. It is for her by grace that *anything is*— most crucially the intellectual soul in its own existence, even though it find itself lost in a dark wood.

That is the mystery she engages in such a surrogate person as her Rayber in *The Violent Bear It Away.* Rayber, formed as surrogate person is imagined as self-constricted by reason in denial of his own intuitive nature, leaving him self-destructive through what he sees as his limited "natural" inclination — an effect of evolution. How reasonable to him, this substitute for Cause, he not having yet confronted a logical consequence whereby he must declare himself an "accident of nature." That he is haunted by loving the good allows no accounting by his reason as reduced to a mere "logicism" dominated by pervasive Positivistic theory. How contrary, Rayber's response to those trees he owns that "stood rising above him, majestic and aloof, as if they belonged to an order that had never budged from its first allegiance in the days of creation." (And note here the poet's *as if,* an indirection speaking the poet's certainty of a truth put conditionally to the attention of our own reason in observing Rayber's response to trees.) Rayber's response? "Quickly he reduced the whole wood in probable board feet into a college education for the boy [Tarwater]." In maintaining this rationalistic separation of nature from grace (nature reduced to temporal convenience) what can Rayber make of that inherent inclination in himself to love the good? The good stands evident in the trees as "majestic and aloof," unbudging from "first allegiance in the days of creation." No wonder then that Rayber is disturbed in such a fleeting moment of con-union. He knows as his actual experience that "Anything he looked at too long could bring … on a horrifying love." That thing could be, not necessarily majestic and aloof trees, but "a stick or a stone, the line of a shadow, the absurd old man's walk of a starling crossing the sidewalk," out of which experience rises in him "a morbid surge of the love that terrified him" because "completely irrational and abnormal." Rayber must conclude this as irrational and abnormal, though lacking sufficient authority in reason for that judgment. Out of his willful self-diminution as an intellectual soul it is an effect evidencing an encroaching, inherited, a "naturalistic" madness for him. That is the fictional circumstance which

O'Connor, her novel made, remarks of Rayber as "the purest love I have ever dealt with" (letter to "A," March 5, 1960). "It is because of its terrifying purity that Rayber has to destroy it," she says, to which she adds an anti-climactic, challenging conclusion, "Very interesting," suggestive of a meditation necessary to this deepened mystery which for her is the Incarnation, a continuous presence sustaining Rayber or trees or stones or starlings *all* "the days of creation."

The story, once it is fixed in a certainty as *this* made thing, is surrendered into creation by the maker. Insofar as it is good as a well-made object, the degree of perfection lies in its having been well-wrought in an accord with material "determined and presupposed" in Thomas' phrase. Once surrendered by the poet, it may subsequently serve any person's intellect through his own prudence in becoming, on a plane differing from his aesthetic pleasure in response to its *claritas*. Differing as well from that more restricted prudence required of the poet in the act of making — that prudence whereby matter and form are consonantly effected in a con-union by form through the limits of the poet's gifts as maker. That service beyond art's limits allows yet another possibility in an additional dimension to the story, for which the poet may take no credit. It may feed a becoming of the audience as it has fed the becoming of the poet, as art collaterally and not primarily the cause of becoming. Hence O'Connor's declaration that she "does not write the best she can for the sake of art but for the sake of returning [her] talent to the invisible God to use or not use as he sees fit." The corollary would require of the reader as well a return of gifts in response to the good, of which one is this story. That use, she recognizes, is possible in the larger arena of a particular person's becoming (poet or reader) toward his proper end as *homo viator*. But that is a concern larger than and improper to her responsibility as maker. It is in this respect, then, that the well-made work may or may not serve prudence within the moral arena in which persons *become*. It may do so or not through a grace given or withheld, or so O'Connor (or Thomas) would add, as God might or might not use the made thing in his love for his created person.

In this arena, prudence wedded to humility in *homo viator* may bear him on his way, sustaining the natural habit of his becoming out of his given essence toward his proper end. (Many are the means in God's mysterious ways to that sustaining other than by art, though art is most variously significant since man is by his given nature a maker, an "artist," in his acts of serving nature as steward.) Prudence in this plane of intellectual action always requires reason's attempt to judge the truth of things, including even the fixity of a story, by which judgment the story may indeed be seen to witness truth implicitly actual as reality within the range of creation, art's *possible* dependent upon truth. Such a witness is a property to the artifact, since despite its fixity it depends *from* matter actual, which matter exists as created and sustained in the continuing act of Love to things. Dame Julian of Norwich is granted grace to see this in that small hazel-nut which does not fall to nothingness, as Rayber himself sees in a terror of mercy which he cannot endure in a stick or stone or starling. Wonder of wonders, then: any thing in any place at any time is an actuality. It *is*. It is to this mystery of existential reality that O'Connor speaks in saying that "all is the Incarnation," she seeing Plato's *many* as having been created actual and not as shadows of Idea. Not to see this truth for her is to be removed to a distance from reality here and now in fruitless pursuit of Idea as created property of reason, thus endangering *homo viator* as spiritual creature. That is the danger most challenging to the prophetic poet in an age that becomes increasingly oblivious or indifferent to man's proper end.

How restive became so many of the poets of the early 20th century, rejecting their "Romantic" fathers of the 19th but nevertheless holding fast to the "romantic" principle shared by both Rationalist and Romantic — namely, a faith in an intellectual autonomy which distances intellect itself from reality. Some of them (Ezra Pound we have suggested an exemplum, as is Emerson) are self-elected as volunteer legislators of mankind.[5] Having enlisted in that concern, and affected by doctrines of deterministic materialism as the principle suited to an illusional common good, they find themselves increasingly reduced to "proving" the materialistic principle by their art in order to command popular consent. (Hence Emerson's dependence upon "fact.") At least intuitively, however, some of them recognize that the attempt is destructive to art, though not many of our recent poet fathers could bring sufficient reason to bear effectively in the refutation of Modernist thought in its growing power to project varied illusions of new Edens. (How void of substance proves Emerson's *fact*.) And so some of those poets began to commit themselves as artists to art as a subspecies of Positivistic science, as we have suggested of the "Naturalist" poets.

By subscription to Positivism, the poet declares art's role subordinate in service to the Positivistic reconstitution of moral, social, economic transformation by systematic order. How quickly, in this process, are persons reduced by abstraction to "individuals," the popular shibboleth we have emphasized in its Modernist deceptions of the popular spirit, the compensation for which is a sentimentality in the name of the "common good." Whether such an artist be committed to pornography (let us say) as a means of "freeing" persons from "Puritanical hang-ups" or committed to art as establishing what is but an obverse of pornography, a new "Puritan" principle intent upon perfecting autonomous freedom under the auspices of the "State," there is on either hand that pronounced intention to a salving under the rubric of the "common good," lest the popular spirit prove restive. At least such is the usual excuse as principle to activist revolutions, whether made in the name of pornography or political tyranny. By such intention, the argument that art is to be deployed to a specific revolutionary cause as if made "moral" by the intent, the strategy is to a seduction of the popular spirit. Whether enlisted by the "puritan" tyrant or the pornographer there can but follow denigrations of the good of things in themselves. On either hand what is promised is the "freedom" of the individual to pursue desires. Such perversions of the nature of art reduce art itself to tract, whose burden is a reformation to ends social, political, even pseudo-religious as in New Age Paganism. The perversion is made vague by deliberate or naïve indiscrimination, by a reductionist inclusiveness as collective power or to individual absolute freedom. The proper aesthetic objection to pornography is that it lacks artfulness in that the form violates its matter, as if art's action determined with absolute authority the moral appropriateness to freedom of the excesses of appetite. As sexual excess, the end for pornography is the obverse of ascetic Manichaeanism. But on either hand there is an excess of denial of things in themselves. For Thomas (and for O'Connor) the intention proper to the artist *as artist* must remain steady against such perversions. First, last, and always — the responsibility of the activist intellect is to the good of any thing loved ordinately. That is an abiding principle not to be subordinated in the act of making toward ends contrary to art's own nature as properly derived through that property of the person as maker as an intellectual soul.

This is not to say that the poet is thereby committed to "art for art's sake" in reaction to these perversions, that too a most vaporous surface shibboleth popularized at the end of the 19th century which fails to engage the true nature of art. The commitment to the good of the thing to be made allows only the foolish artist to suppose himself responsible to art itself as if it were the ultimate good, a mirror error to that error which would prove, "positivistically" demonstrate by art the virtues of Christian mercy and justice. By his commitment as artist, the poet is always enjoined to the limits to his making, whether he recognize or not the reality of art's limits according to its nature as an action of the intellectual soul. As maker, the poet is neither omniscient nor omnipotent — his made thing depending always upon limits of givennesses, a truth he must reiterate. It is in this respect that the poet's responsibility is circumscribed in the limits of his own given nature as *this* person. By implication, if not by his reason's recognition then, he engages a complex of limits by the act of selecting necessary matter in relation to his inherent gifts of discovering possible form. That is the hard-learned lesson to the idealist poets wavering in their idealism toward submitting (for the "common good") toward programmatic formulae such as those notorious ones out of Marxist determinism or even out of some religious Phariseeism.

The inevitable end of such submission establishes political or religious tyranny, to the growing regret of some poets, as is especially evident in the political sphere in the 20th century. Even so, many gifted artists then subscribed to temporal good as ultimate (whether to a Hitler's or a Stalin's demands). They discovered (if they lived long enough) that they were required to distort their gifts in support of a worship of an evolving idol, usually some systematized image of the State. If they refused to do so, they could but be seen by a tyrant as subversive rivals to his absolute authority, an authority that must be maintained for cumulative power under the auspices of some new god, most popularly called the "State." Alternately, through sentimental Nihilism, they must establish a more private liberty equally cannibalistic of being. The shibboleth *patriotism* on the one hand or *freedom of conscience* on the other become code words to alternate concerns. When some of those poets refuse to adapt the "science" of their callings as artists to the political or social or economic control of the tyrannical state and its sciences of power, rejecting the gnostically predetermined ends to their making through a "pure" system devoted to an ideology, that refusal may cost them either their freedom or their lives. (Solzhenitsyn as artist became their celebrated surrogate for a brief moment of the poet as enemy to Modernist "progress," not only in the U.S.S.R. but among enclaves of intellectuals in the U.S.A.)

George Orwell, with some safety of distance from Stalin, wrote both his *1984* and *Animal Farm* with a wit intending to purge the Western popular spirit of its sentimentality about tyranny. But consider at what risk beyond Orwell's is evident in Solzhenitsyn, in his *One Day in the Life of Ivan Denisovich.* There is to this point as well Pasternak's *Dr. Zhivago,* which O'Connor finds "a great book," though initially suspicious of its Western reputation "because Pasternak was a 'good' Russian" to Western enthusiasts she observes. Much taken with the novel, she writes Dr. Spivey (November 16, 1958), delighted by words spoken by Zhivago: "Art has two constants, two unending concerns: it always meditates on death and thus creates life. All great, all genuine art resembles and continues the Revelation of St. John." What a kindred soul to her own. She follows this quotation with the observation that "Perhaps it is right that this should have been wrung out of Russia. I can't fancy its being wrung out of America right now." Even so, we have been arguing that something close akin to this recognition she has herself "wrung out" of circumstances to her as a Southern Catholic in America — wrung out of the local in a seemingly unpromising here and now in the vicinity of Andalusia.

We must of course recognize once more that, in making these observations about the artist's responsibility to the good of his artifact as primary to his calling as artist, even by that proper devotion it does not necessarily follow that the thing he makes is therefore good in its fixed certainty. For though one's calling is as poet, and though he make with humility and piety — with a "right reason" — it need not follow that a poem or story or play will therefore be a good one in respect to its informing of matter. We must insist once more on a self-evident: some poems are more perfect as "artifacts" than others, and they are so regardless of the poet's perfection as person. As "hillbilly" Thomist, Flannery O'Connor is attuned to this distinction. She may, in responding to John Hawkes, confess herself "a Thomist three times removed," glossing the phrase parenthetically: "(A Thomist three times removed is one who doesn't read Latin or St. Thomas but gets it by osmosis." She of course reads St. Thomas steadily, though not in Latin.) This, following her suggestion that Hawkes himself takes "the diabolical" as "the divine," overlooking her own Thomistic recognition to the contrary, since "Fallen spirits are of course still spirits, and I suppose the Devil teaches most of the lessons that lead to self-knowledge." Even the self-knowledge of the prophetic poet.

As for her not reading St. Thomas, we know the contrary. In a moment of excitement two years before this exchange with Hawkes she writes "A," Christmas Day of 1959: "I have found a lucky find for me in St. Thomas' sections of the *Summa* and the *De Veritate* on prophecy…. St. Thomas says that prophetic vision is dependent on the *imagination* of the prophet, not his moral life; and that there is a distinction that must be made between having prophetic vision and the proclamation of the same." The "proclamation" depends upon the gifts in the prophet as suited to his clear articulation of what he sees, the *truth* he sees being independent of both his seeing and of his gifts in witness to that truth — whether by St. Thomas as prophetic philosopher or O'Connor as prophetic poet. Many of those "called" as critics, whether critics of art or of philosophy in her own moment, appear more intent upon reputation than concerned to be governed by truth itself. She observes this confusion most immediately in academic criticisms of art that are increasingly given to establishing provinces of specializations in aesthetic territories — art itself reduced to the service of a critical industry and so losing prophetic immediacy to truth itself. (This a corollary to the teaching of "creative writing" void of vision.) That such "professional" self-interest is destructive of art is a suspicion that Flannery O'Connor expresses with some irritation, as in her response to an "English Teacher" from her hospital bed, June 6, 1964, he apparently in pursuit of symbolism in her early story "Greenleaf." He raises questions seeking her approval. Why call the protagonist "Mrs. May"? She answers: "As for Mrs. May [in "Greenleaf"], I must have named her that because I knew some English teacher would write and ask me why. I think you folks sometimes strain the soup too thin…."

There was that other stinging response to the questions raised in a critical address to a story as if it were a "frog in a bottle." And we have heard her more public words in her defense of "The Regional Writer" — that is, the writer engaged here and now with making out of personal responsibility as artist is likely to be faulted. For "no matter how favorable all the critics of New York may be, they are an unreliable lot" when it comes to "interpreting Southern literature to the world." (She rather certainly means her own "Southern literature.") It might be quite otherwise were such critics devoted, as is she, to the perfection of their peculiar gifts as critics — not for criticism's sake nor for its advantage to a flourishing of the self in a community of selves as bound in a Modernist faith in autonomy as primary authority over truth. For the critic as well as the poet is responsible for a prudential humility in his making. O'Connor's is a wary eye on "New York" critics or poets, which epithet, let us repeat, speaks not exclusively to a local geography but to those "Yankees of the spirit" of whom Allen Tate speaks. They are always with us as are the poor — whether discovered resident in New York or Atlanta — or in Milledgeville.

12

Getting Dusty, Even Muddy, in the Swamp of the Self

"The fact is that the materials of the fiction writer are the humblest. Fiction is about everything human and we are made of dust, and if you scorn getting yourself dusty, then you shouldn't try to write fiction. It's not a grand enough job for you."

— Flannery O'Connor, "The Nature and Aim of Fiction"

In our epigraph, Flannery O'Connor is warning the would-be writer of what might seem to them a tediousness necessary in dealing with the detail of precise words responsive to given material as experienced, the labor required of the writer in making a story's action sufficiently "incarnate" by form in an accord with matter. How demanding of him as novelist that he must select "every word for a reason, every detail for a reason, every incident for a reason," and then must arrange them all "in a certain time-sequence for a reason." Alas, art proves to require the exacting labor of "reason in making." Perhaps one had best write stories then, rather than a novel, since the novel "requires a more massive energy. For those of us who want to get the agony over in a hurry, the novel is a burden and a pain." It is made in the sweat of one's brow, and not without the complications of getting "dusty" in doing so. Indeed, getting dusty while sweating might even lead the maker of a novel (or even of a story) to get all muddy, immersed as he must become in the human condition as the most essential matter to his story or novel.

Playful admonition to would-be writers, such a testimony as this is out of her own experiences. But though playful in manner, she is serious in an intent to honor the responsibility to making required of the story-writer. In the mode of serious witness, she adds that "There is no excuse for anyone to write fiction for public consumption unless he has been called to do so by the presence of a gift. It is the nature of fiction not to be good for much unless it is good in itself." It is in the surrender to the making, whereby the thing made is at last "good in itself," that the risk lies. It is a risk beyond the tediousness of that craftsmanship which is so often accompanied by boredom to the would-be writer who may or may not have a gift. In her perspective, gift speaks a responsibility in which is implicit the "agony" of labor toward perfection, even of a suffering in that action which she understands in relation to her faith as an inheritance from Adam. It is a participation as steward, designated in its limits by inherent gifts. But it is labor not alien to any maker, being consequent upon that ancient fallenness called Original Sin as O'Connor would have it. In making a thing good in itself through the sweat of the brow, the person experiences a current kinship with that ancient Adam, a kinship which she believes we all share equally, perhaps as the only "egalitarian" property of our possessions as persons. That is a dimension to writing stories or poems seemingly far removed from the excited sentimental anticipations of the neophytes to whom she speaks, they busily caught up in the "writing courses" proliferating in the academy. (This essay, "The Nature and Aim of Fiction," is a composite made by the editors of *Mystery and Manners* from several talks O'Connor made to would-be writers in academic settings, so that it evidences her repeated message to would-be writers.)

There is, O'Connor knows, a principle beyond the concerns for an efficient fiction being taught and demanded in academic laboratories — in "workshops" — as the pursuit of technique. The more fundamental necessity to her labor is that felt balance out of a governing vision, the absence of which leaves the short story (she says) "in danger of dying of competence." And so she attempts to speak out of her own vision to an age skeptical of such mystery. Hence her remarking the uses of the "naturalistic" in relation to art. "In a strictly naturalistic work the detail is there because it is natural to life, not because it is natural to the work.... Art is selective, and its truthfulness is the truthfulness of the essential that creates movement." It is a movement in a dramatic work in imitation of the action of human nature, experienced as the actualities of our intellectual movement in being "naturally" responsive in a perception of things — even those sometimes shockingly reported second-hand in the evening newspaper. She is touching upon that Thomistic vision whereby the "essential" is perceived as flowing out of things in themselves, out of and through the particularities in becoming, thence into the larger movement of confluent things which we call reality. That is to say, the going-on-ness of individual things commingles as "nature," upon which art's "naturalistic work" depends through the poet's selectivity.

It is in this limit to the gifted writer — the limits of the antecedently actual as experienced — that governs the consequences in art of the maker's choice. The writer discovers not only his dependence upon creation but must discover a manner of appropriating, of selecting and ordering in reason's making, by an imaginative discovery. For that allows by his choice of matter a consonant form to the selectively chosen matter. And if there is that more tedious responsibility to craftsmanship, to the accommodation of form and matter at the level of writing as a reasoned "science," it is at this juncture that he must also give consent to the truth antecedently inherent to the selected matter — lest he impose form superficially. Reality is the ground that feeds his vision as artist, out of which it may prove at once spiritually exhilarating but perhaps also even spiritually dangerous. How could it be otherwise, since the matter to the writer of a story or novel (or poem) has as its primary source "everything human." But that is a human nature *fallen*? How quaint a declaration! It was in this recognition that a Goethe or a Dostoevsky will declare that no human action is so foreign to his own potential, so that in making a Faust or a Raskolnikov "incarnate" through art, he as poet must not involve himself in a possibility most "personal" to him, and therefore at some possible risk to himself as person.

Not that such risk is unique to the artist, of course, since it is consequent upon our common human nature as fallen. But we encounter in the artist, especially in the poet, a fear that the devil lurks in his inkwell, leading to Chaucer's retraction of his work or to Hawthorne's defense against Puritan suspicions that the poet no less than fiddlers may be in league with the devil. In order to make, through calling forth by reason an imaginative form as a thing which is good in itself, seems to require a presumptuous intrusion upon the created good that already exists, a presumption not always disavowed by the poet. Rather certainly for Flannery O'Connor, there is at least a necessary risk to the poet of getting himself "dusty" by an imaginative descent as it were into fallen human nature. He may even risk getting muddy as well through that sweat of labor in making out of his own fallenness as shared, as *human*. Hence that remark to Hawkes — he skeptical of the Devil's existence as actual rather than merely a fictional convenience: "Fallen spirits are of course still spirits, and I suppose the Devil teaches most of the lessons that lead to self-knowledge." This is not an easy responsibility of the poet to talk about in an age rejecting the vision of the human which O'Connor would bear witness to. And so only by a sort of indirection of her art may she speak toward that mystery, for those with ears to hear or eyes to see. For the most part in the audience she recognizes as hers, ear and eye now may be somewhat damaged from a randomness of intellectual habit, stay taking spectacle as essence as a nonbelieving audience. To the hard of hearing, she says, therefore she must shout; for the almost blind, she must draw large and startling pictures.

She will say that "fiction is an incarnational art," dependent upon that "essential" reality that allows the seeming (the imagined) "enfleshment" of a character by signs, by the poet's *word*. It is at this juncture of action in making that she engages her own vision of the incarnational action required of her. Thus, "when you write fiction you are speaking *with* character and action, not *about* character and action." And that is the condition whereby the writer may get himself dusty. How crucial the distinction, made by so lowly a "grammatical" element as the prepositions *with* and *about* in her rendering of Keats's principle of "negative capability." It is in their mistaking the distinction she makes that some of her critics, for instance, took her to be but a satirist using local "naturalistic" details kept at distance by irony, thus writing "*about* character." They miss thereby her close proximity *with* her character and his action. She is not writing *about* in order to distance herself from her characters' "provincial" nature in order to be satirical about them in the dissociation of herself as person from them.

She declares her manner of deportment in making as a participation *with* the essential human matter of her drama, with *fallen* human nature manifest in current culture in the vicinity of Andalusia. How appealing at the level of theory, this concept of negative capability, though as well tempting to a sentimentality in art, a danger much feared by 20th century poets — James Joyce and the early Eliot our instances. But there is also underneath that sentimentality as symptom of decayed sentiment a darker danger recognized by O'Connor, in response to which she returns often to insist on evil as actual. There is a necessary risk to the poet nevertheless, which O'Connor acknowledges in suggesting the Devil as preparing the ground for grace in her own fiction. We have suggested these dangers inherent to negative capability in the poet. We have remarked John Keats, who by his consenting participation in union with things finds himself increasingly engulfed by melancholy, drawn toward spiritual despair. And by juxtaposition we have posed another "Keats": Gerard Manley Hopkins, whose consenting participation with things unlike for Keats opens to Hopkins by grace that larger vision O'Connor shares with him. And we have as well suggested even darker dangers to "negative capability." How endangering to Marlowe or Goethe a Faust. How spiritually unsettling to Dostoevsky a Raskolnikov, and more especially an Ivan Karamazov.

And so, when O'Connor speaks to would-be writers of the necessity to them of getting "dusty" in their labors of making, she has in mind more than tedious labor of crafts-manship. To that recognition, she reminds us of evil as actual, knowing that the Devil is in the writer's inkwell as elsewhere, and so requiring a courage in the maker to command his mode through manner despite the Devil. From quill and ink, through objective correlatives recovered in a negative capability — but out of a "felt balance" undismayed by the realities of evil at war with the good, the poet may make his poem. Such "metaphysical" concerns for the poet as himself a person, pursued so variously by terms from the poets themselves. *Vision* in art, *presence* of the poet in his words, explored under rubrics such as *negative capability* and *objective correlatives* in quest of a reunification of *dissociated sensibilities*: these speak challenging dangers to the poet as person that are hardly if ever addressed in "writers workshops," as O'Connor was aware from her own experiences. She knows nevertheless the intimacy to her spirit as person which is required in participating *with,* in consent to the *possible* which lies potential in common human nature. There is a possible likeness, this is to say, between Flannery and her Haze or Misfit. Her labor of making and remaking *Wise Blood,* then, is not merely a matter of selecting every word, detail, incident and ordering them to an effected form as if her concern is for mechanical perfections. Having mastered mechanically the technique required as if following Edgar Allen Poe's "science" of making in his "Philosophy of Composition," the would-be poet has not thereby gained the vision O'Connor believes necessary. Craftsmanship is important to her, of course, but she faults that mastering of technique as if it alone were sufficient to a good story. The mechanics alone speak a mechanical poet lacking spiritual participation in his making. Lacking vision, even though proficient to an overplus of technique, his art dies of its own mechanical competence if lacking the "additive" of vision. That competence at mid–20th century became more and more dear in critical accountancies, especially in more radical "New Critics" who became fascinated by technique as the measure of art, they addressing a story (as O'Connor objected) as if it were "a frog in a bottle." That manner of address as critical mode of analysis will have lost touch with a father of the New Criticism we know in his early spiritual "novel" now recognized but only vaguely remembered, the *Confessions* of St. Augustine. In it is discovered a way of seeing for Augustine as *homo viator* and poet, he having lost vision in treating things as "frog" parts. They begin to shout to him through their beauty a Beauty past change.

More is necessary than technique managed by reason alone, O'Connor argues out of St. Augustine and St. Thomas, out of St. John of the Cross and other companionable presences to her. One needs as poet the "violence of a single-minded respect for the truth" as writer she says of her own deportment as writer. It is a respect for truth shared by O'Connor even with a Haze Motes, both in quest of the *possible* truth she already believes implicit as actual in human nature. That *possible*, contingently potential to man, includes realities of both good and evil. A most dangerous undertaking, then, this surrender to "possible" actions "*with* a character." One might well sympathize with that old Puritan suspicion focused again and again on the problematic calling of the poet as discontent with mere homily. (John Locke urges parents who discover this inclination in their children to beat it out of them early, especially an attraction to poetry. And we have hinted as possible that Flannery's mother bears similar suspicion.) There is often an alarmed rejection of art by Puritan simplifications out of the discomforting truth undeniable to art's own validity when it engages that scandal of beauty. But it is that very *pied* beauty O'Connor recognizes as intricately related to the Incarnation though denied by Puritan antipathy to "nature" itself.

Hence in part her sympathetic friendship to Hawthorne in his recognizing this as well. She declares to the contrary that "all is the Incarnation," and sees art as "incarnational" therefore always rich with sensual elements involving human response to creation through the mediating senses. To be therefore by sign imagistically appropriated to an imaginative making. The Puritan, in his simplification, will be suspicious of both wine and bread in the end, sacramental "art" held in suspicion. Such things delighting the senses are to be taken as also speaking a delight deeper than the senses to an O'Connor, contrary to the severe worldliness of Puritan sensibilities that would control things actual to the senses. Otherwise (the Puritan comes to fear) spiritual discomfort — as if beauty were self-evidently diabolical by its very nature. The body endangers us to the worldly, as Hawthorne's Puritan Governor Endicott declares, his sword drawn, in "The Maypole of Merrymount." And there lingers a shadow of Endicott in Hawthorne's near neighbor Emerson as a secular "divine" out of that tradition, Emerson declaring he will no longer participate in sacraments involving the bread and wine as actually present to the senses, his a secularization of nature by denying grace to it.

Flannery O'Connor is of a different party, then, sharing with particular visionary writers in her risks as writer — from Dante down to Walker Percy. She feels an almost personal affinity with Hawthorne, suffering as he did in such close proximity to the likes of Emerson — escaping out his own back door to avoid encounter with that self-confident sage on one occasion (one anecdote O'Connor remarks). She recognizes, if cautious in the recognition, her affinity as well with Dostoevsky, that dark Russian "romantic" who is as alarmed as Hawthorne has become (they being contemporaries) by the emerging Modernist doctrines. Dostoevsky witnesses those doctrines leading to violent Nihilistic disruptions, differing in spectacle from their slower evolution in seemingly less violent manifestations in the American intelligentsia. That "progress" does not escape Hawthorne, he intuitively responding to a spiritual violence though not accompanied by high spectacle at his moment, mid–19th century, just before a general letting of blood (1861–65). Many of this intelligentsia by the 1930s, more loudly in a "revolutionary" rhetoric, were at last welcoming the brave new world inherited through the Nihilistic adaptations of Western 18th century thought by Russian (and German) intelligentsia.

Dostoevsky anticipates T. S. Eliot's *Waste Land* in his later work, we remarked, turning from the shallow, more "naturalistic" fictions he published up to the 1860s, his turning being signaled conspicuously by *Notes from Underground* (the hidden "underground" of a detached consciousness). After that work his deportment as poet is forever changed. (His *Notes from Underground* proves interesting analogue to Eliot's famous "Love Song of J. Alfred Prufrock.") In his turning, Dostoevsky will see as more evident Tolstoy's growing Manichaean terror. For if we pose Dostoevsky as a Russian Hawthorne waking in reaction to spiritual decay, we might discover in the later Tolstoy something of a Russian Emerson. Tolstoy adapts Kantian "pure" reason, not toward pragmatic transcendentalism in the direction Emerson takes Kantian thought, but toward a radical Manichaean rejection of creation itself. Progressively, Tolstoy suffers a terror in response to creation, to the point of his own spiritual collapse in self-condemnation as a great sinner beyond rescue — because he writes fiction. For any fiction requires a "sensual" necessity of images from things sensed. How is he to escape the curse of being "incarnate" if he is to purify his soul? After *Anna Karenina*, Tolstoy writes arresting fictions, but he suffers excruciatingly in doing so each time, since his stories by their very existence in relation to creation stand an accusation of his sinfulness. His fiction he believes increasingly condemns him, a story well-made evidence that he is already damned.

The danger to the poet, then, may prove more than an illusion of risk in participating "*with* a character" in the realities of human nature. As for that danger, O'Connor will speak of it elsewhere with ironic humor out of her experiences: "You discover your audience at the same time and in the same way that you discover your subject; but it is an added blow" (*Mystery and Manners,* "On Her Own Work"). She is not much interested in Tolstoy she confesses, but is much engaged by that Russian Hawthorne, Dostoevsky, though also cautious in recognizing any affinity to him. She remarks in a letter to "A" (March 10, 1956) that it is "hard to make your adversaries real people unless you recognize yourself in them — in which case, if you don't watch out they cease to be adversaries. I don't know if that was Dostoevsky's trouble or not." She reads with interest and recommends Guardini's "things on Dostoevsky," concerned by Dostoevsky's "using the Inquisition as a figure for the whole [Roman] Church." Meanwhile, through firm faith she is confident of surviving her own risk of consent to the realities of actual persons whom she recognizes as at dangerous spiritual risk though recognizing herself in them. Dostoevsky, we ventured, might be endangered by his Ivan Karamazov or Raskolnikov, as she by Haze Motes or her Misfit, the danger becoming that any agents of evil may "cease to be adversaries." As poet, her own species of "negative capability" is necessary to the borrowing of the realities of persons to make incarnate fictional characters, surrogate persons with possible intellectual spiritual actions. She makes such borrowings as well in believing that no person is beyond the possibility of rescue through grace, since no person can be "poorer than dead." He may at last even be in an ultimate moment rescued if he does not reject proffered grace at death.

So long as yet alive, hope abides in love. Meanwhile, the dramatic immediacy necessary to make a story good in itself, though its being good may depend upon human fallenness acknowledged, requires an imaginative immediacy to the making in a suspension of faith's certainty by the poet in participating *with* a surrogate person, a character. Not therefore abandoning a faith vesting O'Connor as person with hope — with that continuing "felt balance" necessary to the good of the thing she is making. A considerable and delicate challenge to reason, but it makes possible to O'Connor her sharing in dramatic contingency with a character (a suffering with) as if he were a person very like herself. There is in her always this sense of shared *suffering-with,* making believable a character's worldly actions as he wavers on the cusp of spiritual despair, that death of the soul. He might very possibly slide into the volcanic, centripetal destruction of the self through love turned cannibalistic as self-love. But then he may also be recovered — may even become a prophet beyond his local reputation as a Misfit destructive of "social" order. And, as we have also suggested, it is this suffering-with by O'Connor which allows her humor in a consent of recognizing kinship. For "you recognize yourself in them."

It is in this participation of the poet in a *possible* ultimate destruction of the soul that she recognizes how foolish the easy expectation often demanded of her by her reader: a demand for a false rescue of the reader — or a false damnation — through a surrogate person. To take that distortion as reality might allow a making for book club selection, she will say ironically. But to do so is to be tempted to presume as poet the power of a false grace — the determined rescue of or judgment of her surrogate person — violating the actual realities of contingencies to a person's journeying as *homo viator.* That temptation to please thoughtless expectations might, for instance, tempt one to suggest by false art even the utter damnation of a character, usurping Justice thereby. Or there may be attempted an unjustified rescue of a character in violation of the limits of art, as if art were a sufficient instrument of Mercy. This is a point of risk at which the poet may take himself as creator, not maker, and in doing so become victim of a sentimentality whose end is the elevation of himself to the "Artist as Savior." That epithet may thus bear in it pretensions of a self-elevation beyond human nature. It may well be a severe irony in such distortion that the Artist as Savior can pretend to such rescue not as an agent of grace, but as ready source of the highly-marketable opiate, sentimentality, encouraging in his audience not a suffering in love *with*, but a distorted self-love pandering *to*.

Such sentimentality in the poet, O'Connor suggests to her readers, may condition the reader to expectation of that instant damnation or instant salvation by a story's denouement, since her readers have "forgotten … the cost" to our Redeemer in that inclusive redemptive act of grace, the Incarnation, in a Revelation to restive man of his fallen uncertainty in the Crucifixion. Such the Spectacle of Action which the Misfit laments not having witnessed: the Crucifixion, Resurrection, Ascension, a spectacle he holds necessary to belief in the Incarnation. Meanwhile, we have lost or diluted to psychological conveniences any "sense of evil" as actual to human will by discarding these mysteries, O'Connor believes. We are left disabled in our response to mysteries of grace as beyond reason's comprehension, though commanding reason to remove obstacles to that grace. Dangerous country indeed, this surface swamp of the psychological, which swamps the poet must nevertheless make recognizable in order to recall the Modernist "self" to the known but forgotten things deeper than the psychological; recall him, that is, to the reality of his intellectual soul. In celebrating reality (which is not so simple as a *proving* of that reality by science, testing by the will)—we lift up complex creation in all its manifestations—but especially fallen human nature. That is an office of the prophetic poet to community—his making more believable by art the reality of *homo viator* as person potential to fulfillment. Reality is more than the surface swamp of perceived reality, which taken as but spectacle is always a possible quicksand. Despite such truth, Emerson would have us through *facts* commanded skate that surface. By facts as intellectual pontoon of an ingenious manufacture (created by autonomous reason), we may skate that surface swamp toward some imagined Eden. That has been the promise enlarged upon out of Emerson's formulation of a Modernist self-rescue, progressively sold to the popular spirit in this new age of the theorist-consumer.

By her art, O'Connor tests that faith in autonomy. And so (such is our argument's burden here), there may be for the Christian poet a very personal risk as poet. He is likely to get "dusty" in doing so, perhaps even become muddy by the sweat of his making a thing good in itself out of matter which is undeniably not good in itself: human nature *fallen*. That was the lesson learned by Dostoevsky in his attempt to make as his protagonist what he called at inception "the positively good man," only to discover that there is "nothing in the world more difficult to do, and especially now"—*now* being the 1860s.[1] In the end, Raskolnikov of *Crime and Punishment* is easier to make believable as surrogate person than Prince Myshkin of *The Idiot* as a "positively good man" from inception as a character. Prince Myshkin as protagonist is the greater challenge, demanding the poet's tampering with the "naturally" of his good man. As surrogate person Prince Myshkin proves necessarily less than naturally good, unable to be freed of Original Sin by the poet's fancy. That initial failure of Dostoevsky to see himself in Myshkin is a mistake Flannery O'Connor would not make, this attempt to make believable an innocent, good man. Such a creature (in an understate-

ment) is hard to find indeed. Her Haze Motes in the parabola of his actions describes a journey more closely parallel to Raskolnikov's than to Myshkin's. How arresting to us, then, to
hear O'Connor declare as her sense of the possible for Haze that he may at last be a saint.
And by her speculative testimony, we may be reminded that in the conclusion of Dostoevsky's *Crime and Punishment*, Raskolnikov in his 19th century gulag seems about to enter
upon a journey not unlike that of Haze in Haze's final hours, Dostoevsky's final sentences
suggesting a growing *suffering with* by his protagonist out of his sense of guilt and sorrow
which perhaps may issue for him in hope.

There is an apocryphal story about *Wise Blood* that may have amused Flannery, providing a wry evidence of her own success perhaps in her figuring of Haze as surrogate person akin to us — though through habitual sentimentality we might resist such an association. A kinsman a few miles from Andalusia is said to have checked out cousin Mary
Flannery's new novel *Wise Blood* from the public library. But, having read it, the cousin returned it — in a brown paper sack. Mary Flannery perhaps seemed to have crossed the line,
perhaps even to have become numbered among lost souls for such pornography. But she
had certainly not written one of that new species of novel being demanded by some from
within the Church, "fictional apologetics ... light Catholic summer reading," a fiction given
to instant "uplift." Required to write such, for her, would be to Baudlerize reality, particularly that reality of human nature inclined to participate in evil at the expense of possible
good — that participation called sinfulness, about which so much is said in homilies before
Sunday brunch. (As for personal endangerment by evil in human nature, why the obligation to every person to confession, contrition, amendment if sin does not exist in his will?)

We have emphasized the poet's difficulty in dealing with human nature in its fundamental reality as seen from the perspective of a hillbilly Thomist, Flannery O'Connor. What
that poet knows is a necessity to empathy for the human condition of fallenness — a "suffering-with" — a lesson learned from that ancient but ever-present example that so scandalized the Pharisees and long confused the learning Apostles. One must know, in that openness to sinners called love, the state of the sinner through an intimacy of love. Indeed, John
Keats in his concern for "negative capability" was truly concerned for this openness, though
he could not name it fully. One regrets in retrospect most especially that he did not know
St. Francis of Assisi, more present to him than he could know when he talks of pecking about
the gravel with the sparrow in an intimacy of love for a creature through that manner he
calls negative capability. That is the openness in what St. Thomas would call con-naturality with things created. And that is the moment O'Connor presents in its terror to her Rayber when he sees "the absurd old man's walk of a starling crossing the sidewalk." Or we may
regret that Keats did not hear St. Thomas's exposition of Keats's response to things as a response of the "possible" intellect, the *intellectus possibilis* — an openness of intuitive intellect
as mode, then to be complemented by the rational mode in response to the actuality of things
as intuitively loved toward the possible visionary understanding which Hopkins witnesses
as pied beauty.

It is nevertheless a challenge of a different sort to respond to the nightingale's song
through negative capability and to respond to a person far gone in his sinfulness. The necessity does not, however, require neutrality toward evil in such circumstances to the poet,
but rather his suspension of judgment of the evildoer in respect to his possible end. What
a challenge to O'Connor as poet, then, to make a Haze Motes fictionally "incarnate" in
contingency to his becoming. For Haze by his rational intent to willfulness rejects love,

systematically pursuing a mechanical lust in O'Connor's rendering of him as surrogate person, as a "character." He is posed as intent to prove that *love* and *lust* are at once the same and meaningless, since the only truth is that there is no truth. In that intent to scandalize God by committing sin, his rational argument is that there is no such thing as sin and that therefore he is logically "clean" when he commits so-called sin. And his position depends in his faith that there is no God. What he has not yet recognized is that he does not intend to scandalize the people of Taulkinham but God, while vehemently, violently denying that God exists.

Haze's is an evolving system of belief which leads him from mechanical lust in a rejection of love to the mechanical murder (his Edsel the self-justifying murder weapon) of Onnie Jay Holy (Hoover Shoates). Onnie Jay Holy: self-proclaimed "Holy John" to Haze's Church of Christ without Christ, but that self-called prophet does not believe in unbelief with single-minded passion. How challenging to the poet, having imagined such a possible human willfulness to move *with* empathy (O'Connor's preposition) as if she were within Haze, *as if* in an essential nearness to him. As if she has set aside her own identity as person in a devotion to the good of the thing she would make — Haze as the surrogate person demanded by her art, her choice of what Thomas calls the given "material" to the form imagined out of that material. For, insofar as Haze Motes is imagined consonant to the truth of possible human actions out of free will, his radical rejection of God is a possible human material founded in the truth of human nature itself. As such, it is matter suited to a form imagined in particularities. The poet would make Haze consonant with such actual possibility of a person as a surrogate person, thus serving the good of the thing made (*Wise Blood*) out of the truth of human falseness.

For us, then, more than for Haze's empathetic summoner Flannery O'Connor, that surrogate person Haze may be seen as an enticing reflection of "our broken condition." This is a phrase O'Connor uses in speaking specifically of her Misfit. In our broken condition we find reflected "the face of the devil we are possessed by," endangering us by that recognition if accepted incautiously — if accepted that is as no longer adversary but a comforting friend such as that familiar stranger accompanying young Tarwater. That is the danger whereby the Adversary, and his legion in whom we recognize ourselves as fallen (as O'Connor suggests), no longer appear as manifestations "to be adversaries" here and now. That is a truth concerning Modernist decay of sensibilities which Baudelaire remarks in one of his prefaces to *Flowers of Evil*: how clever of the Devil to convince us that he does not exist. If we side with the Misfit in his spiritual state as if it were a state as spiritually fixed within the story itself, we may be seduced by our own reflection in it, inclined to possible evil as Narcissus was trapped by his own image in a still pool. For the Misfit, we may thus fail to notice, in defending his evil against Modernist denials of evil's existence is not thereby freed of the Devil but may become the Devil's subtle instrument. Lest we be too tempted to approve of evil in such circumstances, the "sorry" spectacles of evil suggested by the Misfit's companions Hiram and Bobby Lee as banal presences of evil stays our consent somewhat. They are recognizable, that is, as adolescent "red necks." For who among us sees himself in Hiram or Bobby Lee?

We remember here once more that old objection to Milton's Satan of *Paradise Lost*— that Satan becomes a sympathetic victim as protagonist, the implication being that Milton as poet has allowed himself to be seduced into Satan's party. That is a critical argument out of sentimentality against which C. S. Lewis makes his persuasive argument, *A Preface to Paradise Lost,* 1942. In O'Connor's small version of a Paradise Lost to her Misfit, Hiram and Bobby Lee as "good ole boys" in the story remind us that the Misfit in the story's resolution is suspended in a fixed spiritual moment, a peculiar dilemma to him as he reacts to the old woman's gesture of love that may eventually resolve his arrest, O'Connor will suggest, he becoming the prophet he was meant to be: he shoots her. In that moment in which he shoots the old woman the Misfit has experienced love actual, a refutation of his long doubting of love on the ground that he was not present in that actual moment of Revelation two thousand years ago, an actual witness to the Resurrection. (The Misfit's suspension will be concentrated by O'Connor in Tarwater's moment of drowning and baptizing Bishop simultaneously.) In the prelude to this moment of arrest, the Misfit knows he has been robbed of his humanity by a Modernist dogma that would determine social order by rejecting both good and evil, though he lacks such terms to argue what he knows. All that has been left to him with certainty, then, is the evil to which he clings as denied by Modernism, defending it with a ruthless and calculated violence — calculated in being largely an arbitrary violence against a false social order. Until, that is, his evil is confronted by a seemingly arbitrary love — by a love unwarranted, manifest in the old woman's sacrificial gesture. That is the gesture which may become (in O'Connor's speculative musing) "a great crow-filled tree in the Misfit's heart, ... enough of a pain to him to turn him into the prophet he was meant to become."

The "meaning" hovering that intellectual action in the Misfit, executed in spectacles of physical violence, suggests evil as dependent upon the good and by its very presence (when recognized as evil) a proof of the existence of the good. But that is a subtle reality indeed, affecting our understanding of the Devil's role in O'Connor's fiction. It speaks as well the peculiar danger to the poet in his empathetic act of incarnating Dostoevsky's Raskolnikov or Shakespeare's Iago or any radical spiritual Misfit — a danger as O'Connor was acutely aware that might make one's adversary appealing because so believable, and in being believable seemingly companionable. In addressing that danger in "The Fiction Writer and His Country," her challenge to the writer from within his actual country of personhood, she remarks that "What leads the writer to his salvation [as a believer who writes] may lead a reader into sin, and the Catholic writer who looks at the possibility directly looks the Medusa in the face and is turned to stone." That threatening stasis must be broken by action, setting aside the moral rectitude of the reader as but secondary concern to the primary one for the good of the thing being made. Even so in the very making O'Connor acknowledges that other presence. For "the devil accomplishes a good deal of groundwork that seems to be necessary before grace is effective," both in actual life and therefore in a story. (*Effective* in being persuasive of grace as *possible,* as evil is persuasive of the good.) If, in our participation in creation as persons, we "need a sense of evil which sees the devil as a real spirit," we must in that arena to our life require of him that he name himself, not as "vague evil" but as "specific personality." For an empathy for the tempted person to possession must not dissolve into an empathy for the devil. Otherwise, we lose our own identity to the Devil, such is the subtlety of evil.

In riddling the stories themselves as they reflect the reality of evil, care is to be taken. She would not "equate the Misfit with the devil" in a final account, a summary simplification. He is rather a "prophet gone wrong" through the devil's subtle cleverness. We heard her insist, concerning "Tarwater's friend" in the lavender car, "I certainly do mean [him] to be the Devil." The difficulty she has as storywriter is to be persuasive in artfully echoing the

reality of evil and of the Evil One as a presence within actual realities to our spiritual nature as persons. In consequence, the Devil as a fictional presence depends from the reality
of the Devil as himself actual in O'Connor's view, the Church confirming him actual to her.
That is a difficulty with which her reason must contend in making fiction in an age believing to its imprudent convenience that the truth is only relativistic, since (in logic's
justification of relativity) there is no such thing as a Good God, without which God, Evil
could not exist. *Good* and *evil* as terms borrowed from now antiquated social history signify only in relation to *convenience,* and *convenience* only in relation to *power. Ergo,* the relativism of *good* and *evil.* But O'Connor's primary subject is the battle between good and
evil within each person, in which battle relativism is ally to evil as actual. Her discovery of
her audience as denying the realities of this battle has been an "added blow" to her she acknowledges. A part of that "blow" is the recognition of encroaching vagueness in our sensibilities when *feeling* supercedes *thought,* a most considerable challenge to her as maker of
stories. We define personal responsibility for our intellectual actions as resting in how we
feel, and we may not feel good about ourselves after reading her stories. If it makes us feel
good it is good. In such ambiance of feeling, how unlikely that we now remember in pray-
ing that prayer to the Father which Jesus taught, we say "deliver us from evil." It is a phrase
in its actual ("historical") context of that teaching a plea that we be delivered from the "Evil
One." Though that prayer is almost universally known to her audience, it is difficult to share
a recognition with her audience that evil exists as a proximate agency to us of the Evil One
as that prayer suggests. It proves even more challenging to share a recognition of the good
as more than the moment's convenience. How is she to make persuasive, then, that other
Presence, the Holy Ghost, as both actual and proximate to us, antecedently necessary to
our existence into which would intrude in petty antipathy to the Good that Evil One?
Good, if taken as relative convenience to the person as himself sovereign over being itself,
allows conclusion that evil may be rationalized as a relative good. How subtle the Devil as
Sophist, declaring to himself "Evil, be thou my Good," as Milton has him say.

Insofar as the Devil prepares a fictional grounding of her character's actions, it is (she
suggests) a preparation for the possible action of grace through the Holy Ghost's active love.
Hers is a strange "country" to Modernist sensibilities, stranger to those sensibilities than any
science fiction. A fictional character as a spiritual entity by her reckoning of truth may remove obstacles to grace in his actions in the unfolding story. For O'Connor he may do so
possibly through that first Presence in the fiction — that of the Holy Ghost, the last to be
recognized by a character. (Remember Asbury of "The Enduring Chill.") It is this Lord and
Giver of life upon Whom depends her fictional character (in a secondary way in that her
matter depends from that Causing Reality). It is He who sustains the life which the Devil
would take away from the person through the person's will consenting to evil. That is the
reality of that little world, the person, which sets as dramatically possible the tensional circumstance of any story "worth the telling," O'Connor will say. Her audience might grant
it only as a fictional metaphor, spun by fancy just as is that pretense that the Devil is actual. From her view as prophet of distances that partial suspension of disbelief suggests her
audience closer to evil in fallenness than it can recognize. Her use of fancy is a fictional strategy, an *as if* made dependent from the actual, but supposed only as a fancy by the audience — only a "metaphorical" embellishment rather than an indicative in subjunctive disguise as it is for O'Connor. For her not a subjunctive fancy in an indirection but an echo
of actual evil as dependent upon actual good.

Given an audience either oblivious to or skeptical of metaphorical truth — of a Saving Grace — that proves a most formidable challenge to any poet as a believing Christian. How ironic for O'Connor that evil, not yet forced to name itself, should be so familiar to us though nameless is more comfortable to the Modernist consciousness (the spirit of the age) than is Good, as Baudelaire recognized and as Hawthorne and Dostoevsky know as poets engaging Evil as actual. And as Young Tarwater will come to recognize as he makes his way toward the sleeping Modernist children in the City of Man at the conclusion of *The Violent Bear It Away.*

O'Connor's audience is not much given to such metaphysical vision, though accepting an *as if,* a play of "fancy," whereby one holds only imaginatively the Devil. O'Connor herself holds the Devil imaginatively but believing she may do so only because in dependence upon the good, as created. Evil is actual, dependent upon a *created good,* a proposition intellectually discomforting to a non-believer. Evil "so-called" then is more acceptable as a name for relative inconvenience, accidental in nature. So Rayber argues. If O'Connor's audience is the one Baudelaire speaks of in that preface to his *Flowers of Evil,* her fictional Devil nevertheless proves intriguing even to a non-believer. Once upon a time, Baudelaire says, we found it more difficult "to love God than to believe in Him." But nowadays, God being dead by denial, "it is more difficult for people … to believe in the Devil than to love him. Everyone smells him and no one believes in him. Sublime subtlety of the Devil" as so much loved through our feeling.

From O'Connor's perspective we recognize that both the Holy Ghost and the Devil are real presences, borrowed implicitly in borrowing human nature fallen through Original Sin as the matter of fiction. Characters inevitably partake of that reality, or so O'Connor believes, in some degree of imperfection as person. For the *actual* affects *possible* reflections in surrogate persons, in fictional *personae.* In an age which has rejected this as a reality of human nature, O'Connor becomes the more committed to "the violence of a single-minded respect for the truth," and for this truth in particular as affecting fiction. And so Flannery O'Connor finds herself as person called through her gifts as poet to engage a double responsibility with her reason. She must continue unwavering in her faith lest she become lost as person. She is required, that is, to a rectitude as person through reason. She must maintain the virtues of prudence and humility toward her own final end. But she must also, out of that primary responsibility to herself as a person whose proper end is Beatitude, respect her *proximate* responsibility as prophetic steward of her gifts. Nor may she in her art set aside evil as a proximate reality to her making, dealing as she must with human nature. Only by facing evil directly (making the Devil name himself) may she fulfill her peculiar gift as a prophetic poet *now* making *this* story.

The good of the story she is making must be in accord with the limits of art, and therefore it requires of her a risk of herself as person to the making. She does not "scorn" getting herself "dusty" by engaging evil, protected in the openness of a faith in her givenness as person in whom lies a potential stewardship, her "talent." Her gifts involve for her, toward their perfection, virtues in service to her actions of making. *Prudence* and *humility,* in their particular offices to her deportment as complementary, govern the limits of her reason in making — in relation both to her own *becoming* as person and to her *making* of an artifact. Through a making thus governed, she *becomes* more and more *this* person, within the limits we now remember but do not comprehend as Mary Flannery O'Connor. She, believing in the intricate and sustaining grace through which things are the things they are (including that most complex of created creatures, herself), must attempt to order by reason the possible in human nature as dramatic art.

In doing so, however, she must not partake of a Jansenistic determinism as it were. For O'Connor, both the Protestant and the Jansenist are tempted to avoid that encounter in this world in which the contingencies between lesser and greater good complicate the journey and so often baffle reason. She writes Dr. Spivey (November 16, 1958) that "the Protestant temper" tends to approach "the spiritual directly instead of through matter"—i.e., instead of through the hazards of things in themselves as actual in form and matter, disallowing that egalitarian reduction of things as solution to the dilemma of proportionate good in orders of being. How much simpler it seems to reduce "nature" by conquest, and in respect to spiritual unrest even reject that singular "nature" in a species of Manichaean spiritual assault on Heaven, setting creation aside. It is in the dilemma to reason of impinging "nature" that arises the Puritan fear of nature itself, the fear given violent manifestation in Hawthorne's "Maypole of Merrymount." In that story, the Lord and Lady of the May celebrate their woodland marriage till confronted by (in Hawthorne's phrase) "the Puritain of Puritains," Governor Endicott himself, tyrannically disrupting the festivities. As Hawthorne concludes of the encounter, Endicott took "the wreath of roses from the ruin of the Maypole, and threw it, with his own gauntleted hand, over the heads of the Lord and Lady of the May ... a deed of prophecy." It is a deed of prophecy, Hawthorne says in reflective retrospect, for "As the moral gloom of the Puritan world overpowers all systematic gayety, even so was their home of wild mirth made desolate amid the sad forest."

The Jansenist solution to such threatening pagan inclinations to gaiety? In the letter just cited, O'Connor adds that, as for Jansenism, "I like Pascal but I don't think the Jansenist influence is healthy in the Church," for "Jansenism doesn't seem to breed so much a love of God as a love of asceticism." We need only reflect a moment to discover asceticism in an extremity as a species of Manichaeanism, as O'Connor sees. Out of each (either Puritanism or Jansenism) we might fear there rises a false deference to grace itself, attempting to escape the dragon at the crossroads lest the cost of encounter be too great — perhaps even for grace. Deferring the risks of *suffering with,* either the Puritan or the Jansenist species of asceticism would avoid the reality of the abiding contingency to human nature in its "natural" circumstances, that travail with evil in a quest of the good. Yet always, ascetic or not, the pilgrim must make his way past that dragon lying always in contingencies by the way though he deny that dragon. It is in recognition of evil's relation to the good *in the will itself,* affecting the person's manner of taking impinging "nature," that obstacles to grace may be removed "on the way."

Put more directly in respect to O'Connor's calling as artist as she understands it, she must avoid dependence as maker upon grace as *deus ex machina* to her art, as if thereby to escape getting dusty in her labor of making. But she must do so without denying the reality of that mystery called grace, separating it from the challenge of circumstantial nature. How is she to resolve this dilemma of an effecting grace as possibly operative in art's drama (because inherent to reality), but without reducing grace to a device rescuing her art by a simplistic — even a sentimental — resolution? How is she, to put the difficulty in an old formulation, to affirm an operative grace encompassing all creation, including artifacts, without reducing grace itself to *deus ex machina* convenient to resolving drama's tension in the artifact she makes? As finite creature, she confronts the dangers of presumption on the one hand, but on the other the danger of blasphemy should she suppose her own words as rendered to be sufficiently efficacious to rectitude — as if thereby commanding grace even to the making of a story. How tempting to become too-confident in pretense to an authority as maker — to force by art the rescue of her agents as if the Word itself were both contained and controlled by fiction's word. One must go slowly in this delicate endangerment of one's own word — go word by word — seeking to maintain by the word a felt balance suited to both her art and her person. It must be a balance which does not violate reality itself, but most crucially she must not violate herself as *this* person through a presumptuous authority. How comforting, then, to find words other than her own that confirm her understanding of art's delicate demands and limits, and most especially when that confirmation is from the Church's great doctor, St. Thomas.

Thomas addresses the poet's dilemma in making, teaching with a care she would herself emulate as maker. Again and again, the truth the poet embraces by a felt balance: the relation of art's exemplars (artifacts) to truth is as *made* things, in that they depend from the *realities* of things antecedently created. A mystery in things themselves whispers to intellect, mediating a message in witness: "He made us." For created things, St. Thomas says (*Summa Theologica*, I, q. 14, a. 8, ad 3) "are midway between God's knowledge and our knowledge, for we receive our knowledge from things that are caused by God's knowledge." We may not as intellectual soul incarnate presume to go "directly instead of through matter," as do those Puritans O'Connor has in mind in her phrase. Nor may we presume a purging of incarnate nature through ascetic extremes in denying our given nature — selectively. There is mystery in existing things spoken by the limit of each thing in itself (including the poet), to be accepted by the prudential person, a mystery *understood* only through faith — never fully *comprehended* by his reason. Nor can art resolve that disproportionality between God's comprehension, whereby created things are, and a partial knowing by God's image, man. Man's understanding exceeds his knowing through habits of faith, hope, and charity, those virtues themselves reminding him that he is not comprehensive — is not autonomous. It is in the deportment of those virtues, learned in response to created things, that O'Connor herself knows as deeper than rational explication an actual Presence in the very material she must choose from, her choosing consonant to that Presence toward bringing a thing into being by her imagined form. Deeper than reason, that Presence cannot be "proved" by a story. Nevertheless, "All," she says, "is the Incarnation." That Presence is therefore inherent to the form she discovers in echoing possible actions of diverse human persons and things — ranging from Rayber's sticks and old man starling to that imagined idiot child Bishop, including Rayber himself as surrogate person no less than Old Tarwater. Such imagined things allow a possible form, an "incarnation" by art, out of "created things" as manifest spectacle. So says St. Thomas. They are perceived as "singular" in themselves in that they *are*. And they are actual because *created*. And foremost among such singularities, the most enigmatic as actual to intellect itself, are persons in their discrete reciprocal responses to that actuality. The mystery of myself, so easily divided against myself! What a marvel is lowly man! Man's peculiar office in this recognition he discovers is *making* in that he is resident steward to creation as image of God. Therefore it is through his making, when spiritually alert to his responsibility as steward, that he discovers the thing he makes to be a consequent effect of his own action — an action of making echoing Creating Love creating. For he is by his very nature an image of that Creating Love as maker and not a creator.

In this understanding the poet enlarges metaphysically his understanding of himself as poet. There lies a difference between the actuality of his made thing and his own actu-

ality as person, though his made thing is in a limited sense some image of himself in a secondary proportionality. As he is image of his Creator so, his thing if but distantly, speaks
his presence in it, as John Paul II reminds us in his letter to artists. As maker of a thing now
become actual (which was *not* but now *is*), he discovers that thing to be nevertheless dependent upon antecedent "material" realities since he cannot create *ex nihilo*. But one of those
antecedent realities is himself, upon whom the existence of the made thing depends as its
proximate agent. That dependence speaks to him his own subordinate, disproportionate,
office as called to making. The thing he makes is a thing different, even when he makes a
drama out of his own essential nature as person and may do so arrestingly — tempted to confuse himself thereby with his Creator. For how easily out of an enthusiasm for his thing well-
made may he mistake himself to be absolute god to the made thing — at least an "Artist" as
exceptional from humanity. By its beauty, which he has called into being by form, his made
thing draws him into temptation out of his awe in responding to it, then to wonder through
reason at his own "creative" gifts. Francoise Gilot, one of Picasso's mistresses, in her memoir of their relationship recalls their discussion of Cubism. "You see, one of the fundamental points about Cubism is this: Not only did we try to displace reality; reality was no longer
in the object. Reality was in the painting. When the Cubist painter said to himself, 'I will
paint a bowl,' he set out to do it with the full realization that a bowl in the painting has
nothing to do with a bowl in real life." And Joyce's Stephen Dedalus holds that doctrine
sacred as poet before Picasso, a doctrine widely abroad in the first quarter of the 20th century. Of course, as Flannery O'Connor would remind us, this Modernist presumption of
an autonomous "creation" by the poet tempted Adam and Eve to presume themselves as the
"gods" — beyond good and evil.

How inevitable a metaphor to the poet, his taking the things he makes as his "children," conceived and born as they seem out of his intellect as their womb, "embodiment"
by his words — presuming his word the Word as if begotten not made. But they are not his
children in an *essential* begetting despite a metaphorical likeness. Hence reason's requiring
a most careful awareness of unlikeness in such things. That is a likeness remarked by St.
Thomas, most carefully proscribed in metaphorical limit. The made thing (the purported
"child" of intellect), though singular in itself is nevertheless Thomas says "fixed and certain." To the contrary, in life actual, a child *is* in a *becoming*. Yet in this unlikeness, by the
very fixity and certainty of the artifact, there seems to fall upon art as an intellectual discipline a shadow of determinism, not that of the maker as agent in making but antecedently
resident in the matter chosen by the artist as deemed suited to his peculiar gifts. Carelessly
taken, that fixity of limit will seem most evident in the matter selected, not in the poet's
intentionality of choice. His act of selection seems to hint nevertheless his own Jansenist
participation. For the imagined form when made actual in a thing (an artifact), in relation
to the matter selected from reality to a fixity, seems to suggest either that the poet forces the
possible upon selected materials in his own species of art's determinism, or that perhaps the
poet himself is but an instrument used in a larger determinism — by a force not yet recognized nor named. That latter possibility is the argument Socrates pursues in Plato's *Ion*, the
poet suggested by Socrates to be a blind proximate force to the making of a poem. Such,
indeed, will become a "romantic" defense by the poet when he declares himself seized by
"inspiration" to a spontaneous "making," disallowing reason's participation, a most spectacular phenomenon in an extremity that movement called Dada.[2]

What is denied in such a deterministic view of the poet is his own free will, through which he consents or not to his limits. He is neither omniscient nor omnipotent as poet. If he does not consent to limit, he may take that Jansenistic position, substituting his own intellect for God's in a deterministic intent to justify form. But an impasse confronts free will even so, "wills in conflict," in an irony whereby the poet at once desires a fixity and certainty of his own will as determining the thing he makes, inflexible in respect to discovery through his act of making. That very desire becomes disoriented, refusing recognition of the mystery of grace in the givenness of things as affecting the becoming of intellect in the act of making. Thus the reality of free will in man, itself a mystery larger than his own reason, may entangle reason's concern for an ultimate end in making, determined antecedently by the will before the act of making. In that intellectual disarray, committed to an intentional determinism by willfulness to an imposition of form, how easily confused may become *reason* with *omniscience*. It is only prudential humility that allows resolving the encounter of such an intellect with its made thing, removing thereby obstacles to grace supportive of making. By that removal of obstacles there may follow a contingent safe-passage of the poet as *homo viator* into the reality of his dual citizenship in two countries. That would be a citizenship enlarged, understood within human limits but never comprehended with intellectual certainty and fixity since intellect continues in its becoming. On his way, *homo viator* continues actual and becoming. The danger of losing this understanding of his personal mystery (encouraged by the dragon, by the way) is that he may presume an insistent determination by his will of his own end — as if will were itself the ultimate lord of grace. (As a maker presuming himself creator, this is the intellectual process formulated by Jean-Paul Sartre.)

Such a forcing might be anticipated as more likely to the believing artist out of his conviction, whether the believing secular naturalist or the orthodox Christian believer such as Flannery O'Connor. And because she speaks of her work so often in terms of *good* and *evil* as resolved only by *grace,* her very language has been used to suggest her a determinist out of Church dogma by some critics. Walker Percy took note of this tendency in the critical reception of her work as a Christian writer, as he faced that criticism of himself also. It becomes a repeated theme of his essays in his concern with his own calling as novelist. Especially, then, he emphasizes his own necessity to an indirection. For terms like *good, evil, grace* or *soul* are best avoided, he says, since they have now been relegated to the attic of our language, Percy lamenting the loss of those terms as now stored in the attic of our age's decaying house.[3] O'Connor, though subtle in her art and so partaking of Percy's principle of indirection, is nevertheless more resolute in recovering such terms. They speak for her the reality of any person's confronting circumstance at whatever crossroads of self-awareness. She will insist on the hidden presence of the Holy Ghost and of the Devil in conflict within the individual consciousness of every person, therefore for her inescapably implicit in characters as surrogate persons in her fictions. That metaphysical aspect of art she argues (both by direct argument and by art in its indirection) is a dimension of the dramatic action of a character like Haze Motes. Evil made palpable through art's spectacle speaks by indirection a grace possible.

What freedom has the Christian writer then? That is the question put to O'Connor, a question still mused upon in critical response to her work. How odd nevertheless that in a dogmatic naturalism as a faith constrictive of art (from her perspective), supported by Positivistic science and philosophy as dogma to that faith, there seems a less critical uneasiness about that "deterministic" position as forcing the writer by a dogma held in secular faith.

A reason for that failure no doubt is that Modernist faith has vested itself in existence as self-evidently accidental and not to be questioned under penalty of epithet — a principal one, "provincial" arrest in antiquated cultural residue. The "mystery" attending this secular faith holds in its fascinated reason a residue of its own: a presumption that though intellect must therefore be an accident, it has evolved into an independent power, a blossoming of an evolved self-consciousness out of random accidents in the span of accidental eons. Such is a faith which requires the necessity that intellect deny grace to nature in Positivistic denials of any givenness. For givenness raises as conspicuous question the mystery of a Giver. By the rigor of denial, intellect may seem to set aside the reduction of itself by its willful intention of a self-creation out of the presumed cumulative accidents of a cosmos that has no beginning and no end, Positivism a late descendent of Zeno's logic.

Whatever the philosophical or theological or scientific foundations upon which the artist's beliefs are founded, Thomas observes in addition a less controversial self-evident truth: Once made, the artifact is *certain* and *fixed* when at last surrendered by its maker into the vast confluence of existing things as *this* now particular made thing. It must be dealt with intellectually as actual in itself, but it is not simply actual, it is undeniably fixed. There is no *becoming* in an artifact. And so, given the fixity of the poem or story as the thing it is, the very fixity yields to us a recognition of whatever good it may speak through its perfection, the artifact suspended in fixed and certain stasis as the thing it is. Thomas suggests that by that fixity and certainty, it allows no "room for counsel on account of [its] certitude." But as any literary critic knows, it "lives" by our own intellectual response to it, thus inhabited in the active and changing intellect as a fixed and certain resident of intellect, a waystation to intellectual becoming. Thus it is in intellect's response to its very fixity that *this* poem as *text* is to be accepted as a limiting resting ground to an intellectual becoming — to an aesthetic response subject to reason's speculation.

It is out of a revolution founded in this truth of art's limited givenness as fixed and certain that there arose recently a self-doomed critical movement, now withered but for a moment topically celebrated in the academy: Deconstruction, a latter-day echo of the Tower of Babel. How could it not wither, given its dominant principle as a dead-end of Cartesian Idealism? That new movement held that a text is infinite *in itself* to the uses of speculative intellect of the critic, and precisely so because it is fixed and certain. Those concepts (*fixed* and *certain*) are imaginatively translated to *inert,* whereby the text is assumed infinitely susceptible to a present speculative intellect as matter to whatever wished-for speculative ends. This is the point at which "literary" criticism arrives out of the aesthetic dead end already reached by French Symbolism, that old movement as devoted to the poem as a mirror of the poet's or reader's "self," convenient to the radical subjectivity whose eventual end is solipsism. Cartesian Idealism, from Descartes to the Deconstructionists, accepts and then glorifies intellect's various strategies for its separation from reality. Any existence may then be declared necessarily dependent upon the "self" as themselves illusional, as but shadows cast by a burning self-consciousness. That is the position arrived at out of Descartes, with considerable assistance from Kant in his pursuit of "pure reason" as the ideal flame in the illusion of consciousness, as if a flame removed from all save its purified self. That flame casts shadows in the newest cave of the "self," in an intentional inversion of Plato's allegory of the cave. (That is the inversion which Walker Percy will make satiric play of in Binx Bolling's fascinations with movies in *The Moviegoer.*)

What the Thomist suspects in response to such intellectual pretense is that intellect has begun to suffer, since Descartes, an aberrant cancer. The symptoms are revealed in the intellectual address to that which is other than self-consciousness, whereby *words* attempt to arrest all save the self in a fixity and a certainty. Thus all other than self-awareness would be made as a vehicle to intellect's private transport to a speculative transcendental certainty. That transport is dreamed possible through a divorce of self-awareness from reality by "pure" reason. If philosophy seems suitably manipulative of the word to such an end, even more may art prove so — the ordered words a spent residue of reality as an illusion. (Remember Picasso's bowl in Cubist art.) For the artist (the poet as increasingly isolated from community and at first desperate to embrace "nature" over community) declares out of desperation the possibility of transcending both community and nature through a discharge of a fixity of his words as self-propulsion. Words (or Picasso's painting) seem his most reliable fuel for the "space ship" of the self in its quest of a transcendental freedom beyond all reality. How lowly in contrast, St. Thomas' address. For Thomas to the contrary explores the word as born of an intellectual "inception" through the senses from actual things experienced, intellect in its becoming dependent therefore upon the actuality of experienced things, in themselves antecedent to an inception of truths. But when the word is divorced from existential reality by "Puritanical" abstraction, severing nature from the word, Thomas argues, there is severed as well the Word from any word. And thus is to be born that new destructive species of Manichaeanism of which we have spoken, arrived at through sterilizing *being* by the arbitrary fixity of the word, whether as a *fact* for Positivistic science or as a *sign* magically spawned by the imagination of the poet. Nominalism would thus have its way with reality. No longer is the word residual in its relation to things. It is rather declared a prime matter as if created by intentional intellect Nominalistically, to be directed to the service of an autonomous intent which is itself justified on the presumption that intellect's present action is the only reality. (We will remember this strategy as ancient. It is that strategy which St. Augustine engages with devastating reason against those he calls "the skeptics of the academy," intellectual Sophists.)

We shall presently have occasion to explore this strategy as adapted by James Joyce's Stephen Dedlaus as poet. Stephen appropriates and distorts St. Thomas to his arrogant intent. Stephen fascinates his academic dean on this question, presumably his Jesuit director, by his strategy of manipulation. "For my purpose," Stephen says, "I can work on at present by the light of one or two ideas of Aristotle and Aquinas." Stephen's "working on" Aristotle and Aquinas is prelude to that radical position we spoke of as Deconstruction in recent criticism as famous for its fifteen minutes in the academy as the 20th century closes. Joyce's *Portrait of the Artist as a Young Man* opened that very "literary" century, suggestive of a parabola in this temporal span from Joyce to the Deconstructionists through which intellect through fancy presumes to godhead. But it is a strategy anticipated by Coleridge with some alarm, he warning the poet of it in his *Biographia Literaria* as the confusion of *imagination* and *fancy*. While the "Imagination" of human intellect, says Coleridge, in its "primary" nature is "the living power and prime agent of all human perception" — the very *created* nature of human intellect as St. Thomas would rather put it — there is also imagination in a secondary nature which coexists with the "conscious will." That primary Imagination Coleridge says is "a repetition in the finite mind of the eternal act of creation in the infinite I AM." But then, alas, there is also *fancy* as unlike Imagination. Contrary to imagination, fancy has "no other counters to play with, but fixities and definites." It is "no other than a mode of memory emancipated from the order of time and space," deployed by the will in pursuit of an arbitrary intent. If we put Coleridge's point as Thomas might, such a deployment by fancy of remembered experiences of things denies the *becoming* upon which spectacle depends and therefore dependent upon that reality of things to art's uses. By fancy may be intended (Picasso says) "that a bowl in [a] painting has nothing to do with a bowl in real life"—art divorced from "life" in "creating" a ghost—a shadow—of the artist in act as an illusionist, as a magician denying any *given* to his magic. That is a Cartesian arrogance rising to prominence in the intelligentsia of the 20th century, becoming conspicuous in the disoriented popular spirit and allowing its worship of celebrity.

Walker Percy will argue in his "The Fateful Rift: The San Andreas Fault in the Modern Mind" (*Signposts in a Strange Land*) that it is not the poet or philosopher alone who suffers a fiery cancer erupting in intellect and making it conspicuous as "The Modern Mind" (another of his essays on the theme). Through fancy's having overwhelmed imagination the rift occurs, widening in the 20th century mind. A conflagration seems to Percy ubiquitous in whole peoples as a "popular spirit" in consequence, the heated lava of the self let loose. And so both Percy and O'Connor recognize this willful error as opening intellect to such a malady, in spectacular phenomena of the dissociation of thought and feeling. It is through this willful denial for instance that the fixity of a text becomes a principle adapted by prying fixed words away from reality, leaving words as but inert stones in the created world's rubble with which the will may build whatever cathedral to its own worship as a "self" it desires. What we begin to discover on the threshold of our own new millennium is not a catharsis in art but a fortress of dead words shored against reality. A place devised as no-place, upon which to "stand" as if thereby transcending all reality. Of course words, signposts in the *desert* of reality as they seem to us at this juncture of our journeying, themselves prove already challenging to that illusional retreat from reality. Shall these stones live? Already, they speak beyond the intended neutrality from reality supposed enacted by them. They echo the reality of those things existing in themselves as actual, even that bowl, never quite purged of that ambiguous mystery called existential reality which includes even the intellect itself, despite Picasso's intent.

In natural things there is a *becoming* rather than a *fixity,* then, and that very changeableness of things calls forth more and more our fixed signs in quest of an orientation beyond deracinated intellect's dilemmas. How comforting, if but for a moment, the fixity of *a* word as if assuring and demonstrating certainty. It is the certitude which Joyce's Stephen will long for, calling it an intellectual aesthetic state, "stasis." How then reconcile intellect to the inescapable and self-evident aspect of reality as created, as "natural," and by its nature "becoming?" For it is the very "becoming-ness" of things that stirs in us the desire for certainty, at risk of Keatsian melancholy. And so the artifact as a thing *fixed* may turn intellect upon itself, tempting as a conundrum which hints art's powers of fixity—as if by art we might arrest any "becoming" of any created entity, a flower or a person or a nightingale's song. It is this conundrum which leads some poets to declare art the only possible salvation, an evangelical argument for which there is that often-cited fixed poem, William Butler Yeats's "Sailing to Byzantium." "Once out of nature," the poem's voice declares toward certitude, "I shall not take/ My bodily form from any natural thing." For only existence as an artifact is acceptable in that it escapes becoming. It is this conundrum as well that leads the critic (the Deconstructionist for instance) to make of art—of Yeats's poem—his own private jungle-gym for the exercise of ego in pursuit of an intellectual eternal youth. But the conundrum remains unresolved: *this* person is self-evidently distinguished from his made thing — the poem or story in our present concern. He indeed ceases. Yeats is now dead, as was Keats before him.

There lies the gnawing mystery which Thomas addresses toward resolution in distinguishing *maker* from *creator,* the person as intellectual soul incarnate from God the Creator in Whom there is no becoming. In whom there is no shadow of turning. A self-evident to common sense as a point for reason's departure: By art's certitude in the artifact, fixed and beyond changeableness in its nature, the made thing exists independent of both its maker and its audience. Does that fixity therefore determine *truth* itself? If so, the maker becomes the causal agent of truth and may very likely conclude himself to be the god of truth. That proves the continuing temptation to *homo viator* since Adam, spoken by the dramatic parable of Haze Motes in *Wise Blood.* It is as well the temptation to the philosopher no less than to the poet as he may attempt a fixed system of metaphysical certainty. It is the temptation to the scientist in his ordering facts as deducted from reality to a fixity of formulae, whereby the Word is his own word. Which is to say that such a temptation is common to man in his fallen nature as St. Thomas would say. By his "calling," the person may be drawn by answering the call into an illusion of his own power to rescue *being* from *becomingness,* through the authority of his will's intent, assumed as if the determiner of truth itself and first cause of any fixity. His instruments of signs (of which our actual machines are one form) provide power to an intention over being, that ground of the "becomingness" of things properly addressed by stewardship. We may recognize this danger to the poet often evident in the "Romantic" poet. But we may observe as well that his fixed made thing (his poem) seems often ripe with a pathos out of him, ambiently witnessing his presence in the fixity of the poem. Pathos speaks the poet's recognition that his has been a failed intent. His own becoming proves unaffected, unrescued, by any certainty of his art. Thus art's promise of immortality proves always a false promise, and by pathos signaled as known by the poet in the very attempt. By contrast to its fixity, his own becoming continues unaffected, tempting him (in Keats's phrase) to be "half in love with easeful death."

This is to say that the poem as instrument to the "Romantic" intellect is intended in the making, through prospect of a fixed certitude, to be some rescue of the poet from nature's decay. It is an intent based in forlorn hope. A John Keats in this attempt only exacerbates his melancholy. For by that intent the poet must ignore the "counsel" of reality concerning art's limits, thus becoming entrapped in art's limits, confounded by illusion. One might summon not only a Keats, but as we suggested his successor William Butler Yeats. Or a James Joyce. Or we might even recall that the young Shakespeare long ago argues his sonnet a rescue, once it is made and fixed and certain. He would confer immortality upon his Beloved by fancy. How confident that voice in Sonnet 18 that he as poet by his words may rescue his Beloved from death. She shall have a fixed presence to any ears that hear or eyes that see in the long becomings of generation. But then a falling away — she is immortal at least "So long as men can breathe, or eyes can see." But Shakespeare, no longer the artist as young man intending seduction, in making his late plays seems hardly comforting, as we discover in that most melancholy of his plays at his own life's end, his *Tempest.*

In the last lines of that last play, in the "Epilogue" to *The Tempest,* the poet himself now an old man, seems almost coequal with time as he speaks in the person of Prospero. His is a painfully poignant farewell to art's inadequacy. Now he lacks "Spirits to enforce, art to enchant," being forced to confess at last that "my ending is despair," unless …

"Unless I be relieved by prayer,/ Which pierces so, that it assaults/ Mercy itself, and frees all faults." Art's certitude can rest in the poet himself only proximately — in a moment already fading as he speaks his words. How uncertain of continuance. If art abides, it does so in a consequent reality that contains it as in itself fixed and certain, to the changing actual time and place — a museum perhaps. The artifact appears as itself only ironically "immortal" in the confluence of becomings at a moment in a time, at a place, the poet long dead. The finite nature of the poet as intellectual creature proves hardly rescued from his finitude, short of a Mercy prayed for. As poet he has, through reason, selected and ordered, drawn forth a form suited by fixity to the chosen matter he has taken, and taken from what he knows are most marvelous things in their discrete becoming. But these are things themselves doomed, as it may seem especially to a melancholy poet out of his own relentless becoming. I should have been a pair of ragged claws, scuttling across the floor of silent seas — or so the poet might say on the brink of despair in his self-awareness. For what the poet makes as if in rescue of its maker is most uncertain. In the "Romantic" inclination, there lies a Jansenistic determinism at work, but it rests as cause in the poet, not in any Jansenistic God other than he. This, though for a moment the poet by his action of making may presume himself to a "grace" in a thing (his poem) as if "created" by reason's autonomous omnipotence. But he must return at last to his sole self. The actions appear to be made by turning matter *against* matter itself in an imaginative attempt to deny imagination as an inherent given to his nature as person. (Coleridge declares the poet's "primary Imagination" a "repetition in the finite mind of the eternal act of creation in the infinite I AM.") As for Shakespeare, the artist as a young man at his making of sonnets when older and wiser must deal with art's limits as insufficient to his desire for immortality. How hauntingly poignant that last play, his *Tempest,* in this recognition.

Such "Romantic" poets as those we have summoned, from Shakespeare and Milton to Yeats and Joyce and Eliot, prove cautionary examples to Flannery O'Connor, even as she learns from some of them the craft necessary to her making, learning especially from Joyce. Craft serves the fixity of the made thing, the craft itself however an intellectual action fluid till the made thing is surrendered beyond an active making *now.* Such are art's limits as already anticipated by the artist's act of selecting his matter. By the artist's selectivity, we have argued, there occurs implicitly a fixity of limit to the possible form he would imaginatively "incarnate" out of chosen matter into an existing story or poem. That fixed certitude as the end of his making, the poet must eventually concede, does not either *cause* the existence of truth itself as echoed in his made thing, nor necessarily conform to preexistent truth of the material chosen to his making in his imagined possible form. His gifts of making, a conformation of matter and form, distort the given in an intent by the maker to force form out of his reason's failure. That suggests will gone astray in transgression of truth itself. As a critic might put it, the made thing thus exposes a false witness of the *possible,* differing from a true witness by form and matter, for instance witness to the falseness of a Haze in denying truth.

We may recall to the point that intellectual flaw in Sophocles' Oedipus as surrogate person in *Oedipus Rex* as like a similar flaw in Haze Motes as he engages paradox, dramatically revealed by Flannery O'Connor as lying within the intensity of Haze's own will to an integrity. Haze in his flawed spiritual state struggles for recovery, and in that struggle he moves by indirection in spectacles of actions speaking a movement which appears contrary to the end he would dictate through willfulness. He attempts to commit sin to prove it doesn't exist for instance. Thus the "wills in conflict" through which he comes to a recognition that his power to control and establish his own integrity fails because he fails in initial consent to the grace always pending as Mercy. He comes at last to see himself as "unclean" in his moment of turning toward the true way as pilgrim. In this respect, we shall presently consider a relation between the concept of *epiphany* as understood differently by James Joyce and Flannery O'Connor, presented quite differently by them in the fixities of their made stories. In doing so, we shall keep in mind that in Joyce's fictions there is evident a "Jansenist determinism" which Flannery O'Connor would avoid. It is a difference out of a significant disparity between them in their concepts of the nature of persons. Flannery O'Connor recognizes herself as an agent to the fixity of her made thing, but her own power as agent she knows to be more problematic in respect to "revelation" in an agent character. She is a servant of grace through making more than an intentional agent of grace in the making of an artifact. Joyce's inclination is to the contrary. He would be the willful agent of a grace *as artist,* in service to a radical intent of controlling absolutely art itself. His is a poet's pride in his autonomy, which declares *non servium,* Stephen Dedalus' motto as artist, and no accidental motto put into Stephen's mouth in relation to his maker James Joyce.

If the certitude and fixity extant in the made thing devolves from the proximate action of the artist as maker, then the maker as person in the very act of his making may be endangered by presumption that the certitudes and fixities of his art are themselves Revelation to be credited to him as "Artist." That is the source of an old disquiet for poets, various of whom come to suspect out of disappointment that it has rather been the devil as proximate and very active presence in their ink pots than their own superiority over being. If so, then their intended self-salvation through art is turned upside down. How reassuring as exorcist, then, St. Thomas. In his *Summa Contra Gentiles* (Book IV, 11, 14) he reminds us that "since the likeness of the artifact existing in the mind of the artist is the principle of the operation which constitutes the artifact [as *actualized,* as *made*], the likeness [in the mind] is related to the artifact as an exemplar to that [which is] exemplified; but the likeness of a natural thing conceived in our intellect [by contrast] is related to the thing whose likeness it is as to its *beginning,* for our act of understanding takes its *beginning* from the senses which are changed by natural things." There is a limited contingent relation of the artifact "in the mind" to the fixity effected in a making by art, both in a relation to the conception in intellect of a natural thing. And the imagined artifact is therefore dependent in relation to the *enveloping* arena of reality upon which the poet's making depends. That art thing, then, as fixed and certain depends from the arena within which is revealed the becoming of things to intellect because they are created, and as fixed and certain differs essentially.

In dramatic art's imitation of the *action* of nature as *possible,* the *possible* as imagined in relation to the *actual* is refined to a fixity and certainty in the made thing. Even so, form imagined as possible is induced from that borrowed reality, selected out of the arena of actual "becomings" of things — of actual persons *in transit* by their intellectual action. The distinction here is between a possible *form imagined* by the poet and *form known* by him as a person to be actual in things — known through his senses in reasoned responses to the pre-existent created things experienced as actual. Out of nature, essential form speaks to intellect in revealing something of the discrete nature of the thing in itself as truth incepted. Thus it is through an imagining (an *imaging* by *intent,* in relation to images known from actual things) that the poet explores his prospects of an "in-forming" of the Aristotelian and Thomistic "possible or probable" through his chosen matter. There is an imagined "likeness of the artifact" before its actuality as made, first "existing in the mind," which at the incepting of that likeness in an actual thing made fixed and certain is still fluid in its inception. It is in a becoming of a *possible* in intellect itself. But always there lies behind that likeness not yet made the precedent actual of nature as the source of depending matter to an "in-forming" of an actual artifact. In response by reason, the imagined "likeness in intellect" of a possible is actively modulated toward an accord with reality itself.

We have here introduced often this distinction made by Aristotle in his *Poetics* between the *actual* and the *possible* or *probable*, for which distinction Thomas will give us as resolving for the speculative reason the inclusive action of grace in nature. The actual is engaged by reason as a "history" of the known in the mind, serving a poet's quest imaginatively of a possible form as pursued by his own speculative reason in making. It is *imaged* speculatively in the mind. By the art of words, form is *drawn from* history (the antecedently actual reality of things as known) into a fixity of the artifact in relation to the imagined form. This action of making will therefore necessarily echo (by the form imaginatively revealed in the made thing) such forms as are already known through the senses, modified by reason under universal concepts (*beauty, truth, good, evil,* and the like). Concepts consistent with the orders of being, arrived at through speculative reason, prepare that complex of the possible in intellect itself, that "likeness" in the mind of which the artifact is made in its image. What we recognize here is an intellectual *becoming* which we may express figuratively as a tuning the finite intellect by a likeness incepted imaginatively to proper accord with things created by the Perfect Knower. Here lies coincident support of Eternal Reason to finite reason in the intellectual action of making which is anterior to the artifact as fixed and certain when made. Eternal Reason, comprehensive knowing, is active Love, creating and sustaining existential reality. It is in this respect then that intellect by its act of making *becomes* in its potentialities toward fulfillment. How often we observe this in the poet, his coming at last into his own "voice."

If Thomas examines the nature of the *becoming* of an intellectual soul incarnate with precisions of terms directed by his speculative reason, the poet may argue like truths in a mode quite different from the philosopher. We have seen this along our way in juxtapositions of O'Connor to Thomas, intending to suggest their accord in sharing a common vision though their modes differ. In respect to Thomas' philosophical concerns for the actions of intellect in making, we find O'Connor's similar concern as poet put quite differently but complementary. Both are concerned with the becoming of the intellectual soul out of its experiences of things known, but in that concern O'Connor expresses our current general difficulties complicated by relativistic denials centering upon the moment's convenience to *homo viator* in an age of unbelief. How much closer to their audience are St. Thomas and Dante, though in differing modes engaging that audience of the 13th century, than Flannery O'Connor can be. St. Thomas explores evil in relation to the good, on experiential knowledge more commonly shared, arguing nature existing intimately through grace in being. Dante counterpoints evil in Hell with the good in Paradise, and with a vision held in common with St. Thomas' metaphysics, and commonly accessible to the intended audiences—whether that of the scholastic at Paris or the emerging humanist in Florence. But for neither St. Thomas nor Dante does the reality of good and evil seem in question. Flannery's shared vision with them as experientially known some six hundred years later proves disturbing and baffling to her own audience, or at least to those she suggests herself aware of as her audience. But why so disturbed?

O'Connor suggests her work unsettling to her audience because her mode (that of the indirection of the "grotesque") reflects in an unsettling way to her audience its own spiritual displacement, intuitively known to it but not named by reason. It is an audience baffled because it lacks both unified sensibilities, having breathed a Modernist contamination of the intellectual air for so long, and the names for the causes of its symptomatic angst. If sensing intuitively its own essential displacement in response to Haze Motes or the Misfit or Mr. Head, it lacks terms steadying reason to some recognition of cause in a spiritual displacement, terms like *sin* or *grace* or *evil* the proper names but the realities now so remote by denial as to seem altogether forgotten. If remembered, such names are likely taken as but fancy's game with terms. What can that audience make of the actual "freak" in nature, if he is not taken as but an object suited to sentimentality in self-vindication of the self. And so in her talk "The Teaching of Literature" she remarks that "The freak in modern fiction is usually disturbing to us because he keeps us from forgetting that we share in his state."

It is by encounter of a ghost of ourselves, then, that we are disturbed, that ghost a metaphor put explicitly in her exploration of "Some Aspects of the Grotesque in Southern Literature." "Ghosts can be fierce and instructive," she says. "They can cast strange shadows, particularly in our literature. In any case, it is when the freak can be sensed as a figure for our essential displacement that he attains some depth in our literature." He does so as fallen, and he is fallen through his will's consent to intellectual distortions of reality. And so that is the "Country" for the "fiction Writer" (to adapt one of her titles) in which, "No matter what form the dragon may take, it is of this mysterious passage past him, or into his jaws, that stories of any depth will always be concerned to tell." The country besieged by the old dragon, again, is that of a discrete consciousness of this intellectual soul. And that is Thomas' concern in his exploration of the actions of *homo viator*. The soul fallen, but seeking the right way: that concerns him as philosopher. It concerns O'Connor as poet as well, so that she will say (in "The Novelist and Believer"): "The serious writer has always taken the flaw in human nature for his starting place, usually the flaw in an otherwise admirable character." In an Oedipus for example. But for the believer (O'Connor), each person is potentially "admirable" in that he may perfect the limits of his gift through a right will, gaining an integrity as person. If this be true for O'Connor as a "Believer," then her Haze Motes or Mr. Head or Mrs. Turpin are potentially admirable for her, insofar as they may possibly be perfected in their limits through an openness to grace. Each is *this* intellectual soul incarnate as created by Love Itself and may therefore move toward integrity, sorting their own wills in conflict toward recovery of the "true way" as Dante and St. Thomas call it.

Thomas' speculative pursuit of metaphysics; O'Connor's pursuit of a thing made good by the integrity of her own devotion to the good of the story she makes in the light of eternity: Both engage the mystery of *becoming* of the intellectual soul incarnate toward being "in tune with the world" (in Josef Pieper's phrase). As a person so becoming, intellect may discover initially *con-naturality with* created things, a participation with things as having in common that they all exist. That attunement to things has as a corollary effect intellect's becoming out of reason's attuning will to things in themselves as known intuitively. And that may lead to a recovered recognition of another con-naturality in the person's given nature, shared with the Cause of beings. That is, through complementary modes of intuitive and rational intellect, the person moves closer to understanding the mystery of his having been created "in the image of God." St. Thomas says, in regard to this intellectual attunement of the soul to created limits, that intellect's recovery from deracination is made through the "natural law" as the gift inherent to finite intellect in relation to man's existing in the image of God. That is a bonding of intellect's reason to the Eternal Reason as *connatural*, established in finite understanding of and actions of stewardship through a habit of making. Thus reason affirms its own con-naturality to Eternal Reason by its very created nature and in relation to its con-naturality to things created, is known as self-evident in the actual existence of itself and of all else. But by humility, reason avoids presumption of its own Godhead — understanding as it must its unlikeness according to Thomas' principle of proportionality, not only to all things created but to that Causing Love in which it exists as image through reason.

Actual form of things, then, is perceived by the senses in relation to the "becomings" of things perceived in their particularities, becomings differing from a story's fixity of a possible form. We may compare and contrast within this distinction science and art: Formulae derived from abstract fact is an attempt at a fixity by definition in a science of things as actual, in order to steady the pursuit by that intellectual (the scientist) as he *becomes* toward an understanding. But if such abstracted form should be believed by dislocated faith to be an absolute knowing, through Positivistic philosophy for instance, *science* turns quickly into a *scientism* of gnostic presumption. It dwells on doctrine with a spiritual intensity tempting to self-apotheosis through a power diverted to serve its own intellectual intentionality. Alas, that is a direction taken by much Modernist science, the error which Walker Percy repeatedly objects to — himself a scientist before becoming the poet as diagnostician of intellectual scientism.

Art's concern for form is with that possible or probable — to be recognized by the artist as limited by the actual, the actual *being* of things he knows from experiences of their becomings. The artist in using reason in his making therefore must know art not *conclusive* about reality. It is precisely here that the poet discovers himself in the most dangerous ground not only to his art but to himself as person, we have suggested, especially so if he conclude himself creator rather than maker — an intellectual error he may share with the Positivistic scientist. That is the dangerous intellectual ground which O'Connor (and Percy) especially suspect the Positivistic scientist of ignoring (in the interest of intellectual convenience) in the presence of mystery in creation. In our own moment, both these wayfarers now dead (O'Connor and Percy), the error is more blatantly evident in those Positivistic geneticists who, as "poets" liberated by fancy, would reconstitute being itself. How insistent their promises that they will create a nature corrected of Rayber's "mistakes of nature." But how ancient the presumption from O'Connor's perspective. Adam aside, this is intellectually troubling ground at the center of the *personal* for Dante no less than for O'Connor, leading Dante to make himself protagonist of his *Divine Comedy*. It is at the center as personal to Dostoevsky or Eliot, requiring elaborate maskings of the *personal* in their art in self defense.

Thomas speaks to this relation of man as image of his creator in a joyful affirmation reiterated here. He says (*Theologica*, I-II, q. 91, Reply Objection 2): "Among all others [i.e., among all other *created* things], the rational creature [man] is subject to divine providence in the most excellent way, insofar as it partakes of a share of providence, being provident both for itself and for others. Thus it has a share of the Eternal Reason, whereby it has a natural inclination to its proper act and end." It is this very "participation of the eternal law in the rational creature" that is called "natural law." As participant in the Eternal Reason, then, man as maker acts in stewardship to "all others" (Thomas's phrase), doing so through that gift *inherent to reason itself* which Thomas calls natural law — a gift actualized by active reason and so made actual in the intellectual soul in contrast to the instance of angelic knowledge in Thomas's argument. It is thus through the discursiveness of reason as proper to man's nature that man partakes of the "Eternal Reason," though by his fallenness a considerable labor is required to that partaking. That is the lesson which Dante the Pilgrim must learn, first under the tutelage of that most rational poet Virgil. Through "natural" experience recovered to understanding by his reason, Dante must labor on his journeying through Hell and then up Purgatory Mountain.

That gift of participation in the eternal law through natural law *actualizes* intellect, Thomas argues. It does so through discursive actions of rational response to knowing intuitively, truth received from particular things through the senses. That is a knowing of *form* held by intellect as truth about a thing as singularly engaged by the discrete intellect out of a con-union of intellect and thing in response to the *inherent* accidents (not *random* accidents) of the now known thing — out of the particularities of the thing as perceived through the senses. By that *singular* engagement, become cumulative in intellect through sequential experiences of things, reason attempts through aggregate orderings some purchase upon universals. Such is the epistemological nature of man as rational creature advanced by St. Thomas. Through the intellectual action peculiar to a person, he comes to share in a "personal" relation with pre-existing actualities of creation, with things as existing in themselves. For the person there occurs a communion (a *con-union*) with a thing, but as well with the Cause of creation insofar as truth is mediated to him by things. He shares by operative reason with his Cause *through* the nature of created things as himself incarnate. It is in this respect that man as "imaginative" creature — whether scientist, philosopher, or poet — pursues universals, the end of which pursuit within creation is an understanding of his own existence whereby he may order himself as pilgrim toward eternity. What he pursues is a simple unity as intellectual soul incarnate. From St. Thomas' perspective, what the pilgrim pursues is Beatitude, that simple unity of perfection through grace as a limited intellectual soul incarnate — a state of perfection beyond the discursiveness in its given nature as intellectual soul. That is a suggestion in Dante's visionary resolution of his *Divine Comedy* in his final canto, his attempt to anticipate that promise that in Beatitude we see god "face to face." He as pilgrim is overwhelmed by the TRUE LIGHT of the Trinity in that fleeting vision of the Good "on which the will is bent," as he puts it, that good which speaks all else "outside it incomplete." That Blinding Light is Complement, is the Completer of things as Love. Dante's vision attends the long pursuit by will which St. Thomas engages as our proper nature in *becoming,* we ourselves by grace providential through a reason, a "share of the Eternal Reason, whereby [the rational creature] has a natural inclination to [his] proper act [in a progress of becoming to perfection of given limit] and end [i.e., Beatitude]. That "participation of the eternal law in the rational creature," St. Thomas concludes, "is called natural law." Particular to the rational creature as rational, natural law is as well inclusive of all things by virtue of the proportionate particularity from Love whereby each thing is the thing it is — from sandstone to Einstein. (The citations are to Thomas' *Summa Theologica*, I-II, q. 91, a. 2.)

As discursive rational creature, man's proper nature is unfolded to him in his acts of providential becoming, when in accord with the "natural law" specific to him whereby he is *this* person. Through reason shared with Eternal Reason, in an accord with his proper nature as *this* person (shared in an accord with becoming with the limits of Love whereby we are), the person *becomes*. Thomas reminds us of the mediation of things to that becoming, resolving somewhat the disparity between finite reason and Eternal Reason. The disparity is mediated through the senses as perception of things in themselves. That is a point Thomas reminds us of rather early in his *Summa Theologica* (I, q. 14, a. 3, ad 3). "Created things are midway between God's knowledge and our knowledge, for we receive our knowledge from things that are caused by God's knowledge"—from things through the senses. St. Augustine, in a recovery from memory of his moment of recognition of this truth, his moment of an epiphany to himself as intellectual soul hears things cry out a fulfillment in his knowing of things through their beauty, their beauty declaring the Abiding Beauty of their common cause. "He made us!'"

We ourselves encounter such moments again and again, our memory of actual experiences declares, though not many recognizing what we have truly experienced. For how common to the "popular spirit" of any time or place — desert or jungle — a response to perceived "beauties of nature"— a popular phrase in many tongues giving common consent to the most varied beauties of things. A recent poet at last turning from his self-centered skepticism as surprised by joy — C. S. Lewis — in an accord with St. Augustine and St. Thomas speaks to this point. He speaks more in the mode of that pilgrim poet St. Augustine than of Thomas, suggesting that "but for our body one whole realm of God's glory — all that we receive through the senses — would go unpraised. For the beasts can't appreciate it and the angels are, I suppose, pure intelligencies." Enough, this recognition of our participation as rational creature with Divine Reason through the mediation of things, to suggest to the poet that (Lewis adds) "the 'beauties of nature' are a secret God has shared with us alone," perhaps one of the reasons "why we were made — and why the resurrection of the body is an important doctrine."

In this understanding of natural law in relation to, as a gift *in*, the rational creature we may better recognize ourselves as pilgrim in quest of the true way, seeking as already anticipated if yet unnamed self-discovery as an intellectual soul called by Love through things experienced to a proper end. Through grace, we may answer that calling by our becoming, in "natural inclination' to the good. On that way occur moments of epiphany, anticipatory of a possibility of Beatitude. Ah, that morning rose whose beauty is for a Blake or a Keats canker bitten. But it speaks to Hopkins or O'Connor, as it did to Dante, of that entwined beauty Dante glimpses through vision — that Celestial Rose entwined in its limited perfection by Creation seen in Eternal Light of Love. As a vision fleetingly perceived by Dante Heaven is Multifoliate, Multiscented, Multicolored, yet in a simplicity of perfection beyond *multi*— known at last beyond all partial blindness of the senses and at last no longer known as but through a glass darkly. For Dante there is that figure for epiphany, a full swarming of souls in harmony with Perfect Beauty in a trans-mortal vision. That is the vision Dante bravely attempts as poet in resolving his great poem, his "Multifoliate Rose" in which the Beatified Person and Beauty are one. Our recent Dante, T. S. Eliot, in closing his own poems in a patient spiritual peace at last, echoes Dame Julian of Norwich and Dante. "All manner of thing shall be well," in his anticipation that "the tongues of fire" of Pentecost will be seen beyond his limits of finitude in a perfection, all those "tongues of flame ... in-folded/ Into the crowned knot of fire" when the "fire and the rose are one."

In this context we have recalled once more the turning point of St. Augustine's conversion. It occurs when he is at last able to "hear" things speaking truth to him through his senses in justification of the good of creation itself, because God "made us," pied beauty cries. (And here by *justification* we mean a balance in the accountancy of intellect toward things known, a proportionate love of things as one "realm of God's glory' which otherwise save for man "would go unpraised" C. S. Lewis suggests.) Thus things in themselves refute his old Manichaean suspicion of creation as evil. Given the implicit limit to the imagination's service on the person's journeying, this is a first testing moment to the intellectual soul of its capacity to move beyond any self-limited response which confines the pilgrim to the senses in a growing hopelessness instead of moving toward universals as understood by a reason in accord through things with Eternal Reason. Intellect may thus guide the pilgrim into that larger country of spirit that lures O'Connor's Francis Marion Tarwater, a country larger than either the particulars or the universals that open reason to mystery as they may be known through that confluence of created things called the *universe* or the *cosmos*. That is the testing which John Keats could not survive, as he has witnessed to us in his poignant *Odes,* our attention particularly to his "Ode to a Nightingale." He is left in spiritual failure, lamenting that "the fancy cannot cheat so well as she is famed to do, deceiving elf." It is the same testing which O'Connor dramatizes in her young Tarwater, his gradual acceptance of that far country which is always so near, after his strenuous resistance to that spirit of Love infused in creation itself. At last consenting, Tarwater punctuates his becoming by his violent resistance to consent — a spiritual stuttering in his intellectual action as it were. Until, at last, overwhelmed by his own growing right will, he begins to speak that necessity of a "Yes" to Love that was resisted by his Uncle Rayber. Not that Tarwater is beyond that stuttering at last. But his is a "Yes" far other than that pathos of an Anna Karenina's "Yes" leading her to the abyss of despair in Tolstoy's great "Romantic" novel about love, or of Joyce's mischievous rendering of his Penelope as an Anna in *Ulysses,* his Mrs. Marion Tweedy Bloom. Molly Bloom's "Yes" is a prolonged uninterrupted "Yes" to her lover in the Joycean flood of spoken imagery celebrative of the sensual body in the moment of the sexual act, in that celebrated *tour de force* by Joyce as poet which anticipates the mode of the whole of *Finnegans Wake.*

Keats, having experienced a genuine epiphany only to realize that it is "fast fading," attempts by imaginative action to arrest it in a fixity and certainty of imagery by his art. That attempt failing, he laments the inadequacy to the poet of his "fancy" (the imagination). But Keats's dilemma, put in a Thomistic perspective and especially in respect to art as an effect of imaginative action, reveals that such "fixity and certainty" of actual things that Keats desires as a spiritual creature cannot be sufficiently effected by art. His is that "Romantic" attempt at self-rescue by imaginative action, as if art might be made salvific of the soul by the will's imaginative intent. Self-rescue in a desperate moment fails, the poet discovering himself once more lost in creation as a "dark wood," reduced to his "sole self." In the issue, it is not the imagination which is the deceiving elf, but the will's intent to such a rescue through an intentionality, undertaken as either naïve in the face of reality or in a secret intent that is determined to a self-empowerment on the presumption of intellectual autonomy.

Thus the person by either manner is self-deceived in the attempt to divorce *form* itself from created reality by imaginative action, in order to build a trans-reality as sufficient refuge from his own created and becoming nature. It is an attempt to assume the office of grace through intellect in an illusion that grace may thus be separated from the reality of things and appropriated by will. And most damaging effect of all is a separation of grace from his own nature, his willfulness decisive obstacle to grace. As a species of self-deception, the attempt (ironically) from the Thomistic perspective is to transcend that person's own created nature as *this* person, as if thereby to gain an imagined country disjoined from reality itself. Joyce's Stephen, unlike Keats, has a certain leisure of intellectual action to that attempt, Keats as physician knowing his death immanent, coughing over his manuscript. Stephen as surrogate poet (by Joyce's choice imitative somewhat of Keats) has leisure as an "intellectual" to set himself aside from early decay in the presumed immortality of youth, gradually ignoring his own becoming as other than his own willed perfection. In nature as fallen, death appears an inevitable obstacle to the illusion of an eternal existence in art, despite any poet's error as "young man." For art is insufficient to overcome actual worldly death, however well-made the poet's artifact as sepulcher or memorial urn. Inevitably the poet becomes a sod, as Keats laments. The made thing must at last prove sufficient only to his ashes, though his name be emblazoned on it. Keats becomes not only aware of this inevitable failure but deeply saddened by it to a point of spiritual despair. He accepts despair in recognition of his own impotence, unable to move out of that arrest.

We shall presently turn to Joyce's figure of the Keatsian "Romantic" poet, dramatically deployed by Joyce as echoing to the person John Keats and by a *counterpoint* to Keats's intellectual actions. Joyce's artist as a "young man" moves in an intellectual arrogance of intellect, an echoing unlikeness to Keats, as if he might by will alone force his own self-rescue as Keats has failed to do as person. Stephen would adapt, by intellectual reductionism, that phenomenon to the soul, the *epiphany,* as a concept reduced from its orthodox sense to the control of his own will as but psychological. He would make will psychological, therefore subservient to art. Meanwhile, as Thomas would suggest to us in forewarning, form as drawn from given matter by finite intellect through its imaginative action is form quite specific and so quite limited. It is sufficient to the "fixity and certainty" of *this* artifact, but insufficient to the rescue of the artificer. Joyce as maker of his surrogate person Stephen we may anticipate as himself also closely akin to his Stephen in a belief in aesthetic self-rescue, though at his life's end Joyce becomes troubled over whether as poet he has been only a poet of "fancy" rather than of "imagination" as Coleridge distinguishes those terms. Meanwhile, O'Connor recognizes, *making* by intellectual action reveals a faint but true echo in that form of the artist himself as person, as incarnate within a connaturality with both things and the Cause of things, whereby the poet as an intellectual soul as incarnate is finite in all properties of his being and so insufficient to self-rescue. So limited, as but *image* of his Creator, he must at last prove insufficient causal agent of the grace necessary to his rescue. And O'Connor, reading Joyce, sees this presence of Joyce in his work. She will express in sadness that he appears, through that presence in his work, entrapped as spiritual creature in a spiritual *stasis*, not self-rescued by and to aesthetic *stasis* in art as Stephen dreams to be his end as poet.

13

Moral and Dramatic
Problematics of Metaphor

*"The Christian writer will feel that in the greatest depth of vision, moral judgment
will be implicit and that when we are invited to represent the country according to survey, what we are asked to do is to separate mystery from manners and judgment from
vision, in order to produce something a little more palatable to the modern temper.... In
the greatest fiction, the writer's moral sense coincides with his dramatic sense, and I see
no way for it to do this unless his moral judgment is part of the very act of seeing and he
is free to use it."*

— Flannery O'Connor, "The Fiction
Writer & His Country"

*"The Almyers whom Hawthorne saw as a menace have multiplied. Busy cutting down
human imperfection, they are making headway also on the raw material of good. Ivan
Karamazov cannot believe, as long as one child is in torment; Camus' hero cannot accept
the divinity of Christ, because of the massacre of the innocents. In this popular pity, we
mark our gain in sensibility and our loss of vision. If other ages felt less, they saw more,
even though they saw with the blind, prophetical, unsentimental eye of acceptance,
which is to say, of faith."*

— Flannery O'Connor, "Introduction"
to *A Memoir of Mary Ann*

Form, known in intellect as a truth derived from experience; form, projected imaginatively as possible or probable truth in *this* artifact. Between the two borders lies the country proper to man as steward to the pre-existing creation, endured by his nature in being
both providential to himself as given existence by Love and charged thereby as providential to "all others" of creation. That is the country challenging to Flannery O'Connor most
personally, giving rise to her recognition of the necessity to her of a "felt balance" in transit through it. We find her engaging that necessity within the country of her own intellect.
She does so meditatively, and on occasion speaks of that country from her perspective as
person, to some audience that has solicited her as she becomes increasingly "famous" as a
maker of stories. In "The Fiction Writer and His Country," her Thomistic position is implicit, though she does not summon him so overtly in this early talk as presently she shall.
She suggests here a difficulty as story-writer in relation to her audience which Dante with
his audience did not have to deal with so radically as she must. Nevertheless theirs is a com-

mon engagement: they imaginatively project grotesque figurings of the human soul. She says, "When you assume that your audience holds the same beliefs you do, you can relax a little and use more normal means of talking to it; when you have to assume that it does not, then you have to make your vision apparent by shock — to the hard of hearing you shout, and for the almost blind you draw large and startling figures."

In such remarks, she is very much aware that she addresses an audience that does not share her beliefs. This essay, among her earliest reflections, had been solicited by Granville Hicks of *The Saturday Review of Literature* for a book he was editing, *The Living Novel: A Symposium* (1957).[1] She responds to Hicks's request, knowing that he regards her as a "Southern Christian" writer, and therefore an anomaly in those post–World War II days. She is aware as well of sharing with recent and contemporary writers in common difficulties concerning that possible country within the country of spectacle from which she draws. Conrad and Dostoevsky are in her mind as companionable in the problem — Conrad the seafarer; Dostoevsky a wayfarer rather centrally concerned in his making with Petersburg as somewhat analogous to Haze Motes's "Taulkinham." And then there is that threatening Dixie Limited on fiction's track, Faulkner, much closer home and immensely celebrated as a "Southern" writer. Conrad, Dostoevsky, Faulkner: as various as they are in their uses of the concrete and immediate as gathered out of their local experiences, each speaks to a commonness of human nature, which for O'Connor is the nature of man as intellectual soul incarnate.

She holds the recognition steadily, believing as well that by our very given nature as fallen we must engage that old dragon that is always at hand. In her statement for Hicks's book, she concludes with that epigraph we have cited, used as epigraph for her *A Good Man Is Hard to Find*: "St. Cyril of Jerusalem, in instructing catechumens, wrote: 'The dragon sits by the side of the road, watching those who pass. Beware lest he devour you. We go to the Father of Souls, but it is necessary to pass by the dragon.'" She adds for her skeptical listeners as a challenge, "No matter what form the dragon may take, it is of this mysterious passage past him, or into his jaws, that stories of any depth will always be concerned to tell." Then to her reader as catechumen, an encouraging note in conclusion: "It requires considerable courage at any time, in any country, not to turn away from the storyteller." Southern and Catholic (O'Connor), Slavic and Orthodox (Dostoevsky), skeptical and wandering a waste world (Conrad): as diverse as they are, their stories when well-made draw us toward the mystery of the waiting dragon.

Dostoevsky is especially appealing to Flannery O'Connor as we have made apparent (suggesting him by analogy as another "Southern" writer). He, too, uses the local to make fictionally incarnate characters who appear to us "grotesque" more often than not. For both Dostoevsky and O'Connor such characters are resonantly spiritual, however battered in their spirituality. Her later discussion of Ivan Karamazov in relation to Hawthorne (in her "Introduction" to *A Memoir of Mary Ann*) speaks awareness of parallels between Ivan and her Haze Motes. No doubt she would be amused, if perhaps a little saddened or even irritated, by Tolstoy as person, so differing in his response to the spiritual reality engaged by Dostoevsky. For as great an artist as he is (Tolstoy is masterful in treating the concrete), we have suggested that after *Anna Karenina* he becomes haunted by a sense of his own damnation because of his gifts as poet. As imaginative maker, he cannot *not* write, as if writing stories were a disease. But to write he has no choice but to depend for his *matter* upon existential reality — upon actual things adjoining and participating with him in existence, a knowledge to him as intellectual soul received through his body. In self-defense, he becomes more and more a Manichaean. His soul, he becomes convinced, is entrapped by his body. Tolstoy can see nothing in "nature" as good, except the peasant, who by poverty and because unlearned Tolstoy substitutes for Christ.

The peasant in Tolstoy's imaginative projection of him is not recognized by Tolstoy as a "fictional" distortion in his polemical argument. Thus for him the peasant's personhood is even better than Christ's, a position he argues which leads him at last to be excommunicated from the Orthodox Church. Tolstoy resists seeing it as possible that the peasant has in him a Haze Motes or a Misfit. And so by denial of human nature to the peasant Tolstoy removes him as an idol from a world he declares corrupt. Meanwhile, Tolstoy himself feels trapped. He is, after all, Count Tolstoy, holding estate, honored in the social hierarchy by a title, and celebrated worldwide as a writer of fiction. The peasant's intellect is to be envied then as not perverted by knowledge out of recent Western philosophy, as Tolstoy's had been. And what a virtue, the peasant's poverty. It is out of this delusion that Tolstoy becomes a radical Manichaean, though his gifts as poet are constant reminder to him of his earthly nature, speaking to him therefore by his misunderstanding his pending damnation because he is cursed through his body. Of all the suffering Tolstoy heaps upon his devoted wife, Sonya — she having hand-copied revisions of *War and Peace* four times, among others — this spiritual inclination to wild depression is Sonya's most constant burden, given her piety as Orthodox Christian. She attempts rescue of a doubting Tolstoy from his depression, sometimes fueling anger in him because he feels cursed by being a writer, entrapped in the world of the senses. Meanwhile, Sonya fiercely defends him as a great writer to be honored for his art. As for Tolstoy in his gnawing spiritual agony, he had been affected early by his fascination with Kant, unable even later to exorcise a Kantian dream of pure transcendence through reason. Thus the ground prepared to Tolstoy's thought by a Kantian transcendentalism with its Manichaean temptations. But as well, he elects kinship with those more ancient fundamentalist transcendentalists who pronounced creation evil. His is that old heresy (as the Orthodox Church declares by an excommunication still maintained) which O'Connor remarks again and again as widely lingering in the popular spirit of her own time. But O'Connor remarks as well that progressive version of Manichaeanism which by intellectual reductionism appropriates creation to gnostic ends, requiring as a principle that it deny the soul's existence. This becomes an upside down species of Manichaeanism, a secularized "religion" in which material reality is first declared accidental (*evil* a term disallowed) as is the so-called "soul" as but an illusion, born out of physiological biochemical accident but mistaken as soul when only "psychological" consciousness. Materialism is the only acceptable doctrine — out of infinite accident with no beginning or end.

O'Connor does not refer often to Tolstoy, nor at all to that aspect of his ancient Manichaean faith which makes him see as a curse his gifts as writer. She reports her reading interests to her friend "A," speaking a special interest in Dostoevsky, Turgenev, Chekhov, and Gogol, but "not Tolstoy so much." But closer home there were those New England Puritans who left Hawthorne both upset and bemused by their own incipient Manichaeanism to whom she is attuned through Hawthorne's "romances." Hawthorne also presents that new species of Manichaeanism — the Almyers — who since Hawthorne (O'Connor says) have made "headway ... on the raw material of good," that "raw material" of materialistic doctrine established by Positivism. Insofar as O'Connor is a "Southern" writer, she may appear in the shadow cast by that living presence in her day, William Faulkner. In our present context, Faulkner is in one limited respect akin to the early Tolstoy, the poet of *War and Peace,* in that like that early Tolstoy Faulkner engages cultural history as his matter, shying away from the spiritual implications that are for O'Connor the centering concern in her version of "Southern" fiction. Faulkner does wrestle with the relation of good and evil, but largely in *historical* causes that is a matter of the historical "South." For Faulkner, in his response to the matter a Stoical endurance unto death is the virtue to be celebrated.

Between the two Russians — Tolstoy and Dostoevsky — O'Connor finds herself more closely attuned to Dostoevsky, who reacts scornfully to Tolstoy's Manichaeanism, even as he shares with that great contemporary in rejecting the Modernist doctrines imported into Russian thought through the literary salons at Moscow — Voltaire and Diderot having been especially celebrated there as carriers of that Western disease. O'Connor shares an awareness of the intellectual and spiritual dislocations made popular to the intelligentsia by both the Puritan and the Rationalistic (sometimes concomitant) distortions of reality, that buried relation shared between 18th century Puritanism and 18th century Rationalism. Because not mutually recognized as binding them together, the kinship requires further reflection. As a prophet of distances, Flannery O'Connor responds to both, recognizing in her response her own kindred spirit in Dostoevsky. She shares with Dostoevsky in rejecting that curious relationship between Puritan and Rationalist, the intellectual denial of the nature of creation itself as necessarily good.[2] Theirs, as poets, is not an interest in the sweep of history such as that in *War and Peace* that interests Tolstoy and Faulkner as makers of fictions. Dostoevsky's concern, as is O'Connor's, is with the embattlement of consciousness within which grace struggles with evil. Given this as the arena of Tolstoy's own personal spiritual suffering, we are tempted to remark Tolstoy seen from their perspectives as a person sharing kinship with such fictional figurings of the grotesque as a Haze Motes or perhaps even of the Misfit as a prophet gone wrong. In Tolstoy's recollections, usually insistently forced upon his long-suffering wife whom he burdened with his diaries, Tolstoy was prone to dwell on his own past sins, some of them violent, including rape.

Tolstoy's is a malady of spirit which Dostoevsky recognizes, while recognizing as well his own endangerment within the creation which Tolstoy seemed unable to sort as a good fed upon by evil, besieged by evil. With such a celebrity as Tolstoy constant before him, a competitive presence being universally praised by the worldwide media now beginning to declare Tolstoy a saint, Dostoevsky himself increasingly "preaches" the expiation possible through "suffering." His figure of Raskolnikov in *Crime and Punishment* makes that point, Raskolnikov slowly accepting the necessity of suffering to his spiritual benefit. Earlier Raskolnikov has been an arrogant secular Manichaean like Ivan Karamazov (just ahead for Dostoevsky after *Crime and Punishment*). But Raskolnikov as intellectual is more nearly a Russian Haze Motes or a Tarwater as largely unlettered, unsophisticated, attempting to create good out of evil by acts of murder. *Suffering* is Dostoevsky's emerging theme in *Crime and Punishment,* after his incisive exposé of Modernist man in *Notes from Underground* (a work profitably juxtaposed we have suggested to that portrait of Modernist man in spiritual arrest, Eliot's J. Alfred Prufrock). Dostoevsky's theme of suffering will become embraced as suited to sweeping fictions by Southern writers a hundred years after him. Remember Jack Burden's engagement of existence as the "Great Twitch" in Robert Penn Warren's *All the King's Men* as one instance.

It is a theme prominent in Faulkner as well. Faulkner's epithet in praise of this virtue in certain characters is that they "endure," though Faulkner is wary of suggesting as the end of enduring a spiritual expiation. They endure by a Stoical survival alone as their seeming justification, as in the several comedies treating the Snopses. Those characters suffer the world in accumulating adversity, responding with a wiliness seen as admirable, however much disturbing the spectacles of endurance to a reader's residual moral sense in the Modernist climate. (One of Faulkner's admirers of course not so disturbed.) Some survive beyond all odds, though Faulkner will not invoke as a possible cause *grace* as a presence enabling both the suffering and the enduring. We might note as well that many of Faulkner's sufferers are "peasants," culturally trapped as it were by history in a thematic kinship to Tolstoy, so that Faulkner's matter to his making is largely cultural history, a history which he accepts as a determining adversary in challenges to an endurance by his surrogate persons. Unlike O'Connor, then, Faulkner treats religion as an element of residual culture in the consciousness of a character, largely a residue of history. It is not a theme speaking any desire in Faulkner himself running deeper than either nature or history may account for.

On this point, reflection may reveal something of both Faulkner and O'Connor as "Southern" writers, the concern here not to judge them as writers of fiction but to distinguish between their visions of man as *homo viator*. From very early, O'Connor resisted comparison to Faulkner, remarking that the "presence of Faulkner in our midst makes a great difference in what the writer can and cannot permit himself to do" as a "Southern" writer. She adds, as we remember, a Faulknerian metaphor: "Nobody wants his mule and wagon stalled on the same track the Dixie Limited is roaring down." As for their differences in understanding man as a creature in the midst of nature, trailing a history with him willy-nilly, we might compare Faulkner's Joe Christmas of *Light in August* to characters we know from Flannery O'Connor. By that comparison we discover quite a difference in their address to the mystery of existence in respect to their readings of human nature. Remembering O'Connor's Haze Motes or her Misfit, or especially young Tarwater, we may imagine how differently she might have treated Faulkner's own famous victim Joe Christmas. In such a speculative suggestion we, of course, take an imaginative liberty, in a risk similar to the speculations about their characters made by both Faulkner and O'Connor on the evidence of their fictional presences to us as seemingly fixed and certain. Faulkner will speculate on his characters' fates as if they were persons larger than surrogates, as if continuing beyond the confines of his fiction — speculations suggesting how real they are to him. And we heard O'Connor rather positive in her defenses of the Misfit as a prophet gone wrong who may recover to his calling further down a road left yet untraveled by fiction after he kills that grandmother in response to her gesture of love.

Faulkner presents Joe Christmas as a fated victim, the accidents of his life defining and confining his life, seemingly determining his inevitable end. Joe is presented as victim of local cultural tradition. Faulkner does so metaphorically, borrowing radical counterpoint to his Joe Christmas from the New Testament "biography" of Jesus, underlining thereby ironic correspondences. Joe is illegitimate, his mother dying at his birth. His father was killed by his mother's father. (His father had appeared locally as a circus hand, wandering into the story's Mississippi place and fathering Joe.) Abandoned at an orphanage on Christmas Eve, Joe had been given his name. He is raised by religious fanatics as foster parents, kills his foster father and then wanders the South for years, only to return to the place from which he had set out, Faulkner's Jefferson. There he becomes the lover of Joanna Burden, who carries their child in whom his "black blood" seals Joe's fate, he at last brutally killed.

In such stark summary, the correspondence of Joe Christmas to Christ seem underlined by radical, historical aspects of his fated life as a *homo viator*, pointed metaphorically by a secular aspect of Jesus' "biography." Joe's crucifixion is hardly commensurate with the New Testament "history" of Jesus as revealed to be the Son of God, so that *Light in August* bears a heavy burden of irony—sometimes bordering on the cynical, given the enveloping cultural context (Jefferson, Mississippi) in which Christianity itself seems taken by Faulkner largely as but a cultural tradition. Not that these correspondences have been overlooked by literary explications. The burden of the fiction itself, and consequently much of the explication of it, seems to suggest the correspondences more nearly those of a "metaphysical" metaphor, but in that metaphor the implications of spiritual mystery are largely irrelevant. Metaphor instead allows irony as a dramatic effect, this perspective holds, without any necessary dependence upon Revelation as a reality as it is for Flannery O'Connor. In Faulkner, one has little sense that Christ is to be understood as a reality. For O'Connor, Revelation speaks at first an implicit and then explicit Presence of the Son of the living God, as we discover Him through faith. Hence "All is the Incarnation" she affirms. It is rather as if Faulkner borrows "myth," as Joyce does in *Ulysses,* to a metaphorical ordering of his art. For neither Joe Christmas, nor the other characters of *Light in August*—though all are palpably "Southern"—seem to be "Christ-haunted"—that aspect of "Southerness" which O'Connor engages constantly.

The uses of violence in *Light in August* and *The Violent Bear It Away* seem at first far removed from each other in respect to that level of history's spectacle we think of as out of the recent history of the South, the context Faulkner provides Joe Christmas. We nevertheless recognize potentially like characters but as seen differently by their makers. Consider Joe Christmas and Young Tarwater—in respect to their fictional presences to us through the gifted incarnations by the two writers. Both surrogate characters are at the surface largely cultural flotsam in respect to *spectacle*. But Faulkner's Joe Christmas in his imagined history would be for O'Connor the point of a departure to explore his spiritual depths. Joe as presented by Faulkner elicits (from O'Connor's point of vision) only a popular pity, closely akin to that elicited by a Camus hero, or so she might say. "Camus' hero," she says in her "Introduction to *A Memoir of Mary Ann,* "cannot accept the divinity of Christ, because of the massacre of the innocents." Here in Faulkner, the "innocent" victim of history is Joe Christmas, eliciting a "popular pity" which, though marking "our gain in sensibility," reveals as well "our loss in vision" from O'Connor's perspective. In "Novelist and Believer," O'Connor asks, "What Christian novelist could compare his concern to Camus'?" Instead as readers, she says, we find ourselves looking "in much of the fiction of our time for a kind of sub-religion which expresses its ultimate concern in images that have not yet broken through to show any recognition of God who has revealed himself."

Such is the "popular pity" signifying a generally lost vision which could once reach deeper than cultural history, deeper than Faulkner's arresting imagery of *homo viator* as if a victim of history—which limited vision Faulkner shares with Camus (and with the early Tolstoy) as a "sub-religion." In this respect we have lost that spiritual depth O'Connor believes implicit in the very spectacle borrowed from the actual world of persons such as Faulkner uses to make Joe Christmas stirring to our sensibilities. The distinction here suggested reveals a difference in Faulkner's and O'Connor's perceptions of such marginal social persons as borrowed surrogate persons to their fictional dramas. Indeed, we might discover a sense of kinship with Camus to be a conscious awareness in Faulkner, given his express admiration of Camus. (Jean-Paul Sartre responds to Faulkner's work in critical essays that take Faulkner to be of Sartre's own company as agnostic Existentialist — Faulkner more comfortable with Camus.) In this vein of our speculative aside, then, we might imagine on the other hand Faulkner's approach to O. E. Parker of O'Connor's "Parker's Back." He might treat Parker as a victim of historical, cultural deprivation — suited perhaps to the milieux of *As I Lay Dying*. So we might speculate in reading her story alongside Faulkner's "Dry September." At the level of history, of spectacle — at the level of concrete presence of each protagonist as "driven" within a recognizable cultural place — there are certain "naturalistic" likenesses between the two "Southern" writers.

Yet O'Connor's manner of engaging a similar matter is in response to resonances of a mystery in things quite different from the historical resonances to which Faulkner responds. For Faulkner, there is little suggestion of spiritual hope lingering in or for his protagonist, as there is in O'Connor's Parker for instance in contrast to Joe Christmas. O'Connor suggests out of her faith that her character has arrived at his lowest worldly point, but that is a point in which a vision enabling grace seems to become possible. For her, there is a spiritual reality underlying what will otherwise be seen only as a depressing "naturalistic" cultural surface of reality, which therefore leaves the art by such limited vision with a depressing pathos in resolution as reflected in the "incarnated" matrix of a story. For her, a character as struggling intellect, embattled by temptations to evil as he is pulled away from the good, reaches a point where pathos may be dissolved by a tragedy beyond pity's easy sentiment — with some hint of comic rescue, *comic* in Dante's sense. It is this dimension to a spiritual action possible in a character that might be lost to the critic unsympathetic to O'Connor's vision, leaving him to conclude that her characters are at last consumed by despair — a judgment she rejects. In an interview by Gerard E. Sherry (*Critic,* June–July, 1963), she says, "My characters are described as despairing only by superficial critics. Very few of my characters despair, and those who do, don't reflect my views. You have to get the writer's view by looking at the novel as a whole." Or (we add) by looking at the body of a writer's work as a whole.

One might make as a judgment of Faulkner's characters that he leaves them at the cusp of the void, threatened by despair, relieved for a reader (and for Faulkner perhaps) by a comic deportment sometimes wild in its spectacles. Their Stoical *endurance* seems to leave them hopeless of rescue, save through a self-valued honor as recognized, not by their impinging world but only by the enduring self. Endurance is *private* to the Stoic, whatever his cultural circumstances. And indeed for the Stoic as "puritan" there is virtue intensified by the world's not knowing. Stoicism by its very nature is a private virtue and the more virtuous when the least professed. Walker Percy attempts that solution to his own disquiet as Southerner, finding it inadequate. Long before his first novel (*The Moviegoer* in 1961), he published the essay we cited called "Stoicism in the South" (1956), an act of putting Stoicism aside. In the essay he engages "Southern Stoicism" not only as he had known it so closely in his "Uncle Will" (William Alexander Percy), but as he recognized himself as a beginning writer standing in Faulkner's shade. For Faulkner threads this classical Stoicism into several of his works, novels and stories alike, his Gavin Stevens a rich instance. Gavin, summarizing his life at one point as lawyer and judge, says: "I am happy I was given the privilege of meddling with impunity in other people's affairs without doing any harm by belonging to that avocation [the law] whose acolytes have been absolved in advance for holding justice above truth," a sardonic and private self-judgment.[3]

Rather certainly, then, Faulkner does not locate his virtue of endurance at that "peculiar" crossroads which O'Connor calls the one at which she operates as writer, where "time and place and eternity somehow meet." Faulkner recognizes the parameters of good and evil in historical, and thus in social, manifestations, but seems wary of any intersection by eternity that speaks man himself a spiritual creature. He sticks closely to a point on the horizontal plane of history and nature, his mastery of that plane justly celebrated. On that plane the past intersects the present in tensional traumas to a consciousness in its present cultural context, at a present moment as affected by history. That is Faulkner's limited perspective as prophet as he explores his "postage stamp" world, Yoknapatawpha, Mississippi. And it is in this respect that he is most akin to Tolstoy's larger mapping of the Russian world in *War and Peace*. To this point (and by means of an anachronistic metaphor), how Faulknerian is Tolstoy's "Epilogue" to his great novel, and especially so as Faulkner may have heard sympathetic echoes of his own position in that "Part Two" of Tolstoy's "Epilogue" which begins, "The subject of history is the life of nations and of mankind. To perceive directly and encompass in words, that is, to describe the life of a single people much less that of mankind, would appear to be impossible."[4] It is, indeed, Tolstoy's engaging early this "impossible" attempt to encompass "the life and nations of mankind" that leads Flaubert (in a letter to Turgenev, shared with Tolstoy) to fault it a weakness in that otherwise most admirable novel *War and Peace*.

How cautiously wise, therefore, to commit oneself as writer to a small postage stamp arena of history. Such a challenge is daunting enough without risking the attempt through metaphysical concerns larger than a history dramatized as the present's encounter of its own past — in present contingent moments of worldly action by characters imaginatively summoned to encounter. More manageable, Faulkner's attempt to "encompass in words" limited to a local people their history-haunted circumstances than to attempt to engage them as Christ-haunted as does O'Connor. And so Faulkner early and late is more closely akin in his vision to the Tolstoy of *War and Peace* than to O'Connor. We nevertheless recognize that within his limited plane and beyond his intentions, Faulkner nevertheless reflects abundantly the mystery of being which O'Connor will insist is inevitable in serious fiction, even though that fiction may be made out of a confirmed secular rationalism by a poet. Indeed, it is so of Tolstoy to his growing discomfort as we have suggested, who begins to believe himself in danger in those later fictions by his pleasure in the good of things necessary to his art. It cannot be otherwise, O'Connor would say, insofar as such a writer is concerned "above all with an accurate reproduction of the things that most immediately concern man." For by that limited concern he is captive to proximate good through a love *native* to him because he is an intellectual soul incarnate. In devotion to the good of his made thing, such a writer will witness what he as this person makes of God's good creation, whether he himself believe in God or not. That is her steady position. And in respect to Faulkner's own approach to this mystery within concrete nature, we know it especially evident in moving elegiac lament for the mystery of suffering, arrestingly reflected in his Ike McCaslin's devotions to "nature" in *Go Down, Moses*.[5]

Since fiction necessarily depends upon the concrete world as perceived by the senses, the ancient Manichaean can not comfortably write or read fiction. Hawthorne is aware of the Puritan's severe disapproval, feeling the ghosts of his Puritan fathers still with him and severely disapproving of his attempt as a writer of "Romances." He declares his *Scarlet Letter* to be such a work, and in the prologue to that novel called "The Custom-House," dated from within his own local small country, Salem, Hawthorne's concerns he declares are centered around the "town-pump." Nevertheless, Hawthorne hears his restive forefathers from their graves nearby: "A writer of story-books! What kind of business in life, — what mode of glorifying God, or being serviceable to mankind in his day and generation, — may that be? Why, the degenerate fellow might as well have been a fiddler!" What O'Connor sees in Hawthorne, herself a descendent of Hawthorne in that she writes spiritual "Romances," is that this Puritan Manichaean spirit proves ruthless in its intellectual reduction of nature itself, fearful of nature's temptations. She sees as well that these surviving Manichaeans have been followed by the Almyers (of "The Birthmark") who are intent on reconstituting nature as serviceable to mankind, rejecting any collateral glorification of God.[6]

Hawthorne has observed this transformation underway in his neighbor, Ralph Waldo Emerson, as we observed. It is with an uneasy irony that Hawthorne in his introduction to his famous novel *The Scarlet Letter* remarks these "compliments bandied between my great-grandsires and myself, across the gulf of time!" An irony lies in his recognition that there are "strong traits of their nature" that "have intertwined themselves with mine," though an Emersonian reductionism is hardly tempting. If the old Puritans were not Christ-haunted in responding to nature and discomforted by its speaking Revelation, as O'Connor believes her "Southerners" to be, they were certainly "God-haunted," with that incipient Manichaean dimension to spiritual concerns that seeks intellectual relief in declaring this world evil. For Flannery O'Connor there is a difference between New England and the Southern fundamentalist. The New England Puritan's inclination is toward God as an abstraction to be engaged by a reason in response to faith in God. The response of a Southern fundamentalist is as "Christ-haunted" by the Incarnation. Her Haze Motes is "a Christian *malgre lui*," who "innocent of theory," pursues an integrity "in his trying with such vigor to get rid of the ragged figure [Christ] who moves from tree to tree in the back of his mind," O'Connor's observations about Haze in her prefatory note to the reissue of *Wise Blood*. Hawthorne finds himself, as both Christ-haunted and by his Puritan inheritance God-haunted, in what seemed increasingly to him a desert such as that one in which that later New England Puritan descendent, T. S. Eliot, will come to himself. Eliot responds in part to Hawthorne at first as but a "psychological" writer, at that point of response Eliot a liberated "Unitarian" in his sensibilities who, like James, is wary of Hawthorne's insistence on the reality of sin, Hawthorne a story-writer akin to fiddle-player in a newly progressive, pragmatic age. Meanwhile, Hawthorne from that older New England perspective might prove to be of the devil's party, or so such a severe Manichaean as Governor Endicott of "The Maypole of Merrymount" would insist. (So too on the other hand will he be charged by the intellectually liberated, as O'Connor has been charged, as "anti-intellectual," a hovering suspicion in Henry James that Hawthorne is not sufficiently culturally sophisticated.) But Hawthorne's Puritan Manichaeans would not recognize so clearly as Tolstoy did the conclusions required of a Manichaean inclination, Tolstoy inclined first to suicide and then to but a rhetorical intellectual suicide in rejecting the world's body into his ripe old age. Tolstoy, fleeing Sonya and all his family as well as all other worldly entrapments, escapes anonymously, taking with him the opening books of *The Brothers Karamazov* out of the rejected world. He will die in a remote train station at the small settlement of Astapovo, but not before descended upon by official Russia and by the "news media" of the day who sent dispatches worldwide on his daily decline. There were as well his divided family fighting for possession of him. Given the circumstances, and except for the level of spectacle and notoriety over his impending death, one might find Hawthorne's sad eulogy for his Young Goodman Brown ironically appropriate to Tolstoy's final encounter of the relation of evil to good: "when he had lived long, and was borne to his grave [Tolstoy carried back home at Yasnaya Polyana] a hoary corpse, followed by [Sonya], an aged woman, and children and grandchildren, a goodly procession, besides neighbors not a few [from worldwide], they carved no hopeful verse upon his tombstone, for his dying hour was gloom."

The Puritan purveyors of that inclination to reject creation as if necessarily evil, we have suggested, eventually found rescue in a shuffling of creation to their own convenience as secularist Modernists, in a reverse Manichaeanism whereby "nature" must be subdued by the force derived from *facts* turned instrumental to a conquest of nature to correct its "errors." That is more dependably (more pragmatic) solution than arguments from the pulpit about a Golden Heaven and the fires of Hell over which the spider soul is suspended on its tenuous web, the body. Tolstoy saw — though he could not consent to the actions required by his recognition — that only by an absolute rejection of the world might he escape his fancied endangerment. He meditated suicide seriously, as he also seriously considered self-castration as a resolution of one of his dilemmas of the flesh — meanwhile fathering a baker's dozen of children and continuing to write arresting fiction. Tolstoy's severe remedies seem not to have been generally recognized as but logical extensions of Manichaeanism by some of the Puritan fathers, save perhaps by that ascetic development out of Puritanism which we now remember as the Shaker Movement. And how ironic that a principal legacy of that movement should be that severely beautiful furniture, now largely housed in museums as a detritus of history, though occasionally used to appoint stunningly "sheik" residences by affluent patrons of "folk" art.

Concurrent with that retreat from the world by the Shakers, now somewhat sentimentally treated as cultural history on educational television, some of the Puritans become transmogrified into Modernist secular Manichaeans, emerging into a power over both nature and the social community. (President Charles Eliot of Harvard set that as a national goal, now largely accomplished.) It becomes possible by a rejection of the spiritual dimension of grace in nature as did the Shakers but to quite different ends. Diametric rejections of the good evidenced by creation: most proximately potential to fulfillment in the rejecting person — a severe spiritualism denying the body; a severe materialism, nestled in the body and denying the soul. How challenging to our reflection to pose a Shaker against Hugh Hefner and his "Playboy Philosophy" as opposites but committed against creation on the same principle: the desacralization of things in themselves from being good because created. The one, by pursuit of a pure selflessness just shy of suicide, though devoted to generational suicide; the other, a concentrated selfishness whose idol of worship is his own appetitive nature born of flesh, but no less devoted to generational suicide than his Shaker counter. Both intellectually awkward: a Hefner proving one dead end of but a shifted perspective by inverting Manichaeanism in a new heretical puritanism in worship of the "self." Yet in this new perspective, turned toward a pragmatism serving a "pure" selfishness, the disciple of inversion is not freed by obsession with himself as incarnate. More tellingly, neither is he freed of his given nature as spiritual creature, though free to deny that property in his nature as spiritual. (*Intellect* as *mind* effected by the *physical* brain replaces intellectual soul in the self-centered reckoning.) With an intellectual awkwardness of fact sheered from nature and imbued with ultimate authority over nature by mind, *fact* can but become an abstract idol to the worship of the possessive self. It is under the emerging pragmatic necessity to separate grace from nature that there rises the necessity of a new scholasticism, that of Positivistic logic, charged to execute a systemization of fact in order to make easier a command of power over nature. (How "Shaker-like" the Puritan severity in some Positivists.) Even so, the body of the "self" remains a concentrating arena within which nature must be conquered, catered to (in Walker Percy's terms) by the *theorist* by his subverting the popular spirit to *consumerism* as if justifying a popular consent to the theorist's collected power over nature.

As for the writer in this progress of history, if he be converted to Positivism he will more and more depend upon sensual knowledge at the level of spectacle, increasingly refusing any temptation to vision of the spiritual implications in *things* themselves, though in moments of nostalgia he may experience a minor (i.e., a psychological) epiphany over passing beauty. There follows in the train of Naturalistic art an emerging Positivistic "scholasticism" based largely in the dogmas of Evolutionary theory and supported by the new psychology attending that dogma (principally remembered as out of Freud and Jung in the unfolding). Influenced by these emerging sciences, some writers of fiction were converted by that dogma. Those (O'Connor remarks) are dependent upon a "sub-religion" that requires a limited vision of reality contained by "images" sufficient to the established dogma — image taken from spectacle and held as if essence. But those necessary images are, though limited as spectacle, necessarily gathered as a fictional matter from a reality actually experienced. And therefore (from O'Connor's perspective) fictions may therefore speak something deeper than the writer may recognize present in his own words.

O'Connor insists this inevitable, insofar as the writer is devoted to "an accurate reproduction of the things that most immediately concern man." And she asserts it with confidence, herself held by a "mystery unresolved" in creation but known as a mystery consequent upon her own givenness as an embodied spiritual creature. That mystery is stirred by a knowing response to the resonance of things actually experienced, yielding truths to be held actively by reason out of experiences. Thus images of the truths of things become resident in reflective thought. And so she must conclude that the longer she looks at a particular object, the more of the world is revealed to her through it. Thought dwells upon things known now and in the moment or day or year past through the offices of reason, whether the person is called as philosopher or scientist — but most especially if he is called as poet. Truths intuitively known to any calling set mystery echoing in intellect, in response to which echoing there begins a journeying of creation by the pilgrim *homo viator* as intellectual soul, through whatever peculiar gifts to faring the way are his as *this* person. Such is O'Connor's response in recognizing her particular calling, leading her to an emphatic rejection of the separation of grace from nature as a willful violation of reality — a violation of created things but most tellingly a violation reciprocal in that it effects a reduction of the separating self-victim, the pilgrim intellectual soul.

What a writer will discover in answering his calling, she says to her undergraduate and faculty audience at a small middle Georgia college, is that "the meaning of a story does not begin except at a depth where adequate motivation and adequate psychology and the various determinations have been exhausted." It is at such a point that the writer discovers himself on the threshold of unresolved mystery, on the threshold of a "country" mysteriously inherent to the actual concrete country spoken to him through his senses, in which proximate country he is presently a resident — in which he lives and breathes and has his being. The proximate country, insistently contingent to him through his senses as this particular person, may tempt him to cling to it, becoming "worldly." By that pressing contingency perceived through the senses, he may mistake himself as citizen only of *this* place at *this* time.

At such a point, O'Connor adds, "Such a writer will be interested in possibility rather than probability," echoing Aristotle's *possible or probable* as distinguishing art from history's *actual*. This is to suggest that at such a point the writer in his concern for the good of the thing he struggles to make must suspend judgment, turning from a judgmental *probability* to hope born of *possibility*. Otherwise, he may attempt to force the unresolved mystery to reveal hidden depths by the command of his art — art forcing a *probable* conclusion by judgmental intentionality. Even the scientist may allow *probability* too forcefully in his anticipation of hope, intruding as his own judgmental determinism of intent upon whatever species of the *possible* confronting his speculative wonder. Thus may be flawed whatever "experiment" he has in mind speculatively. We make this analogy of scientist to poet to recall a reality: a similitude between them is out of the ground common to both in their human nature — whether responding to contingency in pursuit of a resolution of certainty as scientist or as poet in speculative wonder of the possible.

The writer whom O'Connor describes in her Wesleyan College talk is a self-portrait, though she speaks of "him" (as have we) in the third person. "He will be interested in characters who are forced out to meet evil and grace and who act on trust beyond themselves — whether they know very clearly what it is they act upon or not." That this is a characterization of herself as poet is evident from the sentence that follows. "To the modern mind, this kind of character, and his creator are typical Don Quixotes, tilting at what is not there," at windmills as if they were giants but enemy. It is a tilting that seems reaction to illusions to that current popular spirit, since both evil and grace are concepts touching no reality for the Modernist sensibilities. These two realities enjoin and test her faith though denied as real by that Modernist mind she finds dominant, the mind which has declared God dead and has convinced the popular spirit of God's death as timely in the interest of a progress over nature. Here we must observe that, if on this occasion O'Connor speaks of herself as "creator" of such characters, we remember the circumstances of her informal and diverse audience as part of an educational system given to a flattery of students as "creative." In more formal concerns, and later than this early venture, she clearly understands the necessary distinction we have made. She is maker not creator — a distinction implicit here as well. It is at about the time of her local talk that she remarks (in a letter to "A," January 13, 1956) that "the moral basis of Poetry is the accurate naming of the things of God," that old responsibility of Adam now devolved upon the poet. In that vein of thought she had remarked earlier (to "A," December 8, 1955) the intellectual failures of her characters in "Good Country People." "Mrs. Hopewell is a realist but not a poet, whereas Hulga has tried to be a poet without being a realist. Where the poet and the realist are truly combined you have St. Catherine of Genoa maybe." If we remember St. Catherine as devoted to those souls suffering the miseries of the flesh — a Mother Teresa of her day — we might anticipate that Saint as likely patron to such a writer as O'Connor, who gets herself "dusty" in reality itself out of her own felt balance of responsibility. Even so, she would reject, even scoff at, any suggestion of saintliness in her, she taking herself as an apprentice to such saints in her stewardship of her peculiar gifts as writer.

Such a writer as she, by her surrender to the *possible* in her act of making and with a confident dependence upon the actual as known from her own experience, makes her characters "incarnate" in fictions. But they are not studied imitations of actual persons. Art does not imitate nature, she hears St. Thomas insist. She well understands his point (emphasized by Jacques Maritain in his *Art and Scholasticism*) that the artist properly imitates the *action* of nature — not nature itself in its "historic" manifestations as known through the senses. It is in this distinction that one discovers two truths about art. By his actions of making — in imitating the *actions* of nature as imaginatively recognized through actual things — the poet imitates as well but at a proportionate remove those actions of God as Creator whereby things as actual *are*. The analogy of making to creating requires the distinction Thomas explores as *proportionality*, reminding us that the poet unlike God does not create *ex nihilo*, whether in respect to either his matter or the "possible" form he draws from given chosen matter out of the world's largesse. Nevertheless the intellectual action of *informing* matter recalls that proportionate sharing with Providence in the poet's effecting a thing — the artifact — which does not exist before his action. He makes by reason's accord to Eternal Reason. In the Thomistic epistemology of this action by intellect, the intuitive intellect responds to things in themselves through an openness of love toward things as good — a natural action — thereby receptive to the truth of the *particular* thing. In that communion — that *conunion* as Thomas argues — lies the forming of, an *in-forming of*, intellect itself. In a complementary action of response to what is intuitively known — a response to the specific *essential* nature of a concrete thing held in intellect as a truth corresponding to essence. Reason moves toward universals out of cumulative experience of truths, discovering the *possible* along that way. Thus by the will's consent to the complementary and continuing conjunction of intuition and reason as modes of intellectual action, understanding becomes possible out of the actually known.

In that complementary response to the truth of things known by intellect — the *informing* of intellect whereby it becomes actual out of potentiality to its becoming — the rational mode orders known truths in speculative response to creation. The nature of this intellectual *becoming* is addressed by St. Thomas in thirteen articles of Question 79, Part I of his *Summa Theologica*, from which we here draw argument to our concern for the poet's discovery of an integral relation of his moral sense to his dramatic sense, an integration out of his responsibilities as *this* person to a deportment proper to him according to his specific gifts. The poet in his dramatic concern engages the *possible* actions of persons. In respect to reason in making out of coincidences of these intellectual senses (senses here the orientation of intellectual power) Thomas remarks the speculative reason's primary concern. It is "the consideration of truth," not first "to operation," though operation may follow such consideration (Article 11). The crucial distinction obtains in relation to practical intellectual actions lest "operation" supercede moral responsibility to truth itself. Truth reduced to service of instrumental action, in disregard of moral responsibility, will distort both the person and the truth. That is a distortion by speculative reason which issues in that philosophy, Pragmatism, out of the Modernist separations of grace from nature. In respect to speculative intellect as speculative in obedience to truth, it is in an obedience to truth that "by extension [speculative reason] becomes practical," a deportment we have argued which requires a proportionate extension as governed by prudential humility.

It is by intellect's own action (intellect being substantive but not material) that it *conceives* in response to the truths known. The issue of this intellectual conception is its own *word*, as substantive but not material. (Science's instruments are insufficient to the measure of the actuality of an active *thought* effecting a *concept*, those instruments measuring the neurological "impulses" as *effects* of thought.) Nor does it follow that concept in its actuality may not be flawed, since concept is susceptible to being a "mistake [in intellectual] nature" — a mistake of a finite intellectual soul. That *word* as actual in intellect (by a degree of perfection) may be born from intellect in the spectacle of a sign, though as a sign external to intellect, a sign is by indirection dependent upon essence of things in themselves as intellectually incepted as truth. The effected *word* in intellect, then, is antecedent to the action of extension in the practical actions of making—as for instance an articulation (a sign) of that intellectual word as conceived, extended beyond the discrete intellect itself—"birthed" as sign. And in respect to that concern, considering that the *word* advanced practically into creation (as we are here attempting) requires a distinction lest in our pursuit of a universal—a common understanding of operative intellect—we should reduce any particular intellect itself to an identity in collective intellects, that Averroist error distorting the uniqueness of persons.

On this point as well we remember Thomas' observation at the outset of his Question 79 "Of Intellectual Powers." The "intellectual soul is sometimes called intellect, as from its chief power," Thomas then adducing St. Augustine to the concept of *intellectual soul* from Augustine's *De Trinita* where he says (in Thomas' summary) "the mind is spirit and essence." But it is an *essential intellectual soul* discrete in itself—the very thing it is in *this* manifestation—that concerns both Augustine and Thomas. In this regard we might say that intellectual understanding is thus effected as a word *in intellect,* an active gestation of truths known from particular things embodied in an enlarging, gestating vision as word—as concept nurtured from inceptions within intellect. It is here that intellect (in a complementary "parenting" of incepted truth through the intuitive openness to good and the rational nurturing of truth by reason) gains visions of the *possible* as implicit in actual contingencies to actual things as intuitively known by experience.

In such understanding lies another necessary distinction: between, first of all, *accidents* as inherent to the essence of an actual thing, responded to through those inherent accidents in a thing's essential nature, received by an intuitive openness to the good or truth. The response of the intuitive is initiated by *spectacle* of inherent accidents as in a confluence of things perceived. But it is crucial to distinguish *accidents* as spectacle from those inherent accidents, lest reason arrest intellect's limited response to only the surface of things at the level of the confluence of things—that surface we call *spectacle* upon which Emerson advises us to "skate." It is accident so arrested that leads reason to mistake accident itself for essence. Thus follows a reductionist reception of things through which *accident* is understood as random. Divorced from the nature of a thing as existing through grace, accident as random defines for reason the limited arena allowed to reason. It does so by will's separation of grace from nature. What occurs out of such an arrest is a premature "extrapolation," a premature act of reason in a speculative distortion whereby the general confluence of things in themselves (all creation) is denied the essential nature to discrete things as constituting that body of creation. By that distortion reason may conclude that random accident speaks only randomness. In that speculative reductionism as extended by Positivism, all creation will be declared random accident, either by an intentional strategy of will to dominance over being or through the intellectual error of misunderstanding particularities of things as random and dissociated from the essence of the thing itself.

Such then our own speculative attempt upon the nature of intellect in its pursuit of universals through reason. In Thomas' distinctions, intellect is not a vague cloud enclosing all intellectual souls in a commonness of a reduction to intellect as "over soul," tempting presumption of transcendence by will—the error Thomas refutes in the Averroists. For Thomas, each person is *this* intellectual soul incarnate—discrete in particularities blossoming to our recognition as the accidents inherent to this specific nature of this person. But, in that each person shares in *being* (in existing as created) within the orders of creation as a *human* being, there are common limits also shared within confluent creation by the intellectual soul. Though particular and discrete, that soul shares with things existing in properties other than intellectual. Truths gathered to concept by the intellectual soul may speak therefore a limited commonness in *being*. Here in respect to the nature of intellect itself as discrete lies an aspect of commonness to all creation to be understood through reason. In an understanding of the complementary modes of the intellectual soul as intuitive and rational, within the common limits of discursiveness common to persons, we may as persons approach some understanding of what Thomas means in declaring that "art is reason in making." We do so through diverse arts, diversely appropriate to discrete persons as makers in quest of accommodation within a commonness to things created, in quest of a felt balance in creation as intellectual souls in quest of community: con-union.

It is within the concern of this present speculative venture into the nature of intellectual act that we may understand the intellectual soul's moral sense in relation to its specific sense of its peculiar art of making. In respect to the poet, to his dramatic sense in relation to his moral, we must consider that by the intellectual act of intuitively responding to experienced thing (to which reason seeks accommodation in speculative action toward universals) what the poet knows is in response to the actuality of a thing (to a thing *essential* in being the thing it is). What is known is a truth of the thing corresponding in some degree to that essential nature of the thing—always a partial truth of its essence. Truth for the intellectual soul, this is to say, is *partial* in that finite intellect cannot *comprehend* a thing in the sense we say God comprehends it. It is in relation to truth known that the person's moral sense is properly operative in his intellectual actions as a person in perfecting his calling. O'Connor, aware of this reality to her own knowing (though she does not put it with our present Thomistic argument) asserts unequivocally that her moral sense of responsibility as person requires of her as poet "the violence of a single-minded respect for the truth," as she puts it in her concern for "The Nature and Aim of Fiction." She knows it a moral responsibility, but she knows as well that it will not follow from a coincidence of her moral and dramatic senses that as poet she is responsible for the moral rectitude of any person other than herself. Because her responsibility centers in the moral responsibility to her gifts as poet, in the light of truths intellectually known, she must not presume through those gifts a responsibility as savior of her reader. We discover this understanding already hers from her earliest public essay, "The Fiction Writer and His Country," that essay commissioned by Granville Hicks.

Granville Hicks is one of her "Northern" readers committed to Modernist principles, and it is to him in part that she suggests in her essay for his collection that "The Christian writer will feel that in the greatest fiction, the writer's moral judgment will be implicit." Indeed in her view of that concern she makes the point we dwelt on earlier: "In the greatest fiction, the writer's moral sense coincides with his dramatic sense." It does so because "his moral judgment is part of the very act of seeing." On this same principle, the critic (if a Modernist skeptic adversarial in response to her vision) will exercise his own moral judgment as part of his own "act of seeing," though he deny any moral intent. Nevertheless as either artist or critic, if the person is "concerned above all" with an accurate reproduction of things known with an immediacy to them, especially those natural forces that he feels control his destiny, he may "transcend the limitations of his narrow vision." He will do so though he be one of those "New York" critics she skewers.

James Joyce himself would deny the moral as implicit to his own fiction and requiring moral judgment. But for O'Connor *art* is inescapably morally dramatic by the making, therefore implicating the poet in relation to created good by his very act of informing. In his own limited vision responding to mystery, Joyce may nevertheless truncate that vision as it were, denying at last O'Connor's insistence upon Revelation as ultimate to our moral sense — inevitable to our nature though by willfulness we embrace diminishment as intellectual soul, becoming of the Devil's party rather than toward a potential good as *this* person. Thus Joyce must modify the orthodox sense of *epiphany* to the limits of the psychological. In doing so he elects exile from his Irish Catholicism, though there remains that cultural residue of Thomistic argument in his memory which contributes so largely as matter to his fictions. Revelation for him is an illusion believed by the "folk" of Dublin, at least by many of them, in Joyce's perspective on his recollections of his early childhood and youth. That is young Stephen's conclusion certainly. And if through Stephen, Joyce distances himself by an ironic wit, Stephen nevertheless proves a surrogate person in the fiction rather closer to Joyce as person than the art can obscure. That is, the challenge to Joyce of the "personal" as matter to his art proves very like the challenge to Eliot in his own witty disguises of the "personal" such as we recognize in his "Love Song of J. Alfred Prufrock."

Young Stephen, about to exile himself, confesses to his friend Cranley that he no longer communicates at the altar, Cranley putting to him as the reason that he does so the fear that "the host ... may be the body and blood of the son of god and not a wafer of bread." For if it is the body of Christ, Stephen would feel he must as poet submit in a prudent humility destructive of his arrogant presumption as creator poet. (Here lies a point of correspondence between Stephen and the Misfit.) Yes, says Stephen, that is his fear. But he quickly adds that he fears many things — equally "dogs, horses, firearms, the sea, thunderstorms, machinery, the country roads at night" — along with that elevated Host. He fears existence itself because he "imagines" that "there is a malevolent reality behind those things I say I fear." But most especially, he fears partaking of the Mass lest he fall victim to "the chemical action which would be set up in my soul by a false homage to a symbol behind which are massed twenty centuries of authority and veneration." But he will not turn Protestant, he says scornfully. He has "lost his faith," but not his "self-respect" and so will not "forsake an absurdity which is logical and coherent and ... embrace one which is illogical and incoherent." Joyce himself chooses exile from church, country, family, but those are categories of the same matter with which he must "incarnate" his form. He rejects the Incarnation as actual, though the cultural residue of "twenty centuries of authority and veneration" support it as a reality. Though declared an absurdity, those "twenty centuries of authority" nevertheless feed him as poet in creating his own world, in which world he seeks refuge — the world of art.

We shall presently explore this difference in Joyce's two countries — that of nature and that of art — more explicitly, but first let us see what O'Connor means by "the very act of seeing," in the light of Thomas' exploration of the intellectual act. That is a point of concern which she has pursued before a congenial audience at Wesleyan a few miles from Andalusia, an audience largely "Southern." It is this "seeing" as it relates to her mode of the grotesque that she wishes to engage. Such a writer as herself, she says in that local talk, is drawn by mystery, but that does not mean that she can "slight the concrete." As Thomas would assure her (though she does not here invoke him), "Fiction begins where human knowledge begins — with the senses — and every fiction writer is bound by this fundamental aspect of his medium." It is only in consequence of experiences of actual things (particularly of actual persons) that such a writer finds himself in possession of truths that have been gathered initially through the senses, though those truths already point toward the mystery yet unresolved to his understanding — that anything *is*. St. Augustine's moment of epiphany and turning comes — we have recalled — when he at last hears those things "that stand around the doors of [his] flesh" shouting "He made us!" In this respect Flannery seems not to have been so hard of hearing as Augustine in his youth. She discovers early confirmation of this point of departure for fiction as lying *within* the concrete, evident in the writers she admired. Hawthorne puts his own concern for the concrete metaphorically as centering about the "town-pump." She recognizes that Hawthorne as writer is sometimes tempted toward peremptory resolution of mystery through allegory in a sign's leaping beyond the town-pump immediacy — one may suppose almost out of his frustration with an increasingly unresponsive audience as much as out of a failure of craftsmanship. She will also have learned from Joyce, who is a consummate user of the concrete world of the senses, though reluctant to concede grace operative in his experiences. She learns with caution, not with skepticism, recognizing that Joyce's tendency is to empty the concrete of its resonant mystery in a pursuit of art as ultimate authority. For Joyce as poet inclines to art as a private, autonomous means to a transcendence through limited "psychological" accommodation to the concrete world.

Joyce is, with this difference noted, unquestionably superbly gifted in capturing the concrete world at the level of the senses through the subtlety of his signs. It is here that O'Connor recognizes a kinship in their common point of departure from the concrete world. And she is deeply appreciative of his skill as craftsman in capturing that world, learning from him much of that necessary craft of selecting suitable "objective correlatives." But she sees Joyce as poet shying from that "moral basis of Poetry" which requires of the poet "the accurate naming of the things of God" as *of* God — that recognition following reason's "consideration of truth" in Thomas' phrase. Hence her remark to Father McCown on Joyce's attempted avoidance of the concrete world's dependence from its Creator. Joyce, she says, "can't get rid of it no matter what he does," her "it" being his "hunger for a Catholic completeness of life."

If Joyce shies away from the "moral basis of Poetry" as O'Connor suggests of him, he does so through an elaborately subtle intellectual dissociation of himself as poet from the matter necessary to his making. In the very long exploration of the poet as hero (Joyce's *Stephen Hero*, the text which Joyce reduces to his *Portrait of the Artist as a Young Man*), Stephen proves Joyce's "aesthetic" surrogate, a "fictional" character worked cleverly in a rational dissociation from reality in the interest of his art. By that fictional version of logical (dialectical) dissociation, Stephen projects the self-empowerment of the poet by his signs. Young Stephen as a detached observer of human persons in their natural actions speculates by adapting St. Thomas to ends quite other than those Thomas sees. Stephen's is a studiedly dialectical engagement of questions projected against lesser intelligences like his schoolmate Lynch. (See especially Chapter V of the *Portrait*). At that point in his self-evolution as artist Stephen argues that art must not excite desire, Lynch responding with an anecdote in refutation: "... one day I wrote my name in pencil on the backside of the Venus of Praxiteles in the museum. Was that not desire?" No, not for "normal natures," says Stephen, reminding Lynch of his having earlier given another autobiographical testimony, Lynch reporting that as a boy "in that charming Carmelite school" he had eaten "pieces of dried

cowdung." So much for *desire* as peculiar to normal or even subnormal natures. After all
(says Stephen) "we are all animals, I also am an animal," though as poet Stephen "desires"
to transcend that sad estate. As for Lynch's scribbling his name on the Venus, that was "simply a reflex action of the nerves," having naught to do with the poet's concern for the true
absolute, *beauty*.

   Not that Stephen expects the somewhat rowdy and gauche Lynch to comprehend the
argument. Stephen speaks rather as if to convince himself, turning to St. Thomas as of equal
intelligence for his point of departure, quoting Thomas: "*Pulcra sunt quae visa placent.*" The
beautiful is that which when seen, pleases. "This word," says Stephen, "though it is vague,
is clear enough to keep away good and evil, which excite desire and loathing" in this animal man, good and evil being concepts relevant to animal nature. It is by *beauty* that we
escape beyond the arena of the kinetic limits of animal nature. That is, beauty effects not
"simply a reflex action of the nerves." Indeed, the beauty "expressed by the artist cannot
awaken in us an emotion which is kinetic or a sensation which is purely physical." Instead,
it awakens or induces "an esthetic stasis, an ideal pity or an ideal terror, a stasis called forth,
prolonged and at last dissolved by what I call the rhythm of beauty." Therefore, "Art ... is
the human disposition of sensible or intelligible matter for an esthetic end." For Stephen,
eureka! This is his discovery of the secret of the poet's power beyond his animal limits. Freed
of such limits by that power the artist through signs creates 'beauty," whereby he is enabled
"to keep away good and evil" in triumph over intrusive creation itself as responded to by
animal nature. Thus the poet frees art itself of what O'Connor vows impossible, a removal
of the "moral basis of Poetry" as her phrase puts it in her remarking Joyce's intent.

   For Joyce, insofar as Stephen speaks his aesthetic position, the stasis in consciousness
as beauty's effect is quite removed from a kinesis whereby the person as animal is immersed
in concrete reality as himself a palpable and actual entity, a body ensouled. Stasis is a state
of suspense *out of* the participation in concrete reality, but effected by a Holy Ghost of
the poet's own devising and commanded by sign, namely *beauty*. What Stephen avoids,
of course (as O'Connor is aware) is that beauty blossoms out of the con-naturality of a
person with things in themselves as actual in existing, as Thomas would have it. Beauty is
both in and out of this *connunion* with things, so that beauty pleases the person when
he sees it in things. Gerard Manley Hopkins will put the point in such of his poems as "Pied
Beauty," by indirection, in a recognition as poet of what we might call a blooming in the
poet's own *becoming* in response to the beautiful. Thus beauty fleets in the becoming of a
thing (Heats' rose), things yield only a "pied" beauty to perception. It speaks thereby *toward* a perfection of the perceiver of things aided by beauty, as St. Augustine declares in the
passage we have cited. "My question was the gaze I turned on them; the answer was their
beauty" — the beauty with which "they cried out with a mighty voice, 'He made us!'" In
Hopkins's view (or O'Connor's) the ultimate end of beauty is that stasis of perfection called
Beatitude as it is for St. Augustine, beauty's perfection of the person at last past change
in Beatitude.

   For O'Connor, then, there would be a certain irony in Joyce's aesthetics in relation to
his lingering "hunger for a Catholic completeness of life" as she phrases it. She perceives it
in his work, however much he (or his Stephen) struggle to command matter to created beauty
as evidencing the poet independent of moral obligation to truth itself as any larger than a
subjective convenience to the poet. Art's matter, indeed, is derived from the actuality the
person knows through a "kinetic" response to things in themselves, signaled by beauty in

things. Stephen's "ideal pity" or "ideal terror" are possible only in that never-never land of a Kantian "pure reason," that pure ideal pity or terror freed of the concrete reality of things. Kant himself admits (as that good Thomist Jacques Maritain points out) that he has fabricated this illusion of pure reason, knowingly posited as illusion by Kant in pursuit of his own intellectual stasis of his reason. And so as poet, O'Connor accepts the necessity of getting herself "dusty" in the "kinetic" arena Stephen denies relevant to beauty. By openness to the nitty-gritty of being she as intellectual soul accepts her own incarnate nature, through which nature pity and terror are more real than ideal to the intellectual soul. In that acceptance of limits as poet, she moves toward mystery out of awe, that initiating awe confronting reason so disturbingly by the intellectual soul's experience of things as actual: that *anything* should *be*! Her wonder then demands reason's active response. She is drawn into but through that concrete world.

By Joyce's very gift for concreteness to the contrary, he seems rather to attempt to put a safe distance between himself and that world as if, lest he fail in that self-protection, he might be drawn too deeply into the mystery of existence. About that mystery, he had learned knowledgeable formulations in his Jesuit training, developing a skeptical irony against it.[7] But, as Stephen puts it, it is nevertheless a necessary point of departure, given that man is primarily an "animal." Though only an absurdity, Thomistic argument is nevertheless "an absurdity which is logical and coherent"—perhaps comparable to a Kantian point of departure as animal toward "pure reason" but preferable in being more logical and coherent. For out of Kant emerges what Jacques Maritain calls "an *acosmic-idealit* ethics" devised through the separation of positive from natural law. Thus "things in themselves cannot be grasped in Kant's system," says Maritain, Stephen's "kinetic" concern thus necessarily put aside by "pure reason." (See Maritain's argument in his *An Introduction to the Basic Problems of Moral Philosophy*, 1950.)

For O'Connor, a second point follows from Thomistic argument: though by his act of making the poet echoes analogically the Creative act of God, it is but an echo by his reason in response to his intuitive sense of his origin as created. As echo of "pure" sound in things actual, his reason is connatural to things and to Eternal Reason as well, requiring of reason its recognition of the disproportion between creating and making—between that pure and perfect Act of Love whereby the poet *is* and therefore participates in the Eternal Reason by the poet's limited act, possible to him by as a finite intellectual soul. The poet (as is true of every person as maker) exercises his givenness therefore by making—the givenness of his limited nature unique because as *this* person he is created "in the image of God," his Creator. As intellect in act, the poet may reflect properly (though only by a limited degree) that Absolute Love whereby he is. But he may do so only through a right will. Yet how easily he may force *probability* by willfulness, as if reality were to be made actual by his own reason when that reason is freed from humility's and prudence's governance. Required to that intention: a presumption of absolute empowerment as autonomous intellect, an illusion of unlimited willed intent. *Homo viator* may thus suppose himself creator, whereby *truth* and *beauty*, the *good* itself, are decreed as dependent upon his own agency.

We have seen such reason becoming ungoverned in Emerson, whose arguments continue with us yet, echoed in the words of the late Lewis Mumford in formulating a principle of intent for his "Technics and Human Development": "I shall develop the view that man is pre-eminently a mind-making, self-mastering, and self-designing animal; and the primary locus of all his activities lies first in his own organism, and in the social organization through which it finds fuller expression. Until man made something of himself he could make little of the world around him." Emerson and his intellectual offspring Mumford as philosophers? Or a young Stephen Dedlaus as poet? But these actual persons and Joyce's surrogate person Stephen in their image are but recent advocates of a curse as ancient as Eden, a curse always as immediate to any person as fallen man, wherever and whenever he sojourns in this present "place." The corrective to a person as maker, in O'Connor's contrary position, lies in the surrender through love to the good of the thing being made, in an imitation of that ineffable *action* of Love as Creator whereby the poet himself exists as *this* person: whereby all else he may know in sojourning as *homo viator* exists. That transcendent Love is reflected to him by indirection out of encompassing nature, the most fundamental action shared by things, including himself: *becoming*. That truth requires of him as intellectual maker of poems or arguments about the concrete world an "accurate naming of the things of God," O'Connor asserts. That is a human action in extension of speculative reason which speaks through things made an openness of the maker to the possible good of the thing he is making. And, as O'Connor recognized at once, if he makes as a poet, he must attempt that openness to things which John Keats names in his now famous phrase as "negative capability," an act of surrendering love to the possible good which O'Connor speaks of as a "suffering with."

What Keats could not himself recognize, as we have said (though he recognized his own inclination to and faith in "negative capability" as poet), is the nature of his encounter of an inherent mystery within the concrete world to be recognized by reason in love as intuitive intellect. It is a mystery calling to him that he give an "accurate" naming in witness to the loved thing of God. The action of love in such making imitates the action of transcendent Love whereby the thing named exists in itself as created. It is the dark side of the mystery of "becoming" which arrests Keats on the surface of the existential world, in a spiritual stasis, tempting him to misname that thing he sees as darkened in his seeing the thing. It is not becoming but un-becoming in spectacle of decay, himself thereby coming to a spiritual arrest. *Becoming*, then, can speak to him only *death* as oblivion. From that arrest the only consuming truth is *death*. In the Thomistic vision to the contrary, it is an inclination *through* the good of things beyond temporal stasis that can dissolve the false name *death*. Thomas speaks of that *spiritual* becoming as our inclination out of given nature toward the Cause of things, whose name is Unchanging Love. As a hillbilly Thomist, then, Flannery O'Connor recognizes that, given her kinship to Adam, as poet her responsibility is an "accurate naming of the things of God." That exercise was set for Adam as steward in the garden: to give "names to all cattle, and to the fowl of the air and to every beast of the field"— before there was even Eve, before the fall.

The poet's action in making, then, may be an action of love of the good in the intuitive openness to the good, echoing however faintly man's capacity for love before the fall. By that "remembering" may be removed those obstacles to *grace* occasioned in fallen man by the fall. Or so St. Thomas or Flannery O'Connor might understand the spiritual progress possible in a moral obligation to givenness despite Original Sin. That love is an action speaking to the most profound of spiritual expectations in this little fallen world, man: *hope*. For these companionable journeymen (Thomas and O'Connor), the action effects the spiritual *becoming* in them as persons, a transforming toward a perfection of their discretely given natures as persons. Out of a desire moved by hope, the response to things in themselves, that openness of love reaches deeper than the surface of action as first revealed in an "adequate motivation and adequate psychology and the various determinations," to borrow to the point O'Connor's description of the limits of the writer professing commitment as but a "naturalist." But alas, what might be dreamed by such a naturalist, in a science of the merely "adequate," is the illusion that man's biochemical nature is the limit of his nature — as Emerson or Lewis Mumford would limit it. By such a false dream, spiritual openness beyond surfaces of existential reality is inhibited, losing by delay any hope of that country of Eternity hinted by the mystery of things in themselves here and now. That is the country which, as Pieper remarks of it, "does not just 'adjoin'" present reality of things but permeates things here and now. Entry into that country in hope is young Tarwater's prospect at novel's end, though he lacks rational acts of naming what he now knows, so that Tarwater must continue to deal here and now with the *terror* of Mercy. He is as man contingent in fallenness through his becoming, contingent as well to grace. How distant this terror of Mercy from Stephen Dedalus' dream of "an ecstatic stasis, an ideal pity or an ideal terror ... prolonged [by the poet] and at last dissolved by ... the rhythm of beauty" as salvific of animal man.

Such is the level (a depth in mystery), O'Connor says, at which meaning may begin to emerge in art, as it may in any art governed by a response to that engulfing mystery of Mercy which runs deeper in us than any science's measure can justify as the limited ways of our nature when measured by the limiting laws of biophysics. Even, we must observe, when measured by our own words as poet or philosopher, though such pilgrims may be gifted in a science of naming the things of God by "objective correlatives" deployed by prosody's metaphor, or by systems deployed by logic in any quest for metaphysical vision. Not Descartes nor Kant, not Joyce nor Eliot, capture *comprehensively* the root of mystery of being in its Cause. Nor does St. Thomas or O'Connor. Our witness of failure despite desire we have seen in John Keats's despair. Though he discovers in himself a gift — a manner made possible through grace to intellect — his "Negative Capability" — it cannot rescue him from his "sole self." It is (Thomas might argue) nevertheless a mode of ordinate response as a person to things which is to be properly perfected as a habit — a love toward things elicited to the habitual by the good in things. In a becoming out of that habit, the person may act at last beyond the arrested spiritual stasis which Joyce's young Stephen assumed sufficient to his own self-rescue through his art. "Negative capability" is therefore a gift to the person as a mode of intellectual action, crucial to the person as poet, out of which he sings his namings. It is that mode Thomas would name the *intuitive*, in response to which the person is required active uses of reason in making.

By the poet's naming he sings a visionary insight in which we may all rejoice through understanding in consent with him. And as we may come thereby to a joy in which is also sorrow, we understand in sorrow Keats's attempted surrender of love as having failed him, leaving him consumed by melancholy from a failure of full surrender through "negative capability" to that calling of the things con-natural to him as person. ("We are not he, but he created us.") Again and again, Keats almost "escapes" self-centeredness, almost forgets himself in a love *toward,* becomes almost spiritually opened *through* things in themselves. That *towardness* is stirred in him by a native desire implicit to his nature, a longing speaking exile. Hence, in this context of our concern, there is help to our own understanding if we counterpoint to Keats, Gerard Manley Hopkins's negative capability witnessed in his poetry, as in that great sonnet, "The Windhover" read alongside the "Ode to a Nightingale." Again and again, Keats in failing finds himself returned to his "sole self," disappointed in the moment's fleeting vision as not continuous for him. The nightingale's transporting song is already "one moment past" as he comes to words, and it is at last faded beyond "the near meadows, over the still stream,/ Up the hill-side" till "buried deep/ In the next valley-glades." Keats "feels" left in self-isolation from existence itself, wondering whether he had experienced a daydream out of wishful thinking or had received a true vision, uncertain in his response.

How spiritually naïve, this arrested desire for a transport maintained by the grace of a "fancy" uninterrupted, continuous — obscuring the immediate miracle of actual grace to this actual consciousness named John Keats in *this* moment. Though "forlorne" he is neverthe-less himself continuous in his own being though "fast fading" to the point of death. He is yet sustained most intimately by Love itself, though not recognizing that truth. It is as if Keats expects both an instant and a continuous rescue into an abiding perfection here and now, in a Beatitude of a continuous transport by the nightingale's song. Such the "Roman-tic" failure through "fancy," and one O'Connor herself recognizes pervasive of desire in the popular spirit that confronts her as poet. She responds to that expectation as a sentimental-ity born of fancy, on one occasion doing so with a piercing precision, rejecting the pathos inevitable to the "Romantic" false expectation. She cuts to the depths of that misunderstand-ing, remarking something in us, she says, both "as storytellers and as listeners to stories, that demands the redemptive act, that demands that what falls at least be offered the chance to be restored." But the reader in her day "looks for that motion," having forgotten its cost, wanting "either his senses tormented or his spirits raised. He wants to be transported, in-stantly, either to mock damnation or a mock innocence." It is by an attempt to startle a reader out of this naiveté about his spiritual arrest that she presents those large and startling figur-ings of *homo viator* to readers she finds almost blind, almost deaf. She confronts them fiction-ally with those "freaks" who reflect to us our own "essential displacement," she says.

There are moments of transformation like that Keats makes famous, his communion through the bird-song in that "one moment past," but ah, how fleeting. *Now,* that moment seems already lost from this next moment's *now.* In that manner, lost moments are less cel-ebrated than clung to with growing desperation, the person unreleased from a premature end of his limits of becoming, a becoming whose end appears only resolved by oblivion. There had been that mystical epiphany, surely for Keats. But when he returns from that vi-sion to an impinging nature, he can see the vision only waking as dreamed of lost Eden out of his present decay. He remembers nevertheless having come to a possible threshold, an opening upon that larger country ruled by Love, desired if not believed. From that epiphany, whose memorial is his "Ode to a Nightingale," he turns, no longer poet. He sees himself a sole-self isolated within the withering desert of nature's decay. The glimpse of a garden from within that "natural" world he will now concluded must have been an illusion born of de-sire. (His "Ode to Melancholy" is even closer to despair, there seeing death's oblivion in the April rose, April for him no less than for the early Eliot the cruelest month.) Insofar as Keats's experience had been actual, it was so only as history past. Desire as a reality, stirring his in-tellectual soul, has tricked him to project a fantasy of transcendence, unable to experience the dimension of the transcendent within the continuing reality here and now in pied beauty. That is a country within and yet larger than, sustaining of, the very concrete world he can take as evidencing only an inevitable decay into an oblivion called death. Sad epiphany, that of the Romantic poet, however cheerfully he may whistle in the gathering darkness.

And if ourselves Modernists in this deracination from reality, we can but share this disoriented — these "dissociated" — sensibilities. If we remember this as a real experience of a real John Keats, a man who is unable to resolve through prudential humility the mystery of his own existence despite moments of epiphany, we may with an enlarged understanding engage the ambiguous concept *epiphany* as it has been variously experienced as a reality of human nature by Romantic poets from Keats to Yeats, from Coleridge as intellectual poet concerned with reason to Joyce and the early Eliot as "rational" poets. Nineteenth century literature, down to World War I, struggled to recover from unsettled sensibilities which had by osmotic feeling radically affected the "popular spirit" through literature. (I have explored this spiritual deracination in *Romantic Confusions of the Good: Beauty as Truth, Truth Beauty*, 1997.) We have anticipated that Flannery O'Connor's understanding of this concept (*epiphany*) as significantly different from Joyce's rationalized use of it as a fictional device. Joyce limits that device by his limited Modernist readings of *homo viator*, his version of a Romantic inclination commanded by the strict logic of his reason in a "Romantic" self-protection which he sets in relation to a psychology of thought, experience (as his Stephen asserts) by the person as animal. Both Joyce and O'Connor take point of departure in St. Thomas' address to beauty's relation in nature to beauty in art. But an epiphany for O'Connor is an effect of grace in things in themselves responded to by the intellectual soul. An epiphany in that consciousness is for her more than a psychological dawning of recognition effected by neural response to the impinging naturalistic and cultural circumstances upon a fictional character, in imitation by limited psychological effects used to an aesthetic end as the end-all of art.

In his pursuit of the concept as viable to his making, Joyce takes his initial departure in a Romantic such as Keats, in whose Odes the "epiphany" returns Keats again and again to his "sole-self," with an emotional effect in his art of pathos, the sad music of his very personal melancholy. (How apt a clue this is to the dramatic parabola of Joyce's Irish men and women — especially women — in his *Dubliners*.) Joyce pursues the conditions of self-awareness in his Keatsean character, Stephen Dedalus, who of course differs significantly from Keats. As a would-be poet, Stephen is "scholastically" educated but resolutely intent upon his own "metaphysical way" from the outset, a way for which he will adapt a rational system, despite its "absurdity," from St. Thomas to his own intellectual authority as a creator of Beauty. Beauty for Stephen as for Keats overcomes "every other consideration," indeed obliterating "all consideration," he will say in that portrait of him drawn for us by Joyce. Stephen argues that a possible authority exercised in the purity of firm intent of intellect as autonomous. Unlike Keats, then, Stephen needs no friend to send him three or four books of philosophy from which he might discover a metaphysical way, as Keats writes back to London from his retreat to Margate sands with that request. Thoroughly schooled in Thomism, Stephen adapts Thomas' "absurdity" of belief in Revelation to his purposes. With it he would dramatize a "revelation" to man as an animal existing in naturalistic and cultural circumstances. Stephen may thereby assume himself creator and not maker.

Young Stephen is a John Keats with a difference, then, confident in the power of his intellect as truth's creator and monitor. Keats, trained in the science of medicine, is haunted by nature's inevitable decay, the spectacle of decay as the ghost of nothingness in nature, death itself an oblivion already settling upon him as he knows, being tubercular. Thus nature, though loved, is deceitful, eroding all joys of response to the beauty of things in themselves. For always comes the undeniable destiny of individual things: decay. Keats's circumstance as intellectual poet, then, lacks the advantage of a honed reason such as that enjoyed by young Stephen, who (through Joyce as his maker) has honed reason as a razor in Jesuit arguments based in Thomism. It is out of this advantage in his "education" that Stephen will declare himself justified in rejecting the necessary conclusions of reason as adumbrated by St. Thomas. Thomas' conclusion, after all, is dependent upon faith in the light of Revelation. Thus as a "young man" Stephen has shunned the shadow of decay that haunts Keats, in doing so rejecting the Revelation central to Thomism. He believes himself thus enabled through pride to his own autonomy as creator.

Stephen, in this prideful ambition as Creator, cannot accept being a maker rather than creator. He wills not to be "beholden" to that grace of givenness permeating all nature, but most of all himself as person. What Stephen ignores or suppresses is the particularly and self-evidently *actual* in experience itself that is his very own by grace: his given nature cries out the truth he refuses. Hence O'Connor's remark that Joyce himself can never escape "a hunger for a Catholic completeness of life," a shadow on Young Stephen as artist which is deepened in Joyce's *Ulysses*. From a first reading of Joyce's Romantic novel (the *Portrait* a dead-end of the Romantic Movement one might argue), though it has been celebrated as the opening of a "Modern" literature, is rather a portrait of a dead-end of Romanticism in art. We may well suspect John Keats a likely figure whom Joyce has somewhat in mind in adapting Stephen to certify the autonomy of the intellectual imagination of the poet beyond the Romantic impasse. But, just as Dostoevsky discovers failure in his attempt to portray a "perfectly good man" in Prince Myshkin (*The Idiot*) only to discover the incarnating matter necessary to the attempt serves only to reveal that to be an impossibility given Original Sin, so Joyce in unfolding his perfectly good artist as an autonomous young man free of Original Sin closes his *Portrait of the Artist* with his Stephen a "sole-self," attempting impressionistically a conversation with himself in a private diary. How consonant that dead end with the implications of the truth about human nature itself, and how expected in that light Joyce's necessity to pursue Stephen much further in *Ulysses*. Stephen in *The Portrait* rather too confidently finds fancy no cheating elf. That is the Joycean strategy of escaping "Romanticism," as if an 18th century Rationalism might rescue 19th century Romanticism's "feeling" through a system of consistent logical intentionality of Kantian "reason." From our perspective we may call it rather an intellectual action of *fancy,* and thereby suggest once more a distinction Keats seems not to have been able to make, though acquainted with Coleridge as one of his immediate literary fathers. We anticipate it as well to be a distinction Joyce himself knew but deliberately set aside. For Joyce, the strategy of fancy is adapted and justified out of a new science a-borning in his day: a psychological realism increasingly limited in its parameters of consciousness to those of biological science. Such is the limited arena to this emerging "science" of psychology, however rationally pursued by William James at Harvard as the 19th century turns into the 20th century. It has been a science evolved under the auspices of President Charles Eliot as the godfather of the "New Religion" he preaches out of Darwinian theory, a religion which is to be effected by a radical reconstitution of the American academic curriculum itself. Again, see President Eliot's "Religion of the Future," his lecture in 1909 to the Summer School of Theology at Harvard, to which we have alluded and shall. Out of William James as pragmatic realist, through systematic specializations of that "new religion" of consciousness proposed by Harvard's President Eliot as based in Darwinian theory, there proliferated in the 20th century psychological systems in formulae for a necessary WD-40 to lubricate the mechanical brain — systems as products marketed under various brand names. Again, however, we emphasize: This acerbic judgment of the effects of reductionist theories translated into psychological systems does not deny psychological phenomena. It is rather a judgment in emphasis of the psychological phenomena as but symptomatic. Flannery O'Connor herself emphasizes the psychological as a point of departure to her making, but she insists it such a point toward dramatizing the deeper spiritual disorder in a "psyche" as the cause of the symptomatics. The psychological symptom is for her a spectacle of the mystery of the "psyche," a term in its older meaning for the *intellectual soul,* not a sign of a merely mechanical disorder in the individual as a biological machine.

If such an intellectual context is decisive to Joyce as poet, it perhaps means that Joyce, unlike O'Connor, is made the more wary of those depths of mystery in the "psyche" on which she insists that a story must be built. Certainly it must be so for her if it is a story she is making. And in support of our speculative suggestion that Joyce is wary of that mystery whereby grace is coextensive with nature, we recall and shall revert to Eugene Jolas, Joyce's French friend during his self-exile in Paris, who records Joyce's late uncertainty about a presumption of autonomy as poet. Jolas reports that in the 1930s Joyce "became more and more absorbed by meditations on the imaginative creation."[8] It is in this last decade of his life that Joyce turns back, but not to St. Thomas who had been important to the aesthetics he adumbrates through Stephen. He turns instead to the Romantics, especially concerned with Coleridge, who had stood at a fork in art's road that confronts Romanticism with a choice. Before the aesthetic Sphinx, Coleridge spoke as influenced by German Idealism (and so somewhat affected by Kant, as Tolstoy a little later than Coleridge was to be radically affected by a residual Kantianism to the point of Manichaeanism). Coleridge puzzles the intuitive and rational mode of intellectual journeying, though without recourse to either St. Thomas' epistemology or his terms. He insists nevertheless on a distinction between *imagination* and *fancy* in his *Biographia Literaria.* The passage which we introduced earlier was made famous in the academy by the mid–20th century in academic concerns for literary criticism as emphasized in Modern letters in reactions to a disquiet with that 19th century Romanticism. The 19th century Romanticism from our "progressive" remove by mid-century appeared as heavily evidencing a "dissociation of sensibilities." It was this interest stirred in some of our literary criticism by academic minds within the "humanities" who began to view the Romantic mind with an increasing alarm as having become deracination from reality, prompting those Romantic fathers sometimes to excessive reactions against reason itself, lacking as did those fathers the reasoned science psychology as rescue.

The solutions to the increasing sense of "selves" as "alienated" from reality had tended meanwhile toward a distorted elevation of intuition among the "Romantics," who were themselves smarting under the increasing assault from a scientific rationalism rapidly established with the authority of facts out of Enlightenment Rationalism in 19th century science. It was that rationalism which provided its own myth as if an established science: Darwinian Evolutionary Theory. Out of that myth, under the aegis of President Eliot at Harvard, specialization in sciences through pragmatic curricula had begun to invade the humanities — beginning with those "soft" humanities so appealing to the popular spirit such as sociology, which adapted the emerging science of psychology to its uses (as opposed to biological physics and chemistry which would be summoned later in declaring through Positivistic science Stephen Dedalus' "literary" assertion that man is but an animal. Any uses of philosophy or history as formerly humanistic instead of mechanistic or animalistic must submit within the province of Positivism. Nor is art to be allowed to speak beyond man's animalistic or mechanistic nature save through an implicit or direct admission of art as but "fancy's" creature. Such Positivistic limits were the more easily prescribed when the emerging "New Criticism" began to turn more and more scientific in its own address to the literary text as if with philosophical authority. (See Gilson's *Linguistics and Philosophy: An Essay on the Philosophical Constants of Language*.) In the issue, not only the old time religion and old time philosophy were being routed, but poetry as well. Or so it now appears if we look closely at current academic curricula.

Perhaps Rousseau had been the moment's Moses to Romanticism, leading literature into its desert exile. (At one point, Coleridge himself became enthusiastic about a "return to nature," considering joining a group intending a commune in the American "jungle," Florida, as an awaiting tropical paradise.) Not the least of those emerging sciences, becoming increasingly evident even among Romantic intellectuals in the 19th century and into the 20th, was already growing out of scientific determinism's intense devotion to reductions of man to mere animal, that science of psychology which emerged with authority to the popular spirit to calm it from uneasy response to mystery. Psychology, metaphorically put, became Positivism's "Holy Ghost." And "psychology" quickly replaced "theology" as authority speaking man's proper end, especially at President Eliot's Harvard. It becomes a science in a Positivistic aspect. And so between Coleridge and the emergence of Joyce, psychology increasingly will declare possible a rescue to art itself from its "Romantic" dead end. Dramatic art in particular increased its dependence upon that new science, at the expense of the older sense of the "spiritual" at the heart of drama. (The popular spirit is now more aware of the "Oedipal Complex" than of Sophocles' Oedipus.) It was within this emerging climate to art that Henry James would find it somewhat embarrassing that his predecessor of such a notable talent, Hawthorne, had become so concerned with the problem of "sin," a flaw in Hawthorne's reason in an otherwise impressive work, *The Scarlet Letter,* which therefore lacks "realism." That was a sufficient forewarning to the poet to seek a new "realism," that of the social and psychological manifestations of community as evolved out of existence as accidental. For that new doctrine established by Positivistic reduction of the mystery of existences, the Darwinian myth became crucial to support power over being by the "popular spirit." Positivism, after all, obviates the moral problematic in the seemingly necessary metaphor to popular consent once in the keep of the poet, dramatic contingencies to the person thus obfuscated in his new faith in science as obviating both philosophy and art save as subservient minions to Positivistic authority over the popular spirit.

In the light of these speculative concerns for the Rationalist's and the Romantic's "dissociations of sensibilities" — the separation of thought and feeling we have been exploring — perhaps we may better consider James Joyce's *Portrait of the Artist as a Young Man*. It presents Stephan Dedalus led astray by a rationalistic appropriation of fancy as intellect's instrument in pursuit of "pure" Beauty. How fascination, then, O'Connor's counterpointing of Joyce's novel by her "portrait of the realist of distances as a young man," Francis Marion Tarwater in violent pursuit of Heaven. Likenesses and unlikenesses to be meditated upon.